Memoirs
of
SERVICE AFLOAT

Eng'd by H.B. Hall, Jr. N.Y.

Raphael Semmes

ADM.ᵈ R. SEMMES.

Kelly Piet & Cᵒ Baltimore.

Memoirs
of
SERVICE AFLOAT

DURING THE
WAR BETWEEN THE STATES

BY

ADMIRAL RAPHAEL SEMMES, CSN

Captain of the *CSS Alabama*

Illustrated with Original Engravings

**The
Blue & Grey
Press**

Memoirs of Service Afloat

Manufactured in the United States of America

ISBN 1-55521-177-1

TO THE MEMORY

Sailors and Soldiers of the Southern States,

WHO LOST THEIR LIVES, IN THE WAR BETWEEN THE STATES
IN DEFENCE OF THE LIBERTIES WHICH HAD BEEN
BEQUEATHED TO THEM BY THEIR FATHERS,
THIS VOLUME IS RESPECTFULLY
AND AFFECTIONATELY
INSCRIBED BY

THE AUTHOR.

PREFACE.

A NUMBER of publications have appeared, first and last, concerning the author and his career, as was naturally to have been expected. The *Alabama* was the first steamship in the history of the world — the defective little *Sumter* excepted — that was let loose against the commerce of a great commercial people. The destruction which she caused was enormous. She not only alarmed the enemy, but she alarmed all the other nations of the earth which had commerce afloat, as they could not be sure that a similar scourge, at some future time, might not be let loose against themselves. The *Alabama*, in consequence, became famous. It was the fame of steam. As a matter of course, she attracted the attention of the book-makers — those cormorants ever on the lookout for a "speculation." A number of ambitious *literateurs* entered the seductive field. But it was easier, as they soon found, to enter the field than to explore it, and these penny-a-liners all made miserable failures, — not even excepting the London house of Saunders, Otley & Co., to whom the author was induced to loan his journals, in the hope that something worthy of his career might be produced. To those who have chanced to see the "Log of the *Sumter* and *Alabama*," produced by that house, it will be unnecessary to say that the author had no hand in its preparation. He did not write a line for it, nor had he any interest whatever in the sale of it, as the loan of his journals had been entirely gratuitous. So far as his own career was concerned, the author would gladly have devolved the labor of the historian on other shoulders, if this had been possible. But it did not seem to be possible, after the experiments that had been made. With all the facilities afforded the London house referred to, a meagre and barren record was the result. The cause is sufficiently obvious. The cruise of a ship is a biography. The ship becomes a personification. She not only

"Walks the waters like a thing of life,"

but she speaks in moving accents to those capable of interpreting her. But her interpreter must be a seaman, and not a landsman. He must not only be a seaman, he must have made the identical cruise which he undertakes to describe. It will be seen, hence, that the career of the author was a sealed book to all but himself. A landsman could not even interpret his journals, written frequently in the hieroglyphics of the sea. A line, or a bare mark made by himself, which to other eyes would be meaningless would for him be fraught with the inspiration of whole pages.

Besides, the *Alabama* had an inside as well as an outside life. She was a microcosm. If it required a seaman to interpret her as to her outside life, much more did it require one to give an intelligible view of the little world that she carried in her bosom. No one but an eye-witness, and that witness himself a sailor, could unveil to an outside world the domestic mysteries of the every-day life of Jack, and portray him in his natural colors, as he worked and as he played. The following pages may, therefore, be said to be the first attempt to give anything like a truthful picture of the career of the author upon the high seas, during the late war, to the public. In their preparation the writer has discarded the didactic style of the historian, and adopted that of memoir writing, as better suited to his subject. This style gave him more latitude in the description of persons and events, and relieved him from some of the fetters of a mere writer of history. There are portions of the work, however, purely historical, and these have been treated with the gravity and dignity which became them. In short, the author has aimed to produce what the title of his book imports — an historical memoir of his services afloat during the war. That his book will be generally read by the Northern people he does not suppose. They are scarcely in a temper yet to read anything he might write. The wounds which he has inflicted upon them are too recent. Besides, men do not willingly read unpalatable truths of themselves. The people of America being sovereign, they are like other sovereigns,— they like those best who fool them most, by pandering to their vices and flattering their foibles. The author, not being a flatterer, cannot expect to be much of a favorite at the court of the Demos.

A word now as to the feeling with which the author has written. It has sometimes been said that a writer of history should be as phlegmatic and unimpassioned as the judge upon the bench. If the reader desires a dead history, in other words, a history devoid of the true spirit of history, the author assents to the remark. But if he desires a living, moving, breathing picture of events — a *personam* instead of a *subjectam*, the picture must not be undertaken by one who does not feel something of that which he writes. Such a terrible war as that through which we have passed could not be comprehended by a stolid, phlegmatic writer, whose pulse did not beat quicker while he wrote. When all the higher and holier passions of the human heart are aroused in a struggle — when the barbarian is at your door with the torch of the incendiary in one hand, and the up-lifted sword of diabolical revenge in the other, — *feeling* is an important element in the real drama that is passing before the eyes of the beholder. To attempt to describe such a drama with the cold words of philosophy, is simply ridiculous. If the acts be not described in words suited to portray their infamy, you have a lie instead of history. Nor does it fol-low that feeling necessarily overrides judgment. All pas-sions blind us if we give free rein to them; but when they are held in check, they sharpen, instead of obscuring the intellect. In a well-balanced mind, feeling and judgment aid each other; and he will prove the most successful histo-rian who has the two in a just equipoise. But though the author has given vent occasionally to a just indignation, he has not written in malice. He does not know the meaning of the word. He has simply written as a Southern man might be supposed to think and feel, treading upon the toes of his enemies as tenderly as possible. If he has been occasionally plain-spoken, it is because he has used the English language, which calls a rogue a rogue, notwithstanding his disguises. When the author has spoken of the Yankee and his "grand moral ideas," he has spoken rather of a well-known type than of individual men. If the reader will bear these remarks in mind as he goes along, he will find them a key to some of the passages in the book. In describing natural phenomena, the author has ventured upon some new suggestions. He submits these with great diffidence. Meteorology is yet a new science, and many developments of principles remain to be made.

ANCHORAGE, NEAR MOBILE, ALA.,
  December, 1868.

CONTENTS.

CONTENTS.

CONTENTS.

CONTENTS.

CONTENTS.

CONTENTS.

MEMOIRS OF SERVICE AFLOAT.

CHAPTER I.

A BRIEF HISTORICAL RETROSPECT.

THE disruption of the American Union by the war of 1861 was not an unforeseen event. Patrick Henry, and other patriots who struggled against the adoption of the Federal Constitution by the Southern States, foretold it in burning words of prophecy; and when that instrument was adopted, when the great name and great eloquence of James Madison had borne down all opposition, Henry and his compatriots seemed particularly anxious that posterity should be informed of the manly struggle which they had made. Henry said, "The voice of tradition, I trust, will inform posterity of our struggles for freedom. If our descendants be worthy of the name of Americans, they will preserve, and hand down to the latest posterity, the transactions of the present times; and though I confess my explanations are not worth the hearing, they will see I have done my utmost to preserve their liberty."

The wish of these patriotic men has been gratified. The record of their noble deeds, and all but inspired eloquence, has come down to posterity, and some, at least, of their descendants, "worthy of the name of Americans," will accord to them the foremost rank in the long list of patriots and sages who illustrated and adorned our early annals.

But posterity, too, has a history to record and hand down. We, too, have struggled to preserve our liberties, and the liberties of those who are to come after us; and the history of that struggle must not perish. The one struggle is but the complement of the other, and history would be incomplete if either were omitted. Events have vindicated the wisdom of Henry, and those who struggled with him against the adoption of the Federal Constitution. Events will equally vindicate the wisdom of Jefferson Davis, and other Confederate patriots, who endeavored to preserve that Constitution, and hand it down, unimpaired, to their posterity.

The wisdom of a movement is not always to be judged by its success. Principles are eternal, human events are transitory, and it sometimes takes more than one generation or one revolution to establish a principle. At first sight, it may appear that there is some discordance between Patrick Henry and Jefferson Davis, as the one struggled against the adoption of the Constitution, and the other to preserve it. But they were, in fact, both engaged in a similar struggle; the object of both being to preserve the sovereignty of their respective States. Henry did not object so much to the nature of the partnership, into which his State was about to enter, as to the the nature of the partners with whom she was about to contract. He saw that the two sections were dissimilar, and that they had different and antagonistic interests, and he was unwilling to trust to the *bona fides* of the other contracting party. " I am sure," said he, "that the dangers of this system are real, when those who have no similar interests with the people of this country are to legislate for us — when our dearest interests are to be left in the hands of those whose advantage it will be to infringe them."

The North, even at that early day, was in a majority in both houses of Congress; it would be for the advantage of that majority to infringe the rights of the South; and Henry, with much more knowledge of human nature than most of the Southern statesmen of his era, refused to trust that majority. This was substantially the case with Jefferson Davis and those of us who followed his lead. We had verified the distrust of Henry. What had been prophecy with him, had become history with us. We had had experience of the fact, that our partner-States of the North, who were in a majority, had trampled upon the rights of the Southern minority, and we desired, as the only remedy, to dissolve the partnership into which Henry had objected to entering — not so much because

of any defect in the articles of copartnership, as for want of
faith in our copartners.

This was the wisdom of Jefferson Davis and his compatriots, which, I say, will be vindicated by events.   A final separation of these States must come, or the South will be perma-
nently enslaved.   We endeavored to bring about the separation, and we sacrificed our fortunes, and risked our lives to
accomplish it.   Like Patrick Henry, we have done our
"utmost to preserve our liberties;" like him, we have failed,
and like him, we desire that our record shall go down to such
of our posterity as may be "worthy of the name of Americans."

The following memoirs are designed to commemorate a few
of the less important events of our late struggle; but before I
enter upon them, I deem it appropriate to give some "reason
for the faith" that was in us, of the South, who undertook the
struggle.   The judgment which posterity will form upon our
actions will depend, mainly, upon the answers which we
may be able to give to two questions: First, Had the South the
right to dissolve the compact of government under which it
had lived with the North? and, secondly, Was there sufficient
reason for such dissolution?   I do not speak here of the right
of revolution—this is inherent in all peoples, whatever may
be their form of government.   The very term "revolution"
implies a forcible disruption of government, war, and all the
evils that follow in the train of war.   The thirteen original
Colonies, the germ from which have sprung these States, exercised the right of revolution when they withdrew their allegiance from the parent country.   Not so with the Southern
States when they withdrew from their copartnership with the
Northern States.   They exercised a higher right.   They did
not form a part of a consolidated government, as the Colonies
did of the British Government.   They were sovereign, equally
with the Northern States, from which they withdrew, and
exercised, as they believed, a peaceful right, instead of a right
of revolution.

Had, then, the Southern States the peaceful right to dissolve
the compact of government under which they had lived with
the North?   A volume might be written in reply to this ques-

tion, but I shall merely glance at it in these memoirs, referring the student to the history of the formation of the old Con federacy, prior to the adoption of the Constitution of the United States; to the "Journal and Debates of the Convention of 1787," that formed this latter instrument; to the debates of the several State Conventions which adopted it, to the "Madison Papers," to the "Federalist," and to the late very able work of Dr. Bledsoe, entitled "Is Davis a Traitor?" It will be sufficient for the purpose which I have in view—that of giving the reader a general outline of the course of reasoning, by which Southern men justify their conduct in the late war—to state the leading features of the compact of government which was dissolved, and a few of its historical surroundings, about which there can be no dispute.

The close of the War of Independence of 1776 found the thirteen original Colonies, which had waged that war, sovereign and independent States. They had, for the purpose of carrying on that war, formed a league, or confederation, and the articles of this league were still obligatory upon them. Under these articles, a Federal Government had been established, charged with a few specific powers, such as conducting the foreign affairs of the Confederacy, the regulation of commerce, &c. At the formation of this Government, it was intended that it should be perpetual, and was so declared. It lasted, notwithstanding, only a few years, for peace was declared in 1783, and the *perpetual* Government ceased to exist in 1789. How did it cease to exist? By the *secession* of the States.

Soon after the war, a convention of delegates met at Annapolis, in Maryland, sent thither by the several States, for the purpose of devising some more perfect means of regulating commerce. This was all the duty with which they were charged. Upon assembling, it was found that several of the States were not represented in this Convention, in consequence of which, the Convention adjourned without transacting any business, and recommended, in an address prepared by Alexander Hamilton, that a new convention should be called at Philadelphia, with enlarged powers. "The Convention," says Hamilton, "are more naturally led to this conclusion, as in their reflections on the subject, they have been induced to

think, that the power of regulating trade is of such comprehensive extent, and will enter so far into the great system of
the Federal Government, that to give it efficacy, and to obviate
questions and doubts concerning its precise nature and limits,
may require a corresponding adjustment in other parts of the
Federal system. That these are important defects in the system of the Federal Government is acknowledged by the acts
of those States, which have concurred in the present meeting.
That the defects, upon closer examination, may be found greater
and more numerous than even these acts imply, is at least, so far
probable, from the embarrassments which characterize the present state of our national affairs, foreign and domestic, as may
reasonably be supposed to merit a deliberate and candid discussion, in some mode which will unite the sentiments and
counsels of all the States."

The reader will observe that the Government of the States,
under the Articles of Confederation, is called a "Federal Government," and that the object proposed to be accomplished by the
meeting of the new Convention at Philadelphia, was to *amend*
the Constitution of that *Government*. Northern writers have
sought to draw a distinction between the Government formed
under the Articles of Confederation, and that formed by the
Constitution of the United States, calling the one a league, and
the other a government. Here we see Alexander Hamilton
calling the Confederation a government—a Federal Government. It was, indeed, both a league and a government, as it
was formed by sovereign States; just as the Government of
the United States is both a league and a government, for the
same reason.

The fact that the laws of the Confederation, passed in pursuance of its League, or Constitution, were to operate upon the
States ; and the laws of the United States were to operate upon
the *individual citizens* of the States, without the intervention
of State authority, could make no difference. This did not
make the latter more a government than the former. The difference was a mere matter of detail, a mere matter of machinery — nothing more. It did not imply more or less absolute sovereignty in the one case, than in the other. Whatever
of sovereignty had been granted, had been granted *by the States*,
in both instances.

The new Convention met in Philadelphia, on the 14th of May, 1787, with instructions to devise and discuss "all such *alterations,* and *further* provisions as may be necessary to render the Federal Constitution adequate to the exigencies of the Union." We see, thus, that the very Convention which framed the Constitution of the United States, equally called the Articles of Confederation a Constitution. It was, then, from a Constitutional, Federal Government, that the States seceded when they adopted the present Constitution of the United States! A Convention of the States assembled with powers only to amend the Constitution; instead of doing which, it abolished the old form of government altogether, and recommended a new one, and no one complained. As each State formally and deliberately adopted the new government, it as formally and deliberately seceded from the old one; and yet no one heard any talk of a breach of faith, and still less of treason.

The new government was to go into operation when nine States should adopt it. But there were thirteen States, and if nine States only acceded to the new government, the old one would be broken up, as to the other four States, whether these would or not, and they would be left to provide for themselves. It was by no means the voluntary breaking up of a compact, *by all the parties to it.* It was broken up piece-meal, each State acting for itself, without asking the consent of the others; precisely as the Southern States acted, with a view to the formation of a new Southern Confederacy.

So far from the movement being unanimous, it was a long time before all the States came into the new government. Rhode Island, one of the Northern States, which hounded on the war against the Southern States, retained her separate sovereignty for two years before she joined the new government, not uttering one word of complaint, during all that time, that the old government, of which she had been a member, had been unduly broken up, and that she had been left to shift for herself. Why was this disruption of the old government regarded as a matter of course? Simply because it was a league, or treaty, between sovereign States, from which any one of the States had the right to withdraw at any time, without consulting the interest or advantage of the others.

But, say the Northern States, the Constitution of the United States is a very different thing from the Articles of Confederation. It was formed, not by the States, but by the people of the United States in the aggregate, and made all the States one people, one government. It is not a compact, or league between the States, but an instrument under which they have surrendered irrevocably their sovereignty. Under it, the Federal Government has become the paramount authority, and the States are subordinate to it. We will examine this doctrine, briefly, in another chapter.

CHAPTER II.

THE NATURE OF THE AMERICAN COMPACT.

THE two principal expounders of the Constitution of the United States, in the North, have been Daniel Webster and Joseph Story, both from Massachusetts. Webster was, for a long time, a Senator in Congress, and Story a Justice of the Supreme Court of the United States. The latter has written an elaborate work on the Constitution, full of sophistry, and not always very reliable as to its facts. The great effort of both these men has been to prove, that the Constitution is not a compact between the States, but an instrument of government, formed by the *people* of the United States, as contradistinguished from the States. They both admit, that if the Constitution were a compact between the States, the States would have a right to withdraw from the compact — all agreements between States, in their sovereign capacity, being, necessarily, of no more binding force than treaties. These gentlemen are not always very consistent, for they frequently fall into the error of calling the Constitution a compact, when they are not arguing this particular question; in short, it is, and it is not a compact, by turns, according to the use they intend to make of the argument. Mr. Webster's doctrine of the Constitution, chiefly relied on by Northern men, is to be found in his speech of 1833, in reply to Mr. Calhoun. It is in that speech that he makes the admission, that if the Constitution of the United States is a compact between the States, the States have the right to withdraw from it at pleasure. He says, "If a league between sovereign powers have no limitation as to the time of duration, and contains nothing making it perpetual, it subsists only during the good pleasure of the parties, although no violation be complained of. If in the opinion of either party it be violated, such party may say he will no longer fulfil its obligations, on his part, but will consider the whole league or compact as at an end, although it might be one of its stipulations that it should be perpetual."

In his "Commentaries on the Constitution," Mr. Justice Story says, "The obvious deductions which may be, and indeed have been drawn, from considering the Constitution a *compact between States*, are, that it operates as a mere treaty, or convention between them, and has an obligatory force no longer than suits their pleasure, or their consent continues." The plain principles of public law, thus announced by these distinguished jurists, cannot be controverted. If sovereign States make a compact, although the object of the compact be the formation of a new government for their common benefit, they have the right to withdraw from that compact at pleasure, even though, in the words of Mr. Webster, "it might be one of its stipulations that it should be perpetual."

There might, undoubtedly, be such a thing as State merger; that is, that two States, for instance, might agree that the sovereign existence of one of them should be merged in the other. In which case, the State parting with its sovereignty could never reclaim it by peaceable means. But where a State shows no intention of parting with its sovereignty, and, in connection with other States, all equally jealous of their sovereignty with herself, only delegates a part of it — never so large a part, if you please — to a common agent, for the benefit of the whole, there can have been no merger. This was eminently the case with regard to these United States. No one can read the "Journal and Debates of the Philadelphia Convention," or those of the several State Conventions to which the Constitution was submitted for adoption, without being struck with the scrupulous care with which all the States guarded their sovereignty. The Northern States were quite as jealous, in this respect, as the Southern States. Next to Massachusetts, New Hampshire has been, perhaps, the most fanatical and bitter of the former States, in the prosecution of the late war against the South. That State, in her Constitution, adopted in 1792, three years after the Federal Constitution went into operation, inserted the following provision, among others, in her declaration of principles: "The people of this Commonwealth have the sole and exclusive right of governing them-selves as a free, sovereign, and independent State; and do, and forever hereafter shall exercise and enjoy every power, jurisdiction, and right which is not, or may not hereafter be, by them, expressly delegated to the United States."

Although it was quite clear that the States, when they adopted the Constitution of the United States, reserved, by implication, all the sovereign power, rights, and privileges that had not been granted away — as a power not given is necessarily withheld — yet so jealous were they of the new government they were forming, that several of them insisted, in their acts of ratification, that the Constitution should be so amended as explicitly to declare this truth, and thus put it beyond cavil in the future. Massachusetts expressed herself as follows, in connection with her ratification of the Constitution: "As it is the opinion of this Convention, that certain amendments and alterations in said Constitution would remove the fears, and quiet the apprehensions of the good people of the Commonwealth, and more effectually guard against an undue administration of the Federal Government, the Convention do, therefore, recommend that the following alteration and provisions be introduced in said Constitution: First, that it be explicitly declared, that all powers not delegated by the aforesaid Constitution are reserved to the several States, to be by them exercised."

Webster and Story had not yet arisen in Massachusetts, to teach the new doctrine that the Constitution had been formed by the *"People of the United States,"* in contra-distinction to the people of the States. Massachusetts did not speak in the name of any such people, but in her own name. She was not jealous of the remaining people of the United States, as fractional parts of a whole, of which she was herself a fraction, but she was jealous of them as *States;* as so many foreign peoples, with whom she was contracting. The powers not delegated were to be reserved to those *delegating* them, to wit: the *"several States;"* that is to say, to each and every one of the States.

Virginia fought long and sturdily against adopting the Constitution at all. Henry, Mason, Tyler, and a host of other giants raised their powerful voices against it, warning their people, in thunder tones, that they were rushing upon destruction. Tyler even went so far as to say that "British tyranny would have been more tolerable." So distasteful to her was the foul embrace that was tendered her, that she not only recommended an amendment of the Constitution, similar to that which was recommended by Massachusetts, making explicit reservation of her sovereignty, but she annexed a condition to her ratification, to the effect that she retained the right to withdraw the powers which she had granted, "whenever the same shall be perverted to her injury or oppression."

North Carolina urged the following amendment—the same, substantially, as that urged by Virginia and Massachusetts: "That each State in the Union shall respectively [not aggregately] retain every power, jurisdiction, and right which is not by this Constitution delegated to the Congress of the United States, or to the departments of the Federal Government."

Pennsylvania guarded her sovereignty by insisting upon the following amendment: "All the rights of sovereignty which are not, by the said Constitution, expressly and plainly vested in the Congress, shall be deemed to remain with, and shall be exercised by the several States in the Union." The result of this jealousy on the part of the States was the adoption of the 10th amendment to the Constitution of the United States as follows: "The powers not delegated to the United States, by the Constitution, nor prohibited by it to the States, are reserved to the States, or to the people."

It is thus clear beyond doubt, that the States not only had no intention of merging their sovereignty in the new government they were forming, but that they took special pains to notify each other, as well as their common agent, of the fact. The language which I have quoted, as used by the States, in urging the amendments to the Constitution proposed by them, was the common language of that day. The new government was a federal or confederate government—in the "Federalist," it is frequently called a "Confederation"—which had been created by the States for their common use and benefit; each State taking special pains, as we have seen, to declare that it retained all the sovereignty which it had not expressly granted away. And yet, in face of these facts, the doctrine has been boldly declared, in our day, that the Constitution was formed by the people of the United States in the aggregate, as one nation, and that it has a force and vitality independent of the States, which the States are incompetent to destroy! The perversion is one not so much of doctrine as of history. It is an issue of fact which we are to try.

It is admitted, that if the fact be as stated by our Northern brethren, the conclusion follows: It is, indeed, quite plain, that if the States did not create the Federal Constitution, they cannot destroy it. But it is admitted, on the other hand, by both Webster and Story, as we have seen, that if they did create it, they may destroy it; nay, that any one of them may destroy it as to herself; that is, may withdraw from the compact at pleasure, with or without reason. It is fortunate for us of the South that the issue is so plain, as that it may be tried by the record. Sophistry will sometimes overlie reason and blind men's judgment for generations; but sophistry, with all its ingenuity, cannot hide a fact. The speeches of Webster and the commentaries of Story have been unable to hide the fact of which I speak; it stands emblazoned on every page of our constitutional history.

Every step that was taken toward the formation of the Constitution of the United States, from its inception to its adoption, was taken by the States, and not by the people of the United States in the aggregate. There was no such people known as the people of the United States, in the aggregate, at the time of the formation of the Constitution. If there is any such people now, it was formed by the Constitution. But this is not the question. The question now is, who formed the Constitution, not what was formed by it? If it was formed by the States, admit our adversaries, it may be broken by the States.

The delegates who met at Annapolis were sent thither by the States, and not by the people of the United States. The Convention of 1787, which formed the Constitution, was equally composed of members sent to Philadelphia by the States. James Madison was chosen by the people of Virginia and not by the people of New York; and Alexander Hamilton was chosen by the people of New York, and not by the people of Virginia. Every article, section, and paragraph of the Constitution was voted for, or against, by States; the little State of Delaware, not much larger than a single county of New York, off-setting the vote of that great State.

And when the Constitution was formed, to whom was it submitted for ratification? Was there any convention of the people of the United States in the aggregate, as one nation, called for the purpose of considering it? Did not each State, on the contrary, call its own convention? and did not some of the States accept it, and some of them refuse to accept it? It was provided that when nine States should accept it, it should go into operation; was it pretended that the vote of these nine States was to bind the others? Is it not a fact, on the contrary, that the vote of eleven States did *not* bind the other two? Where was that great constituency, composed of the people of the United States in the aggregate, as one nation, all this time?

"But," say those who are opposed to us in this argument, "look at the instrument itself, and you will see that it was framed by the people of the United States, and not by the States. Does not its Preamble read thus: 'We, the people of the United States, in order to form a more perfect Union, &c., do ordain and establish this Constitution for the United States of America'?" Perhaps there has never been a greater literary and historical fraud practised upon any people, than has been attempted in the use to which these words have been put. And, perhaps, no equal number of reading and intelligent men has ever before submitted so blindly and docilely to be imposed upon by literary quackery and the legerdemain of words, as our fellow-citizens of the North have in accepting Webster's and Story's version of the preamble of the Constitution.

A brief history of the manner, in which the words, "We, the people," &c., came to be adopted by the Convention which framed the Constitution, will sufficiently expose the baldness of the cheat. The only wonder is, that such men as Webster and Story should have risked their reputations with posterity, on a construction which may so easily be shown to be a falsi-

fication of the facts of history.   Mr. Webster, in his celebrated
speech in the Senate, in 1833, in reply to Mr. Calhoun, made
this bold declaration: "The Constitution itself, in its very
front, declares, that it was ordained and established by the
people of the United States in the aggregate!"   From that
day to this, this declaration of Mr. Webster has been the chief
foundation on which all the constitutional lawyers of the North
have built their arguments against the rights of the States as
sovereign copartners.

   If the Preamble of the Constitution stood alone, without the
lights of contemporaneous history to reveal its true character,
there might be some force in Mr. Webster's position; but, unfortunately for him and his followers, he has *misstated a fact.*
It is not true, as every reader of constitutional history must
know, that the Constitution of the United States was ordained
by the people of the United States in the aggregate; nor did
the Preamble to the Constitution *mean to assert* that it was true.
The great names of Webster, and Story have been lent to a
palpable falsification of history, and as a result of that falsification, a great war has ensued, which has sacrificed its heca-
tomb of victims, and desolated, and nearly destroyed an entire
people. The poet did not say, without reason, that "words are
things."   Now let us strip off the disguises worn by these word-
mongers, and see where the truth really lies.   Probably some
of my readers will learn, for the first time, the reasons which
induced the framers of the Constitution to adopt the phraseology, "We, the people," &c., in the formation of their Preamble to that instrument.   In the original draft of the Constitution, the States, by name, were mentioned, as had been done
in the Articles of Confederation.   The States had formed the
old Confederation, the States were equally forming the new
Confederation; hence the Convention naturally followed in their
Preamble the form which had been set them in the old Constitution, or Articles.   This Preamble, purporting that the work
of forming the new government was being done by the States,
remained at the head of the instrument *during all the delibera-*
tions of the Convention, and no one member ever objected to it.
It expressed a fact which no one thought of denying.   It is
thus a fact beyond question, not only that the Constitution

was framed by the States, but that the Convention so proclaimed in *"front of the instrument."*

Having been framed by the States, was it afterward adopted, or "ordained and established," to use the words of Mr. Webster, by the people of the United States, in the aggregate, and was this the reason why the words were changed? There were in the Convention several members in favor of submitting the instrument to the people of the United States in the aggregate, and thereby accomplishing their favorite object of establishing a consolidated government — Alexander Hamilton and Gouverneur Morris among the number. On the "Journal of the Convention," the following record is found: "Gouverneur Morris moved that the reference of the plan [i. e. of the Constitution] be made to one General Convention, chosen and authorized by the people, to consider, amend, and establish the same." Thus the question, as to who should "ordain and establish" the Constitution, whether it should be the people in the aggregate, or the people of the States, was clearly presented to the Convention. How did the Convention vote on this proposition? The reader will perhaps be surprised to learn, that the question was not even brought to a vote, for want of a second; and yet this is the fact recorded by the Convention.

The reader who has read Mr. Madison's articles in the "Federalist," and his speeches before the Virginia Convention, in favor of the ratification of the Constitution, will perhaps be surprised to learn that he, too, made a somewhat similar motion. He was not in favor, it is true, of referring the instrument for adoption to a General Convention of the whole people, alone, but he was in favor of referring it to such a Convention, in connection with Conventions to be called by the States, thus securing a joint or double ratification, by the people of the United States in the aggregate, and by the States; the effect of which would ·have been to make the new government a still more complex affair, and to muddle still further the brains of Mr. Webster and Mr. Justice Story. But this motion failed also, and the Constitution was referred to the States for adoption.

But now a new question arose, which was, whether the Constitution was to be "ordained and established" by the legislatures of the States, or by the people of the States in Convention. All were agreed, as we have seen, that the instrument should be referred to the States. This had been settled; but there were differences of opinion as to how the States should act upon it. Some were in favor of permitting each of the States to choose, for itself, how it would ratify it; others were in favor of referring it to the legislatures, and others, again, to the people of the States in Convention. It was finally decided that it should be referred to Conventions of the people, in the different States.

This being done, their work was completed, and it only remained to refer the rough draft of the instrument to the "Committee on Style," to prune and polish it a little — to lop off a word here, and change or add a word there, the better to conform the language to the sense, and to the proprieties of grammar and rhetoric. The Preamble, as it stood, at once presented a difficulty. All the thirteen States were named in it as adopting the instrument, but it had been provided, in the course of its deliberations by the Convention, that the new government should go into effect if nine States adopted it. Who could tell which these nine States would be? It was plainly impossible to enumerate all the States — for all of them might not adopt it — or any particular number of them, as adopting the instrument.

Further, it having been determined, as we have seen, that the Constitution should be adopted by the people of the several States, as contra-distinguished from the legislatures of the States, the phraseology of the Preamble must be made to express this idea also. To meet these two new demands upon the phraseology of the instrument, the Committee on Style adopted the expression, "We, the people of the United States," — meaning, as every one must see, "We, the people of the several States united by this instrument." And this is the foundation that the Northern advocates of a consolidated government build upon, when they declare that the people of the United States in the aggregate, as one nation, adopted the Constitution, and thus gave the fundamental law to the States, instead of the States giving it to the Federal Government.

It is well known that this phrase, "We, the people," &c., be

came a subject of discussion in the Virginia ratifying Convention.   Patrick Henry, with the prevision of a prophet, was,
as we have seen, bitterly opposed to the adoption of the Constitution.   He was its enemy *a l'outrance*.   Not having been a
member of the Convention, of 1787, that framed the instrument, and being unacquainted with the circumstances above
detailed, relative to the change which had been made in the
phraseology of its Preamble, he attacked the Constitution on
the very ground since assumed by Webster and Story, to wit:
that the instrument itself proclaimed that it had been "ordained and established" by the people of the United States in
the aggregate, instead of the people of the States.   Mr. Madison replied to Henry on this occasion.   Madison had been in
the Convention, knew, of course, all about the change of
phraseology in question, and this was his reply: "The parties
to it [the Constitution] were the people, but not the people as
composing one great society, but the people as composing
thirteen sovereignties.   If it were a consolidated government,"
continued he, "the assent of a majority of the people would
be sufficient to establish it.   But it was to be binding on the
people of a State only by their own separate consent."   There
was, of course, nothing more to be said, and the Virginia
Convention adopted the Constitution.

Madison has been called the Father of the Constitution.
Next to him, Alexander Hamilton bore the most conspicuous
part in procuring it to be adopted by the people.   Hamilton,
as is well known, did not believe much in republics; and
least of all did he believe in federal republics.   His great
object was to establish a consolidated republic, if we must
have a republic at all.   He labored zealously for this purpose, but failed.   The States, without an exception, were
in favor of the federal form; and no one knew better than
Hamilton the kind of government which had been established.

Now let us hear what Hamilton, an unwilling, but an honest
witness, says on this subject.   Of the eighty-five articles in the
"Federalist," Hamilton wrote no less than fifty.   Having failed
to procure the establishment of a consolidated government, his
next great object was, to procure the adoption by the States of

the present Constitution, and to this task, accordingly, he now addressed his great intellect and powerful energies. In turning over the pages of the "Federalist," we can scarcely go amiss in quoting Hamilton, to the point that the Constitution is a compact between the States, and not an emanation from the people of the United States in the aggregate. Let us take up the final article, for instance, the 85th. In this article we find the following expressions: "The compacts which are to embrace thirteen distinct States in a common bond of amity and Union, must necessarily be compromises of as many dissimilar interests and inclinations." Again: "The moment an alteration is made in the present plan, it becomes, to the purpose of adoption, a new one, and must undergo a new decision of each State. To its complete establishment throughout the Union, it will, therefore, require the concurrence of thirteen States."

And again: "Every Constitution for the United States must, inevitably, consist of a great variety of particulars, in which thirteen *Independent States* are to be accommodated in their interests, or opinions of interests. * * * Hence the necessity of moulding and arranging all the particulars which are to compose the whole in such a manner as to satisfy all the *parties to the compact*." Thus, we do not hear Hamilton, any more than Madison, talking of a "people of the United States in the aggregate" as having anything to do with the formation of the new charter of government. He speaks only of States, and of compacts made or to be made by States.

In view of the great importance of the question, whether it was the people of the United States in the aggregate who "ordained and established" the Constitution, or the States,— for this, indeed, is the whole *gist* of the controversy between the North and South,—I have dwelt somewhat at length on the subject, and had recourse to contemporaneous history; but this was scarcely necessary. The Constitution itself settles the whole controversy. The 7th article of that instrument reads as follows: 'The ratification of the Conventions of nine States shall be sufficient for the establishment of the Constitution between the States so ratifying the same." How is it possible to reconcile this short, explicit, and unambiguous provision with the theory I am combating? The Preamble, as explained by the Northern consolidationists, and this article, cannot possibly stand together.   It is not possible that the people of the United States in the aggregate, as one nation, "ordained and established" the Constitution, and that the States ordained and established it at the same time; for there was but one set of Conventions called, and these Conventions were called by the States, and acted in the names of the States.

Mr. Madison did, indeed, endeavor to have the ratification made in both modes, but his motion in the Convention to this effect failed, as we have seen.   Further, how could the Constitution be binding only between the States that ratified it, if it was not ratified — that is, not "ordained and established" — by them at all, but by the people of the United States in the aggregate?   As remarked by Mr. Madison, in the Virginia Convention, a ratification by the people, in the sense in which this term is used by the Northern consolidationists, would have bound all the people, and there would have been no option left the dissenting States.   But the 7th article says that they shall have an option, and that the instrument is to be binding only *between such of them as ratify it.*

With all due deference, then, to others who have written upon this vexed question, and who have differed from me in opinion, I must insist that the proof is conclusive that the Constitution is a compact between the States; and this being so, we have the admission of both Mr. Webster and Justice Story that any one of the States may withdraw from it at pleasure.

CHAPTER III.

FROM THE FOUNDATION OF THE FEDERAL GOVERNMENT DOWN TO 1830, BOTH THE NORTH AND THE SOUTH HELD THE CONSTITUTION TO BE A COMPACT BETWEEN THE STATES.

ONE of the great difficulties in arguing the question of the relative power of the States and of the Federal Government, consists in the fact that the present generation has grown up under the shadow of the great Federal monster, and has been blinded by its giant proportions. They see around them all the paraphernalia and power of a great government — its splendid capital, its armies, its fleets, its Chief Magistrate, its legislature, and its judiciary — and they find it difficult to realize the fact, that all this grandeur is not self-created, but the offspring of the States.

When our late troubles were culminating, men were heard frequently to exclaim, with plaintive energy, "What! have we no government capable of preserving itself? Is our Government a mere rope of sand, that may be destroyed at the will of the States?" These men seemed to think that there was but one government to be preserved, and that that was the Government of the United States. Less than a century had elapsed since the adoption of the Constitution, and the generation now on the theatre of events had seemingly forgotten, that the magnificent structure, which they contemplated with so much admiration, was but a creature of the States; that it had been made by them for their convenience, and necessarily held the tenure of its life at sufferance. They lost sight of the fact that the State governments, who were the creators of the Federal Government, were the governments to be preserved, if there should be any antagonism between them and the Federal Government; and that their services, as well as their sympathies, belonged to the former in preference to the latter. What with the teachings of Webster and Story, and a host of satellites, the dazzling splendor of the Federal Government, and the overshadowing and corrupting influences of its power, nearly a whole generation in the North had grown up in ignorance of the true nature of the institutions, under which they lived.

This change in the education of the people had taken place since about the year 1830; for, up to that time, both of the great political parties of the country, the Whigs as well as the Democrats, had been State-Rights in doctrine. A very common error has prevailed on this subject. It has been said, that the North and the South have always been widely separated in their views of the Constitution; that the men of the North have always been consolidationists, whilst the men of the South have been secessionists. Nothing can be farther from the truth. Whilst the North and the South, from the very commencement of the Government, have been at swords' points, on many questions of mere construction and policy,—the North claiming that more ample powers had been granted the Federal Government, than the South was willing to concede,—there never was any material difference between them down to the year 1830, as to the true nature of their Government. They all held it to be a federal compact, and the Northern people were as jealous of the rights of their States under it, as the Southern people.

In proof of this, I have only to refer to a few of the well-known facts of our political history. Thomas Jefferson penned the famous Kentucky Resolutions of '98 and '99. The first of those resolutions is in these words: "*Resolved*, That the several States comprising the United States of America are not united on the principles of unlimited submission to their general Government; but that by a compact, under the style and title of the Constitution of the United States, and of amendments thereto, they constitute a general Government for special purposes; and that whensoever the general Government assumes undelegated powers, its acts are unauthoritative, void and of no force; that to this compact each State acceded as a State, and is an integral party, its co-States forming, as to itself, the other party; that the government created by this compact

was not made the exclusive or final judge of the extent of
the powers delegated to itself, since that would have made
its discretion, not the Constitution, the measure of its powers,
but that, as in all cases of compact among persons having
no common judge, each party has an equal right to judge
for itself, as well of infractions, as of the mode and measure of
redress."

It is unnecessary to quote the other resolution, as the above
contains all that is sufficient for my purpose, which is to show
that Mr. Jefferson was a secessionist, and that *with this record*
he went before the American people as a candidate for the Presidency, with the following results: In 1800 he beat his opponent, John Adams, who represented the consolidationists of
that day, by a majority of 8 votes in the Electoral College.
In 1804, being a candidate for re-election, he beat his opponent
by the overwhelming majority of 162, to 14 votes. In the
Northern States alone, Mr. Jefferson received 85 votes, whilst
in the same States his opponent received but 9. This was
a pretty considerable indorsement of secession by the Northern States.

In 1808, Mr. Madison, who penned the Virginia Resolutions
of '98, similar in tenor to the Kentucky Resolutions, became
a candidate for the Presidency, and beat his opponent by a
vote of 122 to 47; the Northern majority, though somewhat
diminished, being still 50 to 39 votes. Mr. Madison was re-
elected in 1812, and in 1816, James Monroe was elected President by a vote of 183 to his opponent's 34; and more than
one half of these 183 votes came from the Northern States.
In 1820, Mr. Monroe was re-elected over John Quincy Adams,
of Massachusetts, by a majority of 231 votes to 13. Besides
Monroe and Adams, Crawford and Jackson were also candidates, but these two latter received only 11 votes between
them. This last election is especially remarkable, as showing
that there was no opposition to Jefferson's doctrine of State-
Rights, since *all* the candidates were of that creed. The
opposition had been so often defeated, and routed in former
elections, that they had not strength enough left to put a candidate in the field.

John Quincy Adams succeeded Mr. Monroe, and his State-.

Rights doctrines are well known. He expressed them as follows: "The indissoluble link of union between the people of the several States of this confederated nation, is, after all, not in the *right*, but in the *heart*. If the day should ever come (may heaven avert it) when the affections of the people of these States shall be alienated from each other; when the fraternal spirit shall give way to cold indifference, or *collision of interests shall fester into hatred*, the bands of political association will not long hold together parties, no longer attracted by the magnetism of conciliated interests, and kindly sympathies; and *far better will it be for the people of the dis-united States to part in friendship with each other, than to be held together by constraint.* Then will be the time for reverting to the precedents, which occurred at the formation, and adoption of the Constitution, to form again a more perfect union, by dissolving that which could no longer bind, and to leave the separated parts to be reunited *by the law of political gravitation to the centre.*"

General Jackson succeeded Mr. Adams in 1828, and was re-elected in 1832. It was during his administration that the *heresy* was first promulgated by Mr. Webster, that the Constitution was not a compact between the States, but an instrument of government, " ordained, and established," by the people of the United States, in the aggregate, as one nation. With respect to the New England States in particular, there is other and more pointed evidence, that they agreed with Mr. Jefferson, and the South down to the year 1830, on this question of State rights, than is implied in the Presidential elections above quoted. Massachusetts, the leader of these States in intellect, and in energy, impatient of control herself, has always sought to control others. This was, perhaps, but natural. All mankind are prone to consult their own interests. Selfishness, unfortunately, is one of the vices of our nature, which few are found capable of struggling against effectually.

The New England people were largely imbued with the Puritan element. Their religious doctrines gave them a gloomy asceticism of character, and an intolerance of other men's opinions quite remarkable. In their earlier history as colonists, there is much in the way of uncharitableness and persecution, which a liberal mind could wish to see blotted out. True to these characteristics, which I may almost call instincts, the New England States have always been the most refractory States of the Union. As long as they were in a minority, and hopeless of the control of the Government, they stood strictly on their State rights, in resisting such measures as were unpalatable to them, even to the extremity of threatening secession; and it was only when they saw that the tables were turned, and that it was possible for them to seize the reins of the Government, that they abandoned their State-Rights doctrines, and became consolidationists.

One of the first causes of the dissatisfaction of the New England States with the General Government was the purchase of Louisiana, by Mr. Jefferson, in 1803. It arose out of their jealousy of the balance of power between the States. The advantages to result to the United States from the purchase of this territory were patent to every one. It completed the continuity of our territory, from the head waters of the Mississippi, to the sea, and unlocked the mouths of that great river. But Massachusetts saw in the purchase, nothing more than the creation of additional Southern States, to contest, with her, the future control of the Government. She could see no authority for it in the Constitution, and she threatened, that if it were consummated, she would secede from the Union. Her Legislature passed the following resolution on the subject: "*Resolved*, That the annexation of Louisiana to the Union, transcends the Constitutional power of the Government of the United States. It formed a new Confederacy, to which the States [not the people of the United States, in the aggregate] united by the former compact, are not bound to adhere."

This purchase of Louisiana rankled, for a long time, in the breast of New England. It was made, as we have seen, in 1803, and in 1811 the subject again came up for consideration; this time, in the shape of a bill before Congress for the admission of Louisiana as a State. One of the most able and influential members of Congress of that day from Massachusetts was Mr. Josiah Quincy. In a speech on this bill, that gentlemen uttered the following declaration: "If this bill passes, it is my deliberate opinion that it is virtually a dissolution of the Union; that it will free the States from their moral obligation, and as it will be the right of all, so it will be the duty of some definitely to prepare for separation, amicably if they can, violently if they must."

Time passed on, and the difficulties which led to our War of 1812, with Great Britain, began to rise above the political horizon. Great Britain began to impress seamen from New England merchant ships, and even went so far, at last, as to take some enlisted men from on board the United States ship of war Chesapeake. Massachusetts was furious; she insisted that war should be declared forthwith against Great Britain. The Southern States, which had comparatively little interest in this matter, except so far as the federal honor was concerned, came generously to the rescue of the shipping States, and war was declared. But the first burst of her passion having spent itself, Massachusetts found that she had been indiscreet; her shipping began to suffer more than she had anticipated, and she began now to cry aloud as one in pain. She denounced the war, and the Administration which was carrying it on; and not content with this, in connection with other New England States, she organized a Convention, at Hartford, in Connecticut, with a view to adopt some ulterior measures. We find the following among the records of that Convention: "Events may prove, that the causes of our calamities are deep, and permanent. They may be found to proceed not merely from blindness of prejudice, pride of opinion, violence of party spirit, or the confusion of the times; but they may be traced to implacable combinations, of individuals, *or of States*, to monopolize office, and to trample, without remorse, upon the rights and interests of the commercial sections of the Union. Whenever it shall appear, that these causes are radical, and permanent, *a separation by equitable arrangement, will be preferable to an alliance, by constraint, among nominal friends but real enemies, inflamed by mutual hatred, and jealousy, and inviting, by intestine divisions, contempt and aggressions from abroad.*" Having recorded this opinion of what should be the policy of the New England States, in the category mentioned, the "Journal of the Convention" goes on to declare what it considers the right of the States, in the premises. "That acts of Congress, in violation of the Constitution, are absolutely void, is an indisputable position. It does not, however, consist with the respect, from a *Confederate State* toward the General

Government, to fly to open resistance, upon every infraction of the Constitution. The mode, and the energy of the opposition should always conform to the nature of the violation, the intention of the authors, the extent of the evil inflicted, the determination manifested to persist in it, and the danger of delay. But in case of deliberate, dangerous, and palpable infractions of the Constitution, *affecting the sovereignty of the State,* and liberties of the people, it is not only the right, but the *duty,* of each State *to interpose its authority* for their protection, in the manner best calculated to secure that end. When emergencies occur, which are either beyond the reach of judicial tribunals, or too pressing to admit of the delay incident to their forms, *States,* which have no common umpire, *must be their own judges,* and *execute their own decisions.*" These proceedings took place in January, 1815. A deputation was appointed to lay the complaints of New England before the Federal Government, and there is no predicting what might have occurred, if the delegates had not found, that peace had been declared, when they arrived at Washington.

It thus appears, that from 1803–4 to 1815, New England was constantly in the habit of speaking of the dissolution of the Union—her leading men deducing this right from the nature of the compact between the States. It is curious and instructive, and will well repay the perusal, to read the "Journal of the Hartford Convention," so replete is it with sound constitutional doctrine. It abounds in such expressions as these: "The constitutional compact;" "It must be the duty of the State to watch over the rights *reserved,* as of the United States to exercise the powers *which were delegated;*" the right of conscription is "not delegated to Congress by the Constitution, and the exercise of it would not be less dangerous to their liberties, than hostile to the *sovereignty of the States.*" The odium which has justly fallen upon the Hartford Convention, has not been because of its doctrines, for these were as sound, as we have seen, as the Virginia and Kentucky Resolutions of '98 and '99, but because it was a secret conclave, gotten together, *in a time of war,* when the country was hard pressed by a foreign enemy; the war having, in fact, been undertaken for the benefit of the very shipping States which were threatening to dissolve the Union on account of it.

Mr. John Quincy Adams, the sixth President of the United States, himself, as is well known, a Massachusetts man, speaking of this dissatisfaction of the New England States with the Federal Government, says: "That their object was, and had been, for several years, a dissolution of the Union and the establishment of a separate Confederation, he knew from unequivocal evidence, although not provable in a court of law; and that in case of a civil war, the aid of Great Britain, to effect that purpose, would be assuredly resorted to, as it would be indispensably necessary to their design." See Mr. Adams' letter of Dec. 30th, 1828, in reply to Harrison Gray Otis and others.

We have thus seen, that for forty years, or from the foundation of the Federal Government, to 1830, there was no material difference of opinion between the sections, as to the nature of the league or compact of government which they had formed. There was this difference between the sections, however. The South, during this entire period of forty years, had substantially controlled the Government; not by force, it is true, of her own majorities, but with the aid of a few of the Northern States. She was the dominant or ruling power in the Government. During all this time, she conscientiously adhered to her convictions, and respected the rights of the minority, though she might have wielded her power, if she had been so inclined, to her own advantage.

Constitutions are made for the protection of minorities, and she scrupulously adhered to this idea. Minorities naturally cling to the guarantees and defences provided for them in the fundamental law; it is only when they become strong, when they throw off their pupilage, and become majorities, that their principles and their virtues are really tested. It is in politics, as in religion—the weaker party is always the tolerant party. Did the North follow this example set her by the South? No; the moment she became strong enough, she recanted all the doctrines under which she had sought shelter, tore the Constitution into fragments, scattered it to the winds; and finally, when the South threw herself on the defensive, as Massachusetts had threatened to do, in 1803 and 1815, she subjugated her.

What was the powerful motive which thus induced the North to overthrow the government which it had labored so

assiduously with the South to establish, and which it had construed in common with the South, for the period of forty years?
It was the motive which generally influences human conduct;
it was the same motive which Patrick Henry had so clearly
foreseen, when he warned the people of Virginia against entering into the federal compact; telling them, that interested
majorities never had, in the history of the world, and never
would respect the rights of minorities.

The great "American System," as it has been called, had in
the meantime arisen, championed by no less a personage than
Henry Clay of Kentucky. In 1824, and again in 1828, oppressive tariffs had been enacted for the protection of New
England manufacturers. The North was manufacturing, the
South non-manufacturing. The effect of these tariffs was to
shut out all foreign competition, and compel the Southern con-
sumer to pay two prices for all the textile fabrics he consumed,
from the clothing of his negroes to his own broadcloth coats.
So oppressive, unjust, and unconstitutional were these acts
considered, that South Carolina nullified them in 1830. Immediately all New England was arrayed against South Carolina.
An entire and rapid change took place in the political creed
of that section. New England orators and jurists rose up to
proclaim that the Constitution was not a compact between the
States. Webster thundered in the Senate, and Story wrote
his "Commentaries on the Constitution." These giants had a
herculean task before them; nothing less than the falsifying
of the whole political history of the country, for the previous
forty years; but their barren and inhospitable section of the
country had been touched by the enchanter's wand, and its
rocky hills, and sterile fields, incapable of yielding even a
scanty subsistence to its numerous population, were to become
glad with the music of the spindle and the shuttle; and the
giants undertook the task! How well they have accomplished
it, the reader will see, in the course of these pages, when,
toward the conclusion of my narrative, he will be called upon
to view the fragments of the grand old Constitution, which has
been shattered, and which will lie in such mournful profusion
around him; the monuments at once of the folly and crimes
of a people, who have broken up a government — a free government — which might else have endured for centuries.

CHAPTER IV.

WAS SECESSION TREASON?

A FEW more words, and we shall be in a condition to answer the question which stands at the head of this chapter. Being a legal question, it will depend entirely upon the constitutional right the Southern States may have had to withdraw from the Union, without reference to considerations of expediency, or of moral right; these latter will be more appropriately considered, when we come to speak of the causes which impelled the Southern States to the step. I have combated many of the arguments presented by the other side, but a few others remain to be noticed.

It has been said, that, admitting that the Constitution was a federal compact, yet the States did in fact cede away a part of their sovereignty, and from this the inference has been deduced, that they no longer remained sovereign for the purpose of recalling the part, which had been ceded away. This is a question which arises wholly under the laws of nations. It is admitted, that the States were independent sovereignties, before they formed the Constitution. We have only, therefore, to consult the international code, to ascertain to what extent the granting away of a portion of their sovereignty affected the remainder. Vattel, treating of this identical point, speaks as follows: "Several sovereign and independent States may unite themselves together by a perpetual confederacy, without ceasing to be, each individually, a perfect State. They will, together, constitute a federal republic; their joint deliberations will not impair the sovereignty of each member, though they may, in certain respects, *put some restraint upon the exercise of it*, in virtue of *voluntary* engagements." That was just what the American States did, when they formed the Federal Constitution; they put some voluntary restraint upon their sovereignty, for the furtherance of a common object.

If they are restrained, by the Constitution, from doing certain things, the restraint was self-imposed, for it was they who ordained, and established the instrument, and not a common superior. They, each, agreed that they would forbear to do certain things, if their copartners would forbear to do the same things. As plain as this seems, no less an authority than that of Mr. Webster has denied it; for, in his celebrated argument against Mr. Calhoun, already referred to, he triumphantly exclaimed, that the States were not sovereign, because *they were restrained of a portion of their liberty by the Constitution.* See how he perverts the whole tenor of the instrument, in his endeavor to build up those manufactories of which we spoke in the last chapter. He says: "However men may think this ought to be, the fact is, that *the people of the United States* have chosen to *impose control* on State sovereignty. There are those, doubtless, who wish that they had been left without restraint; but the Constitution has ordered the matter differently. To make war, for instance, is an exercise of sovereignty, but, the Constitution declares that no State shall declare war. To coin money is another act of sovereign power; but no State is at liberty to coin money. Again; the Constitution says, that no sovereign State shall be so sovereign, as to make a treaty. These prohibitions, it must be confessed, are a control on the State sovereignty of South Carolina, as well as of the other States, which does not arise from her feelings of honorable justice."

Here we see, plainly, the germ of the monstrous heresy that has riven the States asunder, in our day. The "people of the United States," a common superior, ordained and established the Constitution, says Mr. Webster, and imposed restraints upon the States! However some might wish they had been left without restraint, the Constitution has "*ordained it differently!*" And the ostrich stomach of the North received, and digested this monstrous perversion of the plainest historical truth, in order that the spindle might whirr on, and the shuttle dance from side to side of the loom.

Following the idea of Mr. Webster, that the people of the

United States gave constitutional law to the States, instead of
receiving it from them, Northern writers frequently ask, in
what part of the Constitution, is the doctrine of secession found?
In no part.   It was not necessary to put it there.   The States
who formed the instrument, delegated certain powers to the
Federal Government, retaining all others.   Did they part, with
the right of secession?   Could they have parted with it, without consenting to a merger of their sovereignty?   And so far
from doing this, we have seen with what jealous care they protested against even the implication of such a merger, in the
10th amendment to the Constitution.   If the power was not
parted with, by explicit grant, did it not remain to them, even
before the 10th amendment was adopted, and still more, if
possible, after it was adopted?

   To make it still more apparent, that the common understanding among the Fathers of the Constitution was, that this
right of secession was reserved, it is only necessary to refer to
what took place, during the transition from the old to the new
government.   The thirteen original States seceded, as we have
seen, from the Articles of Confederation, not unanimously, or
all together, but one by one, each State acting for itself, without consulting the interests, or inclinations of the others.   One
of the provisions of those Articles was as follows: "Every
State shall abide by the determination of the United States,
in Congress assembled, in all questions, which, by this Confederation, are submitted to them; and the Articles of this
Confederation shall be inviolably observed by every State, and
the Union shall be *perpetual;* nor shall any alteration, at any
time hereafter. be made in any of them, unless such alteration
be agreed to, in a Congress of the United States, and be afterward confirmed *by the legislature of every State.*"

   Now, it is a pertinent, and instructive fact, that no similar
provision of perpetuity was engrafted in the new Constitution.
There must have been a motive for this — it could not have
been a mere accidental omission — and the motive probably
was, that the Convention of 1787 were ashamed to attempt, a
second time, to bind sovereign States, by *a rope of sand,* which
they, themselves, were in the act of pulling asunder.   It was in
accordance with this understanding, that both New York and

Virginia, in their ratifications of the new Constitution, expressly reserved to themselves the right of secession; and no objection was made to such conditional ratifications. The reservations made by these States enure, as a matter of course, to the benefit of all the States, as they were all to go into the new Union, on precisely the same footing.

In the extract from Mr. Webster's speech, which has been given above, it is alleged among other things, that the States are not sovereign, because they cannot make treaties; and this disability also has been urged as an argument against secession. The disability, like others, was self-imposed, and, as any one may see, was intended to be binding on the States only so long as the contract which they were then forming should endure. The Confederate States respected this obligation while they remained in the Federal Union. They scrupulously forbore from contracting with each other until they had resumed, each for itself, their original sovereignty; they were then not only free to contract with each other, but to do and perform all the other acts enumerated by Mr. Webster; the act of declaring war included, even though this war should be against their late confederates.

The truth is, the more we sift these arguments of our late enemies, the less real merit there appears in them. The facts of history are too stubborn, and refuse to be bent to conform to the new doctrines. We see it emblazoned on every page of American history for forty years, that the Constitution was a compact between the States; that the Federal Government was created, by, and for the benefit of the States, and possessed and could possess no other power than such as was conferred upon it by the States; that the States reserved to themselves all the powers not granted, and that they took especial pains to guard their sovereignty, in terms, by an amendment to the Constitution, lest, by possibility, their intentions in the formation of the new government, should be misconstrued.

In the course of time this government is perverted from its original design. Instead of remaining the faithful and impartial agent of all the States, a faction obtains control of it, in the interests of some of them, and turns it, as an engine of oppression, against the others. These latter, after long and patient suffering, after having exhausted all their means of defence, within the Union, withdraw from the agent the powers which they had conferred upon him, form a new Confederacy, and desire "to be let alone."   And what is the consequence? They are denounced as rebels and traitors, armies are equipped, and fleets provided, and a war of subjugation is waged against them.   What says the reader?   Does he see rebellion and treason lurking in the conduct of these States?   Are they, indeed, in his opinion, in face of the record which he has inspected, so bereft of their sovereignty, as to be incapable of defending themselves, except with halters around the necks of their citizens?

Let us examine this latter question of halters for a moment. The States existed before the Federal Government; the citizens of the States owed allegiance to their respective States, and to none others.   By what process was any portion of this allegiance transferred to the Federal Government, and to what extent was it transferred?   It was transferred by the States, themselves, when they entered into the federal compact, and not by the individual citizens, for these had no power to make such a transfer.   Although it be admitted, that a citizen of any one of the States may have had the right to expatriate himself entirely—and this was not so clear a doctrine at that day —and transfer his allegiance to another government, yet it is quite certain, that he could not, *ex mero motu*, divide his allegiance.   His allegiance then was transferred to the Federal Government, by his State, whether he would or not.

Take the case of Patrick Henry, for example.   He resisted the adoption of the Federal Constitution, by the State of Virginia, with all the energies of an ardent nature, solemnly believing that his State was committing suicide.   And yet, when Virginia did adopt that Constitution, he became, by virtue of that act, a citizen of the United States, and owed allegiance to the Federal Government.   He had been born in the hallowed old Commonwealth.   In the days of his boyhood he had played on the banks of the Appomattox, and fished in its waters.   As he grew to man's estate, all his cherished hopes, and aspirations clustered around his beloved State.   The bones of his ancestors were interred in her soil; his loves, his joys, his sorrows were all centred there. In short, he felt the inspiration of patriotism, that noble sentiment which nerves men to do, and dare, unto the death, for their native soil. Will it be said, *can* it be said, without revolting all the best feelings of the human heart, that if Patrick Henry had lived to see a war of subjugation waged against his native State, he would have been a traitor for striking in her defence? Was this one of the results which our ancestors designed, when they framed the federal compact? It would be uncharitable to accuse them of such folly, and stupidity, nay of such cruelty. If this doctrine be true, that secession is treason, then our ancestors framed a government, which could not fail to make traitors of their descendants, in case of a conflict between the States, and that government, let them act as they would.

It was frequently argued in the "Federalist," and elsewhere, by those who were persuading the States to adopt the Federal Constitution, that the State would have a sufficient guarantee of protection, in the love, and affection of its citizens—that the citizen would naturally cling to his State, and side with her against the Federal Government—that, in fact, it was rather to be apprehended that the Federal Government would be too weak, and the States too strong, for this reason, instead of the converse of the proposition being true. It was not doubted, in that day, that the primary and paramount allegiance of the citizen was due to his State, and, that, in case of a conflict between her and the Federal Government, his State would have the right to withdraw his allegiance, from that Government. If it was she who transferred it, and if she had the right to transfer it, it follows beyond question, that she would have the right to withdraw it. It was not a case for the voluntary action of the citizen, either way; he could not, of his own free will, either give his allegiance to the Federal Government, or take it away.

If this be true, observe in what a dilemma he has been placed, on the hypothesis that secession is treason. If he adheres to the Federal Government, after his State has withdrawn his allegiance from that Government, and takes up arms against his State, he becomes a traitor to his State. If he adheres to his State, and takes up arms against the Federal

Goverment, he becomes a traitor to that Government.   He is thus a traitor either way, and there is no helping himself.   Is this consistent with the supposed wisdom of the political Fathers, those practical, common sense men, who formed the Federal Constitution?

The mutations of governments, like all human events, are constantly going on.   No government stands still, any more than the individuals of which it is composed.   The only difference is, that the changes are not quite so obvious to the generation which views them.   The framers of the Constitution did not dare to hope that they had formed a government, that was to last for-ever.   Nay, many of them had serious misgivings as to the result of the *experiment* they were making.   Is it possible, then, that those men so legislated, as to render it morally cer-tain, that if their experiment should fail, their descendants must become either slaves or traitors?   If the doctrine that seces-sion is treason be true, it matters not how grievously a State might be oppressed, by the Federal Government; she has been deprived of the power of lawful resistance, and must regain her liberty, if at all, like other enslaved States, at the hazard of war, and rebellion.   Was this the sort of experiment in govern-ment, that our forefathers supposed they were making?   Every reader of history knows that it was not.

CHAPTER V.

ANOTHER BRIEF HISTORICAL RETROSPECT.

IN the previous chapters, I have given a brief outline of the history and formation of the Federal Constitution, proving, by abundant reference to the Fathers, and to the instrument itself, that it was the intention of the former to draft, and that they did draft, a *federal compact* of government, which compact was " ordained, and established," by the States, in their sovereign capacity, and not by the people of the United States, in the aggregate, as one nation. It resulted from this statement of the question, that the States had the legal, and constitutional right to withdraw from the compact, at pleasure, without reference to any cause of quarrel. Accordingly, nothing has yet been said about the causes which impelled the Southern States to a separation, except indeed incidentally, when the tariff system was alluded to, as the motive which had induced Massachusetts and the other Northern States, to change their State-Rights doctrine.

It was stated in the opening chapter, that the judgment which posterity will form, upon the great conflict between the sections, will depend, mainly, upon the answers which we may be able to give to two questions: First, Had the South the right to dissolve the compact of government, under which it had lived with the North? and secondly, Was there sufficient ground for this dissolution? Having answered the first question—imperfectly, I fear, but yet as fully, as was consistent, with the design of these pages—I propose now to consider, very briefly, the second. I would gladly have left all this preliminary work to other, and abler pens, but I do not consider that the memoirs of any actor in the late war, who, like myself, was an officer in the old service, and who withdrew from that service, because of the breaking out of the war—or rather because of the secession of his State—would be complete without, at least, a brief reference to the reasons, which controlled his judgment.

The American Constitution died of a disease, that was inherent in it. It was framed on false principles, inasmuch as the attempt was made, through its means, of binding together, in a republican form of government, two dissimilar peoples, with widely dissimilar interests. Monarchial governments may accomplish this, since they are founded on force, but republican governments never. Austria, and Russia, pin together, in our day, with their bayonets, many dissimilar peoples, but if a republic should make the attempt, that moment it must, of necessity, cease to be a republic, since the very foundation of such a government is the consent of the governed. The secession of the Southern States was a mere corollary of the American proposition of government; and the Northern States stultified themselves, the moment they attempted to resist it. The consent of the Southern States being wanted, there should have been an end of the question.

If the Northern States were not satisfied to let them go, but entertained, on the contrary, a desire to restrain them by force, this was a proof, that those States had become tired of the republican form, and desired to change it. But they should have been honest about it; they should have avowed their intentions from the beginning, and not have waged the war, as so many republics, endeavoring to coerce other republics, into a forced union with them. To have been logical, they should have obliterated the State boundaries, and have declared all the States—as well the Northern States, as the Southern—so many counties of a consolidated government. But even then, they could not have made war upon any considerable number of those counties, without violating the fundamental American idea of a government—the consent of the governed. The right of self-government was vindicated in the Declaration of Independence, in favor of three millions of the subjects of Great Britain. In the States of the Southern Confederacy, there were eight millions.

The American Republic, as has been said, was a failure, because of the antagonism of the two peoples, attempted to be bound together, in the same government. If there is to be but a single government in these States, in the future, it cannot be a republic. De Toqueville saw this, thirty years ago. In his "Democracy in America" he described these States, as "more like hostile nations, than rival parties, under one government."

This distinguished Frenchman saw, as with the eye of intuition, the canker which lay at the heart of the federal compact. He saw looming up, in the dim distance, the ominous, and hideous form of that unbridled, and antagonistic Majority, which has since rent the country in twain—a majority based on the views, and interests of one section, arrayed against the views, and interests of the other section. "The majority," said he, "in that country, exercises a prodigious, actual authority, and a moral influence which is scarcely less preponderant; no obstacles exist, which can impede, or so much as retard its progress, or which can induce it to heed the complaints of those whom it crushes upon its path. * * * This state of things is fatal, in itself, and dangerous for the future. * * * If the free institutions of America are ever destroyed, that event may be attributed to the unlimited authority of the majority. * * * Anarchy will then be the result, but it will have been brought about by despotism."

Precisely so; liberty is always destroyed by the multitude, in the name of liberty. Majorities within the limits of constitutional restraints are harmless, but the moment they lose sight of these restraints, the many-headed monster becomes more tyrannical, than the tyrant with a single head; numbers harden its conscience, and embolden it, in the perpetration of crime. And when this majority, in a free government, becomes a faction, or, in other words, represents certain classes and interests to the detriment of other classes, and interests, farewell to public liberty; the people must either become enslaved, or there must be a disruption of the government. This result would follow, even if the people lived under a consolidated government, and were homogenous: much more, then, must it follow, when the government is federal in form, and the States are, in the words of De Toqueville, "more like hostile nations, than rival parties, under one government." These States are, and indeed always have been rival nations.

The dissimilarity between the people of the Northern, and

the people of the Southern States has always been remarked upon, by observant foreigners, and it has not escaped the attention of our own historians. Indeed it could not be otherwise, for the origin of the two sections has been diverse. Virginia, and Massachusetts were the two original germs, from which the great majority of the American populations has sprung; and no two peoples, speaking the same language, and coming from the same country, could have been more dissimilar, in education, taste, and habits, and even in natural instincts, than were the adventurers who settled these two colonies. Those who sought a new field of adventure for themselves, and affluence for their posterity, in the more congenial climate of the Chesapeake, were the gay, and dashing cavaliers, who, as a class, afterward adhered to the fortunes of the Charleses, whilst the first settlers of Massachusetts were composed of the same materials, that formed the "Praise-God-Barebones" parliament of Cromwell.

These two peoples, seem to have had an instinctive repugnance, the one to the other. To use a botanical phrase, the Puritan was a seedling of the English race, which had been unknown to it before. It had few, or none of the characteristics of the original stock. Gloomy, saturnine, and fanatical, in disposition, it seemed to repel all the more kindly, and generous impulses of our nature, and to take a pleasure in pulling down everything, that other men had built up; not so much, as its subsequent history would seem to show, because the work was faulty, as because it had been done by other hands than their own. They hated tyranny, for instance, but it was only because they were not, themselves, the tyrants; they hated religious intolerance, but it was only when not practised by themselves.

Natural affinities attracted like unto like. The Cavalier sought refuge with the Cavalier, and the Puritan with the Puritan, for a century, and more. When the fortunes of the Charleses waned, the Cavaliers fled to Virginia; when the fortunes of Cromwell waned, the Puritans fled to Massachusetts. Trade occasionally drew the two peoples together, but they were repelled at all other points. Thus these germs grew, step by step, into two distinct nations. A different civilization was naturally developed in each.   The two countries were different in climate, and physical features—the climate of the one being cold and inhospitable, and its soil rugged, and sterile, whilst the climate of the other was soft, and genial, and its soil generous, and fruitful.   As a result of these differences of climate, and soil, the pursuits of the two peoples became different, the one being driven to the ocean, and to the mechanic arts, for subsistence, and the other betaking itself to agriculture.

Another important element soon presented itself, to widen the social, and economical breach, which had taken place between the two peoples—African slavery.   All the Colonies, at first, became slaveholding, but it was soon found, that slave labor was unprofitable in the North, where the soil was so niggard, in its productions, and where, besides, the white man could labor.   One, by one, the Northern States got rid of their slaves, as soon as they made this discovery.   In the South, the case was different.   The superior fertility of the soil, and the greater geniality of the climate enabled the planter to employ the African to advantage; and thus slave labor was engrafted on our system of civilization, as one of its permanent features.

The effect was, as before remarked, a still greater divergence between the two peoples.   The wealth of the South soon began to outstrip that of the North.   Education and refinement followed wealth.   Whilst the civilization of the North was coarse, and practical, that of the South was more intellectual, and refined.   This is said in no spirit of disparagement of our Northern brethren; it was the natural, and inevitable result of the different situations of the two peoples.   In the North, almost every young man was under the necessity, during our colonial existence, of laboring with his own hands, for the means of subsistence.   There was neither the requisite leisure, nor the requisite wealth to bring about a very refined system of civilization.   The life of a Southern planter on the other hand with his large estates, and hundreds of vassals, with his profuse hospitality, and luxurious style of living, resembled more that of the feudatories of the middle ages, than that of any modern gentleman out of the Southern States.

It is not my object to express a preference for either of these modes of civilization—each, no doubt, had its advantages, and disadvantages—but to glance at them, merely, for the purpose of showing the dissimilarity of the two peoples; their uncongeniality, and want of adaptation, socially, the one to the other With social institutions as wide asunder as the poles, and with their every material interest antagonistic, the separation of the two peoples, sooner or later, was a logical sequence.

As had been anticipated by Patrick Henry, and others, the moment the new government went into operation, parties began to be formed, on sectional interests and sectional prejudices. The North wanted protection for her shipping, in the way of discriminating tonnage dues, and the South was opposed to such protection. The North wanted a bank, to facilitate their commercial operations; the South was opposed to it. The North wanted protection for their manufactures, the South was opposed to it. There was no warrant, of course, for any of these schemes of protection in the Federal Constitution; they were, on the contrary, subversive of the original design of that instrument. The South has been called aggressive. She was thrown on the defensive, in the first Congress, and has remained so, from that day to this. She never had the means to be aggressive, having been always in a minority, in both branches of the Legislature. It is not consistent with the scope of these memoirs, to enter, at large, into the political disputes which culminated in secession. They are many, and various, and would fill volumes. It will be sufficient to sketch the history of one or two of the more important of them.

The "American System," of which Mr. Clay, of Kentucky, became the champion, and to which allusion has already been made, became the chief instrument of oppression of the Southern States, through a long series of years. I prefer to let a late distinguished Senator, from the State of Missouri, Mr. Benton, tell this tale of spoliation. On the slavery question, Mr. Benton was with the North, he cannot, therefore, be accused of being a witness unduly favorable to the South. In a speech in the Senate, in 1828, he declared himself, as follows: "I feel for the sad changes, which have taken place in the South, during the last fifty years. Before the Revolution, it was the seat of wealth, as well as hospitality. Money, and all it commanded, abounded there. But how is it now? All this is reversed. Wealth has fled from the South, and settled in regions north of the Potomac; and this in the face of the fact, that the South, in four staples alone, has exported produce, since the Revolution, to the value of eight hundred millions of dollars; and the North has exported comparatively nothing. Such an export would indicate unparalleled wealth, but what is the fact? In the place of wealth, a universal pressure for money was felt—not enough for current expenses—the price of all property down—the country drooping, and languishing—towns and cities decaying—and the frugal habits of the people pushed to the verge of universal self-denial, for the preservation of their family estates. Such a result is a strange, and wonderful phenomenon. It calls upon statesmen to inquire into the cause. Under Federal legislation, the exports of the South have been the basis of the Federal revenue. * * * *Virginia, the two Corolinas, and Georgia, may be said to defray three-fourths, of the annual expense of supporting the Federal Government;* and of this great sum, annually furnished by them, nothing, or next to nothing is returned to them, in the shape of Government expenditures. That expenditure flows in an opposite direction—it flows northwardly, in one uniform, uninterrupted, and perennial stream. *This is the reason why wealth disappears from the South and rises up in the North. Federal legislation does all this.* It does it by the simple process of eternally taking from the South, and returning nothing to it. If it returned to the South the whole, or even a good part, of what it exacted, the four States south of the Potomac might stand the action of the system, but the South must be exhausted of its money, and its property, by a course of legislation, which is forever taking away, and never returning anything. Every new tariff increases the force of this action. No tariff has ever yet included Virginia, the two Carolinas, and Georgia, except to increase the burdens imposed upon them."

This picture is not overdrawn; it is the literal truth. Before the war the Northern States, and especially the New England States, exported next to nothing, and yet they "blossomed as the rose." The picturesque hills of New England were dotted with costly mansions, erected with money, of which the Southern planters had been despoiled, by means of the tariffs of which Mr. Benton spoke. Her harbors frowned with forti- fications, constructed by the same means. Every cove and inlet had its lighthouse, for the benefit of New England ship- ping, three fourths of the expense of erecting which had been paid by the South, and even the cod, and mackerel fisheries of New England were *bountied*, on the bald pretext, that they were nurseries for manning the navy.

The South resisted this wholesale robbery, to the best of her ability. Some few of the more generous of the Northern rep- resentatives in Congress came to her aid, but still she was overborne; and the curious reader, who will take the pains to consult the "Statutes at Large," of the American Congress, will find on an average, a tariff for every five years recorded on their pages; the cormorants increasing in rapacity, the more they devoured. No wonder that Mr. Lincoln when asked, "why not let the South go?" replied, "Let the South go! *where then shall we get our revenue ?*"

This system of spoliation was commenced in 1816. The doctrine of protection was not, at first, boldly avowed. A heavy debt had been contracted during the war of 1812, with Great Britain, just then terminated. It became necessary to raise revenue to pay this debt, as well as to defray the current expenses of the government, and for these laudable purposes, the tariff of 1816 was enacted. The North had not yet be- come the overshadowing power, which it has become in our day. It was comparatively modest, and only asked, that, in adjusting the duties under the tariff, such *incidental* protection, as might not be inconsistent with the main object of the bill, to wit, the raising of revenue, should be given to Northern manufactures. It was claimed that these manufactures had sprung up, *sua sponte*, during the war, and had materially aided the country in prosecuting the war, and that they would languish, and die, unless protected, in this incidental manner. This seemed but just and reasonable, and some of the ablest of our Southern men gave their assent to the pro- position; among others, Mr. Calhoun of South Carolina, and Mr. Clay of Kentucky.

The latter, in particular, then a young member of the House of Representatives, espoused the Northern side of the controversy, and subsequently became known, as we have seen, as the father of the system. Much undeserved obloquy has been thrown upon Mr. Clay, for this supposed abandonment of his section. The most that he claimed, was that a temporary protection, of a few years' duration only, should be given to these infant manufactures, until they should become self-sustaining. In later life, when he saw the extent to which the measure was pushed, he did, indeed recoil from it, as Mr. Calhoun, with keener intellect, had done, years before. The wedge, being thus entered, was driven home by the insatiable North.

In less than twenty years, or during the early part of General Jackson's administration, the public debt was paid off, and it became necessary to reduce the tariffs, to prevent a plethora in the public treasury; but the North, by this time, had "waxed fat," and like the ox in the scriptures, began to kick. From incidental protection, it advanced, boldly, to the doctrine of "*protection, for the sake of protection*"—thus avowing the unjust doctrine, that it was right to rob one section, for the benefit of the other; the pretence being the general good— the "general welfare" clause of the Constitution as well as the expression "We, the people," in the Preamble, being invoked to cover the enormity. Under the wholesale system of spoliation, which was now practised, the South was becoming poorer, and poorer. Whilst her abundant cotton crops supplied all the exchanges of the country, and put in motion, throughout the North, every species of manufacturing industry, from the cut-nail, which the planter put in the weather-boarding of his house, to the coach in which his wife, and daughters took an airing, it was found, that, from year to year, mortgages were increasing on her plantations, and that the planter was fast becoming little better, than the overseer of the Northern manufacturer, and the Northern merchant. A statesman of England once declared, that "not so much as a hob-nail should be manufactured, in America." The colonial dependence, and vassalage meant to be proclaimed by this expression, was now strictly true, as between the North, and the South. The South was compelled to purchase her hob-nails, in the North, being excluded by the Northern tariffs, from all other markets.

South Carolina, taking the alarm at this state of things, resorted as we have seen, to nullification, in 1832. The quarrel was compromised in 1833, by the passage of a more moderate tariff, but the North still growing, in strength, and wealth, disregarded the compromise, in 1842, and enacted a more oppressive tariff than ever. From this time onward, no attempt was made to conciliate the South, by the practice of forbearance, and justice, and the latter sank, hopelessly, into the condition of a tributary province to her more powerful rival.

All this was done under a federal compact, formed by sovereign States, for their common benefit! Thus was the prophecy of Patrick Henry verified, when he said: "But I am sure, that the dangers of this system [the Federal Constitution] are real, when those who have no similar interest with the people of this country [the South] are to legislate for us — when our dearest rights are to be left, in the hands of those, whose advantage it will be to infringe them." And thus also, was verified the declaration of Charles Cotesworth Pinkney, of South Carolina: "If they [the Southern States] are to form so considerable a minority, and the regulation of trade is to be given to the general Government, they will be nothing more than overseers of the Northern States."

CHAPTER VI.

THE QUESTION OF SLAVERY, AS IT AFFECTED SECESSION.

GREAT pains have been taken, by the North, to make it appear to the world, that the war was a sort of moral, and religious crusade against slavery. Such was not the fact. The people of the North were, indeed, opposed to slavery, but merely because they thought it stood in the way of their struggle for empire. I think it safe to affirm, that if the question had stood upon moral, and religious grounds alone, the institution would never have been interfered with.

The Republican party, which finally brought on the war, took its rise, as is well known, on the question of extending slavery to the Territories — those inchoate States, which were finally to decide the vexed question of the balance of power, between the two sections. It did not propose to disturb the institution in the States; in fact, the institution could do no harm there, for the States, in which it existed, were already in a hopeless minority. The fat, Southern goose could not resist being plucked, as things stood, but it was feared that if slavery was permitted to go into the Territories, the goose might become strong enough to resist being plucked. If proof were wanted of this, we have it, in the resolution passed by the Federal Congress, after the first battle of Manassas, in the first year of the war, as follows: " *Resolved*, That the war is not waged on our part, in any spirit of oppression, or for any purpose of conquest, or for interfering with the rights, or *established institutions of these States*, but to defend, and maintain the supremacy of the Constitution, and to preserve the Union, *with all the dignity and rights of the several States unimpaired.*"

In 1820, in the admission of Missouri into the Union, the North and the South had entered into a compromise, which provided, that slavery should not be carried into any of the Territories, north of a given geographical line. This compromise was clearly violative of the rights of the South, for the Territories were common property, which had been acquired, by the blood, and treasure, of the North and the South alike, and no discrimination could justly be made between the sections, as to emigration to those Territories; but discrimination would be made, if the Northern man could emigrate to all of them, and the Southern man to those of them only that lay South of the given line. By the passage of the Kansas-Nebraska bill, introduced into the House of Representatives, in 1854 by Mr. Stephen A. Douglas, this unjust compromise was repealed; the repealing clause declaring, that the Missouri Compromise "being inconsistent with the principles of non-intervention, by Congress, with slavery in the States, and Territories, as recognized by the legislation of 1850, commonly called the Compromise Measures, is hereby declared inoperative, and void; it being the true intent, and meaning of this act, not to legislate slavery into any Territory, or State, nor to exclude it therefrom, but to leave the people thereof perfectly free to form, and regulate their domestic institutions, subject only to the Constitution of the United States."

Nothing would seem more just, than the passage of this act, which removed the restriction which had been put upon a portion of the States, threw open the Territories to immigration from all the States, alike, and left the question of local government, the question of slavery included, to be decided by the inhabitants of the Territories themselves. But this act of justice, which Mr. Douglas had had the address and ability to cause to be passed, was highly distasteful to the Northern people. It was not consistent with their views of empire that there should be any more Southern Slave States admitted into the Union. The Republican party, which, up to that time, had made but little headway, now suddenly sprang into importance. and at the next elections in the North, swept every thing before it. The Northern Democratic members of Congress who had voted for the hated measure, were beaten by over whelming majorities, and Republicans sent in their places; and the Republican Convention which assembled at Chicago in 1860, to nominate a candidate for the Presidency, adopted

as one of the "planks of its platform"—to use a slang political phrase of the day—the principle that slavery should thereafter be excluded from the Territories; not only from the Territories North of the geographical line, of the Missouri Compromise, but from all the Territories! The gauntlet of defiance was thus boldly thrown at the feet of the Southern States.

From 1816 to 1860, these States had been plundered by
tariffs, which had enriched the North, and now they were told
without any circumlocution, that they should no longer have
any share in the Territories. I have said that this controversy,
on the subject of slavery, did not rest, in the North, on any
question of morals or religion. The end aimed at, in restrict-
ing slavery to the States, was purely political; but this end
was to be accomplished by means, and the Northern leaders
had the sagacity to see, that it was all-important to mix up
the controversy, *as a means*, with moral, and religious questions. Hence they enlisted the clergy in their crusade against
the South; the pulpit becoming a rostrum, from which to
inflame the Northern mind against the un-Godly slave-holder;
religious papers were established, which fulminated their
weekly diatribes against the institution; magazine literature,
fiction, lectures, by paid itinerants, were all employed, with
powerful effect, in a community where every man sets himself
up as a teacher, and considers himself responsible for the
morals of his neighbor. The contumely and insult thus heaped
upon the South were, of themselves, almost past endurance, to
say nothing of the wrongs, under which she suffered. The
sectional animosity which was engendered by these means, in
the North, soon became intense, and hurried on the catastrophe
with railroad speed.

Whilst the dispute about slavery in the Territories was drawing to a focus, another, and if possible, a still more exciting
question, had been occupying the public mind — the rendition
of fugitive slaves to their owners. Our ancestors, in the Convention of 1787, foreseeing the difficulty that was likely to
arise on this subject, insisted that the following positive provision, for their protection, should be inserted in the Constitution: "No person held to service, or labor, in one State,
under the laws thereof, escaping into another, shall, in con-

sequence of any law, or regulation therein, be discharged from such service, or labor; but shall be delivered up, on claim of the party to whom such service, or labor may be due."

In 1793, a law, called the fugitive slave law, had been passed, for the purpose of carrying out this provision of the Constitution. This law was re-enacted, with some alterations, the better to secure the object in question, in 1850. Neither of those laws was ever properly executed in the North. It soon became unsafe, indeed, for a Southern man to venture into the North, in pursuit of his fugitive slave. Mr. Webster sought, in vain, in the latter part of his life, when he seemed to be actuated by a sense of returning justice to the South, to induce his countrymen to execute those laws, and he lost much of his popularity, in consequence. The laws were not only positively disobeyed, but they were formally nullified by the Legislatures of fourteen of the Northern States; and penalties were annexed to any attempt to execute them. Mr. Webster, in speaking on this subject, says: "These States passed acts defeating the law of Congress, as far as it was in their power to defeat it. Those of them to whom I refer, not all, but several, nullified the law of 1793. They said in effect, 'We will not execute it. No runaway slave shall be restored.' Thus the law became a dead letter. But here was the Constitution, and compact still binding; here was the stipulation, as solemn as words could form it, and which every member of Congress, every officer of the General Government, every officer of the State government, from governors down to constables, is sworn to support. It has been said in the States of New York, Massachusetts, and Ohio, over and over again, that the law shall not be executed. That was the language in conventions, in Worcester, Massachusetts; in Syracuse, New York, and elsewhere. And for this they pledged their lives, their fortunes, and their sacred honors. Now, gentlemen, these proceedings, I say it upon my professional reputation, are distinctly treasonable. And the act of taking Shadrick [a fugitive slave] from the public authorities, in Boston, and sending him off, was an act of clear treason." Great outcry was raised against South Carolina when she nullified the tariff law of 1830, passed in clear violation of the spirit of the Constitution; here we see fourteen States nullifying an act, passed to carry out an express provision of the same instrument, about which there was not, and could not be any dispute.

Let us again put Mr. Webster on the witness stand, and hear what he says, was the effect of this wholesale nullification by the Northern States of this provision of the Constitution. "I do not hesitate," says he, "to say, and repeat, that if the Northern States refuse wilfully, and deliberately to carry into effect that part of the Constitution, which respects the restoration of fugitive slaves, the South would be no longer bound to keep the compact. *A bargain broken on one side is broken on all sides.*" That was spoken like Daniel Webster, the able jurist, and just man, and not like the Daniel Webster, whom I have before quoted, in these pages, as the casuist, and the sophist. The reader cannot fail to see what a full recantation we have here, of Mr. Webster's heresy, of 1833, when he contended that the Constitution had been "ordained and established," by the people of the United States, in the aggregate, as one nation.

Mr. Webster now calls the States, the parties to the instrument, and claims that the infraction of it, by some of the States, releases the others from their obligations under it. It is then, after all, it seems, a *federal compact;* and if it be such, we have the authority of Mr. Webster, himself, for saying that the States may withdraw from it, at pleasure, without waiting for an infringement of it, by their co-States.

But the Southern States did not desire to withdraw from it, without reason. They were sincerely attached to the Union. and were willing to suffer, and endure much rather than that it should be destroyed. They had stood, shoulder to shoulder, with the North in two wars against the mother country, and had freely spent their wealth, and shed their blood in defence of the common rights. They had rushed to the defence of New England, in the war of the Revolution, and had equally responded to her call in 1812, in defence of her shipping interest.

Mr. Madison relied much upon these ties, as a common bond of union. When Patrick Henry and other Southern patriots were warning their people against the new alliance, proposed

to them in the Federal Constitution, he spoke the following
fervid language in reply to them, in one of the numbers of the
"Federalist." "Hearken not to the unnatural voice, which
tells you, that the people of America, knit together, as they
are, by so many natural cords of affection, can no longer live
together as members of the same family; can no longer continue mutual guardians of their mutual happiness.   *   *   *
No, my countrymen, shut your ears against this unhallowed language.   Shut your hearts against the poison which it conveys.
The kindred blood which flows in the veins of American citizens, the mingled blood which they have shed in defence of
their sacred rights, consecrate their union, and excite horror at
the idea of their becoming aliens, rivals, enemies."   Much of
this feeling still lingered in the bosoms of Southern men.
They were slow to awaken from this dream of delusion.   A
rude and rough hand had been necessary to disenchant them.
But they were compelled, in spite of themselves, to realize the
fact at last, that they had been deceived, and betrayed into the
federal compact, that they might be made slaves.   Like an
unhappy bride, upon whose brow the orange-wreath had been
placed, by hands that promised tenderness, and protection, the
South had been rudely scorned, and repelled, and forced, in
tears, and bitter lamentation, to retract the faith which she had
plighted.   To carry still further our simile; like the deceived,
and betrayed bride, the least show of relenting, and tenderness
was sufficient to induce the South to forgive, and to endeavor
to forget.

The history of our unhappy connection with the North is
full of compromises, and apparent reconciliations—prominent
among which was the compromise of 1833, growing out of the
nullification of South Carolina, on the tariff question; and the
compromise of 1850, in which it was promised, that Congress
should not interfere with the question of slavery, either in the
States, or Territories.   The South, like the too credulous
bride, accepted these evidences of returning tenderness, in good
faith; the North, like the coarse and brutal husband, whose
selfishness was superior to his sense of justice, withdrew them,
almost as soon as made.   The obnoxious laws which had

been modified, or repealed, under these compromises, were re-enacted with additional provocations, and restrictions.

So loth was the South to abandon the Union, that she made strenuous efforts to remain in it, even after Mr. Lincoln had been elected President, in 1860. In this election, that dreaded sectional line against which President Washington had warned his countrymen, in his Farewell Address, had at last been drawn; in it,—"the fire-bell of the night,"—which had so disturbed the last days of Jefferson, had been sounded. There had, at last, arisen a united North, against a united South. Mr. Lincoln had been placed by the Chicago Convention on a platform so purely sectional, that no Southern State voted, or could vote for him. His election was purely geographical; it was tantamount to a denial of the co-equality of the Southern States, with the Northern States, in the Union, since it drove the former out of the common Territories. This had not been a mere party squabble—the questions involved had been *federal*, and *fundamental*. Notwithstanding which, some of the Southern States were not without hope, that the North might be induced to revoke its verdict. Mr. Crittenden, of Kentucky, introduced into the Senate, a series of resolutions, which he hoped would have the effect of restoring harmony; the chief feature of which was, the restoration of the Missouri Compromise, giving the Southern States access to the Territories south of a geographical line. Although this compromise was a partial abandonment of the rights of the South, many of the ablest, and most influential statesmen of that section, gave in their adhesion to it; among others, Mr. Jefferson Davis. The measure failed.

Various other resolutions, looking to pacification, were introduced into both houses of Congress; but they failed, in like manner. The border Slave States aroused to a sense of their danger—for by this time, several of the Gulf States had seceded—called a Convention in the city of Washington, to endeavor to allay the storm. A full representation attended, composed of men, venerable for their years, and renowned for their patriotic services, but their labors ended also in failure; Congress scarcely deigned to notice them. In both houses of Congress the Northern faction, which had so recently triumphed in the election of their President, was arrayed in a solid phalanx of hostility to the South, and could not be moved an inch. The Puritan leaven had at last "leavened the whole loaf," and the descendants of those immigrants who had come over to America, in the *May Flower*, feeling that they had the power to crush a race of men, who had dared to differ with them in opinion, and to have interests separate and apart from them, were resolved to use that power in a way to do no discredit to their ancestry. Rebels, when in a minority, they had become tyrants, now that they were in a majority.

Nothing remained to the South, but to raise the gantlet which had been thrown at her feet. The Federal Government which had been established by our ancestors had failed of its object. Instead of binding the States together, in peace, and amity, it had, in the hands of one portion of the States, become an engine of oppression of the other portion. It so happened, that the slavery question was the issue which finally tore them asunder, but, as the reader has seen, this question was a mere means, to an end. The end was empire, and we were about to repeat, in this hemisphere, the drama which had so often been enacted in the other, of a more powerful nation crushing out a weaker.

The war of the American sections was but the prototype of many other wars, which had occurred among the human race. It had its origin in the unregenerated nature of man, who is only an intellectual wild beast, whose rapacity has never yet been restrained, by a sense of justice. The American people thought, when they framed the Constitution, that they were to be an exception to mankind, in general. History had instructed them that all other peoples, who had gone before them, had torn up paper governments, when paper was the only bulwark that protected such governments, but then they were the *American* people, and no such fate could await *them*. The events which I have recorded, and am about to record, have taught them, that they are no better—and perhaps they are no worse—than other people. It is to be hoped that they will profit by their dear-bought experience, and that when they shall have come to their senses, and undertake to lay the foundation of a new government, they will, if they design to essay another republic, eliminate all discordant materials. The experiment of trusting to human honesty having failed, they must next trust to human interests—the great regulator, as all philosophy teaches, of human nature. They must listen rather to the philosophy of Patrick Henry, than to that of James Madison, and never attempt again to bind up in one sheaf, with a withe of straw, materials so discordant as were the people of the North, and the people of the South.

CHAPTER VII.

THE FORMATION OF THE CONFEDERATE GOVERNMENT, AND THE RESIGNATION OF OFFICERS OF THE FEDERAL ARMY AND NAVY.

AS I am not writing a history of the war, but only of a very small portion of the war, it cannot be expected that I will follow events in a connected train. I have detained the reader, so far, as to give him a continuous, though hasty glance, of the causes of the war, but having brought him down to the final rupture of the sections, I must leave him to supply for himself many a link, here and there, in the broken chain, as we proceed. Let him imagine then that the Southern States have seceded — the gallant little State of South Carolina setting her larger, and more powerful sisters, the example, on the 20th December, 1860 — and that they have met at Montgomery, in Alabama, by their delegates in Congress, to form a new Confederacy; that a Provisional Government has been formed and that Mr. Jefferson Davis has been elected President, and Mr. Alexander H. Stephens Vice-President.

The time had now come for the officers of the old Army, and Navy to make their election, as to which of the two Governments they would give their adhesion. There were no such questions then, as rebellion, and treason in the public mind. This was a Federal after-thought, when that Government began to get the better of us in the war. The Puritan, if he had been whipped, would have been a capital secessionist, and as meek, and humble as we could have desired. He would have been the first to make a "perpetual" alliance with us, and to offer us inducements to give him the benefits of our trade. After the first drubbing we gave him, at Manassas, he was disposed to be quite reasonable, and the Federal Congress passed the conciliatory resolution I have quoted in a previous chapter, intimating to us, that if we would come back, slavery should be secure in the States, and our "rights and dignity" remain unimpaired. But as he gained strength, he gained courage, and as the war progressed, and it became evident that we should be beaten, he began to talk of traitors, and treason.

As a general rule, the officers both of the Army, and the Navy sided with their respective States; especially those of them who were cultivated, and knew something of the form of government, under which they had been living. But even the profession of arms is not free from sordid natures, and many of these had found their way into both branches of the public service. Men were found capable of drawing their swords against their own firesides, as it were, and surrendering their neighbors, and friends to the vengeance of a government, which paid them for their fealty. Some, with cunning duplicity, even encouraged their former messmates, and companions who occupied places above them, to resign, and afterward held back themselves. Some were mere soldiers, and sailors of fortune, and seemed devoid of all sensibility on the subject, looking only to rank and pay. They were open to the highest bidder, and the Federal Government was in a condition to make the highest bids. Some of the Southern men of this latter class remained with the North, because they could not obtain the positions they desired in the South; and afterward, as is the fashion with renegades, became more bitter against their own people than even the Northern men.

Civil war is a terrible crucible through which to pass character; the dross drops away from the pure metal at the first touch of the fire. It must be admitted, indeed, that there was some little nerve required, on the part of an officer of the regular Army, or Navy, to elect to go with his State. His profession was his only fortune; he depended upon it, for the means of subsisting himself and family. If he remained where he was, a competency for life, and promotion, and honors probably awaited him; if he went with the South, a dark, and uncertain future was before him; he could not possibly better his condition, and if the South failed, he would have thrown away the labor of a life-time. The struggle was hard in other respects. All professions are clannish. Men naturally cling together, who have been bred to a common pursuit; and this remark is particularly applicable to the Army, and the Navy. West Point, and Annapolis were powerful bonds to knit together the hearts of young men.   Friendships were there formed, which it was difficult to sever, especially when strengthened by years of after-association, in common toils, common pleasures, and common dangers.   Naval officers, in particular, who had been rocked together in the same storm, and had escaped perhaps from the same shipwreck, found it very difficult to draw their swords against each other.   The flag, too, had a charm which it was difficult to resist.   It had long been the emblem of the principle that all just governments are founded on the consent of the governed, vindicated against our British ancestors, in the War of the Revolution, and it was difficult to realize the fact that it no longer represented this principle, but had become the emblem of its opposite; that of coercing unwilling States, to remain under a Government, which they deemed unjust and oppressive.

Sentiment had almost as much to do with the matter, as principle, for there clustered around the "old flag," a great many hallowed memories, of sacrifices made, and victories won.

The cadet at West Point had marched and countermarched under its folds, dreaming of future battle-fields, and future honors to be gained in upholding and defending it; and the midshipman, as he gazed upon it, in some foreign port, flying proudly from the gaff-end of his ship, had drunk in new inspiration to do and to dare, for his country.   Many bearded men were affected almost to tears, as they saw this once hallowed emblem hauled down from the flag-staves, of Southern forts, and arsenals.   They were in the condition of one who had been forced, in spite of himself, to realize the perfidy of a friend, and to be obliged to give him up, as no longer worthy of his confidence or affection.   General Robert E. Lee has so happily expressed all these various emotions, in a couple of letters, which he wrote, contemporaneously, with his resignation from the Federal Army, that I give them to the reader. One of these letters is addressed to General Winfield Scott, and the other to General Lee's sister.

ARLINGTON, VA., April 20, 1861.

GENERAL: — Since my interview with you on the 18th instant, I have felt that I ought not longer to retain my commission in the army. I therefore tender my resignation, which I request you will recommend for acceptance. It would have been presented at once. but for the struggle which it has cost me to separate myself from a service, to which I have devoted all the best years of my life, and all the ability I possessed. During the whole of that time — more than a quarter of a century — I have experienced nothing but kindness from my superiors, and the most cordial friendship from my comrades. To no one, General, have I been as much indebted as yourself, for uniform kindness and consideration, and it has always been my ardent desire to merit your approbation. I shall carry to the grave the most grateful recollection of your kind consideration, and your name and fame will always be dear to me.

Save in defence of my native State, I never desire to draw my sword. Be pleased to accept my most earnest wishes for the continuance of your happiness and prosperity, and believe me most truly yours,

R. E. LEE.

Lieutenant-General WINFIELD SCOTT,
Commanding United States Army.

ARLINGTON, VA., April 20, 1861.

MY DEAR SISTER: — I am grieved at my inability to see you * * * I have been waiting "for a more convenient season," which has brought to many before me deep and lasting regrets. Now we are in a state of war which will yield to nothing. The whole South is in a state of revolution, into which Virginia after a long struggle, has been drawn, and *though I recognize no necessity for this state of things,* and would have forborne and pleaded to the end, for redress of grievances, real or supposed, yet in my own person I had to meet the question, *whether I should take part against my native State.* With all my devotion to the Union, and the feeling of loyalty, and duty of an American citizen, I have not been able to make up my mind to raise my hand against my relatives, my children, my home. I have therefore resigned my commission in the army, and save in defence of my native State, with the sincere hope that my services may never be needed, I hope I may never be called on to draw my sword.

I know you will blame me, but you must think as kindly of me as you can, and believe that I have endeavored to do what I thought right. To show you the feeling and struggle it has cost me, I send a copy of my letter to General Scott, which accompanied my letter of resignation. I have no time for more. * * * May God guard and protect you, and yours, and shower upon you every blessing is the prayer of your devoted brother.

R. E. LEE.

In the winter of 1860, I was stationed in the city of Washington, as the Secretary of the Lighthouse Board, being then a commander in the United States Navy, and was an observer of many of the events I have described. I had long abandoned all hope of reconciliation between the sections. The public mind, North and South, was in an angry mood, and the day of compromises was evidently at an end. I had made up my mind to retire from the Federal service, at the proper moment, and was only waiting for that moment to arrive.

Although I had been born in the State of Maryland, and was reared on the banks of the Potomac, I had been, for many years, a resident citizen of Alabama, having removed to this State, in the year 1841, and settled with my family, on the west bank of the Perdido; removing thence, in a few years, to Mobile. My intention of retiring from the Federal Navy, and taking service with the South, in the coming struggle, had been made known to the delegation in the Federal Congress from Alabama, early in the session of 1860–1. I did not doubt that Maryland would follow the lead of her more Southern sisters, as the cause of quarrel was common with all the Southern States, but whether she did or not, could make no difference with me now, since my allegiance, and my services had become due to another State.

The month of February, 1861, found me still at the city of Washington. The following extract from a letter written by me to a Southern member of the Federal Congress, temporarily absent from his post, will show the state of mind in which I was looking upon passing events. "I am still at my post at the Light-House Board, performing my routine duties, but listening with an aching ear and beating heart, for the first sounds of the great disruption which is at hand." On the 14th of that month, whilst sitting quietly with my family, after the labors of the day, a messenger brought me the following telegram:—

MONTGOMERY, Feb. 14, 1861.

SIR:— On behalf of the Committee on Naval Affairs, I beg leave to request that you will repair to this place, at your earliest convenience. Your obedient servant,

C. M. CONRAD, *Chairman.*

Commander RAPHAEL SEMMES, *Washington, D. C.*

Here was the sound for which I had been so anxiously listening. Secession was now indeed a reality, and the time had come for me to arouse myself to action. The telegram threw my small family-circle into great commotion. My wife, with the instincts of a woman, a wife, and a mother, seemed to realize, as by intuition, all the dangers and difficulties that lay before me. She had been hoping without hope, that I would not be subjected to the bitter ordeal, but the die was now cast, and with a few tears, and many prayers she nerved herself for the sacrifices, and trials that she knew were before her. Her children were to be withdrawn from school, her comfortable home broken up, and she was to return, penniless, to her people, to abide with them the fortunes of a bloody, and a doubtful war. The heroism of woman! how infinitely it surpasses that of man. With all her gentleness, and tenderness, and natural timidity, in nine cases in ten, she has more nerve than the other sex, in times of great emergency. With a bleeding and bursting heart, she is capable of putting on the composure, and lovely serenity of an angel, binding up the wounds of a husband or son, and when he is restored to health and vigor, buckling on his sword anew, and returning him to the battle-field. Glorious women of the South! what an ordeal you have passed through, and how heroically you have stood the trying test. You lost the liberty which your husbands, sires, and sons struggled for, but only for a period. The blood which you will have infused into the veins of future generations will yet rise up to vindicate you, and "call you blessed."

The telegram reached me about four o'clock, P.M., and I responded to it, on the same evening as follows:

WASHINGTON, Feb. 14, 1861.
Hon. C. M. CONRAD, Chairman of the Committee on Naval Affairs, Congress of the Confederate States:—Despatch received; I will be with you immediately.   Respectfully, &c.,
R. SEMMES.

The next morning, I repaired, as usual, to the office of the Light House Board, in the Treasury building, General John A. Dix being then the Secretary of the Treasury, and *ex officio*

President of the Board, and wrote the following resignation of my commission, as a Commander in the United States Navy:

WASHINGTON, D. C., Feb. 15, 1861.

SIR:—I respectfully tender through you, to the President of the United States, this, the resignation of the commission which I have the honor to hold as a Commander in the Navy of the United States. In severing my connection with the Government of the United States, and with the Department over which you preside, I pray you to accept my thanks for the kindness which has characterized your official deportment towards me.

I have the honor to be very respectfully your obedient servant,

RAPHAEL SEMMES,
Commander U. S. Navy.

Hon. ISAAC TOUCEY, *Secretary of the Navy,*
Washington, D. C.

On the same day, I received the following acceptance of my resignation:—

NAVY DEPARTMENT, Feb. 15, 1861.

SIR:—Your resignation as a Commander in the Navy of the United States, tendered in your letter of this date, is hereby accepted.   I am respectfully your obedient servant,

I. TOUCEY.

RAPHAEL SEMMES, *Esq., late Commander*
U. S. Navy, Washington.

A few days previously to my resignation, by the death of a lamented member of the Light-House Board, I had been promoted from the Secretaryship, to a Membership of that Board, and it now became necessary for me to inform the Board officially, of my being no longer a member of it, which I did in the following communication:—

WASHINGTON, D. C., Feb. 16, 1861.

SIR:—I have the honor to inform you, that I have resigned my commission, as a Commander in the Navy of the United States, and that, as a consequence, I am no longer a member of the Light-House Board. In severing thus my connection with the Board, at which I have had the honor to hold a seat, since the 17th of November, 1858, I desire to say to the members, individually, and collectively, that I shall carry with me to my home in the South, a grateful recollection of the amenities, and courtesies which have characterized, on their part, our official intercourse.

I am very respectfully your obedient servant,

RAPHAEL SEMMES.

Commander T. A. JENKINS, *U. S. N.,*
Secretary Light-House Board, Washington.

I left in the Light-House Board, a South Carolinian, and a Virginian, both of whom were too loyal to their places, to follow the lead of their States. The South Carolinian has been rewarded with the commission of a Rear-Admiral, and the Virginian with that of a Commodore. The presence of these gentlemen in the Board may account for the fact, that my letter was not even honored with an acknowledgment of its receipt.

I have said that there was no talk at this time, about traitors, and treason. The reader will observe how openly, and as a matter of course, all these transactions were conducted. The seceded States had been several months in getting their Conventions together, and repealing, with all due form, and ceremony, the ordinances by which the Federal Constitution had been accepted. Senators, and members of the House of Representatives of the Federal Congress had withdrawn from their seats, under circumstances unusually solemn, and impressive, which had attracted the attention of the whole country. Mr. Jefferson Davis, in particular, had taken leave of a full Senate, with crowded galleries, in a speech of great dignity and power, in the course of which he said: "We will invoke the God of our Fathers, who delivered them from the power of the Lion, to protect us from the ravages of the Bear; and thus putting our trust in God, and in our own firm hearts, and strong arms, we will vindicate the right as best we may."

As the resignation of each officer of the Army, and Navy went in, it was well understood what his object was, and yet we have seen, that up to this period, the Government accepted them all, and permitted the officers to depart to their respective States. It was not known, as yet, to what extent the disintegration might go, and it was not safe therefore to talk of treason. "The wayward sisters" might decide to go in a body, in which event it would not have been *policy* to attempt to prevent them, or to discuss questions of treason with them. The Secretary of the Navy did not think of arresting me, for telegraphing to the Congress of the Confederate States, that I would be with it, immediately; nor did he, though he knew my purpose of drawing my sword against the Federal Government, if necessary, refuse to accept my resignation. Nay, President Buchanan had decided that he had no power under the

Federal Constitution, to coerce a State; though, like a weak old man as he had now become, he involved himself afterward in the inconsistency of attempting to hold possession of the ceded places within the limits of the States which had withdrawn from the Union. It could not but follow, logically, from the premise, that there was no power in the Federal Constitution to coerce a State, that the State had the right to secede; for clearly any one may do that which no one has the right to prevent him from doing.

It was under such circumstances as these, that I. dissolved my connection with the Federal Government, and returned to the condition of a private citizen, with no more obligation resting upon me, than upon any other citizen. The Federal Government, itself, had formally released me from the contract of service I had entered into with it, and, as a matter of course, from the binding obligation of any oath I had taken in connection with that contract. All this was done, as the reader has seen, before I moved a step from the city of Washington; and yet a subsequent Secretary of the Navy, Mr. Gideon Welles, has had the hardihood and indecency of accusing me of having been a "*deserter* from the service." He has deliberately put this false accusation on record, in a public document, in face of the facts I have stated—all of which were recorded upon the rolls of his office. I do not speak here of the clap-trap he has used about "treason to the flag," and the other stale nonsense which he has uttered in connection with my name, for this was common enough among his countrymen, and was perhaps to have been expected from men smarting under the castigation I had given them, but of the more definite and explicit charge, of "*deserting from the service*," when the service, itself, as he well knew, had released me from all my obligations to it.

Another charge, with as little foundation, has been made against myself, and other officers of the Army and Navy, who resigned their commissions, and came South. It has been said that we were in the condition of *élèves* of the Federal Government, inasmuch as we had received our education at the military schools, and that we were guilty of ingratitude to that Government, when we withdrew from its service. This slander has no doubt had its effect, with the ignorant masses, but it can scarcely have been entertained by any one who has a just conception of the nature of our federal system of government. It loses sight of the fact, that the States are the creators, and the Federal Government the creature; that not only the military schools, but the Federal Government itself belongs to the States. Whence came the fund for the establishment of these schools? From the States. In what proportion did the States contribute it? Mr. Benton has answered this question, as the reader has seen, when he was discussing the effect of the tariffs under which the South had so long been depleted. He has told us, that four States alone, Virginia, the two Carolinas and Georgia, defrayed three fourths of the expenses of the General Government; and taking the whole South into view, this proportion had even increased since his day, up to the breaking out of the war.

Of every appropriation, then, that was made by Congress for the support of the military schools, three fourths of the money belonged to the Southern States. Did these States send three fourths of the students to those schools? Of course not —this would have been something like justice to them; but justice to the Southern States was no part of the scheme of the Federal Government. With the exception of a few cadets, and midshipmen "at large," whom the President was authorized to appoint—the intention being that he should appoint the sons of deceased officers of the Army and Navy, but the fact being that he generally gave the appointment to his political friends —the appointments to these schools were made from the several States, in proportion to population, and as a matter of course, the North got the lion's share. But supposing the States to have been equally represented in those schools, what would have been the result? Why, simply that the South not only educated her own boys, but educated three fourths of the Northern boys, to boot. Virginia, for instance, at the same time that she sent young Robert E. Lee to West Point, to be educated, put in the public treasury not only money enough to pay for his education, and maintenance, but for the education and maintenance of three Massachusetts boys! How ungrateful of Lee, afterward, being thus a charity scholar of the North, to draw his sword against her.

CHAPTER VIII.

AUTHOR PROCEEDS TO MONTGOMERY, AND REPORTS TO
THE NEW GOVERNMENT, AND IS DISPATCHED NORTH-
WARD, ON A SPECIAL MISSION.

ON the evening of the 16th of February, the day after I had
resigned my commission, I took a sorrowful leave of my
family, and departed for Montgomery, by the way of Fredericksburg and Richmond. Virginia and North Carolina had
not yet seceded, and anxious debates were going on, on the
all-absorbing question, in each town and village in these two
States, through which I passed. It was easy to see, that the
great majority of the people were with the extreme South, in
this her hour of need, but there were some time-servers and
trimmers, who still talked of conciliation, and of guarantees.
They inquired eagerly after news from Washington, at all the
stations at which the train stopped, and seemed disappointed
when they found we had nothing more to tell them, than they
had already learned through the telegraph.

On the evening of the 18th, I entered the level tract of pine
lands between West Point, and Montgomery. The air had
become soft, and balmy, though I had left a region of frosts,
and snow, only two days before. The pine woods were on fire
as we passed through them, the flames now and then running
up a lightwood tree, and throwing a weird and fitful glare upon
the passing train. The scene was peculiarly Southern, and
reminded me that I was drawing near my home, and my people,
and I mechanically repeated to myself the words of the poet:

> "Breathes there a man with soul so dead,
> Who never to himself hath said,
> This is my own, my native land!"

And my heart, which up to that moment, had felt as though a
heavy weight were pressing upon it, began to give more vigor-

ous beats, and send a more inspiring current through my veins.
Under this happy influence I sank, as the night advanced, and
the train thundered on, into the first sound sleep which had
visited my weary eyelids, since I had resigned my commission,
and read at the foot of the letter accepting my resignation, my
name inscribed as plain "Esq." This night-ride, through the
burning pine woods of Alabama, afterward stood as a great
gulf in my memory, forming an impassable barrier, as it were,
between my past, and my future life. It had cost me pain to
cross the gulf, but once crossed, I never turned to look back.
When I washed and dressed for breakfast, in Montgomery, the
next morning, I had put off the old man, and put on the new.
The labors, and associations of a lifetime had been inscribed
in a volume, which had been closed, and a new book, whose
pages were as yet all blank, had been opened.

My first duty was to put myself in communication with Mr.
Conrad, the chairman of the Committee of Naval Affairs.
Several naval officers had preceded me to the seat of the new
government, and others were arriving. It was agreed that
there should be a special meeting on the next day, in joint
session, of the two committees — on military and naval affairs.

The Confederate Congress was in session in the State Capitol, and about noon, I repaired thither to witness the spectacle.
They did me the honor to admit me to the floor, and upon casting my eyes over the august assembly, I recognized a number
of familiar faces. General Howell Cobb of Georgia was the
President; Toombs, Crawford, and other distinguished men
were there from the same State. Curry, McRae, Robert H.
Smith and other able men were there from Alabama. In
short the Congress was full of the best talent of the South.
It was by far the best Congress that ever assembled under the
new government. It was a convention as well as a Congress,
since it was charged with the establishment of a Provisional
Government. Every one realized the greatness of the crisis
that was upon us, and hence the very best men in the community had been selected to meet the emergency. The harmony
of the body was equal to its ability, for, in the course of a few
weeks, it had put the complicated machinery of a government
in motion, and was already taking active measures for defence,

in case the Federal power should decide upon making war upon us.

Mr. Davis, the Provisional President, had preceded me to the capital, only a few days, and my next step was to call upon him. I had known him in the city of Washington. He received me kindly, and almost the first question which he asked me, was whether I had disembarrassed myself of my Federal commission. I replied to him that I had done so, as a matter of course, before leaving Washington, and that my allegiance henceforth belonged to the new government, and to the Southern people. He seemed gratified at this declaration, and entered into a free, and frank conversation with me, on the subject of the want of preparation for defence, in which he found our States, and the great labor that lay before us, to prepare for emergencies. Congress, he said, has not yet had time to organize a navy, but he designed to make immediate use of me, if I had no objection. I told him that my services were at his command, in any capacity he thought fit to employ them. He then explained to me his plan of sending me back to the city of Washington, and thence into the Northern States, to gather together, with as much haste as possible, such persons, and materials of war as might be of most pressing necessity.

The persons alluded to, were to be mechanics skilled in the manufacture, and use of ordnance, and rifle machinery, the preparation of fixed ammunition, percussion caps, &c. So exclusively had the manufacture of all these articles for the use of the United States, been confined to the North, under "the best government the world ever saw," that we had not even percussion caps enough to enable us to fight a battle, or the machines with which to make them, although we had captured all the forts, and arsenals within our limits, except Fort Sumter and Fort McRae. The President was as calm and unmoved as I had ever seen him, and was living in a very simple, and unpretending style at the Exchange Hotel. He had not yet selected all his Cabinet; nor indeed had he so much as a private secretary at his command, as the letter of instructions which he afterward presented me, for my guidance, was written with his own hand. This letter was very full, and precise, frequently descending into detail, and manifesting an acquaintance with bureau duties, scarcely to have been expected from one who had occupied his exalted positions.

On the next day, I attended the joint-session of the two committees above named. These committees were composed, as was to have been expected, of some of the best men of the Congress. Conrad, Crawford, Curry, and the brilliant young Bartow of Georgia were present, among others whose names I do not now recall. But few naval officers of any rank had as yet withdrawn from the old service; Rousseau, Tattnall, Ingraham, and Randolph were all the captains; and Farrand, Brent, Semmes, and Hartstone were all the commanders. Of these there were present before the committees, besides myself, Rousseau, Ingraham, and Randolph; Major Wm. H. Chase, late of the engineers of the Federal Army, was also present. Randolph commanded the Navy Yard at Pensacola, and Chase the military defences. We discussed the military and naval resources of the country, and devised such means of defence as were within our reach — which were not many — to enable us to meet the most pressing exigences of our situation, and separated after a session of several hours. I can do no more, of course, than briefly glance at these things, as I am not writing, as before remarked, the history of the war.

The next morning I called again on the President, received my instructions, and departed Northward on the mission which had been assigned me. I will be brief in the description of this mission also. I stopped a day at Richmond, and examined the State Arsenal, in charge of Capt. Dimmock, and the Tredegar Iron Works; having been especially enjoined to report upon the present, and future capacity of these works for the casting of cannon, shot, shells, &c. The establishment had already turned its attention in this direction, and I was gratified to find that it was capable of almost indefinite enlargement, and that it could be made a most valuable auxiliary to us. The reader will see how confidently we already reckoned upon the support of Virginia.

Reaching Washington again, I visited the Arsenal, and inspected such of its machinery as I thought worth my notice, particularly an improved percussion-cap machine which I found in operation. I also held conferences with some me-

chanics, whom I desired to induce to go South.   Whilst I
was in Washington Mr. Abraham Lincoln, the newly elected
President of the United States, arrived, for the purpose of being
inaugurated.   Being purely a sectional President, and feeling
probably that he had no just right to rule over the South, he
had come into the city by night, and in disguise, afraid to trust
himself among a people of whom he claimed to be Chief Magistrate.   Poor old General Winfield Scott was then verging
toward senility, and second childhood, and had contributed no
little, perhaps, to Mr. Lincoln's alarm.   He had been gathering together troops for some days, in the Federal capital, for
the purpose of inaugurating, amid bayonets, a President of the
United States.   It had been the boast of the American people,
heretofore, that their Presidents did not need guards, but trusted
wholly for their security, to the love, and confidence of their
constituents, but the reign of peace, and good will was at an
end, and the reign of the bayonet was to ensue.   The rumbling of artillery through the streets of Washington, and the
ring of grounded arms on the pavements, had sounded the
death-knell of liberty in these States for generations.   Swarms
of visitors from far and near, in the North and West, had
flocked to Washington, to see *their* President inaugurated, and
were proud of this spectacle of arms; too stupid to see its fearful significance.

The auspicious day, the 4th of March, at length arrived,
and whilst the glorious pageant is being prepared; whilst the
windows and the house-tops along Pennsylvania Avenue are
being thronged with a motley population of men and women,
come to see the show; whilst the President elect, in a hollow
square of bayonets, is marching toward the Capitol, the writer
of these pages, having again taken leave of his family, was
hurrying away from the desecration of a capital, which had
been ceded by a too credulous Maryland, and Virginia, and
which had been laid out by Washington.   As I left the Baltimore depot, extra trains were still pouring their thousands
into the streets of Washington.   I arrived in New York, the
next day, and during the next three weeks, visited the West
Point Academy, whither I went to see a son, who was a cadet
at the Institution, and who afterward became a major of light

artillery, in the Confederate service; and made a tour through the principal work-shops of New York, Connecticut, and Massachusetts.

I found the people everywhere, not only willing, but anxious to contract with me. I purchased large quantities of percussion caps in the city of New York, and sent them by express without any disguise, to Montgomery. I made contracts for batteries of light artillery, powder, and other munitions, and succeeded in getting large quantities of the powder shipped. It was agreed between the contractors and myself, that when I should have occasion to use the telegraph, certain other words were to be substituted, for those of military import, to avoid suspicion.

I made a contract, conditioned upon the approval of my Government, for the removal to the Southern States, of a complete set of machinery for rifling cannon, with the requisite skilled workmen to put it in operation. Some of these men, who would thus have sold body, and soul to me, for a sufficient consideration, occupied high social positions, and were men of wealth. I dined with them, at their comfortable residences near their factories, where the music of boring out cannon, accompanied the clatter of the dishes, and the popping of champagne-corks; and I had more than one business interview with gentlemen, who occupied the most costly suites of apartments at the Astor House in New York City. Many of these gentlemen, being unable to carry out their contracts with the Confederate States because of the prompt breaking out of the war, afterward obtained lucrative contracts from the Federal Government, and became, in consequence, intensely *loyal*. It would be a *quasi* breach of honor to disclose their names, as they dealt with me, pretty much as conspirators against their government are wont to deal with the enemies of their government, secretly, and with an implied confidence that I would keep their secret. It is accordingly safe.

In the mean time, the great revolution was progressing. Abraham Lincoln had delivered his inaugural address, with triple rows of bayonets between him, and the people to whom he was speaking; in which address he had puzzled his hearers, and was no doubt puzzled himself, as to what he really meant,

He was like President Buchanan; now he saw it, and now he didn't. He would not coerce the States, but he would hold on to the ceded places within their limits, and collect the public revenue. Texas, and Arkansas went out whilst I was in New York. The bulletin-boards at the different newspaper offices were daily thronged by an unwashed multitude, in search of some new excitement. The Northern public was evidently puzzled. It had at first rather treated secession as a joke. They did not think it possible that the Southern people could be in earnest, in dissolving their connection with a people, so emniently proper as themselves; but they now began to waver in this opinion. Still they forbore any decided demonstration. Like sensible men they preferred waiting until they could see how large a bull they were required to take by the horns.

Toward the latter part of my stay in New York I received the following letter from the Hon. Stephen R. Mallory, who had been appointed Secretary of the Navy, which branch of the public service had been organized since I had left Montgomery:

CONFEDERATE STATES OF AMERICA,
NAVY DEPT., MONTGOMERY, ALA., March 13, 1861.
COMMANDER RAPHAEL SEMMES.

SIR:— With the sanction of the President, I am constrained to impose upon you duties connected with this Department, in addition to the important trusts with which you are charged; but I do so, upon the express understanding, that they are not to interfere with the performance of your special duties. I have received reliable information, that two, or more steamers, of a class desired for immediate service, may be purchased at, or near New York; steamers of speed, light draught, and strength sufficient for at least one heavy gun. When I say to you, that they are designed to navigate the waters, and enter the bays, and inlets of the coast, from Charleston to the St. Mary's, and from Key West, to the Rio Grande, for coast defence; that their speed should be sufficient to give them, at all times, the ability to engage, or evade an engagement; and that eight or ten-inch guns, with perhaps two thirty-twos, or if not, two of smaller calibre should constitute their battery, your judgment will need no further guide. Be pleased, should your other important engagements permit, to make inquiries, in such manner as may not excite special attention, and give me such details as to cost, character, &c., as you may deem important.

Under these instructions I made diligent search in the waters of New York, for such steamers as were wanted, but none could be found. The river, and Long Island Sound boats were mere shells, entirely unfit for the purposes of war, and it was difficult to find any of the sea-going steamers, which combined the requisite lightness of draught, with the other qualities desired.

March was now drawing to a close, the war-cloud was assuming darker, and more portentous hues, and it soon became evident that my usefulness in the North was about to end. Men were becoming more shy of making engagements with me, and the Federal Government was becoming more watchful. The New York, and Savannah steamers were still running, curiously enough carrying the Federal flag at the peak, and the Confederate flag at the fore; and in the last days of March, I embarked on board one of them, arriving in Montgomery on the 4th of April, just eight days before fire was opened upon Fort Sumter. During the short interval that elapsed between my arrival, and my going afloat, I was put in charge of the Light-House Bureau; the Confederate Congress having, upon my recommendation, established a Bureau, with a single naval officer at its head, instead of the complicated machinery of a Board, which existed in the old Government. I had barely time to appoint the necessary clerks, and open a set of books, before Fort Sumter was fired upon, and the tocsin of war was sounded.

CHAPTER IX.

THE COMMISSIONING OF THE SUMTER, THE FIRST CON-FEDERATE STATES' SHIP OF WAR.

FORT Sumter surrendered on the 13th of April. The next day was a gala day in Montgomery. We had driven an insolent enemy from one of the strongest positions in the South, and the people were all agog to hear the news. A large Confederate flag was displayed from a balcony of the War Office, and the Hon. L. P. Walker, the Secretary of War, announced in a brief speech, to the assembled multitude below, amid repeated cheering, and the waving of hats, and handkerchiefs, the welcome tidings. The Union men, who have become so numerous since the war, had, if any of them were in the city, slunk to their holes, and corners, and the air was redolent, alone, of Southern patriotism, and Southern enthusiasm.

The driving of the enemy from Charleston harbor, decided the fate of Virginia, which had been trembling in the balance for some days. The grand old State could no longer resist her generous impulses. Under a proclamation of President Lincoln the martial hosts of an enraged and vindictive North were assembling, to make war upon her sisters, and this was enough—her ordinance of secession was passed, by a very gratifying majority. Patrick Henry had become a prophet, and the beautiful, and touching apostrophe of James Madison to the "kindred blood," and the "mingled blood" of the American people, which was given to the reader a few pages back, had proved to be the mere chimera of an excited imagination.

The effect of the surrender of Sumter in the North was beyond conception. A prominent leader of the public press of that section had said of the American flag:—

"Tear down that flaunting lie,
    Half-mast the starry flag,
    Insult no sunny sky
    With hate's polluted rag."

Instantly, and as if by the touch of a magician's wand, the polluted rag became the rallying cry of the whole Northern people, and of none more so, than of the very men who had thus denounced it. But there was method in this madness; the rag had only been polluted whilst it was the emblem of good faith between the North, and the South; whilst, in other words, it prevented the mad fanatics of the North from violating that slave property, which *their* ancestors had promised *our* ancestors, in the solemn league and covenant of the Constitution, should forever remain inviolate.

But now that the rag, instead of being an obstacle, might be made the means of accomplishing their designs, it was no longer necessary to pull it down. The moment it was fired upon, it became, in their eyes, a new flag, and the symbol of a new faith. It was no longer to represent the federative principle, or to protect the rights of States; it was henceforth to wave over yelling, and maddened majorities, whose will was to be both Constitution, and law. Strange that the thinking portion of the Northern people did not see this; strange that the hitherto conservative Democratic party did not see it. Or was it that the whole North had been wearing a mask, and that the mask was now no longer available, or desirable, to hide their treachery?

Perhaps the future historian, in calmer moments, when the waves of passion engendered by the late storm shall have sunk to rest, will be better able to answer this question. For the present it is sufficient to record the fact, mortifying, it must be confessed, to poor human nature, that all our quondam friends, without so many as half a dozen exceptions in a whole nation—I speak, of course, of prominent men—went over to the common enemy. The very men who had stood, shoulder to shoulder, with us, in resisting Northern aggression, who had encouraged us with pen, and voice, to resist, if need be, unto the death, who promised in case of secession, to stand between us, and the march of Northern armies of invasion, instantly, and without even the salvo to their consciences of circumlocution, changed their political faith of a life-time, and became, if not straight-out Republicans, at least blatant War Democrats.

The reader cannot be at a loss to account for this change. It was caused by the purest, and most refined selfishness. Next to the love of wealth, the love of office may be said to be the distinguishing passion of the American people. In the hands of a skilful office-seeker, patriotism is a mere word with which to delude the ignorant masses, and not a sentiment, or a creed, to be really entertained. Our allies in the North were very patriotic, whilst there were still hopes of preserving the Union, and along with it the prospect of office, by the aid of the Southern people, but the moment the Southern States went out, and it became evident that they would be politically dead, unless they recanted their political faith, it was seen that they had no intention of becoming martyrs. Their motto, on the contrary, became *sauve qui peut*, and the d—l take the hindmost; and the banks of the new political Jordan were at once crowded with a multitude anxious to be dipped in its regenerating waters!

As the tidings of these doings in the North were flashed to us, over the wires, in Montgomery, it became evident to me, that the Light-House Bureau was no longer to be thought of. It had become necessary for every man, who could wield a sword, to draw it in defence of his country, thus threatened by the swarming hordes of the North, and to leave the things of peace to the future.

I had already passed the prime of life, and was going gently down that declivity, at whose base we all arrive, sooner or later, but *I thanked God*, that I had still a few years before me, and vigor enough of constitution left, to strike in defence of the right. I at once sought an interview with the Secretary of the Navy, and explained to him my desire to go afloat. We had, as yet, nothing that could be called a navy; not a ship indeed, if we except a few river steamers, that had been hastily armed by some of the States, and turned over, by them, to the Navy Department. The naval officers, who had come South, had brought with them nothing but their poverty, and their swords; all of them who had been in command of ships, at the secession of their respective States, having, from a sense of honor, delivered them back to the Federal Government.

If a sense of justice had presided at the separation of the States, a large portion of the ships of the Navy would have been turned over to the South; and this failing to be done, it may be questionable whether the Southern naval officers, in command, would not have been justified in bringing their ships with them, which it would have been easy for them to do. But, on the other hand, they had been personally intrusted with their commands, by the Federal Government, and it would have been treason to a military principle, if not to those great principles which guide revolutions, to deliver those commands to a different government. Perhaps they decided correctly — at all events, a military, or naval man, cannot go very far astray, who abides by the point of honor.

Shortly before the war-cloud had arisen so ominously above the political horizon, I had written a letter to a distinguished member of the Federal Congress from the South, in reply to one from himself, giving him my views as to the naval policy of our section, in case things should come to a crisis. I make no apology to the reader for presenting him with the following extract from that letter, bearing upon the subject, which we have now in hand. "You ask me to explain what I mean, by an irregular naval force. I mean a well-organized system of private armed ships, called privateers. If you are warred upon at all, it will be by a commercial people, whose ability to do you harm will consist chiefly in ships, and shipping. It is at ships and shipping, therefore, that you must strike; and the most effectual way to do this, is, by means of the irregular force of which I speak. Private cupidity will always furnish the means for this description of warfare, and all that will be required of you will be to put it under sufficient legal restraints, to prevent it from degenerating into piracy, and becoming an abuse. Even New England ships, and New England capital would be at your service, in abundance. The system of privateering would be analogous to the militia system on the land. You could have a large irregular sea force, to act in aid of the regular naval force, so long as the war lasted, and which could be disbanded, without further care or expense, at the end of the war."

Wealth is necessary to the conduct of all modern wars, and

I naturally turned my eyes, as indicated in the above letter, to the enemy's chief source of wealth.   The ingenuity, enterprise, and natural adaptation of the Northern people to the sea, and seafaring pursuits, had enabled them, aided by the vast resources, which they had filched, under pretence of legislation, from the South, to build up, in the course of a very few years, a commercial marine that was second only to that of Great Britain, in magnitude and importance.

The first decked vessel that had been built in the United States, was built by one Adrian Block, a Dutch skipper, on the banks of the Hudson, in 1614, and in 1860, or in less than two centuries and a half, the great Republic was competing with England, the history of whose maritime enterprise extended back a thousand years, for the carrying trade of the world!   This trade, if permitted to continue, would be a powerful means of sustaining the credit of the enemy, and enabling him to carry on the war.   Hence it became an object of the first necessity with the Confederate States, to strike at his commerce.   I enlarged upon this necessity, in the interview I was now holding with Mr. Mallory, and I was gratified to find that that able officer agreed with me fully in opinion.

A Board of naval officers was already in session at New Orleans, charged with the duty of procuring, as speedily as possible, some light and fast steamers to be let loose against the enemy's commercial marine, but their reports up to this time, had been but little satisfactory.   They had examined a number of vessels, and found some defects in all of them. The Secretary, speaking of the discouragement presented by these reports, handed me one of them, which he had received that morning, from the Board.   I read it, and found that it described a small propeller steamer, of five hundred tons burden, sea-going, with a low-pressure engine, sound, and capable of being so strengthened as to be enabled to carry an ordinary battery of four, or five guns.   Her speed was reported to be between nine, and ten knots, but unfortunately, said the Board, she carries but five days' fuel, and has no accommodations for the crew of a ship of war.   She was, accordingly, condemned.   When I had finished reading the report, I turned to the Secretary, and said, "Give me that ship; I think I can make her answer the purpose." My request was at once acceded to, the Secretary telegraphed to the Board, to receive the ship, and the clerks of the Department were set at work, to hunt up the necessary officers, to accompany me, and make out the proper orders. And this is the way in which the Confederate States' steamer *Sumter*, which was to have the honor of being the first ship of war to throw the new Confederate flag to the breeze, was commissioned. I had accepted a stone which had been rejected of the builders, and which, though, it did not afterward become the "chief corner-stone of the temple," I endeavored to work into the building which the Confederates were then rearing, to remind their posterity that they had struggled, as Patrick Henry and his contemporaries had struggled before them, "in defence of their liberties."

The next day, the chief clerk of the Navy Department handed me the following order:

CONFEDERATE STATES OF AMERICA, }
NAVY DEPARTMENT, MONTGOMERY, April 18, 1861. }

SIR: — You are hereby detached from duty as Chief of the Light-House Bureau, and will proceed to New Orleans, and take command of the steamer *Sumter* (named in honor of our recent victory over Fort Sumter). The following officers have been ordered to report to you, for duty: Lieutenants John M. Kell, R. T. Chapman, John M. Stribling, and Wm. E. Evans; Paymaster Henry. Myers; Surgeon Francis L. Galt; Midshipmen, Wm. A. Hicks, Richard F. Armstrong, Albert G. Hudgins, John F. Holden, and Jos. D. Wilson. I am respectfully your obedient servant,

S. R. MALLORY, *Secretary of the Navy.*
Commander RAPHAEL SEMMES.

The reader will observe that I am addressed as a "commander," the rank which I held in the old service. The Navy Department, in consultation with the President, had adopted the rule of accepting all the officers who chose to come to us from the old Navy — as the Federal Navy began now to be called — without increase of rank; and in arranging them on the Navy-list, their old *relative* rank was also preserved. This rule had two good effects; it did not tempt any officer to come to us, moved by the hope of immediate promotion, and it put us all on an equal footing, in the future race for honors.

I had been living in Montgomery as a bachelor, at the house

of Mr. Wm. Knox, an old friend — my family having gone
to spend some time with a beloved brother, in Maryland, until
I could see, by the light of events, what final disposition to
make of it.   It did not occupy me long, therefore, to make my
preparations for departure, in obedience to my orders.   I took
a respectful, and affectionate leave of the officers of the government, with whom I had been associated, and embarked on
the afternoon of the same day on which I had received my
orders, on board the steamer *Southern Republic* for Mobile.
At Mobile I fell in with Lieutenant Chapman, one of the officers who had been detailed to report to me, and he, being a
minute-man like myself, took a hasty leave of a young wife,
and we continued our journey together.

I found Mobile, like the rest of the Confederacy, in a great
state of excitement.   Always one of the truest of Southern
cities, it was boiling over with enthusiasm; the young merchants had dropped their daybooks and ledgers, and were
forming, and drilling companies, by night and by day, whilst
the older ones were discussing questions of finance, and anxiously casting about them, to see how the Confederate Treasury
could be supported.   The Battle House, at which I stopped
for a few hours, previous to taking the steamer for New Orleans, was thronged with young men in military costume, and
all seemed going "as merrily as a marriage-bell."   Alas! my
poor young countrymen, how many of you had disappeared
from the scene, when I next returned among you, near the
close of the war, and how many poor mothers there were, weeping
for the sons that were not.   But your gallant and glorious
record! — that, at least, remains, and must remain forever; for
you have inscribed your names so high on the scroll of fame,
that the slanderous breath of an ungenerous foe can never
reach them.

I arrived in New Orleans, on Monday, the 22d of April, and
at once put myself in communication with the commanding
naval officer, the venerable Lawrence Rousseau, since gone to
his long home, full of years, and full of honors.   Like a true
son of the South he had obeyed the first call of his fatherland,
the State of Louisiana, and torn off the seal from the commission of a Federal captain, which he had honored for forty

years. I will not say, "peace to his ashes," for the spirit of a
Christian gentleman, which animated his frame during life, has
doubtless received its appropriate reward; nor will I say
aught of his name, or fame, for these are embalmed in the
memories of his countrymen. He was my friend, and in that
name "friend" I pronounce his eulogy. On the same day of
my arrival, in company with Lieutenant Chapman, I inspected,
and took possession of my new ship. I found her only a dismantled packet-ship, full of upper cabins, and other top-hamper,
furniture, and crockery, but as unlike a ship of war as possible.
Still, I was pleased with her general appearance. Her lines
were easy, and graceful, and she had a sort of saucy air about
her, which seemed to say, that she was not averse to the service on which she was about to be employed.

CHAPTER X.

THE PREPARATION OF THE SUMTER FOR SEA——SHE DROPS DOWN BETWEEN THE FORTS JACKSON, AND ST. PHILIP—— RECEIVES HER SAILING ORDERS——LIST OF OFFICERS.

A GREAT change was apparent in New Orleans since I had last visited it. The levée in front of the city was no longer a great mart of commerce, piled with cotton bales, and supplies going back to the planter; densely packed with steamers, and thronged with a busy multitude. The long lines of shipping above the city had been greatly thinned, and a general air of desolation hung over the river front. It seemed as though a pestilence brooded over the doomed city, and that its inhabitants had fled before the fell destroyer. The *Sumter* lay on the opposite side of the river, at Algiers, and I crossed over every morning to superintend her refitment. I was sometimes detained at the ferry-house, waiting for the ferry-boat, and on these occasions, casting my eyes up and down the late busy river, it was not unfrequent to see it without so much as a skiff in motion on its bosom.

But this first simoon of the desert which had swept over the city, as a foretaste of what was to come, had by no means discouraged its patriotic inhabitants. The activity of commerce had ceased, it is true, but another description of activity had taken its place. War now occupied the thoughts of the multitude, and the sound of the drum, and the tramp of armed men were heard in the streets. The balconies were crowded with lovely women in gay attire, to witness the military processions, and the Confederate flag in miniature was pinned on almost every bosom. The enthusiasm of the Frenchman had been most easily and gracefully blended with the stern determination of the Southern man of English descent; the consequence of which was, that there was more demonstrative patriotism in New Orleans, than in any other of our Southern cities. Nor was this patriotism demonstrative only, it was deep and real, and was afterward sealed with some of the best Creole blood of the land, poured out, freely, on many a desperate battle-field. Alas! poor Louisiana. Once the seat of wealth, and of a gay and refined hospitality, thy manorial residences are deserted, and in decay, or have been levelled by the torch of the incendiary; thy fruitful fields, that were cultivated by the contented laborer, who whistled his merriment to his lazy plow, have been given to the jungle; thy fair daughters have been insulted, by the coarse, and rude Vandal; and even thy liberties have been given in charge of thy freedmen; and all this, because thou wouldst thyself be free!

I now took my ship actively in hand, and set gangs of mechanics at work to remove her upper cabins, and other top-hamper, preparatory to making the necessary alterations. These latter were considerable, and I soon found that I had a tedious job on my hands. It was no longer the case, as it had been in former years, when I had had occasion to fit out a ship, that I could go into a navy-yard, with well-provided work-shops, and skilled workmen ready with all the requsite materials at hand to execute my orders. Everything had to be improvised, from the manufacture of a water-tank, to the " kids, and cans" of the berth-deck messes, and from a gun-carriage to a friction-primer. I had not only to devise all the alterations but to make plans, and drawings of them, before they could be comprehended. The main deck was strengthened, by the addition of heavy beams to enable it to support the battery; a berth-deck was laid for the accommodation of the crew; the engine, which was partly above the water-line, was protected by a system of wood-work, and iron bars; the ship's rig was altered so as to convert her into a barkentine, with square-sails on her fore and main-masts; the officers' quarters, including my own cabin, were re-arranged; new suits of sails were made, and new boats constructed; hammocks and bedding were procured for the crew, and guns, gun-carriages, and ammunition ordered. Two long, tedious months were consumed in making these various alterations, and additions. My battery was to consist of an eight-inch shell gun, to be pivoted amidships, and of four light thirty-two pounders, of thirteen cwt. each, in broadside.

The Secretary of the Navy, who was as anxious as myself that I should get to sea immediately, had given me all the assistance in his power, readily acceding to my requests, and promptly filling, or causing to be filled, all my requisitions. With the secession of Virginia we had become possessed of a valuable depot of naval supplies, in the Norfolk Navy Yard. It was filled with guns, shot, shell, cordage, and everything that was useful in the equipment of a ship, but it was far away from New Orleans, and such was the confusion along the different lines of railroad, that it was difficult to procure transportation. Commander Terry Sinclair, the active ordnance officer of the yard, had early dispatched my guns, by railroad, but weeks elapsed without my being able to hear anything of them. I was finally obliged to send a lieutenant in search of them, who picked them up, one by one, as they had been thrown out on the road-side, to make room for other freight. My gun-carriages I was obliged to have constructed myself, and I was fortunate enough to obtain the services of a very ingenious mechanic to assist me in this part of my duties — Mr. Roy, a former employee of the Custom-House, within whose ample walls he had established his work-shop. He contrived most ingeniously, and constructed out of railroad iron, one of the best carriages (or rather, slide and circle) for a pivot-gun, which I have ever seen. The large foundry of Leeds & Co. took the contract for casting my shot, and shells, and executed it to my satisfaction.

Whilst all these various operations are going on, we may conveniently look around us upon passing events, or at least upon such of them as have a bearing upon naval operations. President Davis, a few days after the secession of Virginia, and when war had become imminent, issued a proclamation for the purpose of raising that irregular naval force, of which I have spoken in a previous page. Parties were invited to apply for letters-of-marque and reprisal, with a view to the fitting out of privateers, to prey upon the enemy's commerce. Under this proclamation several privateers — generally light-draught river-steamers, with one or two small guns each — were hastily prepared, in New Orleans, and had already brought in some prizes captured off the mouths of the Mississippi. Even this small demonstration seemed to surprise, as well as alarm the Northern government, for President Lincoln now issued a proclamation declaring the molestation of Federal vessels, on the high seas, by Confederate cruisers, *piracy.* He had also issued a proclamation declaring the ports of the Confederacy in a state of blockade. The mouths of the Mississippi were to be sealed on the 25th of May.

The European governments, as soon as it became evident, that the two sections were really at war, took measures accordingly. Great Britain took the lead, and declared a strict neutrality between the combatants. It was of the essence of such a declaration, that it should put both belligerents on the same footing. This was apparently done, and the cruisers of both sections were prohibited, alike, from taking their prizes into British ports. I shall have something to say of the unequal operation of this declaration of neutrality, in a future part of these memoirs; for the present it is only necessary to state, that it acknowledged us to be in possession of belligerent rights. This was a point gained certainly, but it was no more than was to have been expected. Indeed, Great Britain could do nothing less. In recognizing the war which had broken out between the sections, as a war, and not as a mere insurrection, she had only followed the lead of Mr. Lincoln himself. Efforts had been made it is true, both by Mr. Lincoln, and his Secretary of State, to convince the European governments that the job which they had on their hands was a small affair; a mere family quarrel, of no great significance.

But the truth would not be suppressed, and when, at last, it became necessary to declare the Confederate ports in a state of blockade, and to send ships of war thither, to enforce the declaration, the sly little game which they had been playing was all up with them. A blockade was an act of war, which came under the cognizance of the laws of nations. It concerned neutrals, as well as belligerents, and foreign nations were bound to take notice of it. It followed that there could not be a blockade without a war; and it equally followed, that there could not be a war without at least two belligerent parties to it. It will thus be seen, that the declaration of neutrality of Great Britain was a logical sequence of Mr. Lincoln's, and Mr. Seward's own act. And yet with sullen, and singular inconsistency, the Northern Government has objected from that day to this, to this mere routine act of Great Britain. So much was this act considered, as a matter of course, at the time, that all the other powers of the earth, of sufficient dignity to act in the premises, at all, followed the example set them by Great Britain, and issued similar declarations; and the four years of bloody war that followed justified the wisdom of their acts.

We may now return to the equipment of the *Sumter*. A rendezvouz had been opened, and a crew had been shipped for her, which was temporarily berthed on board the receiving ship, *Star of the West*, a transport-steamer of the enemy, which had been gallantly captured by some Texans, and turned over to the Navy. New Orleans was full of seamen, discharged from ships that had been laid up, and more men were offering themselves for service, than I could receive. I had the advantage, therefore, of picking my crew, an advantage which no one but a seaman can fully appreciate. My lieutenants, surgeon, paymaster, and marine officer had all arrived, and, with the consent of the Navy Department, I had appointed my engineers—one chief, and three assistants— boatswain, carpenter, and sailmaker. My provisions had been purchased, and were ready to be put on board, and my funds had already arrived, but we were still waiting on the mechanics, who, though doing their best, had not yet been able to turn the ship over to us. From the following letter to the Secretary of the Navy, inclosing a requisition for funds, it will be seen that my demands upon the department were quite moderate, and that I expected to make the *Sumter pay her own expenses*, as soon as she should get to sea.

NEW ORLEANS, May 14, 1861.

SIR:—I have the honor to inclose, herewith, a requisition for the sum of $10,000, which I request may be remitted to the paymaster of the *Sumter*, in specie, for use during my contemplated cruise. I may find it necessary to coal several times, and to supply my crew with fresh provisions, &c., before I have the opportunity of replenishing my military chest from the enemy.

The ammunition remained to be provided, and on the 20th of May, I dispatched Lieutenant Chapman to the Baton Rouge Arsenal, which had been captured a short time before, for the purpose of procuring it, under the following letter of instructions :

NEW ORLEANS, May 20, 1861.

SIR :— You will proceed to Baton Rouge, and put yourself in communication with the commander of the C. S. Arsenal, at that point, for the purpose of receiving the ammunition, arms, shot, shell, &c., that may be required for the supply of the C. S. steamer *Sumter*, now fitting for sea at this port. It is presumed that the proper orders [which had been requested] have been, or will be dispatched from Montgomery, authorizing the issue of all such articles, as we may need. Should this not be the case, with regard to any of the articles, it is hoped that the ordnance officer in charge will not hesitate to deliver them, as it is highly important that the *Sumter* should not be detained, because of any oversight, or informality, in the orders of the War Department. Be pleased to present the accompanying requisition to Captain Booth, the superintendent, and ask that it may be filled. The gunner will be directed to report to you, to accompany you to Baton Rouge, on this service.

The reader will thus perceive that many difficulties lay in the way of equipping the *Sumter* ; that I was obliged to pick up one material here, and another there, as I could best find it, and that I was not altogether free from the routine of the "Circumlocution Office," as my requisitions had frequently to pass through many hands, before they could be complied with.

About this time, we met with a sad accident in the loss of one of our midshipmen, by drowning. He, with other young officers of the *Sumter*, had been stationed, temporarily, on board the receiving ship, in charge of the *Sumter's* crew, whilst the latter ship was still in the hands of the mechanics. The following letter of condolence to the father of the young gentleman will sufficiently explain the circumstances of the disaster

NEW ORLEANS, May 18, 1861.

SIR :— It becomes my melancholy duty to inform you, of the death, by drowning, yesterday, of your son, Midshipman John F. Holden, of the C. S. steamer *Sumter*. Your son was temporarily attached to the receiving ship (late *Star of the West*) at this place, whilst the *Sumter* was being prepared for sea, and whilst engaged in carrying out an anchor, in a boat belonging to that ship, met his melancholy fate, along with three of the crew, by the swamping of the boat, in which he was embarked. I offer you, my dear sir, my heartfelt condolence on this sad bereavement. You have lost a cherished son, and the Government a valuable and promising young officer.

W. B. HOLDEN, ESQ., *Louisburg, Tenn.*

War had begun, thus early, to demand of us our sacrifices. Tennessee had not yet seceded, and yet this ardent Southern youth had withdrawn from the Naval Academy, and cast his lot with his section.

A few extracts from my journal will now, perhaps, give the reader a better idea of the progress of my preparations for sea, and of passing events, than any other form of narrative. *May 27th.*—News received this morning of the appearance, at Pass à L'Outre, yesterday, of the U. S. steamer *Brooklyn.* and of the establishment of the blockade. Work is progressing satisfactorily, and I expect to be ready for sea, by Sunday next.

News of skirmishing in Virginia, and of fresh arrivals of Northern troops, at Washington, *en route* for that State. The Federal Government has crossed the Potomac, in force, and thus inaugurated a bloody, and a bitter war, by the invasion of our territory. So be it — we but accept the gantlet, which has been flung in our faces. The future will tell a tale not unworthy of the South, and her glorious cause.

Monday, May 30th. My patience is sorely tried by the mechanics. The water-tanks for the *Sumter* are not yet completed. The carriage for the 8-inch gun was finished, to-day, and we are busy laying down the circles for it, and cutting the holes for the fighting-bolts. The carriages for the 32-pounders are promised us, by Saturday next, and also the copper tanks for the magazine. Our ammunition, and small arms arrived, yesterday, from Baton Rouge. Besides the *Brooklyn*, at the Passes, we learn, to-day, that the *Niagara*, and *Minnesota*, two of the enemy's fastest, and heaviest steamships have arrived, to assist in enforcing the blockade, and to lie in wait for some ships expected to arrive, laden with arms and ammunition, for the Confederacy. *May 31st.*—The tanks are at last finished, and they have all been delivered, to-day. Leeds & Co. have done an excellent job, and I shall be enabled to carry three months' water for my crew. We shall now get on, rapidly, with our preparations.

Saturday, June 1st, finds us not yet ready for sea! The tanks have all been taken on board, and stowed; the gun carriages for the 32s will be finished on Monday. The circles for the 8-inch gun have been laid down, and the fighting-bolts are ready for placing. On Monday I shall throw the crew on board, and by Thursday next, I shall, *without doubt* be ready for sea. We are losing a great deal of precious time. The enemy's flag is being flaunted in our faces, at all our ports by his ships of war, and his vessels of commerce are passing, and repassing, on the ocean, in defiance, or in contempt of our power, and, as yet, we have not struck a blow.

At length on the 3d of June, I was enabled to put the *Sumter*, formally, in commission. On that day her colors were hoisted, for the first time—the ensign having been presented to me, by some patriotic ladies of New Orleans—the crew was transferred to her, from the receiving ship, and the officers were ordered to mess on board. The ship was now hauled off and anchored in the stream, but we were delayed two long and tedious weeks yet, before we were finally ready. During these two weeks we made a trial trip up the river, some ten or twelve miles. Some of the principal citizens were invited on board, and a bright, and beautiful afternoon was pleasantly spent, in testing the qualities of the ship, the range of her guns, and the working of the gun-carriages; the whole ending by a collation, in partaking of which my guests were kind enough to wish me a career full of "*blazing* honors."

I was somewhat disappointed in the speed of my ship, as we did not succeed in getting more than nine knots out of her. There was another great disadvantage. With all the space I could allot to my coal-bunkers, she could be made to carry no more than about eight days' fuel. We had masts, and sails, it is true, but these could be of but little use, when the coal was exhausted, as the propeller would remain a drag in the water, there being no means of hoisting it. It was with such drawbacks, that I was to take the sea, alone, against a vindictive and relentless enemy, whose Navy already swarmed on our coasts, and whose means of increasing it were inexhaustible.

But the sailor has a saying, that "Luck is a Lord," and we trusted to luck.

On the 18th of June, after all the vexatious delays that have been described, I got up my anchor, and dropped down to the Barracks, below the city a short distance, to receive my powder on board, which, for safety, had been placed in the State magazine. At 10.30 P. M. of the same day, we got up steam, and by the soft and brilliant light of a moon near her full, threw ourselves into the broad, and swift current of the Father of Waters, and ran rapidly down to the anchorage, between Fort Jackson, and Fort St. Philip, where we came to at 4 A. M. In the course of the day, Captain Brand, an ex-officer of the old Navy, and now second in command of the forts, came on board to make us the ceremonial visit; and I subsequently paid my respects to Major Duncan, the officer in chief command, an ex-officer of the old Army. These gentlemen were both busy, as I found upon inspecting the forts, in perfecting their batteries, and drilling their men, for the hot work that was evidently before them. As was unfortunately the case with our people, generally, at this period, they were over-confident. They kindly supplied some few deficiencies, that still remained in our gunner's department, and I received from them a howitzer, which I mounted on my taffarel, to guard against boat attacks, by night.

I remained three days at my anchors between the forts, for the purpose of stationing, and drilling my crew, before venturing into the presence of the enemy; and I will take advantage of this lull to bring up some matters connected with the ship, which we have hitherto overlooked. On the 7th of June, the Secretary of the Navy—the Government having, in the mean time, removed to Richmond—sent me my sailing orders, and in my letter of the 14th of the same month, acknowledging their receipt, I had said to him: "I have an excellent set of men on board, though they are nearly all green, and will require some little practice, and drilling, at the guns, to enable them to handle them creditably. Should I be fortunate enough to reach the high seas, you may rely upon my implicit obedience of your instructions, 'to do the enemy's commerce the greatest injury, in the shortest time.'"

Here was a model of a letter of instruction—it meant "burn, sink, and destroy," always, of course, within the limits prescribed by the laws of nations, and with due attention to the laws of humanity, in the treatment of prisoners. The reader will see, as we progress, that I gave the "implicit obedience" which had been promised, to these instructions, and that if greater results were not accomplished, it was the fault of the *Sumter*, and not of her commander. In the same letter that brought me my sailing orders, the Secretary had suggested to me the propriety of adopting some means of communicating with him, by cipher, so that, my despatches, if captured by the enemy, would be unintelligible to him. The following letter in reply to this suggestion, will explain how this was arranged: "I have the honor to enclose herewith a copy of 'Reid's English Dictionary,' a duplicate of which I retain, for the purpose mentioned in your letter of instructions, of the 7th instant. I have not been able to find in the city of New Orleans, 'Cobb's Miniature Lexicon,' suggested by you, or any other suitable dictionary, with but a single column on a page. This need make no difference, however. In my communications to the Department, should I have occasion to refer to a word in the copy sent, I will designate the first column on the page, A, and the second column, B. Thus, if I wish to use the word 'prisoner,' my reference to it would be as follows: 323, B, 15; the first number referring to the page, the letter to the column, and the second number to the number of the word from the top of the column." By means of this simple, and cheap device, I was enabled, at all times, to keep my dispatches out of the hands of the enemy, or, in other words, prevent him from interpreting them, when I had anything of importance to communicate.

Before leaving New Orleans, I had, in obedience to a general order of the service, transmitted to the Navy Department, a Muster Roll of the officers, and men, serving on board the *Sumter*. Her crew, as reported by this roll, consisted of ninety-two persons, exclusive of officers. Twenty of these ninety-two persons were marines—a larger guard than was usual for so small a ship. The officers were as follows:

Commander.—Raphael Semmes.

Lieutenants.—John M. Kell; Robert T. Chapman; John M. Stribling; William E. Evans.

Paymaster.—Henry Myers.

Surgeon.—Francis L. Galt.

1st Lieutenant of Marines.—B. Howell.

Midshipmen.—William A. Hicks; Albert G. Hudgins; Richard F. Armstrong; Joseph D. Wilson.

Engineers.—Miles J. Freeman; William P. Brooks; Matthew O'Brien; Simeon W. Cummings.

Boatswain.—Benjamin P. Mecasky.

Gunner.—Thomas C. Cuddy.

Sailmaker.—W. P. Beaufort.

Carpenter.—William Robinson.

Captain's Clerk.—W. Breedlove Smith.

Commissions had been forwarded to all the officers entitled to receive them, and acting appointments had been given by me to the warrant officers. It will thus be seen, how formally all these details had been attended to. These commissions were to be our warrants for what we were to do, on the high seas.

And now the poor boon will be permitted to human nature, that before we launch our frail bark, on the wild sea of adventure, before us, we should turn our thoughts, homeward, for a moment.

> " 'And is he gone?'—on sudden solitude
> How oft that fearful question will intrude!
> 'T was but an instant past—and here he stood!
> And now!'—without the portal's porch she rushed,
> And then at length her tears in freedom gushed;
> Big, bright, and fast, unknown to her they fell;
> But still her lips refused to send 'farewell!'
> For in that word—that fatal word—howe'er
> We promise—hope—believe—there breathes despair."

Such was the agony of many a fair bosom, as the officers of the *Sumter* had torn themselves from the embraces of their families, in those scenes of leave-taking, which more than any other, try the sailor's heart. Several of them were married men, and it was long years before they returned to the homes which they had made sad by their absence.

CHAPTER XI.

AFTER LONG WAITING AND WATCHING, THE SUMTER RUNS
THE BLOCKADE OF THE MISSISSIPPI, IN OPEN DAYLIGHT,
PURSUED BY THE BROOKLYN.

WHILST we were lying at our anchors between the forts, as described in the last chapter, Governor Moore of Louisiana, who had done good service to the Confederacy, by seizing the forts, and arsenals in his State, in advance of secession, and the Hon. John Slidell, lately returned from his seat in the Federal Senate, and other distinguished gentlemen came down, on a visit of inspection to the forts. I went on shore to call on them, and brought them on board the *Sumter* to lunch with me. My ship was, by this time, in excellent order, and my crew well accustomed to their stations, under the judicious management of my first lieutenant, and I took pleasure in showing these gentlemen how much a little discipline could accomplish, in the course of a few weeks. Discipline!—what a power it is everywhere, and under all circumstances; and how much the want of it lost us, as the war progressed. What a pity the officers of our army did not have their respective commands, encircled by wooden walls, with but a "single monarch to walk the peopled deck."

Just at nightfall, on the evening of the 21st of June, I received the following despatch from the commanding officer of the forts:

CAPTAIN:—I am desired by the commanding officer to state, that the *Ivy*—this was a small tender of the forts, and letter-of-marque —reports that the *Powhatan* has left, in pursuit of two ships, and that he has a telegram from Pass à L'Outre, to the effect, that a boat from the *Brooklyn* had put into the river and was making for the telegraph station, where she was expected to arrive within a few minutes.

The *Powhatan* was blockading the Southwest Pass, and it was barely possible that I might get to sea, through this pass, if a pilot could be at once procured; and so I immediately ordered steam to be raised, and getting up my anchor, steamed down to the Head of the Passes, where the river branches into its three principal outlets. Arriving here, at half past ten P. M. I dispatched a boat to the light house, for a pilot; but the keeper *knew nothing* of the pilots, and was unwilling to come on board, himself, though requested. The night wore away, and nothing could be done.

The telescope revealed to us, the next morning, that the *Powhatan* had returned to her station. From the sullen, and unsatisfactory message, which had been returned to me, by the keeper of the light-house, I began to suspect that there was something wrong, about the pilots; and it being quite necessary that I should have one constantly, on board, to enable me to take advantage of any temporary absence of the enemy's cruisers, without having to hunt up one for the emergency, I dispatched the *Ivy*, to the pilots' station, at the Southwest Pass, in search of one. This active little cruiser returned in the course of a few hours, and reported that none of the pilots were willing to come on board of me! I received, about the same time, a telegraphic despatch from the Southwest Pass, forwarded to me through Major Duncan, which read as follows: "Applied to the Captain of the Pilots' Association for a pilot for the *Sumter*. He requested me to state, that there are no pilots on duty now!" "So ho! sits the wind in that quarter," thought I—I will soon set this matter right. I, at once, sent Lieutenant Stribling on board the *Ivy*, and directed him to proceed to the Pilots' Association, and deliver, and see executed the following written order:

> C. S. Steamer Sumter, Head of the Passes, ¦
> June 22, 1861. ¦
>
> Sir:—This is to command you to repair on board this ship, with three or four of the most experienced pilots of the Bar. I am surprised to learn, that an unwillingness has been expressed, by some of the pilots of your Association, to come on board the *Sumter;* and my purpose is to test the fact of such disloyalty to the Confederate States. If any man disobeys this summons I will not only have his Branch taken from him, but I will send an armed force, and arrest, and bring him on board.

This order had the desired effect, and in the course of the afternoon, Lieutenant Stribling returned, bringing with him, the Captain of the Association, and several of the pilots. I directed them to be brought into my cabin, and when they were assembled, demanded to know the reason of their late behavior. Some stammering excuses were offered, which I cut short, by informing them that one of them must remain on board constantly, and that they might determine for themselves, who should take the first week's service; to be relieved at the end of the week, by another, and so on, as long as I should find it necessary. One of their number being designated, I dismissed the rest. The reader will see how many faithful auxiliaries, Admiral Farragut afterward found, in the Pilots' Association of the mouths of the Mississippi, when he made his famous ascent of the river, and captured its great seaport. Nor was this defection confined to New Orleans. The pilots along our whole Southern coast were, with few exceptions, Northern men, and as a rule they went over to the enemy, though pretending, in the beginning of our troubles, to be good secessionists. The same remark may be applied to our steamboat men, of Northern birth, as a class. Many of them had become domiciled in the South, and were supposed to be good Southern men, until the crucial test of self-interest was applied to them, when they, too, deserted us, and took service with the enemy.

The object of the *Brooklyn's* boat, which, as we have seen, pulled into the telegraph station at Pass à L'Outre, just before we got under way from between the forts, was to cut the wires, and break up the station, to prevent intelligence being given me of the movements of the blockading fleet. I now resorted to a little retaliation. I dispatched an officer to the different light-houses, to stave the oil-casks, and bring away the lighting apparatus, to prevent the enemy's shipping from using the lights. They were of great convenience, not only to the ships employed on the blockade, but to the enemy's transports, and other ships, bound to and from the coast of Texas. They could be of no use to our own blockade-runners, as the passes of the Mississippi, by reason of their long, and tortuous, and frequently shifting channels, were absolutely closed to them.

The last letter addressed by me to the Secretary of the Navy, before escaping through the blockade, as hereinafter described, was the following:

C. S. STEAMER SUMTER, HEAD OF THE PASSES,
June 30, 1861.

SIR:—I have the honor to inform the Department that I am still at my anchors at the "Head of the Passes"—the enemy closely investing both of the practical outlets. At Pass à L'Outre there are three ships, the *Brooklyn*, and another propeller, and a large side-wheel steamer; and at the Southwest Pass, there is the *Powhatan*, lying within half a mile of the bar, and not stirring an inch from her anchors, night or day. I am only surprised that the *Brooklyn* does not come up to this anchorage, which she might easily do—as there is water enough, and no military precautions, whatever, have been taken to hold the position—and thus effectually seal all the passes of the river, by her presence alone; which would enable the enemy to withdraw the remainder of his blockading force, for use elsewhere. With the assistance of the *Jackson*, Lieutenant Gwathmey, and the *McRae*, Lieutenant Huger—neither of which has, as yet, however, dropped down—I could probably hold my position here, until an opportunity offers of my getting to sea. I shall watch, diligently, for such an opportunity, and have no doubt, that sooner or later, it will present itself. I found, upon dropping down to this point, that the lights at Pass à L'Outre, and South Pass had been strangely overlooked, and that they were still being nightly exhibited. I caused them both to be extinguished, so that if bad weather should set in—a gale from the south-east, for instance—the blockading ships, having nothing to "hold on to," will be obliged to make an offing. At present the worst feature of the blockade of Pass à L'Outre is, that the *Brooklyn* has the speed of me; so that even if I should run the bar, I could not hope to escape her, unless I surprised her, which with her close watch of the bar, at anchor near by, both night and day, it will be exceedingly difficult to do. I should be quite willing to try speed with the *Powhatan*, if I could hope to run the .gantlet of her guns, without being crippled; but here again, unfortunately, with all the buoys, and other marks removed, the bar which she is watching is a perfectly blind bar, except by daylight. In the meantime, I am drilling my green crew, to a proper use of the great guns, and small arms. With the exception of a diarrhœa, which is prevailing, to some extent, brought on by too free use of the river water, in the excessive heats which prevail, the crew continues healthy.

Nothing in fact surprised me more, during the nine days I lay at the Head of the Passes, than that the enemy did not attack me with some of his light-draught, but heavily armed steamers, or by his boats, by night. Here was the *Sumter*, a

small ship, with a crew, all told, of a little over a hundred
men, anchored only ten, or twelve miles from the enemy, without a gun, or an obstruction between her and him; and yet no
offensive movement was made against her. The enemy watched
me closely, day by day, and bent all his energies toward preventing my escape, but did not seem to think of the simple
expedient of endeavoring to capture me, with a superior force.
In nightly expectation of an assault, I directed the engineer to
keep the water in his boilers, as near the steam-point as possible, without actually generating the vapor, and sent a patrol
of boats some distance down the Southwest Pass; the boats
being relieved every four hours, and returning to the ship, at
the first streaks of dawn. After I went to sea, the enemy did
come in, and take possession of my anchorage, until he was
driven away by Commodore Hollins, in a little nondescript
ram; which, by the way, was the first ram experiment of the
war. The reader may imagine the tedium, and discomforts of
our position, if he will reflect that it is the month of June, and
that at this season of the year, the sun comes down upon the
broad, and frequently calm surface of the Father of Waters,
with an African glow, and that clouds of that troublesome
little insect the mosquito tormented us, by night and by day.
There was no sleeping at all without the mosquito bar, and I
had accordingly had a supply sent down for all the crew.
Rather than stand the assaults of these little *picadores*, much
longer, I believe my crew would have run the gantlet of the
whole Federal Navy.

My diary will now perhaps give the reader, his clearest conception of the condition of things on board the *Sumter*, for the
remaining few days that she is to continue at her anchors.

Tuesday, June 25th. — A sharp thunder-storm at half-past three
A. M., jarring and shaking the ship with its crashes. The very
flood-gates of the heavens seem open, and the rain is descending on our decks like a cataract. Clearing toward ten o'clock.
Both blockading ships still at their anchors. The British
steam sloop *Jason* touched at the Southwest Pass, yesterday,
and communicated with the *Powhatan*. We learn by the newspapers, to-day, that the enemy has taken possession of Ship
Island, and established a blockade of the Sound. The ana-

conda is drawing his folds around us. We are filling some shell, and cartridges to-day, and drilling the crew at the battery.

Wednesday, June 26th.— Cloudy, with occasional rain squalls, which have tempered the excessive heats. The *Ivy* returned from the city to-day, and brought me eighty barrels of coal. Sent the pilot, in the light-house keeper's boat, to sound the S. E. bar, an unused and unwatched outlet to the eastward of the South Pass—in the hope that we may find sufficient water over it, to permit the egress of the ship. The Federal ships are keeping close watch, as usual, at both the passes, neither of them having stirred from her anchor, since we have been at the "Head of the Passes."

Thursday, June 27th.—Weather sultry, and atmosphere charged with moisture. Pilot returned this afternoon, and reports ten and a half feet water on the S. E. bar. Unfortunately the *Sumter* draws twelve feet; so we must abandon this hope.

Saturday, June 29th.— A mistake induced us to expend a little coal, to-day, uselessly. The pilot having gone aloft, to take his usual morning's survey of the "situation," reported that the *Brooklyn* was nowhere to be seen! Great excitement immediately ensued, on the decks, and the officer of the watch hurried into my cabin with the information. I ordered steam to be gotten up with all dispatch, and when, in the course of a very few minutes, it was reported ready—for we always kept our fires banked—the anchor was tripped, and the ship was under way, ploughing her way through the turbid waters, toward Pass à L'Outre. When we had steamed about four miles down the pass, the *Brooklyn* was seen riding very quietly at her anchors, *in her usual berth near the bar.* Explanation: The *Sumter* had dragged her anchor during the night, and the alteration in her position had brought a clump of trees between her, and the enemy's ship, which had prevented the pilot from seeing the latter! With disappointed hopes we had nothing to do, but to return to our anchors, and watch and wait. In half an hour more, the sailors were lounging idly about the decks, under well spread awnings; the jest, and banter went round, as usual, and save the low hissing and singing of the

steam, which was still escaping, there was nothing to remind
the beholder of our recent disappointment. Such is the
school of philosophy in which the seaman is reared. Our
patience, however, was soon to be rewarded.

Early on the next morning, which was the 30th of June, the
steamer, *Empire Parish*, came down from the city, and coming
alongside of us, put on board some fresh provisions for the
crew, and about one hundred barrels of coal, which my thought-
ful, and attentive friend, Commodore Rousseau, had sent down
to me. Having done this, the steamer shoved off, and proceeded
on her trip, down Pass à L'Outre, to the pilots' station, and
lighthouse. It was a bright Sunday morning, and we were
thinking of nothing but the usual muster, and how we should
get through another idle day. In the course of two or three
hours, the steamer returned, and when she had come near us,
she was seen to cast off a boat, which she had been towing,
containing a single boatman—one of the fishermen, or oyster-
men so common in these waters. The boatman pulled rapidly
under our stern, and hailing the officer of the deck, told him,
that the *Brooklyn* had gone off in chase of a sail, and was no
longer in sight. The crew, who had been "cleaning themselves," for Sunday muster, at once stowed away their bags;
the swinging-booms were gotten alongside, the boats run up,
and, in ten minutes, the steam was again hissing, as if impatient of control. The men ran round the capstan, in "double-
quick," in their eagerness to get up the anchor, and in a few
minutes more, the ship's head swung off gracefully with the
current, and, the propeller being started, she bounded off like
a thing of life, on this new race, which was to decide whether
we should continue to stagnate in midsummer, in the marshes
of the Mississippi, or reach those "glad waters of the dark
blue sea," which form as delightful a picture in the imagination of the sailor, as in that of the poet.

Whilst we were heaving up our anchor, I had noticed the
pilot, standing near me, pale, and apparently nervous, and agitated, but, as yet, he had said not a word. When we were
fairly under way, however, and it seemed probable, at last, that
we should attempt the blockade, the fellow's courage fairly
broke down, and he protested to me that he knew nothing of

the bar of Pass à L'Outre, and durst not attempt to run me over. "I am," said he, "a S. W. bar pilot, and know nothing of the other passes." "What," said I, "did you not know that I was lying at the Head of the Passes, for the very purpose of taking any one of the outlets through which an opportunity of escape might present itself, and yet you dare tell me, that you know but one of them, and have been deceiving me." The fellow stammered out something in excuse, but I was too impatient to listen to him, and, turning to the first lieutenant, ordered him to hoist the "Jack" at the fore, as a signal for a pilot. I had, in fact, resolved to attempt the passage of the bar, from my own slight acquaintance with it, when I had been a light-house inspector, rather than forego the opportunity of escape, and caused the Jack to be hoisted, rather as a matter of course, than because I hoped for any good result from it. The *Brooklyn* had not "chased out of sight," as reported — she had only chased to the westward, some seven or eight miles, and had been hidden from the boatman, by one of the spurs of the Delta. She had probably, all the while, had her telescopes on the *Sumter;* and as soon as she saw the black smoke issuing from her chimney, and the ship moving rapidly toward the pass, she abandoned her chase, and commenced to retrace her steps.

We had nearly equal distances to run to the bar, but I had the advantage of a four-knot current. Several of my officers now collected around me, and we were discussing the chances of escape. "What think you of our prospect," said I, turning to one of my lieutenants, who had served a short time before, on board the *Brooklyn,* and knew well her qualities. "Prospect, sir! not the least in the world — there is no possible chance of our escaping that ship. Even if we get over the bar ahead of her, she must overhaul us, in a very short time. The *Brooklyn* is good for fourteen knots an hour, sir." "That was the report," said I, "on her trial trip, but you know how all such reports are exaggerated; ten to one, she has no better speed, if so good, as the *Sumter.*" "You will see, sir," replied my lieutenant; "we made a passage in her, only a few months ago, from Tampico to Pensacola, and averaged about thirteen knots the whole distance."

Here the conversation dropped, for an officer now came to report to me that a boat had just shoved off from the pilots' station, evidently with a pilot in her. Casting my eyes in the given direction, I saw a whale-boat approaching us, pulled by four stout blacks, who were bending like good fellows to their long ashen oars, and in the stern sheets was seated, sure enough, the welcome pilot, swaying his body to, and fro, as his boat leaped under the oft-repeated strokes of the oars, as though he would hasten her already great speed. But more beautiful still was another object which presented itself. In the balcony of the pilot's house, which had been built in the very marsh, on the margin of the river, there stood a beautiful woman, the pilot's young wife, waving him on to his duty, with her handkerchief. We could have tossed a biscuit from the *Sumter* to the shore, and I uncovered my head gallantly to my fair countrywoman. A few moments more, and a tow-line had been thrown to the boat, and the gallant young fellow stood on the horse-block beside me.

As we swept past the light-house wharf, almost close enough to touch it, there were other petticoats fluttering in the breeze, the owners of which were also waving handkerchiefs of encouragement to the *Sumter*. I could see my sailors' eyes brighten at these spectacles, for the sailor's heart is capacious enough to love the whole sex, and I now felt sure of their nerves, in case it should become necessary to tax them. Half a mile or so, from the light-house, and the bar is reached. There was a Bremen ship lying aground on the bar, and there was just room, and no more, for us to pass her. She had run out a kedge, and had a warp attached to it that was lying across the passage-way. The crew considerately slackened the line, as we approached, and in another bound the *Sumter* was outside the bar, and the Confederate flag was upon the high seas! We now slackened our speed, for an instant — only an instant, for my officers and men all had their wits about them, and worked like good fellows — to haul the pilot's boat alongside, that he might return to the shore. As the gallant young fellow grasped my hand, and shook it warmly, as he descended from the horse-block, he said, "Now, Captain, you are all clear; give her h—ll, and let her go!"

We had now nothing to do, but turn our attention to the

enemy. The *Brooklyn*, as we cleared the bar, was about three and a half, or four miles distant; we were therefore just out of reach of her guns, with nothing to spare. Thick volumes of smoke could be seen pouring from the chimneys of both ships; the firemen, and engineers of each evidently doing their best. I called a lieutenant, and directed him to heave the log. He reported our speed to be nine, and a half knots. Loth to believe that we could be making so little way, through the yet turbid waters, which were rushing past us with great apparent velocity, I directed the officer to repeat the experiment; but the same result followed, though he had paid out the line with a free hand. I now sent for the engineer, and, upon inquiry, found that he was doing his very best — "though," said he, "there is a little drawback, just now, in the 'foaming' of our boilers, arising from the suddenness with which we got up steam; when this subsides, we may be able to add half a knot more."

The *Brooklyn* soon loosed, and set her sails, bracing them sharp up on the starboard tack. I loosed and set mine, also. The enemy's ship was a little on my weather quarter, say a couple of points, and had thus slightly the weather-gauge of me. As I knew I could lay nearer the wind than she, being able to brace my yards sharper, and had besides, the advantage of larger fore-and-aft sails, comparatively, stay-sails, try-sails, and a very large spanker, I resolved at once to hold my wind, so closely, as to compel her to furl her sails, though this would carry me a little athwart her bows, and bring me perhaps a little nearer to her, for the next half hour, or so. A rain squall now came up, and enveloped the two ships, hiding each from the other. As the rain blew off to leeward, and the *Brooklyn* reappeared, she seemed fearfully near to us, and I began to fear I should realize the foreboding of my lieutenant. I could not but admire the majesty of her appearance, with her broad flaring bows, and clean, and beautiful run, and her masts, and yards, as taunt and square, as those of an old time sailing frigate. The stars and stripes of a large ensign flew out from time to time, from under the lee of her spanker, and we could see an apparently anxious crowd of officers on her quarter-deck, many of them with telescopes directed toward us. She had, evidently, I thought, gained upon us, and I expected every moment to hear the whiz of a shot; but still she did not fire.

I now ordered my paymaster to get his public chest, and papers ready for throwing overboard, if it should become necessary. At this crisis the engineer came up from below, bringing the welcome intelligence that the "foaming" of his boilers had ceased, and that his engine was "working beauti-fully," giving the propeller several additional turns per minute. The breeze, too, favored me, for it had freshened considerably; and what was still more to the purpose, I began to perceive that I was "eating" the *Brooklyn* "out of the wind"; in other words, that she was falling more and more to leeward. I knew, of course, that as soon as she fell into my wake, she would be compelled to furl her sails. This she did in half an hour or so afterward, and I at once began to breathe more freely, for I could still hold on to my own canvas. I have witnessed many beautiful sights at sea, but the most beautiful of them all was when the *Brooklyn* let fly all her sheets, and halliards, at once, and clewed up, and furled, in man-of-war style, all her sails, from courses to royals. We now began to gain quite perceptibly on our pursuer, and at half-past three, the chase was abandoned, the baffled *Brooklyn* retracing her steps to Pass à l'Outre, and the *Sumter* bounding away on her course seaward.

We fired no gun of triumph in the face of the enemy — my powder was too precious for that — but I sent the crew aloft, to man the rigging, and three such cheers were given for the Con-federate flag, "that little bit of striped bunting," that had waved from the *Sumter's* peak during the exciting chase, as could pro-ceed only from the throats of American seamen, in the act of defying a tyrant — those cheers were but a repetition of many such cheers that had been given, by our ancestors, to that other bit of "striped bunting" which had defied the power of Eng-land in that olden war, of which our war was but the logi-cal sequence. The reader must not suppose that our anxiety was wholly allayed, as soon as we saw the *Brooklyn* turn away from us.

We were, as yet, only a few miles from the land, and our coast was swarming with the enemy's cruisers. Ship Island

KELLY, PIET & CO. PUBLISHERS.

LITH BY A.HOEN & CO. BALTº

The Sumter running the blockade of **Pass** à l'Outre, by the enemy's Ship Brooklyn, on the 30th June, 1861

was not a great way off, and there was a constant passing to and fro, of ships-of-war between that island and the passes of the Mississippi, and we might stumble upon one of these at any moment. "Sail ho!" was now shouted from the mast-head. "Where away!" cried the officer of the deck. "Right ahead," said the look-out. A few minutes only elapsed, and a second sail was descried, "broad on the starboard bow." But nothing came of these spectres; we passed on, seaward, without so much as raising either of them from the deck, and finally, the friendly robes of night enveloped us. When we at length realized that we had gained an offing; when we began to feel the welcome heave of the sea; when we looked upon the changing aspect of its waters, now darkening into the deepest blue, and breathed the pure air, fresh from the Gulf, untainted of malaria, and untouched of mosquito's wing, we felt like so many prisoners who had been turned loose from a long and painful confinement; and when I reflected upon my mission, to strike for the right! to endeavor to sweep from the seas the commerce of a treacherous friend, who had become a cruel and relentless foe, I felt, in full force, the inspiration of the poet: —

> "Ours the wild life in tumult still to range,
> From toil to rest, and joy in every change.
> Oh, who can tell? Not thou, luxurious slave,
> Whose soul would sicken o'er the heaving wave;
> Not thou, vain lord of wantonness and ease,
> Whom slumber soothes not — pleasures cannot please;
> Oh, who can tell, save he whose heart hath tried,
> And danced in triumph o'er the waters wide,
> The exulting sense — the pulse's maddening play,
> That thrills the wanderer of that trackless way?
> * * * * * * * * * Death!
> Come when it will — we snatch the life of life;
> When lost — what recks it — by disease or strife?
> Let him who crawls, enamored of decay,
> Cling to his couch, and sicken years away;
> Heave his thick breath, and shake his palsied head;
> Ours! the fresh turf, and not the feverish bed;
> While gasp by gasp he falters forth his soul,
> Ours, with one pang — one bound — escapes control.
> His corpse may boast its wan and narrow cave,
> And they who loathed his life, may gild his grave:
> Ours are the tears, though few, sincerely shed,
> When ocean shrouds and sepulchres our dead."

CHAPTER XII.

BRIEF SKETCH OF THE OFFICERS OF THE SUMTER — HER
FIRST PRIZE, WITH OTHER PRIZES, IN QUICK SUCCES-
SION — HER FIRST PORT.

CAPTAIN POOR, the commander of the *Brooklyn*, was
greatly censured by his Government, for permitting the
escape of the *Sumter*. It was even hinted that there had been
treason, in the engine room of the *Brooklyn*, as one or more
of the engineers had been heard to express sentiments favorable to the South. There was no truth, of course, in this
report. It had its origin in the brain of a people, who, having
become traitors, themselves, to their former principles, were
ready to suspect, and to impute treason to every one else. The
greatest offence which had been committed by Captain Poor,
was that he had probably permitted his cupidity to draw him
away from his station. He had chased a prize, in his eagerness to clutch the prize-money, a little too far — that was all.
But in this, he sinned only in common with his countrymen.
The thirst of gain, as well as the malignity of hate, seemed, from
the very first days of the war, to have seized upon a majority
of the Northern people. The Army, and the Navy, professions
hitherto held honorable, did not escape the contamination. They
were soon found, first plundering, and then maliciously burning private houses. The spectacle of cotton-thieving was more
than once presented by the highest dignitaries of the two services — the Admiral quarrelling with the General, as ignoble
rogues are wont to quarrel, as to which rightly pertained the
booty.

The evening of the escape of the *Sumter* was one of those
Gulf evenings, which can only be *felt*, and not described. The
wind died gently away, as the sun declined, leaving a calm,
and sleeping sea, to reflect a myriad of stars. The sun had
gone down behind a screen of purple, and gold, and to add to

the beauty of the scene, as night set in, a blazing comet, whose tail spanned nearly a quarter of the heavens, mirrored itself within a hundred feet of our little bark, as she ploughed her noiseless way through the waters. As I leaned on the carriage of a howitzer on the poop of my ship, and cast a glance toward the quarter of the horizon whence the land had disappeared, memory was busy with the events of the last few months. How hurried, and confused they had been! It seemed as though I had dreamed a dream, and found it difficult, upon waking, to unite the discordant parts. A great government had been broken up, family ties had been severed, and war — grim, ghastly war — was arraying a household against itself. A little while back, and I had served under the very flag which I had that day defied. Strange revolution of feeling, how I now hated that flag! It had been to me as a mistress to a lover; I had looked upon it with admiring eyes, had dallied with it in hours of ease, and had had recourse to it, in hours of trouble, and now I found it false! What wonder that I felt a lover's resentment?

My first lieutenant now approached me, and touching my elbow, said, "Captain, had we not better throw this howitzer overboard? it can be of no further service to us, and is very much in the way." My waking dream was dissolved, on the instant, and I returned at once to the duties of the ship. I assented to the lieutenant's proposition, and in a few minutes more, the poop was cleared of the incumbrance. It was the howitzer — a heavy, awkward, iron field-piece with huge wheels — which we had received on board, when we lay between the forts, as a protection against the enemy's boats. The rest of the night, to a late hour, was devoted to lashing, and otherwise securing such heavy articles, as were likely to be thrown from their places, by the rolling of the ship; getting the anchors in-board and stowing them, and, generally, in making the ship snug. I turned in after a day of excitement, and slept too soundly to continue the day-dream from which I had been aroused by my first lieutenant.

The sun rose in an unclouded sky, the next morning, with a gentle breeze from the south-west, or about abeam; our course being about south-east. The look-out at the mast-head, after

having carefully scanned the horizon in every direction, informed the officer of the deck, that there was nothing in sight.
The awnings were soon spread, and the usual routine of a man-
of-war, at sea, commenced. The crew was mustered, in clean
apparel, at quarters, at nine o'clock, and a division of guns
was exercised, the rest of the crew being dispersed in idle
groups about the deck ; the old salts overhauling their bags,
and seeing that their tobacco, and soap, and needles, and thread
were all right for the cruise, and the youngsters discussing
their recent escape. At noon, we found ourselves in latitude
26° 18', and longitude 87° 23'. I had provided myself with
two excellent chronometers, before leaving New Orleans, and
having had much experience as a master, I was always enabled,
when the sun was visible, at the proper hours, to fix my position within from a quarter, to half a mile, or, what is the same
thing, within from one to two seconds of time. I appointed
my junior lieutenant, navigating officer, *pro forma*, but always
navigated my ship, myself. I had every confidence in the
ability of my young lieutenant, but I always found, that I
slept better, when surrounded by danger, after I had fixed the
position of my ship, by my own observations.

We held on our course, during the rest of this day, without
the least incident to break in upon the monotony — not so
much as a sail having been descried in any direction ; not that
we were in want of excitement, for we had scarcely regained
our equilibrium from the excitement of the previous day.
An occasional swash of the sea against the ship's sides, the
monotonous beating of time by her propeller, an occasional
order from the officer of the deck, and the routine "calls" of
the boatswain's whistle, as dinner, or grog was piped, were the
only sounds audible, beyond the usual hum of conversation
among the crew.

If the reader will permit me, I will avail myself of this interval of calm before the storm, to introduce to him some of my
officers. This is indeed but a courtesy due him, as he is to be
a passenger in our midst. On the afternoon of our escape
from the *Brooklyn*, the officers of the ward-room were kind
enough to invite me to drink a glass of wine with them, in
honor of our success, and I will avail myself of this occasion,

to make the presentations. I am seated at one end of the long mess-table, and my first lieutenant at the other. The first lieutenant, as the reader has already been informed, by an inspection of the *Sumter's* muster-roll, is from Georgia. John McIntosh Kell is a descendant from one of the oldest families in that State, having the blood of the McIntoshes in his veins, through one branch of his ancestors. He was bred in the old Navy, and my acquaintance with him commenced when he was in trouble. He was serving as a passed midshipman, on board the old sailing sloop *Albany*, and being ordered, on one occasion, to perform what he considered a menial duty, he resisted the order. Some of his brother passed midshipmen were in the same category. A court-martial resulted, and, at the request of the young gentlemen, I defended them. The relation of counsel, and client, as a matter of course, brought us close together, and I discovered that young Kell had in him, the making of a man. So far from being a mutineer, he had a high respect for discipline, and had only resisted obedience to the order in question, from a refined sense of gentlemanly propriety. The reader will see these qualities in him, now, as he sits opposite me. He has developed since the time I speak of, into the tall, well-proportioned gentleman, of middle age, with brown, wavy hair, and a magnificent beard, inclining to red. See how scrupulously neat he is dressed, and how suave, and affable he is, with his associates. His eye is now beaming gentleness, and kindness. You will scarcely recognize him, as the same man, when you see him again on deck, arraigning some culprit, "at the mast," for a breach of discipline. When Georgia seceded, Lieutenant Kell was well on his way to the commander's list, in the old Navy, but he would have scorned the commission of an admiral, if it had been tendered him as the price of treason to his State. To have brought a Federal ship into the waters of Georgia, and ravaged her coasts, and fired upon her people, would have been, in his eyes, little less than matricide. He forthwith resigned his commission, and joined his fortunes with those of his people. When it was decided, at Montgomery, that I was to have the *Sumter*, I at once thought of Kell, and, at my request, he was ordered to the ship — Commodore Tattnall, with

whom he had been serving on the Georgia coast, giving him
up very reluctantly.

Seated next to myself, on my right hand, is Lieutenant
Robert T. Chapman. This gentleman is from Alabâma; he is
several years younger than Kell, not so tall, but stouter, in
proportion. His complexion, as you see, is dark, and he has
jet-black hair, and eyes—the latter remarkable for their brilliancy, and for a twinkle of fun, and good humor. Chapman
is the life of the mess-table; always in a pleasant mood, and
running over with wit and anecdote. Though he has a fashion, as you see, of wearing his hair closely cropped, he is the
very reverse of a round-head, being a *preux chevalier*, as ready
for the fight as the dance, and having a decided preference for
the music of the band, over that of "Old Hundred." He is
the second lieutenant, and has, consequently, the easiest berth
among the sea lieutenants, being relieved from the drudgery
of the first lieutenant, and exempt from the calls for extra duty,
that are sometimes made upon the junior lieutenant. When
his watch is over, and his division drilled, he is a gentleman
at large, for the rest of the day. You see by his build—a
slight inclination to corpulency—that he is fond of his ease,
and that he has fallen as naturally into the place of second
lieutenant, as if it had been cut out for him on purpose. He
also was bred in the old Navy, and was found to be of the
pure metal, instead of the dross, when the touchstone of
secession came to be applied to separate the one from the
other.

At Lieutenant Kell's right hand, sits Lieutenant John M.
Stribling, the third lieutenant, and a native of the glorious little
State of South Carolina. He is of medium height, somewhat
spare in build, with brown hair, and whiskers, and mild and
expressive blue eyes; the mildness of the eye only dwelling
in it, however, in moments of repose. When excited at the
thought of wrong, or oppression, it has a peculiar stare of firmness, as much as to say,

> "This rock shall fly,
> From its firm base as soon as I."

Stribling was also an *élève* of the old Navy, and, though tied

LIEUT. R. T. CHAPMAN

LIEUT. W. E. EVANS

ENG. M. J. FREEMAN

LIEUT. J. M. KELL

SURG. F. GALT

PAYMASTER H. MYERS

LIEUT. J. M. STRIBLING

Eng⁴ by H.B. Hall, Jr N.Y.

Kelly, Piet & Co. Baltimore

to it, by cords that were hard to sever, he put honor above place, in the hour of trial, and came South.

Next to Stribling, sits Lieutenant William E. Evans, the fourth and junior lieutenant of the ship. He is not more than twenty-four years of age, slim in person, of medium height, and rather delicate-looking, though not from ill health. His complexion is dark, and he has black hair, and eyes. He has a very agreeable, *riante* expression about his face, and is some-what given to casuistry, being fond of an argument, when occasion presents itself. He is but recently out of the Naval Academy, at Annapolis, and like all new graduates, feels the freshness of academic honors. He is a native of South Caro-lina, and a brother of General Evans of that State, who so greatly distinguished himself, afterward, at the battle of Manassas, and on other bloody fields.

If the reader will now cast his eye toward the centre of the table, on my right hand, he will see two gentlemen, both with black hair and eyes, and both somewhat under middle size, conversing together. These are Dr. Francis L. Galt, the Sur-geon, and Mr. Henry Myers, the Paymaster, both from the old service; the former a native of Virginia, and the latter a native of South Carolina ; and opposite these, are the Chief Engineer, and Marine Officer,—Mr. Miles J. Freeman, and Lieutenant B. How-ell, the latter a brother-in-law of Mr. Jefferson Davis, our honored President. I have thus gone the circuit of the ward-room. All these officers, courteous reader, will make the cruise with us, and if you will inspect the adjoining engraving, and are a judge of character, after the rules of Lavater and Spurz-heim, you will perceive in advance, how much reason I shall have to be proud of them.

We may now take up our narrative, from the point at which it was interrupted, for the purpose of these introductions. Day passed into night, and with the night came the brilliant comet again, lighting us on our way over the waste of waters. The morning of the second of July, our second day out, dawned clear, and beautiful, the *Sumter* still steaming in an almost calm sea, with nothing to impede her progress. At eight A. M. we struck the north-east trade-wind, and made sail in aid of steam, giving orders to the engineer, to make the most of his fuel, by carrying only a moderate head of steam. Toward

noon, a few trade squalls passed over us, with light and refreshing showers of rain; just enough to cause me to take shelter,
for a few moments, under the lee of the spanker. At noon,
we observed in latitude 23° 4′ showing that we had crossed
the tropic—the longitude being 86° 13′. The reader has
seen that we have been steering to the S. E., diminishing both
latitude, and longitude, and if he will look upon the chart of
the Caribbean Sea, he will perceive, that we are approaching
Cape San Antonio, the south end of the island of Cuba; but he
can scarcely conjecture what sort of a cruise I had marked out
for myself. The Secretary of the Navy, in those curt sailing
orders which we have already seen, had considerately left me
carte blanche as to cruising-ground, but as I was "to do the
greatest injury to the enemy's commerce, in the shortest time,"
the implication was, that I should, at once, throw myself into
some one of the chief thoroughfares of his trade. I accordingly set my eye on Cape St. Roque, in Brazil, which may be
said to be the great turning-point of the commerce of the
world. My intention was to make a dash, of a few days, at the
enemy's ships on the south side of Cuba, coal at some convenient point, stretch over to Barbadoes, coal again, and then
strike for the Brazilian coast. It is with this view, that the
Sumter is now running for the narrow outlet, that issues from
the Gulf of Mexico, between Cape Antonio, and the opposite
coast of Yucatan. I shaped my course for the middle of this
passage, but about midnight, made the light of Cape Antonio
right ahead, showing that I had been drifted, northward, by a
current setting, at the rate of from three fourths of a mile, to a
mile per hour. We drew off a little to the southward, doubled
the Cape, with the light still in view, and at nine o'clock, the
next morning, we found ourselves off Cape Corrientes.

The weather had now become cloudy, and we had a fresh
trade-wind, veering from E. to E. S. E., with some sea on. At
meridian, we observed in latitude 21° 29′, the longitude being
84° 06′. Running along the Cuban coast, between it and the
Isle of Pines, of piratical memory, at about three in the after
noon, the cry of "Sail ho!" was heard from the mast-head, for
the first time since we had left the mouths of the Mississippi.
The look-out, upon being questioned, said that he saw two

sail, and that they were both right ahead. We came up with them, very rapidly, for they were standing in our direction, and when we had approached within signal distance, we showed them the English colors. The nearest sail, which proved to be a brig, hoisted the Spanish colors, and, upon being boarded, was found to be from Cadiz, bound for Vera Cruz. She was at once permitted to proceed. Resuming our course, we now stood for the other sail, which, by this time, there was no mistaking; she being plainly American, although she had not yet shown her colors. A gun soon brought these to the peak; when, as I had expected, the stars and stripes unfolded themselves, gracefully, to the breeze. Here was our first prize, and a most welcome sight it was. The capture, I find, upon looking over my notes, was recorded in a few lines, barren of all incident, or remark, except only that the doomed ship was from the "Black Republican State of Maine;" but I well recollect the mingled impressions of joy, and sadness, that were made upon me by the event. The "old flag," which I had been accustomed to worship, in my youth, had a criminal look, in my eyes, as it ascended to the peak of that ship. How strangely we sometimes invest mere inanimate things with the attributes of life! When I had fired the gun, as a command to the stranger to heave to, and show his colors, I had hauled down the English, and hoisted my own flag. The stars and stripes seemed now to look abashed in the presence of the new banner of the South; pretty much as a burglar might be supposed to look, who had been caught in the act of breaking into a gentleman's house; but then the burglar was my relative, and had erst been my friend — how could I fail to feel some pity for him, along with the indignation, which his crime had excited? The boarding officer soon returned from the captured ship, bringing with him the master, with his papers. There were no knotty points of fact or law to embarrass my decision. There were the American register, and clearance, and the American character impressed upon every plank and spar of the ship. Nothing could exceed the astonishment of the master, who was rather a mild, amiable-looking gentleman, not at all disposed to go either into hysterics, or the heroics. "A clap of thunder in a cloudless sky could not have surprised me more," said he to me as I overhauled his papers, "than the appearance of the Confederate flag in these seas." "My duty is a painful one," said I, "to destroy so noble a ship as yours, but I must discharge it without vain regrets; and as for yourself, you will only have to do, as so many thousands have done before you, submit to the fortunes of war — yourself and your crew will be well treated on board my ship." The prize bore the name of *The Golden Rocket,* was a fine bark, nearly new, of about seven hundred tons, and was seeking, in ballast, a cargo of sugar in some one of the Cuban ports. Boats were dispatched to bring off the crew, and such provisions, cordage, sails, and paints as the different departments of my ship stood in need of, and at about ten o'clock at night, the order was given to apply the torch to her.

The wind, by this time, had become very light, and the night was pitch-dark — the darkness being of that kind, graphically described by old sailors, when they say, you may cut it with a knife. I regret that I cannot give to the reader the picture of the burning ship, as it presented itself to the silent, and solemn watchers on board the *Sumter* as they leaned over her hammock rails to witness it. The boat, which had been sent on this errand of destruction, had pulled out of sight, and her oars ceasing to resound, we knew that she had reached the doomed ship, but so impenetrable was the darkness, that no trace of either boat, or ship could be seen, although the *Sumter* was distant only a few hundred yards. Not a sound could be heard on board the *Sumter*, although her deck was crowded with men. Every one seemed busy with his own thoughts, and gazing eagerly in the direction of the doomed ship, endeavoring, in vain, to penetrate the thick darkness. Suddenly, one of the crew exclaimed, "There is the flame! She is on fire!" The decks of this Maine-built ship were of pine, calked with old-fashioned oakum, and paid with pitch; the wood-work of the cabin was like so much tinder, having been seasoned by many voyages to the tropics, and the forecastle was stowed with paints, and oils. The consequence was, that the flame was not long in kindling, but leaped, full-grown, into the air, in a very few minutes after its first faint glimmer had been seen. The boarding officer, to do his work more effectually, had applied the torch simultaneously in three places, the cabin, the mainhold, and the forecastle; and now the devouring flames rushed up these three apertures, with a fury which nothing could resist. The burning ship, with the *Sumter's* boat in the act of shoving off from her side; the *Sumter* herself, with her grim, black sides, lying in repose like some great sea-monster, gloating upon the spectacle, and the sleeping sea, for there was scarce a ripple upon the water, were all brilliantly lighted. The indraught into the burning ship's holds, and cabins, added every moment new fury to the flames, and now they could be heard roaring like the fires of a hundred furnaces, in full blast. The prize ship had been laid to, with her main-topsail to the mast, and all her light sails, though clewed up, were flying loose about the yards. The forked tongues of the devouring element, leaping into the rigging, newly tarred, ran rapidly up the shrouds, first into the tops, then to the topmast-heads, thence to the topgallant, and royal mast-heads, and in a moment more to the trucks; and whilst this rapid ascent of the main current of fire was going on, other currents had run out upon the yards, and ignited all the sails. A top-gallant sail, all on fire, would now fly off from the yard, and sailing leisurely in the direction of the light breeze that was fanning, rather than blowing, break into bright, and sparkling patches of flame, and settle, or rather silt into the sea. The yard would then follow, and not being wholly submerged by its descent into the sea, would retain a portion of its flame, and continue to burn, as a floating brand, for some minutes. At one time, the intricate net-work of the cordage of the burning ship was traced, as with a pencil of fire, upon the black sky beyond, the many threads of flame twisting, and writhing, like so many serpents that had received their death wounds. The mizzen-mast now went by the board, then the fore-mast, and in a few minutes afterward, the great main-mast tottered, reeled, and fell over the ship's side into the sea, making a noise like that of the sturdy oak of the forests when it falls by the stroke of the axeman

By the light of this flambeau, upon the lonely and silent sea, lighted of the passions of bad men who should have been our brothers, the *Sumter*, having aroused herself from her dream of vengeance, and run up her boats, moved forward on her course.

The captain of the *Golden Rocket* watched the destruction of his ship from the quarter-deck of the *Sumter*, apparently with the calm eye of a philosopher, though, doubtless, he felt the emotions which the true sailor always feels, when he looks upon the dying agonies of his beloved ship, whether she be broken up by the storm, or perish in any other way.

The flag! what was done with the "old flag"? It was marked with the day, and the latitude and longitude of the capture, and consigned to the keeping of the signal quarter-master, who prepared a bag for its reception; and when this bag was full, he prepared another, and another, as the cruise progressed, and occasion required. It was the especial pride of this veteran American seaman to count over his trophies, and when the weather was fine, he invariably asked permission of the officer of the deck, under pretence of damage from moths, to "air" his flags; and as he would bend on his signal-halliards, and throw them out to the breeze, one by one, his old eye would glisten, and a grim smile of satisfaction would settle upon his sun-burned, and weather-beaten features. This was our practice also on board the *Alabama*, and when that ship was sunk in the British channel, in her engagement with the enemy's ship *Kearsarge*, as the reader will learn in due time, if he has the patience to follow me in these memoirs, we committed to the keeping of the guardian spirits of that famous old battle-ground, a great many bags full of "old flags," to be stored away in the caves of the sea, as mementos that a nation once lived whose naval officers prized liberty more than the false memorial of it, under which they had once served, and who were capable, when it became

"Hate's polluted rag,"

of tearing it down.

The prisoners—what did we do with them? The captain was invited to mess in the ward-room, and when he was afterward landed, the officers generously made him up a purse to supply his immediate necessities. The crew was put into a mess by themselves, with their own cook, and was put on a footing, with regard to rations, with the *Sumter's* own men.

We were making war upon the enemy's commerce, but not upon his unarmed seamen. It gave me as much pleasure to treat these with humanity, as it did to destroy his ships, and one of the most cherished recollections which I have brought out of a war, which, in some sense, may be said to have been a civil war, is, that the "pirate," whom the enemy denounced, with a pen dipped in gall, and with a vocabulary of which decent people should be ashamed, set that same enemy the example, which he has failed to follow, *of treating prisoners of war, according to the laws of war.*

CHAPTER XIII.

RAPID WORK — SEVEN PRIZES IN TWO DAYS. — THE SUMTER MAKES HER FIRST PORT, AND WHAT OCCURRED THERE.

WE burned the *Golden Rocket*, as has been seen, on the 3d of July. The next day was the "glorious Fourth" — once glorious, indeed, as the day on which a people broke the chains of a government which had bound them against their will, and vindicated the principle of self-government as an *inalienable* right; but since desecrated by the same people, who have scorned, and spat upon the record made by their fathers, and repudiated, as a heresy fraught with the penalties of treason, the inalienable right for which their fathers struggled. The grand old day belonged, of right, to us of the South, for we still venerated it, as hallowed by our fathers, and were engaged in a *second* revolution, to uphold, and defend the doctrines which had been proclaimed in the *first*, but we failed to celebrate it on board the *Sumter*. We could not help associating it with the "old flag," which had now become a sham and a deceit; with the wholesale robberies which had been committed upon our property, and with the villification and abuse which had been heaped upon our persons by our late co-partners, for a generation and more. The Declaration of Independence had proved to be a specious mask, under which our loving brethren of the North had contrived to draw us into a co-partnership with them, that they might be the better enabled, in the end, to devour us. How could we respect it, in such a connection? Accordingly, the Captain of the *Sumter* was not invited to dine in the ward-room, on the time-honored day, nor was there any extra glass of grog served to the crew, as had been the custom in the old service.

The weather still continued cloudy, with a few rain squalls

passing with the trade wind, during the morning. I had turned into my cot, late on the previous night, and was still sleeping soundly, when, at daylight, an officer came below to inform me, that there were two sails in sight from the mast-head. We were steaming, as before, up the south side of Cuba, with the land plainly in sight, and soon came close enough to distinguish that the vessels ahead were both brig-antines, and probably Americans. There being no occasion to resort to *ruse*, or stratagem, as the wind was light, and there was no possibility of the ships running away from us, we showed them at once the Confederate colors, and at the same time fired a blank cartridge to heave them to. They obeyed our signal, promptly, and came to the wind, with their foretop-sails aback, and the United States colors at their peaks. When within a few hundred yards, we stopped our engine, and lowered, and sent a boat on board of them — the boarding officer remaining only a few minutes on board of each, and bringing back with him, their respective masters, with their ships' papers. Upon examination of these, it appeared that one of the brigantines was called the *Cuba*, and the other the *Machias;* that they were both laden with sugar and molasses, for English ports, and that they had recently come out of the port of Trinidad-de-Cuba. Indeed the recency of their sail-ing was tested, by the way in which their stern-boats were gar-landed, with festoons of luscious bananas, and pine-apples, and by sundry nets filled with golden-hued oranges — all of which was very tempting to the eyes and olfactories of men, who had recently issued from a blockaded port, in which such luxuries were tabooed. The cargoes of these small vessels being neu-tral, as certified by the papers — and indeed of this there could be little doubt, as they were going from one neutral port to another — I could not burn the vessels as I had done the *Golden Rocket,* and so after transferring prize crews to them, which occupied us an hour or two, we took them both in tow, and steamed away for Cienfuegos — it being my intention to test the disposition of Spain toward us, in this matter of taking in prizes. England and France had issued procla-mations, prohibiting both belligerents, alike, from bringing prizes into their ports, but Spain had not yet spoken, and

I had hopes that she might be induced to pursue a different course.

Nothing worthy of note occurred during the rest of this day; we steamed leisurely along the coast, making about five knots an hour. Finding our speed too much diminished, by the towage of two heavily laden vessels, we cast off one of them — the *Cuba* — during the night and directed the prize-master to make sail, and follow us into port. The *Cuba* did not rejoin us, and we afterward learned through the medium of the enemy's papers, that she had been recaptured by her crew. I had only sent a midshipman and four men on board of her as a prize crew; and the midshipman incautiously going aloft, to look out for the land, as he was approaching his port, and a portion of his prize crew proving treacherous — they were not native Americans I am glad to say — he was fired upon by the master, and crew of the brig, who had gotten possession of the revolvers of the prize crew, and compelled to surrender, after defending himself the best he could, and being wounded in one or two places. The vessel then changed her course and made haste to get out of the Caribbean Sea.

The morning of the fifth dawned cloudy, with the usual moderate trade-wind. It cleared toward noon, and at two P. M. we crossed the shoal off the east end of the *Jardinillos* reef, in from seven to five fathoms of water. The sea, by this time, had become quite smooth, and the rays of a bright sun penetrated the clear waters to the very bottom of the shoal, revealing everything to us, as clearly as though the medium through which we were viewing it were atmosphere instead of water. Every rock, sea-shell, and pebble lying at the bottom of the sea were distinctly visible to us, and we could see the little fish darting into their holes, and hiding-places, as the steamer ploughed her way through their usually quiet domain. It was quite startling to look over the side, so shallow did the waters appear. The chart showed that there was no danger, and the faithful lead line, in the hands of a skilful seaman, gave us several fathoms of water to spare, and yet one could hardly divest himself of the belief, that at the next moment the steamer would run aground.

Crossing this shoal, we now hauled up N. E. by N., for the Cienfuegos lighthouse. As we approached the lights, we descried two more sail in the south-east, making an offing with all diligence, to which we immediately gave chase. They were eight or nine miles distant from the land, and to facilitate our pursuit, we cast off our remaining tow, directing the prize-master to heave to, off the lighthouse, and await our return. We had already captured three prizes, in twenty-four hours, and, as here were probably two more, I could perceive that my crew were becoming enamoured of their business, pretty much as the veteran fox-hunter does in view of the chase. They moved about with great alacrity, in obedience to orders; the seamen springing aloft to furl the sails like so many squirrels, and the firemen below sending up thick volumes of black smoke, from their furnaces. The *Sumter*, feeling the renewed impulse of her engines, sprang forward in pursuit of the doomed craft ahead, as if she too knew what was going on. We had just daylight enough left to enable us to accomplish our purpose; an hour or two later, and at least one of the vessels might have escaped. Coming up, first with one, and then the other, we hove them to, successively, by "hail," and brought the masters on board. They both proved to be brigantines, and were American, as we had supposed:— one, the *Ben. Dunning*, of Maine, and the other, the *Albert Adams*, of Massachusetts. They had come out of the port of Cienfuegos, only a few hours before, were both sugar laden, and their cargoes were documented as Spanish property. We hastily threw prize crews on board of them, and directed the prize masters to stand in for the light, still in sight, distant about twelve miles, and hold on to it until daylight. It was now about ten P. M. Some appeal was made to me by the master of one of the brigantines, in behalf of his wife and a lady companion of hers, who were both invalids from the effects of yellow fever, which they had taken in Cienfuegos, and from which they were just convalescing. I desired him to assure the ladies, that they should be treated with every tenderness, and respect, and that if they desired it, I would send my surgeon to visit them; but I declined to release the captured vessel on this account.

We now stood in for the light ourselves, and letting our steam go down, to the lowest point consistent with locomotion, lay off, and on, until daylight. The next morning dawned beautiful, and bright, as a tropic morning only can dawn. We were close in under the land, and our prizes were lying around us, moving to and fro, gracefully, to preserve their positions. The most profuse, and luxuriant vegetation, of that peculiarly dark green known only to the tropics, ran down to the very water's edge; the beautiful little stream, on which Cienfuegos lies, disembogued itself at the foot of the lighthouse perched on a base of blackened limestone rock; and the neat, white fort, that sat a mile or two up the river, was now glistening in the rays of the sun, just lifting himself above the central range of mountains. The sea breeze had died away during the night, and been replaced by the land breeze, in obedience to certain laws which prevail in all countries swept by the trade-winds; and this land breeze, blowing so gently, as scarce to disturb a tress on the brow of beauty, came laden with the most delicious perfume of shrub and flower.

But, "what smoke is that we perceive, coming down the river?" said I, to the officer of the deck. "I will see in a moment," said this active young officer, and springing several ratlines up the rigging, to enable him to obtain a view over the intervening foliage, he said, "There is a small steam-tug coming down, with three vessels in tow, two barks and a brig." "Can you make out the nationality of the ships in tow?" I inquired. "Plainly," he replied, "they all have the American colors set." Here was a piece of unlooked-for good fortune. I had not reckoned upon carrying more than three, or four prizes into port, but here were three others. But to secure these latter, a little management would be necessary. I could not molest them, within neutral jurisdiction, and the neutral jurisdiction extended to a marine league, or three geographical miles from the land. I immediately hoisted a Spanish jack at the fore, as a signal for a pilot, and directed the officer of the deck, to disarrange his yards, a little, cock-billing this one, slightly, in one direction, and that one, in another, and to send all but about a dozen men below, to give the strangers the idea that we were a common merchant steamer, instead of a ship

of war. To carry still further the illusion, we hoisted the Spanish
merchant flag. But the real trouble was with the prizes — two of
these must surely be recognized by their companions of only the
day before! Luckily my prize masters took the hint I had
given them, and hoisted their respective flags, at the fore, for
a pilot also. This mystified the new-comers, and they concluded that the two brigantines, though very like, could not
be the same. Besides, there was a third brigantine in company,
and she evidently was a new arrival. And so they came on,
quite unsuspiciously, and when the little steamer had towed
them clear of the mouth of the harbor, she let them go, and
they made sail. The fellows worked very industriously, and
soon had their ships under clouds of canvas, pressing them out
to get an offing, before the sea breeze should come in. The
steam-tug, as soon as she had let go her tows, came alongside
the *Sumter*, and a Spanish pilot jumped on board of me, asking me in his native tongue, if I desired to go up to town;
showing that my ruse of the Spanish flag had even deceived
him. I replied in the affirmative, and said to him, pleasantly,
"but I am waiting a little, to take back those ships you have
just towed down." "Diablo!" said he, "how can that be; they
are *Americanos del Norte*, bound to Boston, and *la Nueva York!*"
"That is just what I want," said I, "we are *Confederados*, and
we have *la guerra* with the *Americanos del Norte!*" "*Caram-
ba!*" said he, "that is good; give her the steam quick, Captain!" "No, no," replied I, "wait a while. I must pay due
respect to your Queen, and the Captain-General; they command in these waters, within the league, and I must wait until
the ships have passed beyond that." I accordingly waited
until the ships had proceeded some five miles from the coast,
as estimated both by the pilot, and myself, when we turned the
Sumter's head seaward, and again removed the leash. She was
not long in pouncing upon the astonished prey. A booming
gun, and the simultaneous descent of the Spanish, and ascent
of the Confederate flag to the *Sumter's* peak, when we had
approached within about a mile of them, cleared up the mystery of the chase, and brought the fugitives to the wind. In
half an hour more, their papers had been examined, prize
crews had been thrown on board of them, and they were

standing back in company with the *Sumter*, to rejoin the other prizes.

I had now a fleet of six sail, and when the sea breeze set in next morning, which it did between nine and ten o'clock, I led into the harbor, the fleet following. The three newly captured vessels were the bark *West Wind*, of Rhode Island; the bark *Louisa Kilham*, of Massachusetts, and the brigantine *Naiad*, of New York. They had all cargoes of sugar, which were covered by certificates of neutral property. When the *Sumter* came abreast of the small fort, which has already been noticed, we were surprised to see the sentinels on post fire a couple of loaded muskets, the balls of which whistled over our heads, and to observe them making gestures, indicating that we must come to anchor. This we immediately did ; but the prizes, all of which had the United States colors flying, were permitted to pass, and they sped on their way to the town, some miles above, as they had been ordered. When we had let go our anchor, I dispatched Lieutenant Evans to the fort, to call on the Commandant, and ask for an explanation of his conduct, in bringing us to. The explanation was simple enough. He did not know what to make of the new-born Confederate flag. He had never seen it before. It did not belong to any of the nations of the earth, of which he had any knowledge, and we might be a buccaneer for aught he knew. In the afternoon, the Commandant himself came on board to visit me, and inform me, on the part of the Governor of Cienfuegos, with whom he had communicated, that I might proceed to the town, in the *Sumter*, if I desired. We drank a glass of wine together, and I satisfied him, that I had not come in to carry his fort by storm — which would have been an easy operation enough, as he had only about a corporal's guard under his command — or to sack the town of Cienfuegos, after the fashion of the Drakes, and other English sea-robbers, who have left so vivid an impression upon Spanish memory, as to make Spanish commandants of small forts, cautious of all strange craft.

It had only been a week since the *Sumter* had run the blockade of New Orleans, and already she was out of fuel ! having only coal enough left for about twenty-four hours steaming. Here was food for reflection. Active operations which would require the constant use of steam, would never do; for, by-and-by, when the enemy should get on my track, it would be easy for him to trace me from port to port, if I went into port once a week. I must endeavor to reach some cruising-ground, where I could lie in wait for ships, under sail, and dispense with the use of steam, except for a few hours, at a time, for the purpose of picking up such prizes, as I could not decoy within reach of my guns. I was glad to learn from the pilot, that there was plenty of coal to be had in Cienfuegos, and I dispatched Lieutenant Chapman to town, in one of the ship's cutters, for the double purpose of arranging for a supply, and communicating with the Governor, on the subject of my prizes, and the position which Spain was likely to occupy, during the war. The following letter addressed by me to his Excellency will explain the object I had in view in coming into Cienfuegos, and the hopes I entertained of the conduct of Spain, whose important island of Cuba lay, as it were, athwart our main gateway to the sea—the Gulf of Mexico.

CONFEDERATE STATES STEAMER SUMTER, }
ISLAND OF CUBA, July 6, 1861. }

SIR: — I have the honor to inform you, of my arrival at the port of Cienfuegos, with seven prizes of war. These vessels are the brigantines *Cuba,** *Machias, Ben. Dunning, Albert Adams,* and *Naiad;* and barks *West Wind,* and *Louisa Kilham,* property of citizens of the United States, which States, as your Excellency is aware, are waging an aggressive and unjust war upon the Confederate States, which I have the honor, with this ship under my command, to represent. I have sought a port of Cuba, with these prizes, with the expectation that Spain will extend to the cruisers of the Confederate States, the same friendly reception that, in similar circumstances, she would extend to the cruisers of the enemy; in other words, that she will permit me to leave the captured vessels within her jurisdiction, until they can be adjudicated by a Court of Admiralty of the Confederate States. As a people maintaining a government *de facto,* and not only holding the enemy in check, but gaining advantages over him, we are entitled to all the rights of belligerents, and I confidently rely upon the friendly disposition of Spain, who is our near neighbor, in the most important of her colonial possessions, to receive us with equal and even-handed justice, if not with the sympathy which our identity of interests and policy, with regard to an important social and industrial institution, are so well calculated to inspire. A rule which would

* The *Cuba* was hourly expected to arrive, but, as the reader has seen, was recaptured, and did not make her appearance.

exclude our prizes from her ports, during the war, although it should be applied, in terms, equally to the enemy, would not, I respectfully suggest, be an equitable, or just rule. The basis of such a rule, as indeed, of all the conduct of a neutral during war, is equal and impartial justice to all the belligerents, without inclining to the side of either; and this should be a substantial and practical justice, and not exist in terms merely, which may be deceptive. Now, a little reflection will, I think, show your Excellency that the rule in question — the exclusion of the prizes of both belligerents from neutral ports — cannot be applied in the present war, without operating with great injustice to the Confederate States. It is well known to your Excellency, that the United States are a manufacturing and commercial people, whilst the Confederate States are an agricultural people. The consequence of this dissimilarity of pursuits was, that at the breaking out of the war, the former had within their limits, and control, almost all the naval force of the old government. This naval force they have dishonestly seized, and turned against the Confederate States, regardless of the just claims of the latter to a large proportion of it, as tax-payers, out of whose contributions to the common Treasury it was created. The United States, by this disseizin of the property of the Confederate States, are enabled, in the first months of the war, to blockade all the ports of the latter States. In this condition of things, observe the *practical* working of the rule I am discussing, whatever may be the seeming fairness of its terms. It will be admitted that we have equal belligerent rights with the enemy. One of the most important of these rights, in a war against a commercial people, is that which I have just exercised, of capturing his property, on the high seas. But how are the Confederate States to enjoy, to its full extent, the benefit of this right, if their cruisers are not permitted to enter neutral ports, with their prizes, and retain them there, in safe custody, until they can be condemned, and disposed of? They cannot send them into their own ports, for the reason already mentioned, viz. : that those ports are hermetically sealed by the agency of their own ships, forcibly wrested from them. If they cannot send them into neutral ports, where are they to send them? Nowhere. Except for the purpose of destruction, therefore, their right of capture would be entirely defeated by the adoption of the rule in question, whilst the opposite belligerent would not be inconvenienced by it, at all, as all his own ports are open to him. I take it for granted, that Spain will not think of acting upon so unjust, and unequal a rule.

But another question arises, indeed has already arisen, in the cases of some of the very captures which I have brought into port. The cargoes of several of the vessels are claimed, as appears by certificates found among the papers, as Spanish property. This fact cannot, of course, be verified, except by a judicial proceeding, in the Prize Courts of the Confederate States. But if the prizes cannot be sent either into the ports of the Confederate States, or

into neutral ports, how can this verification be made? Further —
suppos.ng there to be no dispute about the title to the cargo, how
is it to be unladen, and delivered to the neutral claimant, unless
the captured ship can make a port? Indeed, one of the motives
which influenced me in making a Spanish colonial port, was the
fact that these cargoes were claimed by Spanish subjects, whom I
was desirous of putting to as little inconvenience as possible, in the
unlading and reception of their property, should it be restored to
them, by a decree of the Confederate Courts. It will be for your
Excellency to consider, and act upon these grave questions, touching alike the interests of both our governments.

I have the honor to be, &c., &c.,

RAPHAEL SEMMES.

I did not expect much to grow immediately out of the
above communication. Indeed, as the reader will probably
surmise, I had written it more for the eye of the Spanish Pre-
mier, than for that of the Governor of a small provincial town,
who had no diplomatic power, and whom I knew to be timid,
as are all the subordinate officers of absolute governments. I
presumed that the Governor would telegraph it to the Captain-
General, at Havana, and that the latter would hold the subject
in abeyance, until he could hear from the Home Government.
Nor was I disappointed in this expectation, for Lieutenant Chapman returned from Cienfuegos, the next morning, and brought
me intelligence to this effect.

To dispose of the questions raised, without the necessity of
again returning to them, the reader is informed, that Spain, in
due time, followed the lead of England and France, in the matter of excluding prizes from her ports; and that my prizes
were delivered — to whom, do you think, reader? You will
naturally say, to myself, or my duly appointed agent, with instructions to take them out of the Spanish port. This was the
result to be logically expected. The Captain-General had received them, in trust, as it were, to abide the decision of his
Government. If that decision should be in favor of receiving
the prizes of both belligerents, well; if not, I expected to be
notified to take them away. But nothing was further, it seems,
from the intention of the Captain-General, than this simple and
just proceeding; for as soon as the Queen's proclamation was
received, he deliberately handed back all my prizes to their
original owners! This was so barefaced a proceeding, that

it was necessary to allege some excuse for it, and the excuse given was, that I had violated the neutral waters of Cuba, and captured my three last prizes within the marine league—my sympathizing friend, the Spanish pilot, and an English sailor, on board the tug, being vouched as the respectable witnesses to the fact! Such was the power of Spanish gold, and Yankee unscrupulousness in the use of it. When I heard of these transactions a few months afterward, I planned a very pretty little quarrel between the Confederate States and Spain, in case the former should be successful in establishing their independence. Cuba, I thought, would make us a couple of very respectable States, with her staples of sugar and tobacco, and with her similar system of labor; and if Spain refused to foot our bill for the robbery of these vessels, we would foot it ourselves, at her expense. But poor old Spain! I ought perhaps to forgive thee, for thou wast afterward kicked, and cuffed by the very Power to which thou didst truckle—the Federal steamers of war making a free use of thy coast of the "Ever Faithful Island of Cuba," chasing vessels on shore, and burning them, in contempt of thy jurisdiction, and in spite of thy remonstrances. And the day is not far distant, when the school-ma'am and the carpet-bag missionary will encamp on thy plantations, and hold joint conventicles with thy freedmen, in the interests of Godliness, and the said ma'am and missionary.

Great excitement was produced, as may be supposed, by the arrival of the *Sumter*, with her six prizes, at the quiet little town of Cienfuegos. Lieutenant Chapman was met by a host of sympathizers, and carried to their club, and afterward to the house of one of the principal citizens, who would not hear of his spending the night at a hotel, and installed as his honored guest. Neighbors were called in, and the night was made merry, to a late hour, by the popping of champagne-corks and the story, and the song; and when the festivities had ceased, my tempest-tossed lieutenant was laid away in the sweetest and whitest of sheets, to dream of the eyes of the houries of the household, that had beamed upon him so kindly, that he was in danger of forgetting that he was a married man. For weeks afterward, his messmates could get nothing out of him, but something about Don this, and Doña that. There was a hurrying to and fro, too, of the stewards, and mess boys, as the cutter in which he returned, came alongside of the ship, for there were sundry boxes, marked Bordeaux, and Cette, and sundry baskets branded with anchors; and there were fruits, and flowers, and squalling chickens to be passed up.

The principal coffee-house of the place had been agog with wonders; the billiard-players had rested idly on their cues, to listen to Madam Rumor with her thousand tongues—how the fort had fired into the *Sumter*, and how the *Sumter* had fired back at the fort, and how the matter had finally been settled by the *Pirata* and the *Commandante*, over a bottle of champagne. Yankee captains, and consignees, supercargoes, and consuls passed in, and out, in consultation, like so many ants whose nest had been trodden upon, and nothing could be talked of but freights, and insurance, with, and without the war risk; bills of lading, invoices, consul's certificates to cover cargoes, and last, though not least, where the d—l all the Federal gunboats were, that this Confederate hawk should be permitted to make such a flutter in the Yankee dove-cot.

CHAPTER XIV.

THE SUMTER ON THE WING AGAIN—IS PUT UNDER SAIL
FOR THE TIME—REACHES THE ISLAND OF CURAÇOA,
AND IS ONLY ABLE TO ENTER AFTER A DIPLOMATIC
FIGHT.

FROM what has been said in the last chapter, the reader will have observed how anxious I was to conform my conduct, in all respects, to the laws of war. My hope was, that *some* of the nations of the earth, at least, would give me an asylum for my prizes, so that I might have them formally condemned by the Confederate States Prize Courts, instead of being obliged to destroy them. It was with this hope, that I had entered the port of Cienfuegos, as the reader has seen; and it was in furtherance of this object, that I now drew up the following appointment of a Prize Agent, who had come well recommended to me, as a gentleman of integrity and capacity.

C. S. STEAMER SUMTER, CIENFUEGOS, }
July 6, 1861. }

SIR:—You are hereby appointed Prize Agent, for, and in behalf of the Confederate States of America, of the following prizes, to wit: The *Cuba, Machias, Ben. Dunning, Albert Adams, Naiad, West Wind,* and *Louisa Kilham,* and their cargoes, until the same can be adjudicated, by the Prize Courts of the Confederate States, and disposed of by the proper authorities. You will take the necessary steps for the safe custody of these prizes, and you will not permit anything to be removed from, or disturbed on board of them. You will be pleased, also, to take the examinations of the master, and mate of each of these vessels, before a notary, touching the property of the vessels, and cargoes; and making a copy thereof, to be retained in your own possession, you will send, by some safe conveyance, the originals, addressed to "The Judge of the Confederate States District Court, New Orleans, La."

I have the honor to be, &c.,

RAPHAEL SEMMES.

Señor Don MARIANO DIAS.

During the day, the steam-tug towed down from the town, for me, a couple of lighters, containing about one hundred tons of coal, five thousand gallons of water, and some fresh provisions for the crew. It was necessary that we should prepare for sea, with some dispatch, as there was a line of telegraph, from Cienfuegos to Havana, where there were always a number of the enemy's ships of war stationed. As a matter of course, the U.'S. Consul at Cienfuegos .had telegraphed to his brother Consul, in Havana, the arrival of the *Sumter,* in the first ten minutes after she had let go her anchor; and as another matter of course, there must already be several fast steamers on their way, to capture this piratical craft, which had thus so unceremoniously broken in upon the quiet of the Cuban waters, and the Yankee sugar, and rum trade. I had recourse to the chart, and having ascertained at what hour these steamers would be enabled to arrive, I fixed my own departure, a few hours ahead, so as to give them the satisfaction of finding that the bird, which they were in pursuit of, had flown. My excellent first lieutenant came up to time, and the ship was reported ready for sea before sunset, or in a little more than twenty-four hours, after our arrival.

To avoid the coal dust, which is one of the pests of a steamer, and the confusion, and noise which necessarily accompany the exceedingly poetic operation of coaling, I landed, as the sun was approaching the western horizon, in company with my junior lieutenant and sailing-master, for a stroll, and to obtain sights for testing my chronometers, as well. Having disposed of the business part of the operation first, in obedience to the old maxim; that is to say, having made our observations upon the sun, for time, we wandered about, for an hour, and more, amid the rich tropical vegetation of this queen of islands, now passing under the flowering acacia, and now under the deep-foliaged orange-tree, which charmed two senses at once — that of smell, by the fragrance of its young flowers, and that of sight, by the golden hue of its luscious and tempting fruit. We had landed abreast of our ship, and a few steps sufficed to put us in the midst of a dense wilderness, of floral beauty, with nothing to commune with but nature. What a contrast there was between this peaceful, and lovely scene, and the life we had led for the last week! We almost loathed to go back to the dingy walls, and close quarters of our little craft, where everything told us of war, and admonished us that a life of toil, vexation, and danger lay before us, and that we must bid a long farewell to rural scenes, and rural pleasures. As we still wandered, absorbed in such speculations as these, unconscious of the flight of time, the sound of the evening gun came booming on the ear, to recall us to our senses, and retracing our steps, we hurriedly re-embarked. That evening's stroll lingered long in my memory, and was often recalled, amid the whistling, and surging of the gale, and the tumbling, and discomforts of the ship.

I had been looking anxiously, for the last few hours, for the arrival of our prize brigantine, the *Cuba*, but she failed to make her appearance, and I was forced to abandon the hope of getting back my prize crew from her. I left with my prize agent, the following letter of instructions for the midshipman in command of the *Cuba*.

CONFEDERATE STATES STEAMER SUMTER, ⎱
CIENFUEGOS, July 7, 1861. ⎰

SIR:—Upon your arrival at this place, you will put the master, mate, and crew of the *Cuba* on *parole*, not to serve against the Confederate States, during the present war, unless exchanged, and release them. You will then deliver the brigantine to the Governor, for safe custody, until the orders of the Captain-General can be known in regard to her. I regret much that you are not able to arrive in time, to rejoin the ship, and you must exercise your judgment, as to the mode in which you shall regain your country. You will, no doubt, be able to raise sufficient funds for transporting yourself, and the four seamen who are with you, to some point in the Confederate States, upon a bill of exchange, which you are hereby authorized to draw, upon the Secretary of the Navy. Upon your arrival within our territory, you will report yourself to that officer. Your baggage has been sent you by the pilot.

Midshipman A. G. HUDGINS.

I did not meet Mr. Hudgins, afterward, until as a rear admiral, I was ordered to the command of the James River fleet, in the winter of 1864. He was then attached to one of my ships, as a lieutenant. On the retreat from Richmond, I made him a captain of light artillery, and he was paroled with me, at Greensboro', North Carolina, in May 1865. How he has settled with my friend, the Spanish pilot, who agreed with *me* that the prizes which I captured, off Cienfuegos, were *five* miles from the land, and with the Northern claimants, and the Captain-General of Cuba, that they were less than *three* miles from it, about his baggage, I have never learned.

Everything being in readiness for sea, on board the *Sumter*, and the officers having all returned from their visits to the town, at eleven P. M., we got under way, and as the bell struck the midnight hour, we steamed out of the harbor, the lamps from the light-house throwing a bright glare upon our deck, as we passed under its shadow, close enough to "have tossed a biscuit" to the keeper; so bold is the entrance of the little river. The sea was nearly calm, and the usual land breeze was gently breathing, rather than blowing. Having given the course to the officer of the deck, I was glad to go below, and turn in, after the excitement, and confusion of the last forty-eight hours. When some seven or eight miles from the land, we lost the land breeze, and were struck by the sea breeze, nearly ahead, with some force. We steamed on, all the next day, without any incident to break in upon the monotony, except a short chase which we gave to a brigantine, which proved, upon our coming up with her, to be Spanish. Between nine, and ten o'clock in the evening, we passed the small islands of the *Caymans*, which we found to be laid down in the charts we were using, some fifteen or sixteen miles too far to the westward. As there is a current setting in the vicinity of these islands, and as the islands themselves are so low, as to be seen with difficulty, in a dark night,—and the night on which we were passing them was dark,—I make this observation, to put navigators on their guard.

The morning of the ninth of July dawned clear, and beautifully, but as the sun gained power, the trade-wind increased, until it blew half a gale, raising considerable sea, and impeding the progress of the ship. Indeed, so little speed did we make, that the island of Jamaica, which we had descried with the first streaks of dawn, remained in sight all day; its blue mountains softened but not obliterated by the distance as the evening set in. The sea was as blue as the mountains, and the waves seemed almost as large, to our eyes, as the little steamer plunged into, and struggled with them, in her vain attempt to make headway. All the force of her engine was incapable of driving her at a greater speed than five knots. The next day, and the day after were equally unpropitious. Indeed the weather went from bad, to worse, for now the sky became densely overcast, with black, and angry-looking clouds, and the wind began to whistle through the rigging, with all the symptoms of a gale. We were approaching the hurricane season, and there was no telling at what moment, one of those terrible cyclones of the Caribbean Sea might sweep over us. To add to the gloominess of the prospect, we were comparatively out of the track of commerce, and had seen no sail, since we had overhauled the Spanish brigantine.

As explained to the reader, in one of the opening chapters, it was my intention to proceed from Cuba, to Barbadoes, there recoal, and thence make the best of my way to Cape St. Roque, in Brazil, where I expected to reap a rich harvest from the enemy's commerce. I was now obliged to abandon, or at least to modify this design. It would not be possible for me to reach Barbadoes, with my present supply of coal, in the teeth of such trade-winds, as I had been encountering for the last few days. I therefore determined to bend down toward the Spanish Main; converting the present head-wind, into a fair wind, for at least a part of the way, and hoping to find the weather more propitious, on that coast. It was now the thirteenth of July, and as we had sailed from Cienfuegos, on the seventh, we had consumed six out of our eight days' supply of fuel. Steaming was no longer to be thought of, and we must make some port under sail. The Dutch island of Curaçoa lay under our lee, and we accordingly made sail for that island. The engineer was ordered to let his fires go down, and uncouple his propeller that it might not retard the speed of the ship, and the sailors were sent aloft to loose the topsails.

This was the first time that we were to make use of our sails, unaided by steam, and the old sailors of the ship, who had not bestridden a yard for some months, leaped aloft, with a will, to obey the welcome order. The race of sailors has not yet entirely died out, though the steamship is fast making sad havoc with it. There is the same difference between the old-time sailor, who has been bred in the sailing-ship, and the modern sailor of the steamship, that there is between the well-trained fox-hound, who chases Reynard all day, and the cur that dodges a rabbit about, for half an hour or so. The sailing-ship has a romance, and a poetry about her, which is thoroughly killed by steam. The sailor of the former loves, for its own sake, the howling of the gale, and there is no music so sweet to his ear, as the shouting of orders through the trumpet of the officer of the deck, when he is poised upon the topsail-yard, of the rolling and tumbling ship, hauling out the "weather ear-ring." It is the *ranz de vache*, which recalls the memory of his boyhood, and youth, when under the tutelage of some foster-father of an old salt, he was taking his first lessons in seamanship.

It used to be beautiful to witness the rivalry of these children of the deep, when the pitiless hurricane was scourging their beloved ship, and threatening her with destruction. The greater the danger, the more eager the contest for the post of honor. Was there a sail to be secured, which appeared about to be torn into ribbons, by the gale, and the loose gear of which threatened to whip the sailor from the yard; or was there a topmast to be climbed, which was bending like a willow wand under the fury of the blast, threatening to part at every moment, and throw the climber into the raging, and seething caldron of waters beneath, from which it would be impossible to rescue him, Jack, noble Jack was ever ready for the service. I have seen an old naval captain, who had been some years retired from the sea, almost melt into tears, as he listened to the musical "heaving of the lead" by an old sailor, in the "chains" of a passing ship of war.

But steam, practical, commonplace, hard-working steam, has well-nigh changed all this, and cut away the webbing from the foot of the old-time sailor. Seamanship, evolutions, invention, skill, and ready resource in times of difficulty, and danger, have nearly all gone out of fashion, and instead of reefing the topsails, and club-hauling, and box-hauling the ship, some order is now sent to the engineer, about regulating his fires, and paying attention to his steam-gauges. Alas! alas! there will be no more Nelsons, and Collingwoods, and no more such venerable "bulwarks upon the deep," as the *Victory*, and the

Royal Sovereign. In future wars upon the ocean, all combatants will be on the dead level of impenetrable iron walls, with regard to dash, and courage, and with regard to seamanship, and evolutions, all the knowledge that will be required of them, will be to know how to steer a nondescript box toward their enemy.

Our first night under canvas, I find thus described, in my journal: "Heavy sea all night, and ship rolling, and tumbling about, though doing pretty well. The propeller revolves freely, and we are making about five knots." The next day was Sunday, and the weather was somewhat ameliorated. The wind continued nearly as fresh as before, but as we were now running a point free, this was no objection, and the black, angry clouds had disappeared, leaving a bright, and cheerful sky. A sail was seen on the distant horizon, but it was too rough to chase. This was our usual muster-day, but the decks were wet, and uncomfortable, and I permitted my crew to rest, they having scarcely yet recovered from the fatigue of the last few days.

There is, perhaps, no part of the world where the weather is so uniformly fine, as on the Spanish Main. The cyclones never bend in that direction, and even the ordinary gales are unknown. We were already beginning to feel the influence of this meteorological change; for on Monday, the 15th of July, the weather was thus described in my journal: "Weather moderating, and the sea going down, though still rough. Nothing seen. In the afternoon, pleasant, with a moderate breeze, and the clouds assuming their usual soft, fleecy, trade-wind appearance." The next day was still clear, though the wind had freshened, and the ship was making good speed.

At nine A. M. we made the land, on the starboard bow, which proved to be the island of Oruba, to leeward, a few miles, of Curaçoa. For some hours past, we had been within the influence of the equatorial current, which sets westward, along this coast, with considerable velocity, and it had carried us a little out of our course, though we had made some allowance for it. We hauled up, a point, or two, and at eleven A. M. we made the island of Curaçoa, on the port bow. We doubled the northwest end of the island, at about four P. M. and hauling up on the

south side of it we soon brought the wind ahead, when it became necessary to put the ship under steam again, and to furl
the sails.

The afternoon proved beautifully bright, and clear; the sea
was of a deep indigo-blue, and we were all charmed, even with
this barren little island, as we steamed along its bold, and
blackened shores, of limestone rock, alongside of which the
heaviest ship might have run, and throwing out her bow and
stern lines, made herself fast with impunity, so perpendicularly deep were the waters. Our average distance from the
land, as we steamed along, was not greater than a quarter of a
mile. There were a few stunted trees, only, to be seen, in the
little ravines, and some wild shrubbery, and sickly looking
grass, struggling for existence on the hills' sides. A few goats
were browsing about here, and there, and the only evidence of
commerce, or thrift, that we saw, were some piles of salt, that
had been raked up from the lagoons, ready for shipment. And
yet the Dutch live, and thrive here, and have built up quite a
pretty little town — that of St. Anne's, to which we were bound.
The explanation of which is, that the island lies contiguous to
the Venezuelan coast, and is a free port, for the introduction
of European, and American goods, in which a considerable
trade is carried on, with the main land.

We arrived off the town, with its imposing battlements
frowning on either side of the harbor, about dusk, and immediately hoisted a jack, and fired a gun, for a pilot. In the
course of half an hour, or so, this indispensable individual
appeared, but it was too late, he said, for us to attempt the
entrance, that night. He would come off, the first thing in the
morning, and take us in. With this assurance we rested satisfied, and lay off, and on, during the night, under easy steam.
But we were not to gain entrance to this quaint little Dutch
town, so easily, as had been supposed. We were to have here
a foretaste of the trouble, that the Federal Consuls were to give
us in the future. We have already commented on the love of
office of the American people. There is no hole, or corner of
the earth, into which a ship can enter, and where there is a
dollar to be made, that has not its American Consul, small or
large. The smallest of salaries are eagerly accepted, and, as a

consequence, the smallest of men are sometimes sent to fill these places. But the smaller the place, the bigger were the cocked hats and epaulettes the officials wore, and the more brim-full were they of patriotism.

At the time of which I am writing, they called one Wm. H. Seward, master, and they had taken Billy's measure to a fraction. They knew his tastes, and pandered to them, accordingly. His circular letters had admonished them, that, in their intercourse with foreign nations, they must speak of our great civil war, as a mere *rebellion*, that would be suppressed, in from sixty, to ninety days; insist that we were not entitled to belligerent rights, and call our cruisers, "corsairs," or "pirates." Accordingly, soon after the pilot had landed, from the *Sumter*, carrying with him to the shore, the intelligence that she was a Confederate States cruiser, the Federal Consul made his appearance at the Government-House, and claimed that the "pirate" should not be permitted to enter the harbor; informing his Excellency, the Governor, that Mr. Seward would be irate, if such a thing were permitted, and that he might expect to have the stone, and mortar of his two forts knocked about his ears, in double quick, by the ships of war of the Great Republic.

This bold, and defiant tone, of the doughty little Consul, seemed to stagger his Excellency; it would not be so pleasant to have St. Anne's demolished, merely because a steamer with a flag that nobody had seen before, wanted some coal; and so, the next morning, bright and early, he sent the pilot off, to say to me, that "the Governor could not permit the *Sumter* to enter, having received recent orders from Holland to that effect." Here was a pretty kettle of fish! The *Sumter* had only one day's fuel left, and it was some distance from Curaçoa, to any other place, where coal was to be had. I immediately sent for Lieutenant Chapman, and directed him to prepare himself for a visit to the shore; and calling my clerk, caused him to write, after my dictation, the following despatch to his Excellency: —

CONFEDERATE STATES STEAMER SUMTER, ⎫
OFF ST. ANNE'S, CURAÇOA, July 17, 1861. ⎬

HIS EXCELLENCY GOVERNOR CROL:—

I was surprised to receive, by the pilot, this morning, a message from your Excellency, to the effect that this ship would not be permitted to enter the harbor, unless she was in distress, as your Excellency had received orders from his Government not to admit vessels of war of the Confederate States of America, to the hospitality of the ports, under your Excellency's command. I most respectfully suggest that there must be some mistake here; and I have sent to you the bearer, Lieutenant Chapman, of the Confederate States Navy, for the purpose of an explanation. Your Excellency must be under some misapprehension as to the character of this vessel. She is a ship of war, duly commissioned by the government of the Confederate States, which States have been recognized, as belligerents, in the present war, by all the leading Powers of Europe, viz. :—Great Britain, France, Spain, &c., as your Excellency must be aware.

It is true, that these Powers have prohibited both belligerents, alike, from bringing prizes into their several jurisdictions ; but no one of them has made a distinction, either between the respective prizes, or the cruisers, themselves, of the two belligerents — the cruisers of both governments, unaccompanied by prizes, being admitted to the hospitalities of the ports of all these great Powers, on terms of perfect equality. In the face of these facts, am I to understand from your Excellency, that Holland has adopted a different rule, and that she not only excludes the prizes, but the ships of war, themselves, of the Confederate States? And this, at the same time, that she admits the cruisers of the United States; thus departing from her neutrality, in this war, ignoring the Confederate States, as belligerents, and aiding and abetting their enemy? If this be the position which Holland has assumed, in this contest, I pray your Excellency to be kind enough to say as much to me in writing.

When this epistle was ready, Chapman shoved off for the shore, and a long conference ensued. The Governor called around him, as I afterward learned, all the dignitaries of the island, civil and military, and a grand council of State was held. These Dutchmen have a ponderous way of doing things, and I have no doubt, the gravity of this council was equal to that held in New Amsterdam in colonial days, as described by the renowned historian Diederick Knickerbocker, at which Woutter Van Twiller, the doubter, was present. Judging by the time that Chapman was waiting for his answer, during which he had nothing to do but sip the most delightful mint juleps—for these islanders seemed to have robbed old Virginia of some of her famous mint patches—in company with an admiring crowd of friends, the councillors must have "smoked and talked, and smoked again;" pondered with true Dutch gravity, all the arguments, *pro* and *con*, that were offered, and weighed my despatch, along with the "recent order from Holland," in a torsion balance, to see which was heaviest.

After the lapse of an hour, or two, becoming impatient, I told my first lieutenant, that as our men had not been practised at the guns, for some time, I thought it would be as well to let them burst a few of our eight-inch shells, at a target. Accordingly the drum beat to quarters, a great stir was made about the deck, as the guns were cast loose, and pretty soon, whiz! went a shell, across the windows of the council-chamber, which overlooked the sea; the shell bursting like a clap of rather sharp, ragged thunder, a little beyond, in close proximity, to the target. Sundry heads were seen immediately to pop out of the windows of the chamber, and then to be withdrawn very suddenly, as though the owners of them feared that another shell was coming, and that my gunners might make some mistake in their aim. By the time we had fired three or four shells, all of which bursted with beautiful precision, Chapman's boat was seen returning, and thinking that our men had had exercise enough, we ran out and secured the guns.

My lieutenant came on board, smiling, and looking pleasantly, as men will do, when they are bearers of good news, and said that the Governor had given us permission to enter. We were lying close in with the entrance, and in a few minutes more, the *Sumter* was gliding gracefully past the houses, on either side of her, as she ran up the little canal, or river, that split the town in two. The quays were crowded with a motley gathering of the townspeople, men, women, and children, to see us pass, and sailors waved their hats to us, from the shipping in the port. Running through the town into a landlocked basin, in its rear, the *Sumter* let go her anchor, hoisted out her boats, and spread her awnings, — and we were once more in port.

CHAPTER XV.

THE SUMTER AT CURAÇOA—HER SURROUNDINGS—
PREPARATIONS FOR SEA, AND DEPARTURE—THE
CAPTURE OF OTHER PRIZES—PUERTO CABELLO, AND
WHAT OCCURRED THERE.

THE *Sumter* had scarcely swung to her anchors, in the
small land-locked harbor described, before she was surrounded by a fleet of bum-boats, laden with a profusion of
tropical fruits, and filled with men, and women, indifferently
—the women rather preponderating. These bum-boat women
are an institution in Curaçoa; the profession descends from
mother to daughter, and time seems to operate no change
among them. It had been nearly a generation since I was last
at Curaçoa. I was then a gay, rollicking young midshipman, in
the " old " Navy, and it seemed as though I were looking upon
the same faces, and listening to the same confusion of voices
as before. The individual women had passed away, of course,
but the bum-boat women remained. They wore the same
parti-colored handkerchiefs wound gracefully around their
heads, the same gingham or muslin dresses, and exposed similar, if not the same, bare arms, and unstockinged legs. They
were admitted freely on board, with their stocks in trade, and
pretty soon Jack was on capital terms with them, converting
his small change into fragrant bananas, and blood-red oranges,
and replenishing his tobacco-pouch for the next cruise. As
Jack is a gallant fellow, a little flirtation was going on too
with the purchasing, and I was occasionally highly amused at
these joint efforts at trade and love-making. No one but a
bum-boat woman is ever a sailor's *blanchiseuse, et par consequence*
a number of well-filled clothes'-bags soon made their appearance, on deck, from the different apartments of the ship, and
were passed into the boats alongside.

These people all speak excellent English, though with a drawl, which is not unmusical, when the speaker is a sprightly young woman. Jack has a great fondness for pets, and no wonder, poor fellow, debarred, as he is, from all family ties, and with no place he can call his home, but his ship; and pretty soon my good-natured first lieutenant had been seduced into giving him leave to bring sundry monkeys, and parrots on board, the former of which were now gambolling about the rigging, and the latter waking the echoes of the harbor with their squalling. Such was the crowd upon our decks, and so serious was the interruption to business, that we were soon obliged to lay restrictions upon the bum-boat fleet, by prohibiting it from coming alongside, except at meal-hours, which we always designated by hoisting a red pennant, at the mizzen. It was curious to watch the movements of the fleet, as these hours approached. Some twenty or thirty boats would be lying upon their oars, a few yards from the ship, each with from two to half a dozen inmates, eagerly watching the old quartermaster, whose duty it was to hoist the pennant; the women chattering, and the parrots squalling, whilst the oarsmen were poising their oars, that they might get the first stroke over their competitors in the race. At length, away goes the flag! and then what a rushing and clattering, and bespattering until the boats are alongside.

In an hour after our anchor had been let go, the business of the ship, for the next few days, had all been arranged. The first lieutenant had visited a neighboring ship-yard, and contracted for a new foretop-mast, to supply the place of the old one which had been sprung; the paymaster had contracted for a supply of coal, and fresh provisions, daily, for the crew, and for having the ship watered; the latter no unimportant matter, in this rainless region, and I had sent an officer to call on the Governor, *with my card*, being too unwell to make the visit, in person. Upon visiting the shore the next day, I found that we were in a *quasi* enemy's territory, for. besides the Federal Consul before spoken of, a Boston man had intrenched himself in the best hotel in the place, as proprietor, and was doing a thriving business, far away from "war's alarms," and a New Yorker had the monopoly of taking all the phizes of the staid old Dutchmen

—"John Smith, of New York, Photographer," hanging high above the artist's windows, on a sign-board that evidently had not been painted by a Curaçoan.   Mr. Smith had already taken an excellent photograph of the *Sumter*, which he naively enough told me, was intended for the New York illustrated papers.   If I had had ever so much objection, to having the likeness of my ship hung up in such a "rogues' gallery," I had no means of preventing it.   Besides, it could do us but little damage, in the way of identification, as we had the art of disguising the *Sumter* so that we would not know her, ourselves, at half a dozen miles distance.

I was surprised, one morning, during our stay here, whilst I was lounging, listlessly, in my cabin, making a vain attempt to read, under the infliction of the caulkers overhead, who were striking their caulking-irons with a vigor, and rapidity, that made the tympanum of my ears ring again, at the announcement that Don somebody or other, the private secretary of President Castro, desired to see me.   The caulkers were sent away, and his Excellency's private secretary brought below. President Castro was one of those unfortunate South American chiefs, who had been beaten in a battle of ragamuffins, and compelled to fly his country.   He was President of Venezuela, and had been deprived of his office, before the expiration of his term, by some military aspirant, who had seated himself in the presidential chair, instead, and was now in exile in Curaçoa, with four of the members of his cabinet.   The object of the visit of his secretary was to propose to me to reinstate the exiled President, in his lost position, by engaging in a military expedition, with him, to the mainland.

Here was a chance, now, for an ambitious man!   I might become the Warwick of Venezuela, and put the crown on another's head, if I might not wear it myself.   I might hoist my admiral's flag, on board the *Sumter*, and take charge of all the piraguas, and canoes, that composed the Venezuelan navy, whilst my colleague mustered those men in buckram, so graphically described by Sir John Falstaff, and made an onslaught upon his despoiler.   But unfortunately for friend Castro, I was like one of those damsels who had already plighted her faith to another, before the new wooer appeared — I was not in the market. I listened courteously, however, to what the secretary had to say; told him, that I felt flattered by the offer of his chief, but that I was unable to accept it. "I cannot," I continued, "consistently with my obligations to my own country, engage in any of the revolutionary movements of other countries." "But," said he, "Señor Castro is the *de jure* President of Venezuela, and you would be upholding the right in assisting him; — can you not, at least, land us, with some arms and ammunition, on the main land?" I replied that, "as a Confederate States officer, I could not look into *de jure* claims. These questions were for the Venezuelans, themselves, to decide. The only government I could know in Venezuela was the *de facto* government, for the time being, and *that*, by his own showing, was in the hands of his antagonists." Here the conversation closed, and my visitor, who had the bearing and speech of a cultivated gentleman, departed. The jottings of my diary for the next few days, will perhaps now inform the reader, of our movements, better than any other form of narrative.

July 19th.—Wind unusually blustering this morning, with partial obscuration of the heavens. The engineers are busy, overhauling and repairing damages to their engine and boilers; the gunner is at work, polishing up his battery and ventilating his magazine, and the sailors are busy renewing ratlines and tarring down their rigging. An English bark entered the harbor to-day from Liverpool.

July 20th.— Painting and refitting ship; got off the new foretopmast from the shore. It is a good pine stick, evidently from our Southern States, and has been well fashioned. The monthly packet from the island of St. Thomas arrived, to-day, bringing newspapers from the enemy's country as late as the 26th of June. We get nothing new from these papers, except that the Northern bee-hive is all agog, with the marching and countermarching of troops.

July 21st.— Fresh trade-winds, with flying clouds — atmosphere highly charged with moisture, but no rain. This being Sunday, we mustered and inspected the crew. The washerwomen have decidedly improved the appearance of the young officers, the glistening of white shirt-bosoms and collars having been somewhat unusual on board of the *Sumter*, of late.

The crew look improved too, by their change of diet, and the use of antiscorbutics, which have been supplied to them, at the request of the surgeon; though some of them, having been on shore, "on liberty," have brought off a blackened eye.   No matter — the more frequently Jack settles his accounts, on shore, the fewer he will have to settle on board ship, in breach of discipline.   We read, at the muster, to-day, the finding and sentence of the first court-martial, that has sat on board the *Sumter*, since she reached the high seas.

July 22d.— Warped alongside a wharf, in the edge of the town, and commenced receiving coal on board.   Refitting, and repainting ship.   In the afternoon, I took a lonely stroll through the town, mainly in the suburbs.   It is a quaint, picturesque old place, with some few modern houses, but the general air is that of dilapidation, and a decay of trade.   The lower classes are simple, and primitive in their habits, and but little suffices to supply their wants.   The St. Thomas packet sailed, to-day, and, as a consequence, the Federal cruisers, in and about that island, will have intelligence of our whereabouts, in four or five days.   To mislead them, I have told the pilot, and several gentlemen from the shore, *in great confidence*, that I am going back to cruise on the coast of Cuba.   The packet will of course take that intelligence to St. Thomas.

July 23d.— Still coaling, refitting and painting.   Weather more cloudy, and wind not so constantly fresh, within the last few days.   Having taken sights for our chronometers, on the morning after our arrival, and again to-day, I have been enabled to verify their rates.   They are running very well.   The chronometer of the *Golden Rocket* proves to be a good instrument.   We fix the longitude of Curaçoa to be 68° 58′ 30″, west of Greenwich.

July 24th.—Sky occasionally obscured, with a moderate trade-wind.   Our men have all returned from their visits to the shore, except one, a simple lad named Orr, who, as I learn, has been seduced away, by a Yankee skipper, in port, aided by the Boston hotel-keeper, and our particular friend, the consul.   As these persons have tampered with my whole crew, I am gratified to know, that there has been but one traitor found among them.

We had now been a week in Curaçoa, during which time, besides recruiting, and refreshing my crew, I had made all the necessary preparations for another cruise. The ship had been thoroughly overhauled, inside and out, and her coal-bunkers were full of good English coal. It only remained for us to put to sea. Accordingly, at twelve o'clock precisely, on the day last above mentioned, as had been previously appointed, the *Sumter*, bidding farewell to her new-made friends, moved gracefully out of the harbor—this time, amid the waving of handkerchiefs, in female hands, as well as of hats in the hands of the males; the quay being lined, as before, to see us depart. The photographer took a last shot at the ship, as she glided past his sanctum, and we looked with some little interest to the future numbers of that "Journal of Civilization," vulgarly yclept "Harper's Weekly," for the interesting portrait; which came along in due time, accompanied by a lengthy description, veracious, of course, of the "Pirate."

Curaçoa lies a short distance off the coast of Venezuela, between Laguayra, and Puerto Cabello, and as both of these places had some commerce with the United States, I resolved to look into them. The morning after our departure found us on a smooth sea, with a light breeze off the land. The mountains, back of Laguayra, loomed up blue, mystic, and majestic, at a distance of about thirty miles. and the lookout, at the mast-head, was on the *qui vive* for strange sails. He had not to wait long. In the tropics, there is very little of that bewitching portion of the twenty-four hours, which, in other parts of the world, is called twilight. Day passes into night, and night into day, almost at a single bound. The rapidly approaching dawn had scarcely revealed to us the bold outline of the coast, above mentioned, when sail ho! resounded from the mast-head. The sail bore on our port-bow, and was standing obliquely toward us. We at once gave chase, and at half-past six A. M., came up with, and captured the schooner *Abby Bradford*, from New York, bound for *Puerto Cabello*.

We knew our prize to be American, long before she showed us her colors. She was a "down-East," fore-and-aft schooner, and there are no other such vessels in the world. They are

as thoroughly marked, as the Puritans who build them, and
there is no more mistaking the "cut of their jib." The little
schooner was provision laden, and there was no attempt to
cover her cargo. The news of the escape of the *Sumter* had
not reached New York, at the date of her sailing, and the few
privateers that we had put afloat, at the beginning of the war,
had confined their operations to our own, and the enemy's
coasts. Hence the neglect of the owners of the *Bradford*, in
not providing her with some good English, or Spanish certificates, protesting that her cargo was neutral. The "old flag"
was treated very tenderly on the present occasion. The
"flaunting lie," which Mr. Horace Greeley had told us, should
"insult no sunny sky," was hauled down, and stowed away in
the quartermaster's bag described a few pages back.

The *Bradford* being bound for Puerto Cabello, and that
port being but a short distance, under my lee, I resolved to
run down, with the prize, and try my hand with my friend
Castro's opponent, the *de facto* President of Venezuela, to see
whether I could not prevail upon him, to admit my prizes into
his ports. I thought, surely, an arrangement could be made
with some of these beggarly South American republics, the revenue of which did not amount to a cargo of provisions, annually, and which were too weak, besides, to be worth kicking by
the stronger powers. What right had *they*, thought I, to be
putting on the airs of nations, and talking about acknowledging other people, when they had lived a whole generation,
themselves, without the acknowledgment of Spain.

But, as the reader will see, I reckoned without my host. I
found that they had a wholesome fear of the Federal gunboats, and that even their cupidity could not tempt them to be
just, or generous. If they had admitted my prizes into their
ports, I could, in the course of a few months, have made those
same ports more busy with the hum and thrift of commerce,
than they had ever been before; I could have given a new
impulse to their revolutions, and made them rich enough to
indulge in the luxury of a *pronunciamiento*, once a week. The
bait was tempting, but there stood the great lion in their
path—the model Republic. The fact is, I must do this model
Republic the justice to say, that it not only bullied the little

South American republics, but all the world besides. Even old John Bull, grown rich, and plethoric, and asthmatic and gouty, trembled when he thought of his rich argosies, and of the possibility of Yankee privateers chasing them.

Taking the *Bradford* in tow, then, we squared away for Puerto Cabello, but darkness came on before we could reach the entrance of the harbor, and we were compelled to stand off and on, during the night—the schooner being cast off, and taking care of herself, under sail. The *Sumter* lay on the still waters, all night, like a huge monster asleep, with the light from the light-house, on the battlements of the fort, glaring full upon her, and in plain hearing of the shrill cry of "*Alerta!*" from the sentinels. So quietly did she repose, with banked fires, being fanned, but not moved, by the gentle land-breeze that was blowing, that she scarcely needed to turn over her propeller during the night, to preserve her relative position with the light. There was no occasion to be in a hurry to run in, the next morning, as no business could be transacted before ten, or eleven o'clock, and so I waited until the sun, with his broad disk glaring upon us, like an angry furnace, had rolled away the mists of the morning, and the first lieutenant had holy-stoned his decks, and arranged his hammock-nettings, with his neat, white hammocks stowed in them, before we put the ship in motion.

We had, some time before, hoisted the Confederate States flag, and the Venezuelan colors were flying from the fort in response. The prize accompanied us in, and we both anchored, within a stone's throw of the town, the latter looking like some old Moorish city, that had been transported by magic to the new world, *gallinazos*, and all. Whilst my clerk was copying my despatch to the Governor, and the lieutenant was preparing himself, and his boat's crew, to take it on shore, I made a hasty *reconnoissance* of the fort, which had a few iron pieces, of small calibre mounted on it, well eaten by rust, and whose carriages had rotted from under them. The following is a copy of my letter to his Excellency.

CONFEDERATE STATES STEAMER SUMTER, }
PUERTO CABELLO, July 26, 1861. }

HIS EXCELLENCY, THE GOVERNOR :—

I have the honor to inform your Excellency of my arrival at this place, in this ship, under my command, with the prize schooner, *Abby Bradford*, in company, captured by me about seventy miles to the northward and eastward. The *Abby Bradford* is the property of citizens of the United States, with which States, as your Excellency is aware, the Confederate States, which I have the honor to represent, are at war, and the cargo would appear to belong, also, to citizens of the United States, who have shipped it, on consignment, to a house in *Puerto Cabello*. Should any claim, however, be given for the cargo, or any part of it, the question of ownership can only be decided by the Prize Courts of the Confederate States. In the meantime, I have the honor to request, that your Excellency will permit me to leave this prize vessel, with her cargo, in the port of Puerto Cabello, until the question of prize can be adjudicated by the proper tribunals of my country. This will be a convenience to all parties ; as well to any citizens of Venezuela, who may have an interest in the cargo, as to the captors, who have also valuable interests to protect.

In making this request, I do not propose that the Venezuelan government shall depart from a strict neutrality between the belligerents, as the same rule it applies to us, it can give the other party the benefit of, also. In other words, with the most scrupulous regard for her neutrality, she may permit both belligerents to bring their prizes into her waters ; and, of this, neither belligerent could complain, since whatever justice is extended to its enemy, is extended also to itself. * * * [Here follows a repetition of the facts with regard to the seizure of the Navy by the Federal authorities, and the establishment of the blockade of the Southern ports, already stated in my letter to the Governor of Cienfuegos.] * * * Thus, your Excellency sees, that under the rule of exclusion, the enemy could enjoy his right of capture, to its full extent — all his own ports being open to him — whilst the cruisers of the Confederate States could enjoy it, *sub modo*, only ; that is, for the purpose of destroying their prizes. A rule which would produce such unequal results as this, is not a just rule (although it might, in terms, be extended to both parties), and as equality and justice, are of the essence of neutrality, I take it for granted, that Venezuela will not adopt it.

On the other hand, the rule admitting both parties, alike, with their prizes into your ports, until the prize courts of the respective countries could have time to adjudicate the cases, would work equal and exact justice to both ; and this is all that the Confederate States demand.

With reference to the present case, as the cargo consists chiefly of provisions, which are perishable, I would ask leave to sell them, at public auction, for the benefit of " whom it may concern," deposit-

ing the proceeds with a suitable prize agent, until the decision of
the court can be known. With regard to the vessel, I request that
she may remain in the custody of the same agent, until condemned
and sold.

When the *Sumter* entered *Puerto Cabello*, with her prize, she
found an empty harbor, there being only two or three coasting
schooners anchored along the coast; there was a general dearth
of business, and the quiet little city was panting for an excitement. A bomb-shell, thrown into the midst of the stagnant
commercial community, could not have startled them more,
than the rattling of the chain cable of the *Sumter* through her
hawse-hole, as she let go her anchor; and when my missive
was handed to the Governor, there was a racing, and chasing
of bare-footed orderlies, that indicated a prospective gathering
of the clans, similar to the one which had occurred at Curaçoa.
A grand council was held, at which the Confederate States had
not the honor to be represented.

That the reader may understand the odds against which we
now had to struggle, he must recollect, that all these small
South American towns are, more or less, dependent upon
American trade. The New England States, and New York
supply them with their domestic cottons, flour, bacon, and
notions; sell them all their worthless old muskets, and damaged ammunition, and now and then, smuggle out a small craft
to them, for naval purposes. The American Consul, who is
also a merchant, represents not only those "grand moral ideas,"
that characterize our Northern people, but Sand's sarsaparilla,
and Smith's wooden clocks. He is, *par excellence*, the big dog
of the village. The big dog was present on the present occasion, looking portentous, and savage, and when he ope'd his
mouth, all the little dogs were silent. Of course, the poor
Sumter, anchored away off in the bay, could have no chance
before so august an assemblage, and, pretty soon, an orderly
came down to the boat, where my patient lieutenant was waiting, bearing a most ominous-looking letter, put up in true
South American style, about a foot square, and bearing on it,
"Dios y Libertad."

When I came to break the seal of this letter, I found it to
purport, that the Governor had not the necessary *funciones*, to
reply to me, diplomatically, but that he would *elevate* my de-

spatch, to the *Supreme* Government; and that, in the mean time, I had better take the *Abby Bradford* and get out of *Puerto Cabello*, as soon as possible! This was all said, very politely, for your petty South American chieftain is

"As mild a mannered man, as ever cut a throat,"

but it was none the less strong for all that. The missive of the Governor reached me early, in the afternoon, but I paid not the least attention to it. I sent the paymaster on shore, to purchase some fresh provisions, and fruits, for the crew, and gave such of the officers " liberty," as desired it. The next morning I sent a prize crew on board the *Bradford*, and determined to send her to New Orleans. Being loth to part with any more of my officers, after the experience I had had, with the prize brig *Cuba*, I selected an intelligent quartermaster, who had been mate of a merchantman, as prize-master. My men I could replace—my officers I could not. The following letter of instructions was prepared for the guidance of the prize-master:

CONFEDERATE STATES STEAMER SUMTER,
OFF PUERTO CABELLO, July 26, 1861.
QUARTERMASTER AND PRIZE-MASTER. EUGENE RUHL:
You will take charge of the prize schooner, *Abby Bradford*, and proceed with her, to New Orleans — making the land to the westward of the passes of the Mississippi, and endeavoring to run into Barrataria Bay, Berwick's Bay, or some of the other small inlets. Upon your arrival, you will proceed to the city of New Orleans, in person, and report yourself to Commodore Rousseau, for orders. You will take especial care of the accompanying package of papers, as they are the papers of the captured schooner, and you will deliver them, with the seals unbroken, to the judge of the Prize Court, Judge Moise. You will batten down your hatches, and see that no part of the cargo is touched, during the voyage, and you will deliver both vessel, and cargo, to the proper law officers, in the condition in which you find them, as nearly as possible.

I availed myself of this opportunity, to address the following letter to Mr. Mallory, the Secretary of the Navy; having nothing very important to communicate, I did not resort to the use of the cipher, that had been established between us.

CONFEDERATE STATES STEAMER SUMTER, ⎱
PUERTO CABELLO, July 26, 1861. ⎰

SIR:—Having captured a schooner of light draught, which, with her cargo, I estimate to be worth some twenty-five thousand dollars, and being denied the privilege of leaving her at this port, until she could be adjudicated, I have resolved to dispatch her for New Orleans, in charge of a prize crew, with the hope that she may be able to elude the vigilance of the blockading squadron, of the enemy, and run into some one of the shoal passes, to the westward of the mouth of the Mississippi, as Barrataria, or Berwick's Bay. In great haste, I avail myself of this opportunity to send you my first despatch, since leaving New Orleans. I can do no more, for want of time, than barely enumerate, without describing events.

We ran the blockade of Pass à L'Outre, by the *Brooklyn*, on the 30th of June, that ship giving us chase. On the morning of the 3d of July, I doubled Cape Antonio, the western extremity of Cuba, and, on the same day, captured, off the Isle of Pines, the American ship, *Golden Rocket*, belonging to parties in Bangor, in Maine. She was a fine ship of 600 tons, and worth between thirty and forty thousand dollars. I burned her. On the next day, the 4th, I captured the brigantines *Cuba* and *Machias*, both of Maine, also. They were laden with sugars. I sent them to Cienfuegos, Cuba. On the 5th of July, I captured the brigs *Ben. Dunning*, and *Albert Adams*, owned in New York, and Massachusetts. They were laden, also, with sugars. I sent them to Cienfuegos. On the next day, the 6th, I captured the barks *West Wind*, and *Louisa Kilham*, and the brig *Naiad*, all owned in New York, Rhode Island, and Massachusetts. I sent them, also, to Cienfuegos.

On the same day, I ran into that port, myself, reported my captures to the authorities, and asked leave for them to remain, until they could be adjudicated. The Government took them in charge, until the Home Government should give directions concerning them. I coaled ship, and sailed, again, on the 7th. On the 17th I arrived at the Island of Curaçoa, without having fallen in with any of the enemy's ships. I coaled again, here—having had some little difficulty with the Governor, about entering—and sailed on the 24th. On the morning of the 25th, I captured, off Laguayra, the schooner *Abby Bradford*, which is the vessel, by which I send this despatch. I do not deem it prudent to speak, here, of my future movements, lest my despatch should fall into the hands of the enemy. We are all well, and "doing a pretty fair business," in mercantile parlance, having made nine captures in twenty-six days.

The *Bradford* reached the coast of Louisiana, in due time, but approaching too near to the principal passes of the Mississippi, against which I had warned her, she was re-captured, by one of the enemy's steamers, and my prize crew were made prisoners, but soon afterward released, though they did not rejoin me. I am thus particular, in giving the reader an account of these, my first transactions, for the purpose of showing him, that I made every effort to avoid the necessity of destroying my prizes, at sea; and that I only resorted to this practice, when it became evident that there was nothing else to be done. Not that I had not the right to burn them, under the laws of war, when there was no dispute about the property — as was the case with the *Golden Rocket*, she having had no cargo on board — but because I desired to avoid all possible complication with neutrals.

Having dispatched the *Bradford*, we got under way, in the *Sumter*, to continue our cruise. We had scarcely gotten clear of the harbor, before a sail was discovered, in plain sight, from the deck. The breeze was light, and she was running down the coast, with all her studding sails set. Her taunt and graceful spars, and her whitest of cotton sails, glistening in the morning's sun, revealed at once the secret of her nationality. We chased, and, at the distance of full seven miles from the land, came up with, and captured her. She proved to be the bark *Joseph Maxwell*, of Philadelphia, last from Laguayra, where she had touched, to land a part of her cargo. The remainder she was bringing to Puerto Cabello. Upon inspection of her papers, I ascertained that one-half of the cargo, remaining on board of her, belonged to a neutral owner, doing business in Puerto Cabello.

Heaving the bark to, in charge of a prize crew, beyond the marine league, I took her master on board the *Sumter*, and steaming back into the harbor, sent Paymaster Myers on shore with him, to see if some arrangement could not be made, by which the interests of the neutral half-owner of the cargo could be protected; to see, in other words, whether *this* prize, in which a Venezuelan citizen was interested, would not be permitted to enter, and remain until she could be adjudicated. Much to my surprise, upon the return of my boat, the paymaster handed me a written *command* from the Governor, to bring the *Maxwell* in, and deliver her to him, until the *Venezuelan courts* could determine whether she had been captured within the marine league, or not! This insolence was refreshing. I scarcely knew whether to laugh, or be angry at it. I

believe I indulged in both emotions. The *Sumter* had not let go
her anchor, but had been waiting for the return of her boat, under
steam. She was lying close under the guns of the fort, and we
could see that the tompions had been taken out of the guns,
and that they were manned by some half-naked soldiers. Not
knowing but the foolish Governor might order his commandant to fire upon me, in case I should attempt to proceed to sea,
in my ship, before I had sent a boat out to bring in the *Maxwell*, I beat to quarters, and with my crew standing by my
guns, steamed out to rejoin my prize. When I had a little
leisure to converse with my paymaster, he told me, that the
Federal consul had been consulted, on the occasion, and that
the nice little *ruse* of the Governor's order had been resorted
to in the hope of intimidating me. I would have burned the
Maxwell, on the spot, but, unfortunately, as the reader has seen,
she had some neutral cargo on board, and this I had no right to
destroy. I resolved, therefore, to send her in ; not to the Confederate States, for she drew too much water to enter any,
except the principal ports, and these being all blockaded, by
steamers, it was useless for her to make the attempt. The
following letter of instructions to her prize-master, will show
what disposition was made of her.

CONFEDERATE STATES STEAMER SUMTER,
AT SEA, July 27, 1861.

MIDSHIPMAN AND PRIZE-MASTER WM. A. HICKS : —

You will take charge of the prize bark, *Joseph Maxwell*, and
proceed, with her, to some port on the south side of the island of
Cuba, say St. Jago, Trinidad, or Cienfuegos. I think it would be
safest for you to go into Cienfuegos, as the enemy, from the very
fact of our having been there, recently, will scarcely be on the look
for us a second time. The steamers which were probably sent
thither from Havana in pursuit of the *Sumter* must, long since,
have departed, to hunt her in some other quarter.

Upon your arrival, you will inform the Governor, or Commandant of the Port, of the fact, state to him that your vessel is the
prize of a ship of war, and not of a privateer, and ask leave for
her to remain in port, in charge of a prize agent, until she can be
adjudicated by a prize court of the Confederate States. Should he
grant you this request, you will, if you go into Cienfuegos, put the
vessel in charge of *Don Mariano Dias*, our agent for the other
prizes; but should you go into either of the other ports, you will
appoint some reliable person to take charge of the prize, but
without power to sell, until further orders — taking from him a

bond, with sufficient sureties for the faithful performance of his duties.

Should the Governor decline to permit the prize to remain, you will store the cargo, with some responsible person, if permitted to land it, taking his receipt therefor, and then take the ship outside the port, beyond the marine league, and burn her. Should you need funds for the unlading and storage of the cargo, you are authorized to sell so much of it as may be necessary for this purpose. You will then make the best of your way to the Confederate States, and report yourself to the Secretary of the Navy. You will keep in close custody the accompanying sealed package of papers, being the papers of the captured vessel, and deliver it, in person, to the Judge of the Admiralty Court, in New Orleans. The paymaster will hand you the sum of ,one hundred dollars, and you are authorized to draw on the Secretary of the Navy for such further sum as you may need, to defray the expenses of yourself, and crew, to the Confederate States.

I had not yet seen the proclamation of neutrality by Spain, and the reader will perceive, from the above letter, that I still clung to the hope that that Power would dare to be just, even in the face of the truckling of England and France. The master of the *Maxwell* had his wife on board, and the sea being smooth, I made him a present of one of the best of his boats, and sent him and his wife on shore in her. He repaid my kindness by stealing the ship's chronometer, which he falsely told the midshipman in charge of the prize I had given him leave to take with him. At three P. M., taking a final leave of *Puerto Cabello*, there being neither waving of hats or handkerchiefs, or regrets on either side, we shaped our course to the eastward, and put our ship under a full head of steam.

CHAPTER XVI.

THERE was a fresh trade-wind blowing, and some sea on,
as the *Sumter* brought her head around to the eastward,
and commenced buffeting her way, again, to windward. She
had, in addition, a current to contend with, which sets along
this coast in the direction of the trade-wind, at the rate of
about a knot an hour. We were steaming at a distance of
seven or eight miles from the land, and, as the shades of evening closed in, we descried a Federal brigantine, running down
the coast—probably for the port we had just left—hugging
the bold shore very affectionately, to keep within the charmed
marine league, within which she knew she was safe from capture. We did not, of course, molest her, as I made it a point
always to respect the jurisdiction of neutrals, though never so
weak. I might have offended against the sovereignty of Venezuela, by capturing this vessel, with impunity, so far as Venezuela was herself concerned, but then I should have committed an offence against the laws of nations, and it was these
laws that I was, myself, looking to, for protection. Besides,
the Secretary of the Navy, in preparing my instructions, had
been particular to enjoin upon me, not only to respect the
rights of neutrals, but to conciliate their good will.

As we were running along the land, sufficiently near for its
influence to be felt upon the trade-winds, it became nearly calm
during the night, the land and sea breezes, each struggling for
the mastery, and thus neutralizing each other's forces. The

steamer sprang forward with renewed speed, and when the day dawned the next morning, we were far to windward of Laguayra. The sun rose in a sky, without a cloud, and the wind did not freshen, as the day advanced, so much as it had done the day before. The mountains of Venezuela lay sleeping in the distance, robed in a mantle of heavenly blue, numerous sea-birds were on the wing, and the sail of a fishing-boat, here and there, added picturesqueness to the scene. At half-past nine, we gave chase to a fore-and-aft schooner, which proved to be a Venezuela coaster.

In the afternoon, we passed sufficiently near the island of Tortuga, to run over some of its coral banks. The sun was declining behind the yet visible mountains, and the sea breeze had died away to nearly a calm, leaving the bright, and sparkling waters, with a mirrored surface. We now entered upon a scene of transcendent beauty, but the beauty was that of the deep, and not of the surface landscape. The reader is familiar with the history of the coral insect, that patient little stone-mason of the deep, which, though scarcely visible through the microscope, lays the foundations of islands, and of continents. The little coralline sometimes commences its work, hundreds of fathoms down in the deep sea, and working patiently, and laboriously, day and night, night and day, week after week, month after month, year after year, and century after century, finally brings its structure to the surface.

When its tiny blocks of lime-stone, which it has secreted from the salts of the sea, have been piled so high, that the tides now cover the structure, and now leave it dry, the little toiler of the sea, having performed the functions prescribed to it by its Creator, dies, and is entombed in a mausoleum more proud than any that could be reared by human hands. The winds, and the clouds now take charge of the new island, or continent, and begin to prepare it for vegetation, and the habitation of man, and animals. The Pacific Ocean, within the tropics is, *par excellence*, the coral sea, and the navigator of that ocean is familiar with the phenomenon, which I am about to describe. In the midst of a clear sky, the mariner sometimes discovers on the verge of the horizon, a light, fleecy cloud, and as he sails toward it, he is surprised to find that it scarcely alters its position. It rises a little, and a little higher, as he approaches it, pretty much as the land would appear to rise, if he were sailing toward it, but that is all. He sails on, and on, and when he has come near the cloud, he is surprised to see under it, a white line of foam, or, maybe a breaker, if there is any undulation in the sea, in a spot where all is represented as deep water on his chart. Examining with his telescope, he now discovers, in the intervals of the foam, caused by the rising and falling of the long, lazy swell, a coral bank, so white as scarcely to be distinguished from the seething and boiling foam. He has discovered the germ of a new island, which in the course of time, and the decrees of Providence, will be covered with forests, and inhabited by men, and animals.

The cloud, as a sort of "pillar by day," has conducted him to the spot, whilst it has, at the same time, warned him of his danger. But the cloud — how came it there, why does it remain so faithfully at its post, and what are its functions? One of the most beautiful of the phenomena of tropical countries is the alternation, with the regularity of clock-work, of the land and sea breezes; by day, the sea breeze blowing toward the land, and by night the land breeze blowing toward the sea. The reason of this is as follows. The land absorbs heat, and radiates it, more rapidly than the sea. The consequence is, that when the sun has risen, an hour or two, the land becomes warmer than the surrounding sea, and there is an in-draught toward it; in other words, the sea breeze begins to blow. When, on the contrary, the sun has set, and withdrawn his rays from both land and sea, and radiation begins, the land, parting with its absorbed heat, more rapidly than the sea, soon becomes cooler than the sea. As a consequence, there is an out-draught from the land; in other words, the land breeze has commenced to blow. The reader now sees how it is, that the "pillar by day" hangs over the little coral island; the bank of coral absorbing heat by day more rapidly than the surrounding sea, there is an in-draught setting toward it, and as the lazy trade-winds approach it, they themselves become heated, and ascend into the upper air. There is thus a constantly ascending column of heated atmosphere over these banks. This ascending column of atmosphere, when it reaches a certain point, is condensed into cumuli of beautiful, fleecy clouds, often piled up in the most fantastic and gorgeous shapes. It is thus that the cloud becomes stationary. It is ever forming, and ever passing off; retaining, it may be, its original form, but its nebulæ constantly changing.

When a cooler blast of trade-wind than usual comes along, the condensation is more rapid, and perfect, and showers of rain fall. The sea-birds are already hovering, in clouds, over the inchoate little island, fishing, and wading in its shallow waters, and roosting on it, when they can get a sufficient foothold. Vegetation soon ensues, and, in the course of a few more ages, nature completes her work.

But to return from this digression, into which we were led by a view of the coral bank over which we were passing. The little insect, which is at work under our feet, has not yet brought its structure sufficiently near the surface, to obstruct our passage over it. We are in five or six fathoms of water, but this water is so clear, that we are enabled to see the most minute object, quite distinctly. We have "slowed" the engine the better to enjoy the beautiful sub-marine landscape; and look! we are passing over a miniature forest, instinct with life. There are beautifully branching trees of madrepores, whose prongs are from one to two feet in length, and sometimes curiously interlaced. Each one of the branches, as well as the trunk, has a number of little notches in it. These are the cells in which the little stone-mason is at work. Adhering to the branches of these miniature trees, like mosses, and lichens, you see sundry formations that you might mistake for leaves. These are also cellular, and are the workshops of the little masons. Scattered around, among the trees, are waving the most gorgeous of fans, and, what we might call sea-ferns, and palms. These are of a variety of brilliant colors, purple predominating.

Lying on the smooth, white sand, are boulders of coral in a variety of shapes—some, like the domes of miniature cathedrals; some, perfectly spherical; some, cylindrical. These, and the trees, are mostly of a creamy white, though occasionally, pink, violet, and green are discovered. As the passage

of the steamer gives motion to the otherwise smooth sea, the
fans, ferns, and palms wave, gracefully, changing their tints
as the light flashes upon them, through the pellucid waters
The beholder looks entranced, as though he were gazing upon
a fairy scene, by moonlight; and to add to the illusion, there
is a movement of life, all new to the eye, in every direction.
The beautiful star-fish, with its five points, as equally, and
regularly arranged, as though it had been done by the rule of
the mathematician, with great worm-like molluscs, lie torpid
on the white sand. Jelly-fish, polypi, and other nondescript
shapes, float about in the miniature forest; and darting hither
and thither, among the many-tinted ferns, some apparently in
sport, and some in pursuit of their prey, are hundreds of little
fishes, sparkling, and gleaming in silver, and gold, and green,
and scarlet.

The most curious of these is the parrot-fish, whose head is
shaped like the beak of the parrot, and whose color is light
green. How wonderfully full is the sea of animal life! All
this picture is animal life; for what appears to be the vegetable
portion of this sub-marine landscape, is scarcely vegetable at
all. The waving ferns, fans, and palms are all instinct with
animal life. The patient little toiler of the sea, the coralline
insect, is busy with them, as he is with his limestone trees.
He is helping on their formation by his secretions, and it is
difficult to say what portion of them is vegetable, what, mineral, and what, animal.

I had been an hour, and more, entranced by the fairy sub-
marine forest, and its denizens, which I have so imperfectly
described, when the sun sank behind the Andes, and night
threw her mantle upon the waters, changing all the sparkling
colors of forest, and fish, to sombre gray, and admonishing me,
that it was time to return to every-day life, and the duties of
the ship. "Let her have the steam," said I to the officer of the
deck. as I arose from my bent posture over the ship's rail;
and, in a moment more, the propeller was thundering us along
at our usual speed.

At eleven P. M., we were up with the island of Margarita,
and as I designed to run the passage between it, and the main
land, I preferred daylight for the operation; and so, sounding

in thirty-two fathoms of water, I hove the ship to, under her trysails for the night, permitting her steam to go down.   The, next day, the weather still continued clear and pleasant, the trade-wind being sufficiently light not to impede our head-way, for we were steaming, as the reader will recollect, nearly head to wind.   We had experienced but little adverse current during the last twenty-four hours, and were making very satisfactory progress.   I was now making a passage, rather than cruising, as a sail is a rare sight, in the part of the ocean I was traversing.

At meridian we passed that singular group of islands called the Frayles—*Anglice*, friars—jutting up from the sea in cones of different shapes, and looking, at a distance, not unlike so many hooded monks.   With the exception of a transient fisherman, who now and then hauls up his boat out of the reach of the surf, on these harborless islands, and pitches his tent, made of his boat's sail, for a few days of rest and refresh-ment, they have no inhabitants.

July 30th.—"Thick, cloudy weather, with incessant, and. heavy rains; hauling in for the coast of Venezuela, near the entrance to the Gulf of Paria.   So thick is the weather, that to 'hold on to the land,' I am obliged to run the coast within a mile, and this is close running on a coast not minutely sur-veyed."   So said my journal.   Indeed the day in question was a memorable one, from its scenery, and surroundings.   Few landscapes present so bold, and imposing a picture as this part of the South American coast.   The Andes here rise abruptly out of the sea, to a great height.   Our little craft running along their base, in the bluest and deepest of water, looked like a mere cockle-shell, or nautilus.   Besides the torrents of rain, that were coming down upon our decks, and through which, at times, we could barely catch a glimpse of the majestic, and sombre-looking mountains, we were blinded by the most vivid flashes of lightning, simultaneously with which, the roll-ing and crashing of the thunder deafened our ears.   I had stood on the banks of the Lake of Geneva, and witnessed a storm in the Alps, during which Byron's celebrated lines occurred to me.   They occurred to me more forcibly here, for literally —

"Far along
From peak to peak, the rattling crags among,
Leaps the live thunder! Not from one cloud,
But every mountain now had found a tongue,
And Jura answers, through her misty shroud,
Back to the joyous Alps, who call to her aloud!"

That word "joyous" was well chosen by the poet, for the mountains did indeed seem to rejoice in this grand display of nature. Of wind there was scarcely any — what little there was, was frequently off the land, and even blew in the direction opposite to that of the trade-wind. We were in the rainy season, along this coast, and all the vegetable kingdom was in full luxuriance. The cocoanut, and other palms, giving an Eastern aspect to the scenery, waved the greenest of feathery branches, and every shrub, and almost every tree rejoiced in its flower. It was delightful to inhale the fragrance, as the whirling aërial current brought us an occasional puff from the land.

On board the ship, we looked like so many half-drowned rats. The officer of the deck, trumpet in hand, was ensconced, to his ears, in his india-rubber pea jacket, his long beard looking like a wet mop, and little rills of rain trickling down his neck, and shoulders, from his slouched "Sou'wester." The midshipman of the watch had taken off his shoes, and rolled up his trousers, and was paddling about in the pools on deck, as well pleased as a young duck. And as for the old salt, he was in his element. There was plenty of fresh water to wash his clothes in, and accordingly the decks were filled with industrious washers, or rather scrubbers, each with his scrubbing-brush, and bit of soap, and a little pile of soiled duck frocks and trousers by his side.

The reader has been informed, that we were running along the coast, within a mile of it, to enable us to keep sight of the land. The object of this was to make the proper landfall for running into the Gulf of Paria, on which is situated the Port of Spain, in the island of Trinidad, to which we were bound. We opened the gulf as early as nine A. M., and soon afterward identified the three islands that form the *Bocas del Drago*, or dragon's mouth. The scenery is remarkably bold and striking at the entrance of this gulf or bay. The islands rise to the height of mountains, in abrupt and sheer precipices, out of the now muddy waters — for the great Orinoco, traversing its thousands of miles of alluvial soil, disembogues near by. Indeed, we may be said to have been already within the delta of that great stream.

Memory was busy with me, as the *Sumter* passed through the Dragon's Mouth. I had made my first cruise to this iden-tical island of Trinidad, when a green midshipman in the Federal Navy. A few years before, the elder Commodore Perry — he of Lake Erie memory — had died of yellow fever, when on a visit, in one of the small schooners of his squadron, up the Orinoco. The old sloop-of-war *Lexington*, under the command of Commander, now Rear-Admiral Shubrick, was sent to the Port of Spain to bring home his remains. I was one of the midshipmen of that ship. A generation had since elapsed. An infant people had, in that short space of time, grown old and decrepid, and its government had broken in twain. But there stood the everlasting mountains, as I remem-bered them, unchanged! I could not help again recurring to the poet: —

> " Man has another day to swell the past,
>   And lead him near to little but his last;
>   But mighty Nature bounds as from her birth.
>   The sun is in the heavens, and life on earth;
>   Flowers in the valley, splendor in the beam,
>   Health on the gale, and freshness in the stream.
>   Immortal man! behold her glories shine,
>   And cry, exulting inly, 'they are thine!'
>   Gaze on, while yet thy gladdened eye may see;
>   A morrow comes when they are not for thee:
>   And grieve what may above thy senseless bier,
>   Nor earth, nor sky shall yield a single tear;
>   Nor cloud shall gather more, nor leaf shall fall,
>   Nor gale breathe forth one sigh for thee, for all;
>   But creeping things shall revel in their spoil,
>   And fit thy clay to fertilize the soil."

We entered through the Huevo passage — named from its egg-shaped island — and striking soundings, pretty soon after-ward, ran up by our chart and lead-line, there being no pilot-boat in sight. We anchored off the Port of Spain a little after

mid-day — an English merchant brig paying us the compliment of a salute.

I dispatched a lieutenant to call on the Governor. The
orders of neutrality of the English government had already
been received, and his Excellency informed me that, in accordance therewith, he would extend to me the same hospitality
that he would show, in similar circumstances, to the enemy;
which was nothing more, of course, than I had a right to expect. The Paymaster was dispatched to the shore, to see about
getting a supply of coal, and send off some fresh provisions
and fruit for the crew; and such of the officers as desired went
on liberty.

The first thing to be thought of was the discharge of our
prisoners, for, with the exception of the Captain, whom I had
permitted to land in *Puerto Cabello*, with his wife, I had the
crew of the *Joseph Maxwell*, prize-ship, still on board. I had
given these men, eight in number, to understand that they
were hostages, and that their discharge, their close confinement, or their execution, as the case might be, depended upon
the action of their own Government, in the case of the *Savannah* prisoners. The reader will probably recollect the case to
which I allude. President Lincoln, of the Federal States, in
issuing his proclamation of the 15th of April, 1861, calling
out 75,000 troops to revenge the disaster of Fort Sumter,
inserted the following paragraph: —

" And I hereby proclaim, and declare, that, if any person, under
the pretended authority of said States, or under any other pretence,
shall molest a vessel of the United States, or the persons, or cargo
on board of her, such persons will be held amenable to the laws of
the United States, for the prevention, and punishment of piracy."

On the 6th of May following, the Congress of the Confederate States, passed the following act, in reply, as it were, to this
manifesto of Mr. Lincoln: —

"*Whereas*, The earnest efforts made by this Government, to establish friendly relations between the Government of the United States,
and the Confederate States, and to settle all questions of disagree-
ment between the two Governments, upon principles of right, equity,
justice, and good faith, have proved unavailing, by reason of the
refusal of the Government of the United States to hold any inter-

course with the Commissioners appointed by this Government, for the purposes aforesaid, or to listen to any proposal they had to make, for the peaceful solution of all causes of difficulty between the two Governments; and *whereas*, the President of the United States of America has issued his proclamation, making requisition upon the States of the American Union, for 75,000 men, for the purpose, as therein indicated, of capturing forts, and other strong-holds within the jurisdiction of, and belonging to the Confederate States of America, and raised, organized, and equipped a large military force, to execute the purpose aforesaid, and has issued his other proclamation, announcing his purpose to set on foot a block-ade of the ports of the Confederate States; and *whereas*, the State of Virginia has seceded from the Federal Union, and entered into a convention of alliance, offensive and defensive, with the Confederate States, and has adopted the Provisional Constitution of said States, and the States of Maryland, North Carolina, Tennessee, Kentucky, Arkansas and Missouri have refused, and it is believed, that the State of Delaware, and the inhabitants of the Territories of Arizona, and New Mexico, and the Indian Territory, south of Kansas will refuse to co-operate with the Government of the United States, in these acts of hostility, and wanton aggression, which are plainly intended to overawe, oppress, and finally subjugate the people of the Con-federate States; and *whereas*, by the acts, and means aforesaid, war exists between the Confederate States, and the Government of the United States, and the States and Territories thereof, excepting the States of Maryland, North Carolina, Tennessee, Kentucky, Arkan-sas, Missouri, and Delaware, and the Territories of Arizona, and New Mexico, and the Indian Territory south of Kansas: THEREFORE,

"SEC. 1. *The Congress of the Confederate States of America do enact,* That the President of the Confederate States is hereby au-thorized to use the whole land, and naval force of the Confederate States, to meet the war thus commenced, and to issue to private armed vessels, commissions, or letters-of-marque, and general repri-sal, in such form, as he shall think proper, under the seal of the Con-federate States, against the vessels, goods, and effects of the Govern-ment of the United States, and of the citizens, or inhabitants of the States, and Territories thereof, except the States and Territories hereinbefore named. *Provided,* however, that the property of the enemy, (unless it be contraband of war,) laden on board a neutral vessel, shall not be subject to seizure, under this Act; and *pro-vided further,* that the vessels of the citizens, or inhabitants of the United States, now in the ports of the Confederate States, except such as have been since the 15th of April last, or may hereafter be, in the service of the Government of the United States, shall be allowed thirty days, after the publication of this Act, to leave said ports, and reach their destination; and such vessels, and their car-goes, excepting articles contraband of war, shall not be subject to capture, under this Act, during said period, unless they shall pre-viously have reached the destination for which they were bound, on leaving said ports."

Among the private armed vessels which took out commissions under this Act, was the schooner *Savannah*, formerly a
pilot-boat out of Charleston. She carried one small gun, and
about twenty men. During the month of June, this adventurous little cruiser was captured by the U. S. brig *Bainbridge*,
and her crew were hurried off to New York, confined in cells,
like convicted felons, and afterward brought to trial, and *convicted of piracy*, under Mr. Lincoln's proclamation. I had informed myself of these proceedings from newspapers captured
on board the enemy's ships, and hence the announcement I had
made to the prisoners of the *Joseph Maxwell*. The reader may
imagine the delight of those men, and my own satisfaction, as
well, when my lieutenant brought back with him, from the
shore, after his visit to the Governor, an American newspaper,
of late date, stating that the *Savannah* prisoners had been
released from close confinement, and were to be treated as
prisoners of war. I was stretching a point, in undertaking
retaliation of this serious character without instructions from
my Government, but the case was pressing, and we of the *Sumter* were *vitally* interested in the issue. The commission of the
Savannah, though she was only a privateer, was as lawful as
our own, and, judging by the abuse that had already been
heaped upon us, by the Northern newspapers, we had no reason
to expect any better treatment, at the hands of well-paid New
York District-Attorneys, and well-packed New York juries.

I was gratified to learn, as I did soon afterward, that my
Government had taken a proper stand on this question. President Davis, as soon as he heard of the treatment to which the
Savannah prisoners had been subjected, wrote a letter of remonstrance to President Lincoln, threatening retaliation, if he dared
execute his threat of treating them as pirates. In that letter
so worthy of the Christian statesman, and so opposite to the
coarse fulminations of the enemy, Mr. Davis used the following expressions: "It is the desire of this Government so to
conduct the war, now existing, as to mitigate its horrors, as far
as may be possible; and with this intent, its treatment of the
prisoners captured by its forces has been marked, by the greatest humanity, and leniency, consistent with public obligation.
Some have been permitted to return home, on *parole*, others to

remain at large, under similar conditions, within the Confederacy, and all have been furnished with rations for their subsistence, such as are allowed to our own troops. It is only since the news has been received, of the treatment of the prisoners taken on the *Savannah*, that I have been compelled to withdraw those indulgences, and to hold the prisoners taken by us, in strict confinement. A just regard to humanity, and to the honor of this Government, now requires me to state, explicitly, that, painful as will be the necessity, this Government will deal out to the prisoners held by it, the same treatment, and the same fate, as shall be experienced by those captured on the *Savannah;* and if driven to the terrible necessity of retaliation, by your execution of any of the officers, or crew of the *Savannah*, that retaliation will be extended so far, as shall be requisite to secure the abandonment of a practice, unknown to the warfare of civilized men, and so barbarous, as to disgrace the nation which shall be guilty of inaugurating it."

Shortly before the conviction of the *Savannah* prisoners, a seaman named Smith, captured on board the privateer *Jefferson Davis*, was tried, and convicted of piracy, in Philadelphia. There were fourteen of these men, in all, and the following order from Mr. Benjamin, the Acting Secretary of War of the Confederate States, to General Winder, in charge of Federal prisoners, in Richmond, will show how much in earnest President Davis was, when he wrote the above letter to President Lincoln:—

"SIR: — You are hereby instructed to choose, by lot, from among the prisoners of war, of highest rank, one who is to be confined in a cell appropriated to convicted felons, and who is to be treated, in all respects, as if such convict, and to be held for execution, in the same manner as may be adopted by the enemy for the execution of the prisoner of war, Smith, recently condemned to death in Philadelphia.

"You will, also, select thirteen other prisoners of war, the highest in rank of those captured by our forces, to be confined in cells, reserved for prisoners accused of infamous crimes, and will treat them as such, so long as the enemy shall continue so to treat the like number of prisoners of war, captured by them at sea, and now held for trial in New York as pirates.

"As these measures are intended to repress the infamous attempt now made by the enemy, to commit judicial murder on prisoners of war, you will execute them, strictly, as the mode best calculated to prevent the commission of so heinous a crime."

The list of hostages, as returned by General Winder, was as follows: Colonels Corcoran, Lee, Cogswell, Wilcox, Woodruff, and Wood; Lieutenant-Colonels Bowman, and Neff; Majors Potter, Revere, and Vogdes, and Captains Ricketts, McQuade, and Rockwood. These measures had the desired effect; the necessity, that the Federal Government was under of conciliating the Irish interest, contributing powerfully thereto — Colonel Corcoran, the first hostage named, being an Irishman of some note and influence, in New York. President Lincoln was accordingly obliged to take back his proclamation, and the Savannah prisoners, and Smith, were put on the footing of prisoners of war. But this recantation of an attempted barbarism had not been honestly made. It was not the generous taking back of a wrong principle, by a high-minded people. The tiger, which had come out of his jungle, in quest of blood, had only been driven back by fear; his feline, and bloodthirsty disposition would, of course, crop out again, as soon as he ceased to dread the huntsman's rifle. Whilst we were strong, but little more was heard of "pirates," and "piracy," except through Mr. Seward's long-winded and frantic despatches to the British Government, on the subject of the *Alabama,* but when we became weak, the slogan was taken up again, and rung, in all its changes, by an infuriated people.

To return now to the *Sumter.* Our decks were crowded with visitors, on the afternoon of our arrival; some of these coming off to shake us warmly by the hand, out of genuine sympathy, whilst others had no higher motive than that of mere curiosity. The officers of the garrison were very civil to us, but we were amused at their diplomatic precaution, in coming to visit us in *citizens' dress.* There are no people in the world, perhaps, who attach so much importance to matters of mere form and ceremony, bluff and hearty as John Bull is, as the English people. Lord Russell had dubbed us a "so-called" government, and this expression had become a law to all his subordinates; no official visits could be exchanged, no salutes reciprocated, and none other of the thousand and one courtesies of red-tapedom observed toward us; and, strange to say, whilst all this nonsense of form was being practised, the substance of nationality, that is to say, the acknowledgment that we possessed belligerent rights, had been frankly and freely accorded to us. It was like saying to a man, "I should like, above all things, to have you come and dine with me, but as you hav n't got the right sort of a dining-dress, you can't come, you know!" Some ridiculous consequences resulted from this etiquette of nations. Important matters of business frequently remained unattended to, because the parties could not address each other officially. An *informal* note would take the place of an official despatch.

The advent of the *Sumter* invariably caused more, or less commotion, in official circles; the small colonial officials fearing lest she might complicate them with their governments. There was now another important council to be held. The opinion of the "law-officers of the crown" was to be taken by his Excellency, upon the question, whether the *Sumter* was entitled to be coaled in her Majesty's dominions. The paymaster had found a lot of indifferent coal, on shore, which could be purchased at about double its value, but nothing could be done until the "council" moved; and it is proverbial that large bodies like provincial councils, move slowly. The Attorney-General of the Colony, and other big wigs got together, however, after due ceremony, and, thanks to the fact, that the steamer is an infernal machine of modern invention, they were not very long in coming to a decision. If there had been anything about a steamer, in Coke upon Littleton, Bacon, or Bracton, or any other of those old fellows who deal in black letter, I am afraid the *Sumter* would have been blockaded by the enemy, before she could have gotten to sea. The *pros* and *cons* being discussed — I had too much respect for the calibre of certain guns on shore, to throw any shells across the windows of the council-chamber — it was decided that coal was not contraband of war, and that the *Sumter* might purchase the necessary article in the market.

But though she might purchase it, it was not so easy to get it on board. It was hard to move the good people on shore. The climate was relaxing, the rainy season had set in, and there was only negro labor to be had, about the wharves and quays. We were four tedious days in filling our coal-bunkers. It had rained, off and on, the whole time. I did not visit the

shore, but I amused myself frequently by inspecting the magnificent scenery by which I was surrounded, through an excellent telescope. The vegetation of Trinidad is varied, and luxuriant beyond description. As the clouds would break away, and
the sun light up the wilderness of waving palms, and other tropical trees and plants of strange and rich foliage, amid which
the little town lay embowered, the imagination was enchanted
with the picture.

The emancipation of the slave ruined this, as it did the other
West India islands. As a predial laborer, the freedman was
nearly worthless, and the sugar crop, which is the staple, went
down to zero. In despair, the planters resorted to the introduction of the coolie; large numbers of them have been
imported, and under their skilful and industrious cultivation,
the island is regaining a share of its lost prosperity.

A day or two after my arrival, I had a visit from the master of a Baltimore brig, lying in the port. He was ready for
sea, he said, and had come on board, to learn whether I would
capture him. I told him to make himself easy, that I should
not molest him, and referred him to the act of the Confederate
Congress, declaring that a' state of war existed, to show him
that, as yet, we regarded Maryland as a friend. He went
away rejoicing, and sailed the next day.

We had, as usual, some little refitting of the ship to do.
Off *Puerto Cabello*, we had carried away our main yard, by
coming in contact with the *Abby Bradford*, and the first lieutenant having ordered another on our arrival, it was now towed
off, and gotten on board, fitted, and sent aloft.

Sunday, August 4th. — Morning calm and clear. The chimes
of the church-bells fall pleasantly and suggestively on the ear.
An American schooner came in from some point, up the bay,
and anchored well in shore, some distance from us, as though
distrustful of our good faith, and of our respect for British neutrality. Being all ready for sea, at half-past ten A. M., I gave
the order to get up steam; but the paymaster reporting to me
that his vouchers were not all complete, the order was countermanded, and we remained another day.

Her Majesty's steam-frigate *Cadmus* having come in, from
one of the neighboring islands, I sent a lieutenant on board to

call on her captain. This was the first foreign ship of war to which I had extended the courtesy of a visit, and, in a few hours afterward, my visit was returned. I had, from this time onward, much agreeable intercourse with the naval officers of the several nations, with whom I came in contact. I found them much more independent, than the civil, and military officers. They did not seem to care a straw, about *de factos*, or *de jures*, and had a sailor's contempt for red tape and unmeaning forms. They invariably received my officers, and myself, when we visited their ships, with the honors of the side, appropriate to our rank, without stopping to ask, in the jargon of Lord Russell, whether we were "So-Called," or Simon Pure. After the usual courtesies had passed between the lieutenant of the *Cadmus* and myself, I invited him into my cabin, when, upon being seated, he said his captain had desired him to say to me, that, as the *Sumter* was the first ship of the Confederate States he had fallen in with, he would take it, as a favor, if I would show him my commission. I replied, " Certainly, but there is a little ceremony to be complied with, on your part, first." " What is that? " said he. " How do I know," I rejoined, " that you have any *authority* to demand a sight of my commission —the flag at your peak may be a cheat, and you may be no better than you take me for, a ship of war of some hitherto unknown government—you must show me *your* commission first." This was said, pleasantly, on my part, for the idea was quite ludicrous, that a large, and stately steam-frigate, bearing the proud cross of St. George, could be such as I had hypothetically described her. But I was right as to the point I had made, to wit, that one ship of war has no right to demand a sight of the commission of another, without first showing her own. Indeed, this principle is so well known among naval men, that the lieutenant had come prepared for my demand, having brought his commission with him. Smiling, himself, now, in return, he said: "Certainly, your request is but reasonable ; here is her Majesty's commission," unrolling, at the same time, a large square parchment, beautifully engraved with nautical devices, and with sundry seals, pendent therefrom. In return, I handed him a small piece of coarse, and rather dingy Confederate paper, at the bottom of which was inscribed

the name of Jefferson Davis. He read the commission carefully, and when he had done, remarked, as he handed it back
to me, "Mr. Davis's is a smooth, bold signature." I replied
"You are an observer of signatures, and you have hit it exactly, in the present instance. I could not describe his character to you more correctly, if I were to try—our President
has all the smoothness, and polish of the ripe scholar and
refined gentleman, with the boldness of a man, who dares
strike for the right, against odds."

Monday, August 5th.—Weather clear, and fine. Flocks of
parrots are flying overhead, and all nature is rejoicing in the
sunshine, after the long, drenching rains. Far as the eye can
reach, there is but one sea of verdure, giving evidence, at once,
of the fruitfulness of the soil, and the ardor of the sun. At
eleven A. M., Captain Hillyar, of the *Cadmus*, came on board,
to visit me, and we had a long and pleasant conversation on
American affairs. He considerately brought me a New York
newspaper, of as late a date, as the 12th of July. "I must
confess," said he, as he handed me this paper, "that your
American war puzzles me—it cannot possibly last long."
"You are probably mistaken, as to its duration," I replied; "I
fear it will be long and bloody. As to its being a puzzle, it
should puzzle every honest man. If our late co-partners had
practised toward us the most common rules of honesty, we
should not have quarrelled with them; but we are only defending ourselves against robbers, with knives at our throats."
"You surprise me," rejoined the Captain; "how is that?"
"Simply, that the machinery of the Federal Government,
under which we have lived, and which was designed for the
common benefit, has been made the means of despoiling the
South, to enrich the North;" and I explained to him the
workings of the iniquitous tariffs, under the operation of
which the South had, in effect, been reduced to a dependent
colonial condition, almost as abject, as that of the Roman
provinces, under their proconsuls; the only difference being,
that smooth-faced hypocrisy had been added to robbery, inasmuch as we had been plundered under the forms of law.

"All this is new to me, I assure you," replied the Captain;
"I thought that your war had arisen out of the slavery ques-

tion." "That is a common mistake of foreigners. The enemy has taken pains to impress foreign nations with this false view of the case. With the exception of a few honest zealots, the canting, hypocritical Yankee cares as little for our slaves, as he does for our draught animals. The war which he has been making upon slavery, for the last forty years, is only an interlude, or by-play, to help on the main action of the drama, which is Empire; and it is a curious coincidence, that it was commenced about the time the North began to rob the South, by means of its tariffs. When a burglar designs to enter a dwelling, for the purpose of robbery, he provides himself with the necessary implements. The slavery question was one of the implements employed, to help on the robbery of the South. It strengthened the Northern party, and enabled them to get their tariffs through Congress; and when, at length, the South, driven to the wall, turned, as even the crushed worm will turn, it was cunningly perceived by the Northern men, that 'No Slavery' would be a popular war-cry, and hence they used it. It is true, we are defending our slave property, but we are defending it no more than any other species of our property — it is all endangered, under a general system of robbery. We are, in fact, fighting for independence. Our forefathers made a great mistake, when they warmed the Puritan serpent in their bosom; and we, their descendants, are endeavoring to remedy it."

The Captain now rose to depart. I accompanied him on deck, and when he had shoved off, I ordered the ship to be gotten under way — the fires having been started some time before, the steam was already up. The *Sumter*, as she moved out of the harbor of the Port of Spain, looked more like a comfortable passenger steamer, bound on a voyage, than a ship of war, her stern nettings, and stern and quarter boats being filled with oranges, and bananas, and all the other luscious fruits that are produced so abundantly in this rich tropical island. Other luxuries were added, for Jack had brought, on board, one or two more sad-looking old monkeys, and a score more of squalling parrots.

CHAPTER XVII.

ON THE WAY TO MARANHAM — THE WEATHER AND THE
WINDS — THE SUMTER RUNS SHORT OF COAL, AND IS
OBLIGED TO "BEAR UP" — CAYENNE AND PARAMARIBO,
IN FRENCH AND DUTCH GUIANA — SAILS AGAIN, AND
ARRIVES IN MARANHAM, BRAZIL.

WE passed out of the Gulf of Paria, through the eastern,
or Mona passage, a deep strait, not more than a third of
a mile in width, with the land rising, on both sides, to a great
height, almost perpendicularly. The water of the Orinoco
here begins to mix with the sea-water, and the two waters, as
they come into unwilling contact, carry on a perpetual struggle, whirling about in small circles, and writhing and twisting
like a serpent in pain.

We met the first heave of the sea at about two o'clock in
the afternoon, and turning our head again to the eastward, we
continued to run along the mountainous and picturesque coast
of Trinidad, until an hour or two after nightfall. The coast
is quite precipitous, but, steep as it is, a number of negro
cabins had climbed the hill-sides, and now revealed their presence to us by the twinkle of their lights, as the shades of evening fell over the scene. These cabins were quite invisible,
by daylight, so dense was the foliage of the trees amid which
they nestled. This must, indeed, be the very paradise of the
negro. The climate is so genial, that he requires little or no
clothing, and bountiful Nature supplies him with food, all the
year round, almost unasked. In this land of the sun, a constant succession of fruits is pendent from the trees, and the
dwellers in the huts beneath their sheltering arms, have only
to reach out their hands when hunger presses. I was reminded,
by this scene, of a visit I had once made to the island of St.
Domingo, and of the indolence in which the negro lives in

that soft and voluptuous climate. I landed at the bay of Samana, from the ship of war to which I was attached, and taking a stroll, one evening, I came upon the hut of an American negress. Some years before, Boyer, the President of the island, had invited the immigration of free negroes, from the United States. A colony from the city of Baltimore had accepted his invitation, and settled at Samana. In the course of a very few years, all the men of the colony had run off, and found their way back, in various capacities, on board of trading vessels, to the land of their birth; leaving their wives and daughters behind to shift for themselves. The negro woman, whose hut I had stumbled upon, was one of these grass widows. She had become quite old, but was living without apparent effort. The cocoanut waved its feathery branches over her humble domicil, and the juicy mango and fragrant banana hung within tempting reach. A little plot of ground had been picketed in with crooked sticks, and in this primitive garden were growing some squashes and watermelons, barely visible under the rank weeds. I said to her, " My good woman, you don't seem to have much use for the plough or the hoe in your garden." "La! master," said she, "no need of much work in this country — we have only to put in the seed, and the Lord, *he* gives the increase."

In time, no doubt, all the West India islands will lapse into just such luxuriant wildernesses, as we were now coasting along, in the *Sumter*. Amalgamation, by slow, but sure processes, will corrupt what little of European blood remains in them, until every trace of the white man shall disappear. The first process will be the mulatto; but the mulatto, as the name imports, is a mule, and must finally die out; and the mass of the population will become pure African. This is the fate which England has prepared, for some of her own blood, in her colonies. I will not stop here to moralize on it. If we are beaten in this war, what will be our fate in the Southern States? Shall we, too, become mongrelized, and disappear from the face of the earth? Can this be the ultimate design of the Yankee? The night was quite light, and taking a fresh departure, at about ten P. M., from the east end of Trinidad, we passed through the strait between it and the island

of Tobago, and soon afterward emerged from the Caribbean
Sea, upon the broad bosom of the South Atlantic. Judging
by the tide rips, that were quite visible in the moonlight,
there must have been considerable current setting through
this strait, to the westward. The next day the weather was
still fine, and the wind light from about E. N. E., and
the *Sumter* made good speed through the smooth sea. At
about ten A. M. a sail was descried, some twelve or fourteen
miles distant. She was away off on our port beam, running before the trade-wind, and I forbore to chase. As before remarked, I was not now cruising, but anxious to make
a passage, and could not afford the fuel to chase, away from
the track I was pursuing, the few straggling sail I might
discover in this lonely sea. Once in the track of commerce,
where the sails would come fast and thick, I could make
up for lost time. At noon, we observed in latitude 9° 14′;
the longitude, by chronometer, being 59° 10′.

Wednesday, August 7th. — Weather clear, and delightful, and
the sea smooth. Nothing but the broad expanse of the ocean
visible, except, indeed, numerous flocks of flying-fish, which
we are flushing, now and then like so many flocks of par-
tridges, as we disturb the still waters. These little creatures
have about the flight of the partridge, and it is a pretty sight
to see them skim away over the billows with their transparent
finny wings glistening in the sun, until they drop again into
their "cover," as suddenly as they rose. Our crew having been
somewhat broken in upon, by the sending away of so many
prize crews, the first lieutenant is re-arranging his watch and
quarter-bills, and the men are being exercised at the guns, to
accustom them to the changes which have become necessary, in
their stations. Officers and men are enjoying, alike, the fine
weather. With the fore-castle, and quarter-deck awnings
spread, we do not feel the heat, though the sun is nearly perpendicular at noon. Jack is "overhauling" his clothes'-bag, and
busy with his needle and thread, stopping, now and then, to
have a "lark" with his monkey, or to listen to the prattle of
his parrot. The boys of the ship are taking lessons, in knot-
ting, and splicing, and listening to the "yarn" of some old salt,
as he indoctrinates them in these mysteries. The midshipmen

have their books of navigation spread out before them, and slate in hand, are discussing sine and tangent, base, and hypothenuse. The only place in which a lounger is not seen is the quarter-deck. This precinct is always sacred to duty, and etiquette. No one ever presumes to seat himself upon it, not even the Commander. Here the officer of the deck is pacing, to and fro, swinging his trumpet idly about, for the want of something to do. But hold a moment! he has at last found a job. It is seven bells (half-past eleven) and the ship's cook has come to the mast, to report dinner. The cook is a darkey, and see how he grins, as the officer of the deck, having tasted of the fat pork, in his tin pan, and mashed some of his beans, with a spoon, to see if they are done, tells him, "that will do." The Commander now comes on deck, with his sextant, having been informed that it is time to "look out for the sun." See, he gathers the midshipmen around him, each also with his instrument, and, from time to time, asks them what "altitude they have on," and compares the altitude which they give him with his own, to see if they are making satisfactory progress as observers. The latitude being obtained, and reported to the officer of the deck, that officer now comes up to the Commander, and touching his hat, reports twelve o'clock, as though the Commander did n't know it already. The Commander says to him, sententiously, "make it so," as though the sun could not make it so, without the Commander's leave. See, now what a stir there is about the hitherto silent decks. Since we last cast a glance at them, Jack has put up his clothes'-bag, and the sweepers have "swept down," fore and aft, and the boatswain having piped to dinner, the cooks of the different messes are spreading their "mess-cloths" on the deck, and arranging their viands. The drum has rolled, "to grog," and the master's mate of the spirit-room, muster-book in hand, is calling over the names of the crew, each man as his name is called, waddling up to the tub, and taking the "tot" that is handed to him, by the "Jack-of-the-dust," who is the master-mate's assistant. Dinner now proceeds with somewhat noisy jest and joke, and the hands are not "turned to," that is, set to work again, until one o'clock.

We have averaged, in the last twenty-four hours, eight knots

and a half, and have not, as yet, experienced any adverse current, though we are daily on the lookout for this enemy; latitude 8° 31'; longitude 56° 12'. In the course of the afternoon,
a brigantine passing near us, we hove her to, with a blank cartridge, when she showed us the Dutch colors. She was from
Dutch Surinam, bound for Europe. Toward nightfall, it became quite calm, and naught was heard but the thumping of
the ship's propeller, as she urged her ceaseless way through
the vast expanse of waters.

August 8th. — Weather still beautifully clear, with an occasional rain squall enclosing us as in a gauze veil, and shutting
out from view for a few minutes, at a time, the distant horizon. The wind is light, and variable, but always from the
Eastern board; following the sun as the chariot follows the
steed. We are making good speed through the water, but
we have at length encountered our dreaded enemy, the great
equatorial current, which sets, with such regularity, along
this coast. Its set is about W. N. W., and its drift about
one knot per hour. Nothing has been seen to-day. The
water has changed its deep blue color, to green, indicating
that we are on soundings. We are about ninety miles from
the coast of Guiana. The sun went down behind banks, or
rather cumuli of pink and lilac clouds. We are fast sinking
the north polar star, and new constellations arise, nightly,
above the southern horizon. Amid other starry wonders, we
had a fine view this evening, of the southern cross; latitude
7° 19'; longitude 53° 04'.

The next day was cloudy, and the direction of the current
was somewhat changed, for its set was now N. W., half N.
This current is proving a serious drawback, and I begin to
fear, that I shall not be able to make the run to Maranham, as
I had hoped. Not only are the elements adverse, but my engineer tells me, that we were badly cheated, in our coal measure,
at Trinidad, the sharp coal-dealer having failed to put on
board of us as many tons as he had been paid for; for which
the said engineer got a rowing. We observed, to-day, in latitude 6° 01' and longitude 50° 48'.

August 10th. — Weather clear, with a deep blue sea, and a
fresh breeze, from the south-east. The south-east trade-winds

have thus crossed the equator, and reached us in latitude 5° north, which is our latitude to-day. I was apprehensive of this, for we are in the middle of August, and in this month these winds frequently drive back the north-east trades, and usurp their place, to a considerable extent, until the sun crosses back into the southern hemisphere. We thus have both wind, and current ahead; the current alone has retarded us fifty miles, or a fraction over two knots an hour; which is about equal to the drift of the Gulf Stream off Cape Hatteras.

Things were beginning now to look decidedly serious. I had but three days of fuel on board, and, upon consulting my chart, I found that I was still 550 miles from my port, current taken into account. It was not possible for the dull little *Sumter* to make this distance, in the given time, if the wind, and current should continue of the same strength. I resolved to try her, however, another night, hoping that some change for the better might take place. My journal tells the tale of that night as follows: —

August 11*th.*—"The morning has dawned with a fresh breeze, and rather rough sea, into which we have been plunging all night, making but little headway. The genius of the east wind refuses to permit even steam to invade his domain, and 'drives us back, with disdain. His ally, the current, has retarded us sixty miles in the last twenty-four hours!" I now no longer hesitated, but directing the engineer to let his fires go down, turned my ship's head, to the westward, and made sail; it being my intention to run down the coast to Cayenne in French Guiana, with the hope of obtaining a fresh supply of fuel at that place. We soon had the studding sails on the ship, and were rolling along to the northward and westward, with more grace than speed, our rate of sailing being only four knots. The afternoon proved to be remarkably fine, and we should have enjoyed this *far niente* change, but for our disappointment. Our chief regret was that we were losing so much valuable time, in the midst of the stirring events of the war.

Hauling in for the coast, in the vicinity of Cape Orange, we struck soundings about nightfall. The sea now became quite smooth, and the wind fell very light during the night—the current, however, is hurrying us on, though its set is not exactly in the right direction. Its tendency is to drive us too far from the coast. The next day, it became perfectly calm, and so continued all day. We were in twenty-three fathoms of water, and could see by the lead line that we were drifting over the bottom at the rate of about two knots an hour. We got out our fishing-lines, and caught some deep sea-fish, of the grouper species. The sea was alive with the nautilus, and the curious sea-nettle, with its warps and hawsers thrown out, and its semi-transparent, gelatinous disc contracting and expanding, as the little animal extracted its food from the water. Schools of fish, large and small, were playing about in every direction, and flocks of sea-gulls, and other marine birds of prey, were hovering over them, and making occasional forays in their midst. During the day, a sail was descried, far in shore, but we were unable to make it out; indeed sails were of the least importance to us now, as we were unable to chase. Just before sunset, we had a fine view of the Silver Mountains, some forty or fifty miles distant, in the south-west.

August 15th. — During the past night, we made the "Great Constable," a small island, off the coast, and one of the landmarks for Cayenne. The night was fine, and moonlit, and we ran in, and anchored about midnight, in fourteen fathoms of water. At daylight, the next morning, after waiting for the passage of a rain-squall, we got under way, and proceeding along the coast, came up with the Remize Islands, in the course of the afternoon, where we found a French pilot-lugger lying to, waiting for us. We were off Cayenne, and the lugger had come out to show us the way into the anchorage. A pilot jumping on board, we ran in, and anchored to the north-west of the "Child" — a small island — in three and a quarter fathoms of water. I could scarcely realize, that this was the famous penal settlement of Cayenne, painted in French history, as the very abode of death, and fraught with all other human horrors, so beautiful, and picturesque did it appear. The outlying islands are high, rising, generally, in a conical form, and are densely wooded, to their very summits. Sweet little nooks and coves, overhung by the waving foliage of strange-looking tropical trees, indent their shores, and invite the fisherman, or pleasure-seeker to explore their recesses. The main land is equally rich in vegetation, and though the sea-coast is low, distant ranges of mountains, inland, break in, agreeably, upon the monotony. A perennial summer prevails, and storms, and hurricanes are unknown. It was here that some of the most desperate and bloodthirsty of the French revolutionists of 1790, were banished. Many of them died of yellow fever; others escaped, and wandered off to find inhospitable graves, in other countries; few of them ever returned to France. Shortly after we came to anchor, the batteries of the town, and some small French steamers of war, that lay in the harbor, fired salutes in honor of the birthday of Louis Napoleon—this being the 15th of August.

The next morning, at daylight, I dispatched Lieutenant Evans, and Paymaster Myers, to the town—the former to call on the Governor, and the latter to see if any coal could be had. Their errand was fruitless. Not only was there no coal to be purchased, but my officers thought that they had been received rather ungraciously. The fact is, we found here, as in Curaçoa, that the enemy was in possession of the neutral territory. There was a Federal Consul resident in the place, who was the principal contractor, for supplying the French garrison with fresh beef! and there were three, or four Yankee schooners in the harbor, whose skippers had a monopoly of the trade in flour and notions. What could the *Sumter* effect against such odds?

In the course of an hour after my boat returned, we were again under way, running down the coast, in the direction of Surinam, to see if the Dutchmen would prove more propitious, than the Frenchmen had done. About six P. M., we passed the "Salut" Islands, three in number, on the summit of one of which shone the white walls of a French military hospital, contrasting prettily with the deep-green foliage of the shade-trees around it. It was surrounded by low walls, on which were mounted some small guns *en barbette*. Hither are sent all the sick sailors, and soldiers from Cayenne.

August 17th.—Morning clear, and beautiful, as usual, in this delightful climate, with a fresh breeze from the south-east. We are now in latitude 6° north, and still the south-east trade-wind is following us—the calm belt having been pushed farther and farther to the northward. We are running along in ten fathoms of water, at an average distance of seven, or eight miles, from the land, with the soundings surprisingly regular. Passed the mouth of the small river Maroni, at noon. At four P. M., ran across a bank, in very muddy water, some fifteen miles to the northward and eastward, of the entrance of this river, with only three fathoms of water on it; rather close shaving on a strange coast, having but six feet of water under our keel. Becoming a little nervous, we "hauled out," and soon deepened into five fathoms. There is little danger of shipwreck, on this coast, however, owing to the regularity of the soundings, and the almost perpetual smoothness of the sea. The bars off the mouths of the rivers, too, are, for the most part, of mud, where a ship *sticks*, rather than *thumps*. Hence, the temerity with which we ran into shallow waters.

Sunday, August 18th. — The south-east wind came to us, as softly, and almost as sweetly, this morning, as if it were "breathing o'er a bed of violets;" but it freshened as the day advanced, in obedience to the mandate of its master, the sun, and we had a fresh breeze, toward nightfall. After passing Post Orange, we ran over another three-fathom bank, the water deepening beyond, and enabling us to haul in toward the coast, as we approached Bram's Point, at the mouth of the Surinam River, off which we anchored, (near the buoy on the bar,) at twenty minutes past five P. M., in four fathoms of water. This being Sunday, as we were running along the coast, we had mustered and inspected the crew, and caused the clerk to read the articles "for the better government of the Navy" to them — the same old articles, though not read under the same old flag, as formerly. This was my invariable practice on the Sabbath. It broke in, pleasantly, and agreeably, upon the routine duties of the week, pretty much as church-going does, on shore, and had a capital effect, besides, upon discipline, reminding the sailor of his responsibility to the laws, and that there were such merciless tribunals, as Courts-Martial, for their enforcement. The very shaving, and washing, and dressing, of a Sunday morning, contributed to the sailor's self-respect. The "muster" gratified, too, one of his passions, as it gave him the opportunity of displaying all those anchors, and stars, which he had so industriously embroidered, in floss silk, on his ample shirt-collar, and on the sleeve of his jacket. We had some dandies on board the *Sumter*, and it was amusing to witness the self-complacent air, with which these gentlemen would move around the capstan, with the blackest, and most carefully polished of pumps, and the whitest, and finest of sinnott hats, from which would be streaming yards enough of ribbon, to make the ship a pennant.

I had had considerable difficulty in identifying the mouth of the Surinam River, so low and uniform in appearance was the coast, as seen from the distance at which we had been compelled to run along it, by the shallowness of the water. There is great similarity between these shelving banks, running off to a great distance, at sea, and the banks on the coast of West Florida. The rule of soundings, on some parts of the latter coast, is a foot to the mile, so that, when the navigator is in ten feet of water, he is ten miles from the land. This is not quite the case, on the coast of Guiana, but on some parts of it, a large ship can scarcely come within sight of the land. A small craft, drawing but a few feet of water, has no need of making a harbor, on either coast, for the whole coast is a harbor—the sea, in bad weather, breaking in from three to five fathoms of water, miles outside of her, leaving all smooth and calm within. There is a difference, however, between the two coasts—the Florida coast is scourged by the hurricane, whilst the Guiana coast is entirely free from storms.

Soon after we came to anchor, as related, we descried a steamer in the west, steering for the mouth of the river. Nothing was more likely than that, by this time, the enemy should have sent some of his fast gun-boats in pursuit of us, and the smoke of a steamer on the horizon, therefore, caused me some uneasiness. I knew that I had not a chivalrous enemy to deal with, who would be likely to give me a fair fight. The captures made by the *Sumter* had not only touched the Yankee in a very tender spot—his pocket—they had administered, also, a well-merited rebuke to his ridiculous self-conceit. It was monstrous, indeed, in his estimation, that any one should have the audacity, in the face of Mr. Lincoln's proclamation of prompt vengeance, to molest one of his ships.

A malignant press, from Maine to Maryland, had denounced the *Sumter* as a pirate, and no quarter was to be shown her. The steamer, now approaching, having been descried, at a great distance, by the curling of her black smoke high into the still air, night set in before she was near enough to be made out.   We could see her form indistinctly, in the darkness, but no certain conclusion could be arrived at as to her size or nationality.   I, at once, caused my fires to be lighted, and, beating to quarters, prepared my ship for action.   We stood at our guns for some time, but seeing, about ten P. M., that the strange steamer came to anchor, some three or four miles outside of us; I permitted the men to leave their quarters, cautioning the officer of the watch, however, to keep a bright lookout, during the night, for the approach of boats, and to call me if there should be any cause for alarm.   As I turned in, I thought things looked a little squally.   If the strange vessel were a mail-steamer, she would, of course, be familiar with the waters in which she plied, and, instead of anchoring outside, would have run boldly into the river without waiting for daylight.   Besides, she had no lights about her, as she approached, and packet steamers always go well lighted up.   That she was a steamer of war, therefore, appeared quite certain; but, of course, it was of no use to speculate upon the chances of her being an enemy; daylight only could reveal that.   In the meantime, the best thing we could do would be to get a good night's rest, so as to rise refreshed for the morning's work, if work there should be.

At daylight, all hands were again summoned to their quarters; and pretty soon the strange steamer was observed to be under way, and standing toward us.   We got up our own anchor in a trice — the men running around the capstan in "double-quick," — and putting the ship under steam, started to meet her.   Neither of us had, as yet, any colors hoisted.   We soon perceived that the stranger was no heavier than ourselves.   This greatly encouraged me, and I could see a corresponding lighting up of the faces of my crew, all standing silently at their guns.   Desiring to make the stranger reveal her nationality to me first, I now hoisted the French colors — a fine new flag, that I had had made in New Orleans.   To my astonishment, and no little perplexity, up went the same colors, on board the stranger! I was alongside of a French ship of war, pretending to be a Frenchman myself! Of course, there was but one thing to be done, and that was, to haul down the French flag and hoist my own, which was done in an instant, when we mutually hailed. A colloquy ensued, when the names of the two ships were interchanged, and we ascertained that the stranger was bound into the Surinam, like ourselves. We now both ran in for the light-ship, and the Frenchman receiving a pilot on board from her, I permitted him to take the lead, and we followed him up the long and narrow channel, having sometimes scarcely a foot of water to spare under our keel.

After we had passed inside of Bram's Point, the tide being out, both ships anchored to wait for the returning flood. I took advantage of the opportunity, and sent a lieutenant to visit the French ship. The *Vulture*, for such was her name, was one of the old-fashioned, side-wheel steamers, mounting only carronades, and was last from Martinique, with convicts on board, for Cayenne. Running short of coal, she was putting into Paramaribo, for a supply. Getting under way again, soon after mid-day, we continued our course up the river. We were much reminded, by the scenery of the Surinam, of that of some of our Southern rivers—the Mississippi, for instance, after the voyager from the Gulf has left the marshes behind him, and is approaching New Orleans. The bottom lands, near the river, are cleared, and occupied by sugar, and other plantations, the back-ground of the picture presenting a dense, and unbroken forest. As we passed the well-known sugar-house, with its tall chimney, emitting volumes of black smoke, and saw gangs of slaves, cutting, and hauling in the cane, the illusion was quite perfect. Nothing can exceed the fertility of these alluvial lands. They are absolutely inexhaustible, yielding crop after crop, in continual succession, without rest or interval; there being no frosts to interfere with vegetation, in this genial climate. Some of the planters' dwellings were tasteful, and even elegant, surrounded by galleries whose green Venetian blinds gave promise of coolness within, and sheltered besides by the umbrageous arms of giant forest-trees. Cattle wandered over the pasture lands, the negroes were well clothed, and there was a general air of abundance, and contentment. Slavery is held by a very precarious tenure, here, and will doubtless soon disappear, there being a strong party, in Holland, in favor of its abolition. Our consort, the *Vulture*, and ourselves anchored almost at the same moment, off the town of Paramaribo, in the middle of the afternoon. There were two, or three American brigantines in the harbor, and a couple of Dutch ships of war. I sent a lieutenant to call on the Governor, and to request permission to coal, and refit; both of which requests were granted, with the usual conditions, viz.: that I should not increase my crew or armament, or receive ammunition on board. The Captain of the *Vulture* now came on board, to return the visit I had made him, through my lieutenant, and the commanding Dutch naval officer also called. But, what was more important, several coal merchants came off to negotiate with my paymaster, about supplying the ship with the very necessary article in which they dealt. The successful bidder for our contract was a *"gentleman of color,"* that is to say, a quadroon, who talked freely about whites, and blacks, always putting himself, of course, in the former category, by the use of the pronoun "we," and seemed to have no sort of objection to our flag, or the cause it was supposed to represent. I wined this "gentleman," along with my other visitors, and though I paid him a remunerative price for his coal, I am under many obligations to him, for his kindness, and assistance to us, during our stay. I take great pleasure in contrasting the conduct and bearing of this person, with those of the Federal Consul, at Paramaribo. This latter gentleman was a Connecticut man, who had probably worn white cravats, and delivered quarter-dollar lectures, in his native village, against slavery, as a means of obtaining an "honest living." Coming to Paramaribo, he had married a mulatto wife, and through her, become a slave-holder. This virtuous representative of "great moral ideas," at once threw himself into the breach, between the *Sumter*, and the coal-market, and did all he could to prevent her from coaling. He was one of Mr. Seward's men, and taking up the refrain about "piracy," went first to the Governor, to see what could be effected, in that quarter. Being told that Holland had followed the lead of the great powers, and recognized the Confederates as belligerents, he next went to our quadroon contractor, and endeavored to bluff him off, by threatening him with the loss of any Yankee trade, that he might possess. Being equally unsuccessful here, he next tried to seduce the lightermen, to prevent them from delivering the coal to us. All would not do, however, the *Sumter*, or what is more likely, the *Sumter's* gold—that talisman that works so many miracles in this virtuous world of ours— was too strong for him, and, pretty soon, the black diamonds —the most precious of jewels to men in our condition—came tumbling into our coal-bunkers. Failing to prevent us from coaling, the little Connecticut official next tampered with the pilot, and endeavored to prevail on him, to refuse to take us to sea. But the pilot was a sailor, with all the generous instincts that belong to his class, and he not only refused to be seduced, but presented me with some local charts of the coast, which I found very useful.

The Consul had his triumph at last, however. When I was fitting out the *Sumter* in New Orleans, a friend, and relative resident in that city, had kindly permitted me to take with me, as my steward, a valuable slave of his who had been brought up as a dining-room servant. Ned was as black as the ace of spades, and being a good-tempered, docile lad, had become my right-hand man, taking the best of care of my cabin, and keeping my table supplied with all the delicacies of the different markets, to which we had had access. He was as happy as the days were long, a great favorite with the crew, and when there was any fun going on, on the forecastle, he was sure to be in the midst of it. But the tempter came along. The Connecticut miscegenist (and slave-holder, at the same time) had seen Ned's shining and happy face going to market, of mornings, and, like the serpent of old, whispered in his ear. One morning Ned was missing, but the market-basket came off, piled up as usual with luxuries for dinner. The lad had been bred in an honest household, and though his poor brain had been bewildered, he was still above theft. His market-basket fully balanced his account. Poor Ned! his after-fate was a sad one. He was taken to the country, by his Mephistophiles, and set at work, with the slaves of that pious Puritan, on a small plantation that belonged to his negro wife. Ned's head was rather too woolly, to enable him to understand much about the abstractions of freedom and slavery, but he had sense enough to see, ere long, that he had been beguiléd, and cheated, by the smooth Yankee; and when, in course of time, he saw himself reduced to yam diet, and ragged clothing, he began, like the prodigal child, to remember the abundance of his master's house, and to long to return to it.   Accordingly, he was missing, again, one fine morning, and was heard of no more in Paramaribo.   He had embarked on board a vessel bound to Europe, and next turned up in Southampton.   The poor negro had wandered off at· a hazard in quest of the *Sumter*, but hearing nothing of her, and learning that the Confederate States steamer *Nashville*, Commander Pegram, was at Southampton, he made his way on board of that ship, and told his tale to the officers.   He afterward found his way to the United States, and died miserably, of cholera, in some of the negro suburbs of Washington City

August 23d. — Weather clear, during the day, but we had some heavy showers of rain, with thunder, and lightning during the night.   We are receiving coal rather slowly — a small lighter-load at a time.   We are making some changes in the internal arrangements of the ship.   Finding, by experience, that we have more tank-room, for water, than is requisite, we are landing a couple of our larger tanks, and extending the bulkheads of the coal-bunkers.   By this means, we shall be enabled to increase our coal-carrying capacity by at least a third, carrying twelve days of fuel, instead of eight.   Still the *Sumter* remains fundamentally defective, as a cruiser, in her inability to lift her screw.

August 24th. — Weather clear, and pleasant, with some passing clouds, and light showers of rain.   The Dutch mail-steamer, from Demerara, arrived, to-day.   We are looking anxiously for news from home, as, at last accounts — July 20th from New York — a battle near Manassas Junction, seemed imminent.   Demerara papers of the 19th of August contain nothing, except that some skirmishing had taken place, between the two armies.   The French steamer-of-war *Abeille* arrived, and anchored near us.

Sunday, August 25th. — Morning cloudy.   At half-past eight

I went on shore to church. The good old Mother has her churches, and clergymen, even in this remote Dutch colony. The music of her choirs is like the "drum-beat" of England; it encircles the earth, with its never-ending melody. As the sun, "keeping company with the hours," lights up, with his newly risen beams, one degree of longitude after another, he awakens the priest to the performance of the never-ending mass. The church was a neat, well-arranged wooden building, of large dimensions, and filled to overflowing with devout worshippers. All the shades of color, from "snowy white to sooty" were there, and there did not seem to be any order in the seating of the congregation, the shades being promiscuously mixed. The preacher was fluent, and earnest in action, but his sermon, which seemed to impress the congregation, being in that beautiful and harmonious language, which we call "low Dutch," was entirely unintelligible to me. The Latin mass, and ceremonies—which are the same all over the world—were, of course, quite familiar, and awoke many tender reminiscences. I had heard, and seen them, in my own country, under the domes of grand cathedrals, and in the quiet retreat of the country house, where the good wife herself had improvised the altar. A detachment of the Government troops was present.

Some Dutch naval lieutenants visited the ship to-day. We learn, by late papers from Barbadoes, politely brought us by these gentlemen, that the enemy's steamer, *Keystone State*, was in that island, in search of us, on the 21st of July. She probably heard, there, of my intention to go back to cruise off the island of Cuba, which, as the reader has seen, I *confidentially* communicated to my friends at Curaçoa, and has turned back herself. If she were on the right track she should be here before this. There was great commotion, too, as we learn by these papers, at Key West, on the 8th of July, when the news reached there of our being at Cienfuegos. Consul Shufeldt, at Havana, had been prompt, as I had foreseen. We entered Cienfuegos on the 6th, and on the 8th, he had two heavy and fast steamers, the *Niagara* and the *Crusader*, in pursuit of us. They, too, seem to have lost the trail.

August 28th.— Bright, elastic morning, with a gentle breeze from the south-east. There was a grand fandango, on shore, last night, at which some of my officers were present. The fun grew "fast and furious," as the night waned, and what with the popping of champagne-corks, and the flashing of the bright eyes of the waltzers, as they were whirled in the giddy dance, my young fellows have come off looking a little red about the eyes, and inclined to be poetical.

Rumors have been rife, for some days past, of a Confederate victory at Manassas. There seems now to be no longer any doubt about the fact. Private letters have been received, from Demerara, which state that the enemy was not only beaten, but shamefully routed, flying in confusion and dismay from the battle-field, and seeking refuge, pell-mell, in the Federal capital. With the exception of the Federal Consul, and Yankee skippers in the port, and a small knot of shop-keepers, interested in the American trade, all countenances are beaming with joy at this intelligence. This splendid victory was won by General Beauregard. McDowell was the commander of the enemy's forces, assisted, as it would seem, by the poor old superannuated Winfield Scott — this renegade soldier lending his now feeble intellect to the Northern Vandal, to assist in stabbing to the heart his mother State — Virginia! Alas! what an ignoble end of a once proud and honored soldier.

August 29th.— We have, at length, finished coaling, after a tedious delay of ten days. A rumor prevailed in the town, yesterday, that there were two enemy's ships of war off the bar — keeping themselves cunningly out of sight, to waylay the *Sumter*. The rumor comes with circumstance, for it is said that the fisherman, who brought the news, supplied one of the ships with fish, and said that the other ship was getting water on board from one of the coast plantations. To-day, the rumor dwindles; but one ship, it seems, has been seen, and she a merchant ship. The story is probably like that of the three white crows.

August 30th.— The pilot having come on board, we got under way, at two P. M., and steamed down to the mouth of the river, where we came to anchor. A ship, going to sea, is like a woman going on a journey — many last things remaining to be attended to, at the moment of departure. I have always found it best, to shove off shore-boats, expel all visitors, "drop down" out of the influences of the port, and send an officer or two back, to arrange these last things. A boat was now accordingly dispatched back to the town, for this purpose, and as she would not return until late in the night, inviting the surgeon and paymaster, and my clerk to accompany me, I pulled on shore, in my gig, to make a visit to an adjoining sugar plantation, that lay close by, tempting us to a stroll under its fine avenues of cocoanut and acacia trees. We were received very hospitably at the planter's mansion, where we found some agreeable ladies, and with whom we stayed late enough, to take tea, at their pressing solicitation. It was a Hollandese household, but all the inmates spoke excellent English. Whilst tea was being prepared, we wandered over the premises, the sugar-house included, where we witnessed all the processes of sugar making, from the expression of the juice from the cane, to the crystallization of the syrup. There were crowds of negroes on the place, old and young, male and female — some at work, and some at play; the players being rather the more numerous of the two classes. The grounds around the dwelling were tastefully laid out, in serpentine walks, winding through a wilderness of rare tropical shrubbery, redolent of the most exquisite of perfumes. True to the Dutch instinct for the water, the river, or rather the bay, for the river has now disembogued into an arm of the sea, washed the very walls of the flower-garden, and the plash, or rather the monotonous fretting of the tiny waves, at their base, formed no unmusical accompaniment to the hum of conversation, as the evening wore away. Among other plants, we noticed the giant maguey, and a great variety of the cactus, that favorite child of the sun. Our visit being over, we took a warm leave of our hospitable entertainers, and pulled on board the *Sumter*, by moonlight, deeply impressed, and softened as well by the harmonies of nature, and feeling as little like "pirates," as possible.

The next morning, having run up our boats, and taken a final leave of the waters of the Surinam, we steamed out to sea, crossing the bar about meridian; the weather being fine, and the wind fresh from the north-east. Having given it out that we were bound to Barbadoes, to look for the *Keystone State*,

we stood north, until we had run the land out of sight, to give
color to this idea, when we changed our course to E., half S.
We ran along, for the next two or three days, on soundings,
with a view to break the force of the current, doubling Cape
Orange, on the 2d of September, and hauling more to the
southward, with the trending of the coast.   On the next day,
we had regained the position from which we had been compelled to bear up, and my journal remarks:—"We have thus
lost three days and a half of steaming, or about fifty tons of
coal, but what is worse, we have lost twenty-three days of
valuable time,—but this time can scarcely be said to have
been wholly lost, either, since the display of the flag of our
young republic, in Cayenne and Paramaribo, has had a most
excellent effect."

Sept. 4th. — Weather fine, with a fresh breeze, from about
E. by S.   During most of the day, we have carried fore and
aft sails, and have made an excellent run, for a dull ship — 175
miles.   We have experienced no current.   We passed the
mouths of the great Amazon, to-day, bearing on its bosom the
waters of a continent.   We were running along in the deepest
and bluest of sea-water, whilst at no great distance from us,
we could plainly perceive, through our telescopes, the turbid
waters of the great stream, mixing and mingling, by slow degrees, with the ocean.   Numerous tide rips marked the uncon-
genial meeting of the waters, and the sea-gull and penguin
were busy diving in them, as though this neutral ground, or
rather I should say, battle-ground, was a favorite resort for
the small fish, on which they prey.   A drift log with sedate
water-fowl seated upon it, would now and then come along,
and schools of porpoises were disporting themselves, now in
the blue, now in the muddy waters.   Unlike the mouths of the
Mississippi, there were no white sails of commerce dotting the
waters, in the offing, and no giant tow-boats throwing their
volumes of black smoke into the air, and, with their huge
side-wheels, beating time to the pulsations of the steam-engine.
All was nature.   The giant stream ran through a wilderness,
scarcely yet opened to civilization.   It disembogues a little
south of the equator, and runs from west to east, nearly
entirely across the continent.

We crossed the equator in the *Sumter*, on the meridian of 46° 40', and sounded in twenty fathoms of water, bringing up from the bottom of the sea, for the first time, some of the sand, and shells of the Southern Hemisphere. We hoisted the Confederate flag, though there were no eyes to look upon it outside of our ship, to vindicate, symbolically, our right to enter this new domain of Neptune, in spite of Abraham Lincoln, and the Federal gun-boats.

September 5th.—Wind fresh from E. S. E. Doubled Cape *Garupi*, during the early morning, and sounded, at meridian, in eight fathoms of water, *without any land in sight*, though the day was clear. Hauled out from the coast a little. At half-past three, P. M., made the island of *San Joao*, for which we had been running, a little on the starboard bow. We now hauled in close with this island, and running along its white sand beach, which reminded us much of the Florida coast, about Pensacola, we doubled its north-eastern end, in six, and seven fathoms of water. Night now set in, and, shaping our course S. E. by S., we ran into some very broken ground—the soundings frequently changing, in a single cast of the lead, from seven to four fathoms. Four fathoms being rather uncomfortably shoal, on an open coast, we again hauled out, until we deepened our water to eight fathoms, in which we ran along, still in very equal soundings, until we made the light on Mount *Itacolomi*, nearly ahead. In half an hour afterward, we anchored in six and a half fathoms of water, to wait for daylight.

When I afterward told some Brazilian officers, who came on board, to visit me, in Marauham, of this eventful night's run, they held up their hands in astonishment, telling me that the chances were a hundred to one, that I had been wrecked, for, many parts of the broken ground over which I had run, were *almost dry*, at low water. Their steamers never attempt it, they said, with the best pilots on board. It is a pity this coast is not better surveyed, for the charts by which I was running, represented it free from danger. The Brazilian is a coral coast, and, as before remarked, all coral coasts are dangerous. The inequality of soundings was due to the greater industry of the little stone-mason, of which we read some pages back, in some spots than in others. This little worker of the sea will sometimes pierce a ship's bottom, with a cone, which it has brought near the surface, from surrounding deep.waters.   As it is constantly at work, the bottom of the sea is constantly changing, and hence, on coral coasts, surveying steamers should be almost always at work.   Having anchored in the open sea, and the sea being a little rough, we found, when we came to heave up our anchor, the next morning, that we brought up only the ring, and a small piece of the shank.   It had probably been caught in the rocky bottom, and broken by the force of the windlass, aided by the pitching of the ship.

There was, much to my regret, no pilot-boat in sight.   The entrance to Maranham is quite difficult, but difficult as it was, I was forced to attempt it.   We rounded safely, the shoals of Mount Itacolomi, and passed the middle ground of the Meio, and I was already congratulating myself that the danger was past, when the ship ran plump upon a sand-bank, and stopped! She went on, at full speed, and the shock, to those standing on deck, was almost sufficient to throw them off their feet.   We had a skilful leadsman in the chains, and at his last cast, he had found no bottom, with eight fathoms of line — all that the speed of the ship would allow him to sink.   Here was a catastrophe!   Were the bones of the *Sumter* to be laid to rest, on the coast of Brazil, and her Commander, and crew to return to the Confederate States, and report to the Government, that they had lost its only ship of war!   This idea flashed through my mind for an instant, but only for an instant, for the work of the moment pressed.   The engineer on duty had stopped his engine, without waiting for orders, as soon as he felt the ship strike, and I now ordered it reversed.   In a moment more the screw was revolving in the opposite direction, and the strong tide, which was running out, catching the ship, on the port bow, at the same time, she swung round to starboard, and slid off the almost perpendicular edge of the bank into deep water, pretty much as a turtle will drop off a log.   The first thing I did was to draw a long breath, and the second was to put on an air of indifference, as if nothing had happened, and tell the officer of the deck, in the coolest manner possible, to "let her go ahead."   We now proceeded more cautiously, under low steam, giving the leadsman plenty of time to get his soundings, accurately. These soon proving very irregular, and there being some fishermen on the coast, half a mile distant, throwing up their arms, and gesticulating to us, as though to warn us of danger, we anchored, and sending a boat on shore, brought one of them off, who volunteered to pilot us up to the town. Upon sounding the pumps, we found that the ship had suffered no damage from the concussion. We anchored in the port of Maranham, in three or four hours afterward, and the Confederate States flag waved in the Empire of Brazil. The Port Admiral sent a lieutenant to call on us, soon after anchoring, and I dispatched one of my own lieutenants, to call on the Governor; returning the Admiral's visit, myself, in the course of the afternoon, at his place of business on shore.

CHAPTER XVIII.

THE SUMTER AT MARANHAM — MORE DIPLOMACY NECES-
SARY — THE HOTEL PORTO AND ITS PROPRIETOR — A
WEEK ON SHORE — SHIP COALS AND SAILS AGAIN.

THE day after our arrival in Maranham, was a day of feast-
ing and rejoicing by the townspeople — all business being
suspended. It was the 7th of September, the anniversary of
the day on which Brazil had severed her political connection
with Portugal — in other words, it was her Independence-day.
The forts and ships of war fired salutes, and the latter were
gayly draped in flags and signals, presenting a very pretty appearance. It is customary, on such occasions, for the ships of
war of other nations, in the port, to participate in the ceremonies and merry-making. We abstained from all participation,
on board the *Sumter*, our flag being, as yet, unrecognized, for
the purposes of form and ceremony. In the evening, a grand
ball was given, at the Government House, by the President of
the Province, to which all the world, except the *Sumter*, was
invited — the etiquette of nations, before referred to, requiring
that she should be ruled out. The only feeling excited in us,
by this official slight, was one of contempt for the silliness of
the proceeding — a contempt heightened by the reflection that
we were a race of Anglo-Saxons, proud of our lineage, and
proud of our strength, frowned upon by a set of half-breeds.
The Government House being situated on the river bank, near
our anchorage, the lights of the brilliantly illuminated halls
and chambers, shone full upon our decks, and the music of the
bands, and even the confused hum of the voices of the merry-
makers, and the muffled shuffling of the dancers' feet, came to
us, very distinctly, to a late hour. The *Sumter* lay dark, and
motionless, and silent, amid this scene of merriment; the only
answer which she sent back to the revellers, being the sonorous

and startling cry, every half hour, of her marine sentinels on post, of "All's well!"

Having suffered, somewhat, in health, from the fatigue and excitement of the last few weeks, I removed on shore the next day, and took up my quarters at the hotel *Porto*, kept by one of those nondescripts one sometimes meets with in the larger South American cities, whose nationality it is impossible to guess at, except that he belongs to the Latin race. My landlord had followed the sea, among his thousand and one occupations, spoke half a dozen languages, and was "running"— to use a slang Americanism—a theatre and one or two fashionable restaurants, in beautifully laid out pleasure-grounds in the suburbs, in addition to his hotel. He drove a pair of fast horses, was on capital terms with all the pretty women in the town, smashed champagne-bottles, right and left, and smoked the best of Havana cigars. The reader will thus see, that being an invalid, and requiring a little nursing, I had fallen into capital hands. Whether it was that *Senhor Porto*— for he had given his own name to his hotel—had chased and captured merchant-ships, in former days, himself, or from some other motive, I could never tell, but he took quite a fancy to me at once, and I rode with him daily, during my stay, behind his fast ponies, and visited all the places of amusement, of which he was the *padron*. The consequence was, that I visibly improved in health, and at the end of the week which I spent with him, returned on board the *Sumter*, quite set up again; in requital whereof, I have permitted the gallant Captain to sit for his portrait in these pages.

My first duty, after being installed in my new apartments on shore, was, of course, to call on the President of the Department—the town of Maranham being the seat of government of the province of the same name. The President declined to see me then, but appointed noon, the next day, to receive me. Soon after I had returned to my hotel, *Senhor Porto* entered my room, to inform me that Captain *Pinto*, of the Brazilian Navy, the commanding naval officer on the station, accompanied by the Chief of Police, had called to see me. "What does this mean?" said I, "the Chief of Police, in our cities, is a very questionable sort of gentleman, and is usually supposed to be on the scent of malefactors." "Oh! he is a very respectable gentleman, I assure you," replied *Porto*, "and, as you see, he has called with the Port Admiral, so that he is in good company, at least. Indeed he is reputed to be the confidential friend of the President." Thus reassured, and making a virtue of necessity, I desired *Porto*, very complacently, to admit the visitors. The Port Admiral had done me the honor to visit me, immediately upon my arrival, and I had returned his visit, so that we were not strangers. He introduced the Chief of Police to me, who proved to be, as *Porto* had represented him, an agreeable gentleman, holding military rank, and, after the two had been seated, they opened their business to me. They had come, they said, on behalf of the President, to present me with a copy of a paper, which had been handed him, by the United States Consul, protesting against my being permitted to coal, or receive any other supplies in the port of Maranham. Oh ho! thought I, here is another of Mr. Seward's small fry turned up. I read the paper, and found it full of ignorance and falsehoods—ignorance of the most common principles of international law, and barefaced misrepresentations with regard to my ship; the whole composed in such execrable English, as to be highly creditable to Mr. Seward's Department. I characterized the paper, as it deserved, and said to the gentlemen, that as I had made an appointment to call on the President, on the morrow, I would take that opportunity of replying to the slanderous document. The conversation then turned on general topics, and my visitors soon after withdrew.

As I rode out, that afternoon, with Porto, he said, "Never mind! I know all that is going on, at the palace, and you will get all the coal, and everything else you want." The pay of the Federal Consul at Maranham, was, I believe, at the time I visited the town, about twelve hundred dollars, per annum. As was to be expected, a small man filled the small place. He was quite young, and with commendable Yankee thrift, was exercising, in the consular dwelling, the occupation of a dentist; the "old flag" flying over his files, false teeth, and spittoons. He probably wrote the despatch, a copy of which had been handed me, in the intervals between the entrance, and exit of his customers. It was not wonderful, therefore, that this semi-diplomat, charged with the affairs of the Great Republic, and with the decayed teeth of the young ladies of Maranham, at one and the same time, should be a little confused, as to points of international law, and the rules of Lindley Murray. That he should misrepresent me was both natural, and Federal.

At the appointed hour, the next day, I called to see his Excellency, the President, and being ushered, by an orderly in waiting, into a suite of spacious, and elegantly furnished apartments, I found Captain Pinto, and his Excellency, both prepared to receive me. We proceeded, at once, to business. I exhibited to his Excellency the same little piece of brownish paper, with Mr. Jefferson Davis's signature at the bottom of it, that I had shown to Captain Hillyer of the *Cadmus* — unasked, however, as no doubts had been raised as to the verity of the character of my ship. I then read to his Excellency an extract or two from the letter of instructions, which had been sent me by the Secretary of the Navy, directing me to pay all proper respect to the territory, and property of neutrals. I next read the proclamations of England and France, acknowledging us to be in the possession of belligerent rights, and said to his Excellency, that although I had not seen the proclamation of Brazil, I presumed she had followed the lead of the European powers — to which he assented. I then "rested my case," as the lawyers say, seeing, by the expression of his Excellency's countenance, that every lick had told, and that I had nothing now to fear. "But, what about coal being contraband of war," said his Excellency, at this stage of the proceeding. "The United States Consul, in the protest addressed to me, a copy of which I sent you, yesterday, by Captain Pinto, and the Chief of Police, states that you had not been permitted to coal, in any of the ports, which you have hitherto visited." The reader will recollect, that, at the British Island of Trinidad, the question of my being permitted to coal had been submitted to the "law officers of the Crown." The newspaper, at that place, had published a copy of the opinion of these officers, and also a copy of the decision of the Gov-

ernor, thereupon.   Having brought a copy of this paper, in my
pocket, for the occasion, I now rejoined to his Excellency:
"The United States Consul has made you a false statement.   I
have coaled, already, in the colonies of no less than three
Powers—Spain, Holland, and England"—and drawing from
my pocket the newspaper, and handing it to him, I continued,
"and your Excellency will find, in this paper, the decision of
the English authorities, upon the point in question—that is to
say, that coal is not contraband of war, and may be supplied
by neutrals to belligerents."   Captain Pinto, to whom his Excellency handed the paper, read aloud the decision, putting it
into very good Portuguese, as he went along, and when he had
finished the reading, his Excellency turned again to me,
and said: "I have no longer any doubts on the question.
You can have free access to the markets, and purchase what-
soever you may desire—munitions of war alone excepted."   I
have been thus particular in describing these proceedings to
the reader, to show him with what sleuth-hound perseverance
I was followed up, by these small consuls, taken from the
political kennel in the Northern States, who never hesitated to
use the most unblushing falsehoods, if they thought these
would serve their purposes better than the truth.   The official
portion of my interview with the President being ended, I
ventured upon some general remarks with regard to the unnatural, and wicked war which was being waged upon us, and
soon afterward took my leave.

In an hour after I had left the President's quarters, my
paymaster had contracted for a supply of coal, and lighters
were being prepared to take it on board.   The sailors were
now permitted to visit the shore, in detachments, "on liberty,"
and the officers wandered about, in twos and threes, wherever
inclination prompted.   We soon found that wherever we
moved, we were objects of much curiosity, the people frequently turning to stare at us; but we were always treated
with respect.   Nothing was thought, or talked of, during our
stay, but the American war.   The Provincial Congress was in
session, and several of its members boarded at the hotel *Porto*.
I found them intelligent, well-informed men.   There were
political parties here, as elsewhere, of course; among others,

as might be expected, in a slave-holding country, there was an abolition party, and this party sympathized with the North. It was very small, however, for it was quite evident, from the popular demonstrations, that the great mass of the people were with us. This state of the public feeling not only rendered our stay, very pleasant, but facilitated us in getting off our supplies. Invitations to the houses of the citizens were frequent, and we had free access to all the clubs, and other places of public resort.

I must not omit to mention here, a very agreeable fellow-countryman, whom we met in Maranham—Mr. J. Wetson, from Texas. He had been several years in Brazil. His profession was that of a steam-engineer, and mill-wright. This worthy young mechanic, full of love, and enthusiasm for his section, loaned the paymaster two thousand dollars, on a bill against the Secretary of the Navy; and during the whole of our stay, his rooms were the head-quarters of my younger officers, where he dispensed to them true Southern hospitality. We were gratified to find him a great favorite with the towns-people, and we took leave of him with regret.

Maranham lies in latitude 2° S. and we visited it, during the dry season; the sun having carried the equatorial cloud-ring, which gives it rain, farther north. We had perpetual sunshine, during our stay, but the heat was tempered by the trade-wind, which blew sometimes half a gale, so that we did not feel it oppressive. Toward night the sea-breeze would moderate, and the most heavenly of bright skies, and most balmy of atmospheres would envelop the landscape. At this witching hour, the beauties of Maranham made their appearance, at the street-doors, and at open windows, and the tinkle of the guitar and the gentle hum of conversation would be heard. Later in the night, there would arise from different parts of the town—somewhat removed from the haunts of the upper-tendom—the rumbling, and jingling of the tambourine, and the merry notes of the violin, as the national fandango was danced, with a vigor, and at the same time with a poetry of motion unknown to colder climes. The wine flowed freely on these occasions, and not unfrequently the red knife of the assassin found the heart's blood of a rival in love; for there are other climes besides those of which the poet sang, where

> " The rage of the vulture, the love of the turtle
> Now melt into sorrow, now madden to crime."

The trade of Maranham is mostly monopolized by Portugal, France, and Spain, though there is some little carried on with the United. States — an occasional ship from New York, or Boston, bringing a cargo of flour, cheap but gaudy furniture, clocks, and domestic cottons, and other Yankee staples, and notions. The shop-keepers are mostly French and Germans. An excellent staple of cotton is produced in the province of Maranham.

On the 15th of September, the *Sumter* was ready for sea, having been refitted, and repainted, besides being coaled, and provisioned; and there being, as usual, according to rumor, a couple of enemy's ships waiting for her outside, we received a pilot on board, and getting up steam, took leave of Maranham, carrying with us many kindly recollections of the hospitality of the people. We swept the sea horizon, with our glasses, as we approached the bar, but the enemy's cruisers were nowhere to be seen, and at three P. M., we were again in blue water; our little craft rising, and falling gently, to the undulations of the sea, as she ploughed her way through it.

The question now was, in what direction should we steer? I was within striking distance of the cruising-ground, for which I had set out — Cape St. Roque; but we had been so long delayed, that we should reach it, if we proceeded thither at all, at a most unpropitious season — the sailing, and steaming qualities of the *Sumter* considered. The trade-winds were sweeping round the Cape, blowing half a gale, on the wings of which the dullest ship would be able to run away from us, if we trusted to sail, alone; and steam, in the present state of my exchequer, was out of the question. I had paid $17.50 per ton for the coal I had taken in, at Maranham, and but for the timely loan of Mr. Wetson, should have exhausted my treasury entirely. The trade-winds would continue to blow, with equal force, until some time in December; they would then moderate, and from that time, onward, until March, we might expect more gentle weather. This, then, was the only season, in which the *Sumter* could operate off the Cape, to advantage.

On the other hand, the calm belt of the equator lay before me—its southern edge, at this season of the year, being in latitude of about 5° N. All the homeward-bound trade of the enemy passed through this calm belt, or used to pass through it before the war, at a well-known crossing. At that crossing, there would be a calm sea, light, and variable winds, and rain. In such weather, I could lie in wait for my prey, under sail, and, if surprise, and stratagem did not effect my purpose, I could, when a sail appeared, get up steam and chase and capture, without the expenditure of much fuel. In this way, with the coal I had on board, I could prolong my cruise, probably, for a couple of months. I did not hesitate long, therefore, between the two schemes. I turned my ship's head to the northward, and eastward, for the calm belt, and before sunset, we had run the coast of Brazil out of sight.

We recrossed the equator, the next day. In five days more, the sun would have reached the equator, when we should have had the grand spectacle, at noon, of being able to sweep him, with our instruments, entirely around the horizon, with his lower limb just touching it, at all points. We could nearly do this, as it was, and so rapidly did he dip, at noon, that we were obliged to watch him, with constant vigilance, to ascertain the precise moment of twelve o'clock.

September 17th.—The sea is of a deep, indigo blue, and we have a bright, and exceedingly transparent atmosphere, with a fresh breeze from the south-east. At half-past eleven A. M., we let the steam go down, uncoupled the propeller, and put the ship under sail. Observed at noon, in latitude 2° 19′ N.; longitude, 41° 29′

For the next few days, we encountered a remarkable easterly current—the current, in this part of the ocean, being almost constantly to the westward. This current—which we were now stemming, for we were sailing toward the north-west—retarded us, as much as fifty miles, in a single day! So remarkable did the phenomenon appear, that if I had noticed it, for but a single day, I should have been inclined to think that I had made some mistake in my observations, or that there was some error in my instrument, but we noticed it, day after day, for four or five days.

Contemporaneously with this phenomenon, another, and even more wonderful one appeared. This was a succession of tide-rips, so remarkable, that they deserve special description.

The *Sumter* lay nearly stationary, during the whole of these phenomena—the easterly current setting her back, nearly as much as she gained under sail. She was in the average latitude of 5° N., and average longitude of 42° W. For the first three days, the rips appeared with wonderful regularity — there being an interval of just twelve hours between them. They approached us from the south, and travelled toward the north. At first, only a line of foam would be seen, on the distant horizon, approaching the ship very rapidly. As it came nearer, an almost perpendicular wall of water, extending east and west, as far as the eye could reach, would be seen, the top of the wall boiling and foaming, like a breaker rolling over a rocky bottom. As the ridge approached nearer and nearer, it assumed the form of a series of rough billows, jostling against, and struggling with each other, producing a scene of the utmost confusion, the noise resembling that of a distant cataract. Reaching the ship, these billows would strike her with such force, as to send their spray to the deck, and cause her to roll and pitch, as though she were amid breakers. The phenomenon was, indeed, that of breakers, only the cause was not apparent — there being no shoal water to account for it. The *Sumter* sometimes rolled so violently in these breakers, when broadside to, that we were obliged to keep her off her course, several points, to bring the sea on her quarter, and thus mitigate the effect. The belt of rips would not be broad, and as it travelled very rapidly — fifteen or twenty miles the hour — the ship would not be long within its influence. In the course of three quarters of an hour, it would disappear, entirely, on the distant northern horizon. So curious was the whole phenomenon, that the sailors, as well as the officers, assembled, as if by common consent, to witness it. "There come the tide rips!" some would exclaim, and, in a moment there would be a demand for the telescopes, and a rush to the ship's side, to witness the curious spectacle. These rips have frequently been noticed by navigators, and discussed by philosophers, but, hitherto, no satisfactory explanation has been given of them. They are like the bores, at the mouths of great rivers; as at the mouth of the Amazon, in the western hemisphere, and of the Ganges, in the eastern; great breathings, or convulsions of the sea, the causes of which elude our research. These bores sometimes come in, in great perpendicular walls, sweeping everything before them, and causing immense destruction of life, and property. I was, at first, inclined to attribute these tide rips to the lunar influence, as they appeared twice in twenty-four hours, like the tides, and each time near the passing of the meridian, by the moon; but, in a few days, they varied their times of appearance, and came on quite irregularly, sometimes with an interval of five or six hours, only. And then the tidal wave, for it is evidently this, and not a current, should be from east to west, if it were due to lunar influence; and we have seen that it travelled from south to north. Nor could I connect it with the easterly current that was prevailing — for it travelled at right angles to the current, and not with, or against it. It was, evidently, due to some pretty uniform law, as it always travelled in the same direction.

We reached the calm belt, on the 24th of September, for, on this day, having lost the south-east trade, we had light and baffling winds from the south-west, and rain-clouds began to muster overhead. On the next day, the weather being in its normal condition of cloud, the welcome cry of "sail ho!" came resounding from the mast-head, with a more prolonged, and musical cadence than usual — the look-out, with the rest of the crew, having become tired of the inactivity of the last few days. All was bustle, immediately, about the decks; and in half an hour, with the sails snugly furled, and the ship under steam, we were in hot pursuit. The stranger was a brigantine, and was standing to the north-west, pursuing the usual crossing of the calm belt, as best he might, in the light winds, that were blowing, sometimes this way, sometimes that. We came up with him quite rapidly, there being scarcely a ripple on the surface of the smooth sea, to impede our progress, and when we had come sufficiently near to enable him to make it out, distinctly, we showed him the enemy's flag. He was evidently prepared with his own flag, for, in less than a minute, the lazy breeze was toying and playing with it, and presently blew it out sufficiently, to enable us to make out the well-known and welcome stars and stripes. We hove him to, by "hail," and hauling down the false colors, and hoisting our own, we sent a boat on board of him, and captured him. He proved to be the *Joseph Parke*, of Boston, last from Pernambuco, and six days out, *in ballast*. The *Parke* had been unable to procure a return cargo; the merchants of Pernambuco having heard of the arrival of the *Sumter*, at Maranham, in rather uncomfortable proximity.

We transferred the crew of the captured vessel to the *Sumter*, replacing it with a prize crew, and got on board from her such articles of provisions, cordage, and sails as we required; but instead of burning her, we transformed her, for the present, into a scout vessel, to assist us in discovering other prizes. I sent Lieutenant Evans on board to command her, and gave him a couple of midshipmen, as watch officers. The following was his commission:—

"Sir:—You will take charge of the prize-brig *Joseph Parke*, and cruise in company with this vessel, until further orders. During the day, you will keep from seven to eight miles, to the westward, and to windward, and keep a bright look-out, from your top-gallant yard, for sails—signalling to us, such as you may descry. Toward evening, every day, you will draw in toward this vessel, so as to be within three, or four miles of her, at dark; and, during the night you will keep close company with her, to guard against the possibility of separation. Should you, however, be separated from her, by any accident, you will make the best of your way to latitude 8° N., and longitude 45° W., where you will await her a reasonable time. Should you not join her again, you will make the best of your way to some port in the Confederate States."

In obedience to these instructions, the *Parke* drew off to her station, and letting our fires go down on board the *Sumter*, we put her under sail, again. Long before night, the excitement of the chase and capture had died away, and things had resumed their wonted course. The two ships hovered about the "crossing," for several days, keeping a bright look-out, but nothing more appeared; and on the 29th of September, the *Parke* having been called alongside, by signal, her prize crew was taken out, and the ship burned, after having been made a target, for a few hours, for the practice of the crew. It was evidently no longer of any use to bother ourselves about the crossing of the calm-belt, for, instead of falling in with a constant stream of the enemy's ships, returning home, from different parts of the world, we had been cruising in it, some ten days, and had sighted but a single sail! We had kept ourselves between the parallels of 2° 30′ N., and 9° 30′ N., and between the meridians of 41° 30′ W., and 47° 30′ W.; and if the reader have any curiosity on the subject, by referring to the map, he will perceive, that the north-western diagonal of the quadrilateral figure, formed by these parallels, and meridians, is the direct course between Cape St. Roque, and New York. But the wary sea-birds had, evidently, all taken the alarm, and winged their way, home, by other routes. I was the more convinced of this, by an intercepted letter which I captured in the letter-bag of the *Parke*, which was written by the master of the ship, *Asteroid*, to his owner, and which ran as follows:—

"The *Asteroid* arrived off this port [Pernambuco], last evening, seventy-five days from Baker's Island, and came to anchor in the outer roads, this morning. I found yours of August 9th, and noted the contents, which, I must say, have made me rather *blue*. I think you had better *insure*, even at the extra premium, as the *Asteroid* is not a *clipper*, and will be a *bon* prize for the Southerners. I shall sail this evening [September 16th, three days before the *Joseph Parke*] and take a *new* route, for Hampton Roads."

The *Asteroid* escaped us, as no doubt many more had done, by avoiding the "beaten track," and taking a new road home; thus verifying, in a very pointed manner, the old adage, that "the longest way round is the shortest way home."

We now made sail for the West India Islands, designing, after a short cruise among them, to run into the French island of Martinique, and coal. We still kept along on the beaten track of homeward-bound ships, but with little expectation of making any prizes, and for some days overhauled none but neutral ships. Many of these had cargoes for the United States, but not having the same motive to avoid me, that the enemy's ships had, they were content to travel the usual highway. Although many of them had enemy's property, on board, they were perfectly safe from molestation—the Confederate States' Government having adopted, as the reader has seen, in its Act declaring, that, by the conduct of the enemy, a state of war existed, the liberal principle, that "Free ships make free goods."

Among the neutrals overhauled by us, was an English brig called the *Spartan*, from Rio Janeiro, for St. Thomas, in the West Indies. We had an exciting chase after this fellow. We pursued him, under United States colors, and as the wind was blowing fresh, and the chase was a "stern-chase," it proved, as usual, to be a long one, although the *Sumter* was doing her best, under both steam and sail. John Bull evidently mistook us for the Yankee we pretended to be, and seemed determined to prevent us from overhauling him, if possible. His brig, as we soon discovered, had light heels, and he made the best possible use of them, by giving her every inch of canvas he could spread. Still, we gained on him, and as we came sufficiently near, we gave him a blank cartridge, to make him show his colors, and heave to. He showed his colors—the English red—but refused to heave to. The unprofessional reader may be informed, that when a merchant-ship is under full sail, and especially when she is running before a fresh breeze, as the *Spartan* was, it puts her to no little inconvenience, to come to the wind. She has to take in her sails, one by one, owing to her being short-handed, and "the clewing up," and "hauling down" occupy some minutes. The captain of the Spartan was loth to subject himself to this inconvenience, especially at the command of the hated Yankee. Coming up a little nearer, we now fired a shotted gun at him, taking care not to strike him, but throwing the shot so near as to give him the benefit of its rather ominous music, as it whistled past. As soon as the smoke from the gun, which obscured him for a moment, rolled away before the breeze, we could see him starting his "sheets," and "halliards," and pretty soon the saucy little *Spartan* rounded to, with her main top-sail to the mast. The reader may be curious to know, why I had been so persistent in heaving to a neutral. The answer is, that I was not sure she was neutral. The jaunty little brig looked rather more American, than English, in all but the flag that was flying at her peak. She had not only the grace and beauty of hull that characterize our American-built ships, but the long, tapering spars on which American ship-masters especially pride themselves. She did, indeed, prove to be American, in a certain sense, as we found her to hail from Halifax, in Nova Scotia. The master of the *Spartan* was in an ill-humor when my boarding-officer jumped on board of him. It was difficult to extract a civil answer from him. "What is the news?" said the boarding-officer. "Capital news!" replied the master; "you Yankees are getting whipped like h—ll; you beat the Derby boys at the Manassas races." "But what's the news from Rio?" now inquired the supposed Yankee boarding-officer. "Well, there's good news from that quarter too—all the Yankee ships are laid up, for want of freights." "You are rather hard upon us, my friend," now rejoined the boarding-officer; "why should you take such an interest in the Confederate cause?" "Simply, because there is a little man fighting against an overgrown bully, and I like pluck."

The *Spartan* being bound to St. Thomas, and we ourselves intending to go, soon, into the West Indies, it was highly important that we should preserve our *incognito*, to which end, I had charged the boarding-officer, to represent his ship as a Federal cruiser, in search of the *Sumter*. The boarding-officer having done this, found the master of the *Spartan* complimentary to the last; for as he was stepping over the brig's side, into his boat, the master said, "I hope you will find the *Sumter*, but I rather think you will hunt for her, as the man did for the tax-collector, hoping all the time he might n't find him."

The weather now, again, became calm, and we had "cat's-paws" from all the points of the compass. The breeze, with which we had chased the *Spartan*, was a mere spasmodic effort of Nature, for we were still in the calm-belt, or, as the sailors expressively call it, the "doldrums." For the next few days, it rained almost incessantly, the heavily charged clouds sometimes settling so low, as scarcely to sweep clear of our mastheads. It did not simply rain; the water fell in torrents, and the lightning flashed, and the thunder rolled, with a magnificence and grandeur that were truly wonderful to witness. In the intervals of these drenching rains, the clouds, like so many half-wrung sponges, would lift themselves, and move about with great rapidity, in every direction — now toward, and now from, each other — convolving, in the most curious disorder, as though they were so many huge, black serpents, writhing and twisting in the powerful grasp of some invisible hand. Anon, a water-spout would appear upon the scene, with its inverted cone, sometimes travelling rapidly, but more frequently at rest. At times, so ominous, and threatening would be the aspect of the heavens, with its armies of black clouds in battle-array, its forked lightning, and crashing thunder, the perfect stillness of the atmosphere, and the rapid flight of scared water-fowl, that a hurricane would seem imminent, until we would cast our eyes upon the barometer, standing unmoved, at near the marking of thirty inches, amid all the signs, and portents around it. In half an hour, sometimes, all this paraphernalia of clouds would break in twain, and retreat, in opposite directions, to the horizon, and the sun would throw down a flood of golden light, and scalding heat upon our decks ; on which would be paddling about the half-drowned sailors. The first lieutenant took advantage of these rains, to fill, anew, his water-tanks, " tenting " his awnings, during the heaviest of the showers, and catching more water than he needed ; and the sailors had another such jubilee of washing, as they had had, when we were running along the Venezuelan coast.

Sunday, September 29th. — Beautiful, clear morning, with a gentle breeze from the south-east, and a smooth sea. At eleven A. M., mustered the crew, and inspected the ship. Latitude, 6° 55′ N. ; longitude, 45° 08′ W. Evening set in, squally, and rainy. Running along to the north-west, under topsails.

October 2d. — This morning, when I took my seat, at the breakfast-table, I was surprised to find a very tempting-looking dish of fried fish set out before me, and upon inquiring of my faithful steward, John, (a Malayan, who had taken the place of Ned,) to what good fortune he was indebted, for the prize, his little black eyes twinkled, as he said, " Him jump aboard, last night ! " Upon further inquiry, I found that it was a small sword-fish, that had honored us with a visit ; the active little creature having leaped no less than fifteen feet, to reach the deck of the *Sumter.* It was lucky that its keen spear did not come in contact with any of the crew during the leap — a loss of life might have been the consequence. The full-grown sword-fish has been known to pierce a ship's bottom, floor-timber and all, with its most formidable weapon.

October 4th. — Weather clear, and beautiful, with trade-clouds, white and fleecy, and a light breeze from the eastward. The bosom of the gently heaving sea is scarcely ruffled. Schools of fish are playing around us, and the sailors have just hauled, on board, a large shark, which they have caught with hook and line. The sailor has a great antipathy to the shark, regarding him as his hereditary enemy. Accordingly, the monster receives no mercy when he falls into Jack's hands. See how Jack is tormenting him now! and how fiercely the monster is snapping, and grinding his teeth together, and beating the deck with his powerful tail, as though he would crush in the planks. He is tenacious of life, and will be a long time in dying, and, during all this time, Jack will be cutting, and slashing him, without mercy, with his long sheath-knife. The comparatively calm sea is covered, in every direction, for miles, with a golden or straw-colored dust. Whence comes it? We are four hundred miles from any land! It has, doubtless, been dropped by the trade-winds, as they have been neutralized over our heads, in this calm belt of the equator, and, in a future page, we shall have further occasion to refer to it. We have observed, to-day, in latitude 8°; the longitude being 46° 58'.

October 11th.—Morning clear and calm, after a couple of days of tempestuous weather, during which the barometer settled a little. Toward noon it clouded up again, and there were squally appearances in the south-east. The phenomenon of the tide-rips has reappeared. Malay John was in luck, again, this morning, a covey of flying-fish having fallen on the deck, last night, during the storm. He has served me a plate full of them for breakfast. The largest of them are about the size of a half-grown Potomac herring, and they are somewhat similar in taste — being a delicate, but not highly flavored fish.

October 14th.— At noon, to-day, we plotted precisely upon the diagonal between St. Roque and New York; our latitude being 8° 31', and longitude 45° 56'. We now made more sail,

and on the 17th of October we had reached the latitude of
11° 37′. From this time, until the 22d, we had a constant
series of bad weather, the barometer settling to 29.80, and the
wind blowing half a gale, most of the time. Sometimes the
wind would go all around the compass, and the weather
would change half a dozen times, in twenty-four hours. On
the last-mentioned day, the weather became again settled, and
being now in latitude 14°, we had passed out of the calm belt,
and began to receive the first breathings of the north-east
trade-wind.

On the 24th, we chased and hove to a French brig, called
La Mouche Noire, from Nantes, bound for Martinique. She
had been out forty-two days, had no newspapers on board, and
had no news to communicate. We boarded her under the
United States flag, and when the boarding-officer apologized
to the master for the trouble we had given him, in heaving him
to, in the exercise of our belligerent right of search, he said,
with an admirable *naiveté*, he had *heard* the United States were
at war, but he did not recollect with whom! Admirable
Frenchman! wonderful simplicity, to care nothing about newspapers, and to know nothing about wars!

On the 25th, we overhauled that *rara avis in mare*, a Prussian ship. The 27th was Sunday; we had a gentle breeze
from the north-east, with a smooth sea, and were enjoying the fine
morning, with our awnings spread, scarcely expecting to be
disturbed, when the cry of "Sail ho!" again rang from the
mast-head. We had been making preparations for Sunday
muster; Jack having already taken down from its hiding-
place his Sunday hat, and adjusted its ribbons, and now being
in the act of "overhauling" his bag, for the "mustering-shirt
and trousers." All these preparations were at once suspended, the firemen were ordered below, there was a passing to
and fro of engineers, and in a few minutes more the welcome
black smoke came pouring out of the *Sumter's* chimney.
Bounding away over the sea, we soon began to raise the strange
sail from the deck. She was a fore-and-aft schooner of that
peculiar model and rig already described as belonging to the
New Englander, and nobody else, and we felt certain, at once,
that we had flushed the enemy. The little craft was "close-

hauled," or, may be, she had the wind a point free, which was
her best point of sailing, had the whitest kind of cotton canvas, and carried very taunt gaff-topsails. We found her exceedingly fast, and came up with her very slowly. The chase
commenced at nine A. M., and it was three P. M. before we were
near enough to heave her to with the accustomed blank cartridge. At the report of our gun — the Confederate States flag
being at our peak — the little craft, which had probably been
in an agony of apprehension, for some hours past, saw that her
fate was sealed, and without further ado, put her helm down,
lowered her foresail, hauled down her flying-jib, drew her jib-
sheet over to windward — and was hove to; the stars and
stripes streaming out from her main-topmast head. Upon
being boarded, she proved to be the *Daniel Trowbridge*, of New
Haven, Connecticut, last from New York, and bound to Demerara, in British Guiana.

This was a most opportune capture for us, for the little craft
was laden with an assorted cargo of provisions, and our own
provisions had been nearly exhausted. With true Yankee
thrift, she had economized even the available space on her deck,
and had a number of sheep, geese, and pigs, on board, for the
Demerara market. Another sail being discovered, almost at
the moment of this capture, we hastily threw a prize crew on
board the *Trowbridge*, and directing her to follow us, sped off
in pursuit of the newly discovered sail. It was dark before
we came up with this second chase. She proved to be an
English brigantine, from Nova Scotia, for Demerara. We now
stood back to rejoin our prize, and banking our fires, and hoisting a light at the peak, the better to enable the prize to keep
sight of us, during the night, we lay to, until daylight. The
next day, and the day after, were busy days, on board the
Sumter, for we devoted both of them, to getting on board provisions, from the prize. The weather proved propitious, the
breeze being gentle, and the sea smooth. We hoisted out the
Tallapoosa — our launch — and employed her, and the quarter-
boats — the gig included, for war admits of little ceremony —
in transporting barrels, bales, boxes, and every other conceiv-
able kind of package, to the *Sumter*. The paymaster was in
ecstasy, for, upon examination, he found the *Trowbridge's* cargo

to be all that he could desire—the beef, pork, canvased hams, ship-bread, fancy crackers, cheese, flour, everything being of the very best quality. We were, indeed, under many obligations to our Connecticut friends. To get at the cargo, we were obliged to throw overboard many articles, that we had no use for, and treated old Ocean to a gayly painted fleet of Connecticut woodenware, buckets, foot-tubs, bath-tubs, wash-tubs, churns. We found the sheep, pigs, and poultry in excellent condition; and sending the butcher on board each evening, we caused those innocents to be slaughtered, in sufficient numbers to supply all hands. Jack was in his glory. He had passed suddenly, from mouldy and worm-eaten bread, and the toughest and leanest of "old horse," to the enjoyment of all these luxuries. My Malayan steward's eyes fairly danced, as he stowed away in the cabin lockers, sundry cans of preserved meats, lobster, milk, and fruits. John was a real artist, in his line, and knew the value of such things; and as he busied himself, arranging his luxuries, on the different shelves, I could hear him muttering to himself, "Dem Connecticut mans, bery good mans—me wish we find him often." We laid in, from the *Trowbridge*, full five months' provisions, and getting on board, from her, besides, as much of the live stock, as we could manage to take care of, we delivered her to the flames, on the morning of the 30th of October. On the same day, we chased, and boarded the Danish brig, *Una*, from Copenhagen, bound to Santa Cruz. Being sixty-six days out, she had no news to communicate. We showed her the United States colors, and when she arrived, at Santa Cruz, she reported that she had fallen in with a Federal cruiser. The brig *Spartan*, which we boarded, a few pages back, made the same report, at St. Thomas; so that the enemy's cruisers, that were in pursuit of us, had not, as yet, the least idea that we had returned to the West Indies.

For the next few days, we chased and overhauled a number of ships, but they were all neutral. The enemy's West India trade seemed to have disappeared almost entirely. Many of his ships had been laid up, in alarm, in his own ports, and a number of others had found it more to their advantage, to enter the public service, as transports. The Federal Government had already entered upon that career of corrupt, and reckless expenditure which has resulted in the most gigantic national debt of modern times. The entire value of a ship was often paid to her owners, for a charter-party, of a few months only; the quartermasters, commissaries, and other public swindlers frequently dividing the spoils, with the lucky ship-owners. Many indifferent vessels were sold to the Federal Navy Department, at double, and treble their value, and agencies to purchase such ships were conferred, by the Secretary, upon relatives, and other inexperienced favorites. The corruptions of the war, soon made the war popular, with the great mass of the people. As has been remarked, in a former page, many of these *nouveau-riche* men, whose love of country, and hatred of "rebels," boiled over, in proportion as their pockets became filled, had offered to sell themselves, and all they possessed, to the writer, when he was in the New England States, as a Confederate States agent. Powder-mills, manufactories of arms and accoutrements, foundries for the casting and boring of cannon, machines for rifling cannon—all were put at his disposal, by patriotic Yankees, on the very eve of the war—for a consideration.

November 2d.—Morning, heavy clouds, with rain, breaking away partially, toward noon, and giving us some fitful sunshine. Sail ho! at early dawn. Got up steam, and chased, and at 7 A. M. came up with, and sent a boat on board of the English brigantine, *Falcon*, from Halifax, for Barbadoes. Banked fires. Latitude 16° 32'; longtitude 56° 55'. Wore ship to the northward, at meridian. Received some newspapers, by the *Falcon*, from which we learn, that the enemy's cruiser *Keystone State*, which, when last heard from, was at Barbadoes, had gone to Trinidad, in pursuit of us. At Trinidad, she lost the trail, and, instead of pursuing us to Paramaribo, and Maranham, turned back to the westward. We learn from the same papers, that the enemy's steam-frigate, *Powhatan*, Lieutenant Porter, with more sagacity, pursued us to Maranham, arriving just one week after our departure. At a subsequent date, Lieutenant—now Admiral—Porter's official report fell into my hands, and, plotting his track, I found that, on one occasion, we had been within forty miles of each other; almost near enough, on a still day, to see each other's smoke.

November 3d.—Weather fine, with a smooth sea, and a light breeze from the north-east. A sail being reported from the mast-head, we got up steam, and chased, and upon coming near enough to make out the chase, found her to be a large steamer. We approached her, very warily, of course, until it was discovered that she was English, when we altered our course, and banked fires. Our live-stock still gives us fresh provisions, and the abundant supply of Irish potatoes, that we received on board, at the same time, is beginning to have a very beneficial effect, upon the health of the crew—some scorbutic symptoms having previously appeared.

Nov. 5th.—Weather fine, with the wind light from the eastward, and a smooth sea. At daylight, a sail was descried in the north-east, to which we immediately gave chase. Coming up with her, about nine A. M., we sent a boat on board of her. She proved to be the English brigantine, *Rothsay*, from Berbice, on the coast of Guiana, bound for Liverpool. Whilst we had been pursuing the *Rothsay*, a second sail had been reported. We now pursued this second sail, and, coming up with her, found her to be a French brigantine, called *Le Pauvre Orphelin*, from St. Pierre (in France) bound for Martinique. We had scarcely turned away from the *Orphelin*, before a third sail was announced. This latter sail was a large ship, standing, close-hauled, to the N. N. W., and we chased her rather reluctantly, as she led us away from our intended course. She, too, proved to be neutral, being the *Plover*, from Barbadoes, for London. The *Sumter* being, by this time out of breath, and no more sails being reported, we let the steam go down, and gave her a little rest. We observed, to-day, in latitude 17° 10′ N.; the longitude being 59° 06′ W. We had shown the United States colors to all these ships to preserve our *incognito*, as long as possible. We found them all impatient, at being "hove to," and no doubt many curses escaped, *sotto voce*, against the d—d Yankee, as our boats shoved off, from their sides. We observed that none of them saluted the venerable "old flag," which was flying at our peak, whereas, whenever we had shown the Confederate flag to neutrals, down went, at once, the neutral flag, in compliment—showing the estimate, which generous seamen, the world over, put upon this ruthless war, which the strong were waging against the weak.

The 6th of November passed without incident.   On the 7th, we overhauled three more neutral ships—the English schooner *Weymouth*, from Weymouth, in Nova Scotia, for Martinique; an English barque, which we refrained from boarding, as there was no mistaking her bluff English bows, and stump top-gallant masts; and a French brig, called the *Fleur de Bois*, last from Martinique, and bound for Bordeaux.   In the afternoon of the same day, we made the islands, first of Marie Galante, and then of Guadeloupe, and the Saints.   At ten P. M., we doubled the north end of the island of Dominica, and, banking our fires, ran off some thirty or forty miles to the south-west, to throw ourselves in the track of the enemy's vessels, homeward bound from the Windward Islands.   The next day, after overhauling an English brigantine, from Demerara, for Yarmouth, we got up steam, and ran for the island of Martinique approaching the town of St. Pierre near enough, by eight P. M., to hear the evening gun-fire.   A number of small schooners and sail-boats were plying along the coast, and as night threw her mantle over the scene, the twinkling lights of the town appeared, one by one, until there was quite an illumination, relieved by the sombre back-ground of the mountain. The *Sumter*, as was usual with her, when she had no work in hand, lay off and on, under sail, all night.   The next morning at daylight, we again got up steam, and drawing in with the coast, ran along down it, near enough to enjoy its beautiful scenery, with its waving palms, fields of sugar-cane, and picturesque country houses, until we reached the quiet little town of Fort de France, where we anchored.

CHAPTER XIX.

THE *Sumter* having sailed from Maranham, on the 15th of
September, and arrived at Martinique, on the 9th of November, had been nearly two months at sea, during all of which
time, she had been actively cruising in the track of the
enemy's commerce. She had overhauled a great many vessels,
but, for reasons already explained, most of these were neutral.
But the damage which she did the enemy's commerce, must
not be estimated by the amount of property actually destroyed.
She had caused consternation, and alarm among the enemy's
ship-masters, and they were making, as we have seen, long and
circuitous voyages, to avoid her. Insurance had risen to a
high rate, and, for want of freights, the enemy's ships — such
of them, at least, as could not purchase those lucrative contracts from the Government, of which I have spoken in a former page — were beginning to be tied up, at his wharves,
where they must rot, unless they could be sold, at a sacrifice,
to neutrals. As a consequence, the little *Sumter* was denounced,
without stint, by the Yankee press. She was called a "pirate,"
and other hard names, and the most summary vengeance was
denounced against her commander, and all who served under
him. Venal scribblers asserted all kinds of falsehoods concerning him, and the elegant pages of "Journals of Civiliza
tion" pandered to the taste of the "b'hoys," in the work-shops,
by publishing malicious caricatures of him. Even the Federal Government denounced him, in grave state papers; Mr.

Welles, the Federal Secretary of the Navy, forgetting his international law, if he ever knew any, and the courtesies, and proprieties of official speech, and taking up in his "annual reports," the refrain of "pirate." This was all very natural, however. Men will cry aloud, when they are in pain, and, on such occasions, above all others, they will be very apt to use the language that is most natural to them — be it gentle, or ungentle. Unfortunately for the Great Republic, political power has descended so low, that the public officer, however high his station, must, of necessity, be little better than the b'hoy, from whom he receives his power of attorney. When mobs rule, gentlemen must retire to private life. Accordingly, the Commander of the *Sumter*, who had witnessed the *facile descensus* of which he has spoken, was not at all surprised, when he received a batch of late Northern newspapers, at seeing himself called hard names — whether by the mob or officials. Knowing his late fellow-citizens well, he knew that it was of no use for them to

> "Strive to expel strong nature, 'tis in vain;
> With redoubled force, she will return again."

Immediately after anchoring, in Fort de France, I sent a lieutenant on shore, to call on the Governor, report our arrival, and ask for the usual hospitalities of the port,— these hospitalities being, as the reader is aware, such as Goldsmith described as welcoming him at his inn, the more cheerfully rendered, for being paid for. I directed my lieutenant to use rather the language of demand — courteously, of course — than of petition, for I had seen the French proclamation of neutrality, and knew that I was entitled, under the orders of the Emperor, to the same treatment, that a Federal cruiser might receive. I called, the next day, on the Governor myself. I found him a very affable, and agreeable gentleman. He was a rear admiral, in the French Navy, and bore the aristocratic name of Condé. Having observed a large supply of excellent coal in the government dock-yard, as I pulled in to the landing, I proposed to his Excellency that he should supply me from that source, upon my paying cost, and expenses. He declined doing this, but said that I might have free access to the market, for this and other supplies. Mentioning that I had a number of prisoners on board, he at once gave me permission to land them, provided the United States Consul, who lived at St. Pierre, the commercial metropolis of the island, would consent to become responsible for their maintenance during their stay in the island. There being no difference of opinion between the Governor and myself, as to our respective rights and duties, our business-matters were soon arranged, and an agreeable chat of half an hour ensued, on general topics, when I withdrew, much pleased with my visit.

Returning on board the *Sumter*, I dispatched the paymaster to St. Pierre — there was a small passenger-steamer plying between the two ports — to contract for coal and some articles of clothing for the crew. Of provisions we had plenty, as the reader has seen. Lieutenant Chapman accompanied him, and I sent up, also, the masters of the two captured ships, that were on board, that they might see their Consul and arrange for their release.

The next day was Sunday, and I went on shore, with **Mr.** Guerin, a French gentleman, who had been educated in the United States, and who had called on board to see me, to the Governor's mass. In this burning climate the church-hours are early, and we found ourselves comfortably seated in our pews as early as eight o'clock. The building was spacious and well ventilated. The Governor and his staff entered punctually at the hour, as did, also, a detachment of troops — the latter taking their stations, in double lines, in the main aisle. A military band gave us excellent sacred music from the choir. The whole service was concluded in three-quarters of an hour. The whites and blacks occupied pews promiscuously, as at Paramaribo, though there was no social admixture of races visible. 1 mean to say that the pews were mixed, though the people were not — each pew was all white or all black; the mulattoes, and others of mixed blood, being counted as blacks. I returned on board for "muster," which took place at the usual hour of eleven o'clock. Already the ship was full of visitors, and I was struck with the absorbed attention with which they witnessed the calling of the names of the crew, and the reading of the articles of war by the clerk. They were evidently not prepared for so interesting a spectacle. The officers were all dressed in bright and new uniforms of navy blue — we had not yet been put in gray, along with the army — the gorgeous epaulettes of the lieutenants flashing in the sun, and the midshipmen rejoicing in their gold-embroidered anchors and stars. The men attracted no less attention than the officers, with their lithe and active forms and bronzed countenances, heavy, well-kept beards, and whitest of duck frocks and trousers. One of my visitors, turning to me, after the muster was over, said, pleasantly, in allusion to the denunciations of us by the Yankee newspapers, which he had been reading, "*Ces hommes sont des pirates bien polis, Monsieur Capitaine.*"

In the afternoon, one watch of the crew was permitted to visit the shore, on liberty. To each seaman was given a sovereign, for pocket-money. They waked up the echoes of the quaint old town, drank dry all the grog-shops, fagged out the fiddlers, with the constant music that was demanded of them, and "turned up Jack" generally; coming off, the next morning, looking rather solemn and seedy, and not quite so *polis* as when the Frenchman had seen them the day before. The United States Consul having come down from St. Pierre to receive his imprisoned countrymen, himself, I caused them all — except three of them, who had signed articles for service on board the *Sumter* — to be parolled and sent on shore to him. Before landing them, I caused them to be mustered on the quarter-deck, and questioned them, in person, as to the treatment they had received on board — addressing myself, especially, to the two masters. They replied, without exception, that they had been well treated, and thanked me for my kindness. From the next batch of Northern newspapers I captured, I learned that some of these fellows had been telling wonderful stories, about the hardships they had endured on board the "pirate" *Sumter*. It will not be very difficult for the reader, if he have any knowledge of the sailor-character, to imagine how these falsehoods had been wheedled out of them. The whole country of the enemy was on the *qui vive* for excitement. The Yankee was more greedy for news than the old Athenian. The war had been a god-send for newspaperdom. The more extraordinary

were the stories that were told by the venal and corrupt newspapers, the more greedily were they devoured by the craving
and prurient multitude. The consequence was, a race between
the newspaper reporters after the sensational, without the least
regard to the truth. The moment a sailor landed, who had
been a prisoner on board the *Sumter*, he was surrounded by
these vampires of the press, who drank him and greenbacked
him until parturition was comparatively easy. The next morning, the cry of "NEWS FROM THE PIRATE SUMTER" rang
sharp and clear upon the streets, from the throats of the news-
boys, and Jack found himself a hero and in print! He had
actually been on board the "pirate," and escaped to tell the
tale! More drinks, and more greenbacks now followed from
his admiring countrymen. Your old salt has an eye to fun, as
well as drinks, and when it was noised about, among the sailors, that some cock-and-a-bull story or other, about the *Sumter*,
was as good as "fractional" for drinks, the thing ran like wild-
fire, and every sailor who landed, thereafter, from that famous
craft, made his way straight to a newspaper office, in quest of
a reporter, drinks, and greenbacks. Such is the stuff out of
which a good deal of the Yankee histories of the late war will
be made.

My paymaster, and lieutenant returned, in good time, from
St. Pierre, and reported that they had found an abundance of
excellent coal, at reasonable rates, in the market, but that the
Collector of the Customs had interposed, to prevent it from
being sold to them. Knowing that this officer had acted without authority, I addressed a note to the Governor, reminding
him of the conversation we had had the day before, and asking him for the necessary order to overrule the action of his
subordinate. My messenger brought back with him the following reply :—

FORT DE FRANCE, November 12, 1861.
TO THE CAPTAIN :—
  I have the honor to send you the enclosed letter, which I ask you
to hand to the Collector of Customs, at St. Pierre, in which I request him to permit you to embark freely, as much coal as you wish
to purchase, in the market. *   *   *
  With the expression of my highest regard for the Captain,
                              MAUSSION DE CONDÉ.

I remained a few days longer, at Fort de France, for the convenience of watering ship, from the public reservoir, and to enable the rest of my crew to have their run on 'shore. Unless Jack has his periodical frolic, he is very apt to become moody, and discontented; and my sailors had now been cooped up, in their ship, a couple of months. This giving of "liberty" to them is a little troublesome, to be sure, as some of them will come off drunk, and noisy, and others, overstaying their time, have to be hunted up, in the grog-shops, and other sailor haunts, and brought off by force. My men behaved tolerably well, on the present occasion. No complaint came to me from the shore, though a good many "bills," for "nights' lodgings," and "drinks," followed them on board. Poor Jack! how strong upon him is the thirst for drink! We had an illustration of this, whilst we were lying at Fort de France. It was about nine P. M., and I was below in my cabin, making preparations to retire. Presently, I heard a plunge into the water, a hail, and almost simultaneously, a·shot fired from one of the sentinels' rifles. The boatswain's-mate's whistle now sounded, as a boat "was called away," and a rapid shuffling of feet was heard overhead, as the boat was being lowered. Upon reaching the deck, I found that one of the firemen, who had come off from "liberty," a little tight, had jumped overboard, and, in defiance of the hail, and shot of the sentinel, struck out, lustily, for the shore. The moon was shining brightly, and an amusing scene now occurred. The boat was in hot pursuit, and soon came upon the swimmer; but the latter, who dived like a duck, had no notion of being taken. As the boat would come up with him, and "back all," for the purpose of picking him up, he would dive under her bottom, and presently would be seen, either abeam, or astern, "striking out," like a good fellow, again. By the time the boat could turn, and get headway once more, the swimmer would have some yards the start of her, and when she again came up with him, the same tactics would follow. The crew, hearing what was going on, had all turned out of their hammocks, and come on deck to witness the fun; and fun it really was for some minutes, as the doubling, and diving, and twisting, and turning went on—the boat now being sure she had him, and now sure she had n't. The fellow finally escaped, and probably a more chop-fallen boat's crew never returned alongside of a ship, than was the *Sumter's* that night. An officer was now sent on shore in pursuit of the fugitive. He had no difficulty in finding him. In half an hour after the performance of his clever feat, the fireman was lying — dead drunk — in one of the *cabarets*, in the sailor quarter of the town. He had had no intention of deserting, but had braved the sentinel's bullet, the shark — which abounds in these waters — and discipline — all for the sake of a glass of grog!

Our time was made remarkably pleasant, during our stay; the inhabitants showing us every mark of respect and politeness, and the officers of the garrison, and of a couple of small French vessels of war, in the port, extending to us the courtesies of their clubs, and mess-rooms. I declined all invitations, myself, but my officers frequently dined on shore; and on the evening before our departure, they returned the hospitalities of their friends, by an elegant supper in the wardroom, at which the festivities were kept up to a late hour. Riding, and breakfast-parties, in the country, were frequent, and bright eyes, peeping out of pretty French bonnets, shone benignantly upon my young "pirates." The war was frequently the topic of conversation, when such expressions as " *les barbares du Nord!* " would escape, not unmusically, from the prettiest of pouting lips. I passed several agreeable evenings, at the hospitable mansion of my friend, Mr. Guerin, the ladies of whose family were accomplished musicians. The sailor is, above all others of his sex, susceptible of female influences. The difference arises, naturally, out of his mode of life, which removes him so often, and so long, from the affections, and refinements of home. After roughing it, for months, upon the deep, in contact only with coarse male creatures, how delightful I found it to sink into a luxurious seat, by the side of a pretty woman, and listen to the sweet notes of her guitar, accompanied by the sweeter notes, still, of her voice, as she warbled, rather than sang some lay of the sea.

In these delightful tropical climates, night is turned into day. The sun, beating down his fierce rays upon heated walls and streets, drives all but the busy merchant and the laborer

in-doors during the day.   Windows are raised, blinds closed
and all the members of the household, not compelled to exer
tion, betake themselves to their *fauteuils*, and luxurious hammocks.   Dinner is partaken of at five or six o'clock, in the
afternoon.   When the sun goes down, and the shades of evening begin to fall, and the first gentle stirring of the trees and
shrubbery, by the land breeze begins to awaken the katydid,
and the myriads of other insects, which have been dozing in
the heat, the human world is also awakened.   The lazy beauty
now arises from her couch, and seeking her bath-room, and
tire-woman, begins to prepare for the *duties of the day*.   She is
coiffed, and arranged for conquest, and sallies forth to the *Place
d'Armes*, to listen to the music of the military bands, if there
be no other special entertainment on hand.   The *Place d'Armes*
of Fort de France is charmingly situated, on the very margin
of the bay, where, in the intervals of the music, or of the hum
of conversation, the ripple of the tide beats time, as it breaks
upon the smooth, pebbly beach.   Ships are anchored in front,
and far away to the left, rises a range of blue, and misty hills,
which are pointed out to the stranger, as the birth-place of the
Empress Josephine.   The statue of the Empress also adorns
the grounds, and the inhabitants are fond of referring to her
history.   I was quite surprised at the throng that the quiet
little town of Fort de France was capable of turning out, upon
the *Place d'Armes ;* and even more at the quality, than the
quantity of the throng.   What with military and naval officers, in their gay uniforms, the multitudes of well-dressed
men and women, the ecclesiastics in the habits of their several
orders, the flower-girls, the venders of fruits, sherbets, and ice-
creams—for the universal Yankee has invaded the colony
with his ice-ships—and the delightful music of the bands, it
would be difficult to find a more delightful place, in which to
while away an hour.

Whilst we were still at Fort de France, a rather startling
piece of intelligence reached us.   A vessel came in, from St.
Thomas, and brought the news, that the English mail-steamer,
Trent, had arrived there from Havana, and reported that Messrs.
Mason and Slidell had been forcibly taken out of her, by the
United States steamer, *San Jacinto,* Captain Wilkes.   A few

days afterward, I received a French newspaper, giving a detailed account of the affair. It was indeed a very extraordinary proceeding, and could not fail to attract much attention. I had known friend Wilkes, in former years, and gave him credit for more sagacity, than this act of his seemed to indicate. "A little learning is a dangerous thing," and the Federal Captain had read, it would seem, just enough of international law to get himself into trouble, instead of keeping himself out of it. He had read of "contraband persons," and of "enemy's despatches," and how it was prohibited to neutrals, to carry either; but he had failed to take notice of a very important distinction, to wit, that the neutral vessel, on the present occasion, was bound from one neutral port to another; and that, as between neutral ports, there is no such thing as contraband of war; for the simple reason that contraband of war is a person, or thing, going to, or from an enemy's country. I was glad to hear this news, of course. The Great Republic would have to stand up to its work, and Great Britain would be no less bound to demand a retraxit. If things came to a deadlock, we might have an ally, in the war, sooner than we expected. It would be a curious revolution of the wheel of fortune I thought, to have John Bull helping us to beat the Yankee, on a point — to wit, the right of self-government — on which we had helped the Yankee to beat Bull, less than a century before. I will ask the reader's permission, to dispose of this little quarrel between Bull and the Yankee, to avoid the necessity of again recurring to it; although at the expense of a slight anachronism.

When the news of Wilkes' exploit reached the United States, the b'hoys went into ecstasies. Such a shouting, and throwing up of caps had never been heard of before. The multitude, who were, of course, incapable of reasoning upon the act, only knew that England had been bearded and insulted; but that was enough. Their national antipathies, and their ridiculous self-conceit had both been pandered to. The newspapers were filled with laudatory editorials, and "plate," and "resolutions," were showered upon unfortunate friend Wilkes, without mercy. If he had been an American Nelson, returning from an American Nile, or Trafalgar, he could not have been received with more honor. State legislatures bowed down before him, and even the American Congress — the House of Representatives; the Senate had not quite lost its wits — gave him a vote of thanks. It was not, perhaps, so much to be wondered at, that the multitude should go mad, with joy, for multitudes, everywhere, are composed of unreasoning animals, but men, who should have known better, permitted themselves to be carried away by the popular hallucination. The Executive Government approved of Captain Wilkes' conduct — the Secretary of the Navy, whose insane hatred of England was quite remarkable, making haste to write the Captain a congratulatory letter. But an awful collapse was at hand. Mr. Seward, as though he already heard the ominous rumbling of the distant English thunder, which was, anon, to break over his head, in tones that would startle him, on the 30th of November — the outrage had been committed on the 7th, — wrote, as follows, to his faithful sentinel, at the Court of London, Mr. Charles Francis Adams.

"We have done nothing, on the subject, to anticipate the discussion, and we have not furnished you with any explanation. We adhere to that course now, because we think it more prudent, that the ground taken by the British Government should be first made known to us, here. It is proper, however, that you should know one fact, in the case, without indicating that we attach much importance to it, namely, that in the capture of Messrs. Mason and Slidell, on board a British vessel, Captain Wilkes having acted without any instructions from the Government, the subject is therefore free from the embarrassment, which might have resulted, if the act had been especially directed by us."

If no "explanation" had been thought of by Mr. Seward, up to this time, it was high time that he was getting one ready, for, on the same day, on which the above despatch was written, Lord John Russell, then charged with the duties of the foreign office, in England, under the administration of Lord Palmerston, wrote as follows, to Lord Lyons, his Minister at Washington:

"Her Majesty's Government, bearing in mind the friendly relations which have long subsisted between Great Britain, and the United States, are willing to believe, that the United States naval officer who committed the aggression, was not acting in compliance with any authority from his Government, or that, if he conceived himself to be so authorized, he greatly misunderstood the

instructions, which he had received. For the Government of the
United States must be fully aware, that the British Government
could not allow such an affront to the national honor, to pass without *full reparation*, and her Majesty's Government are unwilling
to believe that it could be the deliberate intention of the Government of the United States, unnecessarily to force into discussion,
between the two Governments, a question of so grave a character,
and with regard to which, the whole British nation would be sure
to entertain such unanimity of feeling. Her Majesty's Government,
therefore, trust that, when this matter shall have been brought
under the consideration of the Government of the United States,
that Government will, of its own accord, offer to the British Government such redress as alone, could satisfy the British nation,
namely, the liberation of the four gentlemen [the two Secretaries
of Legation were also captured], and their delivery to your lordship, in order that they may again be placed under British protection, and a suitable apology for the aggression, which has been
committed. Should these terms not be offered, by Mr. Seward,
you will propose them to him."

Mr. Seward had no notion of proposing any terms to Lord
Lyons. The shouts of the b'hoys had scarcely yet ceased to
ring in his ears, and it would be an awkward step to take.
Besides, he could have no terms to offer, for the Government
had, in fact, approved of Captain Wilkes' act, through its Secretary of the Navy. The back door, which Mr. Seward inti-
mated to Mr. Adams was open for retreat, when he told him,
that Captain Wilkes' act had not been *authorized* by the Government, was not *honorably* open, for the act had afterward
been *approved* by the Government, and this amounted to the
same thing. Later on the same day on which Earl Russell
wrote his despatch to Lord Lyons he added a postscript to it, as
follows:—

"In my previous despatch of this date, I have instructed you, by
command of her Majesty, to make certain demands of the Government of the United States. Should Mr. Seward ask for delay, in
order that this grave and painful matter should be deliberately considered, you will consent to a delay, *not exceeding seven days*. If,
at the end of that time, no answer is given, or if any other answer
is given, except that of a compliance with the demands of her
Majesty's Government, your lordship is instructed to leave Washington, with all the members of your legation, bringing with you
the archives of the legation, and to repair immediately to London.
If, however, you should be of opinion that the requirements of her

Majesty's Government are substantially complied with, you may report the facts to her Majesty's Government, for their consideration, and remain at your post, until you receive further orders."

This was indeed bringing matters to a focus. Mr. Seward was required to liberate the prisoners, and make an apology, and that *within seven days*. This was putting it rather offensively. It is bad enough to make a man apologize, especially, if he has been "blowing" a short while before, but to tell him that he must do it *at once*, that was, indeed, rubbing the humiliation in. And then, where was the Congress, and the Massachusetts legislature, and Mr. Secretary Welles, and all the "plate," and all the "resolutions"? Posterity will wonder, when it comes to read the elaborate, and lengthy despatch, which Mr. Seward prepared on this occasion, how it was possible for him to prepare it *in seven days*. But it will wonder still more, after having patiently waded through it, to find how little it contains. I cannot deny myself the pleasure of giving a few of its choicest paragraphs to the reader. Do not start! gentle reader, the paragraphs will be short; but short as they are, you shall have the *gist* of this seven days' labor, of the American diplomatist. David wrote *seven* penitential psalms. I wonder if Lord John Russell had a little fun in his eye, when he gave Mr. Seward just *seven* days for *his* penitential performance. But to the paragraphs. Mr. Seward is addressing himself, the reader will observe, to Lord Lyons. After stating the case, he proceeds: —

"Your lordship will now perceive, that the case before us, instead of presenting a merely flagrant act of violence, on the part of Captain Wilkes, as might well be inferred, from the incomplete statement of it, that went up to the British Government, was undertaken as a simple, legal, and customary belligerent proceeding, by Captain Wilkes, to arrest and capture a neutral vessel, engaged in carrying contraband of war, for the uses and benefit of the insurgents."

This point was so utterly untenable, that it is astonishing that Mr. Seward should have thought of defending it. If it were defensible, he ought not to have given up the prisoners, or made an apology; for the law is clear, that contraband of war may be seized, and *taken out of a neutral vessel*, on the high seas. It was not because contraband of war had been taken out of one of their vessels, that Great Britain demanded an apology, but because persons, and things, *not contraband of war*, under the circumstances under which they were found, had been taken out. If the *Trent* had been overhauled in the act of sailing from one of the Confederate ports, blockaded or not blockaded, with Messrs. Mason and Slidell, and their despatches on board, and the *San Jancinto* had taken them out of her, permitting the ship to proceed on her voyage, Great Britain would never have thought of complaining — waiving, for the sake of the present argument, the diplomatic character of the passengers. And why would she not have complained? Simply, because one of her ships had been found with contraband of war, on board, and the least penalty, namely, the seizure of the contraband, that the laws of war imposed upon her, had been exacted. But her ship the *Trent*, neither having sailed from, or being bound for a Confederate port, it matters not whom, or what she might have on board, the question of contraband could not arise, at all; for, as we have seen, it is of the essence of contraband, that the person, or thing should be going to, or from an enemy's port. Wilkes' act being utterly and entirely indefensible, the Federal Government should have saved its honor, the moment the affair came to its notice, by a frank disavowal of it. But, as we have seen, the b'hoys had shouted; Mr. Welles had spoken approvingly; Congress had resolved that their officer was deserving of thanks, and even Mr. Seward, himself, had gloried over the capture of "rebels," and "traitors;" the said "rebels," and "traitors" having frequently, in former years, snubbed, and humbled him in the Senate of the United States. Hence the indecent language, in which he now spoke of them. The reader, having seen that Mr. Seward justified Captain Wilkes' conduct, as a "simple, legal, and customary belligerent proceeding, to arrest and capture a neutral vessel engaged in carrying contraband of war, for the use and benefit of the insurgents," he will be curious to know, on what ground it was, that Mr. Seward based his apology. This ground was curious enough. It was, not that Captain Wilkes had gone too far, but that he had not gone far enough. If, said he, Captain Wilkes had taken the *Trent* into port, for adjudication, instead of letting her go, his justification would be complete, and there would be no apology to make. Adjudication presupposes something to adjudicate; but if there was no contraband of war, on board the *Trent*, what was there to adjudicate? The British Government did not complain, that the question had not been presented for adjudication to the proper prize tribunals, but that their vessel had been boarded, and outraged, without there being any grounds for adjudication, at all. If the *Trent* had been taken into port, a prize-court must have liberated the prisoners. It would then, if not before, have been apparent, that there was no ground for the seizure. The act still remaining to be atoned for, what was there to be gained, by sending the vessel in? It is not denied that, as a rule, neutrals are entitled to have their vessels, when captured, sent in for adjudication, but Mr. Seward knew, very well, that no question of this nature had arisen, between the British Government and himself, and he was only trifling with the common sense of mankind, when he endeavored to turn the issue in this direction.

One cannot help sympathizing with a diplomatist, who being required to eat a certain amount of dirt, gags at it, so painfully, and yet pretends, all the while, that he really likes it, as Mr. Seward does in the following paragraph : —

"I have not been unaware that, in examining this question, I have fallen into an argument, for what seems to be the British side of it, against my own country [what a deal of humiliation it would have saved his country, if he had fallen into this train of argument, before the dirt-pie had been presented to him]. But I am relieved from all embarrassment, on that subject. I had hardly fallen into that line of argument, when I discovered, that I was really defending and maintaining, not an exclusively British interest, but an old, honored, and cherished American cause, not upon British authorities, but upon principles that constitute a large portion of the distinctive policy, by which the United States have developed the resources of a continent, and thus becoming a considerable maritime power, have won the respect and confidence of many nations."

Like an adroit circus-man, the venerable Federal Secretary of State has now gotten upon the backs of two ponies. He continues : —

" These principles were laid down, for us, by James Madison, in 1804 ; when Secretary of State, in the administration of Thomas Jefferson, in instructions given to James Monroe, our minister to England."

These instructions had relation to the old dispute, between the two Governments, about the impressment of seamen from American ships, and were as follows : —

" Whenever property found in a neutral vessel is supposed to be liable, on any ground, to capture and condemnation, the rule in all cases, is, that the question shall not be decided by the captor, but be carried before a legal tribunal, where a regular trial may be had, and where the captor himself is liable for damages, for an abuse of his power. Can it be reasonable then, or just, that a belligerent commander, who is thus restricted, and thus responsible, in a case of mere property, of trivial amount, should be permitted, without recurring to any tribunal, whatever, to examine the crew of a neutral vessel, to decide the important question of their respective allegiances, and to carry that decision into execution, by forcing every individual, he may choose, into a service abhorrent to his feelings, cutting him off from his most tender connections, exposing his mind and person to the most humiliating discipline, and his life, itself, to the greatest danger. Reason, justice, and humanity unite in protesting against so extravagant a proceeding."

Mr. Seward after thus quoting, continues : —

" If I decide this case in favor of my own Government, I must disavow its most cherished principles, and reverse, and forever abandon its essential policy. The country cannot afford the sacrifice. If I maintain these principles, and adhere to that policy, I must surrender the case itself. It will be seen, therefore, that this Government could not deny the justice of the claim presented to us, in this respect, upon its merits. We are asked to do to the British nation, just what we have always insisted, all nations ought to do to us."

That is " coming down with the corn," now, handsomely, but in view of the antecedents of the question, and of the " seven days'" pressure under which Mr. Seward's despatch was written, one cannot help pitying Mr. Seward. We not only pity him, but he absolutely surprises us by the fertility of his imagination, in discovering any resemblance between the Madison precedent, and the case he had in hand. The British Government was not insisting that Mr. Seward should send the *Trent* in for adjudication. It did not mean that there should be any adjudication about the matter, except such as it had itself already passed upon the case. Had it not said to its minister, at Washington, "If, at the end of that time, no answer is given, or, *if any other answer* is given, *except that of a compliance with the demands of her Majesty's Government,* your lordship is instructed to leave Washington, &c."? To be logical, Mr. Seward should have said, "Our officer having made a mistake, by doing a right thing, in a wrong way, namely, by seizing contraband of war, on board a neutral ship, without sending the ship in, for adjudication, we will send the prisoners back to the *Trent,* if you will send the *Trent* into one of our ports for adjudication." But Mr. Seward knew better than to say any such thing, for the simple reason, that this was not the thing which was demanded of him, although he had written a lengthy despatch to prove that it was.

I was in Europe when Mr. Seward's despatch arrived there. Every one was astonished, both at the paper, and the act of humiliation performed by it. The act needed not to be humiliating. A great wrong had been done a neutral. It could be neither justified, nor palliated. A *statesman,* at the head of the Federal State Department, would have made haste to atone for it, before any demand for reparation could be made. To pander to a vitiated public taste, and gain a little temporary *eclat,* by appearing to beard the British lion, hoping that the lion would submit, in silence to the indignity, Mr. Seward committed one of those blunders which was equivalent to a great crime, since it humiliated an entire people, and put on record against them one of those damaging pages that historians cannot, if they would, forget. The following were the closing lines of this famous despatch:—

"The four persons in question are now held in military custody, at Fort Warren, in the State of Massachusetts. They will be cheerfully liberated. Your lordship will please indicate a time, and place, for receiving them."

When I read this paragraph, I experienced two sensations — one, of disappointment at the loss of an ally, with whose aid we would be sure to gain the independence for which we were struggling, and one, of mortification, that an American nation had been so greatly humbled, before an European Power; for though the Federal States were my enemies, as between them and foreign nations, I could not but feel something like family attachment. Whilst I would humble them, and whip them into a sense of justice and decent behavior, myself, I was loth to see strangers kick them, and themselves submit to the kicking.

So very one-sided was the question, which Mr. Seward had permitted himself to argue, with so much zeal, and so little discrimination, that all the principal nations of Europe rallied, as if by common consent, to the side of Great Britain. Russia, France, Spain, and other Powers, all took the same view of the case that Earl Russell had done, and made haste, through their respective ministers at Washington, so to express themselves. I will let France speak for them all. The reasons which influenced the action of the French Government are thus assigned:—

" The desire to contribute to prevent a conflict, perhaps imminent, between two Powers, for which the French Government is animated with sentiments equally friendly, and the duty to uphold, for the purpose of placing the right of its own flag under shelter from any attack, certain principles essential to the security of neutrals, have, after mature reflection, convinced it, that it could not, under the circumstances, remain entirely silent."

The French Minister for Foreign Affairs then goes on to examine the arguments which could be set up in defence of the Federal Captain, concluding as follows:—

"There remains, therefore, to invoke, in explanation of their capture, only the pretext that they were the bearers of official despatches from the enemy ; but this is the moment to recall a circumstance, that governs all this affair, and which renders the conduct of the American cruiser unjustifiable. The *Trent* was not destined to a point belonging to one of the belligerents. She was carrying to a neutral country her cargo and her passengers ; and moreover, it was in a neutral port that they were taken. The Cabinet at Washington could not, without striking a blow at principles, which all neutral nations are alike interested in holding in respect, nor without taking the attitude of contradiction to its own course, up to this time, give its approbation to the proceedings of the commander of the *San Jacinto*. In this state of things, it evidently should not, according to our views, hesitate about the determination to be taken."

The excuse which I have to offer to the reader, for permitting so much of my space to be occupied with this "affair," is, that it deeply interested every Confederate States naval officer, afloat at the time. I, myself, made several passages, in neutral vessels, between neutral ports, and might have been captured with as much propriety, even when passing from Dover to Calais, as Messrs. Mason and Slidell had been.

On the 13th of November, my water-tanks being full, and my crew having all returned from "liberty"—none of them having shown any disposition to desert—we got up steam, and proceeded to the town of St. Pierre, for the purpose of coaling; arriving at the early hour of 8 A. M., and anchoring at the man-of-war anchorage, south of the town. I immediately dispatched a lieutenant to call on the military commandant, accompanied by the paymaster, to make the necessary arrangements for coaling. St. Pierre was quite a different place, from the quiet old town we had left. A number of merchant-ships were anchored in the harbor, and there was quite an air of stir, and thrift, about the quays. Busy commerce was carrying on her exchanges, and with commerce there is always life. There were not so many idle people here, to be awakened from their noon-tide slumbers, by the katydid, as in Fort de France. A number of visitors came off, at once, to see us; rumor having preceded us, and blown the trumpet of our fame, much more than we deserved. Among the rest, there were several custom-house officers, but if these had any office of espionage to perform, they performed it, so delicately, as not to give offence. Indeed they took pains to explain to us, that they had only come on board out of civility, and as a mere matter of curiosity. I never permit myself to be out-done in politeness, and treated them with all consideration.

The Collector of the Customs gave prompt obedience to the Governor's despatch—commanding him not to throw any obstacle in the way of our coaling—by withdrawing the interdict of sale which he had put upon the coal-merchants; and the paymaster returning, after a short absence, with news that he had made satisfactory arrangements with the said merchants, the ship was warped up to the coal-depot, and some thirty tons of coal received, on board, the same afternoon. This was very satisfactory progress. We sent down the fore-yard, for repairs, and the engineer finding some good machinists on shore, with more facilities in the way of shop, and tools, than he had expected, took some of his own jobs, of which there are always more or less, in a steamer, on shore.

As the sun dipped his broad red disk into the sea, I landed with my clerk, and we took a delightful evening stroll, along one of the country roads, leading to the northern end of the island, and winding, occasionally, within a stone's throw of the beach. The air was soft, and filled with perfume, and we were much interested in inspecting the low-roofed and red-tiled country houses, and their half-naked inmates, of all colors, that presented themselves, from time to time, as we strolled on. We were here, as we had been in Maranham, objects of much curiosity, and the curiosity was evinced in the same way, respectfully. Wherever we stopped for water—for walking in this sultry climate produces constant thirst—the coolest "monkeys"—a sort of porous jug, or jar—and calabashes, were handed us, often accompanied by fruits and an invitation to be seated. Fields of sugar-cane stretched away on either hand, and an elaborate cultivation seemed everywhere to prevail. The island of Martinique is mountainous, and all mountainous countries are beautiful, where vegetation abounds. Within the tropics, when the soil is good, vegetation runs riot in very wantonness; and so it did here. The eye was constantly charmed with a great variety of shade and forest trees, of new and beautiful foliage, and with shrubs, and flowers, without number, ever forming new combinations, and new groups, as the road meandered now through a plane, and now through a rocky ravine, up whose precipitous sides a goat could scarcely clamber.

> " As the shades of eve came slowly down,
> The hills were clothed with deeper brown,"

and the twinkle of the lantern at the *Sumter's* peak denoting that her Captain was out of the ship, caught my eye, at one of the turnings of the road, and reminded me, that we had wandered far enough. We retraced our steps just in time to escape a shower, and sat down, upon our arrival on board, to the evening's repast, which John had prepared for us, with appetites much invigorated by the exercise. We found the market-place, situated near the ship, both upon landing and returning, filled with a curious throng, gazing eagerly upon the *Sumter*. This throng seemed never to abate during our stay — it was the first thing seen in the morning, and the last thing at night. The next morning, John brought me off a French newspaper; for St. Pierre is sufficiently large, and prosperous, to indulge in a tri-weekly. With true island marvel, a column was devoted to the *Sumter*, predicating of her, many curious exploits, and cunning devices by means of which she had escaped from the enemy, of which the little craft had never heard, and affirming, as a fact beyond dispute, that her Commander was a Frenchman, he having served, in former years, as a lieutenant on board of the French brig-of-war *Mercure!* I felt duly grateful for the compliment, for a compliment indeed it was, to be claimed as a Frenchman, *by* a Frenchman — the little foible of Gallic vanity considered.

CHAPTER XX.

MANY rumors were now afloat as to the prospective presence, at Martinique, of the enemy's ships of war. It
was known that the enemy's steam-sloop, *Iroquois*, Captain James S. Palmer, had been at the island of Trinidad,
on the second of the then current month of November, whence
she had returned to St. Thomas — this neutral island being
unscrupulously used by the enemy, as a regular naval station,
at which there was always at anchor one or more of his ships
of war, and where he had a coal-depot. St. Thomas was a free
port, and an important centre of trade, both for the West India
Islands and the Spanish Main, and had the advantage, besides,
of being a general rendezvous of the mail-steamers that plied
in those seas. One of these steamers, bound to St. Thomas,
had touched at Martinique, soon after the *Sumter's* arrival
there, and, as a matter of course, we might expect the presence
of the enemy very soon. I used every possible diligence to
avoid being blockaded by the enemy, and twenty-four hours
more would have enabled me to accomplish my purpose, but
the Fates would have it otherwise; for at about two P. M., on
the very next day after the delightful evening's stroll described in the last chapter, the *Iroquois* appeared off the north
end of the island. She had purposely approached the island
on the side opposite to that on which the town of St. Pierre
lies, the better to keep herself out of sight, until the last moment; and when she did come in sight, it was ludicrous to

witness her appearance. Her commander's idea seemingly
was, that the moment the *Sumter* caught sight of him, she
would, if he were recognized, immediately attempt to escape.
Hence it was necessary to surprise her; and to this end, he had
made some most ludicrous attempts to disguise his ship.   The
Danish colors were flying from his peak, his yards were hanging, some this way, some that, and his guns had all been run
in, and his ports closed.   But the finely proportioned, taunt,
saucy-looking *Iroquois*, looked no more like a merchant-ship,
for this disguise, than a gay Lothario would look like a saint,
by donning a cassock.   The very disguise only made the cheat
more apparent.   We caught sight of the enemy first.   He was
crawling slowly from behind the land, which had hidden him
from view, and we could see a number of curious human
forms, above his rail, bending eagerly in our direction.   The
quarter-deck, in particular, was filled with officers, and we were
near enough to see that some of these had telescopes in their
hands, with which they were scanning the shipping in the harbor.   We had a small Confederate States flag flying, and it was
amusing to witness the movements on board the *Iroquois*, the
moment this was discovered.   A rapid passing to and fro of
officers was observable, as if orders were being carried, in a
great hurry, and the steamer, which had been hitherto cautiously creeping along, as a stealthy tiger might be supposed
to skirt a jungle, in which he had scented, but not yet seen a
human victim, sprang forward under a full head of steam.   At
the same moment, down came the Danish and up went the
United States flag.   "There she comes, with a bone in her
mouth!" said the old quartermaster on the look-out; and, no
doubt, Captain Palmer thought to see, every moment, the little
Sumter flying from her anchors.   But the *Sumter* went on coaling, and receiving on board some rum and sugar, as though no
enemy were in sight, and at nine P. M. was ready for sea.   The
men were given their hammocks, as usual, and I turned in,
myself, at my usual hour, not dreaming that the *Iroquois* would
cut up such antics during the night as she did.

During the afternoon, she had run into the harbor,— without
anchoring, however,—and sent a boat on shore to communicate, probably, with her consul, and receive any intelligence

he might have to communicate. She then steamed off, seaward, a mile, or two, and moved to and fro, in front of the port until dark. At half-past one o'clock, the officer of the deck came down in great haste, to say, that the *Iroquois* had again entered the harbor, and was steaming directly for us. I ordered him to get the men immediately to their quarters, and followed him on deck, as soon as I could throw on a necessary garment or two. In a very few minutes, the battery had been cast loose, the decks lighted, and the other preparations usual for battle made. It was moonlight, and the movements of the enemy could be distinctly seen. He came along, under low steam, but, so steadily, and aiming so directly for us, that I could not doubt it was his intention to board us. The men were called to "repel boarders;" and for a moment or two, a pin might have been heard to drop, on the *Sumter's* deck, so silent was the harbor, and so still was the scene on board both ships. Presently, however, a couple of strokes on the enemy's steam gong were heard, and, in a moment more, he sheered a little, and lay off our quarter, motionless. It was as though a great sea-monster had crawled in under cover of the night, and was eying its prey, and licking its chops, in anticipation of a delicious repast. After a few minutes of apparent hesitation, and doubt, the gong was again struck, and the leviathan — for such the *Iroquois* appeared alongside the little *Sumter* — moving in a slow, and graceful curve, turned, and went back whence it came. This operation, much to my astonishment, was repeated several times during the night. Captain Palmer was evidently in great tribulation. He had found the hated "pirate" at last — so called by his own Secretary of the Navy, and by his own Secretary of State. Captain Wilkes had just set him a glorious example of a disregard of neutral rights; and the seven days' penitential psalms had not yet been ordered to be written. If a ship might be violated, why not territory? Besides, the press, the press! a rabid, and infuriate press was thundering in the ears of the luckless Federal Captain. Honors were before him, terrors behind him! But there loomed up, high above the *Sumter*, the mountains of the *French* island of Martinique. Nations, like individuals, sometimes know whom to kick — though they have occasionally to take the kicking back, as we have just seen. It might do, doubtless thought Captain Palmer, to kick some small power, but France! there was the rub. If the *Sumter* were only in Bahia, where the *Florida* afterward was, how easily and securely the kicking might be done? A gallant captain, with a heavy ship, might run into her, cut her down to the water's edge, fire into her crew, struggling in the water, killing, and wounding, and drowning a great many of them, and bear off his prize in triumph! And then, Mr. Seward, if he should be called upon, not by Brazil alone, but by the sentiment of all mankind, to make restitution of the ship, could he not have her run into, by *accident*, in Hampton Roads, and sunk ; and would not this be another feather in his diplomatic cap — Yankee feather though it might be? What is a diplomat fit for, unless he can be a little cunning, upon occasion? The b'hoys will shout for him, if history does not. The reader need no longer wonder at the "backing and filling" of the *Iroquois*, around the little *Sumter ;* or at the sleepless night passed by Captain Palmer.

The next morning, the Governor having heard of what had been done ; how the neutral waters of France had been violated by manœuvre and by menace, though the actual attack had been withheld, sent up from Fort de France the steamer-of-war *Acheron*, Captain Duchatel, with orders to Captain Palmer, either to anchor, if he desired to enter the harbor, or to withdraw beyond the marine league, if it was his object to blockade the *Sumter ;* annexing to his anchoring, if he should choose this alternative, the condition imposed by the laws of nations, of giving the *Sumter* twenty-four hours the start, in case she should desire to proceed to sea. Soon after the *Acheron* came to anchor, the *Iroquois* herself ran in and anchored. The French boat then communicated with her, when she immediately hove up her anchor again! She had committed herself to the twenty-four hours' rule the moment she dropped her anchor ; but being ignorant of the rule, she had not hesitated to get her anchor again, the moment that she was informed of it, and to claim that she was not bound by her mistake. I did not insist upon the point. The *Iroquois* now withdrew beyond the marine league, by day, but, by night, invariably crept in, a mile or two nearer, fearing that she might lose sight of me, and that I might thus be enabled to escape. She kept up a constant communication, too, with the shore, both by means of her own boats, and those from the shore, in violation of the restraints imposed upon her by the laws of nations—these laws requiring, that if she would communicate, she must anchor; when, of course, the twenty-four hours' rule would attach. I had written a letter to the Governor, informing him of the conduct of Captain Palmer, on the first night after his arrival, and claiming the neutral protection to which I was entitled. His Excellency having replied to this letter, through Captain Duchatel, in a manner but little satisfactory to me. I addressed him, through that officer, the following, in rejoinder:—

CONFEDERATE STATES STEAMER SUMTER,
ST. PIERRE, November 22, 1861.

SIR:—I have had the honor to receive your letter of yesterday, in which you communicate to me the views of the Governor of Martinique, relative to the protection of my right of asylum, in the waters of this island; and I regret to say, that those views do not appear to me to come up to the requirements of the international code. The Governor says, that "it does not enter into his intentions, to exercise toward the *Iroquois*, either by night, or by day, so active a *surveillance* as you [I] desire"; and you tell me, that I ought to have "confidence in the strict execution of a promise, made by a commander in the military marine of the American Union, so long as he has not shown to me the evidence that this engagement has not been scrupulously fulfilled." It would appear from these expressions, that the only protection I am to receive against the blockade of the enemy, is a simple promise exacted by you, from that enemy, that he will keep himself without the marine league, the Governor, in the meantime, exercising no watch, by night or by day, to see whether this promise is complied with. In addition to the violations of neutrality reported by me, yesterday, I have, this morning, to report, that one of my officers being on shore, in the northern environs of the town, last night, between eight and nine o'clock, saw two boats, each pulling eight oars, the men dressed in dark blue clothing, with the caps usually worn by the sailors of the Federal Navy, pulling quietly in toward the beach; and that he distinctly heard a conversation, in English, between them — one of them saying to the other, "Look Harry! there she is, I see her,"— in allusion, doubtless, to this ship. These boats are neither more nor less than scout, or sentinel boats, sent to watch the movements, within neutral waters, of their enemy. Now, with all due deference to his Excellency, I cannot see the difference between the violation of the neutrality of these waters, by the enemy's boats, and by his ship; and if no surveillance is to be exercised, either by night or by day, I am receiving very much such protection as the wolf would accord to the lamb.

It is an act of war for the enemy to approach me, with his boats, for the purpose of reconnoissance, or watch, and especially during the night, and I have the same right to demand that he keep his boats beyond the marine league, as that he keep his ship, at that distance. Nor am I willing to rely upon his promise, that he will not infringe my rights, in this particular. If France owes me protection, it is her duty to accord it to me, herself, and not remit me to the good faith, or bad faith, of my enemy; in other words, I respectfully suggest, that it is her *duty*, to exercise *surveillance* over her own waters, both "by night, and by day," when one belligerent is blockading another, in those waters. I have, therefore, respectfully to request, that you will keep a watch, by means of guard boats, at both points of the harbor, to prevent a repetition of the hostile act, which was committed against me last night;* or if you will not do this, that you will permit me to arm boats, and capture the enemy, when so approaching me. It would seem quite plain, either that I should be protected, or be permitted to protect myself. Further: it is in plain violation of neutrality for the enemy to be in daily communication with the shore, whether by means of his own boats, or boats from the shore. If he needs supplies, it is his duty to come in for them; and if he comes in, he must anchor; and if he anchors, he must accept the condition of remaining twenty-four hours after my departure. It is a mere subterfuge for him to remain in the offing, and supply himself with all he needs, besides reconnoitring, me closely, by means of his boats, and I protest against this act also. I trust you will excuse me, for having occupied so much of your time, by so lengthy a communication, but I deem it my duty to place myself right, upon the record, in this matter. I shall seize an early opportunity to sail from these waters, and if I shall be brought to a bloody conflict, with an enemy, of twice my force, by means of signals given to him, in the waters of France, either by his own boats, or others, I wish my Government to know, that I protested against the unfriendly ground assumed by the Governor of Martinique, that 'it does not enter into his intentions, to exercise toward the *Iroquois*, either by night, or by day, so active a surveillance as you [I] desire.'

Mr. Duchatel, *commanding H. I. F. M's steamer Acheron.*"

As the lawyers say, "I took nothing by my motion," with Governor Condé. The United States were strong at sea, and the Confederate States weak, and this difference was sufficient to insure the ruling against me of all but the plainest points, about which there could be no dispute, either of principle, or of fact. Whilst the Governor would probably have protected me, by force, if necessary, against an actual assault, by the *Iroquois*, he had not the moral courage to risk the ire of his master, by offending the Great Republic, on a point about which there could be any question.

The *Iroquois* was very much in earnest in endeavoring to capture me, and Captain Palmer spent many sleepless nights, and labored very zealously to accomplish his object; notwithstanding which, when my escape became known to his countrymen, he had all Yankeeland down on him. It was charged, among other things, by one indignant Yankee captain, that Palmer and myself had been school-mates, and that treachery had done the work. I must do my late opponent the justice to say, that he did all that vigilance and skill could do, and a great deal more, than the laws of war authorized him to do. He made a free use of the neutral territory, and of his own merchant-ships that were within its waters. He had left St. Thomas in a great hurry, upon getting news of the *Sumter*, without waiting to coal. In a day or two after his arrival at St. Pierre, he chartered a Yankee schooner, and sent her to St. Thomas, for a supply of coal; and taking virtual possession of another—a small lumber schooner, from Maine, that lay discharging her cargo, a short distance from the *Sumter*—he used her as a signal, and look-out ship. Sending his pilot on shore, he arranged with the Yankee master—one of your long, lean, slab-sided fellows, that looked like the planks he handled—a set of signals, by which the *Sumter* was to be circumvented.

The anchorage of St. Pierre is a wide, open bay, with an exit around half the points of the compass. The *Iroquois*, as she kept watch and ward over the *Sumter*, generally lay off the centre of this sheet of water. As the *Sumter* might run out either north of her, or south of her, it was highly important that the *Iroquois* should know, as promptly as possible, which of the passages the little craft intended to take. To this end, the signals were arranged. Certain lights were to be exhibited, in certain positions, on board the Yankee schooner, to indicate to her consort, that the *Sumter* was under way, and the course she was running. I knew nothing, positively, of this arrangement. I only knew that the pilot of the *Iroquois* had frequently been seen on board the Yankee. To the mind of a seaman, the rest followed, as a matter of course. I could not know what the precise signals were, but I knew what signals I should require to be made to me, if I were in Captain Palmer's place. As the sequel will prove, I judged correctly.

I now communicated my suspicions to the Governor, and requested him to have a guard stationed near the schooner, to prevent this contemplated breach of neutrality. But the Governor paid no more attention to this complaint, than to the others I had made. It was quite evident that I must expect to take care of myself, without the exercise of any *surveillance*, "by night or by day," by Monsieur Condé. This being the case, I bethought myself of turning the enemy's signals to my own account, and the reader will see, by and by, how this was accomplished.

In the meantime, the plot was thickening, and becoming very interesting, as well to the islanders, as to ourselves. Not only was the town agog, but the simple country people, having heard what was going on, and that a naval combat was expected, came in, in great numbers, to see the show. The crowd increased, daily, in the market-place, and it was wonderful to witness the patience of these people. They would come down to the beach, and gaze at us for hours, together, seeming never to grow weary of the sight. Two parties were formed, the *Sumter* party, and the *Iroquois* party; the former composed of the whites, with a small sprinkling of blacks; the latter of the blacks, with a small sprinkling of whites. The Governor, himself, came up from Fort de France, in a little sail-schooner of war, which he used as a yacht. The Mayor, and sundry councilmen, came off to see me, and talk over the crisis. The young men boarded me in scores, and volunteered to help me whip the *barbare*. I had no thought of fighting, but of running; but of course I did not tell *them* so —I should have lost the French nationality, they had conferred upon me.

The *Iroquois* had arrived, on the 14th of November. It was now the 23d, and I had waited all this time, for a dark night; the moon not only persisting in shining, but the stars looking, we thought, unusually bright. Venus was still three hours high, at sunset, and looked provokingly beautiful, and brilliant, shedding as much light as a miniature moon. To-night —the 23d—the moon would not rise until seven minutes past eleven, and this would be ample time, in which to escape, or be captured. I had some anxiety about the weather, however, independently of the phase of the moon, as in this climate of the gods, there is no such thing as a dark night, if the sky be clear. The morning of the 23d of November dawned provokingly clear. It clouded a little toward noon, but, long before sunset, the clouds had blown off, and the afternoon became as bright, and beautiful, as the most ardent lover of nature in her smiling moods, could desire. But time pressed, and it was absolutely necessary to be moving. Messengers had been sent hither, and thither, by the enemy, to hunt up a reinforcement of gun-boats, and if several of these should arrive, escape would be almost out of the question. Fortune had favored us, thus far, but we must now help ourselves. The *Iroquois* was not only twice as heavy as the *Sumter*, in men, and metal, as the reader has seen, but she had as much as two or three knots, the hour, the speed of her. We must escape, if at all, unseen of the enemy, and as the latter drew close in with the harbor, every night, in fraud of the promise he had made, and in violation of the laws of war, this would be difficult to do. Running all these reasons rapidly through my mind, I resolved to make the attempt, without further delay.

I gave orders to the first lieutenant, to see that every person belonging to the ship was on board, at sundown, and directed him to make all the necessary preparations for getting his anchor, and putting the ship under steam, at eight P. M.—the hour of gun-fire; the gun at the garrison to be the signal for moving. The ship was put in her best sailing trim, by removing some barrels of wet provisions aft, on the quarter-deck; useless spars were sent down from aloft, and the sails all "mended," that is, snugly furled. Every man was assigned his station, and the crew were all to be at quarters, a few minutes before the appointed hour of moving. I well recollect the *tout ensemble* of that scene. The waters of the bay were of glassy smoothness. The sun had gone down in a sky so clear, that there was not a cloud to make a bank of violets, or a golden pyramid of. Twilight had come and gone; the insects were in full chorus — we were lying within a hundred yards of the shore — and night, friendly, and at the same time unfriendly, had thrown no more than a semi-transparent mantle over the face of nature.

The market-place, as though it had some secret sympathy with what was to happen, was more densely thronged than ever, the hum of voices being quite audible. The muffled windlass on board the *Sumter* was quietly heaving up her anchor. It is already up, and the "cat hooked," and the men "walking away with the cat." The engineer is standing, lever in hand, ready to start the engine, and a seaman, with an uplifted axe, is standing near the taffarel, to cut the sternfast. One minute more and the gun will fire! Every one is listening eagerly for the sound. The *Iroquois* is quite visible, through our glasses, watching for the *Sumter*, like the spider for the fly. A flash! and the almost simultaneous boom of the eight o'clock gun, and, without one word being uttered on board the *Sumter*, the axe descends upon the fast, the engineer's lever is turned, and the ship bounds forward, under a full head of steam.

A prolonged, and deafening cheer at once arose from the assembled multitude, in the market-place. Skilful and trusty helmsmen, under the direction of the "master," bring the *Sumter's* head around to the south, where they hold it, so steadily, that she does not swerve a hair's breadth. There is not a light visible on board. The lantern in the captain's cabin has a jacket on it, and even the binnacle is screened, so that no one but the old quartermaster at the "con" can see the light, or the compass. The French steamer-of-war, *Acheron*, lay almost directly in our course, and, as we bounded past her, nearly grazing her guns, officers and men rushed to the side, and in momentary forgetfulness of their neutrality, waved hats and hands at us. As the reader may suppose, I had stationed a quick-sighted and active young officer, to look out for the signals, which I knew the Yankee schooner was to make. This young officer now came running aft to me, and said, "I see them, sir! I see them! — look, sir, there are two red lights, one

above the other, at the Yankee schooner's mast-head." Sure
enough, there were the lights; and I knew as well as the
exhibitor of them, what they meant to say to the *Iroquois*, viz. :
"Look out for the *Sumter*, she is under way, standing south!"

I ran a few hundred yards farther, on my present course,
and then stopped. The island of Martinique is mountainous,
and near the south end of the town, where I now was, the
mountains run abruptly into the sea, and cast quite a shadow
upon the waters, for some distance out. I had the advantage
of operating within this shadow. I now directed my glass
toward the *Iroquois*. I have said that Captain Palmer was
anxious to catch me, and judging by the speed which the *Iroquois* was now making, toward the south, in obedience to her
signals, his anxiety had not been at all abated by his patient
watching of nine days. I now did, what poor Reynard sometimes does, when he is hard pressed by the hounds—I doubled.
Whilst the *Iroquois* was driving, like mad, under all steam, for
the south, wondering, no doubt, at every step, what the d——l
had become of the *Sumter*, this little craft was doing her level-
best, for the north end of the island. It is safe to say, that,
the next morning, the two vessels were one hundred and fifty
miles apart! Poor Palmer! he, no doubt, looked haggard
and careworn, when his steward handed him his dressing-
gown, and called him for breakfast on the 24th of November;
the yell of Actæon's hounds must have sounded awfully distinct in his ears. I was duly thankful to the slab-sided lumberman, and to Governor Condé—the one for violating, and
the other for permitting the violation of the neutral waters of
France—the signals were of vast service to me.

Various little *contre-temps* occurred on board the *Sumter*, on
this night's run. We were obliged to stop some fifteen or twenty
precious minutes, opposite the very town, as we were retracing
our steps to the northward, to permit the engineer to cool the
bearings of his shaft, which had become heated by a little
eccentricity of movement. And poor D., a hitherto-favorite
quartermaster, lost his *prestige*, entirely, with the crew, on this
night. D. had been famous for his sharp sight. It was, indeed, wonderful. When nobody else in the ship could "make
out" a distant sail, D. was always sent aloft, glass in hand, to

tell us all about her. As a matter of course, when the question came to be discussed, as to who the look-out should be, on the occasion of running by the enemy, I thought of D. He was, accordingly, stationed on the forecastle, with the best night-glass in the ship. Poor D.! if he saw one *Iroquois*, that night, he must have seen fifty. Once, he reported her lying right "athwart our fore-foot," and I even stopped the engine, on his report, and went forward, myself, to look for her. She was nowhere to be seen. Now she was bearing down upon our bow, and now upon our quarter. I was obliged to degrade him, in the first ten minutes of the run; and, from that time, onward, he never heard the last of the *Iroquois*. The young foretop-men, in particular, whose duty it was to take the regular look-out aloft, and who had become jealous of his being sent up to their stations, so often, to make out sails, which they could give no account of, were never tired of poking fun at him, and asking him about the *Iroquois*.

The first half hour's run was a very anxious one for us, as the reader may suppose. We could not know, of course, at what moment the *Iroquois*, becoming sensible of her error, might retrace her steps. It was a marvel, indeed, that she had not seen us. Our chimney was vomiting forth dense volumes of black smoke, that ought to have betrayed us, even if our hull had been invisible. I was quite relieved, therefore, as I saw the lights of the town fading, gradually, in the distance, and no pursuer near; and when a friendly rain squall overtook us, and enveloping us in its folds, travelled along with us, for some distance, I felt assured that our run had been a success. Coming up with the south end of the island of Dominica, we hauled in for the coast, and ran along it, at a distance of four or five miles. It was now half-past eleven, and the moon had risen. The sea continued smooth, and nothing could exceed the beauty of that night-scene, as we ran along this picturesque coast. The chief feature of the landscape was its weird-like expression, and aspect of most profound repose. Mountain, hill, and valley lay slumbering in the moonlight; no living thing, except ourselves, and now and then, a coasting vessel close in with the land, that seemed also to be asleep, being seen. Even the town of Rousseau, whose white walls we could see shimmering in the moonlight, seemed more like a city of the dead, than of the living. Not a solitary light twinkled from a window. To add to the illusion, wreaths of mist lay upon the mountain-sides, and overhung the valleys, almost as white, and solemn looking as winding-sheets.

We came up with the north end of Dominica, at about two A. M., and a notable change now took place, in the weather. Dense, black clouds rolled up, from every direction, and amid the crashing, and rattling of thunder, and rapid, and blinding lightning, the rain began to fall in torrents. I desired to double the north end of the island, and to enable me to do this, I endeavored, in sea phrase, to "hold on to the land." The weather was so thick, and dark, at times, that we could scarcely see the length of the ship, and we were obliged often to slow down, and even stop the engine. For an hour or two, we literally groped our way, like a blind man; an occasional flash of lightning being our only guide. Presently the water began to whiten, and we were startled to find that we were running on shore, in Prince Rupert's Bay, instead of having doubled the end of the island, as we had supposed. We hauled out in a hurry. It was broad daylight, before we were through the passage, when we were struck by a strong northeaster, blowing almost a gale. I now drew aft the try-sail sheets, and heading the ship to the N. N. W., went below and turned in, after, as the reader has seen, an eventful night. The sailor has one advantage over the soldier. He has always a dry hammock, and a comfortable roof over his head; and the reader may imagine how I enjoyed both of these luxuries, as stripping off my wet clothing, I consigned my weary head to my pillow, and permitted myself to be sung to sleep by the lullaby chanted by the storm.

We learned from the Yankee papers, subsequently captured, that the *Dacotah*, one of the enemy's fast steam-sloops, of the class of the *Iroquois*, arrived at St. Pierre, the day after we "left"—time enough to condole with her consort, on the untoward event. In due time, Captain Palmer was deprived of his command—the Naval Department of the Federal Government obeying the insane clamors of the "unwashed," as often as heads were called for.

The day after our escape from Martinique was Sunday, and we made it, emphatically, a day of rest — even the Sunday muster being omitted, in consideration of the crew having been kept up nearly all the preceding night. I slept late, nothing having been seen to render it necessary to call me. When I came on deck, the weather still looked angry, with a dense bank of rain-clouds hanging over the islands we had left, and the stiff northeaster blowing as freshly as before. We were now running by the island of Deseada, distant about ten miles. At noon we observed in latitude 16° 12′, and, during the day, we showed the French colors to a French bark, running for Guadeloupe, and to a Swedish brig standing in for the islands. Being in the track of commerce, and the night being dark, we carried, for the first time, our side-lights, to guard against collision. It was a delightful sensation to breathe the free air of heaven, and to feel the roll of the sea once more; and as I sat that evening, in the midst of my officers, and smoked my accustomed cigar, I realized the sense of freedom, expressed by the poet, in the couplet,—

> " Far as the breeze can bear, the billow foam,
> Survey our empire, and behold our home!"

We had no occasion, here, to discuss jurisdictions, or talk about marine leagues; or be bothered by *Iroquois*, or bamboozled by French governors.

Monday, November 25th.— Morning clear, with trade-clouds and a fresh breeze. We are still holding on to our steam, and are pushing our way to the .eastward; my intention being to cross the Atlantic, and see what can be accomplished in European waters. We may be able to exchange the *Sumter* for a better ship. At seven, this morning, we gave chase to a Yankee-looking hermaphrodite brig. We showed her the United States colors, and were disappointed to see her hoist the English red in reply. In the afternoon, a large ship was descried running down in our direction. When she approached sufficiently near, we hoisted again the United States colors, and hove her to with a gun. As she rounded to the wind, in obedience to the signal, the stars and stripes were run up to her peak. The wind was blowing quite fresh, but the master and his papers were soon brought on board, when it appeared that our prize was the ship *Montmorency*, of Bath, Maine, from Newport, in Wales, and bound to St. Thomas, with a cargo of coal, for the English mail-steamers rendezvousing at that island. Her cargo being properly documented, as English property, we could not destroy her, but put her under a ransom bond, for her supposed value, and released her. We received on board from her, however, some cordage and paints; and Captain Brown was civil enough to send me on board, with his compliments, some bottles of port wine and a box of excellent cigars. The master and crew were parolled, not to serve against the Confederate States during the war, unless exchanged.

I began, now, to find that the Yankee masters, mates, and sailors rather liked being parolled; they would sometimes remind us of it, if they thought we were in danger of forgetting it. It saved them from being conscripted, unless the enemy was willing first to exchange them; and nothing went so hard with the enemy as to exchange a prisoner. With cold-blooded cruelty, the enemy had already counted his chances of success, as based upon the relative numbers of the two combatants, and found that, by killing a given number of our prisoners by long confinement—the same number of his being killed by us, by the same process—he could beat us! In pursuance of this diabolical policy, he threw every possible difficulty in the way of exchanges, and toward the latter part of the war put a stop to them nearly entirely. Our prisons were crowded with his captured soldiers. We were hard pressed for provisions, and found it difficult to feed them, and we were even destitute of medicines and hospital stores, owing to the barbarous nature of the war that was being made upon us. Not even a bottle of quinine or an ounce of calomel was allowed to cross the border, if the enemy could prevent it. With a full knowledge of these facts, he permitted his soldiers to sigh and weep away their lives in a hopeless captivity—coolly "calculating," that one Confederate life was worth, when weighed in the balance of final success, from three to four of the lives of his own men!

The enemy, since the war, has become alarmed at the atrocity of his conduct, and at the judgment which posterity will be likely to pass upon it, and has set himself at work, to falsify history, with his usual disregard of truth. Committees have been raised, in the Federal Congress, composed of unscrupulous partisans, whose sole object it was, to prepare the false material, with which to mislead the future historian. Perjured witnesses have been brought before these committees, and their testimony recorded as truth. To show the partisan nature of these committees, when it was moved by some member—Northern member, of course, for there are no Southern members, at this present writing, in the Rump Parliament—to extend the inquiry, so as to embrace the treatment of Southern prisoners, in Northern prisons, the amendment was rejected! It was not the truth, but falsehood that was wanted. Fortunately for the Southern people, there is one little record which it is impossible to obliterate. *More men perished in Northern prisons, where food and medicines were abundant, than in Southern prisons, where they were deficient — and this, too, though the South held the greater number of prisoners. See report of Secretary Stanton.*

CHAPTER XXI.

THE SUMTER PURSUES HER VOYAGE ACROSS THE AT-
LANTIC — CAPTURE AND BURNING OF THE ARCADE,
VIGILANT, AND EBENEZER DODGE — A LEAKY SHIP,
AND A GALE — AN ALARM OF FIRE.

THE morning of the 26th of November dawned clear, with
the wind more moderate, and a smoother sea. A ship of
war being seen to windward, running down in our direction,
we beat to quarters, and hoisted the U. S. colors. She was a
heavy ship, but being a sailing vessel, we had nothing to fear,
even if she should prove to be an enemy. Indeed, it would have
been only sport for us, to fall in with one of the enemy's old time
sailing-frigates. Our agile little steamer, with her single long-
range gun, could have knocked her into pie, as the printers
say, before the majestic old thing could turn round. It was
in the morning watch, when holystones and sand, and scrub-
bing-brushes and soap were the order of the hour, and we
surprised the stranger, consequently, in her morning disha-
bille, for her rigging was filled with scrubbed hammocks, and
a number of well-filled clothes-lines were stretched between
her main and mizzen shrouds. She proved to be Spanish; and
was steering apparently for the island of Cuba. We observed
to-day in latitude 20° 7′; the longitude, as told by our faithful chronometer, being 57° 12′.

By the way, one of my amusements, now, was to wind and
compare a number of chronometers, daily. The nautical instruments were almost the only things, except provisions, and
clothing for the crew, that we could remove from our prizes.
I never permitted any other species of property to be brought
on board. We had no room for it, and could not have disposed
of it, except by violating the laws of neutral nations, and converting our ship into a trader; neither one of which comported
with the duties which I had in hand, viz., the rapid destruc-

tion of the enemy's commerce. I should have had no objection to receiving, on deposit, for safe keeping, any funds that I might have found on board the said prizes, but the beggarly Yankee masters never carried any. A few hundred dollars for ship's expenses was all that was ever found, and sometimes not even this—the master having, generally, an order on his consignee, for what moneys he might need. I sometimes captured these orders, and a stray bill of exchange for a small amount, but of course I could make no use of them. The steamship has not only revolutionized commerce, and war, but exchanges. Long before the arrival of the tardy sailing-ship, at her destined port, with her ponderous cargo, the nimble mail-steamer deposits a duplicate of her invoice, and bill of lading, with the merchant to whom she is consigned; and when the ship has landed her cargo, the same, or another steamer, takes back a bill of exchange, for the payment of the freight.

The masters of my prizes frequently remonstrated against my capturing their chronometers; in some instances claiming them as their own individual property. When they would talk to me about private property, I would ask to whom their ships belonged—whether to a private person, or the Government? They at once saw the drift of the question, and there was an end of the argument. I was making war upon the enemy's commerce—and especially upon the ship, the vehicle of commerce, and the means and appliances by which she was navigated. If her chronometers, sextants, telescopes, and charts were left in possession of the master, they would be transferred to, and used in the navigation of some other ship. The fact that these instruments belonged to other parties, than the ship-owners, could not make the least difference—ship and instruments were all private property, alike, and alike subject to capture. Silly newspaper editors have published a good deal of nonsense, mixed with a good deal of malice, on this subject. It is only their nonsense that I propose to correct—their abuse was something to be expected under the circumstances. Being dependent upon the patronage of ship-owners and ship-masters, for the prosperity of their papers, abuse of the *Sumter*, during the war, came as naturally to them, as whittling a stick.

No prisoner of mine was ever disturbed in the possession of his strictly personal effects. Under this head were included his watch, and his jewelry, as well as his wardrobe. Every boarding-officer had orders to respect these, nor do I believe that the orders were ever violated. I will not detain the reader to contrast this conduct, with the shameful house-burnings, robberies, and pilferings, by both officers and men, that accompanied the march of the enemy's armies, through the Southern States. It would be well for human nature, if the record made by these men, lost to every sense of manliness and shame, could be obliterated; but as the wicked deeds of men live after them, our common history, and our common race will long have to bear the disgrace of their acts.

Soon after passing the Spanish ship, sail ho! was cried from the mast-head, in a sharp, energetic voice, as though the look-out had, this time, scented real game. The chase was one of those well-known schooners, twice before described in these pages, as being unmistakable—hence the energy that had been thrown into the voice of the look-out. She soon came in sight from the deck, when we gave chase. In a couple of hours we had come up with, and hove her to, with a gun. She proved to be the *Arcade*, from Portland, Me., with a load of staves, bound to Guadeloupe, where she intended to exchange her staves for rum and sugar. The owner of the staves had not thought it worth while to certify, that his property was neutral, and so we had no difficulty with the papers. We had not made much of a prize. The little craft was sailed too economically to afford us even a spare barrel of provisions. The number of mouths on board were few, and the rations had been carefully adjusted to the mouths. And so, having nothing to transfer to the *Sumter*, except the master and crew, we applied the torch to her, in a very few minutes. The staves being well seasoned, she made a beautiful bonfire, and lighted us over the seas, some hours after dark.

During the night, the wind lulled, and became variable, and we hauled down the fore and aft sails, and brought the ship's head to the north-east. The prize had no newspapers on board, but we learned from the master, that the great naval expedition, which the enemy had been sometime in preparing, and about which there had been no little mystery, had at last struck at Port Royal, in South Carolina. An immense fleet of ships of war, with thirty-three transports, and an army of 15,000 men, had been sent to capture a couple of mud forts, armed with 24 and 32-pounders, and garrisoned with three or four hundred raw troops. Our next batch of newspapers from New York, brought us the despatches of Commodore Dupont, the commander of this expedition, exceeding in volume any-thing that Nelson or Collingwood had ever written. Plates, and diagrams showed how the approaches had been buoyed, and the order of battle was described, with minute prolixity. I cannot forbear giving to the reader, the names of the ships, that participated in this great naval victory, with their loss in killed and wounded, after an engagement that lasted four mor-tal hours. The ships were the *Wabash*, the *Susquehanna*, the *Mohican*, the *Seminole*, the *Pawnee*, the *Unadilla*, the *Ottawa*, the *Pembina*, the *Isaac Smith*, the *Bienville*, the *Seneca*, the *Curlew*, the *Penguin*, the *Augusta*, the *R. B. Forbes*, the *Poca-hontas*, the *Mercury*, the *Vandalia*, and the *Vixen*—total 19. The killed were 8—not quite half a man apiece; and the seri-ously wounded 6!

November 27th.—Morning thick, with heavy clouds and rain, clearing as the day advanced. Afternoon clear, bright weather, with a deep blue sea, and the trade-wind blowing half a gale from the north-east. At six P. M., put all sail on the ship, and let the steam go down. We had already consumed half our fuel, and it became necessary to make the rest of our way to Europe under sail. Our boilers had been leaking for several days, and the engineer availed himself of the opportunity to repair them. The weather is sensibly changing in tempera-ture. We are in latitude 22° 22′, and the thermometer has gone down to 78°—for the first time, in five months. We have crossed, to-day, the track of the homeward-bound ships, both from the Cape of Good Hope, and Cape Horn, but have seen no sail. We cannot delay to cruise in this track, as we have barely water enough, on board, to last us across the Atlantic.

November 28th.—Weather changeable, and squally—wind frequently shifting during the day, giving indications of ou approach to the northern limit of the trade-wind, crossing which we shall pass into the variables.

November 29th.— Thick, ugly weather — this term ugly being very expressive in the seaman's vocabulary.   The wind is veering, as before, blowing half a gale, all the time, and a cold rain is pouring down, at intervals, causing the sailors to haul on their woollen jackets, and hunt up their long-neglected sou'westers.   We observed in latitude 25° 51′ to-day; the longitude being 57° 36′.

November 30th.— The morning has dawned bright, and beautiful, with a perfectly clear sky.   The boisterous wind of yesterday has disappeared, and we have nearly a calm — the sea wearing its darkest tint of azure.   We are, in fact, in the calm-belt of Cancer, and having no fuel to spare, we must be content to creep through it under sail, as best we may.   A sail has been reported from aloft.   It is a long way off, and we forbear to chase.

December 1st.— Another beautiful, bright, morning, with a glassy sea, and a calm.   This being the first of the month, the sailors are drawing their clothing, and "small stores" from the paymaster, under the supervision of the officers of the different divisions.   The paymaster's steward is the shopman, on the occasion, and he is "serving" a jacket to one, a shirt to another, and a pair of shoes to a third.   His assortment is quite varied, for besides the requisite clothing, he has tobacco, and pepper, and mustard; needles, thimbles, tape, thread, and spool-cotton; ribbons, buttons, jack-knives, &c.   Jack is not allowed to indulge in all these luxuries, *ad lib.*   He is like a school-boy, under the care of his preceptor; he must have his wants approved by the officer of the division to which he belongs. To enable this officer to act understandingly, Jack spreads out his wardrobe before him, every month.   If he is deficient a shirt, or a pair of trousers, he is permitted to draw them; if he has plenty, and still desires more, his extravagance is checked. These articles are all charged to him, at cost, with the addition of a small percentage, to save the Government from loss. When the monthly requisitions are all complete, they are taken to the Captain, for his approval, who occasionally runs his pencil through a *third,* or a *fourth* pound of tobacco, when an inveterate old chewer, or smoker is using the weed to excess; he rarely interferes in other respects. On the present occasion, woollen garments are in demand; Jack, with a prudent forethought, preparing himself for the approaching change in the climate. Much of the clothing, which the sailor wears, is made up with his own hands. He is entirely independent of the other sex, in this respect, and soon becomes very expert with the needle.

The 3d of December brought us another prize. The wind was light from the south-east, and the stranger was standing in our direction. This was fortunate, as we might hope to capture him by stratagem, without the use of steam. The *Sumter*, when not under steam, and with her smoke-stack lowered, might be taken for a clumsy-looking bark. Throwing a spare sail over the lowered smoke-stack, to prevent it from betraying us, we hoisted the French flag, and stood on our course, apparently unconscious of the approaching stranger. We were running free, with the starboard studding-sails set, and when the stranger, who, by this time, had hoisted the United States colors, crossed our bows, we suddenly took in all the studding-sails, braced sharp up, tacked, and fired a gun, at the same moment. The stranger at once hauled up his courses, and backed his main-topsail. He was already under our guns. The clumsy appearance of the *Sumter*, and the French flag had deceived him. The prize proved to be the *Vigilant*, a fine new ship, from Bath, Maine, bound to the guano island of Sombrero, in the West Indies; some New Yorkers having made a lodgment on this barren little island, and being then engaged in working it for certain phosphates of lime, which they called mineral guano. We captured a rifled 9-pounder gun, with a supply of fixed ammunition, on board the *Vigilant*, and some small arms. We fired the ship at three P. M., and made sail on our course. The most welcome part of this capture was a large batch of New York newspapers, as late as the 21st of November. The Yankees of that ilk had heard of the blockade of the "Pirate *Sumter*," by the *Iroquois*, but they had n't heard of Captain Palmer's rueful breakfast on the morning of the 24th of November.

These papers brought us a graphic description of the gallant ram exploit, of Commodore Hollins, of the Confederate Navy, at the mouth of the Mississippi, on the 12th of October. This exploit is remarkable as being the first practical application of the iron-clad ram to the purposes of war. Some ingenious steamboat-men, in New Orleans, with the consent of the Navy Department, had converted the hull of a steam-tug into an iron-clad, by means of bars of railroad iron fastened to the hull of the boat, and to a frame-work above the deck fitted to receive them; a stout iron prow being secured to the bow of the boat, several feet below the water-line. In this curious nondescript, which the enemy likened to a smoking mud-turtle, the gallant Commodore assaulted the enemy's fleet, lying at the old anchorage of the *Sumter*, at the "Head of the Passes," consisting of the *Richmond, Vincennes, Preble,* and *Water Witch.* The assault was made at four o'clock in the morning, and caused great consternation and alarm among the enemy. The *Richmond*, lying higher up the Pass than the other ships, was first assaulted — some of her planks being started, below the water-line, by the concussion of the ram, though the blow was broken by a coal-schooner, which, fortunately for her, was lying alongside. As the ram drew off, a broadside of the *Richmond's* guns was fired into her, without effect. After this harmless broadside, the ships all got under way, in great haste, and fled down the Pass, the ram pursuing them, but Hollins was unable, from the effect of the current, and the speed of the fleeing ships, to get another blow at them. The *Richmond* and the *Vincennes* grounded, for a short time, on the bar, in their hurry to get out, but the former was soon got afloat again. In the confusion and panic of the moment, the *Vincennes* was abandoned by her captain, who left a slow match burning. Commodore Hollins, finding that nothing more could be accomplished, threw a few shells at the alarmed fleet, and withdrew. The *Vincennes*, not blowing up, and the enemy recovering from his panic, her captain was ordered to return to her, and she was finally saved with the rest of the fleet. This little experiment was the *avant courier* of a great change, in naval warfare — especially for harbor and coast defence. The enemy, with his abundant resources, greatly improved upon it, and his "monitor" system was the result.

December 4th.—Weather clear, and becoming cool — thermometer, 76°. We have run some 140 miles to the eastward, during the last twenty-four hours, under sail, and as we are dragging our propeller through the water, I need not tell the reader what a smacking breeze we have had. It is delightful to be making so much easting, under sail, after having been buffeted so spitefully, by the east wind, for the last five months, whenever we have turned our head in that direction. Ten of the crew of the *Vigilant* are blacks, and as our ship is leaking so badly that the constant pumping is fagging to the crew, I have set the blacks at the pumps, with their own consent. The fact is, some of these fellows, who are runaway slaves, have already recognized "master," and whenever I pass them, grin pleasantly, and show the whites of their eyes. They are agreeably disappointed, that they are not "drawn, hung, and quartered," and rather enjoy the change to the *Sumter,* where they have plenty of time to bask in the sun, and the greasiest of pork and beans without stint. In arranging the *Vigilant's* crew into messes, a white bean and a black bean have been placed, side by side, at the mess-cloth, my first lieutenant naturally concluding, that the white sailors of the Yankee ship would like to be near their colored brethren. Cæsar and Pompey, having an eye to fun, enjoy this arrangement hugely, and my own crew are not a little amused, as the boatswain pipes to dinner, to see the gravity with which the darkies take their seats by the side of their white comrades. This was the only mark of "citizenship," however, which I bestowed upon these sons of Ham. I never regarded them as prisoners of war—always discharging them, when the other prisoners were discharged, without putting them under parole.

December 5th.—Weather thick and ugly — the wind hauling to the north, and blowing very fresh for a while. Reefed the topsails. At noon, the weather was so thick, that no observations could be had for fixing the position of the ship — latitude, by dead reckoning, 30° 19′; longitude 53° 02′. During the afternoon and night, it blew a gale from N. E. to E. N. E. Furled the mainsail, and set the reefed trysail instead; and the wind still increasing, before morning we hauled up and furled the foresail. For the next two or three days, we had a series of easterly gales, compelling me to run somewhat farther north than I had intended. We carried very short sail, and most of the time we were shut down below—that is, such of the crew as were not on watch—with tarpaulin-covered hatches, and a cold, driving rain falling almost incessantly. What with the howling of the gale, as it tears through the rigging, the rolling and pitching of the ship, in the confused, irregular sea, and the jog, jog, jog of the pumps, through half the night, I have had but little rest.

December 8th.—This is an anniversary with me. On this day, fifteen years ago, the United States brig-of-war *Somers*, of which I was the commander, was capsized and sunk, off Vera Cruz, having half her crew, of 120 officers and men, drowned. It occurred during the Mexican war. I was left alone to blockade the port of Vera Cruz—Commodore Connor, the commander of the squadron, having gone with his other ships on an expedition to Tampico. There being every appearance of a norther on that eventful morning, I was still at my anchors, under *Isla Verde*, or Green Island, where I had sought refuge the preceding night. Suddenly a sail was reported, running down the northern coast, as though she would force the blockade. It would never do to permit this; and so the little *Somers*—these ten-gun brigs were called coffins in that day—was gotten under way, and under her topsails and courses, commenced beating up the coast, to intercept the stranger. I had gone below, for a moment, when the officer of the deck, coming to the companion-way, called to me, and said that "the water looked black and roughened ahead, as though more wind than usual was coming." I sprang upon deck, and saw, at the first glance, that a norther was upon us. I immediately ordered everything clewed down and brailed up, but before the order could be executed, the gale came sweeping on with the fury of a whirlwind, and in less time than I have been describing the event, the little craft was thrown on her beam-ends, her masts and sails lying flat upon the surface of the sea, and the water pouring in at every hatchway and scuttle. I clambered to the weather side of the ship, and seeing that she must go down in a few minutes, set my first lieutenant at work to extricate the only boat that was available—the weather-quarter boat, all the others being submerged — from her fastenings, to save as much life as possible. This was fortunately done, and the boat being put in charge of a midshipman, the non-combatant officers, as the surgeon and paymaster; the midshipmen, and such of the boys of the ship as could not swim, were permitted to get into her. So perfect was the discipline, though death, within the next ten minutes, stared every man in the face, that there was no rush for this boat. A large man was even ordered out of her, to make room for two lads, who could not swim, and he obeyed the order as a matter of course! This boat having shoved off from the sinking ship, the order was given, "Every man save himself, who can!" whereupon there was a simultaneous plunge into the now raging sea, of a hundred men and more, each struggling for his life. The ship sank out of sight in a moment afterward. We were in twenty fathoms of water. Divesting myself of all my clothing, except my shirt and drawers, I plunged into the sea with the rest, and, being a good swimmer, struck out for and reached a piece of grating, which had floated away from the ship as she went down. Swimming along, with one arm resting on this grating, I felt one of my feet touch something, and, at the same moment, heard a voice exclaiming, "It is I, Captain; it is Parker, the second lieutenant — give me a part of your grating, I am a good swimmer, and we shall get along the better together." I, accordingly, shared my grating with Parker, and we both struck out, manfully, for the shore, distant no more than about a mile; but, unfortunately, the now raging gale was sweeping down parallel with the coast, and we were compelled to swim at right angles with the waves and the wind, if we would save ourselves; for once swept past the coast of the island, and the open sea lay before us, whence there was no rescue!

As we would rise upon the top of a wave, and get a view of the "promised land," the reader may imagine how anxious our consultations were, as to whether we were gaining, or losing ground! In the meantime, the boat, which had shoved off from the ship, as described, had reached the island, half-swamped, and discharging her passengers, and freeing herself from water as soon as possible, pushed out again into the raging caldron of waters, under the gallant midshipman, who had charge of her, in the endeavor to rescue some of the drowning crew. She came, by the merest accident, upon Parker and myself! We were hauled into her more dead than alive, and after she had picked up two, or three others — all that could now be seen — she again returned to the shore. My first lieutenant, Mr. G. L. Claiborne, was saved, as by a miracle, being dashed on shore — he having struck out, in the opposite direction, for the mainland — between two ledges of rock, separated only by a span of sand beach. If he had been driven upon the rocks, instead of the beach, he must have been instantly dashed in pieces. The reader will, perhaps, pardon me, for having remembered these eventful scenes of my life, as I wrote in my journal, on board the leaky little *Sumter*, amid the howling of another gale, *the "eighth day of December."*

On *this* eighth day of December, 1861, however, the record is very different, it being as follows: "At ten A. M. descried a sail from the deck, startlingly close to; so thick has been the weather. The stranger being a bark, taunt-rigged, with sky-sail poles, and under top-sails, we mistook him at first for a cruiser, and raised our smoke-stack, and started the fires in the furnaces. Having done this, we approached him somewhat cautiously, keeping the weather-gauge of him, and showed him the United States colors. He soon hoisted the same. Getting a nearer view of him, we now discovered him to be a whaler. The engineer at once discontinued his "firing up," and the smoke-stack was again lowered, to its accustomed place. Upon being boarded, the bark proved to be the *Eben. Dodge*, twelve days out, from New Bedford, and bound on a whaling voyage to the Pacific Ocean. She had experienced a heavy gale, had sprung some of her spars, and was leaking badly — hence the easy sail she had been under. Although the sea was still very rough, and the weather lowering, we got on board from the prize, some water, and provisions, clothing, and small stores. The supply of pea-jackets, whalers' boots, and flannel over-shirts, which our paymaster had been unable to procure in the West Indies, was particularly acceptable to us, battling, as we now were, with the gales of the North Atlantic, in the month of December. We brought away from her, also, two of her fine whale-boats, so valuable in rough weather; making room for them on deck, by the side of the *Sumter's* launch. The crew of the *Dodge*, consisting of twenty-two persons, made a considerable addition to our small community. We fired the prize at half-past six, P. M., as the shades of evening were closing in, and made sail on our course. The flames burned red and lurid in the murky atmosphere, like some Jack-o'-lantern; now appearing, and now disappearing, as the doomed ship rose upon the top, or descended into the abyss of the waves.

Having now forty-three prisoners on board, and there never being, at one time, so many of the *Sumter's* crew on watch, it became necessary for me to think of precautions. It would be easy for forty-three courageous men, to rise upon a smaller number, sleeping carelessly about the decks, and wrest from them the command of the ship. Hitherto I had given the prisoners the run of the ship, putting no more restrictions upon them, than upon my own men, but this could no longer be. I therefore directed my first lieutenant to put one-half of the prisoners in single irons—that is, with manacles on the wrists only—alternately, for twenty-four hours at a time. The prisoners, themselves, seeing the necessity of this precaution, submitted cheerfully to the restraint—for as such only they viewed it—and not as an indignity.

We received another supply of late newspapers, by the *Dodge*. They were still filled with jubilations over Dupont's great naval victory. We learned, too, that New England had been keeping, with more than usual piety and pomp, the great National festival of "Thanksgiving," which the Puritan has substituted for the Christian Christmas. The pulpit thundered war and glory, the press dilated upon the wealth and resources of the Universal Yankee *Nation*, and hecatombs of fat pigs and turkeys fed the hungry multitudes—pulpit, press, pig, and turkey, all thanking God, that the Puritan is "not like unto other men."

December 10th.—The weather remains still unsettled. The wind, during the last five or six days, has gone twice around the compass, never stopping in the west, but lingering in the east. The barometer has been in a constant state of fluctuation, and there will, doubtless, be a grand climax before the atmosphere regains its equilibrium. These easterly winds are retarding our passage very much, and taxing our patience. Observed, to-day, in latitude 32° 39'; the longitude being 49° 57'.

The next day, the weather culminated, sure enough, in a gale. The barometer began to settle, in the morning watch, and dense black clouds, looking ragged and windy, soon obscured the sun, and spread an ominous pall over the entire heavens. I at once put the ship under easy sail; that is to say, clewed up everything but the topsails and trysails, and awaited the further progress of the storm. The wind was as yet light, but the barometer, which had stood at 29° 70' at eight o'clock, had fallen to 29° 59' by two P. M. The dense canopy of clouds now settled lower and lower, circumscribing more and more our horizon, and presently fitful gusts of wind would strike the sails, pressing the ship over a little. It was time to reef. All hands were turned up, and the close reefs were taken, both in topsails and trysails; the jib hauled down and stowed, and the top-gallant yards sent down from aloft. The squalls increasing in frequency and force, the gale became fully developed by three P. M. The wind, which we first took from about E. S. E., backed to the N. E., but did not remain long in that quarter, returning to east. It now began to blow furiously from this latter quarter, the squalls being accompanied by a driving, blinding rain; the barometer going down, ominously down, all the while.

As the night closed in, an awful scene presented itself. The aspect of the heavens was terrific. The black clouds overhead were advancing and retreating like squadrons of opposing armies, whilst loud peals of thunder, and blinding flashes of lightning that would now and then run down the conductor, and hiss as they leaped into the sea, added to the elemental strife. A streaming scud, which you could almost touch with your hand, was meanwhile hurrying past, screeching and screaming, like so many demons, as it rushed through the rigging. The sea was mountainous, and would now and then strike the little *Sumter* with such force as to make her tremble in every fibre of her frame. I had remained on deck during most of the first watch, looking anxiously on, to see what sort of weather we were going to make. The ship behaved nobly, but I had no confidence in her strength. Her upper works, in particular, were very defective. Her bends, above the main deck, were composed of light pine stanchions and inch plank, somewhat strengthened in the bows. Seeing the fury of the gale, and that the barometer was still settling, I went below about midnight, and turned in to get a little rest, with many misgivings. I had scarcely fallen into an uneasy slumber, when an old quartermaster, looking himself like the demon of the storm, with his dishevelled hair and beard dripping water, and his eyes blinking in the light of his lantern, shook my cot, and said, "We've stove in the starboard bow-port, sir, and the gun-deck is all afloat with water!" Here was what I had feared; unless we could keep the water out of the between-decks, all the upper works, and the masts along with them, would be gone in a trice. I hurried at once to the scene of disaster, but before I could reach it, my energetic and skilful first lieutenant had already, by the aid of some planks and spare spars, erected a barricade that would be likely to answer our purpose.

The gale lulled somewhat in an hour or two afterward, and I now got some sleep. I was on deck again, however, at daylight. The same thick gloom overspread the heavens, the scud was flying as furiously, and as low as before, and the gale was raging as fiercely as ever. But we had one great comfort, and that was *daylight*. We could see the ship and the heavens — there was nothing else visible — and this alone divested the gale of half its terrors. At last, at six A.M., the barometer reached its lowest point, 29.32, which, in the latitude we were in, was a very low barometer. Any one who has watched a barometer under similar circumstances, will understand the satisfaction with which I saw the little tell-tale begin to rise. It whispered to me as intelligibly as if it had been a living thing, "the gale is broken!" We had been lying to, all this time, under a close-reefed main-topsail. We now bore up under a reefed foresail, and kept the ship on her course, east by south. She scudded as beautifully as she had lain to, darting ahead like an arrow, on the tops of the huge waves that followed her like so many hungry wolves, and shaking the foam and spray from her bows, as if in disdain and contempt of the lately howling storm.

December 13*th.*—Weather clear, with passing clouds. Wind
fresh from the south-west, but abating, with a rapidly rising
barometer. The cyclone, for such evidently the late gale was,
had a diameter of from three hundred and fifty to four hundred miles. We took it in its northern hemisphere—the
gale travelling north. Hence it passed over us in nearly its
entire diameter—the vortex at no great distance from us.
Observed in latitude 33° 28′; the longitude being 47° 03′.
Repairing damages. The ship leaks so badly as to require to
be pumped out twice in each watch. During the heaviest of
the gale, the masters and mates of the captured ships offered
their services, like gallant men, to assist in taking care of the
ship. We thanked them, but were sufficiently strong-handed
ourselves.

December 14*th.*—We had an alarm of fire on the berth deck
last night. The fire-bell, sounded suddenly in a sleeping city,
has a startling effect upon the aroused sleepers, but he who
has not heard it, can have no conception of the knell-like
sound of the cry of fire! shouted from the lungs of an alarmed
sailor on board a ship, hundreds of miles away from any land.
It is the suddenness with which the idea of danger presents
itself, quite as much as the extent of the danger, which intimi-
dates. Hence the panics which often ensue, when a ship is
discovered to be on fire. Ships of war, as a rule, are not the
subjects of panics. Discipline keeps all the passions and
emotions under control, as well those which arise from fear, as
from lawlessness. We had no panic on board the *Sumter*,
although appearances were sufficiently alarming for a few
moments. A smoke was suddenly seen arising through one
of the ventilators forward, in the dead hour of the night, when
except the sentry's lantern and the lamp in the binnacle,
there should be no other fire in the ship. The midshipman
of the watch, upon rushing below, found one of the prisoners'
mattresses on fire. The flames were soon smothered, and the
whole danger was over before the ship's crew were fairly
aroused. Some prisoner, in violation of orders, had lighted
his pipe for a smoke, after hours, and probably gone to sleep
with it in his mouth. The prisoner could not be identified,
but there were two sentinels on post, and these in due time
paid the penalty of their neglect.

CHAPTER XXII.

VOYAGE ACROSS THE ATLANTIC PURSUED — CHRISTMAS-
DAY ON BOARD THE SUMTER — CAPE FLY-AWAY, AND
THE CURIOUS ILLUSION PRODUCED BY IT — THE SUM-
TER PASSES FROM THE DESERT PARTS OF THE SEA,
INTO A TRACT OF COMMERCE ONCE MORE — BOARDS A
LARGE FLEET OF SHIPS IN ONE DAY, BUT FINDS NO
ENEMY AMONG THEM — ARRIVAL AT CADIZ.

THE punishment administered to the two delinquent sentinels mentioned in the last chapter, had the most salutary
effect. Seamen are very much like children, requiring the
reins to be tightened upon them from time to time. I made
it a rule on board the *Sumter,* that punishment should follow
the offence, with *promptitude,* and *certainty,* rather than severity; and this excellent rule had already performed marvels, in
the matter of disciplining my ship.

Sunday, December 15th.—A fine bright morning, with a
moderate breeze from the north-west, and the weather just
cool enough to be delightfully bracing. We mustered the
crew this morning, and read the articles of war for the first
time in three weeks, owing to the bad weather. I did not
inspect the ship below, according to custom, the sea being still
rough, and the water ankle-deep on the gun-deck in consequence. Our new prisoners always looked upon the muster
ceremonies on board the *Sumter,* with curiosity, as though
they were surprised to find so much order and discipline, and
so much attention to dress and ceremony, on board the "pirate" of which they had read, and whose "cut" they had so
often admired, in their truth-loving and truth-telling newspapers. The latitude, to-day, is 34°, and the longitude 42° 05′.

We were quite surprised to find so much bad weather in

the parallel, on which we were crossing the Atlantic. I had purposely chosen this parallel, that my little cock-boat of a ship might not be knocked in pieces, by the storms of the North Atlantic, and yet the reader has seen how roughly we have been handled. Nor were the fates more propitious for the next few days. Gale followed gale, with angry skies, and cloud and rain; there sometimes being lightning around the entire horizon, with now rolling, now crashing thunder. I had intended when I left the West Indies to touch at Fayal, in the Azores, for coal and water, but I found these islands so guarded and defended, by the Genius of the storm, that it would require several days of patience and toil, to enable me to reach an anchorage in one of them. I therefore determined to pass them, and haul up for the southern coast of Spain, running finally into Cadiz.

Christmas day was passed by us on the lonely sea, in as doleful a manner as can well be conceived. The weather is thus described in my journal. "Thermometer 63°; barometer 29.80. Heavy rain squalls — weather dirty, with lightning all around the horizon, indicating a change of wind at any moment. Under short sail during the night." The only other record of the day was that we "spliced the main brace;" that is, gave Jack an extra glass of grog. Groups of idle sailors lay about the decks, "overhauling a range of their memories;" how they had spent the last Christmas-day, in some "Wapping," or "Wide Water street," with the brimming goblet in hand, and the merry music of the dance sounding in their ears. Nor were the memories of the officers idle. They clasped in fancy their loved ones, now sad and lonely, to their bosoms once more, and listened to the prattle of the little ones they had left behind. Not the least curious of the changes that had taken place since the last Christmas day, was the change in their own official positions. They were, most of them, on that day, afloat under the "old flag." That flag now looked to them strange and foreign. They had some of their own countrymen on board; not, as of yore, as welcome visitors, but as prisoners. These, too, wore a changed aspect — enemy, instead of friend, being written upon their faces. The two "rival nations," spoken of by De Tocqueville, stood face to face. Nature is

stronger than man. She will not permit her laws to be violated with impunity, and if this war does not separate these
two nations, other wars will. If we succeed in preserving the
principle of State sovereignty — the only principle which can
save this whole country, North and South, from utter wreck
and ruin — all will be well, whatever combinations of particular States may be made, from time to time. The States
being free, liberty will be saved, and they will gravitate naturally, like unto like — the Puritan clinging to the Puritan, and
the Cavalier to the Cavalier. But if this principle be overthrown, if the mad idea be carried out, that all the American
people must be moulded into a common mass, and form one
consolidated government, under the rule of a *majority* — for no
constitution will then restrain them — Constitutional liberty
will disappear, and no man can predict the future — except in
so far, that it is impossible for the Puritan, and the Cavalier to
live together in peace.

On the next day, we witnessed a curious natural illusion.
The look-out called land ho! from the mast-head. The officer
of the watch saw the land at the same time from the deck, and
sent a midshipman below to inform me that we had made "high
land, right ahead." I came at once upon deck, and there, sure
enough, was the land — a beautiful island, with its blue mountains, its plains, its wood-lands, its coast, all perfect. It was
afternoon. The weather had been stormy, but had partially
cleared. The sun was near his setting, and threw his departing rays full upon the newly discovered island, hanging over
it, as a symbol that, for a time, there was to be a truce with
the storm, a magnificent rainbow. So beautiful was the scene,
and so perfect the illusion — there being no land within a
couple of hundred miles of us — that all the crew had come on
deck to witness it; and there was not one of them who would
not have bet a month's pay that what he looked upon was a
reality.

The chief engineer was standing by me looking upon the
supposed landscape, with perfect rapture. Lowering the telescope through which I had been viewing it, I said to him,
"You see, now, Mr. F., how often men are deceived. You
would no doubt swear that that is land." "Why should I not,

sir?" said he. "Simply," rejoined I, "because it is Cape Fly-away." He turned and looked at me with astonishment, as though I were quizzing him, and said, "You surely do not mean to say, Captain, that that is not land; it is not possible that one's senses can be so much deceived." "Like yourself, I should have sworn it was land, if I did not know, from the position of the ship, that there is no land within a couple of hundred miles of us." Reaching out his hand for my glass, I gave it to him, and as he viewed the island through it, I was much amused at his ejaculations of admiration, now at this beauty, and now at that. "Why," said he, "there is the very coast, sand beach and all, with beautiful bays and indentations, as though inviting the *Sumter* to run in and anchor." As the sun sank lower and lower, withdrawing now one ray, and now another, first the rainbow began to disappear, and then the lower strata of the island to grow a little gray, and then the upper, until, as the sun dipped, the whole gorgeous fabric, of mountain, woodland, plain, and coast, was converted into a leaden-colored cloud-bank. The engineer handing me my glass, said, "Captain, I will be a cautious witness hereafter, in a court of justice, when I am questioned as to a fact, which has only been revealed to me through a single sense." "I see," I replied, "that you are becoming a philosopher. Many meta-physicians have maintained that all nature is a mere phantas-magoria, so far as our senses are capable of informing us."

For the last two weeks, we had been crossing a desert tract of the ocean, where a sail is seldom seen. We now began to approach one of the beaten highways, over which a constant stream of travel is passing — the road leading from the vari-ous ports of Europe to the equator and the coast of Brazil, and thence east and west, as may be the destination of the way-farer.

December 28th. — A fine, bright day, with the wind light from the south-west. At daylight, "Sail ho!" came ringing from the mast-head. The sail crossing our bows, we took in our studding-sails, hauled up south-east, to intercept her, and got up steam. Our latitude being 35° 17′, and longitude 20° 53′, we were within striking distance of Cadiz or Gibral-tar, and could afford now to use a little steam. The chase did

not reward us, however, as she proved to be English — being
the ship *Richibucto*, from Liverpool, for Vera Cruz, laden with
salt.   We received from her some English newspapers, which
gave us several items of interesting intelligence.   All England
was in mourning for the death of Prince Albert.   The *Trent*
affair was causing great excitement, and the Confederate States
steamer *Nashville*, Captain Pegram, had arrived at Southampton, having burned a large Yankee ship, the *Harvey Birch*.
This ship having been burned in the English Channel, much
attention was attracted to the act; especially as the ship was
tea-laden, and supposed to be worth near half a million of
dollars.

The next day was rainy, with a light wind from the south-
east.   Only two sails were seen, and to neither of them did we
give chase; but on the morning of the 30th of December, we
fell in with a perfect stream of ships.   "Sail ho!" was shouted
at daylight from the mast-head, and repeated at short intervals,
until as many as twenty-five were reported.   We at once got
up steam, and commenced chasing; but though we chased
diligently, one ship after another, from eight o'clock in the
morning until four in the afternoon, we did not overhaul a
single ship of the enemy!   We actually boarded sixteen sail,
a number of others showing us their colors.   The ships
boarded were of the following nationalities: — Four Dutch,
seven English, two French, one Swedish, one Prussian, one
Hamburg.   Here was quite a representation of the nations of
Europe, and I amused myself taking the vote of these ships,
according to our American fashion, upon the war.   Their sentiments were elicited as follows: — I would first show them the
United States colors, pretending to be a Federal cruiser; I
would then haul down these colors, and show them the Confederate flag.   The result was that but one ship — the Prussian — saluted the United States flag, and that all the other
ships, with one or two exceptions, saluted the Confederate States
flag.   We were then beating the enemy, and the nations of the
earth were worshipping success.

So large a fleet of ships — not being a convoy — so far out
at sea, was quite a curiosity, and may serve to show the landsman how accurately we have mapped out, upon the ocean, the

principal highways of commerce. There were no mile-posts on the road these ships were travelling, it is true, but the road was none the less "blazed" out, for all that—the blazes being on the wind and current charts. The night succeeding this busy day set in cloudy and ugly, with a fresh breeze blowing from the eastward; and so continuous was the stream of ships, all sailing in the contrary direction from ourselves, that we had serious apprehensions of being run over. To guard against this, we set our side-lights, and stationed extra look-outs. Several ships passed us during the night, hurrying forward on the wings of the wind, at a rapid rate, and sometimes coming so close, in the darkness, as almost to make one's hair stand on end. The next morning the weather became clear and beautiful, and the stream of ships had ceased.

The reader may be curious to know the explanation of this current of ships. It is simple enough. They were all Mediterranean ships. At the strait of Gibraltar there is a constant current setting into the Mediterranean. This current is of considerable strength, and the consequence is, that when the wind also sets into the strait — that is to say, when it is from the westward — it is impossible for a sailing-ship to get out of the strait into the Atlantic. She is obliged to come to anchor in the bay of Gibraltar, and wait for a change of wind. This is sometimes a long time in coming—the westerly winds continuing here, not unfrequently, two and three weeks at a time. As a matter of course, a large number of ships collect in the bay, waiting for an opportunity of exit. I have seen as many as a hundred sail at one time. In a few hours after a change of wind takes place, this immense fleet will all be under way, and such of them as are bound to the equator and the coast of Brazil, the United States, West Indies, and South America, will be found travelling the blazed road of which I have spoken; some taking the forks of the road, at their respective branching-off places, and others keeping the main track to the equator. Hence the exodus the reader has witnessed.

Perhaps the reader needs another explanation—how it was, that amid all that fleet of ships, there was not one Yankee. This explanation is almost as easy as the other. Commerce is a sensitive plant, and at the rude touch of war it had contracted its branches. The enemy was fast losing his Mediterranean trade, under the operation of high premiums for war risks.

We began now to observe a notable change in the weather, as affected by the winds. Along the entire length of the American coast, the clear winds are the west winds, the rain-winds being the east winds. Here the rule is reversed; the west winds bringing us rains, and the east winds clear weather. The reason is quite obvious. The east winds, sweeping over the continent of Europe, have nearly all of their moisture wrung out of them before they reach the sea; hence the dryness of these winds, when they salute the mariner cruising along the European coasts. Starting now from the European seas as dry winds, they traverse a large extent of water before they reach the coasts of the United States. During the whole of this travel, these thirsty winds are drinking their fill from the sea, and by the time they reach Portland or Boston, they are heavily laden with moisture, which they now begin to let down again upon the land. Hence, those long, gloomy, rainy, rheumatic, easterly storms, that prevail along our coast in the fall and winter months. The reader has now only to take up the west wind, as it leaves the Pacific Ocean, as a wet wind, and follow it across the American continent, and see how dry the mountains wring it before it reaches the Atlantic, to see why it should bring us fair weather. The change was very curious to us at first, until we became a little used to it.

Another change was quite remarkable, and that was the great difference in temperature which we experienced with reference to latitude. Here we were, in midwinter, or near it, off the south coast of Spain, in latitude 36°, nearly that of Cape Henry at the entrance of the Chesapeake Bay, and unless the weather was wet, we had not felt the necessity of a pea-jacket. Whence this difference? The cause, or causes, whatever they are, must, of course, be local; for other things being equal, the heat should be the same, on the same parallel of latitude, all around the globe which we inhabit. Captain Matthew F. Maury, of the late Confederate States' Navy, to whom all nations accord, as by common consent, the title of Philosopher

of the Seas, accounts for this difference of temperature in the
following manner: "Modern ingenuity has suggested a beautiful mode of warming houses in winter. It is done by means
of hot water. The furnace and the caldron are sometimes
placed at a distance from the apartment to be warmed. It is
so at the Observatory. In this case, pipes are used to conduct
the heated water from the caldron under the Superintendent's
dwelling, over into one of the basement rooms of the Observatory, a distance of one hundred feet. These pipes are then
flared out, so as to present a large cooling surface; after which
they are united into one again, through which the water, being
now cooled, returns of its own accord to the caldron. Thus,
cool water is returning all the time, and flowing in at the bottom of the caldron, while hot water is continually flowing out
at the top. The ventilation of the Observatory is so arranged
that the circulation of the atmosphere through it is led from
this basement room, where the pipes are, to all parts of the
building; and in the process of this circulation, the warmth
conveyed by the water to the basement, is taken thence by the
air, and distributed all over the rooms.

"Now, to compare small things with great, we have, in the
warm waters which are confined in the Gulf of Mexico, just
such a heating apparatus for Great Britain, the North Atlantic,
and Western Europe. The furnace is the torrid zone; the
Mexican Gulf and Caribbean Sea are the caldrons; the Gulf
Stream is the conducting-pipe. From the Grand Banks of
New Foundland to the shores of Europe is the basement — the
hot-air chambers — in which this pipe is flared out so as to present a large cooling surface. Here the circulation of the atmosphere is arranged by nature, and it is such that the warmth
conveyed into this warm-air chamber of mid-ocean is taken up
by the genial west winds, and dispensed in the most benign
manner, throughout Great Britain and the west of Europe.
The maximum temperature of the water-heated air-chamber of
the Observatory, is about 90°. The maximum temperature of
the Gulf Stream is 86°, or about 9° in excess of the ocean temperature due the latitude. Increasing its latitude, 10°, it loses
but 2° of temperature; and after having run three thousand
miles toward the north, it still preserves, even in winter, the
heat of summer.

" With this temperature it crosses the 40th degree of North latitude, and there, overflowing its liquid banks, it spreads it-self out for thousands of square leagues over the cold waters around, and covers the ocean with a mantle of warmth that serves so much to mitigate in Europe, the rigors of winter. Moving now slowly, but dispensing its genial influences more freely, it finally meets the British Islands. By these it is di-vided, one part going into the polar basin of Spitzbergen, the other entering the Bay of Biscay, but each with a warmth con-siderably above the ocean temperature. Such an immense volume of heated water cannot fail to carry with it beyond the seas a mild and moist atmosphere. And this it is which so much softens climates there. We know not, except approxi-mately in one or two places, what the depth or the under temperature of the Gulf Stream may be; but assuming the temperature and velocity, at the depth of two hundred fathoms to be those of the surface, and taking the well-known differ-ence between the capacity of air, and of water for specific heat as the argument, a simple calculation will show that the quan-tity of heat discharged over the Atlantic from the waters of the Gulf Stream in a winter's day would be sufficient to raise the whole column of atmosphere that rests upon France, and the British Islands from the freezing-point to summer heat. Every west wind that blows, crosses the stream on its way to Europe, and carries with it a portion of this heat to temper there the northern winds of winter. It is the influence of this stream upon climates, that makes Erin the 'Emerald Isle of the Sea,' and that clothes the shores of Albion in evergreen robes; while in the same latitude on this side, the coasts of Labrador are fast bound in fetters of ice."

To pursue Captain Maury's theory a little farther: the flow of tepid waters does not cease at the Bay of Biscay, but con-tinues along the coasts of Spain and Portugal, thence along the coast of Africa, past Madeira and the Canaries, to the Cape de Verdes; where it joins the great equatorial current flowing westward, with which it returns again into the Gulf of Mexico. The *Sumter*, being between Madeira and the coast of Spain, was within its influence. One word before I part with my friend Maury. In common with thousands of mariners all

over the world, I owe him a debt of gratitude, for his gigantic
labors in the scientific fields of our profession; for the sailor
may claim the philosophy of the seas as a part of his profession. A knowledge of the winds and the waves, and the laws
which govern their motions is as necessary to the seaman as
is the art of handling his ship, and to no man so much as to
Maury is he indebted for a knowledge of these laws. Other
distinguished co-laborers, as Reid, Redfield, Espy, have contributed to the science, but none in so eminent a degree. They
dealt in specialties—as, for instance, the storm—but he has
grasped the whole science of meteorology—dealing as well in
the meteorology of the water, if I may use the expression, as
in that of the atmosphere.

A Tennesseean by birth, he did not hesitate when the hour
came, "that tried men's souls." Poor, and with a large family,
he gave up the comfortable position of Superintendent of the
National Observatory, which he held under the Federal Government, and cast his fortunes with the people of his State.
He had not the courage to be a traitor, and sell himself for
gold. The State of Tennessee gave him birth; she carried
him into the Federal Union, and she brought him out of
it. Scarcely any man who withdrew from the old service has
been so vindictively, and furiously assailed as Maury. The
nationalists of the North,—and I mean by nationalists, the
whole body of the Northern people, who ignored the rights
of the States, and claimed that the Federal Government was
paramount,—had taken especial pride in Maury and his labors.
He, as well as the country at large, belonged to them. They
petted and caressed him, and pitted him against the philosophers of the world, with true Yankee conceit. They had the
biggest country, and the cleverest men in the world, and Maury
was one of these.

But Maury, resisting all these blandishments, showed, to
their horror, when the hour of trial came, that he was a
Southern gentleman, and not a Puritan. The change of sentiment was instantaneous and ludicrous. Their self-conceit had
received an awful blow, and there is no wound so damaging
as that which has been given to self-conceit. Almost everything else may be forgiven, but this never can. Maury became

at once a "rebel" and a "traitor," and everything else that was vile. He was not even a philosopher any longer, but a hum-bug and a cheat. In science, as in other pursuits, there are rivalries and jealousies. The writer of these pages, having been stationed at the seat of the Federal Government for a year or two preceding the war, was witness of some of the rivalries and jealousies of Maury, on the part of certain small philosophers, who thought the world had not done justice to themselves. These now opened upon the dethroned monarch of the seas, as live asses will kick at dead lions, and there was no end to the partisan abuse that was heaped upon the late Chief of the National Observatory.·

Maury had been a Federal naval officer, as well as philoso-pher, and some of his late *confrères* of the Federal service, who, in former years, had picked up intellectual crumbs from the table of the philosopher, and were content to move in orbits at a very respectful distance from him; now, raised by capricious fortune to *place*, joined in the malignant outcry against him. Philosopher of the Seas! Thou mayest afford to smile at these vain attempts to humble thee. Science, which can never be appreciated by small natures, has no na-tionality. Thou art a citizen of the world, and thy historic fame does not depend upon the vile traducers of whom I have spoken. These creatures, in the course of a few short years, will rot in unknown graves; thy fame will be immortal! Thou hast revealed to us the secrets of the depths of the ocean, traced its currents, discoursed to us of its storms and its calms, and taught us which of its roads to travel, and which to avoid. Every mariner, for countless ages to come, as he takes down his chart, to shape his course across the seas, will think of thee! He will think of thee as he casts his lead into the deep sea; he will think of thee, as he draws a bucket of water from it, to examine its animalculæ; he will think of thee as he sees the storm gathering thick and ominous; he will think of thee as he approaches the calm-belts, and especially the calm-belt of the equator, with its mysterious cloud-ring; he will think of thee as he is scudding before the "brave west winds" of the Southern hemisphere; in short, there is no phe-nomenon of the sea that will not recall to him thine image.

This is the living monument which thou hast constructed for thyself, and which all the rage of the Puritan cannot shake.

December 31st.—The last day of the year, as though it would atone to us for some of the bad weather its previous days had given us, is charming. There is not a cloud, as big as a man's hat, anywhere to be seen, and the air is so elastic that it is a positive pleasure to breathe it. The temperature is just cool enough to be comfortable, though the wind is from the north. At daylight, a couple of sail were reported from aloft, but, as they were at a great distance, and out of our course, we did not chase. Indeed, we have become quite discouraged since our experience of yesterday. A third sail was seen at noon, also at a great distance. These are probably the laggards of the great Mediterranean wind-bound fleet. We observed, to-day, in latitude 35° 22′; the longitude being 16° 27′. It becoming quite calm at eight P. M., I put the ship under steam; being about 490 miles from Cadiz.

January 1st, 1862.—Nearly calm; wind light from the south-west, and sky partially overcast. The sea is smooth, and we are making nine knots, the hour. We made an excellent run during the past night, and are approaching the Spanish coast very rapidly. Nothing seen during the day. At nine P. M. a sail passed us, a gleam of whose light we caught for a moment in the darkness. The light being lost almost as soon as seen, we did not attempt to chase. Latitude 35° 53′; longitude 13° 14′.

On the next day we overhauled a French, and a Spanish ship. It had been my intention, when leaving Martinique, to cruise a few days off Cadiz, before entering the port, and for this purpose I had reserved a three days' supply of fuel; but, unfortunately, the day before our arrival we took another gale of wind, which shook us so severely, that the ship's leak increased very rapidly; the engineer reporting that it was as much as he could do to keep her free, with the bilge pumps, under short steam. The leak was evidently through the sleeve of the propeller, and was becoming alarming. I therefore abandoned the idea of cruising, and ran directly for the land. Night set in before anything could be seen, but having every confidence in my chronometers, I ran without any hesitation for the Light, although we had been forty-one days at sea, without testing our instruments by a sight of land. We made the light—a fine Fresnel, with a red flash—during the mid-watch, and soon afterward got soundings. We now slowed down the engine, and ran in by the lead, until we judged ourselves four or five miles distant from the light, when we hove to. The next morning revealed Cadiz, fraught with so many ancient, and modern memories, in all its glory, though the weather was gloomy and the clouds dripping rain.

> " Fair Cadiz, rising o'er the dark blue sea ! "

as Byron calls thee, thou art indeed lovely! with thy white Moresque-looking houses, and gayly curtained balconies, thy church-domes which carry us back in architecture a thousand years, and thy harbor thronged with shipping. Once the Gades of the Phœnician, now the Cadiz of the nineteenth century, thou art perhaps the only living city that can run thy record back so far into the past.

We fired a gun, and hoisted a jack for a pilot, and one boarding us soon afterward, we steamed into the harbor. The Confederate States' flag was flying from our peak, and we could see that there were many curious telescopes turned upon us, as we passed successively the forts and the different quays lined with shipping. As the harbor opened upon us, a magnificent spectacle presented itself. On our left was the somewhat distant coast of Andalusia, whose name is synonymous with all that is lovely in scenery, or beautiful in woman. One almost fancies as he looks upon it, that he hears the amorous tinkle of the guitar, and inhales the fragrance of the orange grove. Seville is its chief city, and who has not read the couplet,

> " Quien no ha visto Sevilla
> No ha visto maravilla,"

which may be rendered into the vernacular thus :

> " He who hath not Seville seen,
> Hath not seen wonders, I ween."

The landscape, still green in mid-winter, was dotted with villas and villages, all white, contrasting prettily with the groves in which they were embowered. Casting the eye forward, it

rested upon the picturesque hills of the far-famed wine district
of Xeres, with its vineyards, wine-presses, and pack-mules.
Some famous old wine estates were pointed out to us by the
pilot.

We ran through a fleet of shipping before reaching our
anchorage off the main quay, the latter lined on both sides with
market-boats; and as much more shipping lay beyond us. I was,
indeed, quite surprised to find the harbor, which is spacious, so
thronged. It spoke well for the reviving industry of Spain.
With a little fancy one might imagine her still the mistress of
the "Indies," and that these were her galleons come to pour
the mineral treasures of half a world in her lap. All nations
were represented, though the Spanish flag predominated.
Wearing this flag there were many fine specimens of naval
architecture — especially lines of steamships plying between
Cadiz, the West Indies, and South America. A number of
the merchant-ships of different nations hoisted their flags in
honor of the *Sumter* as she passed; and one Yankee ship —
there being three or four of them in the harbor — hoisted hers,
as much as to say, "You see we are not afraid to show it."

CHAPTER XXIII

ANNOYANCE OF THE SPANISH OFFICIALS — SHORT CORRE-
SPONDENCE WITH THE UNITED STATES CONSUL — THE
TELEGRAPH PUT IN OPERATION BY THE OFFICIALS
BETWEEN CADIZ AND MADRID — THE SUMTER IS OR-
DERED TO LEAVE IN TWENTY-FOUR HOURS — DECLINES
OBEDIENCE TO THE ORDER — PRISONERS LANDED, AND
SHIP DOCKED AFTER MUCH ADO — DESERTERS — SUM-
TER LEAVES CADIZ.

THE Spanish officials began to annoy us even before we let
go our anchor — a health officer boarding us, and telling
us that he should have to quarantine us for three days, unless
we could show him a clean bill of health. We told him that
our health was clean enough, but that we had no bill to establish the fact, whereupon he went on shore to consult his
superiors. I sent by him, the following communication to the
United States Consul, whose name was Eggleston : —

> Confederate States Steamer Sumter, ⎱
> Cadiz, January 4, 1862. ⎰
>
> Sir : — I have the honor to inform you, that I have on board this
> ship forty-three prisoners of war — late the crews of a ship, a
> bark, and a schooner, property of citizens of the United States,
> burned by me on the high seas. These men having elected to be
> discharged on *parole*, I am ready to deliver them to you.

Mr. Eggleston, proving to be quite a diplomat, refused to
give me my official title, in replying to my note; and of
course, I could have no further communication with him. In
the afternoon, the Health Officer again came off to inform us
that the important questions, of the cleanness of our health,
and the discharge of our prisoners, had been telegraphed to
Madrid, and that we might soon expect a reply from her
Majesty, the Queen.

The next morning I received, by the hands of the same officer, a peremptory order, from the Military Governor, to proceed to sea, within twenty-four hours! I sat down and wrote him the following reply:—

> CONFEDERATE STATES STEAMER SUMTER, }
> CADIZ, January 5, 1862.   }
>
> SIR:—I have had the honor to receive through the health officer of the port, an order purporting to come from the Government of Spain, directing me to proceed to sea within twenty-four hours. I am greatly surprised at this unfriendly order. Although my Government has not yet been formally recognized by Spain, as a *de jure* government, it has been declared to be possessed of the rights of a belligerent, in the war in which it is engaged, and it is the duty of Spain to extend to my ship the same hospitality that she would extend to a ship of war of the opposite belligerent. It can make no difference that one of the belligerents is a *de jure* nation, and the other a *de facto* nation, since it is only war rights, or such as pertain to belligerents, which we are discussing.
>
> I am aware of the rule adopted by Spain, in common with the other great powers, prohibiting belligerents from bringing their prizes into her ports, but this rule I have not violated. I have entered the harbor of Cadiz, with my single ship, and I demand only the hospitality to which I am entitled by the laws of nations—the Confederate States being one of the *de facto* nations of the earth, by Spain's own acknowledgment, as before stated.
>
> I am sorry to be obliged to add, that my ship is in a crippled condition. She is damaged in her hull, is leaking badly, is unseaworthy, and will require to be docked and repaired before it will be possible for her to proceed to sea. I am therefore constrained, by the force of circumstances, most respectfully to decline obedience to the order which I have received, until the necessary repairs can be made.
>
> Further:—I have on board forty-three prisoners, confined within a small space greatly to their discomfort, and simple humanity would seem to dictate, that I should be permitted to hand them over to the care of their Consul on shore, without unnecessary delay.

Again, the telegraphic wires were put in operation, and my reply to the Military Commandant went up to Madrid. In a few hours a reply came down, giving me permission to land my prisoners, and to remain a sufficient time to put the necessary repairs upon my ship. In the meantime the most offensive espionage was exercised toward me. A guard-boat was anchored near by, which overhauled all shore-boats which passed between the *Sumter* and the shore; and on the evening of my arrival, a Spanish frigate came down from the dock-yard, and anchored near my ship.   There are no private docks in Cadiz, and I was obliged, therefore, to go into one of the government docks for repairs.   Charles Dickens has given us an amusing account of an English Circumlocution Office, but English red tape dwindles into insignificance by the side of Spanish red tape.   Getting into the hands of the Spanish offi-cials was like getting into a Chancery suit.   I thought I should never get out.   The Military Commandant referred me to the Captain of the Port, and the Captain of the Port referred me back to the Military Commandant; until finally they both toge-ther referred me to the Admiral of the Dock-Yard; to whom I should have been referred at first.   In the meantime, engineers and sub-engineers, and other officials whose titles it were tedi-ous to enumerate, came on board, to measure the length of the ship and the breadth of the ship, calculate her tonnage, inspect her boilers, examine into the quantity of water she made during the twenty-four hours, and to determine generally whether we were really in the condition we had represented ourselves to be in, or whether we were deceiving her Majesty and the Min-ister of the Universal Yankee Nation at Madrid, for some sinister purpose.

The permission came for me, at length, to go into dock, and landing our prisoners, we got up steam and proceeded to Carraca, where the docks lie, distant some eight miles east of the city. The Navy Yard at Carraca is an important building-yard; it lies at the head of the bay of Cadiz, and is approached by a long, narrow, and somewhat tortuous channel, well buoyed. The waters are deep and still, and the Yard is, in every other respect, admirably situated.   It reminded us much, in its gen-eral aspect and surroundings, of the Norfolk Navy Yard, in Vir-ginia.   We were not long delayed in entering the dock.   A ship which had occupied the basin assigned to us — there were several of them — was just being let out as we approached, and in the course of an hour afterward, the *Sumter* was high and dry; so rapidly had the operation been performed.   We examined her bottom with much curiosity, after the thumping she had had on the bar at Maranham, and were gratified to find that she had received no material damage.   A small portion

of her copper had been rubbed off, and one of her planks indented, rather than fractured. She was as sound and tight as
a bottle, in every part of her, except in her propeller sleeve.
It was here where the leak had been, as we had conjectured.

To the delight both of the Spanish officials, who were exceedingly anxious to get rid of us, lest we should compromise
them in some way with the Great Republic, of whom they
seemed to be exceedingly afraid, and ourselves, we found that
the needed repairs would be slight. The boilers were a good
deal out of condition, it is true, but as they were capable of
bearing a low pressure of steam, sufficient to take us to sea,
the officials would not listen to my proposals to repair them.
I had one or two interviews, whilst I lay here, with the Dock-
Admiral, whom I found to be a very different man from the
Military Commandant. He was a polite and refined gentleman, expressed much sympathy for our people, and regretted
that his orders were such that he could not make my repairs
more thorough. He expressed some surprise at the back-
down of the Federal Government, in the *Trent* affair, the news
of which had just arrived, and said that he had fully reckoned
upon our having Great Britain as an ally in the war. "Great
Britain seems, herself, to have been of this opinion," said he,
"as she has withdrawn all her ships of war from the Mediterranean station, for service on the American coast, and sent ten
thousand troops to Canada."

From the moment my ship entered within the precinct of the
Spanish Navy Yard, the very d—l seemed to have broken
loose among my crew. With rare exceptions, a common sailor
has no sense of nationality. He commences his sea-going
career at so tender an age, is so constantly at sea, and sails
under so many different flags, that he becomes eminently a
citizen of the world. Although I had sailed out of a Southern
port, I had not half a dozen Southern-born men among the
rank and file of my crew. They were mostly foreigners—
English and Irish preponderating. I had two or three Yankees on board, who had pretended to be very good Southern men, but who, having failed to reap the rich harvest of
prize-money, which they had proposed to themselves, were
now about to develop their true characters. Some of my

boats' crews had visited the shore on duty, and whilst their boats were lying at the pier waiting for the officers to transact their business, the tempter had come along. Sundry Jack-Tars, emissaries of the *diplomatic* Mr. Eggleston, the Federal Consul, had rolled along down the pier, hitching up their trousers, and replenishing their tobacco quids as they came along. "Cadiz is a nice place," said they to my boats' crews, " with plenty of grog, and lots of fun. We have gotten tired of our ships, and are living at free quarters at the Consul's. Come with us, and let us have a jolly good time together." And they did come, or rather go, for, on one single night, nine of my rascals deserted. This was whilst we were still in dock. Being let out of dock, we dropped down to the city, and being afloat again, we were enabled to prevent a general stampede, by the exercise of firmness and vigilance. I directed an officer to be sent in each boat, whenever one should have occasion to communicate with the shore, armed with a revolver, and with orders to shoot down any one who should attempt to desert. Two or three other sailors slipped away, notwithstanding these precautions, but there the matter ended. Hearing that my deserters were harbored by the United States Consul, I addressed the following letter on the subject to the Governor of the city : —

Confederate States Steamer Sumter,
Cadiz, January 16, 1862.

Sir:— I have the honor to inform you, that whilst my ship was in dock at Carraca, nine of my seamen deserted, and I am informed that they are sheltered and protected by the United States Consul. I respectfully request that you will cause these men to be delivered up to me ; and to disembarrass this demand of any difficulty that may seem to attend it, permit me to make the following observations.

1*st*. In the first place, my Government has been acknowledged as a *de facto* government by Spain, and as such it is entitled to all the rights of a belligerent, in its war with the Government of the United States.

2*d*. All the rights and privileges, therefore, which would attach to the flag of the United States, should one of the ships of that country enter this harbor, equally attach to the flag of the Confederate States, mere ceremonial excepted.

3*d*. It has been and is the uniform custom of all nations to arrest, upon request, and to hand over to their proper officers, deserters from ships of war, and this without stopping to inquire into the nationality of the deserter.

4th. If this be the practice in peace, much more necessary does such a practice become in war, since otherwise the operations of war might be tolerated in a neutral territory, as will be seen from my next position.

5th. Without a violation of neutrality, an enemy's consul in a neutral territory cannot be permitted to entice away seamen, from a ship of the opposite belligerent, or to shelter or protect the same: for if he be permitted to do this, then his domicil becomes an enemy's camp in a neutral territory.

6th. With reference to the question in hand, I respectfully submit that the only facts, which your Excellency can take cognizance of, are that these deserters entered the waters of Spain under my flag, and that they formed a part of my crew. The inquiry cannot pass a step beyond, and Spain cannot undertake to decide, as between the United States Consul and myself, to which of us the deserters in question more properly belong. In other words, she has no right to look into any plea set up by a deserter, that he is a citizen of the United States, and not of the Confederate States.

7th. I might, perhaps, admit, that if a Spanish subject, serving under my flag, should escape to the shore, and should satisfy the authorities that he was held by force, either without contract, or in violation of contract, he might be set at liberty, but such is not the present case. The nationality of the deserters not being Spanish, Spain cannot, as I said before, inquire into it. To recapitulate: the case which I present is simply this. Several of the crew serving on board this ship, under voluntary contracts, have deserted, and taken refuge in the Consulate of the United States. To deprive me of the power, with the assistance of the police, to recapture them, would in effect convert the Consulate into a camp, and enable the Consul to exercise the rights of a belligerent in neutral territory. He might cripple me as effectually by this indirect means, as if he were to assault me by means of an armed expedition.

I took precisely what I expected by this remonstrance, that is to say, nothing. I was fighting here, as I had been in so many other places, against odds — the odds being the stationed agents, spies, and pimps of a recognized government. Our Southern movement, in the eyes of Spain, was a mere political revolution, and like all absolute governments, she had no sympathy with revolutionists. It was on this principle that the Czar of Russia had fraternized so warmly with the Federal President.

Another difficulty now awaited the *Sumter.* I had run the blockade of New Orleans, as the reader has seen, with a very slim exchequer; that exchequer was now exhausted, and we had no means with which to purchase coal. I had telegraphed to Mr. Yancey, in London, immediately upon my arrival, for funds, but none, as yet, had reached me, although I had been here two weeks. In the meantime, the authorities, under the perpetual goading of the United States Chargé in Madrid, Mr. Perry, and of Mr. Consul Eggleston, were becoming very restive, and were constantly sending me invitations to go to sea. Before I had turned out on the morning of the 17th of January, an aide-de-camp of the Governor came on board, to bring me a peremptory order from his chief, to depart *within six hours.* I went on shore, for the first time, to have an official interview with the blockhead. I found him, contrary to all Spanish rule, a large, thick-set, bull-necked fellow, with whom, I saw at the first glance, it would be of but little use to reason. I endeavored to make him understand the nature of the case; how it was that a steamer could no more go to sea without fuel, than a sailing-ship without a mast; but he was inexorable. He was, in short, one of those dunder-headed military men, who never look, or care to look, beyond the orders of their superiors. The most that he would undertake to do, was to telegraph to Madrid my statement, that I was out of fuel, but expected momentarily to be supplied with funds to purchase it. He added, however, "but if no reply comes *within the six hours,* you must go to sea." I had retained enough coal on board from my last cruise, to run me around to Gibraltar — a run of a few hours only — and I now resolved to have nothing more to do with Spain, or her surly officials.

I returned on board, without further delay, and gave orders to get up steam, and make all the other necessary preparations for sea. As we were weighing our anchor, an aide-de-camp of the Governor came off in great haste to say, that his Excellency had heard from Madrid in reply to his telegram, and that her Majesty had graciously given me permission to remain another twenty-four hours; but that at the end of that time I must depart without fail. The aide-de-camp added that his Excellency, seeing that we were getting up steam, had sent him off to communicate the intelligence to me verbally, in advance of the official communication of it by letter, which he was preparing. I directed the aide to say to his chief that he needn't bother himself with the preparation of any letter, as I should

not avail myself of her Majesty's gracious permission—she having been a little too ungracious in meting out the hours to me.
He departed, and we got under way. As we passed abreast of
the Government House, a boat shoved off in a great hurry, and
came pulling out to us, with a man standing up in the bow,
shaking a letter at us with great vehemence. It was the letter
the aide-de-camp had spoken of. We paid no attention whatever to the signal, and the boat finding, after some vigorous
pulling, that she could not overtake us, turned back. In half
an hour afterward, we were outside the Cadiz bar, and had
discharged the pilot.

This was the second Spanish experiment we had made in the
Sumter. I never afterward troubled her Majesty, either in her
home ports, or those of any of her colonies. I had learned
by experience that all the weak powers were timid, and
henceforth, I rarely entered any but an English or a French
port. We should have had, during all this controversy, a
Commissioner at the Court of Madrid, one having been dispatched thither at the same time that Mr. Yancey was sent to
London, and Mr. Mann to Brussels, but if there was one there, I
did not receive a line from him. The Federal Chargé seemed
to have had it all his own way. There is no proposition of international law clearer, than that a disabled belligerent cruiser —
and a steamer without coal is disabled—cannot be expelled
from a neutral port, and yet the *Sumter* was, in fact, expelled
from Cadiz. As remarked some pages back, the Demos, and
the Carpet-bagger will revenge us in good time.

We did enjoy some good things in the harbor of Cadiz,
however. One was a superb dinner, given us at the principal
hotel by an English admirer, and another was the market.
The latter is unexcelled in any part of the world. Fine beef
and mutton from Andalusia, fish from the sea, and fruits and
wines from all parts of Spain, were present in profusion.
Although we were in midwinter, there were a variety of vegetables, and luscious oranges and bananas that had ripened in
the open air—all produced by the agency of that Mexican
Gulf heating-apparatus, of which we spoke through the lips
of Professor Maury, a few pages back. Before leaving Cadiz
I saw the first annual report of the Federal Secretary of the

Navy since the breaking out of the war. Old gentleman Welles was eloquent, and denunciatory when he came to speak of the *Sumter*. The vessel was a "pirate," and her commander everything that was odious. The latter "was courageously capturing unarmed merchant-ships, and cowardly fleeing from the Federal steamers sent in pursuit of him." There were six of these ships in full hue and cry after the little *Sumter*, any one of which could have hoisted her in upon deck. At the same time that these denunciations were hurled against the Captain of the *Sumter*, gallant naval officers, wearing Mr. Welles' shoulder-straps, and commanding Mr. Welles' ships, were capturing little coasting-schooners laden with firewood, plundering the houses and hen-roosts of non-combatant citizens along the Southern coast, destroying salt-works, and intercepting medicines going in to our hospitals. But I must be charitable. Mr. Welles was but rehearsing the lesson which he had learned from Mr. Seward. What could *he* know about "pirates" and the laws of nations, who had been one half of his life editing a small newspaper, in a small town in Connecticut, and the other half "serving out" to Jack his frocks and trousers, and weighing out to him his sugar and tea, as Chief of the Bureau of Provisions and Clothing? It was late in life before the old gentleman, on the rising tide of the Demos, had been promoted, and allowance must be made for the defects of his early training.

CHAPTER XXIV.

THE SUMTER OFF CADIZ — THE PILLARS OF HERCULES —
GIBRALTAR — CAPTURE OF THE ENEMY'S SHIPS NEA-
POLITAN AND INVESTIGATOR — A CONFLAGRATION BE-
TWEEN EUROPE AND AFRICA — THE SUMTER ANCHORS
IN THE HARBOR OF GIBRALTAR — THE ROCK; THE
TOWN; THE MILITARY; THE REVIEW AND THE ALA-
MEDA.

THE afternoon was bright and beautiful as the *Sumter*,
emerging from the harbor of Cadiz, felt once more the
familiar heave of the sea. There was no sail in sight over the
vast expanse of waters, except a few small coasting-craft, and
yet what fleets had floated on the bosom of these romantic
waters! The names of Nelson, Collingwood, Jervis, and
others, came thronging upon the memory. Cape St. Vincent
and Trafalgar were both in the vicinity. The sun, as he
approached his setting, was lighting up a scene of beauty,
peace, and tranquillity, and it was difficult to conjure those
other scenes of the storm, and the flying ships, and the belch-
ing cannon, so inseparably connected with those great names.

It was too late to attempt the run to Gibraltar that night,
with the hope of arriving at a seasonable hour, and so we
"held on," in nautical phrase, to the light — that beautiful red
flash which I have before described — until midnight, when we
gave the ship her steam, and turned her head in the direction
of the famous Strait, or Gut, as the sailors sometimes less
euphoniously call it. The weather, in the meantime, had
changed, the wind had died entirely away, and the sea was
calm, but rifts of cloud were passing over the moon, indicating an upper current in the higher atmosphere, that might
portend storm or rain on the morrow. We steamed along the

bold Spanish coast, at a distance of only a few miles, and entered the Strait before daylight, passing the Tarifa light at about five A. M.

The Pillars of Hercules, that for so many centuries bounded the voyages of the ancient mariners, rose abruptly and majestically on either hand of us, softened and beautified by the moonlight. We had the Strait all to ourselves, there being no sail visible. The Genius of the ancient time seemed to hover over the scene, so solemn and mysterious did everything appear. But no! the Genius of the ancient time could not be there, for the quiet waters were broken by the prow of the *steamship*, from a hemisphere of which the Genius had not conceived. And that steamship, what flag did she bear? A flag that neither Phœnician, nor Carthaginian, nor Roman had dreamed of. It had arisen amid the wreck and ruin of a new empire, that had decayed before its time, was floating above a thousand dead nationalities, and was struggling, as the polished Greek had struggled, long centuries before, against the "long-haired" barbarian of the North, who was repeating history by overrunning the fair lands of the South.

We made the light at Gibraltar just as the day was dawning, and, hurried on by the current, moved rapidly up the Strait. Several sail that were coming down the Mediterranean became plainly visible from the deck as the twilight developed into day. We could not think of running into Gibraltar before overhauling these sails; we might, perchance, find an enemy among them, and so we altered our course and gave chase; as so many barks, ancient and modern, heathen, Christian, and Moor had done before us, in this famous old Strait. The telescope soon revealed the secret of the nationality of two of the sails; they being, as plainly as symmetry and beauty of outline, the taper and grace of spars, and whiteness of canvas—produced upon our own cotton-fields—could speak, American. To these, therefore, we directed our attention. It was a couple of hours before we came up with the first of these ships. She was standing over toward the African side of the Strait, though still distant from the land, some six or seven miles. We hoisted our own colors, and fired the usual gun. She hauled up her courses, and backed her maintopsail at

once, and in a moment more, we could see the brightest of
stars and stripes fluttering in the breeze, and glittering, in very
joyousness, as it were, in the rays of the morning's sun; for
the captain of the prize had evidently treated himself to a
new ensign. The cat ran close enough to parley with the
mouse, before she put her paw upon it. The bark, for such
the prize was, proved to be the *Neapolitan*, of Kingston, Mass.,
from Messina, in the island of Sicily, bound for Boston, with
a cargo of fruit, dried and fresh, and *fifty tons of sulphur*. She
had been freshly painted, with that old robber, the bald eagle,
surrounded by stars, gilded on her stern; her decks looked
white and sweet after the morning's ablution which she had
just undergone; her sails were well hoisted, and her sheets
well home; in short, she was a picture to look at, and the cat
looked at her, as a cat only can look at a sleek mouse. And
then only to think, that the sly little mouse, looking so pretty
and so innocent, should have so much of that villanous material called sulphur in its little pouch!

The master stated in his deposition, that the entire cargo
belonged to the British house of Baring Bros., it being consigned to an agent of theirs in Boston. The object of so word-
ing the deposition was, of course, to save the cargo as neutral
property, but as I happened to know that the Boston house
of the Barings, instead of being an agent merely, was a partner
of the London house, the master took nothing by his deposition. Besides, if there had been no doubt as to the British
ownership, sulphur going to an enemy's country is contraband
of war; and in this case the contraband of war was not only
condemnable of itself, but it tainted all the rest of the cargo,
which belonged to the same owner. The master, who was as
strongly marked in his Puritan nationality, as the Israelite is
in the seed of Abraham, feeling himself securely intrenched
behind the Baring Bros., was a little surprised when I told
him that I should burn his ship, and began to expostulate.
But I had no time for parley, for there was another ship demanding my attention; and so, transferring the prisoners from
the doomed ship to the *Sumter*, as speedily as possible, the
Neapolitan was burned; burned in the sight of Europe and
Africa, with the turbaned Moor looking upon the conflagra-

tion, on one hand, and the garrison of Gibraltar and the Spaniard on the other. Previously to applying the torch, we took a small liberty with some of the excellent fruit of the Barings, transferring a number of drums of figs, boxes of raisins and oranges, to the cooks and stewards of the different messes.

We now steamed off in pursuit of the other sail. This second sail proved also to be American, as we had supposed. She was the bark *Investigator*, of Searsport, Maine, from one of the small ports of Spain, bound for Newport, in Wales, with a cargo of iron ore. The cargo being properly documented as British property, we could not destroy her, but were compelled to release her under ransom bond. The capturing and disposing of these two ships had occupied us several hours, during which the in-draught of the Strait had set us some miles to the eastward of the Rock. We now, at half-past two P. M., turned our head in the direction of Gibraltar, and gave the ship all steam. By this time the portent of last night had been verified, and we had an overcast sky, with a strong northwester blowing in our teeth. With the wind and current both ahead, we had quite a struggle to gain the anchorage.

It was half-past seven P. M., or some time after dark, that we finally passed under the shadow of the historical rock, with the brilliant light on Europa Point throwing its beams upon our deck; and it was a few minutes past eight o'clock, or evening gun-fire, when we ran up to the man-of-war anchorage, and came to. We had no occasion to tell the people of Gibraltar who we were. They were familiar with our Cadiz troubles, and had been expecting us for some days; and accordingly, when the signal-man on the top of the Rock announced the appearance of a Confederate States' steamer in the Strait, every one knew that it was the *Sumter*. And when, a short time afterward, it was announced that the little steamer was in chase of a Yankee, the excitement became intense. Half the town rushed to Europa Point and the signal-station, to watch the chase and the capture; and when the flames were seen ascending from the doomed *Neapolitan*, sketch-books and pencils were produced, and all the artists in the crowd went busily to work to sketch the extraordinary spectacle; extraordinary in any age, but still more extraordinary in this.

Here were two civilized nations at war, at the door of a third, and that third nation, instead of mitigating and soften-ing, as much as possible, the barbarities of war, had, by her timidity, caution, or unfriendliness, whichever to the reader may seem more probable, ordered, directed, and decreed that one of the parties should burn all the ships of the other that it should capture! The spectacle of the burning ship which the inhabitants of Gibraltar had witnessed from the top of their renowned rock, was indirectly the work of their own Govern-ment. Why might not this Federal ship, when captured, have been taken into Gibraltar, there to await the disposition which a prize-court should make of her, instead of being burned? Because Great Britain would not permit it. Why might she not have been taken into some other neutral port, for this purpose? Because all the world had followed the lead of Great Britain, the chief maritime power of the earth. Great Britain knew when she issued her orders in council, prohibiting both the belligerents in the American war, from bringing their prizes into her ports, precisely what would be the effect of those orders. She knew that the stronger belligerent would shut out the weaker belligerent from his own ports, by means of a blockade. She knew that if she denied this weaker belliger-ent access to her ports, with his prizes, all the other nations of the earth would follow her lead. And she knew that if this same weaker belligerent should have no ports whatever into which to carry his prizes, he must burn them. Hence the spectacle her people had witnessed from the top of her rock of Gibraltar.

In a few minutes after anchoring, we were boarded by a boat from the English frigate, which had the guard for the day. The officer made us the usual "tender of service" from the Port Admiral. We sent a boat ourselves to report our arrival on board the health ship, and to inquire if there would be any quarantine; and after a *long* day of excitement and fatigue,—for I had not turned in since I left the Cadiz light, the night before—I sought my berth, and slept soundly, nei-ther dreaming of Moor or Christian, Yankee or Confederate. John spread me the next morning a sumptuous breakfast, and brought me off glowing accounts of the Gibraltar market, filled with all the delicacies both of Spain and Morocco. The prize which we had liberated on ransom-bond, followed us in, and was anchored not far from us. There was another large American ship at anchor.

At an early hour a number of English officers, of the garrison and navy, and citizens called on board to see us; and at ten o'clock I went on board the frigate whose boat had boarded us the previous night, to return the commanding naval officer's visit. He was not living on board, but at his quarters on shore, whither I proceeded at two P. M. Landing at the Navy Yard, an orderly conducted me thence to his neat little cottage, perched half way up the rock, and embowered by shade trees, in the most charming little nook possible. I found Captain—now Rear-Admiral—Sir Frederic Warden a very clever specimen of an English naval officer; and we had a pleasant conversation of half an hour together. Having lost one of my anchors, I asked the loan of one from him until I could supply myself in the market. He replied that he had every disposition to oblige me, but that he must first submit the question to the "law officers of the Crown." I said to him playfully, "these 'law officers of the Crown' of yours must be sturdy fellows, for they have some heavy burdens to carry; when I was at Trinidad the Governor put a whole cargo of coal on their shoulders, and now you propose to saddle them with an anchor!" He said pleasantly, in return, "I have not the least doubt of the propriety of your request, but we must walk according to rule, you know." The next morning, bright and early, a boat came alongside, bringing me an anchor.

From Captain Warden's, I proceeded to the residence of the Governor and Military Commander of the Rock, Sir William J. Codrington, K. C. B. His house was in the centre of the town, and I had a very pleasant walk through shaded avenues and streets, thronged with a gayly dressed population, every third man of which was a soldier, to reach it. The same orderly still accompanied me. I was in uniform, and all the sentinels saluted me as I passed; and I may as well mention here, that during the whole of my stay at this military and naval station, my officers and myself received all the honors and courtesies due to our rank. No distinction whatever was drawn, that I

am aware of, between the *Sumter*, and any of the enemy's ships
of war that visited the station, except in the matter of the
national salute. Our flag not being yet recognized, except for
belligerent purposes, this honor was withheld. We dined at
the officers' messes, and they dined on board our ship; the club
and reading-rooms were thrown open to us, and both military
and citizens were particular in inviting us to partake of all the
festivities that took place during our stay.

My conductor, the orderly, stopped before a large stone
mansion on the principal street, where there was a sentinel
walking in front of the door, and in a few minutes I was led
to a suite of large, airy, well-furnished rooms on the second
floor, to await his Excellency. It was Sunday, and he had
just returned from church. He entered, however, almost immediately. I had seen him a hundred times, in the portraits
of half the English generals I had ever looked upon, so peculiarly was he *English* and *military*. He was a polite gentleman
of the old school, though not a very old man, his age being
not more than about fifty-five. Governor Codrington was a
son of the Admiral of the same name, who, as the commander-
in-chief of the combined English, French, and Russian fleets,
had gained so signal a victory over the Turkish fleet, in the
Mediterranean, in 1827, which resulted in the independence of
Greece, and the transfer of Prince Otho of Bavaria to the
throne of that country. His rank was that of a lieutenant-
general in the British army. I reported my arrival to his
Excellency, and stated that my object in visiting Gibraltar was
to repair, and coal my ship, and that I should expect to have the
same facilities extended to me, that he would extend to an
enemy's cruiser under similar circumstances. He assented at
once to my proposition, saying that her Majesty was exceedingly anxious to preserve a strict neutrality in our unhappy
war, without leaning to the one side or the other. "There is
one thing, however," continued he, "that I must exact of you
during your stay, and that is, that you will not make Gibraltar, a station, from which to watch for the approach of your
enemy, and sally out in pursuit of him." I replied, "Certainly not; no belligerent has the right to make this use of the
territory of a neutral. Your own distinguished admiralty

judge, Sir William Scott, settled this point half a century and more ago, and his decisions are implicitly followed in the American States."

The Governor gave me permission to land my prisoners, and they were paroled and sent on shore the same afternoon. We could do nothing in the way of preparing the *Sumter* for another cruise, until our funds should arrive, and these did not reach us until the 3d of February, when Mr. Mason, who had by this time relieved Mr. Yancey, as our Commissioner at the Court of London, telegraphed me that I could draw on the house of Frazer, Trenholm & Co., of Liverpool, for the sum I needed. In the mean time, we had made ourselves very much at home at Gibraltar, quite an intimacy springing up between the naval and military officers and ourselves; whereas, as far as we could learn, the Yankee officers of the several Federal ships of war, which by this time had arrived, were kept at arm's-length, no other than the customary official courtesies being extended to them. We certainly did not meet any of them at the "club," or other public places. I had visited Gibraltar when a young officer in the "old service," and I had often read, and laughed over Marryatt's humorous description of the "Mess" of the garrison in his day; how, after one of their roistering dinners, the naval officers who had been present, would be wheeled down to the "sally-port," where their boats were waiting to take them on board their ships, on wheel-barrows—the following colloquy taking place between the sally-port sentinel (it being now some hours after dark), and the wheeler of the wheel-barrow. Sentinel:—"Who comes there?" Wheeler of wheel-barrow:—"Officer drunk on a wheel-barrow!" Sentinel:—"Pass Officer drunk on a wheel-barrow."

The wheel-barrow days had passed, in the general improvement which had taken place in military and naval habits, but in other respects, I did not find the "Mess" much changed. The military "Mess" of a regiment is like the king; it never dies. There is a constant change of persons, but the "Mess" is ever the same, with its history of this "field," and of that; its traditions, and its anecdotes. Every person who has been in England knows how emphatically dinner is an institution with the English people; with its orthodox hour, the punctual attendance of the guests, the scrupulous attention they pay to dress, and the quantity of wine which they are capable of putting under their vests, without losing sight of the gentlemanly proprieties.

It is still more an institution, if possible, with the garrisons of the colonies. There they do the thing in a business-like way, and the reader will perhaps be curious to know how the young fellows stand such constant wear and tear upon their constitutions. It is done in the simplest manner possible. After a late carouse over night, during which these fellows would drink two bottles to my young men's one, the latter would get up next morning on board the *Sumter* feeling seedy, and dry, and go on shore in quest of "hock and soda-water." Meeting their late companions, they would be surprised to see them looking so fresh and rosy, with an air so jaunty, and a step so elastic. The secret, upon explanation, would prove to be, that the debauchee of the night was the early bird of the morning. Whilst my officers were still lying in uneasy slumbers, with Queen Mab playing pranks with their imaginations, the officer of the "Mess" would be up, have taken his cold shower-bath, have mounted his "hunter," sometimes with, and sometimes without dogs, and would be off scouring the country, and drinking in the fresh morning air, miles away. Not a fume of the liquor of the overnight's debauch would be left by the time the rider got back to breakfast.

On the day after my visit to the Governor, Colonel Freemantle, of the Coldstream Guards, the Governor's aide-de-camp and military secretary, came off to call on me on behalf of the Governor, and to read to me a memorandum, which the latter had made of my conversation with him. There were but two points in this memorandum:—"First: It is agreed that the *Sumter* shall have free access to the work-shops and markets, to make necessary repairs and supply herself with necessary articles, contraband of war excepted. Secondly: The *Sumter* shall not make Gibraltar a *station*, from which to sally out from the Strait, for the purposes of war." I assented to the correctness of the conversation as recorded, and there the official portion of the interview ended. I could not but be amused here, as I had been at other places, at the exceeding scrupulousness of the authorities, lest they should compromise themselves in some way with the belligerents.

I found Colonel Freemantle to be an ardent Confederate, expressing himself without any reserve, and lauding in the highest terms our people and cause. He had many questions to ask me, which I took great pleasure in answering, and our interview ended by a very cordial invitation from him to visit, in his company, the curiosities of the Rock. This is the same Colonel Freemantle, who afterward visited our Southern States during the war, and made the acquaintance of some of our principal military men; writing and publishing a very interesting account of his tour. I met him afterward in London, more of a Confederate than ever. Freemantle was not an exception. The army and navy of Great Britain were with us, almost to a man, and many a hearty denunciation have I heard from British military and naval lips, of the coldness and selfishness of the Palmerston-Russell government.

Gibraltar, being a station for several steam-lines, was quite a thoroughfare of travel. The mixed character of its resident population, too, was quite curious. All the nations of the earth seemed to have assembled upon the Rock, for the purposes of traffic, and as each nationality preserved its costume and its language, the quay, market-place, streets and shops presented a picture witnessed in few, if in any other towns of the globe. The attractions for traffic were twofold: first, Gibraltar was a free port, and, secondly, there were seven thousand troops stationed there. The consequence was, that Christian, Moor, and Turk, Jew and Gentile, had assembled here from all the four quarters of the earth, bringing with them their respective commodities. The London tailor had his shop alongside that of the Moor or Turk, and if, after having been measured for a coat, to be made of cloth a few days only from a Manchester loom, you desired Moorish slippers, or otto of roses, or Turkish embroidery, you had only to step into the next door.

Even the shopmen and products of the far East were there; a few days of travel only sufficing to bring from India, China, and Japan, the turbaned and sandalled Hindoo, the close-shaved and long-queued Chinaman, and the small-statured, deep-brown

Japanese, with their curious stuffs and wares, wrought with as much ingenuity as taste. The market was indeed a curiosity. Its beef and mutton, both of which are very fine, are brought from the opposite Morocco coast, to and from which small steamers ply regularly. But it is the fruits and vegetables that more especially astonish the beholder. Here the horn of plenty seems literally to have been emptied. The south of Spain, and Morocco, both fine agricultural countries, have one of those genial climates which enables them to produce all the known fruits and vegetables of the earth. Whatever you desire, that you can have, whether it be the apple, the pear, or the cherry of the North, or the orange, the banana, or the date of the South. The Spaniards and Moors are the chief market people.

Nor must we forget the fishermen, with their picturesque boats, rigged with their long, graceful latteen yards and pointed sails, that come in laden with the contributions of the sea from the shores of half a dozen kingdoms. Fleets of these little craft crowd the quay day and night, and there is a perfect Babel of voices in their vicinity, as the chaffering goes on for the disposal of their precious freight, much of it still "alive and kicking." By the way, one of the curiosities of this quay, whilst the *Sumter* lay in Gibraltar, was the frequent proximity of the Confederate and the Federal flag. When landing I often ran my boat into the quay-steps, alongside of a boat from a Federal ship of war; the *Kearsarge* and the *Tuscarora* taking turns in watching my movements — one of them being generally anchored in the Bay of Gibraltar, and the other in the Bay of Algeziras, a Spanish anchorage opposite. No breach of the peace ever occurred; the sailors of the two services seemed rather inclined to fraternize. They would have fought each other like devils outside of the marine league, but the neutral port was a powerful sedative, and made them temporarily friends. They talked, and laughed and smoked, and peeled oranges together, as though there was no war going on. But the sailor is a cosmopolite, as remarked a few pages back, and these boats' crews could probably have been exchanged, without much detriment to each other's flag.

Sunday, January 26th. — A charming, balmy day, after the

several days of storm and rain that we have had. At ten A. M., I went on shore to the Catholic church. The military attendance, especially of the rank and file, was very large. I should judge that, at least, two thirds of the troops stationed here are Irish, and there is no distinction, that I can discover, made between creeds. Each soldier attends whatever church he pleases. It is but a few years back, that no officer could serve in the British army without subscribing to the Thirty-Nine Articles — the creed of the "Established Church." After church, I took a stroll "up the Rock," and was astonished to find so much arable soil on its surface. The Rock runs north and south. Its western face is an inclined plane, lying at an angle of about thirty degrees with the sea-level. Ascending gradually from the water, it rises to the height of fifteen hundred feet. From this height, a plummet-line let down from its eastern face would reach the sea without obstruction, so perpendicular is the Rock in this direction. This face is of solid rock.

On the western face, up which I was now walking, is situated near the base, and extending up about half a mile, the town. The town is walled, and after you have passed through a massive gateway in the southern wall, you are in the country. As you approach the Rock from the sea, it matters not from what direction, you get the idea that it is nothing but a barren rock. I now found it diversified with fields, full of clover and fragrant grasses, long, well-shaded avenues, of sufficiently gentle ascent for carriage-drives, beautifully laid-out pleasure-grounds, and well-cultivated gardens. The parade-ground is a level space just outside the southern wall, of sufficient capacity for the manœuvre and review of five thousand men; and rising just south of this is the Alameda, consisting of a series of parterres of flowers, with shade-trees and shrubbery, among which wind a number of serpentine walks. Here seats are arranged for visitors, from which the exercise of the troops in the parade-ground below may be conveniently witnessed. A colossal statue of General Elliot, who defended the Rock in the famous siege that was laid to it in the middle of the last century by the Spaniards, is here erected.

The review of the troops, which takes place, I believe,

monthly, is *par excellence*, the grand spectacle of Gibraltar. I
had the good fortune to witness one of these reviews, and the
spectacle dwells vividly, still, in my imagination. Drill of the
soldiers, singly, and in squads, is the chief labor of the garrison. Skilful drill-sergeants, for the most part young, active,
intelligent men, having the port and bearing of gentlemen, are
constantly at work, morning and afternoon, breaking in the
raw material as it arrives, and rendering it fit to be moulded
into the common mass. Company officers move their companies, to and fro, unceasingly, lest the men should forget
what the drill-sergeant has taught them. Battalion and regi-
mental drills occur less frequently.

These are the labors of the garrison ; now comes the pas-
time, viz., the monthly drill, when the Governor turns out, and
inspects the troops. All is agog, on the Rock of Gibraltar, on
review days. There is no end to the pipe-claying, and brush-
ing, and burnishing, in the different barracks, on the morning
of this day. The officers get out their new uniforms, and
horses are groomed with more than ordinary care. The citizens turn out, as well as the military, and all the beauty and
fashion of the town are collected on the Alameda. On the
occasion of the review which I witnessed, the troops — nearly
all young, fine-looking men — presented, indeed, a splendid
appearance. All the corps of the British army were there,
represented save only the cavalry ; and they were moved
hither and thither, at will ; long lines of them now being tied
into what seemed the most inextricable knots, and now untied
again, with an ease, grace, and skill, which called forth my
constant admiration.

But it was not so much the movements of the military that
attracted my attention, as the *tout ensemble* of the crowd. The
eye wandered over almost all the nationalities of the earth, in
their holiday costumes. The red fez cap of the Greek, the
white turban of the Moor and Turk, and the hat of the Christian, all waved in a common sea of male humanity, and, when
the eye turned to the female portion of the crowd, there was
confusion worse confounded, for the fashions of Paris and
London, Athens and Constantinople, the isles and the continents, all were there ! What with the waving plumes of the

generals, the galloping hither and thither of aides and orderlies, the flashing of the polished barrel of the rifle in the sun,
the music of the splendid bands, and the swaying and surging
of the civic multitude which I have attempted to describe, the
scene was fairly beyond description. A man might dream of
it, but could not describe it.

CHAPTER XXV.

THE SUMTER STILL AT GIBRALTAR — SHIP CROWDED
WITH VISITORS — A RIDE OVER THE ROCK WITH
COLONEL FREEMANTLE — THE "GALLERIES" AND
OTHER SUBTERRANEAN WONDERS — A DIZZY HEIGHT,
AND THE QUEEN OF SPAIN'S CHAIR — THE MONKEYS
AND THE "NEUTRAL GROUND."

THE stream of visitors to the *Sumter* continued for some
days after our arrival. Almost every steamer from
England brought more or less tourists and curiosity-hunters,
and these did us the honor to visit us, and frequently to say
kind words of sympathy and encouragement. Among others,
the Duke of Beaufort and Sir John Inglis visited us, and
examined our ship with much curiosity. The latter, who had
earned for himself the title of the "hero of Lucknow," in that
most memorable and barbarous of all sieges, was on his way
to the Ionian Islands, of which he had recently been appointed
Governor.

January 23d.—Weather clear and pleasant. We received
a visit from Captain Warden to-day, in return for the visit I
had made him upon my arrival. He came off in full uniform,
to show us that his visit was meant to be official, as well as
personal. Nothing would have pleased the gallant captain
better, than to have been able to salute the Confederate States'
flag, and welcome our new republic among the family of nations. We discussed a point of international law while he
was on board. He desired, he said, to call my attention to
the well-known rule that, in case of the meeting of two opposite belligerents in the same neutral port, twenty-four hours
must intervene between their departure. I assented readily
to this rule. It had been acted upon, I told him, by the
Governor of Martinique, when I was in that island—the

enemy's sloop *Iroquois* having been compelled to cruise in the offing for fear of its application to her. I remarked, however, that it was useless for us to discuss the rule here, as the enemy's ships had adroitly taken measures to evade it. "How is that?" he inquired. "Why, simply," I replied, "by stationing one of his ships in Gibraltar, and another in Algeziras. If I go to sea from Gibraltar, the Algeziras ship follows me, and if I go to sea from Algeziras, the Gibraltar ship follows me." "True," rejoined the captain, "I did not think of that." "I cannot say," continued I, "that I complain of this. It is one of those chances in war which perhaps nine men in ten would take advantage of; and then these Federal captains cannot afford to be over-scrupulous; they have an angry mob at their heels, shouting, in their fury and ignorance, 'Pirate! pirate!'"

The Southampton steamer brought us late news, to-day, from London. We are becoming somewhat apprehensive for the safety of Messrs. Mason and Slidell, who, having embarked on board the British steam-sloop *Rinaldo*, at Provincetown, Mass., on the 2d inst., bound to Halifax, distant only a few hundred miles, had not been heard from as late as the 10th inst. A heavy gale followed their embarcation. I received a letter, to-day, too, from Mr. Yancey. He writes despondently as to the action of the European powers. They are cold, distrustful, and cautious, and he has no hope of an early recognition. I am pained to remark here, that this distinguished statesman died soon after his return to the United States. He was one of the able men of the South, who, like Patrick Henry, and John C. Calhoun, seemed to be gifted with the spirit of prophecy; or, rather, to speak more correctly, his superior mental powers, and knowledge of men and of governments, enabled him, like his great predecessors, to arrive at conclusions, natural and easy enough to himself, but which, viewed in the light of subsequent events, seemed like prophecy to his less gifted countrymen. Mr. Yancey much resembled Patrick Henry in the simplicity and honesty of his character, and in the fervidness and power of his eloquence:

January 30th.—A fine, clear day, with the wind from the eastward. Having received a note last evening, from Colonel

Freemantle, informing me that horses would be in readiness for us, this morning, at the Government House, to visit the fortifications, I went on shore the first thing after breakfast, and finding the Colonel in readiness, we mounted, and accompanied by an orderly to take care of our horses, rode at a brisk pace out of the western gate, and commenced our tour of inspection. Arriving at the entrance of the famous "galleries" situated about half-way up the Rock, we dismounted, and dived into the bowels of mother Earth.

The Spaniards have been celebrated above all other people for fortifications. They have left monuments of their patience, diligence, and skill all over the world, wherever they have obtained a foothold. The only other people who have ever equalled them, in this particular, though in a somewhat different way, are the people of these Northern States, during the late war. No Spaniard was ever half so diligent in his handling of stone, and mortar, as was the Yankee soldier in throwing up his "earth-work." His industry in this regard was truly wonderful. If the Confederate soldier ever gave him half an hour's breathing-time, he was safe. With pick and spade he would burrow in the ground like a rabbit. When the time comes for that New-Zealander, foretold by Macaulay, to sit on the ruins of London bridge, and wonder what people had passed away, leaving such gigantic ruins behind them, we would recommend him to come over to these States, and view the miles of hillocks that the industrious Yankee moles threw up during our late war; and speculate upon the genus of the animal gifted with such wonderful instincts.

But to return to our tour of inspection. The famous underground "galleries" of the Rock of Gibraltar, are huge tunnels, blasted and bored, foot by foot, in the living rock, sufficiently wide and deep to admit of the placing, and working of heavy artillery. They are from one third of a mile, to half a mile in length, and there are three tiers of them, rising one above the other; the embrasures or port-holes of which resemble, when viewed from a distance, those of an old-time two-decker. Besides these galleries for the artillery, there have also been excavated in the solid rock, ample magazines, and store and provision rooms, and tanks for the reception of water. These receptacles are kept constantly well supplied with munitions, both *de guerre*, and *de bouche*, so that if the garrison should be driven from the fortifications below, it could retreat to this citadel, close the massive doors behind them, and withstand a siege.

We passed through all the galleries, ascending from one to the other, through a long, rough-hewn stairway—the Colonel frequently stopping, and explaining to me the history of some particular nook or battlement—until we finally emerged into the open air through a port-hole, or doorway at the very top of the Rock, and stood upon a narrow footway or platform, looking down a sheer precipice of fifteen hundred feet upon the sea breaking in miniature waves at the base of the Rock. There was no rail to guard one from the precipice below, and I could but wonder at the *nonchalance* with which the Colonel stepped out upon this narrow ledge, and walked some yards to get a view of the distant coast of Spain, expecting me to follow him. I did follow him, but I planted my feet very firmly and carefully, feeling all the while some such emptiness in the region of the "bread-basket," as Marryatt describes Peter Simple to have experienced when the first shot whistled past that young gentleman in his first naval engagement.

The object of the Colonel, in this flank movement, was to show me a famous height some distance inland, called the "Queen of Spain's Chair," and to relate to me the legend in connection with it. The Rock of Gibraltar has always been the darling of Spain. It has been twice wrested from her, once by the Moors, and once by the English. She regained it from the Moors, when she drove them out of her Southern provinces, after an occupation of eight hundred years! Some of the remains of the old Moorish castles are still visible. Afterward, an English naval captain, returning from some expedition up the Mediterranean, in which he had been unsuccessful, stormed and captured the Rock with a handful of sailors. Spain, mortified beyond measure, at the result, made strenuous efforts to recover it. In 1752 she bent all her energies in this direction, and fitted out large expeditions, by land and by sea, for the purpose. The Queen came down from Madrid to witness the siege, and causing her tent to be pitched near the "Chair," vowed she would never leave it, until she saw the flag of Spain floating once more from the coveted battlements. But General Elliot, with only a small garrison, beat back the immense armaments, and the Spaniards were compelled to raise the siege. But the poor Queen of Spain! what was to become of her, and her vow? English gallantry came to her relief. The Spanish flag was raised for a single day from the Rock, to enable the Queen to descend from her chair! The reader will judge whether this legend was worth the emptiness in the "bread-basket" which I had experienced, in order to get at it.

Descending back through the galleries, to where we had left our horses, we remounted, and following a zigzag path, filled with loose stones, and running occasionally along the edges of precipices, down which we should have been instantly dashed in pieces, if our sure-footed animals had stumbled, we reached the signal-station. On the very apex of the rock, nature seemed to have prepared a little *plateau*, of a few yards square, as if for the very purpose for which it was occupied — that of over-looking the approaches from every direction, to the famous Rock. A neat little box of a house, with a signal-mast and yard, and a small plot of ground, about as large as a pocket-handkerchief, used as a garden, occupied the whole space. Europe, and Africa, the Mediterranean, and the Atlantic were all visible from this eyry. The day was clear, and we could see to great distances. There were ships in the east coming down the Mediterranean, and ships in the west coming through the famous Strait; they all looked like mere specks. Fleets that might shake nations with their thunder, would be here mere cock-boats. The country is mountainous on both sides of the Strait, and these mountains now lay sleeping in the sunshine, covered with a thin, gauzy veil, blue and mysterious, and wearing that air of enchantment which distance always lends to bold scenery.

"We had a fine view of your ship, the other day," said the signal-man to me, "when you were chasing the Yankee. The latter was hereaway, when you set fire to her"—pointing in the direction. "Are there many Yankee ships passing the Rock now?" I inquired. "No. Very few since the war commenced." "It would not pay me, then, to cruise in these seas?" "Scarcely."

As we turned to go to our horses, we were attracted by the appearance of three large apes, that had come out of their lodging-place in the Rock, to sun themselves. These apes are one of the curiosities of the Rock, and many journeys have been made in vain to the signal-station, to see them. The Colonel had never seen them before, himself, and the signal-man congratulated us both on our good fortune. "Those are three old widows," said he, "the only near neighbors I have, and we are very friendly; but as you are strangers, you must not move if you would have a good look at them, or they will run away." He then gave us the history of his neighbors. Years ago there was quite a colony of these counterfeit presentments of human nature on the Rock, but the whole colony has disappeared except these three. "When I first came to the signal-station," continued our informant, "these three old widows were gay, and dashing young damsels, with plenty of sweethearts, but unfortunately for them, there were more males than females, and a war ensued in the colony in consequence. First one of the young males would disappear, and then another, until I at last noticed that there were only four of the whole colony left: one very large old male, and these three females. Peace now ensued, and the old fellow lived apparently very happily with his wives, but no children were born to him, and finally he died, leaving these three disconsolate widows, who have since grown old—you can see that they are quite gray—to mourn his loss." And they did indeed look sad and disconsolate enough. They eyed us very curiously, and when we moved toward our horses, they scampered off. They subsist upon wild dates, and a few other wild fruits that grow upon the Rock.

We passed down the mountain-side to the south end of the Rock, where we exchanged salutations with the General and Mrs. Codrington, who had come out to superintend some repairs upon a country house which they had at this end; and reaching the town, I began to congratulate myself that my long and fatiguing visit of inspection was drawing to a close. Not so, however. These Englishmen are a sort of cross between the Centaur and the North American Indian. They can ride you, or walk you to death, whichever you please; and so Freemantle said to me, "Now, Captain, we will just take a little gallop out past the 'neutral ground,' and then I think I will have shown you all the curiosities." The "neutral ground" was about three miles distant, and "a gallop" out and back, would be six miles! Imagine a sailor who had not been on horseback before, for six months; who had been riding for half a day one of those accursed English horses, with their long stride, and swinging trot, throwing a man up, and catching him again, as if he were a trap-ball; who was galled, and sore, and jaded, having such a proposition made to him! It was worse than taking me out on that narrow ledge of rock fifteen hundred feet above the sea, to look at the Queen of Spain's Chair. But I could not retreat. How could an American, who had been talking of his big country, its long rivers, the immense distances traversed by its railroads and steamboats, and the capacity for endurance of its people in the present war, knock under to an Englishman, and a Coldstream Guardsman at that, on this very question of endurance? And so we rode to the "neutral ground."

This is a narrow strip of territory, accurately set off by metes and bounds, on the isthmus that separates the Rock from the Spanish territory. As its name implies, neither party claims jurisdiction over it. On one side are posted the English sentinels, and on the other, the Spanish; and the *all's-well!* of the one mingles strangely, at night, with the *alerta!* of the other. We frequently heard them both on board the *Sumter*, when the night was still. I got back to my ship just in time for a six o'clock dinner, astonished John by drinking an extra glass of sherry, and could hardly walk for a week afterward.

A day or two after my visit to the Rock, I received a visit from a Spanish naval lieutenant, sent over, as he stated, by the Admiral from Algeziras, to remonstrate with me against the burning of the ship *Neapolitan within Spanish jurisdiction.* The reader who has read the description of the burning of that ship, will be as much astonished as I was at this visit. The Spanish Government owns the fortress of Ceuta, on the

African shore opposite Gibraltar, and by virtue of this ownership claims, as it would appear, jurisdiction for a marine
league at sea, in the neighborhood of the fortress. It was
claimed that the *Neapolitan* had been captured within this
league. The lieutenant having thus stated his case, I demanded to know on what testimony the Admiral relied, to
establish the fact of the burning within the league. He replied that the United States Consul at Gibraltar had made the
statement to the Admiral. Here was the "cat out of the bag"
again; another United States Consul had turned up, with his
intrigues and false statements. The nice little piece of diplomacy had probably been helped on, too, by the commanders
of the Federal ships of war, that had made Algeziras a rendezvous, since I had been anchored in the Bay of Gibraltar.
When the Spanish officer had done stating his case, I said to
him: — "I do not recognize the right of your Admiral to raise
any question with me, as to my capture of the *Neapolitan.*
The capture of that ship is an accomplished fact, and if any
injury has been done thereby to Spain, the Spanish Government can complain of it to the Government of the Confederate
States. It has passed beyond the stage, when the Admiral
and I could manage it, and has become an affair entirely
between our two Governments."

This was all the official answer I had to make, and the lieutenant, whose bearing was that of an intelligent gentleman,
assented to the correctness of my position. I then said to
him: — "But aside from the official aspect of the case, I desire
to show you, that your Admiral has had his credulity played
upon by his informant, the Consul, and whatever other parties
may have approached him on this subject. They have made
false statements to him. It is not only well known to hundreds of citizens of the Rock, who were eye-witnesses of the
burning of the *Neapolitan,* that that vessel was burned at a
distance of from six to seven miles from the African coast,
but I have the testimony of the master of the captured vessel himself, to the same effect." I then sent for my clerk,
whom I directed to produce and read the deposition of the
master, which, according to custom, we had taken immediately upon effecting the capture. In that deposition, after

having been duly sworn, the master had stated that the capture was made about five miles from Europa Point, the
southern extremity of the Rock of Gibraltar. The Strait is
about fourteen miles wide at this point, which would put
the ship, when captured, nine miles from Ceuta! The lieutenant, at the conclusion of the reading, raised both hands,
and with an expressive smile, ejaculated, "*Es possible?*" "Yes,"
I replied, "all things are possible to Federal Consuls, and
other Federal pimps and spies, when the *Sumter* and Yankee
ships are concerned."

CHAPTER XXVI.

THE SUMTER IN TROUBLE — FINDS IT IMPOSSIBLE TO COAL,
BY REASON OF A COMBINATION AGAINST HER, HEADED
BY THE FEDERAL CONSUL — APPLIES TO THE BRITISH
GOVERNMENT FOR COAL, BUT IS REFUSED — SENDS HER
PAYMASTER AND EX-CONSUL TUNSTALL TO CADIZ —
THEY ARE ARRESTED AND IMPRISONED AT TANGIER —
CORRESPONDENCE ON THE SUBJECT — THE SUMTER LAID
UP AND SOLD.

THE *Sumter's* boilers were very much out of condition when
she arrived at Gibraltar, and we had hoped, from the fact
that Gibraltar was a touching-point for several lines of steamers,
that we should find here, machine and boiler shops sufficiently
extensive to enable us to have a new set of boilers made. We
were disappointed in this; and so were compelled to patch up
the old boilers as best we could, hoping that when our funds
should arrive, we might be enabled to coal, and run around to
London or Liverpool, where we would find all the facilities we
could desire. My funds arrived, as before stated, on the 3d of
February, and I at once set about supplying myself with coal.
I sent my first lieutenant and paymaster on shore, and afterward my engineer, to purchase it, authorizing them to pay
more than the market-price, if it should be necessary. The
reader will judge of my surprise when these officers returned,
and informed me that they found the market closed against
them, and that it was impossible to purchase a pound of coal
in any direction!

It has been seen, in the course of these pages, how often I
have had occasion to complain of the conduct of the Federal
Consuls, and one can scarcely conceive the trouble and annoyance which these well-drilled officials of Mr. Seward gave

me. I could not, of course, have complained, if their bearing toward me had been simply that of open enemies. This was to be expected. But they descended to bribery, trickery, and fraud, and to all the other arts of petty intrigue, so unworthy of an honorable enemy. Our Southern people can scarcely conceive how little our non-commercial Southern States were known, in the marts of traffic and trade of the world. Beyond a few of our principal ports, whence our staple of cotton was shipped to Europe, our nomenclature even was unknown to the mass of mere traders. The Yankee Consul and the Yankee shipmaster were everywhere. Yankee ships carried out cargoes of cotton, and Yankee ships brought back the goods which were purchased with the proceeds. All the American trade with Europe was Yankee trade—a ship here and there excepted. Commercial men, everywhere, were thus more or less connected with the enemy; and trade being the breath of their nostrils, it is not wonderful that I found them inimical to me. With rare exceptions, they had no trade to lose with the South, and much to lose with the North; and this was the string played upon by the Federal Consuls. If a neutral merchant showed any inclination to supply the *Sumter* with anything she needed, a runner was forthwith sent round to him by the Federal Consul, to threaten him with the loss of his American—*i. e.* Yankee—trade, unless he desisted.

Such was the game now being played in Gibraltar, to prevent the *Sumter* from coaling. The same Federal Consul, who, as the reader has seen a few pages back, stated in an official letter to the Spanish Admiral, that the *Neapolitan* had been captured within the marine league of the Spanish-African coast, whilst the captain of the same ship had sworn positively that she was distant from it, nine miles, was now bribing and threatening the coal-dealers of Gibraltar, to prevent them from supplying me with coal. Whilst I was pondering my dilemma, I was agreeably surprised, one morning, to receive a visit from an English shipmaster, whose ship had just arrived with some coal on board. He was willing, he said, to supply me, naming his price, which I at once agreed to give him. I congratulated myself that I had at last found an independent Englishman, who had no fear of the loss of Yankee trade, and expressed as much to him. "If there is anything," said he, "of which I am proud, it is just *that thing*, that I am an independent man." It was arranged that I should get up steam, and go alongside of him the next day. In the meantime, however, "a change came o'er the spirit" of the Englishman's dream. He visited the shore. What took place there, we do not know; but the next morning, whilst I was weighing my anchor to go alongside of him, according to agreement, a boat came from the ship of my "independent" friend to say, that I could not have the coal, unless I would pay him double the price agreed upon! He, too, had fallen into the hands of the enemy. The steam was blown off, and the anchor not weighed.

Finding that I could do nothing with the merchants, I had recourse to the Government. There was some coal in the Dock-Yard, and I addressed the following note to my friend, Captain Warden, to see if he would not supply me:—

Confederate States Steamer Sumter,
February 10, 1862.

Sir:—I have the honor to inform you, that I have made every effort to procure a supply of coal, without success. The British and other merchants of Gibraltar, instigated I learn by the United States Consul, have entered into the unneutral combination of declining to supply the *Sumter* with coal on any terms. Under these circumstances I trust the Government of her Majesty will find no difficulty in supplying me. By the recent letter of Earl Russell — 31st of January, 1862 — it is not inconsistent with neutrality, for a belligerent to supply himself with coal in a British port. In other words, this article has been pronounced, like provisions, innoxious; and this being the case, it can make no difference whether it be supplied by the Government or an individual (the Government being reimbursed the expense), and this even though the market were open to me. Much more then may the Government supply me with an innocent article, the market not being open to me. Suppose I had come into port destitute of provisions, and the same illegal combination had shut me out from the market, would the British Government permit my crew to starve? Or suppose I had been a sailing-ship, and had come in dismasted from the effects of a recent gale, and the dock-yard of her Majesty was the only place where I could be refitted, would you deny me a mast? The laws of nations are positive on this last point, and it would be your duty to allow me to refit in the public dock. And if you would not, under the circumstances stated, deny me a mast, on what principle will you deny me coal — the latter being as necessary to a steamer as a mast to a sailing-ship, and both being alike innoxious?

The true criterion is, not whether the Government or an individual may supply the article, but whether the article itself be noxious or innoxious. The Government may not supply me with powder — why? Not because I may have recourse to the market, but because the article itself is interdicted. A case in point occurred when I was in Cadiz recently My ship was admitted into a Government dock, and there repaired. The reasons were, first, the repairs, themselves, were such as were authorized by the laws of nations; and secondly, there were no private docks in Cadiz. So here, the article is innocent, and there is none in the market — or rather none accessible to me, which is the same thing. Why, then, may not the Government supply me? In conclusion, I respectfully request that you will supply me with 150 tons of coal, for which I will pay the cash; or, if you prefer it, I will deposit the money with an agent, who can have no difficulty, I suppose, in purchasing the same quantity of the material from some of the coal-hulks, and returning it to her Majesty's dock-yard."

This application was telegraphed to the Secretary for Foreign Affairs, in London, and after the lapse of a week — for it took the "law-officers of the Crown" a week, it seems, to decide the question — was denied. On the same day on which I wrote the above letter, I performed the very pleasant duty of paying to the Spanish Consul at Gibraltar, on account of the authorities at Cadiz, the amount of the bill which the dock-yard officers at Caracca had rendered me, for docking my ship. The dock-yard Admiral had behaved very handsomely about it. I was entirely destitute of funds. He docked my ship, with a knowledge of this fact, and was kind enough to say that I might pay at my convenience. I take pleasure in recording this conduct on the part of a Spanish gentleman, who held a high position in the Spanish Navy, as a set-off to the coarse and unfriendly conduct of the Military Governor of Cadiz, of whom I have before spoken.

Failing with the British Government, as I had done with the merchants of Gibraltar, to obtain a supply of coal, I next dispatched my paymaster for Cadiz, with instructions to purchase in that port, and ship the article around to me. A Mr. Tunstall, who had been the United States Consul at Cadiz, before the war, was then in Gibraltar, and at his request, I sent him along with the paymaster. They embarked on board a small French steamer plying between some of the Mediterranean ports, and Cadiz. Tangier, a small Moorish town on the opposite side of the Strait of Gibraltar, lies in the route, and the steamer stopped there for a few hours to land and receive passengers, and to put off, and take on freight. Messrs. Myers and Tunstall, during this delay, went up into the town, to take a walk, and as they were returning, were set upon by a guard of Moorish soldiers, and made prisoners! Upon demanding an explanation, they were informed that they had been arrested upon a requisition of the United States Consul, resident in that town.

By special treaties between the Christian powers, and the Moorish and other non-Christian powers on the borders of the Mediterranean, it is provided that the consuls of the different Christian powers shall have jurisdiction, both civil and criminal, over their respective citizens.   It was under such a treaty between the United States and Morocco, that the United States Consul had demanded the arrest of Messrs. Myers and Tunstall, as citizens of the United States, alleging that they had committed high crimes against the said States, on the high seas! The ignorant Moorish officials knew nothing, and cared nothing, about the laws of nations; nor did they puzzle their small brains with what was going on, on the American continent.   All they knew was, that one "Christian dog," had demanded other "Christian dogs," as his prisoners, and troops were sent to the Consul, to enable him to make the arrest as a matter of course.

The Consul, hoping to recommend himself to the mad populace of the United States, who were just then denouncing the *Sumter* as a "pirate," and howling for the blood of all embarked on board of her,—with as little brains as their Moorish allies,—acted like the brute he was, took the prisoners to his consular residence, ironed them heavily, and kept them in close confinement! He guarded them as he would the apple of his eye, for had he not a prize which might make him Consul for life at Tangier?   Alas for human hopes! I have since learned that he was kicked out of his place, to make room for another *Sans Culotte*, even more hungry, and more "truly loil" than himself.

Intelligence of the rich prizes which he had made, having been conveyed by the Consul, to the commanding United

States naval officer, in the Bay of Algeziras, which bay had by this time become a regular naval station of the enemy, that officer, instead of releasing the prisoners at once, as he should have done, on every principle of honor, if not out of regard for the laws of nations, which he was bound to respect and obey, sent the sailing bark *Ino*, one of his armed vessels, to Tangier, which received the prisoners on board, and brought them over to Algeziras — the doughty Consul accompanying them.

There was great rejoicing on board the Yankee ships of war, in that Spanish port, when the Consul and his prisoners arrived. They had blockaded the *Sumter* in the Mississippi, they had blockaded her in Martinique, they had chased her hither and thither; Wilkes, Porter, and Palmer, had all been in pursuit of her, but they had all been baffled. At last, the little Tangier Consul appears upon the scene, and waylaying, not the *Sumter*, but her paymaster, unarmed, and unsuspicious of Yankee fraud, and Yankee trickery, captures him in the streets of a Moorish town, and hurries him over to Algeziras, ironed like a felon, and delivers him to Captain Craven, of the United States Navy, who receives the prisoner, irons and all, and applauds the act!

In a day or two, after the Consul's trophies had been duly exhibited in the Bay of Algeziras; after the rejoicings were over, and lengthy despatches had been written, announcing the capture to the Washington Government, the *Ino* sets sail for Cadiz, and there transfers her prisoners to a merchant-ship, called the *Harvest Home*, bound for the goodly port of Boston.

The prisoners were gentlemen, — one of them had been an officer of the Federal Navy, and the other a Consul, — but this did not deter the master of the Yankee merchant-ship from practising upon them the cruelty and malignity of a cowardly nature. His first act was to shave the heads of his prisoners, and his second, to put them in close confinement, still ironed, though there was no possibility of their escape. The captain of the *Ino*, or of the *Harvest Home*, I am not sure which, — they may settle it between them, — robbed my paymaster of his watch, so as not to be behindhand with their countrymen on the land, who were just then beginning to practise the art of watch and spoon stealing, in which, under the lead of illustrious chiefs, they soon afterward became adepts. I blush, as an American, to be called upon to record such transactions. It were well for the American name, if they could be buried a thousand fathoms deep, and along with them the perpetrators.

At first, a rumor only of the capture and imprisonment of my paymaster, and his companion, reached me. It appeared so extraordinary, that I could not credit it. And even if it were true, I took it for granted, that the silly act of the Federal Consul would be set aside by the commander of the Federal naval forces, in the Mediterranean. The rumor soon ripened, however, into a fact, and the illusion which I had labored under as to the course of the Federal naval officer, was almost as speedily dispelled. I had judged him by the old standard, the standard which had prevailed when I myself knew something of the *personnel* of the United States Navy. But old things had passed away, and new things had come to take their places. A violent, revolutionary faction had possessed itself of the once honored Government of the United States, and, as is the case in all revolutions, coarse and vulgar men had risen to the surface, thrusting the more gentle classes into the background. The Army and the Navy were soon brought under the influence of these coarser and ruder men, and the necessary consequence ensued — the Army and the Navy themselves became coarser and ruder. Some few fine natures resisted the unholy influ ences, but the mass of them went, as masses will always go, with the current.

As soon as the misfortunes of my agents were known to me, I resorted to all the means within my reach, to endeavor to effect their release, but in vain, as they were carried to Boston, and there imprisoned. I first addressed a note to General Codrington, the Governor of Gibraltar, requesting him to intercede with her Britannic Majesty's Chargé, at the Court of Morocco, for their release. This latter gentleman, whose name was Hay, resided at Tangier, where the Court of Morocco then was, and was said to have great influence with it; indeed, to be all-powerful. I then wrote to the Morocco Government direct, and also to Mr. Hay. I give so much of this correspondence below as is necessary to inform the reader of the facts and circumstances of the case, and of the conduct of the several functionaries to whom I addressed myself.

CONFEDERATE STATES STEAMER SUMTER, ⎱
BAY OF GIBRALTAR, February 22, 1862. ⎰

SIR:—I have the honor to ask the good offices of his Excellency, the Governor of Gibraltar [this letter was addressed to the Colonial Secretary, who conducted all the Governor's official correspondence], in a matter purely my own. On Wednesday last, I dispatched from this port, in a French passenger-steamer for Cadiz, on business connected with this ship, my paymaster, Mr. Henry Myers, and Mr. T. T. Tunstall, a citizen of the Confederate States, and ex-United States Consul at Cadiz. The steamer having stopped on her way, at Tangier, and these gentlemen having gone on shore for a walk during her temporary delay there, they were seized by the authorities, at the instigation of the United States Consul, and imprisoned.

A note from Paymaster Myers informs me that they are both heavily ironed, and otherwise treated in a barbarous manner. * * * An occurrence of this kind could not have happened, of course, in a civilized community. The political ignorance of the Moorish Government has been shamefully practised upon by the unscrupulous Consul. I understand that the British Government has a diplomatic agent resident at Tangier, and a word from that gentleman would, no doubt, set the matter right, and insure the release of the unfortunate prisoners. And it is to interest this gentleman in this humane task, that I address myself to his Excellency. May I not ask the favor of his Excellency, under the peculiar circumstances of the case, to address Mr. Hay a note on the subject, explaining to him the facts, and asking his interposition? If any official scruples present themselves, the thing might be done in his character of a private gentleman. The Moorish Government could not hesitate a moment, if it understood correctly the facts, and principles of the case ; to wit: that the principal powers of Europe have recognized the Confederate States, as belligerents, in their war against the United States, and consequently that the act of making war against these States, by the citizens of the Confederate States, is not an offence, political, or otherwise, of which a neutral can take cognizance, &c.

Governor Codrington did kindly and humanely interest himself, and write to Mr. Hay, but his letter produced no effect. In reply to my own note to Mr. Hay, that gentleman wrote me as follows:—

"You must be aware, that her Majesty's Government have decided on observing a strict neutrality, in the present conflict between the Northern and Southern States; it is therefore incumbent on her Majesty's officers, to avoid anything like undue interference in any questions affecting the interests of either party, which do not concern the British Government; and though I do not refuse to accede to your request, to deliver the letter to the Moorish authorities, I think it my duty to signify, distinctly, to the latter, my intention to abstain from expressing an opinion regarding the course to be pursued by Morocco, on the subject of your letter."

In reply to this letter of Mr. Hay, I addressed him the following: —

CONFEDERATE STATES STEAMER SUMTER,
GIBRALTAR, February 25, 1862.

SIR: — I have had the honor to receive your letter of yesterday's date, in reply to mine of the 23d inst., informing me that "You [I] must be aware that her Britannic Majesty's Government have decided on observing a strict neutrality, in the present conflict between the Northern and Southern States; it is therefore incumbent on her Majesty's officers to avoid anything like undue interference in any questions affecting the interests of either party, which do not concern the British Government; and though I do not refuse to accede to your request, to deliver the letter to the Moorish authorities, I think it my duty to signify distinctly to the latter my intention to refrain from expressing an opinion regarding the course to be pursued by Morocco on the subject-matter of your letter."

Whilst I thank you for the courtesy of delivering my letter, as requested, I must be permitted to express to you my disappointment at the course which you have prescribed to yourself, of refraining from expressing any opinion to the Moorish Government, of the legality or illegality of its act, lest you should be charged with undue interference.

I had supposed that the "*Trent* affair," of so recent occurrence, had settled, not only the right, but the duty of the civilized nations of the earth to "interfere," in a friendly manner, to prevent wars between nations. It cannot have escaped your observation, that the course pursued by Europe in that affair, is precisely analogous to that which I have requested of you. In that affair a quarrel arose between the United States, one of the belligerents in the existing war, and Great Britain, a neutral in that war; and instead of "refraining" from offering advice, all Europe made haste to volunteer it to both parties. The United States were told by France, by Russia, by Spain, and other Powers, that their act was illegal, and that they could, without a sacrifice of honor, grant the reparation demanded by Great Britain. Neither the nation giving the advice nor the nation advised, supposed for a moment that there was a breach of neutrality in this proceeding; on the contrary, it was the general verdict of mankind, that the course pursued was not only legal, but eminently humane and proper, as tending to allay excitement, and prevent the effusion of blood.

If you will run a parallel between the *Trent* case, and the case in hand, you will find it difficult, I think, to sustain the reason you have assigned for your forbearance. In that case, the quarrel rel was between a neutral, and a belligerent, as in this case. In that case, citizens of a belligerent State were unlawfully arrested on the high seas, in a neutral ship, by the opposite belligerent, and imprisoned. In this case, citizens of a belligerent State have been unlawfully arrested by a neutral, in neutral territory, and imprisoned. Does the fact that the offence was committed in the former case, by a belligerent against a neutral, and in the latter case, by a neutral against a belligerent, make any difference in the application of the principle we are discussing? And if so, in what does the difference consist? If A strikes B, is it lawful to interfere to preserve the peace, and if B strikes A, is it unlawful to interfere for the same purpose? Can the circumstance, that the prisoners seized by the one belligerent, in the *Trent* affair, were citizens of the other belligerent, alter the application of the principle? The difference, if any, is in favor of the present case, for whilst the belligerent in the former case was compelled to release its enemies, whom, under proper conditions it would have had the right to capture, in the latter case I requested you to advise a neutral to release prisoners, who were not the enemies of the neutral, and whom the neutral could have no right to capture under any circumstances whatever.

Upon further inquiry, I learn that my first impression, that the two gentlemen in question had been arrested under some claim of extradition, was not exactly correct. It seems that they were arrested by Moorish soldiery, upon the requisition of the United States Consul, who claimed to exercise jurisdiction over them, *as citizens of the United States*, under a provision of a treaty common between what are called the non-civilized and the civilized nations. This state of facts does not alter, in any degree, the reasoning applicable to the case. If Morocco adopts the *status* given to the Confederate States by Europe, she must remain neutral between the two belligerents, not undertaking to judge of the nationality of the citizens of either of them, or to decide any other question growing out of the war, which does not concern her own interests. She has no right, therefore, to adjudge a citizen of the Confederate States, to be a citizen of the United States; and not having this right, herself, she cannot convey it by treaty to the United States, to be exercised by their Consul in Tangier.

I trust that you will not understand, that I have written in a tone of remonstrance, or complaint. I have no ground on which to *demand* anything of you. The friendly offices of nations, like those of individuals, must be spontaneous; and if in the present instance, you have not deemed yourself at liberty to offer a word of friendly advice, to a Barbarian Government which has evidently erred through ignorance of its rights and duties, in favor of unfortunate citizens of a Government, in amity with your own, and whose people are connected with your people by so many ties of consanguinity and interest, I have no word of remonstrance to offer. You are the best judge of your own actions.

I never received any reply to this letter from Mr. Hay. The fact that the prisoners were permitted to be delivered up to the enemy, as before stated, is conclusive that he was as good as his word, and "signified distinctly" to the Moorish Government, that he should refrain from giving it any advice on the subject — which, of course, under the circumstances, was tantamount to advising it to do what it did. If he had contented himself with handing in my protest to the Moorish authorities, without any remark whatever, his conduct would not have been so objectionable, but when he made it a point to inform them, as he took pains to tell me he would, that he had no advice to offer them, this was saying to them in effect, "I have no objection to offer to your course;" for it must be borne in mind, that Mr. Hay was a great favorite with the Government to which he was accredited, and was in the constant habit of giving it advice on every and all occasions. The consuls of the different powers resident in Tangier behaved no better than Mr. Hay. A serious commotion among the Christian residents took place, upon the arrest and imprisonment of Messrs. Myers and Tunstall, which would probably have resulted in their release by the Government, but for the interference of these consuls, headed by Mr. Hay. They advised their respective countrymen to disperse, and "refraining distinctly," each and all of them, from giving a word of advice to the perplexed authorities, though implored by the Moors themselves to do so, the latter construed the whole course of Hay and the consuls to mean, that they must comply with the Federal Consul's demand, and hand over the prisoners to him.

The news of this arrest and imprisonment created great excitement in most of the Christian capitals, particularly in London. A formal call was made in the British Parliament, upon the Under Secretary for Foreign Affairs, for an official statement of the facts; but it being rumored and believed, soon afterward, in London, that the prisoners had been released, no steps were taken by the British Government, if any were contemplated, until it was too late. Mr. Mason, our Commissioner in London,.interested himself at once in the matter, but was deceived like the rest, by the rumor. The following extract from a letter written by me to him on the 19th of March will show how the British Government had been bamboozled by some one, although there was a continuous line of telegraph between London and Gibraltar · —

"I have had the honor to receive your letter of the 8th inst. informing me that, as late as the 7th of March, the English Government was under the impression that Paymaster Myers and Mr. Tunstall, had been released from imprisonment; and requesting me to telegraph you, if the contrary should be the fact. This lack of information on the part of the Under Secretary of State is somewhat remarkable, as no rumor has prevailed here, at any time, that these gentlemen had been liberated. On the contrary, the sloop-of-war *Ino*, of the enemy, came into this Bay — Spanish side — on the 28th of February, with the prisoners on board, and sailed with them the next day. On the 6th of March, the *Ino* transferred the prisoners to the enemy's merchant-ship, *Harvest Home*, off Cadiz, which sailed immediately for Boston. You will perceive, from the narration of these facts, that it was unnecessary to telegraph to you, as the prisoners, though they had not been released, had been placed beyond the reach of the British Government through its Charge at Tangier — even if you could have induced that Government to interfere, which I very much doubt.

"You have, of course, been informed through the press, that the Moorish Government was anxious to liberate the prisoners, but that it was bullied into acquiescence, by the truculent Federal Consul, who was backed by a force of forty armed men, landed from the *Ino*, and who threatened to haul down his flag, and quit the country, if his demand was not complied with. A word of advice given, unofficially even, by Mr. Hay, or some one of the consuls present, would have been an act of kindness to the ignorant Moors, in keeping them out of a scrape, as well as to ourselves. As the case now stands, we shall be obliged, as soon as we shall have gotten rid of this Yankee war, to settle accounts with his Majesty of Morocco."

One more letter, and the reader will have full information of this Tangier difficulty. Myers and Tunstall had embarked, as has been stated, under the French flag, and I wrote to Mr. Slidell in Paris, requesting him to call the attention of the French Government to this fact. Having received from him in reply a note informing me that he had done so, I wrote him again as follows: —

"I have had the honor to receive your note of the 8th of March, informing me that you had referred the subject of the capture of Messrs. Myers and Tunstall to Mons. Thouvenal, the French Secretary of State for Foreign Affairs, but that the impression prevailed in Paris that those gentlemen had been liberated. With regard to the latter fact, you will, of course, have been undeceived before this. The prisoners will probably be in Fort Warren, before this reaches you. The French Consul-General at Tangier must have kept his Government badly informed on the subject, since the latter

supposed, as late as the 8th inst., that the prisoners had been liberated.

"I trust that you will be able to make something out of the case.
It is one in which all the Christian powers are interested. If this
precedent is to stand, a French or an English subject may be seized,
to-morrow, upon the simple requisition of a consul, and handed
over to his enemy. And then, as I stated to you, in my first letter,
is not the honor of the French flag involved? It is admitted that,
as between civilized states, this question of the flag would not
arise, the parties having disembarked. But a different set of rules
has been applied to the dealings of the Christian powers, with the
non-Christian, as is shown by this very arrest, under a claim of
jurisdiction by a consul. A Frenchman in Morocco is, by treaty,
under the protection of the French Consular flag. If he commits
an offence, he is tried and punished by his Consul, regardless of the
fact that he is literally within the jurisdiction of Morocco. And
these concessions have been demanded by the Christian nations, for
the security of their subjects.

"A French citizen, on board a French merchant-ship, lying in
the waters of Morocco, would be subject to the same rule. Should,
now, a French traveller, landing in Morocco, *in itinere*, only, from
a French ship, be subject to a different rule? and if so, on what
principle? And if a Frenchman would be protected under these
circumstances—protected because of the flag which has brought
him hither, and not because he is a Frenchman, simply, why may
not Messrs. Myers and Tunstall claim French protection? Though
they were on the soil of Morocco, when arrested, they were there,
in itinere, under the French flag, which not only exterritorialized
the ship, over which it floated, but every one who belonged to the
ship, whether on ship-board or on shore, for the time being.

"But what appears to me most extraordinary in this case, is the
apathy, or rather the fear of their own governments, which was
manifested by the representatives of the Christian powers, on the
occasion of the arrest. A friend of mine, the Captain of an English steam-frigate, on this station, visited Tangier, with his ship, a
day or two only after the occurrence, and he informs me that the
Moorish authorities were sorely perplexed, during the pendency of
the affair, and that they implored the counsel and assistance of the
representatives of the Christian powers, to enable them to solve
the difficulty, but that not one word of advice was tendered." * * *

I was sorry to lose my very efficient paymaster, but there
was no remedy. He was incarcerated for a while, after his
arrival in Boston, but was treated as a prisoner of war, and
was finally released on parole. The Secretary of the Federal Navy directed his stolen watch to be returned to him,
which is worthy of record, as being something exceptional,

but I have never learned whether any punishment was inflicted upon the party committing the theft. Probably not, as by this time, entire Federal armies had become demoralized and taken to plundering.

The *Sumter* was now blockaded by three ships of the enemy and it being impossible for me to coal, I resolved to lay her up, and proceed to London, and consult with my Government as to my future course. I might possibly have had coal shipped to me from London, or some other English port, but this would have involved expense and delay, and it was exceedingly doubtful besides, whether I could elude the vigilance of so many blockading ships, in a slow ship, with crippled boilers. In her best days, the *Sumter* had been a very inefficient ship, being always anchored, as it were, in the deep sea, by her propeller, whenever she was out of coal. A fast ship, propelled entirely by sail-power, would have been better.

When I look back now, I am astonished to find what a struggle it cost me to get my own consent to lay up this old ship. As inexplicable as the feeling is, I had really become attached to her, and felt as if I would be parting forever with a valued friend. She had run me safely through two vigilant blockades, had weathered many storms, and rolled me to sleep in many calms. Her cabin was my bed-room and my study, both in one, her quarter-deck was my promenade, and her masts, spars, and sails, my playthings. I had handled her in all kinds of weather, watching her every motion in difficult situations, as a man watches the yielding and cracking ice over which he is making a perilous passage. She had fine qualities as a sea-boat, being as buoyant, active, and dry as a duck, in the heaviest gales, and these are the qualities which a seaman most admires.

And then, there are other chords of feeling touched in the sailor's heart, at the end of a cruise, besides the parting with his ship. The commander of a ship is more or less in the position of a father of a family. He necessarily forms an attachment for those who have served under him, and especially for such as have developed honorable qualities, and high abilities, and I had a number on board the *Sumter* who had developed both. I only regretted that they had not a wider field for the exercise of their abilities. I had officers serving with me, as lieutenants, who were equal to any naval command, whatever. But, unfortunately for them, our poor, hard-pressed Confederate States had no navy worth speaking of; and owing to the timidity, caution, and fear of neutrals, found it impossible to improvise one. And then, when men have been drenched, and wind-beaten in the same storm, have stood on the deck of the same frail little ship, with only a plank between them and eternity, and watched her battling with the elements, which threaten every moment to overwhelm her, there is a feeling of brotherhood that springs up between them, that it is difficult for a landsman to conceive.

There was another, and if possible, stronger chord which bound us together. In the olden time, when the Christian warrior went forth to battle with the Saracen, for the cross, each knight was the sworn brother of the other. They not only slept in the same tents, endured the same hardships, and encountered the same risks, but their faith bound them together with hooks of steel. Without irreverence be it spoken, we of the Southern States had, too, our faith. The Saracen had invaded our beloved land, and was laying it waste with fire and sword. We were battling for our honor, our homes, and our property; in short, for everything that was dear to the human heart. Yea, we were battling for our blood and our race, for it had been developed, even at this early stage of the war, that it was the design of the Northern hordes that were swarming down upon us, not only to liberate the slave, but to enable him to put his foot upon the neck of his late master, and thus bastardize, if possible, his posterity. The blood of the white man in our veins could not but curdle at the contemplation of an atrocity which nothing but the brain of a demon could have engendered.

Besides my officers, I had many worthy men among my crew, who had stood by me in every emergency, and who looked forward with sorrowful countenances, to the approaching separation. The reader has been introduced to my Malayan steward, John, on several occasions. John's black, lustrous eyes filled with ill-concealed tears, more than once, during the last days of the *Sumter*, as he smoothed the pillow of my cot with a hand as tender as that of a woman, or handed me the choicest dishes at meals.

I had governed my crew with a rigid hand, never overlooking an offence, but I had, at the same time, always been mindful of justice, and I was gratified to find, both on the part of officers and men, an apparent forgetfulness of the little jars and discords which always grow out of the effort to enforce discipline, it matters not how suavely and justly the effort may be made.

Being more or less cut off from communication with the Navy Department, I deemed it but respectful and proper to consult with our Commissioner in London, Mr. Mason, and to obtain his consent before finally laying up the *Sumter*. Mr. Mason agreed with me entirely in my views, and telegraphed me to this effect on the 7th of April. The next few days were busy days on board the *Sumter*. Upon the capture of Paymaster Myers, I had appointed Lieutenant J. M. Stribling Acting Paymaster, and I now set this officer at work, closing the accounts of the ship and paying off the officers and men. The officers were formally detached from the command, as fast as paid off, and they embarked for London, on their way to another ship, or to the Confederate States, as circumstances might determine; and the men, with snug little sums in their pockets, were landed, and as is usually the case with sailors, soon dispersed to the four quarters of the globe; each carrying with him the material for yarn-spinning for the balance of his life.

By the 11th of April we had completed all our preparations for turning over the ship to the midshipman who was to have charge of her, and in two or three days afterward, accompanied by Mr. Kell, my first lieutenant, and several other of my officers, I embarked on board the mail-steamer for Southampton. The following is an extract from the last letter that was written to the Secretary of the Navy from on board the *Sumter*:—

"I now have the honor to report to you, that I have discharged and paid off, in full, all the crew, numbering fifty, with the exception of the ten men detailed to remain by the ship, as servants, and to form a boat's crew for the officer left in charge. I have placed

Midshipman R. F. Armstrong, assisted by Acting Master's Mate
I. T. Hester, in charge of the ship, with provisions and funds for
ten or twelve months, and I have directed all the other officers to
return to the Confederate States, and report themselves to the Department. I will myself proceed to London, and after conferring
with Mr. Mason, make the best of my way home. I trust the Department will see, in what I have done, an anxious desire to advance the best interests of our country, and that it will justify the
responsibility, which, in the best exercise of my judgment, I felt
it my duty to assume, in the difficult circumstances by which I was
surrounded and embarrassed. Enclosed is a copy of my order to
Midshipman Armstrong, and a list of the officers and men left on
board the ship."

A brief summary of the services of the *Sumter,* and of what
became of her, may not be uninteresting to the reader, who has
followed her thus far, in her wanderings. She cruised six
months, leaving out the time during which she was blockaded
in Gibraltar. She captured seventeen ships, as follows: the
*Golden Rocket, Cuba, Machias, Ben. Dunning, Albert Adams,
Naiad, Louisa Kilham, West Wind, Abby Bradford, Joseph
Maxwell, Joseph Parke, D. Trowbridge, Montmorency, Arcade,
Vigilant, Eben Dodge, Neapolitan,* and *Investigator.* It is impossible to estimate the damage done to the enemy's commerce.
The property actually destroyed formed a very small proportion of it. The fact alone of the *Sumter* being upon the seas,
during these six months, gave such an alarm to neutral and
belligerent shippers, that the enemy's carrying-trade began to
be paralyzed, and already his ships were being laid up, or sold
under neutral flags — some of these sales being *bona fide,* and
others fraudulent. In addition to this, the enemy kept five or
six of his best ships of war constantly in pursuit of her, which
necessarily weakened his blockade, for which, at this time, he
was much pressed for ships. The expense to my Government
of running the ship was next to nothing, being only $28,000,
or about the price of one of the least valuable of her prizes.
The *Sumter* was sold in the course of a month or two after
being laid up, and being put under the English flag as a merchant-ship, made one voyage to the coast of the Confederate
States, as a blockade-runner, entering the port of Charleston.
Her new owner changed her name to that of *Gibraltar.* She
was lost afterward in the North Sea, and her bones lie interred
not far from those of the *Alabama.*

CHAPTER XXVII.

WE had been long enough in Gibraltar to make many warm
friends, and some of these came on board the mail-steamer
in which we had taken passage, to take leave of us; among
others, Captain Lambert, R. N., in command of her Majesty's
steam frigate, the *Scylla*, to whom I am much indebted, for warm
sympathy, and many acts of kindness. The captain was the son
of Vice-Admiral Sir Charles Lambert, whose hospitality I had
enjoyed, for a single night, many years before, under peculiar
circumstances. When the United States brig *Somers* was capsized and sunk, off Vera Cruz, and half her crew drowned, as
briefly described some pages back, Sir Charles Lambert, then
a captain, was in command of the sailing frigate *Endymion*,
and it was on board that ship that I was carried, more dead
than alive, on the evening of the fatal disaster. I recollect
distinctly the plight in which I ascended the side of this English frigate. Like a waif which had been picked up from the
sea, I had nothing on me but shirt and trousers, and these, as
well as my hair, were dripping water. I had lost my ship
only an hour or two before, and had witnessed the drowning
of many helpless men, who had struggled in vain for their
lives. My heart was oppressed with the weight of my misfortune, and my strength nearly exhausted. Sir Charles received
me at the foot of the ladder, as I descended to the deck of his

ship, as tenderly, and with as much genuine sympathy and compassion, as if I had been his own son, and taking me into his cabin, had my wants duly cared for. There are said to be secret chords of sympathy binding men together in spite of themselves. I know not how this may be, but I felt drawn toward the son of my benefactor, even before I knew him to be his son. I take this public mode of expressing to both father and son my thanks for the many obligations under which they have placed me.

As the swift and powerful steamer on which we were embarked, moved silently, but rapidly out of the harbor, in the evening twilight, I took a last, lingering look at the little *Sumter*. Her once peopled decks were now almost deserted, only a disconsolate old sailor or two being seen moving about on them, and the little ship herself, with her black hull, and black mast-heads and yards, the latter of which had been stripped of their sails, looked as if she had clad herself in mourning for our departure.

A pleasant passage of a few days carried us rapidly past the coasts of Spain, Portugal, and a portion of France, into the British Channel, and on the sixth day, we found ourselves in Southampton, which I was afterward destined to revisit, under such different circumstances. On the same night I slept in that great Babel, London. I remained in this city during the month of May, enjoying in a high degree, as the reader may suppose, the relaxation and ease consequent upon so great a change in my mode of life. There were no more enemies or gales of wind to disturb my slumbers; no intrusive officers to come into my bed-room at unseasonable hours, to report sails or land discovered, and no half drowned old quartermasters to poke their midnight lanterns into my face, and tell me, that the bow-ports were stove in, and the ship half full of water! If the storm raged without and the windows rattled, I took no notice of it, unless it was to turn over in my bed, and feel all the more comfortable, for my sense of security.

Kell and myself took rooms together, in Euston Square; our windows looking out, even at this early season, upon well-grown and fragrant grasses, trees in leaf, and flowers in bloom, all in the latitude of 52° N.— thanks, as formerly remarked, to our American Gulf Stream. I called at once upon Mr. Mason, whom I had often seen in his seat in the Senate of the United States, as a Senator from the grand old State of Virginia, but whom I had never known personally. I found him a genial Virginia gentleman, with much *bon hommie,* and a great favorite with everybody. In his company I saw much of the society of the English capital, and soon became satisfied that Mr. Davis could not have intrusted the affairs of the Confederacy, to better hands. English hearts had warmed toward him, and his name was the sesame to open all English doors. I soon learned from him the *status* of Confederate States' naval affairs, on the European side of the Atlantic. The gun-boat *Oreto,* afterward the *Florida,* had sailed for Nassau, in the Bahamas, and the new ship being built by the Messrs. Laird at Birken-head, was well on her way to completion. Other contracts were in hand, but nothing tangible had as yet been accomplished under them.

I had also interviews with Commander North, and Com-mander Bullock, agents of the Confederate States Navy Department, for the building and equipping of ships, in these waters. It being evident that there was nothing available for me, I determined to lose no time in returning to the Confed-eracy, and it was soon arranged that I should depart in the steamer *Melita,* an English steamer preparing to take a cargo of arms, ammunition, and clothing to Nassau. This ship belonged to the Messrs. Isaac, brothers, large blockade run-ners, who kindly tendered free passages to myself, and to my first lieutenant, and surgeon, who were to accompany me.

I trust the reader will pardon me—as I hope the family itself will if I intrude upon its privacy—if I mention before leaving London, one of those old English households, immor-talized by the inimitable pen of Washington Irving. One day whilst I was sitting quietly, after breakfast, in my rooms at Euston Square, running over the column of American news, in the "Times," Commander North entered, and in company with him came a somewhat portly gentleman, with an unmis-takable English face, and dressed in clerical garb—not over clerical either, for, but for his white cravat, and the cut of the collar of his coat, you would not have taken him for a clergyman at all. Upon being presented, this gentleman said to me, pleasantly, "I have come to take the Captain of the *Sumter* prisoner, and carry him off to my house, to spend a few days with me." I looked into the genial face of the speaker, and surrendered myself to him a captive at once. There was no mistaking the old time English gentleman—though the gentleman himself was not past middle age—in the open countenance, and kindly expression of my new friend. Making some remarks to him about quiet, he said, "That is the very thing I propose to give you; you shall come to my house, stay as long as you please, go away when you please, and see nobody at all unless you please." I dined with him, the next day, in company with a few Confederate and English friends, and spent several days at his house—the ladies president of which were his mother and maiden sister. I shall return hereafter to this house, as the reader will see. It became, in fact, my English home, and was but little less dear to me than my own home in America. The name of the Rev. Francis W. Tremlett, of the "Parsonage, in Belsize Park, near Hampstead, London," dwells in my memory, and in that of every other Confederate who ever came in contact with him—and they are not few—like a household word.

We embarked on board the *Melita* in the latter part of May. The vessel had already dropped some distance down the Thames, and we went thither to join her by rail; one of the Messrs. Isaac accompanying us, to see us comfortably installed. The *Melita* was to make a *bona fide* voyage to Nassau, having no intention of running the blockade. I was particular to have this point settled beyond the possibility of dispute, so as to bring our capture, if the enemy should undertake it, within the precedent set by the *Trent* case. The *Sumter* having dared to capture and destroy Yankee ships upon the high seas, in defiance of President Lincoln's proclamation, denouncing her as a "pirate," had wounded the ridiculous vanity of the enemy past forgiveness, to say nothing of that other and sorer wound which resulted from the destruction of his property, and he was exceedingly anxious, in consequence, to get hold of me. I was resolved, therefore, that, if another zealous, but indiscreet Captain Wilkes should turn up, that another seven days of penance and tribulation should be imposed upon Mr. Secretary of State Seward. We were not molested, however, and after a pleasant run of about twenty days we entered the harbor of Nassau, about 2 P. M. on the 13th of June, 1862.

On the same evening of our arrival, I was quartered, with my small staff, in the Victoria Hotel, then thronged with guests, Federal and Confederate; for the Yankee, in obedience to his instincts of traffic, had scented the prey from afar, and was here to turn an honest penny, by assisting the Confederates to run the blockade! "It's an ill wind that blows nobody good," and Nassau was a living witness of this old adage. The island of New Providence, of which Nassau is the only town, is a barren limestone rock, producing only some coarse grass, a few stunted trees, a few pine-apples and oranges, and a great many sand-crabs and "fiddlers." Before the war, it was the rendezvous of a few wreckers and fishermen. Commerce it had none, except such as might grow out of the sponge trade, and the shipment of green turtle and conch-shells. The American war which has brought woe and wretchedness to so many of our States, was the wind which blew prosperity to Nassau.

It had already put on the air of a commercial city; its fine harbor being thronged with shipping, and its warehouses, wharves, and quays filled to repletion with merchandise. All was life, bustle, and activity. Ships were constantly arriving and depositing their cargoes, and light-draught steamers, Confederate and English, were as constantly reloading these cargoes, and running them into the ports of the Confederate States. The success which attended many of these little vessels is surprising. Some of them made their voyages, as regularly as mail packets, running, with impunity, through a whole fleet of the enemy's steamers. Notwithstanding this success, however, the enemy was reaping a rich harvest, for many valuable prizes fell into his hands. It soon became a bone of contention among the Federal naval officers, which of them should be assigned to the lucrative commands of the blockading squadrons. The admiral of one of these squadrons would frequently awake, in the morning, and find himself richer, by ten, twenty, or thirty thousand dollars, by reason of a capture made by some one of his subordinates, the night before. This was the "mess of pottage" for which so many unprincipled Southern men, in the Federal Navy, sold their "birthright."

Some of these men are enjoying princely fortunes, but they have purchased these fortunes at the price of treason, and of blood, and by selling into bondage to the stranger, the people of their native States. Whilst poor old Virginia, for example, the "mother of States and statesmen," is wearing the chains of a captive, and groaning under the tortures inflicted upon her, by her hereditary enemy, the Puritan, some of her sons are counting the "thirty pieces of silver" for which they sold her! "Pity 't is, but pity 't is, 't is true." These gentlemen may wrap themselves in as many folds of the "old flag" as they please, and talk as glibly as any Yankee, of the great Federal "nation" which has swallowed up the States, but future generations, if their ignoble names should descend so far down the stream of time, will unwind these folds from about them, as we have unwound from the mummy, its folds of fine linen, and expose the corruption and deformity beneath.

I found several Confederate naval officers at Nassau — among others Commander J. N. Maffitt, who had been assigned to the command of the *Oreto*, afterward to become famous as the *Florida;* and Commander G. T. Sinclair, who had been kind enough, as the reader may recollect, to send me my guns for the *Sumter*, from the Norfolk Navy Yard. Captain Sinclair was recently from the Confederate States, and had brought me a letter from Mr. Mallory, the Secretary of the Navy, which put a material change upon the face of affairs, so far as I was personally concerned. I was directed by this letter, to return to Europe, and assume command of the new ship which was being built on the Mersey, to be called the *Alabama*. My reply to this letter, dated at Nassau, on the 15th of June, will put the reader in possession of this new programme. It is as follows:—

NASSAU, NEW PROVIDENCE, June 15, 1862.

SIR:—I have the honor to inform you of my arrival here, on the 8th inst., in twenty days from London. I found here Lieutenants Maffitt and Sinclair, and have received your letter of May 29th, enclosing a copy of your despatch to me, of May 2d. As you may conclude, from the fact of my being here, the original of the latter communication [assigning me to the command of the *Alabama*] has not reached me; nor indeed has any other communication from the Department, since I left the mouths of the Mississippi, in June, 1861. As you anticipated, it became necessary for me to lay the *Sumter* up, in consequence of my being hemmed in, by the enemy, in a place where it was impossible to put the necessary repairs upon my boilers, to enable me to take the sea again; and where, moreover, it was impossible, without long delay and expense, to obtain a supply of coal. * * * [Here follows a description of the laying up of the ship, which the reader has already seen.]

Upon my arrival in London, I found that the *Oreto* had been dispatched, some weeks before, to this place; and Commander Bullock having informed me that he had your order assigning him to the command of the second ship he was building [the *Alabama*], I had no alternative but to return to the Confederate States for orders. It is due to Commander Bullock to say, however, that he offered to place himself entirely under my instructions, and even to relinquish to me the command of the new ship; but I did not feel at liberty to interfere with your orders.

While in London, I ascertained that a number of steamers were being prepared to run the blockade, with arms and other supplies for the Confederate States, and, instead of dispatching my officers at once for these States, I left them to take charge of the ships mentioned, as they should be gotten ready for sea, and run them in to their several destinations — deeming this the best service they could render the Government, under the circumstances. I came hither, myself, accompanied by my first lieutenant and surgeon — Kell and Galt — a passenger in the British steamer *Melita*, whose cargo of arms and supplies is also destined for the Confederate States. It is fortunate that I made this arrangement, as many of my officers still remain in London, and I shall return thither in time to take most of them with me to the *Alabama*.

In obedience to your order, assigning me to the command of this ship, I will return by the first conveyance to England, where the joint energies of Commander Bullock and myself will be directed to the preparation of the ship for sea. I will take with me Lieutenant Kell, Surgeon Galt, and First Lieutenant of Marines Howell — Mr. Howell and Lieutenant Stribling having reached Nassau a few days before me, in the British steamer *Bahama*, laden with arms, clothing, and stores for the Confederacy. At the earnest entreaty of Lieutenant-Commanding Maffitt, I have consented to permit Lieutenant Stribling to remain with him, as his first lieutenant on board the *Oreto* (*Florida*) — the officers detailed for that vessel not yet having arrived. Mr. Stribling's place on board the *Alabama* will be supplied by Midshipman Armstrong, promoted, whom I will recall from Gibraltar, where I left him in charge of the *Sumter*. It will, doubtless, be a matter of some delicacy, and tact, to get the *Alabama* safely out of British waters, without suspicion, as Mr. Adams, the Northern Envoy, and his numerous satellites in the shape of consuls and paid agents, are exceedingly vigilant in their espionage.

We cannot, of course, think of arming her in a British port; this must be done at some concerted rendezvous, to which her battery, and a large portion of her crew must be sent, in a neutral merchant-vessel. The *Alabama* will be a fine ship, quite equal to encounter any of the enemy's steam-sloops, of the class of the *Iroquois*, *Tuscarora*, and *Dacotah*, and I shall feel much more independent in her, upon the high seas, than I did in the little *Sumter*.

I think well of your suggestion of the East Indies, as a cruising ground, and I hope to be in the track of the enemy's commerce, in those seas, as early as October or November next; when I shall, doubtless, be able to lay other rich "burnt offerings" upon the altar of our country's liberties.

Lieutenant Sinclair having informed me that you said, in a conversation with him, that I might dispose of the *Sumter*, either by laying her up, or selling her, as my judgment might approve, I will, unless I receive contrary orders from you, dispose of her by sale, upon my arrival in Europe. As the war is likely to continue for two or three years yet, it would be a useless expense to keep a vessel so comparatively worthless, so long at her anchors. I will cause to be sent to the *Alabama*, the *Sumter's* chronometers, and other nautical instruments and charts, and the remainder of her officers and crew.

In conclusion, permit me to thank you for this new proof of your confidence, and for your kind intention to nominate me as one of the "Captains," under the new navy bill. I trust I shall prove myself worthy of these marks of your approbation.

I was delayed several very anxious weeks in Nassau, waiting for an opportunity to return to Europe. The *Alabama*, I knew, was nearly ready for sea, and it was all-important that she should be gotten out of British waters, as speedily as possible, because of the espionage to which I have referred. But there was no European-bound vessel in Nassau, and I was forced to wait. Lieutenant Sinclair having had a passage offered him, in an English steamer of war, as far as Halifax, availed himself of the invitation, intending to take the mail-steamer from Halifax for England. As he would probably arrive a week or two in advance of myself, I wrote to Captain Bullock by him, informing him of my having been appointed to the command of the *Alabama*, and requesting him to hurry that ship off to her rendezvous, without waiting for me. I could join her at her rendezvous. As the reader will hereafter see, this was done.

I passed the time of my enforced delay at Nassau, as comfortably as possible. The hotel was spacious and airy, and the sea-breeze being pretty constant, we did not suffer much from the heat. I amused myself, watching from my windows, with the aid of an excellent glass, the movements of the blockade-runners. One of these vessels went out, and another returned, every two or three days; the returning vessel always bringing us late newspapers from the Confederacy. The fare of the hotel was excellent, particularly the fish and fruits, and the landlord was accommodating and obliging. With Maffitt, Kell, Galt, Stribling, and other Confederate officers, and some very pretty and musical Confederate ladies, whose husbands and brothers were engaged in the business of running the blockade, the time would have passed pleasantly enough, but for the anxiety which I felt about my future movements.

Maffitt, in particular, was the life of our household. He knew everybody, and everybody knew him, and he passed in and out of all the rooms, *sans ceremonie*, at all hours. Being a jaunty, handsome fellow, young enough, in appearance, to pass for the elder brother of his son, a midshipman who was to go with me to the *Alabama*, he was a great favorite with the ladies. He was equally at home, with men or women, it being all the same to him, whether he was wanted to play a game of billiards, take a hand at whist, or join in a duet with a young lady — except that he had the good taste always to prefer the lady. Social, gay, and convivial, he was much courted and flattered, and there was scarcely ever a dining or an evening party, at which he was not present. But this was the mere outside glitter of the metal. Beneath all this *bagatelle* and *dolce far niente*, Maffitt was a remarkable man. At the first blast of war, like a true Southerner — he was a North Carolinian by birth — he relinquished a fine property in the city of Washington, which was afterward confiscated by the enemy, resigned his commission in the Federal Navy, and came South, to tender his services to his native State. Unlike many other naval men, he had the capacity to understand the nature of the Government under which he lived, and the honesty to give his allegiance, in a cross-fire of allegiances, where his judgment told him it was due.

He was a perfect master of his profession, not only in its practical, but in its more scientific branches, and could handle his ship like a toy. Brave, cool, and full of resource, he was equal to any and every emergency that could present itself in a sailor's life. He made a brilliant cruise in the *Florida,* and became more famous as a skilful blockade-runner than any other man in the war. This man, whose character I have not at all overdrawn, was pursued by the Yankee, after his resignation, with a vindictiveness and malignity peculiarly Puritan — to his honor be it said. With Maury, Buchanan, and other men of that stamp, who have been denounced with equal bitterness, his fame will survive the filth thrown upon it by a people who seem to be incapable of understanding or appreciating noble qualities in an enemy, and devoid of any other standard by which to try men's characters, than their own sectional prejudices. We should rather pity than contemn men who have shown, both during and since the war, so little magnanimity as our late enemies have done. The savage is full of prejudices, because he is full of ignorance. His intellectual horizon is necessarily limited; he sees but little, and judges only by what he sees. His own little world is *the* world, and he tries all the rest of mankind by that standard. Cruel in war, he is revengeful and implacable in peace. Better things are ordinarily expected of civilized men. Education and civilization generally dispel these savage traits. They refine and soften men, and implant in their bosoms the noble virtues of generosity and magnanimity. The New England Puritan seems to have been, so far as we may judge him by the traits which have been developed in him during and since the war, an exception to this rule. With all his pretensions to learning, and amid all the appliances of civilization by which he has surrounded himself, he is still the same old Plymouth-Rock man, that his ancestor was, three centuries ago. He is the same gloomy, saturnine fanatic; he has the same impatience of other men's opinions, and is the same vindictive tyrant that he was when he expelled Roger Williams from his dominions. The cockatrice's egg has hatched a savage, in short, that refuses to be civilized.

The *Oreto* was in court whilst I was in Nassau; the Attorney-

General of the colony having libelled her for a breach of the British Foreign Enlistment Act. After a long and tedious trial, during which it was proved that she had left England unarmed, and unprovided with a warlike crew, she was released, very much to the gratification of my friend, Maffitt, who had been anxiously awaiting the result of the trial. This energetic officer throwing himself and Stribling on board of her, with such other officers and men as he could gather on short notice, ran the blockade of the enemy's cruisers, the following night, and the next morning found himself on the high seas, with just five firemen, and fourteen deck hands! His hope was to get his armament on board, and after otherwise preparing his ship for sea, to recruit his crew from the neutral sailors always to be found on board the enemy's merchant-ships.

Arriving at Green Key, the rendezvous, which had been concerted between himself, and our agent at Nassau, Mr. J. B. Lafitte, he was joined by a schooner, on board which his battery and stores had been shipped, and forthwith set himself at work to arm and equip his ship. So short-handed was he, that he was obliged to strip off his own coat, and in company with his officers and men, assist at the stay-tackles, in hoisting in his heavy guns. The work was especially laborious, under the ardent rays of an August sun, but they toiled on, and at the end of five days of incessant labor, which well-nigh exhausted all their energies, they were enabled to dismiss their tender, and steam out upon the ocean, and put their ship in commission. The English flag, which the *Oreto* had worn, was hauled down, and amid the cheers of the crews of the two vessels, the Confederate States flag was hoisted to the peak of the *Florida*.

A number of the men by this time, were unwell. Their sickness was attributed to the severity of the labor they had undergone, in the excessive heats that were prevailing. The Captain's steward died, and was buried on the afternoon on which the ship was commissioned. At sunset of that day, Captain Maffitt called Lieutenant Stribling into his cabin, and imparted to him the startling intelligence that the yellow fever was on board! The sick, now constantly increasing in number, were separated from the well, and the quarter-deck became a hospital. There being no surgeon on board, Maffitt was compelled to assume the duties of this officer, in addition to his own, already onerous. He devoted himself with untiring zeal to the welfare of his stricken crew, without intermission, by night or by day. On the fifth day after leaving Green Key, the *Florida* found herself off the little island of Anguila. By this time the epidemic had reduced her working crew to one fireman, and four deck hands.

It was now no longer possible to keep the sea, and Maffitt evading the blockade of the enemy—a happy chance having drawn them off in chase—ran his ship into the port of Cardenas, in the island of Cuba. Here he was received kindly by the authorities and citizens, but as the yellow fever was epidemic on shore, no medical aid could be obtained. Stribling was now dispatched to Havana for a surgeon, and to ship a few men, if possible. Helpless and sad, the suffering little crew awaited his return. One by one, the officers were attacked by the disease, until Maffitt was left almost alone, to nurse, and administer remedies to the patients. But things were not yet at their worst. On the 13th of August, Maffitt was himself attacked. On the afternoon of that day he sent for his clerk, and when the young gentleman had entered his cabin, said to him: "I 've written directions in regard to the sick, and certain orders in relation to the vessel; also some private letters, which you will please take charge of." Upon the clerk's asking him why this was done, he informed him that "he had all the symptoms of yellow fever, and as he was already much broken down, he might not survive the attack." He had made all the necessary preparations for his own treatment, giving minute written directions to those around him how to proceed, and immediately betook himself to his bed—the fever already flushing his cheeks, and parching his veins. There was now, indeed, nothing but wailing and woe on board the little *Florida*.

In two or three days Stribling returned from Havana, bringing with him twelve men; and on the day after his return, Dr. Barrett, of Georgia, hearing of their helpless condition, volunteered his services, and became surgeon of the ship. On the 22d, young Laurens, the captain's son—whilst his father was unconscious—breathed his last; black vomit having assailed him, in twenty-four hours after he had been taken down with the fever; so virulent had the disease now become. He was a fine, brave, promising lad, greatly beloved, and deeply regretted by all. On the 23d, the Third Assistant Engineer died. The sick were now sent to the hospital on shore, and nearly all of them died. Dr. Gilliard, surgeon of a Spanish gun-boat in the harbor, now visited the Captain, and was exceedingly kind to him. On the 24th, a consultation of physicians was held, and it was decided that Maffitt's case was hopeless. But it so happened that the disease just then had reached its crisis, and a favorable change had taken place. The patient had not spoken for three days, and greatly to the surprise of all present, after one of the physicians had given his opinion, he opened his eyes, now beaming with intelligence, and said in a languid voice: "You are all mistaken—I have got too much to do, and have no time to die."

He convalesced from that moment. On the 28th, Major Helm, our agent in Havana, telegraphed that, for certain reasons, the Captain-General desired that the *Florida* would come round to Havana, and remain until the health of her crew should be restored. The Captain-General probably feared that in an undefended port like Cardenas, some violence might be committed upon the *Florida* by the Federal cruisers, in violation of Spanish neutrality. Accordingly, on the 30th the *Florida* got under way, and proceeded for Havana, where she arrived the next day. The reader naturally wonders, no doubt, where the Federal cruisers were, all this time. Maffitt remained here only a day, finding it impossible, owing to the stringent orders of neutrality that were being enforced, to do anything in the way of increasing his crew, or refitting his ship. Getting his ship under way, again on the 1st of September, he now resolved to run into Mobile. At two P. M. on the 4th of that month Fort Morgan was made, when it was found that three of the enemy's cruisers lay between the *Florida* and the bar. Maffitt was assisted on deck, being too weak yet to move without assistance. Having determined that his ship should not fall into the hands of the enemy, he had made suitable preparations for blowing her up, if it should become necessary. He now hoisted the English ensign and pennant, and stood boldly on. His very boldness staggered the enemy. He must certainly be, they thought, an English gunboat. The *Oneida*, the flagship of Commander Preble, the commanding officer of the blockading squadron, attempted to throw herself in the *Florida's* path, first having hailed her and commanded her to stop. But the latter held on her course so determinedly, that the former, to prevent being run down, was obliged to stop, herself, and reverse her engine.

Preble, now undeceived as to the possibility of the *Florida's* being an Englishman, opened fire upon her, as did the other two ships. The *Oneida's* broadside, delivered from a distance of a few yards only, cut away the *Florida's* hammocks, smashed her boats, and shattered some of her spars. The three enemy's vessels now grouped themselves around the daring little craft, and fired broadside after broadside at her, during the chase which ensued. One eleven-inch shell entering the *Florida's* side, only a few inches above the water-line, passed entirely through her, before the fuse had time to explode it. If the enemy had been a little farther off, the *Florida* must have been torn in pieces by the explosion. Another shell entered the cabin. The fore-topmast and fore-gaff were shot away. In short, when it is recollected that she was nearly two hours under this tremendous fire, the wonder is that she escaped with a whole spar, or a whole timber.

Maffitt, meantime, had not cast loose a gun. He had no crew with which to man his battery. What few sailors he had, he had sent below, except only the man at the wheel, that they might be less exposed. But they were not safe, even here, for the shell which we have described as passing through the ship, took off one man's head, and seven others were wounded by splinters. My ex-lieutenant of the *Sumter*, Stribling, merited, on this occasion, the praise I have bestowed on him, in drawing his portrait. He is described by an eyewitness to have been as cool and self-possessed, as if there had been no enemy within a hundred miles of him. To make a long story short, the gallant little *Florida* finally escaped her pursuers, and, in a shattered condition, ran in and anchored near Fort Morgan. As the reader may suppose, her English flag was exchanged for her own stars and bars, as soon as the enemy opened upon her. This was the most daring and gallant running of a blockade that occurred during a war so fruitful of daring and gallant acts. After repairing and refitting his vessel, my gallant friend dashed again through the enemy's fleet, now much increased in numbers, and commenced that career on the high seas, which has rendered his name one of the notable ones of the war. He lighted the seas with a track of fire, wherever he passed, and sent consternation and alarm among the enemy's shipping. A correspondent of a Northern paper, writing from Havana, thus speaks of Maffitt and his craft :—

"The rebel man-of-war, privateer or pirate *Florida*, otherwise known as the *Oreto*, has safely arrived in this port, although she was chased up to the very walls of the Moro Castle by the Mobile blockading squadron, nine in number. The chase was a most exciting one, but, unfortunately, without the result so much to be desired.

"It appears that the pirate Maffitt came out of the port of Mobile with as much impudence as he entered it. The steamer seems to have been well punished with shot and shell from the Federal ships, and it is reported that she lost her first lieutenant, and sixteen men killed by a shell from one of the men-of-war.

    *   *   *   *   *   *

"From reliable information, I am enabled to state, or, rather, I am convinced, that this vessel will sail for the East Indies in a few days. Our Government had better look out for her advent in those waters. Captain Maffitt is no ordinary character. He is vigorous, energetic, bold, quick, and dashing, and the sooner he is caught and hung, the better will it be for the interests of our commercial community. He is decidedly popular here, and you can scarcely imagine the anxiety evinced to get a glance at him."

We may return now to the movements of the writer. After long waiting at Nassau, the *Bahama*, the steamer in which Stribling and Howell had come over from Hamburg, was ready to return, and I embarked on board of her, with my staff, and after a passage of some three weeks, landed in Liverpool, just in time to find that the bird had flown. The *Alabama* had steamed a few days before, for her rendezvous, where, in due time, we will follow her.

CHAPTER XXVIII.

A BRIEF RESUME OF THE HISTORY OF THE WAR, BE-
TWEEN THE COMMISSIONING OF THE SUMTER AND THE
COMMISSIONING OF THE ALABAMA — SECRETARY MAL-
LORY, AND THE DIFFICULTIES BY WHICH HE WAS SUR-
ROUNDED — THE REORGANIZATION OF THE CONFED-
ERATE STATES NAVY.

ALTHOUGH, as before remarked, I design only to write a
history of my own proceedings, during the late war, yet
it will be necessary, to enable the reader to understand these
proceedings correctly, to run a mere thread of the general his
tory of the war along parallel with them. I have done this
up to the date of commissioning the *Sumter*. It will now be
necessary to take up the thread again, and bring it down to
the commissioning of the *Alabama*. I shall do this very
briefly, barely enumerating the principal military events, without attempting to describe them, and glancing very cursorily
at the naval events.

We ran the blockade of the Mississippi, in the *Sumter*, as
has been seen, on the 30th of June, 1861. In July of that
year, the first great battle of Manassas was fought, to which
allusion has already been made. This battle gave us great
prestige in Europe, and contributed very much to the respect
with which the little *Sumter* had been received by foreign
powers. A long military pause now ensued. The enemy had
been so astonished and staggered by this blow, that it took
him some time to recover from its effects. He, however, turned
it to useful account, and set himself at work with great patience, and diligence, at the same time, to collect and thoroughly drill new troops. The victory, on the other hand, had
an unfavorable effect upon our own people, in giving them an

undue impression of their superiority over their enemy, and lulling them into supineness.

During the summer of 1861, two naval expeditions were fitted out, by the enemy, and sent to operate against our coast. The first of these expeditions, under command of Commodore Stringham, captured two hastily constructed, and imperfect earth-works at Hatteras Inlet on the coast of North Carolina, and made a lodgement on Pamlico Sound. The capture of these works, is no otherwise remarkable, in a naval point of view, than for the circumstance that a Confederate States naval officer fell into the hands of the enemy, for the first time during the war. Commodore Samuel Barron, of the Confederate States Navy, commanded the forts, and surrendered, after a gallant resistance, to the overwhelming force which assaulted him, on condition that he should be treated *as a prisoner of war*. The battle of Manassas had occurred to humble the pride, and appeal to the fears of the enemy, and the condition named by Barron was readily assented to. The other naval expedition, under command of Commodore Dupont, captured Port Royal, in South Carolina as mentioned in a former page. The "*Trent* Affair," already described, came off in November, 1861, and Commodore Hollins' attack upon the enemy's fleet at the mouths of the Mississippi, in which he gave him such a scare, occurred, as already related, in October of the same year. This brings us to the close of the first year of the war.

The year 1862 was big with events, which we will, for the most part, merely string on our thread. The Confederates, in the beginning of the year, occupied a position at Bowling Green, in Kentucky, which was seemingly a strong position, with railroad communication, in their rear, with all parts of the South, but they could not hold it, for the simple reason, that the enemy, having command of the western rivers by means of his superior naval force, penetrated into their rear, and thus compelled a retreat. When the enemy, by means of his gunboats, could send armies up the Cumberland and Tennessee Rivers, to the heart of Tennessee and Alabama, it was folly to think of holding Bowling Green, with our limited forces. Our army fell back to Nashville, and even abandoned that city,

after the fall of Forts Henry and Donelson, which were captured by the Federal forces, in February, 1862.

The evacuation of all these points, one after another, and
afterward the loss of Island No. 10, on the Mississippi, and
New Madrid, were serious blows for us. But our disasters
did not end here. The battle of Shiloh followed, in which we
were defeated, and compelled to retreat, after we had, to all
appearance, gained a victory almost complete on the first day
of the fight. Naval disasters accompanied, or followed our
disasters upon the land. Early in 1862, a naval expedition
of the enemy, under the command of Commodore Goldsbor-
ough, entered Pamlico Sound, and captured Roanoke Island.
Commodore Lynch, of the Confederate States Navy, with six
or seven small, ill-armed gunboats, which had been improvised
from light and frail river steamers, assisted in the defence of
the island, but was obliged to withdraw before the superior
forces of the enemy. The enemy, pursuing his advantages,
followed Lynch's retreating fleet to Elizabeth City, in North
Carolina, where he captured or destroyed it.

The enemy was now not only in possession of the western
waters—Vicksburg and Port Hudson alone obstructing his
free navigation of the Mississippi as far down as New Orleans—
but Pamlico and Albemarle Sounds, in North Carolina, and the
bay of Port Royal in South Carolina and Georgia, were open
to him. To complete the circle of our disasters, New Orleans
was captured by Farragut and Porter, in April—the small
Confederate fleet under Commodore John K. Mitchell, making
a gallant but disastrous defence, in which it was totally destroyed, with great loss of life of both officers and men.

Let us turn now to a more pleasing picture; for all was not
disaster for the Confederates, during the year 1862. In March
of that year, the memorable naval engagement occurred in
Hampton Roads, between the Confederate States iron-clad
steamer *Virginia*, and the enemy's fleet, resulting in the destruction, by the *Virginia*, of two of the enemy's wooden
frigates. ·Great consternation and alarm were produced in the
enemy's fleet, and at Fortress Monroe, by Admiral Buchanan
and his armored ship, as well there might be, for the ship was
perfectly invulnerable, and but for her great draught of water,

might have destroyed or driven off the whole Federal fleet.
Our people were greatly elated by this victory, coming as it
did, in the midst of so many disasters. It attracted great attention in Europe, also, as being decisive of the fate of all the
old-time wooden ships, which had, up to that period, composed
the navies of the world. It so happened, that the Federals
had completed the first of their Monitors, at this very time,
and this little iron ship, arriving opportunely, engaged the
Virginia on the second day of the fight. Like her great antagonist, she, too, was invulnerable, and the result was a drawn
battle. From this time onward, the enemy multiplied his
armored ships very rapidly, and it is scarcely too much to say,
that he is almost wholly indebted to them, for his success in
the war.

Another very creditable affair for the Confederates came off
on the 15th of May. In the interval between the fight of the
Virginia, with the enemy's fleet in Hampton Roads, and the
day last named, Norfolk had been evacuated, and the *Virginia*,
which had passed under the command of Commodore Tatnall,
was blown up. The consequence was that the James River
was open to the navigation of the enemy. Taking advantage
of this state of things, five of the enemy's gunboats, two of
which were iron-clad, ascended the river, with intent to reach,
and shell Richmond, if practicable. They met with no serious
obstruction, or any opposition, until they reached Drury's
Bluff. Here the river had been obstructed, and a Confederate
earth-work erected. The earth-work was commanded by Captain Eben Farrand, of the Confederate States Navy, who had
some sailors and marines under him. The Federal fleet having
approached within 600 yards, opened fire upon the fort, which
it kept up for the space of three hours. It was so roughly
handled, however, by Farrand and his sailors, that at the end
of that time, it was obliged to retire, with several of its vessels seriously damaged. No further attempt was made during
the war, to reach Richmond by means of iron-clads; the dose
which Farrand had given them was quite sufficient.

But the greatest of all the triumphs which crowned the Confederate arms during this year of 1862, were the celebrated
campaigns of Stonewall Jackson, in the Shenandoah Valley,

and the seven days' fighting before Richmond. I will barely string these events, as I pass along. Banks, Fremont, and Shields, of the enemy, were all operating in this valley, with forces greatly outnumbering those of Jackson. The latter, by a series of rapid and masterly movements, fell upon his enemies, one after the other, and defeated them all; Banks, in particular, who having been bred to civil life, was devoid of all military training, and apparently wanting, even, in that first and most common requisite of a soldier, courage, flying in disorder, and abandoning to his pursuer all the supplies and *materiel* of a large and well-appointed army. Such frantic efforts did he make to escape from Jackson, that he marched thirty-five miles in a single day; passing through the good old town of Winchester, which he had formerly occupied, with so many signs of trepidation and alarm, that the citizens received him and his troops, with shouts of derisive laughter!

The enemy, after his defeat at Manassas, put General McClellan in command of the Army of the Potomac, and the balance of the year 1861 was devoted, by this officer, to the collecting and drilling of troops. In the spring of 1862, he landed at Fortress Monroe, with a splendidly appointed army of 90,000 men, provided with 55 batteries of artillery, consisting of 350 field pieces. Magruder held him in check, for some time, with 11,000 men, which enabled the Confederate commanders to gather together their forces, for the defence of Richmond. He moved at length, was checked a while at Williamsburg, by Longstreet, but finally deployed his immense forces on the banks of the Chickahominy.

A series of battles now took place, commencing on the 30th of May, and extending through the month of June, which resulted in the raising of the siege, and the total rout and precipitate retreat of the Federal commander. I will barely enumerate these battles, as follows: Seven Pines; Mechanicsville and Beaver Dam; Gaines' Mills; Savage Station; Frazer's Farm; and Malvern Hill;—names sufficient alone to cover the Confederate cause with immortal glory, in the minds of all true men, as the highest qualities of courage, endurance, patriotism, and self-sacrifice, that any men could be capable of, were exhibited on those fields, destined to become classic in American annals.

Following up the defeat of McClellan, by Johnston and Lee, Stonewall Jackson gained his splendid victory of the Second Manassas over Pope; defeating him with great loss, and driving him before him to the gates of Washington. Thus, notwithstanding our disasters in the West and South, an entirely new face had been put upon the war in Virginia. The enemy's capital, instead of Richmond, was in danger, and McClellan was hastily withdrawn from Fortress Monroe, for its defence.

We must now pause, for we have brought the thread of the war down to the commissioning of the *Alabama,* and the reader will see with what forebodings, as well as hopes, we took the sea, in that ship. The war may be said now to have been at its height. Both the belligerents were thoroughly aroused, and a few blows, well struck, on the water, might be of great assistance. I resolved to attempt to strike these blows.

A few words, now, as to the *status* of the Confederate States Navy. As remarked in the opening of these memoirs, the Confederate States had no navy at the beginning of the war, and the South being almost entirely agricultural, with few or no ships, and but little external commerce, except such as was conducted in Northern bottoms, had but very indifferent means of creating one. Whilst the North was one busy hive of manufacturing industry, with its ship-yards and work-shops, resounding, by night and by day, with the busy strokes of the hammer, the adze, and the caulking-iron; whilst its steam-mills and foundries were vomiting forth their thick smoke from their furnaces, and deafening the ears of their workmen by the din of the trip-hammer and the whirr of the lathe; and whilst foreign material of every description was flowing into open ports, the South had neither ship-yards nor work-shops, steam-mills nor foundries, except on the most limited scale, and all her ports were as good as hermetically sealed, so far as the introduction of the heavy materials of which she stood in need was concerned.

It will be seen what a difficult task the Secretary of the Navy had before him, and how unjust are many of the censures that were cast upon him, by persons unconversant with naval affairs. Indeed, it is rather a matter of surprise, that so much was accomplished with our limited means. Work-shops and foundries were improvised, wherever it was possible to establish them; but the great difficulty was the want of the requisite heavy machinery. We had not the means, in the entire Confederacy, of turning out a complete steam-engine, of any size, and many of our naval disasters are attributable to this deficiency. Well-constructed steamers, that did credit to the Navy Department and its agents, were forced to put to sea, and to move about upon our sounds and harbors, with engines disproportioned to their size, and incapable of driving them at a speed greater than five miles the hour.

The casting of cannon, and the manufacture of small arms, were also undertaken by the Secretary, under the direction of skilful officers, and prosecuted to considerable efficiency. But it took time to accomplish all these things. Before a ship could be constructed, it was necessary to hunt up the requisite timber, and transport it considerable distances. Her armor, if she was to be armored, was to be rolled also at a distance, and transported over long lines of railroad, piecemeal; her cordage was to be picked up at one place, and her sails and hammocks at another. I speak knowingly on this subject, as I had had experience of many of the difficulties I mention, in fitting out the *Sumter* in New Orleans. I was two months in preparing this small ship for sea, practising, all the while, every possible diligence and contrivance. The Secretary had other difficulties to contend with. By the time he had gotten many of his ship-yards well established, and ships well on their way to completion, the enemy would threaten the *locus in quo*, by land, and either compel him to attempt to remove everything movable, in great haste, and at great loss, or destroy it, to prevent it from falling into the hands of the enemy. Many fine ships were, in this way, burned on the very eve of completion.

It must be recollected, too, that in the early days of the war, we had no finances. These were to be improvised along with other things. I travelled to the North, on the mission which has been described in these pages, on money borrowed from a private banker. If we had had plenty of funds in the beginning of the war, it is possible that we might have accomplished more than we did, in Europe, in the matter of getting out ships to prey upon the enemy's commerce — that is, in the way of purchase, for it soon became evident, from the experience we had had, in building the *Alabama*, and other ships contracted for by the Navy Department, that we could not rely upon constructing them. The neutral powers became too watchful, and were too much afraid of the Federal power. When the Government did put the Secretary in funds, several months had elapsed, the war had begun, the coast was blockaded, and all the nations of Europe were on the alert.

With reference to the *personnel* of the Navy, a few words will describe the changes which had taken place in its organization, since I last referred to the subject. It will be recollected that it then consisted of but four captains, four commanders, and about thirty lieutenants, and that the writer was the junior, but one, of the four commanders. A considerable accession was made to the navy-list, as Virginia, North Carolina, and other States seceded, and joined their fortunes with those of their more impulsive sisters, the Cotton States. A number of old officers, past service, disdaining to eat the bread of ignoble pensioners upon the bounty of the Northern States, which were seeking to subjugate the States of their birth or adoption, came South, bringing with them nothing but their patriotism and their gray hairs. These all took rank, as has been remarked, according to the positions they had held in the old service. These old gentlemen, whilst they would have commanded, with great credit, fleets and squadrons of well-appointed and well-officered ships, were entirely unsuited for such service as the Confederacy could offer them. It became necessary, in consequence, to re-organize the Navy; and although this was not done until May, 1863, some months after the *Alabama* was commissioned, I will anticipate the subject here, to avoid the necessity of again referring to it. I had been promoted to the rank of captain in the Regular Navy, in the summer of 1862. The Act of May, 1863, established what was called the Provisional Navy; the object being, without interfering with the rank of the officers in the Regular Navy, to cull out from that navy list, younger and more active men, and put them in the Provisional Navy, with increased rank. The Regular Navy became, thus, a kind of retired list, and the Secretary of the

Navy was enabled to accomplish his object of bringing forward younger officers for active service, without wounding the feelings of the older officers, by promoting their juniors over their heads, *on the same list*. As late as December, 1861, we had had no admirals in our Navy. On the 24th of that month, the Act organizing the Navy was so amended, as to authorize the appointment of four officers of this grade. There was but one of these admirals appointed, up to the time of which I am writing—Buchanan, who was promoted for his gallant fight in the *Virginia*, with the enemy's fleet in Hampton Roads. Buchanan, being already an admiral in the Regular Navy, was now transferred to the Provisional Navy, with the same rank; and the captains' list of this latter Navy was so arranged that Barron stood first on it, and myself second. I was thus, the third in rank in the Provisional Navy, soon after I hoisted my pennant on board the *Alabama*. In reviewing these matters, my only regret now is, that the older officers of whom I have spoken, and who made so many sacrifices for principle—sacrifices that have hastened several of them to the tomb, were not made admirals on the regular or retired list. The honors would have been barren, it is true, as no commands, commensurate with the rank, could have been given them, but the bestowal of the simple title would have been a compliment, no more than due to veterans, who had commanded squadrons in the old service, and who had abandoned all for the sake of their States. The reader is now in a condition to accompany me, whilst I describe to him the commissioning of the *Alabama*.

CHAPTER XXIX.

THE LEGALITY OF THE EQUIPMENT OF THE ALABAMA, AND A FEW PRECEDENTS FOR HER CAREER, DRAWN FROM THE HISTORY OF THE WAR OF 1776.

BEFORE I read my commission on the quarter-deck of the *Alabama*, I desire to say a word or two as to the legality of her equipment, and to recall to the recollection of the reader a few of the incidents of the war of the Revolution of 1776, to show how inconsistent our Northern brethren have been, in the denunciations they have hurled against that ship. Mr. Seward, the Federal Secretary of State, and Mr. Charles Francis Adams, who was the United States Minister at the Court of St. James, during the late war between the States, have frequently lost their temper, when they have spoken of the *Alabama*, and denounced her as a "pirate." In cooler moments, when they come to read over the intemperate despatches they have been betrayed into writing, they will probably be ashamed of them themselves; since these despatches not only contradict the truth of history, and set at defiance the laws of nations, but stultify themselves in important particulars.

Great stress has been laid, by both of these gentlemen, on the foreign origin of the *Alabama*, forgetting entirely, not only what was done by their ancestors in the war of 1776, but what was attempted to be done by Mr. Gideon Welles, their own Secretary of the Navy, in the year of grace 1861. I will refresh their memories on both these points, and first, as to the latter. Mr. Welles attempted to do, nothing more nor less than the Confederate States Secretary of the Navy, Mr. Mallory, did in the matter of building the *Alabama*—that is to say, he endeavored to build some *Alabamas* in England himself, but failed! This little episode in the history of the Federal Navy Department is curious, and worthy of being pre-

served as a practical commentary on so much of the despatches of Messrs. Seward and Adams, as relates to the
foreign origin of my ship. The facts were published soon
after their occurrence, and have not been, and cannot be denied. They were given to the public by Mr. Laird, the gentleman who built the *Alabama*, and who was the party with
whom the Federal Navy Department endeavored to treat.

Mr. Laird was a member of the British Parliament, and
having been abused, without stint, as an aider and abettor of
"pirates," by the Northern newspapers, as soon as it became
known that he was the builder of the *Alabama*, he made a
speech in the House of Commons, in defence of himself, in
the course of which he stated the fact I have charged, to wit:
that Mr. Welles endeavored to make a contract with him, for
building some *Federal Alabamas*. Here is so much of his
speech as is necessary to establish the charge: — "In 1861,"
said he, "just after the war broke out, a friend of mine, whom
I have known for many years, was over here, and came to me
with a view of getting vessels built in this country, for the
American Government — the Northern Government. Its agent
in this country made inquiries; plans and estimates were given
to my friend, and transmitted to the Secretary of the American Navy. I will read an abstract from this gentleman's letter, dated the 30th of July, 1861. It is written from Washington, and states: — 'Since my arrival here, I have had frequent interviews with our Department of Naval Affairs, and
am happy to say that the Minister of the Navy is inclined to
have an iron-plated ship built out of the country. This ship
is designed for a specific purpose, to accomplish a definite
object. I send you, herewith, a memorandum handed me
last evening from the Department, with the request that I
would send it to you, by steamer's mail of to-morrow, and
ask your immediate reply, stating if you will agree to
build such a ship as desired, how soon, and for how much, with
such plans and specifications as you may deem it best to
send me.' The extract from the memorandum states, that the
ship is to be finished complete, with guns and everything appertaining. On the 14th of August, I received another letter
from the same gentleman, from which the following is an ex-

tract:— 'I have this morning a note from the Assistant Secretary of the Navy, in which he says, "I hope your friends will tender for the two iron-plated steamers."' After this, the firm with which I was lately connected, having made contracts to a large extent with other persons, stated that they were not in a condition to undertake any orders to be done in so short a time. This was the reply:— 'I sent your last letter, received yesterday, to the Secretary of the Navy, who was very desirous to have you build the iron-plated or bomb-proof batteries, and I trust that he will yet decide to have you build one or more of the gun-boats.'

"I think, perhaps, in the present state of the law in America, I shall not be asked to give the name of my correspondent, but he is a gentleman of the highest respectability. If any honorable member wishes, I shall have no objection in handing the whole correspondence, with the original letters, into the hands of you, sir, [the Speaker of the House,] or of the First Minister of the Crown, in strict confidence, because there are communications in these letters, respecting the views of the American Government, which I certainly should not divulge, and which I have not mentioned or alluded to before. But, seeing the American Government are making so much work about other parties, whom they charge with violating or evading the law, when, in reality, they have not done so, I think it only fair to state these facts."

It thus appears that the Government of the United States preceded us in the English market, having endeavored, a whole year before the *Alabama* was built, to contract with Mr. Laird for the building of iron-plated, and other ships, and that the only reason why the contract was not made, was, that Mr. Laird had taken already so much work in hand that he could not take "any new orders, to be done in so short a time"— as that prescribed by Mr. Welles, for it seems that he was in a hurry. The explanation probably is, that we had offered Mr. Laird better terms than Mr. Welles, and this is the only reason why the *Alabama* was a Confederate, instead of a Federal ship! This speech of Mr. Laird caused no little merriment in the House of Commons, for, as before remarked, the Federal press, knowing nothing of these secret transactions between Mr. Welles and Mr. Laird, had been denouncing the latter for building the *Alabama*, in the coarse and offensive language to which, by this time, it had become accustomed. The disclosures could not but be ludicrous.

To dispose, now, of Mr. Seward's objection, that the *Alabama* was foreign-built. The reader will see, in a moment, that there is nothing in this objection, when he reflects that a ship of war, in the light in which we are considering her, is a *personification*, and not a mere material thing. If her personification be true, and unobjectionable, it matters not of what materials she may be composed, whence those materials may have been drawn, or where they may have been fashioned. It is the commission which a sovereign puts on board a ship, that causes her to personify the sovereign power, and it is obviously of no importance how the sovereign becomes possessed of the ship. It can make no difference to other nations, so far as her character of ship of war is concerned, whether she is fashioned out of the pines of Norway, or of Florida, or whether the copper on her bottom comes from Lake Superior or Peru; or, finally, whether Englishmen, or Frenchmen, or Americans shall have put her frame together, in either of their respective countries. Even if she be built, armed, and equipped in neutral territory, in plain violation of the neutral duty of that territory, she is purged of this offence, so far as her character of ship of war is concerned, the moment she reaches the high seas, and is commissioned.

To apply this reasoning to the Alabama. If it be true, as stated by Mr. Seward, that she was built in England, in violation of the neutrality of that country, this might have subjected her to detention by England, or it might have raised a question between the United States and England; but the ship, having once escaped, and been commissioned, her origin is necessarily lost sight of, and neither England nor any other country can afterward inquire into it. Indeed, there can be no principle of the laws of nations plainer than this, that when a ship is once commissioned by a sovereign power, no other power can look into the antecedents of the ship. From the moment that her commission is read on her quarter-deck, she becomes the personification of the sovereign power, and the sovereign avows himself responsible for all her acts. No one of these acts can be impeached on the ground, that antecedently to her becoming a ship of war, she committed some offence against the laws of nations, or against the municipal law of some particular nation.

This point was settled years before our war, by the Supreme Court of the United States, in the case of the *Santissima Trinidad*. It was alleged that that ship had been fitted out in the United States, in violation of the neutrality laws—during a war between Spain and her colonies—and the question arose whether this invalidated her commission, as a ship of war. Mr. Justice Story delivered the opinion of the court, in the course of which he said:—

"In general, the commission of a public ship, signed by the proper authorities of the nation to which she belongs [the nation to which the *Santissima Trinidad* belonged, was the *de facto* nation of Buenos Ayres] is complete proof of her national character. A bill of sale is not necessary to be produced, nor will the courts of a foreign country inquire into the means by which the title to the property has been acquired. It would be to exert the right of examining into the validity of the acts of the foreign sovereign, and to sit in judgment upon them in cases where he has not conceded the jurisdiction, and where it would be inconsistent with his own supremacy. The commission, therefore, of a public ship, when duly authenticated, so far at least as foreign courts are concerned, imports absolute verity, and the title is not examinable. The property must be taken to be duly acquired, and cannot be controverted. This has been the settled practice between nations, and it is a rule founded in public convenience and policy, and cannot be broken in upon, without endangering the peace and repose, as well of neutral as of belligerent sovereigns.

"The commission in the present case is not expressed in the most unequivocal terms, but its fair import and interpretation must be deemed to apply to a public ship of the government. If we add to this, the corroborative testimony of our own, and the British Consul at Buenos Ayres, as well as that of private citizens, to the notoriety of her claim of a public character, and her admission into our own ports as a public ship, with the immunities and privileges belonging to such a ship, with the express approbation of our own Government, it does not seem too much to assert, whatever may be the private suspicion of a *lurking American interest*, that she must be judicially held to be a public ship of the country, whose commission she bears."

This was a very strong case. The ship had not only been

fitted out in violation of the neutrality laws of the United States, but the court intimates that she might also be American owned; but whether she was or not, was a fact into which the court could not inquire, the commission, in the language of the court, importing "absolute verity."

But it is not true, as we shall see hereafter, that the *Alabama* violated either the laws of nations, or the municipal law of England. The next question which presents itself for our consideration is, Was the *Alabama* properly commissioned by a sovereign power? No question has ever been raised as to the *bona fides*, or form of her commission. Mr. Seward even has not attacked these. Our question, then, will be reduced to this, Was she commissioned by a sovereign power? The answer to this question is, that a *de facto* government is sovereign, for all the purposes of war, and that the Confederate States were a *de facto* government; so acknowledged by the United States themselves, as well as by the other nations of the earth. The United States made this acknowledgment, the moment President Lincoln issued his proclamation declaring a blockade of the Southern ports; and they acted upon the doctrine that we were belligerents during the whole war, by treating with us for the exchange of *prisoners of war*.

This was no concession on their part. We had become strong enough to compel them to this course, in spite of themselves. In other words, we had become strong enough to make *war*, and when this is the case, let us see what Vattel says is the duty of the other party: "The sovereign indeed, never fails to bestow the appellation of 'rebels' on all such of his subjects as openly resist him; but when the latter have acquired sufficient strength to give him effectual opposition, and to oblige him to carry on the war against them, according to the established rules, he must necessarily submit to the use of the term 'civil war.' It is foreign to our purpose in this place, to weigh the reasons which may authorize and justify a civil war. We have elsewhere treated of cases in which subjects may resist their sovereign. Setting, therefore, the justice of the case wholly out of the question, it only remains for us to consider the maxims which ought to be observed in a civil war, and to explain whether the sovereign is, on such occasions, bound to conform to the established laws of war. A civil war breaks the bands of society and government, or at least suspends their force and effect; it produces in the nation two independent parties, which consider each other as enemies, and acknowledge no common judge. These two parties, therefore, must necessarily be considered as constituting, at least for a time, two separate bodies, two distinct societies. Though one of the parties may have been to blame in breaking the unity of the State, and resisting the lawful authority, they are not the less divided in fact. Besides, who shall judge them? Who shall pronounce on which side the right or wrong lies? On earth they have no common superior. They stand, therefore, in precisely the same predicament as two nations, who engage in a contest, and being unable to come to an agreement, have recourse to arms." This was the law of nations as expounded by Vattel more than a century ago. He tells us that when even a revolt or rebellion has acquired sufficient magnitude and strength, to make "effectual opposition to the sovereign," it is the duty of that sovereign to talk of "civil war," and not of "rebellion," and to cease to call his former subjects "rebels." How much more was it the duty of the Northern States, in a war which was a war from the beginning, waged by States against States, with all the forms and solemnities of war, and with none of the characteristics of a secret revolt or rebellion, to treat us as belligerents, even if they denied the *de jures* of our movement? But even according to the law laid down by Vattel, the United States, and the Confederate States stood "precisely in the same predicament," with regard to all the rights, duties, and obligations growing out of the war. That is to say, they were, *quoad* the war, the equals, one of the other, and whatever one of them might do, the other might do.

Hence it follows, that if the United States could build *Alabamas*, and capture the ships of her enemy, so could the Confederate States. And if Mr. Welles, the Federal Secretary of the Navy, could go into the ship-yards on the Mersey, and endeavor to contract for the delivery to him of a ship or ships of war, "to be finished complete," in the words of Mr. Laird's correspondent, "with guns, and everything appertaining," it is difficult to perceive, why Mr. Mallory, the Secretary of the

Confederate States Navy, might not go into the same ship-
yards, and contract for the delivery to him, of an incomplete
ship, without any guns at all!

But further, with reference to the right of the Confederate
States to be regarded as a *de facto* government, invested with all
the rights of war. The Supreme Court of the enemy himself
affirmed this right, early in the war. When the Federal naval
officers — the Southern renegades, who have been before alluded
to, among the rest — began to grow rich by the capture of blockade runners, it became necessary, of course, to condemn the prizes
before they could get hold of their prize-money. Some of these
cases went up to the Supreme Court, on writ of error, and I shall
quote from a case, known as the "Prize Case," reported in 2d Black,
635. This case was decided as early as the December Term,
1862, and Mr. Justice Greer delivered the opinion of the court.
The question arose upon the capture of some English ships
which had attempted to run the blockade. These ships could
not be condemned, unless there was a lawful blockade, which
they had attempted to break; and there could not be a lawful
blockade, unless there was a war, and not a mere insurrection,
as Mr. Seward, with puerile obstinacy, had so long maintained;
and there could not be a war without, at least, two parties to
it, both of whom must be belligerents; and it is of the essence
of belligerency, as has been seen, that the parties belligerent
should be equal, with reference to all the objects of the war.
The vessels were claimed by the neutral owners, on Mr.
Seward's own ground, to wit: that the war, not being a war,
but an insurrection, there could be no such thing as a blockade
predicated of it. Mr. Justice Greer, in delivering the opinion
of the court, among other things said: " It [the war] is not the
less à civil war, with belligerent parties in hostile array, because it may be called an 'insurrection' by one side, and the
insurgents be considered as rebels and traitors. It is not
necessary that the independence of the revolted Province or
State be acknowledged, in order to constitute it a party belligerent in a war, according to the laws of nations. Foreign
nations acknowledge it as a war, by a declaration of neutrality.
The condition of neutrality cannot exist, unless there be two
belligerent parties. In the case of the *Santissima Trinidad*

(7 Wheaton, 337) this court says: 'The Government of the United States has recognized the existence of a civil war between Spain and her colonies, and has avowed her determination to remain neutral between the parties. Each party is, therefore, deemed by us a belligerent, having, so far as concerns us, the sovereign rights of war.'"

The belligerent character of the Confederate States was thus acknowledged by the highest judicial tribunal of the United States, and the prizes were condemned to the captors; and a precedent is cited by the court, in which the United States recognized the right of the revolted Spanish colonies, such as Columbia, Buenos Ayres, and Mexico, who were then in *consimili casu* with the Confederate States, to build and equip *Alabamas* to prey upon Spanish commerce, not as a mere matter of power simply, but in the exercise of the "sovereign rights of war," under the laws of nations.

With regard to the new American republics, thus acknowledged by the United States as belligerents, it will be recollected that one of the first acts of Mr. John Quincy Adams, when he became President of the United States, was to recommend the passage of a law authorizing him to send members to a Congress of all the American States, to be assembled at Panama. Under this law, members of that Congress were actually appointed—though they never proceeded to their destination—and Mr. Clay, then Secretary of State, and who had been among the foremost to advocate the recognition of the independence of the South American republics, prepared an elaborate and eloquent letter of instructions for their guidance, in which he dwelt upon the very principles I am now invoking. The republics, whose ambassadors it was thus proposed to meet, in an *International Congress*, were nothing more than *de facto* governments, like the Confederate States, the independence of neither one of them having been acknowledged, as yet, by Spain.

I may further mention, as a matter of historical notoriety, that it was a common practice for the cruisers of those young republics, to carry their prizes into the ports of the United States, and there have them condemned and sold. The *Santissima Trinidad* referred to in the case from the Supreme Court above quoted, was one of these cruisers, with nothing more behind her than a *de facto* government, and she was held to be a belligerent, and to be possessed, as such, of all the "sovereign rights of war," under the laws of nations. What renders these transactions the more remarkable, in the light of recent events, and in the face of the denunciations which have been hurled against the *Alabama* by the Federal Government, because of her foreign origin, is, that most of these cruisers were, in fact, *American* ships, not only built and equipped in the United States, but officered and manned by citizens of the Northern States, who had gone southward in quest of plunder! Many of these ships were fitted out on speculation, in the United States, and sailed from Boston, New York, Philadelphia, and Baltimore, *fully armed* and *equipped for war*, with enlisted crews on board.

A case of this kind came under my own actual observation. I was serving as a midshipman on board the old sailing sloop-of-war *Erie*. We happened in at the Swedish Island of St. Bartholomew, in the West Indies, during the war between Buenos Ayres and Spain. We were on our way from New York to one of the South American ports, to land General William H. Harrison, afterward President of the United States, who had been appointed, by President John Quincy Adams, Minister to Colombia. In St. Bartholomew we found at anchor a Buenos Ayrean cruiser called the *Federal*. This was a Baltimore-built schooner — Baltimore in those days being famous above all the other American ports, for building fast vessels of this class. Her captain, and all her officers, and a large proportion of her crew, were Americans. This vessel, we ascertained, had boarded an American ship a few days before, and taken from on board of her a portion of her cargo, under the pretence that it was Spanish property. This being in our view a violation of the laws of nations (as whether the property was Spanish or not, we held that "free ships made free goods"), we resolved to commit one of those outrages against neutral rights which have become so common in our day, by seizing the cruiser. Admitting the act of the cruiser to have been wrongful, the argument, so far as her seizure by us was concerned, was all against us, and might have been contained in a "nutshell;" but our captain, if he had ever read any international law, which was exceedingly doubtful, had read it, like Wilkes, wrong end foremost, and "went it blind," being quite sure of popular applause from the b'hoys at home, and standing in no fear of consequences so far as Buenos Ayres was concerned, as she was so weak that the Great Republic might kick her with impunity.

We first demanded her of the Governor of the island, as a "pirate." The Governor replied, that she was a commissioned ship, with a *de facto* government behind her, and that she could not, so long as she retained this character, be guilty of piracy. Further, that if she were a pirate, she was *hostis humani generis*, and Sweden, within whose waters she was, was as competent to deal with her, as the United States. He ended by informing us, that in whatever category the vessel might be placed, being in neutral jurisdiction, she could not be dealt with forcibly by the captain of the *Erie*, and notified us, that if we attempted it, he would fire upon us. The *Federal* was moored under the guns of the fortification which protected the harbor, and the following night, we fitted out a boat expedition, pulled in under cover of the darkness — the night being black and squally — and boarded her, and brought her out; the Governor being as good as his word, and firing upon us, though without effect, as soon as he discovered the movement. This was my first indoctrination in the laws of the sea! and the first occasion on which I ever heard a shot fired in anger. Sweden remonstrated, and the United States apologized, and there the matter ended. I have mentioned the incident to show, that the very cruisers which the Supreme Court of the United States was protecting by its decisions, were nothing more than American vessels, under belligerent flags, holding commissions under *de facto* governments.

But I have another precedent or two, to which to call the attention of the reader. It is a very useful practice for nations to pause occasionally, and look back upon their own history. It teaches them many lessons, which they would not otherwise learn. It shows them how to avoid inconsistencies, and prevents them from becoming dishonest as circumstances change. But, above all, it teaches them that man is a poor, weak crea-

ture, selfish and corrupt, guided by the instincts and inspira-
tions of the moment;· and that his reason—that God-like
attribute, which distinguishes him from the brute—is so fal-
lible, that he rarely sees a truth, if that truth militate against
his supposed interests. It .makes all the difference in the
world, whether a man's bull gores his neighbor's ox, or his
neighbor's bull gores his ox. The Yankee ship-owners and
ship-masters cried out, in pain, as the *Sumter* and *Alabama*
were capturing and destroying their ships, and called both of
these cruisers "pirates." I design now to show how the
Yankee ship-owners and ship-masters, of a generation or two
back, captured and burned English ships, and took great
credit to themselves for their exploits, not dreaming that they
were pirates.

The precedents which I design to cite will be drawn from
the history of the war of 1776; it will be necessary, therefore
to run a brief parallel between that war and the war of 1861,
to show that the precedents established in the former are applicable to the circumstances of, the latter. To lay aside,
entirely, the question of the right of the Southern States to
secede, and to put the war between the States on no higher
ground than that between the Colonies and Great Britain,
which was a mere rebellion, the following parallel appears:—
The original thirteen Colonies, when they formed a part of
the British Government, declared their independence of that
Government. The Confederate States did the same against the
United States. Great Britain made war upon the Colonies in
consequence of this declaration; so did the United States
against the Confederate States. The Colonies claimed and
exercised the rights of war. So did the Confederate States.
The Colonies, in the exercise of these rights, destroyed much
of the commerce of Great Britain. So did the Confederate
States, with regard to the United States. Both the Colonies
and the Confederate States were *de facto* governments, when
this property was destroyed. Now, it can obviously make no
difference that the Colonies achieved their independence, and
that the Confederate States failed to achieve theirs. If what
the Colonies did *was right, when they did it*—that is to say,
when they were still a *de facto* government—what the Con-

federate States did must have been right for the same reason. The acknowledgment of the independence of the Colonies by the parent country, whilst it had the effect to make them so many nations of the earth, could add nothing to any rights they before possessed, as belligerents, for they did not derive these rights from their status *de jure*, but from their status *de facto ;* nor did they derive them from Great Britain, but from the laws of nations. It follows, that if nothing could be added to these rights by the successful termination of the war, so nothing could be taken away from them, by its unsuccessful termination. The parallel thus appears perfect, in every particular, so far as belligerent rights are concerned, and, of course, it is only of these rights that we are now speaking.

With this introduction I proceed to produce the precedents. Mr. James Fenimore Cooper, the Naval Historian of the United States, is the author whom I shall quote, and his authority will certainly not be disputed north of the Potomac. One of the earliest cruises of the war of 1776, was made by Captain, afterward Commodore, John Paul Jones. This gentleman, in command of a vessel called the *Providence,* in the summer of 1776, made a foray among the British fishermen, on the Banks of Newfoundland, taking no less than twelve sail, and returning to Newport, in Rhode Island, at the end of his cruise, having made sixteen prizes in all. The *Alabama* never flew at such small game as this. Although she cruised, as the reader will see a little further on, for some time off these same Banks of Newfoundland, she never deprived a Yankee fisherman of his "catch of cod."

Jones commanded a regular ship of war, but it was the privateers that were the most numerous and destructive. With reference to this class of vessels, the historian tells us that "Most of the Colonies had their respective cruisers at sea or on their own coasts, and the ocean literally began to swarm with privateers from all parts of the country, though New England took the lead in that species of warfare. Robert Morris, in one of his official letters, of a date later than that precise time, remarks that the passion for privateering was so strong in this particular part of the country, that even agriculture was abandoned in order to pursue it."

In another place, the historian tells us, that " As soon as the struggle commenced in earnest, the habits of the people, their aptitude for sea-service, and the advantages of both a public and *private* nature, that were to be obtained from successful cruising, induced thousands to turn their longing eyes to an element that promised so many flattering results.   Nothing but the caution of Congress, which body was indisposed at first to act as if general warfare, instead of a redress of grievances, was its object, prevented a rushing toward the *private cruisers*, that would probably have given the commerce of England a heavier and more sudden blow than it had ever yet received. But a different policy was pursued, and the orders to capture, first issued, were confined to vessels bringing stores and supplies to the British forces in America.   It was as late as November, 1775, before Massachusetts, the colony which was the seat of war, and which may be said to have taken the lead in the revolt, established Courts of Admiralty, and enacted laws for the encouragement of nautical enterprise."

The reader observes, from the above passage, from the historian, how "circumstances alter cases."   The "nautical enterprise " here spoken of, is the same kind of nautical enterprise which has been charged, by virtuous Massachusetts, whose people were in such haste to grow rich by privateering, against the *Alabama*, as "piracy."   The rush was not, it seems, to the ships of war of the regular navy, to fight the battles of the country, but to the privateers, which promised so many "flattering results."   It took a little time to warm the Congress and the people up to their work, but when they were once fairly warmed, they took their jackets off and went at it with a will, as is the wont of us Americans.

Let us dip a little further into Mr. Cooper, and see what more, these staid New Englanders, who now have such a horror of "piracy," did.   "The proceedings in Congress," he continues, "in reference to assailing British commerce, as has been seen, were reserved and cautious.   War not being regularly declared, and accommodation far from hopeless, the year 1775 was suffered to pass away, without granting letters of marque and reprisal, for it was the interest of the nation to preserve as many friends in England as possible.   As the breach widened, this forbearing policy was abandoned, and the summer of 1776 let loose the nautical enterprise of the country upon British commerce. The effect was at first astounding. Never before had England found an enemy so destructive to her trade, and during the first two years of privateering that followed, something like eight hundred sail of merchantmen were captured. After this period, the efforts of the Americans necessarily lessened, while the precautions of the enemy increased. Still these enterprises proved destructive to the end of the war; and it is a proof of the efficiency of this class of cruisers to the last, that small privateers constantly sailed out of the English ports, with a view to make money by recapturing their own vessels; the trade of America at this time, offering but few inducements to such undertakings.

"Among the vessels employed [the historian tells us there were several hundred of them], the *Halker*, the *Black Prince*, the *Pickering*, the *Wild Cat*, the *Vengeance*, the *Marlborough*, in addition to those elsewhere named, were very conspicuous. The *Marlborough* is said to have made twenty-eight prizes in one cruise. Other vessels were scarcely less fortunate. Many sharp actions occurred, and quite as often to the advantage of the cruisers, as to that of the enemy. In repeated instances they escaped from British ships of war, under favorable circumstances, and there is no question that in a few cases they captured them. * * * The English West India trade, in particular, suffered largely by the private warfare of the day. Two and fifty sail, engaged in this branch of the commerce, are stated to have been captured as early as February, 1777. The whole number of captures made by the Americans in this contest, is not probably known, but six hundred and fifty prizes are said to have been gotten into port. Many others were ransomed, and *some were destroyed at sea*. There can be no minute accuracy in these statements, but the injury done to the commerce of Great Britain was enormous, and there can be no doubt, that the constant hazards it ran, had a direct influence in obtaining the acknowledgment of the independence of the United States of America, which great event took place on the 20th of January, 1783."

We thus see how history repeats itself, and how prone men

are to forget history. The "rebel pirates" of the Colonies—
for such they were, if we apply to them the polite nomenclature which became fashionable during our late war—less than
a century ago, were capturing, burning, and otherwise destroying the commerce of Great Britain. The historian dwells
upon the record with pleasure, as an evidence of the patriotism,
and "nautical enterprise" of his countrymen; and this was
but natural in the historian of a commercial people. But
when the commerce of the same people becomes the object of
capture, in a war far more justifiable, than the war of 1776,
since it was waged by sovereign States, in defence of their
very existence, and not a mere rebellion, the cry is changed.
It is the wrong bull now which is goring the ox, and the *Alabama* and her consorts are committing unheard-of crimes and
atrocities.

I call the reader's particular attention to the fact, that some
of the prizes of the Colonial cruisers were "*destroyed at sea.*"
This same act when committed by the *Sumter* and *Alabama*
was barbarous, atrocious! Now let me run a brief parallel
between the times of Paul Jones, by whom some of this burning of British ships was done, and my own, to show how much
less excuse Jones had for such conduct, than I. In Jones' day,
all the commerce of the world was conducted in sailing ships,
and all the navies of the world were also composed of sailing
ships. The consequence was, that there was no such thing
known, as a stringent blockade; for the simple reason, that
every gale of wind which arose, blew off the blockading ships
from before the blockaded ports, and it was, sometimes, days
before they could regain their stations. Besides, it is well
known to readers of American history, that Great Britain did
not, at any time during the Colonial war, attempt to blockade
all the ports of the Colonies. With a coast-line—from the St.
Croix to St. Mary's in Georgia—of fifteen hundred miles, this
would have been impossible, even with her great navy. The
Colonial cruisers had, therefore, at all times during the entire
war, some of their ports open into which to send their prizes.
Still they "*destroyed some of them at sea.*"

Some ninety years now pass away, and a second, and a
greater war ensues for American principles—this time be-

tween the States themselves. In the meantime, the great and powerful steamship has made her appearance upon the scene, revolutionizing not only the commerce of the world, but the navies of the world. During the first months of the war, all the principal ports of the Confederacy were blockaded, and it was not long before every little nook and inlet was either in possession of the enemy, or had one or more ships watching it. These ships were not the old-time sailing ships, dependent upon the winds and the weather for efficiency—they were steamers, independent of both, having the ability "to hold on" to the blockaded port, both by day and by night, with a tenacity little less than that of fate. Though it was possible for fast steam blockade-runners, taking advantage of the darkness, sometimes to elude the vigilance of these patient watchers, it was utterly impossible for a sailing vessel to do so—and with a rare exception, here and there, all my prizes would be sailing ships. Not only were all the Confederate ports thus hermetically sealed to me, but the ports of neutrals had also been closed against me, as the reader has seen, by unfriendly proclamations and orders in council. In short, during my whole career upon the sea, *I had not so much as a single port open to me, into which I could send a prize.*

What was expected of me under these circumstances? I had shown every disposition, as the reader has seen, to avoid the necessity of burning my prizes. I had sent prizes, both into Cuba and Venezuela, with the hope that at least some of the nations of the earth would relent, and let me in; but the prizes were either handed over to the enemy, on some fraudulent pretext, or expelled. Unlike Jones, I had no alternative. There was nothing left for me but to destroy my prizes, and this course had been forced upon me, by the nations of the earth. How senseless and unjust, then, was the clamor raised against me on this subject; especially in the light of the precedents which the enemy himself had set me? Some senseless prints even went so far as to declare that it was in violation of the laws of war; but what is it that newspapers will not say, during such a contest as that through which we have passed, when reason is dethroned by the passions, and no longer sits in the judgment seat? The right to destroy is as perfect, as the right to sell, or make any other disposition of the captured ship. But has a captor the right to destroy before adjudication? the reader may ask. Certainly. The enemy has no right to adjudication at all. Courts of Admiralty are not established for him. He has, and can have no standing in such court. He cannot even enter an appearance there, either in person, or by attorney; and if he could, he would have nothing to show, for his very *status* as an enemy would be sufficient ground for condemning all the property he might claim. It is only neutrals who can claim adjudication, and it is for the benefit of these alone that Courts of Admiralty have been established. And if any neutrals have suffered in the late war, for want of adjudication, the fault is with their own government, and not with the Confederate cruisers, as the reader has just seen. To instance the Cienfuegos cases: what detriment could have arisen to Spain, if she had permitted my prizes to remain within her jurisdiction, in the custody of my own prize agent, until a prize court in New Orleans, or Mobile could have adjudicated them?

CHAPTER XXX.

THE EQUIPMENT OF THE ALABAMA ILLUSTRATED BY
THAT OF SUNDRY COLONIAL CRUISERS, DURING THE
WAR OF 1776 — BENJAMIN FRANKLIN AND SILAS DEANE,
AS CHIEFS OF A NAVAL BUREAU IN PARIS — THE SUR-
PRISE, AND THE REVENGE — WICKES AND CONYNGHAM,
AND PAUL JONES.

"Mutato nomine
De te fabula narratur."

IN the last chapter, I gave some account of the operations
against British commerce, of certain ships of war and
privateers, fitted out in the home ports of the enemy; but as
stress has been laid, as we have already seen, upon the foreign
origin of the *Alabama,* and it has been objected against her,
that her captures were illegal, and piratical, on that account,
it will be incumbent on me to show some cases on this point.
The naval history of the enemy abounds in them, but I will
content myself with adducing only a few, as specimens of the
rest. I design to show that the United States have produced
ships, the very counterparts of the *Alabama,* in every particular, foreign origin and all, and used them with destructive
effect, against the commerce of their enemy. All readers of
American history are familiar with the names of Benjamin
Franklin, Silas Deane, and John Adams, for these distinguished
gentlemen played a very important part on the theatre of the
American Revolution. As they had much to do with the
naval affairs of the Colonies abroad, it is of them and their
doings that I would now speak. They were all Northern
men, were leaders, in their day, of Northern public opinion,
and their memories are justly held in high estimation, both
North and South. I shall vouch them for the legality of the

origin of the *Alabama*, as a ship of war, and justify by their acts, and out of their mouths, all the doings of that ship upon the high seas. I again have recourse to Fenimore Cooper. "The *Reprisal* was the first American man-of-war, that ever showed herself in the other hemisphere. She sailed from home not long after the Declaration of Independence, and appeared in France, in the autumn of 1776, bringing in with her several prizes, and having Dr. Franklin on board as a passenger." It is well known that Silas Deane followed Dr. Franklin soon afterward, and it was not long before these two Commissioners, who were sent to Europe, to look after the interests of the Colonies, just as Messrs. Mason and Slidell were sent, in our day, to look after the welfare of the Confederate States, went to work.

Dr. Franklin, in particular, was a great favorite with the French people. He wore short breeches, with knee-buckles, and silk stockings, and had the portly air, and bearing of a philosopher. Having learned to fly kites when a boy, he had turned the thing to some account when he had gotten to be a man, and was also well known as the author of "Poor Richard's Almanac," a book full of axiomatic wisdom, and wise saws. He had a much better field before him, therefore, than Mr. John Slidell had. "*Tempora mutantur, et nos mutamur in illis;*" and Slidell found that the "philosophers" who had petted Franklin, and the fair women who had played with the tassels of his three-cornered hat, showered bouquets upon him, and talked prettily of the new doctrines of liberty that were just then coming in vogue, had all passed away. Neither philosophy, liberty, or knee-buckles were at all fashionable at the French Court when Slidell arrived there. In short, the people of France had found out that this thing of getting up a revolution for popular rights, however well it might suit other people, did not suit Frenchmen, and they were tired of the matter. They had, since Franklin's day, cut off the head of Louis XVI., played at republics a while, pretty much as children play at card-houses, now setting them up, and now knocking them down again, and having gotten tired of the game, like good children had gone back quietly to their old form of despotism, under Napoleon III., and were content! The sympathy which they had bestowed upon Franklin, and which was productive of so many good results, in our first revolution, had dried up in the second and greater revolution.

Having thus briefly introduced the Commissioners of the Colonies to the reader, let us again look into Cooper, to see what their business was in France, and how they performed it. "In order," says this writer, "to complete the account of the proceedings of the American Commissioners in Paris, so far as they were connected with naval movements during the years 1776 and 1777, it is necessary to come next to the affair of Captain Conyngham, which, owing to some marked circumstances, made more noise than the cruises of the *Reprisal* and *Lexington*, though the first exploits of the latter were anterior as to time, and not of less consequence in their effects. While the Commissioners were directing the movements of Captain Wickes [we will come to these presently] in the manner that has been mentioned, they were not idle in other quarters. A small frigate was building at Nantes, on their account, and there will be occasion to speak of her hereafter, under the name of the *Queen of France.*

"Some time in the spring of 1777, an agent was sent to Dover by the American Commissioners, where he purchased a fine, fast-sailing, English-built cutter, and had her carried across to Dunkirk. Here she was privately equipped as a cruiser, and named the *Surprise.* To the command of this vessel, Captain Gustavus Conyngham was appointed, *by filling up a blank commission* from John Hancock, the President of Congress. This commission bore date, March 1st, 1777, and, it would seem, as fully entitled Mr. Conyngham to the rank of captain in the Navy, as any other that was ever issued by the same authority. Having obtained his officers and crew at Dunkirk, Captain Conyngham sailed on a cruise about the 1st of May, and on the 4th he took a brig called the *Joseph*," &c.

Now, it is to be remarked, with reference to this passage, that the *Alabama*, though built in England, was not armed or equipped there, nor was her crew enlisted there; whilst the *Surprise* was not only "privately equipped as a cruiser," at Dunkirk, a port of France, then at peace with England — for France had not yet joined the Colonies in the war — but she got

all her officers and crew there, many of whom were Frenchmen. And when she got up her anchor for a cruise, still
lying in the waters of France, she was a perfectly armed and
equipped ship of war. She could have engaged an enemy,
immediately upon passing beyond the marine league, whereas
the *Alabama*, when she left the Mersey, was entirely unarmed,
and without an enlisted crew, and could have been taken possession of by an enemy's cruiser as easily as any other merchant-ship. Mr. Seward insisted, with much vehemence, with
the English Government, that the *Alabama* was not entitled to
be regarded as a ship of war, but rather a "British pirate,"
because she had never been in a Confederate port. His latest
form of protest is found in a letter to Lord Stanley, the British
Secretary for Foreign Affairs, of the date of January 12th,
1867, as follows:—

" Lord Stanley excuses the reception of the vessels complained
of in British ports, subsequently to their fraudulent escapes and
armament, on the ground that when the vessels appeared in these
ports, they did so in the character of properly commissioned cruisers
of the Government of the so-styled Confederate States, and that
they received no more shelter, provisions, or facilities, than was
due to them in that character. This position is taken by his lordship in full view of the facts that—with the exception of the *Sumter* and the *Florida*—none of the vessels named were ever found
in any place where a lawful belligerent commission could either be
conferred or received. It would appear, therefore, that, in the
opinion of her Majesty's Government, a British vessel, in order to
acquire a belligerent character against the United States, had only
to leave the British port where she was built, clandestinely, and
to be fraudulently armed, equipped, and manned anywhere in Great
Britain, or in any foreign country, or on the high seas ; and in some
foreign country, or upon the high seas, to set up and assume the
title and privileges of a belligerent, without even entering the so-
called Confederacy, or ever coming within any port of the United
States. I must confess that, if a lawful belligerent character can
be acquired in such a manner, then I am unable to determine by
what different course of proceeding a vessel can become a pirate
and an enemy to the peace of nations."

Had Mr. Seward forgotten, when he wrote the above, the
case of Dr. Franklin's ship, the *Surprise?* It will be recollected, too, that Mr. Adams, the United States Minister at the
Court of London, frequently protested, in his correspondence

with the English Foreign Office, against the Confederates being permitted to have "stationed agents," at Liverpool, and elsewhere in the British dominions, conducting a "Naval Bureau." Had he forgotten the "Naval Bureau" which was conducted in France, by Dr. Franklin and Silas Deane, who were "stationed agents" of the Colonies? How they built, and purchased, and equipped, and commissioned ships, all in neutral territory; even filling up blank commissions sent out to them by the Congress for the purpose?

But to continue with our precedents. The career of the *Surprise* was not a very long one. Having carried some prizes into a French port, in violation of a treaty then existing between France and Great Britain, providing that neither should permit the enemies of the other to bring their prizes into her ports, she was seized by the French authorities, and we hear no more of her. But we do hear more, and that immediately, from the Naval Bureau in Paris, under the guidance of Dr. Franklin and Silas Deane. As soon as the seizure of the *Surprise* became known to the Commissioners, they dispatched one of their agents, a Mr. Hodge, to Dunkirk, where he purchased another cutter, which was fitted with all dispatch, as a cruiser, as the *Surprise* had been. This second vessel was called the *Revenge*, and "Captain Conyngham and his people," to use the words of the historian, were transferred to her. A new commission was given to Conyngham, dated on the 2d of May, 1777, filled up, as before, by the Commissioners, and he soon afterward proceeded to sea under it.

It will be seen with what indulgence, and even connivance the Commissioners were treated by the French authorities. The seizure of the *Surprise* was a mere blind, intended to satisfy England. The ship herself was suffered to pass out of view, but another ship was permitted to be equipped in her stead, and the officers and crew of the old ship were transferred to the new one, with little or no disguise, and the latter was suffered to depart on a cruise without molestation. Here was another ship, which had never been in any port of the Colonies, and which, according to Mr. Seward's vocabulary, was a "pirate." Let us see what she did. "The *Revenge*," continues the historian, "proved exceedingly successful, making prizes daily, and *generally destroying them.* Some of the more valuable, however, were ordered into Spain, where many arrived; their arrival proving of great moment to the agents of the American Government in Europe. It is even affirmed, that the money advanced to Mr. Adams [the Mr. Adams, here spoken of, was John Adams, afterward second President of the United States, the grandfather of Mr. Charles Francis Adams, Federal Minister to England during the war; and the antagonism in which the grandfather, and grandson are placed, in reference to the principles I am discussing, is one of the curious revolutions of history] for travelling expenses, when he arrived in Spain, a year or two later, was derived from this source."

The *Revenge* now disappears from view, as the *Surprise* had done before her, and the historian takes up the *Reprisal*, the ship, as we have seen, which carried Dr. Franklin over to France. "The *Reprisal*, having refitted, soon sailed toward the Bay of Biscay, on another cruise. Here she captured several more vessels, and among the rest a King's packet, that plied between Falmouth and Lisbon. When the cruise was up, Captain Wickes went into Nantes, taking his prizes with him. The complaints of the English now became louder, and the American Ministers were *secretly* admonished of the necessity of using greater reserve. The prizes were directed to quit France, though the *Reprisal*, being leaky, was suffered to remain in port, in order to refit. The former were taken into the offing, and sold, *the state of the times rendering these informal proceedings necessary.* Enormous losses to the captors were the consequences, while it is not improbable, that the gains of the purchasers had their influence *in blinding the local authorities* to the character of the transaction."

Here we see not only a violation of neutrality, but a little bribery going on, these "rebel pirates" having an eye to the "flattering results," spoken of by Mr. Cooper, some pages back. The historian proceeds. "The business appears to have been managed with dexterity, and the proceeds of the sales, such as they were, proved of great service to the agents of the Government, by enabling them to *purchase other vessels.*" We see how capitally those "stational agents," Franklin and Deane, were conducting that "Naval Bureau," against the like of which, in our case, Mr. Adams had so warmly protested. I again quote: "In April, the *Lexington* arrived in France, and the old difficulties were renewed. But the Commissioners at Paris, who had been authorized to equip vessels, appoint officers, and do other matters to annoy the enemy, now planned a cruise that surpassed anything of the sort that had yet been attempted in Europe, under the American flag. Captain Wickes was directed to proceed to sea, with his own vessel and the *Lexington*, and to go directly off Ireland, in order to intercept a convoy of linen ships, that was expected to sail about that time. A cutter of ten guns called the *Dolphin*, that had been detained by the Commissioners, to carry despatches to America, was diverted from her original destination, and placed under the orders of Captain Wickes. The *Dolphin* was commanded by Lieutenant Nicholson, a brother of the senior captain, and a gentleman who subsequently died at the head of the service. Captain Wickes, in command of this light squadron, sailed from Nantes, about the commencement of June, going first into the Bay of Biscay, and afterward entirely around Ireland, sweeping the sea before him, of everything that was not of a force to render an attack hopeless. The linen ships were missed, but many vessels were taken *or destroyed*.

"The sensation produced among the British merchants, by the different cruises in the European sea, that have been recorded in this chapter, is stated in the diplomatic correspondence of the day to have been greater than that produced in the previous war by the squadron of the celebrated Thurot. Insurance rose to an enormous height, and in speaking of the cruise of Captain Wickes, in particular, Mr. Deane observes in one of his letters to Robert Morris, that it 'effectually alarmed England, prevented the great fair at Chester, occasioned insurance to rise, and even deterred the English merchants from shipping in English bottoms, at any rate, so that, in a few weeks, forty sail of French ships were loading in the Thames, on freight, an instance never known before.' In the same letter the Commissioner adds: 'In a word, Conyngham, by his first and second bold expeditions, is become the terror of all the eastern coasts of England and Scotland, and is more dreaded than Thurot was in the late war.'"

This same Captain Conyngham, afterward, while cruising on the American coast, fell into the hands of the enemy. He had, of course, become odious to the English people, and they had denounced him as a "pirate," as our Northern people have denounced the writer of these pages. Conyngham was closely confined, and the English admiral, whose fleet was then stationed in the waters of New York, threatened to send him to England for trial. Let us see what steps the American Congress took in behalf of this "rebel pirate," as soon as it heard of these proceedings. The subject having been brought to its notice, it directed its Secretary, Charles Thompson, to address a letter of remonstrance to the British admiral, threatening retaliation, if he dared to execute his threats. I quote from the journals of Congress:—

"In Congress assembled, July 1799.—A letter of the 17th instant, from Ann Conyngham, and a petition from a number of inhabitants of Philadelphia were read, representing that Captain Gustavus Conyngham, now a prisoner with the enemy, is closely confined, and ordered to be sent to England, and praying that measures may be taken for the security of his person: *Ordered*, That the same be referred to a committee of three. The members chosen, Mr. Morris, Mr. Dickinson, and Mr. Whipple. The committee to whom were referred the petition, and letter respecting Gustavus Conyngham, brought in a report; whereupon, *Resolved*, That the following letter from the Secretary of Congress, be written to the admiral, or other commanding officer of the fleet, or ships of his Britannic Majesty, lying in the harbor of New York, viz.:

"'Sir, I am directed by the Congress of the United States of America to inform you, that they have received evidence that Gustavus Conyngham, a citizen of America, late commander of an armed vessel in the service of the said States, and taken on board of a private armed cutter, hath been treated in a manner contrary to the dictates of humanity, and the practice of *Christian, civilized nations*. I am ordered, in the name of Congress, to demand that good and sufficient reason be given for this conduct, or that the said Gustavus Conyngham be immediately released from his present rigorous, and *ignominious* confinement.

"'With all due respect, I have the honor to be, Sir,
"'Your most obedient and humble servant.'

"*Resolved*, That, unless a satisfactory answer be received to the foregoing letter, on or before the 1st day of August next, the Marine Committee do immediately order to be confined, in close and safe custody, so many persons as they may think proper, in order to abide the fate of the said Gustavus Conyngham. *Ordered,* That the above letter be immediately transmitted to New York, by the Board of War, and that copies of said letter and resolution be delivered to the wife of Conyngham, and the petitioners.

"*Monday, Dec.* 13*th*, 1779. — A memorial of Christopher Hale was read, praying to be exchanged, and to have leave to go to New York, upon his parole, for a few days, to procure a person in his room. *Resolved,* That Mr. Hale be informed, that the prayer of his memorial cannot be granted, until Captain Conyngham is released, as it has been determined that he must abide the fate of that officer."

Conyngham was afterward released. This is the way in which the ancestors of Mr. Seward, and Mr. Charles Francis Adams, took care of their "rebel pirates."

There is one other point in the legal history of the *Alabama,* which it is necessary to notice, and to which I propose to adduce another of those awkward precedents, which I have exhumed from those musty old records, which our Northern brethren seem so thoroughly to have forgotten. It has been charged against the *Alabama,* that her crew was composed mostly of foreigners, and that this was another reason why she was not entitled to be considered as a Confederate States ship of war. Let us look a little into this charge. A sovereign is not only not obliged to account to other nations, for the manner in which he becomes possessed of his ships of war, as we have seen, but he cannot be questioned as to the nativity or naturalization of the persons serving on board of them. It could have been of no sort of consequence to any foreign officer, demanding to see my commission, whether I was a native of England, Germany, or France, or of any other foreign power. All that he could demand of me, in order to satisfy himself that I was entitled to exercise belligerent rights, was a sight of my commission as a *Confederate States naval officer.* Nationality is presumed in all such commissions, and the presumption cannot be inquired into. Mr. Justice Story, in the decision quoted a few pages back, says, as the reader will recollect, that the commission of a ship of war imports such "absolute verity," that it cannot be ·inquired into, or contradicted. It is like proving a fact by a record. No other proof than the production of the record is required, or indeed permitted. The commission of the commander is the commission of his ship. Neither the *Sumter* nor the *Alabama* had any other commission than my own, and the orders assigning me to them. If this be the law with regard to the commander of a ship, *a fortiori*, must it be the law with reference to the subordinate officers and crew.

The writers on international law, without exception, lay down the rule, that a sovereign may enlist foreigners to assist him in his wars; and that the men thus enlisted are entitled to all the protection of belligerents, equally with native citizens. The Swiss foreign legions, so well known in history, are notable illustrations of this doctrine; and no one has ever heard of a Swiss being hung because he served under a foreign flag. Vattel, who has the rare merit of having so thoroughly exhausted all these subjects, that he has left scarcely anything for those who have followed him to say, lays down the doctrine as follows: "Much has been said on the question whether the profession of a mercenary soldier be lawful or not,—whether individuals may, for money, or any other reward, engage to serve a foreign prince in his wars? This question does not appear to me to be very difficult to be solved. Those who enter into such engagements, without the express or tacit consent of their sovereign, offend against their duty as citizens. But if their sovereign leaves them at liberty to follow their inclination for a military life, they are perfectly free in that respect. [Modern nations, and especially the United States, have left their citizens free to expatriate themselves at pleasure.] Now, every free man may join whatever society he pleases, according as he finds it most to his advantage. He may make its cause his own, and espouse its quarrels. He becomes, in some measure, at least for a time, a member of the State in whose service he engages." Again: "The sovereign has no right to compel foreigners; he must not even employ stratagem or artifice, in order to induce them to engage in a contract, which, like all others, should be founded on candor and good faith."

But it was scarcely necessary to quote other authority, on that point, than the authority of the enemy himself. Mr. Secretary Seward knew, at the very time he was denouncing the *Alabama* as a "pirate," because of her having, as he alleged, a British crew on board, that his own Government was filling up its armies, and its navy, too, with hundreds of thousands of raw recruits from Belgium, Germany, and Ireland, and other countries. Nay, more, that by an act of the Federal Congress, these debased and ignorant men, drawn, for the most part, from the idle and thieving classes of their respective countries, were invested, *ipso facto*, upon enlistment, with all the functions and attributes of American citizens — the function of robbery more especially included! With reference to the conduct of the enemy in this particular, I deem it not amiss to introduce a short extract or two, from a speech made by Sir Hugh Cairnes, her Britannic Majesty's Attorney-General, in the House of Commons, on the 12th of May, 1864. The discussion grew out of the case of the Confederate States steamer *Georgia*, which had recently returned to Liverpool, after a cruise. Among other questions discussed was whether the *Georgia* should be excluded from British ports, because of some alleged infraction on her part, of the British Foreign Enlistment Act. In speaking to this question, the Attorney-General, alluding to the insufficiency of the proof in the case, said : —

"The case of the *Kearsarge* was a case of this character. Beyond all question, a considerable amount of recruiting was carried on, at Cork, for the purposes of that ship, she being employed at the time, in our own waters, or very near them, in looking out for the enemy; and she was furnished with a large addition to her crew from Ireland. Upon that being represented to Mr. Adams, he said, as might have been expected, that it was entirely contrary to the wishes of his Government, and that there must be some mistake. The men were afterward relanded, and there can be no doubt that there had been a violation of our neutrality. Nevertheless, we admitted the *Kearsarge* afterward into English waters. We have not excluded her from our ports, and if we had, I think the Government of the United States would have considered that they had some cause of offence.

"But it does not rest here. I see from the paper, that the Honorable Member for Horsham, wants information respecting the enlistment of British subjects for the Federal Army. Now, from all quarters reports reach us, which we cannot doubt to be substantially true, that agents for recruiting for the Federal Army, with, or without the concurrence of the Government, are in Ireland, and engage men under the pretext of employing them on railways and public works, but really with the intention of enlisting them, and that many of these men are so enlisted. In Canada and New Brunswick the same practices prevail. Representations have been made to the United States Government respecting the cases of particular persons, who have been kidnapped into the service, and I feel bound to say that those representations have not met with that prompt and satisfactory attention we might have expected," &c.

The reader thus perceives, that if the *Alabama* enlisted some foreigners to complete her crew, she was only following the example set her, by Mr. Seward himself; but there was this difference between the honorable Secretary of State and the writer. The former resorted to deceit, trickery, and fraud, whilst no man can say of the latter, that he inveigled him on board the *Alabama*.

I will now produce the precedent I spoke of, from those musty old records. It is drawn from the career of that remarkable sea-captain, to whom I have before referred, and with whose history every American is acquainted—I mean, John Paul Jones. The naval engagement, which conferred most honor upon Jones, was that between the *Bon homme Richard*, (named after Dr. Franklin's "Poor Richard," in the almanac, of which this Chief of the Naval Bureau in Paris was the author,) and the British ships *Serapis* and *Countess of Scarborough*. Mr. Cooper thus describes the crew of Jones' ship, picked up at Dunkirk, or Nantes, or some of the other French ports:—

"To manage a vessel of this singular armament and doubtful construction, Commodore Jones was compelled to receive on board a crew of still more equivocal composition. A few Americans were found to fill the stations of sea officers, on the quarter deck, and forward, but the remainder of the people were a mixture of English, Irish, Scotch, Portuguese, Norwegians, Germans, Spaniards, Swedes, Italians, and Malays, with occasionally a man from one of the islands [meaning Sandwich Islands]. To keep this motley crew in order, 135 soldiers were put on board, under the command of some officers of inferior rank. These soldiers, or marines, were recruited at random, and were not much less singularly mixed as to countries, than the regular crew."

I had something of a mixture on board the *Alabama*, but I think Jones decidedly beat me, in the number of nationalities he had the honor to command.

CHAPTER XXXI.

HAVING cleared the way, in the last two chapters, for the
cruise of the *Alabama,* by removing some of the legal
rubbish with which Mr. Seward and Mr. Adams had sought to
encumber her, we are in a condition to put the ship in commission. I was at last accounts in Liverpool, as the reader
will recollect, having just arrived there in the steamer *Bahama,* from Nassau. The *Alabama,* then known as the "290,"
had proceeded, a few days before, to her rendezvous, the island
of Terceira, one of the group of the Azores. The name "290"
may need a word of explanation. The newspapers of the
enemy have falsely charged that the *Alabama* was built by
290 Englishmen, of "rebel" proclivities, and hence, they say,
the name.

One Parson Boynton has written a book, which he calls the
"History of the Navy," but which is rather a biography of
Mr. Secretary Welles, his Assistant Secretary Fox, and several ingenious mechanics. Judging by this attempt, parsons
are rather bad hands to write histories. Speaking of the *Alabama,* this gentleman remarks: "Insultingly, this vessel was
named '290,' to show, by the large number that contributed to
fit her out, how widespread was the English sympathy for the
rebel cause. The *Alabama* was not regarded as a rebel vessel
of war, but as a British pirate, or rather, perhaps, as an English man-of-war, sent forth under the veil of the rebel flag, to

sink and destroy our merchantmen." It is thus seen, that this *history* repeats the stale newspaper slander. Of such stuff the Yankee histories of the war, generally, are made, especially such of them as are written by amateur parsons. The *fact* is, as the reader has seen, that the *Alabama* was built by the Messrs. Laird of Birkenhead, under a contract with the Confederate States, and was paid for out of the Confederate Treasury. She happened to be the 290th ship built by those gentlemen, and *hence* the name.

The *Alabama* had been built in perfect good faith by the Lairds. When she was contracted for, no question had been raised as to the right of a neutral to build, and sell to a belligerent such a ship. The reader has seen that the Federal Secretary of the Navy himself had endeavored, not only to build an *Alabama*, but iron-clads in England. But as the war progressed, the United States, foreseeing the damage which a few fast steamers might inflict on their commerce, took the alarm, and began to insist that neutrals should not supply us, even with unarmed ships. The laws of nations were clearly against them. Their own practice, in all former wars, in which they had been neutrals, was against them. And yet they maintained their ground so stoutly and defiantly, threatening war, if they were not listened to, that the neutral powers, and especially Great Britain, became very cautious. They were indeed bullied—for that is the word—into timidity. To show the good faith which the Lairds had practised throughout, I quote again from the speech made by the senior partner, in the House of Commons:—

"I can only say from all I know, and from all I have heard, that from the day the vessel was laid down, to her completion everything was open and above board, in this country. I also further say, that the officers of the Government had every facility afforded them for inspecting the ship, during the progress of building. When the officers came to the builders, they were shown the ship, and day after day, the customs officers were on board, *as they were when she finally left*, and they declared that there was nothing wrong. *They only left her when the tug left*, and they were obliged to declare, that she left Liverpool *a perfectly legitimate transaction*."

Notwithstanding this practice of good faith, on our part, and our entire innocence of any breach of the laws of nations, or of the British Foreign Enlistment Act, Lord John Russell had been intimidated to such an extent, that the ship came within an ace of being detained. But for the little *ruse* which we practised, of going on a trial-trip, with a party of ladies, and the customs officers, mentioned by Mr. Laird, on board, and not returning, but sending our guests back in a tug, there is no doubt that the *Alabama* would have been tied up, as the *Oreto* or *Florida* had been, in court. She must have been finally released, it is true, but the delay itself would have been of serious detriment to us.

After a few busy days in Liverpool, during which I was gathering my old officers of the *Sumter* around me, and making my financial arrangements for my cruise, with the house of Frazer, Trenholm & Co., I departed on the 13th of August, 1862, in the steamer *Bahama*, to join the *Alabama*. Captain James D. Bullock, of the Confederate States Navy, a Georgian, who had been bred in the old service, but who had retired from it some years before the war, to engage in the steam-packet service, accompanied me. Bullock had contracted for, and superintended the building of the *Alabama*, and was now going with me, to be present at the christening of his bantling. I am indebted to him, as well the Messrs. Laird, for a very perfect ship of her class.

She was of about 900 tons burden, 230 feet in length, 32 feet in breadth, 20 feet in depth, and drew, when provisioned and coaled for a cruise, 15 feet of water. Her model was of the most perfect symmetry, and she sat upon the water with the lightness and grace of a swan. She was barkentine rigged, with long lower masts, which enabled her to carry large fore-and-aft sails, as jibs and try-sails, which are of so much importance to a steamer, in so many emergencies. Her sticks were of the best yellow pine, that would bend in a gale, like a willow wand, without breaking, and her rigging was of the best of Swedish iron wire. The scantling of the vessel was light, compared with vessels of her class in the Federal Navy, but this was scarcely a disadvantage, as she was designed as a scourge of the enemy's commerce, rather than for battle. She was to defend herself, simply, if defence should become necessary. Her engine was of three hundred horse-power, and she had attached an apparatus for condensing, from the vapor of sea-water, all the fresh water that her crew might require. She was a perfect steamer and a perfect sailing-ship, at the same time, neither of her two modes of locomotion being at all dependent upon the other. The reader has seen that the *Sumter*, when her fuel was exhausted, was little better than a log on the water, because of her inability to hoist her propeller, which she was, in consequence, compelled to drag after her. The *Alabama* was so constructed, that in fifteen minutes, her pro-peller could be detached from the shaft, and lifted in a well contrived for the purpose, sufficiently high out of the water, not to be an impediment to her speed. When this was done, and her sails spread, she was, to all intents and purposes, a sailing-ship. On the other hand, when I desired to use her as a steamer, I had only to start the fires, lower the propeller, and if the wind was adverse, brace her yards to the wind, and the conversion was complete. The speed of the *Alabama* was always greatly over-rated by the enemy. She was ordinarily about a ten-knot ship. She was said to have made eleven knots and a half, on her trial trip, but we never afterward got it out of her. Under steam and sail both, we logged on one occa-sion, thirteen knots and a quarter, which was her utmost speed.

Her armament consisted of eight guns; six 32-pounders, in broadside, and two pivot-guns amidships; one on the fore-castle, and the other abaft the main-mast—the former a 100-pounder rifled Blakeley, and the latter, a smooth-bore eight-inch. The Blakeley gun was so deficient in metal, compared with the weight of shot it threw, that, after the first few dis-charges, when it became a little heated, it was of comparatively small use to us, to such an extent were we obliged to reduce the charge of powder, on account of the recoil. The average crew of the *Alabama*, before the mast, was about 120 men; and she carried twenty-four officers, as follows: A Captain, four lieutenants, surgeon, paymaster, master, marine officer, four engineers, two midshipmen, and four master's mates, a Captain's clerk, boatswain, gunner, sailmaker, and carpenter. The cost of the ship, with everything complete, was two hun-dred and fifty thousand dollars.

On the morning of our departure from Liverpool, the *Ba-*

hama had dropped some distance down the Mersey, and we joined her by tug. She had her steam up, and was ready to trip her anchor, the moment we arrived, and in a few minutes after getting on board, we were under way. The tug cheered us, as she turned to steam back to the city, and the cheer was answered lustily by our crew. We were a week on the passage from Liverpool to Terceira; our old friend, Captain Tessier, of the *Bahama*, with whom I had made the passage from Nassau to Liverpool, rendering our time very comfortable. On the morning of the 20th of August, we were on the look-out, at an early hour, for the land, and it was not long before we discovered the island, looking, at first, hazy and indistinct in the distance, but gradually assuming more form and consistency. After another hour's steaming, Porto Praya, our place of rendezvous, became visible, with its white houses dotting the mountain side, and we now began to turn our glasses upon the harbor, with no little anxiety, to see if our ships — for a sailing-ship, with the *Alabama's* battery and stores, had preceded her some days, and should now be with her — were all right. We first caught sight of their spars, and pretty soon, raising their hulls sufficiently for identification, we felt much relieved. Our secret had been well kept, and the enemy, notwithstanding his fine "smelling qualities," had not scented the prey.

In the meantime, our own approach was watched with equal anxiety from the deck of the *Alabama*. We might be, for aught she knew, an enemy's steamer coming in pursuit of her; and as the enemy was in the habit of kicking all the small powers, that had not the means of kicking back, a neutral port, belonging to *effete* old Portugal, would not afford her the least protection. At half-past eleven A. M., we steamed into the harbor, and let go our anchor. I had surveyed my new ship, as we approached, with no little interest, as she was to be not only my home, but my bride, as it were, for the next few years, and I was quite satisfied with her external appearance. She was, indeed, a beautiful thing to look upon. The store-ship was already alongside of her, and we could see that the busy work of transferring her cargo was going on. Captain Butcher, an intelligent young English seaman, who had been bred in the mail-packet service, and who had taken the *Alabama* out from Liverpool, on that trial trip of hers, which has since become historical through the protests of Messrs. Seward and Adams, now came on board of us. He had had a rough and stormy passage from Liverpool, during which he had suffered some little damage, and consumed most of his coal. Considerable progress had been made, in receiving on board from the transport, the battery and stores, and a few days more would suffice to put the ship in a condition for defence.

The harbor of Porto Praya lies open to the eastward, and as the wind was now from that quarter, and blowing rather freshly, a considerable sea had been raised, which rendered it inconvenient, if not unsafe, for the transport and the *Alabama* to continue to lie alongside of each other; which was nevertheless necessary for the transfer of the remainder of the heavy guns. I therefore directed Captain Butcher to get up his anchors immediately, and follow me around to Angra Bay, on the west side of the island, where we should find a lee, and smooth water. This was done, and we arrived at Angra at four o'clock, on the same afternoon. Here the transshipment of the guns and stores was renewed, and here, for the first time, I visited the *Alabama*. I was as much pleased with her internal appearance, and arrangements, as I had been with her externally, but everything was in a very uninviting state of confusion, guns, gun-carriages, shot, and shell, barrels of beef and pork, and boxes and bales of paymaster's, gunner's, and boatswain's stores lying promiscuously about the decks; sufficient time not having elapsed to have them stowed in their proper places. The crew, comprising about sixty persons, who had been picked up, promiscuously, about the streets of Liverpool, were as unpromising in appearance, as things about the decks. What with faces begrimed with coal dust, red shirts, and blue shirts, Scotch caps, and hats, brawny chests exposed, and stalwart arms naked to the elbows, they looked as little like the crew of a man-of-war, as one can well conceive. Still there was some *physique* among these fellows, and soap, and water, and clean shirts would make a wonderful difference in their appearance. As night approached, I relieved Captain

Butcher of his command, and removing my baggage on board, took possession of the cabin, in which I was to spend so many weary days, and watchful nights. I am a good sleeper, and slept soundly. This quality of sleeping well in the intervals of harassing business is a valuable one to the sailor, and I owe to it much of that physical ability, which enabled me to withstand the four years of excitement and toil, to which I was subjected during the war.

There are two harbors called Angra, in Terceira—East Angra, and West Angra. We were anchored in the latter, and the authorities notified us, the next morning, that we must move round to East Angra, that being the port of entry, and the proper place for the anchorage of merchant-ships. We were *playing* merchant-ship as yet, but had nothing to do, of course, with ports of entry or custom-houses; and as the day was fine, and there was a prospect of smooth water under the lee of the island, I got under way, and went to sea, the *Bahama* and the transport accompanying me. Steaming beyond the marine league, I hauled the transport alongside, and we got on board from her the remainder of our armament, and stores. The sea was not so smooth, as we had expected, and there was some little chafing between the ships, but we accomplished our object, without serious inconvenience. This occupied us all day, and after nightfall, we ran into East Angra, and anchored.

As we passed the fort, we were hailed vociferously, in very bad English, or Portuguese, we could not distinguish which. But though the words were unintelligible to us, the manner and tone of the hail were evidently meant to warn us off. Continuing our course, and paying no attention to the hail, the fort presently fired a shot over us; but we paid no attention to this either, and ran in and anchored—the bark accompanying us, but the *Bahama* hauling off, seaward, and lying off and on during the night. There was a small Portuguese schooner of war at anchor in the harbor, and about midnight, I was aroused from a deep sleep, into which I had fallen, after a long day of work and excitement, by an officer coming below, and informing me, very coolly, that the Portuguese man-of-war was firing into us! "The d—l she is," said I;

how many shots has she fired at us?" "Three, sir," replied
the officer. "Have any of them struck us?" "No, sir, none
of them have struck us—they seem to be firing rather wild."
I knew very well, that the little craft would not dare to fire
into us, though I thought it probable, that, after the fashion of
the Chinese, who sound their gongs to scare away their enemies, she might be firing *at* us, to alarm us into going out of
the harbor. I said therefore to the officer, "Let him fire away,
I expect he won't hurt you," and turned over and went to
sleep. In the morning, it was ascertained, that it was not the
schooner at all, that had been firing, but a passing mail steamer
which had run into the anchorage, and fired three signal guns,
to awaken her sleeping passengers on shore—with whom she
departed before daylight.

We were not further molested, from this time onward, but
were permitted to remain and coal from the bark; though
the custom-house officers, accompanied by the British Consul,
paid us a visit, and insisted that we should suspend our operation of coaling, until we had entered the two ships at the custom-house. This I readily consented to do. I now called the
Bahama in, by signal, and she ran in and anchored near us.
Whilst the coaling was going forward, the carpenter, and
gunner, with the assistance of the chief engineer, were busy
putting down the circles or traverses for the pivot guns; and
the boatswain and his gang were at work, fitting side and
train tackles for the broadside guns. The reader can understand how anxious I was to complete all these arrangements.
I was perfectly defenceless without them, and did not know at
what moment an enemy's ship might look in upon me. The
harbor of East Angra, where we were now anchored, was quite
open, but fortunately for us, the wind was light, and from the
S. W., which gave us smooth water, and our work went on
quite rapidly.

To cast an eye, for a moment, now, from the ship to the
shore, I was charmed with the appearance of Terceira. Every
square foot of the island seemed to be under the most elaborate
cultivation, and snug farm-houses were dotted so thickly over
the hill-sides, as to give the whole the appearance of a ram-
bling village. The markets were most bountifully supplied

with excellent beef and mutton, and the various domestic fowls, fish, vegetables, and fruits. My steward brought off every morning in his basket, a most tempting assortment of the latter; for there were apples, plums, pears, figs, dates, oranges, and melons all in full bearing at Terceira. The little town of Angra, abreast of which we were anchored, was a perfect picture of a Portuguese-Moorish town, with its red-tiled roofs, sharp gables, and parti-colored verandas, and veranda curtains. And then the quiet, and love-in-a-cottage air which hovered over the whole scene, so far removed from the highways of the world's commerce, and the world's alarms, was charming to contemplate.

I had arrived on Wednesday, and on Saturday night, we had, by the dint of great labor and perseverance, drawn order out of chaos. The *Alabama's* battery was on board, and in place, her stores had all been unpacked, and distributed to the different departments, and her coal-bunkers were again full. We only awaited the following morning to steam out upon the high seas, and formally put the ship in commission. Saturday had been dark and rainy, but we had still labored on through the rain. Sunday morning dawned bright and beautiful, which we hailed as a harbinger of future success. All hands were turned out at early daylight, and the first lieutenant, and the officer of the deck took the ship in hand, to prepare her for the coming ceremony. She was covered with coal dust and dirt and rubbish in every direction, for we had hitherto had no time to attend to appearances. But by dint of a few hours of scrubbing, inside and out, and of the use of that well-known domestic implement, the holy-stone, that works so many wonders with a dirty ship, she became sweet and clean, and when her awnings were snugly spread, her yards squared, and her rigging hauled taut, she looked like a bride, with the orange-wreath about her brows, ready to be led to the altar.

I had as yet no enlisted crew, and this thought gave me some anxiety. All the men on board the *Alabama*, as well as those who had come out with me, on board the *Bahama*, had been brought thus far, under articles of agreement that were to be no longer obligatory. Some of them had been shipped for one voyage, and some for another, but none of them for service on board a Confederate cruiser. This was done to avoid a breach of the British Foreign Enlistment Act. They had, of course, been undeceived from the day of our departure from Liverpool. *They* knew that they were to be released from the contracts they had made, but *I* could not know how many of them would engage with me for the *Alabama*. It is true I had had a talk with some of the leaders of the crew, who had promised to go with me, and to influence others, but no creature can be more whimsical than a sailor, until you have bound him past recall, unless indeed it be a woman.

The ship having been properly prepared, we steamed out, on this bright Sunday morning, under a cloudless sky, with a gentle breeze from the southeast, scarcely ruffling the surface of the placid sea, and under the shadow of the smiling and picturesque island of Terceira, which nature seemed to have decked specially for the occasion, so charming did it appear, in its checkered dress of a lighter and darker green, composed of corn-fields and orange-groves, the flag of the new-born Confederate States was unfurled, for the first time, from the peak of the *Alabama*. The *Bahama* accompanied us. The ceremony was short but impressive. The officers were all in full uniform, and the crew neatly dressed, and I caused "all hands" to be summoned aft on the quarter-deck, and mounting a gun-carriage, I read the commission of Mr. Jefferson Davis, appointing me a captain in the Confederate States Navy, and the order of Mr. Stephen R. Mallory, the Secretary of the Navy, directing me to assume command of the *Alabama*. Following my example, the officers and crew had all uncovered their heads, in deference to the sovereign authority, as is customary on such occasions; and as they stood in respectful silence and listened with rapt attention to the reading, and to the short explanation of my object and purposes, in putting the ship in commission which followed, I was deeply impressed with the spectacle. Virginia, the grand old mother of many of the States, who afterward died so nobly; South Carolina, Georgia, Alabama, and Louisiana, were all represented in the persons of my officers, and I had some of as fine specimens of the daring and adventurous seaman, as any ship of war could boast.

While the reading was going on, two small balls might

have been seen ascending slowly, one to the peak, and the other to the main-royal mast-head. These were the ensign and pennant of the future man-of-war. These balls were so arranged, that by a sudden jerk of the halliards by which they had been sent aloft, the flag and pennant would unfold themselves to the breeze. A curious observer would also have seen a quartermaster standing by the English colors, which we were still wearing, in readiness to strike them, a band of music on the quarter-deck, and a gunner (lock-string in hand) standing by the weather-bow gun. All these men had their eyes upon the reader; and when he had concluded, at a wave of his hand, the gun was fired, the change of flags took place, and the air was rent by a deafening cheer from officers and men; the band, at the same time, playing "Dixie,"— that soul-stirring national anthem of the new-born government. The *Bahama* also fired a gun and cheered the new flag. Thus, amid this peaceful scene of beauty, with all nature smiling upon the ceremony, was the *Alabama* christened; the name "290" disappearing with the English flag. This had all been done upon the high seas, more than a marine league from the land, where Mr. Jefferson Davis had as much jurisdiction as Mr. Abraham Lincoln. Who could look into the horoscope of this ship — who anticipate her career? Many of these brave fellows followed me unto the close.

From the cradle to the grave there is but a step; and that I may group in a single picture, the christening and the burial of the ship, let the reader imagine, now, some two years to have rolled over — and such a two years of carnage and blood, as the world had never before seen — and, strangely enough, another Sunday morning, equally bright and beautiful, to have dawned upon the *Alabama*. This is her funeral morning! At the hour when the church-goers in Paris and London were sending up their orisons to the Most High, the sound of cannon was heard in the British Channel, and the *Alabama* was engaged in her death-struggle. Cherbourg, where the *Alabama* had lain for some days previously, is connected with Paris by rail, and a large number of curious spectators had flocked down from the latter city to witness, as it proved, her interment. The sun rose, as before, in a cloudless sky, and the sea-breeze has come in over the dancing waters, mild and balmy. It is the nineteenth day of June, 1864. The *Alabama* steams out to meet the *Kearsarge* in mortal combat, and before the sun has set, she has gone down beneath the green waters, and lies entombed by the side of many a gallant craft that had gone down before her in that famous old British Channel; where, from the time of the Norseman and the Danish sea-king, to our own day, so many naval combats have been fought, and so many of the laurel crowns of victory have been entwined around the brows of our naval ancestors. Many of the manly figures who had stood with uncovered heads, and listened with respectful silence to the christening, went down in the ship, and now lie buried with her, many fathoms deep, with no other funeral dirge than the roar of cannon, and the howling winds of the North Sea. Such were the birth and death of the ship, whose adventures I propose to sketch in the following pages.

My speech, I was glad to find, had produced considerable effect with the crew. I informed them, in the opening, that they were all released from the contracts under which they had come thus far, and that such of them as preferred to return to England could do so in the *Bahama*, without prejudice to their interests, as they would have a free passage back, and their pay would go on until they were discharged in Liverpool. I then gave them a brief account of the war, and told them how the Southern States, being sovereign and independent, had dissolved the league which had bound them to the Northern States, and how they were threatened with subjugation by their late confederates, who were the stronger. They would be fighting, I told them, the battles of the oppressed against the oppressor, and this consideration alone should be enough to nerve the arm of every generous sailor. Coming nearer home, for it could not be supposed that English, Dutch, Irish, French, Italian, and Spanish sailors could understand much about the rights or wrongs of nations, I explained to them the individual advantages which they might expect to reap from an enlistment with me. The cruise would be one of excitement and adventure. We had a fine ship under us; one that they might fall in love with, as they would with their sweethearts about Wapping. We should visit many parts of the world, where they would have "liberty" given them on proper occasions; and we should, no doubt, destroy a great many of the enemy's ships, in spite of the enemy's cruisers. With regard to these last, though fighting was not to be our principal object, yet, if a favorable opportunity should offer of our laying ourselves alongside of a ship that was not too heavy for us, they would find me disposed to indulge them.

Finally I came to the finances, and like a skilful Secretary of the Treasury, I put the budget to them, in its very best aspect. As I spoke of good pay, and payment in gold, "hear! hear!" came up from several voices. I would give them, I said, about double the ordinary wages, to compensate them for the risks they would have to run, and I promised them, in case we should be successful, "lots of prize-money," to be voted to them by the Confederate Congress, for the ships of the enemy that they would be obliged to destroy. When we "piped down," that is to say, when the boatswain and his mates wound their "calls" three times, as a signal that the meeting was over, and the crew might disperse, I caused the word to be passed for all those who desired to sign the articles, to repair at once to the paymaster and sign. I was anxious to strike whilst the iron was hot. The *Alabama* had brought out from the Mersey about sixty men, and the *Bahama* had brought about thirty more. I got eighty of these ninety men, and felt very much relieved in consequence.

The *democratic* part of the proceedings closed, as soon as the articles were signed. The "public meeting" just described, was the first, and last ever held on board the *Alabama*, and no other stump speech was ever made to the crew. When I wanted a man to do anything after this, I did not talk to him about "nationalities," or "liberties," or "double wages," but I gave him a rather sharp order, and if the order was not obeyed in "double-quick," the delinquent found himself in limbo. Democracies may do very well for the land, but monarchies and pretty absolute monarchies at that, are the only successful governments for the sea. There was a great state of confusion on board the ship, of course, during the remainder of this day, and well into the night. Bullock and Butcher were both on board assisting me, and we were all busy, as well as the paymaster and clerk, making out half-pay tickets for the sailors' wives and sweethearts, drawing drafts for small amounts payable to relatives and dependants, in different parts of England, for such of the sailors as wanted them, and paying advance-wages to those who had no pay-tickets to leave, or remittances to make. I was gratified to find, that a large proportion of my men left half their pay behind them. "A man, who has children, hath given hostages to fortune," and you are quite as sure of a sailor, who sends half his pay to his wife or sweetheart.

It was eleven P. M. before my friend Bullock was ready to return to the *Bahama*, on his way back to England. I took an affectionate leave of him. I had spent some days with him, at his quiet retreat, in the little village of Waterloo, near Liverpool, where I met his excellent wife, a charming Southern woman, with whom hospitality was a part of her religious faith. He was living in a very plain, simple style, though large sums of public money were passing through his hands, and he has had the honor to come out of the war poor. He paid out moneys in good faith, to the last, even when it was quite evident that the cause had gone under, and there would be no accounts to settle with an Auditor of the Treasury. I had not only had the pleasure of his society during a number of anxious days, but he had greatly assisted me, by his counsel and advice, given with that modesty and reserve which always mark true ability. As soon as the *Bahama* had steamed away, and left me alone, I turned my ship's head to the north-east, set the fore-and-aft sails, and directed the engineer to let his fires go down. The wind had freshened considerably, and there was some sea on. I now turned into an unquiet cot, perfectly exhausted, after the labors of the day, and slept as comfortably as the rolling of the ship, and a strong smell of bilge-water would permit.

CHAPTER XXXII.

THE ALABAMA A SHIP OF WAR, AND NOT A PRIVATEER
—SKETCH OF THE PERSONNEL OF THE SHIP—PUT-
TING THE SHIP IN ORDER FOR SERVICE—SAIL AND
STEAM—THE CHARACTER OF THE SAILOR—THE FIRST
BLOW STRUCK AT THE WHALE FISHERY—THE HABI-
TAT AND HABITS OF THE WHALE—THE FIRST CAP-
TURE.

THE reader has seen in the last chapter, that the *Alabama*
is at length upon the high seas, as a commissioned ship
of war of the Confederate States, her commission having been
signed by Mr. Jefferson Davis, who had all the *de facto* right,
and much more of the *de jure* right, to sign such a commission
than John Hancock, who signed Paul Jones' commission.
The *Alabama* having been built by the Government of the
Confederate States, and commissioned by these States, as a
ship of war, was, in no sense of the word, a *privateer*, which is
a private armed ship belonging to individuals, and fitted out
for purposes of gain. And yet, throughout the whole war,
and long after the war, when she was not called a "pirate"
by the Northern press, she was called a *privateer*. Even high
Government officials of the enemy so characterized her. Many
of the newspapers erred through ignorance, but this misnomer
was sheer malice, and very petty malice, too, on the part of
those of them who were better informed, and on the part of
the Government officials, all of whom, of course, knew better.
Long after they had acknowledged the war, *as a war*, which
carried with it an acknowledgment of the right of the Confederate States to fit out cruisers, they stultified themselves
by calling her "pirate," and "privateer." They were afraid
to speak the truth, in conformity with the facts, lest the de-

struction of their property, for which they hoped ultimately to be paid, should seem to be admitted to have been done under the sanction of the laws of nations. They could as logically have called General Robert E. Lee *a bandit*, as myself a *pirate;* but logic was not the *forte* of the enemy, either during or since the late war.

Before we commence operations, a glance at the *personnel* of the ship may not be uninteresting. If the reader is to embark on the cruise with us, he will very naturally desire to know something of his future shipmates. Having made the cruise in the *Sumter*, he is, of course, acquainted with the officers of that ship, and if, after the fashion of the sailor, he has formed a liking for any of them, he will naturally be inclined to know what became of such of them as did not follow me to the *Alabama*. Of the lieutenants, only one of my old set followed me. Accident separated the rest from me, very much to my regret, and we afterward played different *roles* in the war. The reader has not forgotten Chapman, the second officer of the *Sumter*, who made such a sensation in Cienfuegos, among the fair sex, and who slept in such a sweet pair of sheets at the house of his friend, that he dreamed of them for weeks afterward. Chapman finished the cruise in the *Sumter*, serving everybody else pretty much as he served the Cienfuegos people, whenever he chanced to get ashore. He was always as ready "to tread one measure — take one cup of wine," with a friend, as to hurl defiance at an enemy. He carried the garrison mess at Gibraltar by storm. There was no dinner-party without him. He talked war and strategy with the colonel, fox-hunted with the major, and thrumbed the light guitar, and sang delightful songs, in company with the young captains, and lieutenants, beneath the latticed windows of their lady-loves. It is astonishing, too, the progress he made in learning Spanish, which was attributable entirely to the lessons he took from some bright eyes, and musical tongues, in the neighboring village of San Roque, only a pleasant canter over into Spain, from Gibraltar. Chapman was, unfortunately, going from London to Nassau, in a blockade runner, while I was returning from the latter place to Liverpool, preparatory to joining the *Alabama*. It was thus we missed each other; and the *Alabama* was on the wing so soon afterward, that it was impossible for him to catch her. He served in the *Georgia*, a while, under Captain William Lewis Maury, and, when that ship was laid up and sold, he returned to the Confederate States, and rendered gallant and efficient service, in the last days of the war, in doing what was possible for the defence of Wilmington, against the overwhelming fleet of Porter.

Stribling, the third of the *Sumter*, was assigned by me to Maffitt's command, as already related. He died of yellow fever in Mobile, deeply regretted by the whole service.

Evans, the fourth of the *Sumter*, missed me as Chapman had done, and like Chapman, he took service on board the *Georgia*, and afterward returned to the Confederate States. He served in the naval batteries on the James River, until the evacuation of Richmond.

I took with me to the *Alabama*, as the reader has seen, my old and well-tried First Lieutenant, Kell. He became the first lieutenant of the new ship.

Lieutenant Richard F. Armstrong, of Georgia, whom, as the reader will recollect, I had left at Gibraltar, in charge of the *Sumter*, took Chapman's place, and became second lieutenant. Armstrong was a young gentleman of intelligence and character, and had made good progress in his profession. He was a midshipman at the Naval School, at Annapolis, when the war broke out. Though still a mere boy, he resigned his appointment without hesitation, and came South. He had made the cruise with me in the *Sumter*, and been since promoted.

Midshipman Joseph D. Wilson, of Florida, also an *élève* of Annapolis, and who, like Armstrong, had made the cruise with me in the *Sumter*, and been promoted, took Stribling's place, and became third lieutenant.

My fourth lieutenant in place of Evans was Mr. Arthur Sinclair, who, though not bred in the old service, belonged to one of the old naval families of Virginia, both his father and grandfather having been captains in the United States Navy. These two young gentlemen were also intelligent, and for the short time they had been at sea, well informed in their profession.

LIEUT. A. SINCLAIR.

MAST. J. BULLOCK.

MID'N. C. MAFFIT.

LIEUT. R. F. ARMSTRONG.

LIEUT. B. HOWELL.

MID'N. E. R. ANDERSON.

MAST. MATE. G. T. FULLAM.

Eng'd by H.B.Hall. Jr.N.Y.

Kelly, Piet & Co. Baltimore

My fifth lieutenant was Mr. John Low, of Georgia, a capital seaman, and excellent officer.

Galt, my old surgeon, had accompanied me, as the reader has seen, as did also First Lieutenant Howell, of the marines. Myers, the paymaster of the *Sumter*, was, unfortunately for me, in prison, in Fort Warren, when the *Alabama* was commissioned—the Federal authorities still gloating over the prize they had made, through the trickery of the Consul at Tangier, of one of the "pirate's" officers. In his place I was forced to content myself with a man, as paymaster, who shall be nameless in these pages, since he afterward, upon being discharged by me, for his worthlessness, went over to the enemy, and became one of Mr. Adams' hangers-on, and paid witnesses and spies about Liverpool, and the legation in London. As a preparatory step to embracing the Yankee cause, he married a mulatto woman, in Kingston, Jamaica, (though he had a wife living,) whom he swindled out of what little property she had, and then abandoned. I was quite amused, when I saw afterward, in the Liverpool and London papers, that this man, who was devoid of every virtue, and steeped to the lips in every vice, was giving testimony in the English courts, in the interest of the nation of "grand moral ideas." This was the only recruit the enemy ever got from the ranks of my officers.

To complete the circle of the ward-room, I have only to mention Mr. Miles J. Freeman, the chief engineer of the *Sumter*, who was now filling the same place on board the *Alabama*, and with whom the reader is already acquainted; Dr. Llewellyn, an Englishman from Wiltshire, who having come out in the *Alabama* as surgeon when she was yet a merchant-ship, had been retained as assistant surgeon; and Acting Master Bullock, brother of the captain already named in these pages. My "steerage officers," who are too numerous to be named individually, were a capital set of young men, as were the "forward officers." Indeed, with the exception of the black sheep in the ward-room, with Federal propensities, to whom I have alluded, I had reason to be satisfied with my officers of all grades.

I must not forget to introduce to the reader one humble

individual of the *Alabama's* crew. He was my steward, and
my household would not be complete without him. When I
was making the passage from Nassau to Liverpool, in the *Ba-*
hama, I noticed a pale, rather delicate, and soft-mannered young
man, who was acting as steward on board. He was an obedient, respectful, and attentive major-domo, but, unfortunately,
was rather too much addicted to the use of the wine which he
set on the table, every day, for the guests. Poor Bartelli—I
thus designate him, because of his subsequent sad fate, which
the reader will learn in due time—did not seem to have the
power of self-restraint, especially under the treatment he received, which was not gentle. The captain was rough toward
him, and the poor fellow seemed very much cowed and humbled, trembling when spoken to harshly. His very forlorn-
ness drew me toward him. He was an Italian, evidently of
gentle blood, and as, with the Italians, drinking to intoxication
is not an ineradicable vice, I felt confident that he could be
reformed under proper treatment. And so, when we arrived
at Terceira, I asked Bartelli how he would like to go with me,
as steward, on board the *Alabama*. He seemed to be delighted
with the proposal. "There is one understanding, however,"
I said to him, "which you and I must have: you must never
touch a drop of liquor, on board the ship, on duty. When
you go on shore, 'on liberty,' if you choose to have a little
frolic, that is your affair, provided, always, you come off sober.
Is it a bargain?" "It is, Captain," said he; "I promise you I
will behave myself like a man, if you will take me with you."
The Captain of the *Bahama* had no objection, and Bartelli was
duly installed as my steward. I found him, as I had expected,
a capital servant. He was faithful, and became attached to
me, and kept his promise, under strong temptation; for there
was always in the cabin-lockers of the *Alabama* the best of
wines and other liquors. He took care of my linen like a
woman, washing it himself when we were at sea, and sending
it to some careful laundress when in port. I shall, perhaps,
astonish a great many husbands and heads of families, when I
tell them, that every shirt-button was always in its place, and
that I never had to call for needle and thread under difficulties!
My mess affairs never gave me the least trouble. My table

was always well supplied, and when guests were expected, I could safely leave the arrangements to Bartelli; and then it was a pleasure to observe the air, and grace of manner and speech, with which he would receive my visitors and conduct them into the cabin. Poor Bartelli!

The day after the *Bahama* left us was cloudy, and cheerless in aspect, with a fresh wind and a rough sea. The ship was rolling and tumbling about, to the discomfort of every one, and confusion still reigned on board. Below decks everything was dirt and disorder. Nobody had as yet been berthed or messed, nor had any one been stationed at a gun or a rope. Spare shot-boxes and other heavy articles were fetching way, and the ship was leaking considerably through her upper works. She had been put together with rather green timber, and, having been caulked in England, in winter, her seams were beginning to gape beneath the ardent heats of a semi-tropical climate. I needed several days yet, to put things "to rights," and mould the crew into a little shape. I withdrew, therefore, under easy sail, from the beaten tracks of commerce; and my first lieutenant went to work berthing, and messing, and quartering, and stationing his men. The gun-equipments were completed, and such little alterations made as were found necessary for the easy and efficient working of the battery, and the guns were sealed with blank cartridges, and put in a proper condition for being loaded promptly. We now devoted several days to the exercise of the crew, as well at general, as division, quarters. Some few of the guns' crews had served in ships of war before, and proved capital drill-sergeants for the rest. The consequence was, that rapid progress was made, and the *Alabama* was soon in a condition to plume her wings for her flight. It only remained to caulk our upper works, and this occupied us but a day or two longer.

I was much gratified to find that my new ship proved to be a fine sailer, under canvas. This quality was of inestimable advantage to me, as it enabled me to do most of my work under sail. She carried but an eighteen days' supply of fuel, and if I had been obliged, because of her dull sailing qualities, to chase every thing under steam, the reader can see how I should have been hampered in my movements. I should have been half my time running into port for fuel. This would have disclosed my whereabouts so frequently to the enemy, that I should have been constantly in danger of capture, whereas I could now stretch into the most distant seas, and chase, capture, and destroy, perfectly independent of steam. I adopted the plan, therefore, of working under sail, in the very beginning of my cruise, and practised it unto the end. With the exception of half a dozen prizes, all my captures were made with my screw hoisted, and my ship under sail; and with but one exception, as the reader will see hereafter, I never had occasion to use steam to escape from an enemy.

This keeping of the sea, for three, and four months at a time, had another great advantage — it enabled me to keep my crew under better drill, and discipline, and, in every way, better in hand. Nothing demoralizes a crew so much as frequent visits to port. The sailor is as improvident, and incapable of self-government as a child. Indeed he is regarded by most nations as a ward of the state, and that sort of legislation is thrown around him, which is thrown around a ward in chancery. The moment a ship drops her anchor in a port, like the imprisoned bird, he begins to beat the bars of his cage, if he is not permitted to go on shore, and have his frolic; and when on shore, to carry our simile still further, he is like the bird let out of the cage. He gives a loose rein to his passions, and sometimes plunges so deeply into debauchery, that he renders himself unfit for duty, for days, and sometimes weeks, after he is hunted up and brought on board by the police, which is most frequently the manner in which his captain again gets possession of him. Such is the reckless intemperance into which some of the regular old salts plunge, that I have known them to go on shore, make their way straight to a sailor-boarding-house, which is frequently a dance-house, and always a grog-shop, give what money they have about them to the "landlord," and tell him to keep them drunk as long as it will last, and when they have had the worth of it in a *good, long, big* drunk, to pick them up, and send them off to their ship! The very d—l is to pay, too, when a lot of drunken sailors is brought on board, as every first lieutenant knows. Frequently they have to be knocked down, disarmed of the dangerous sheath-knives which they wear, and confined in irons until they are sober. When that takes place, Jack comes out of the "Brig," his place of confinement, very much ashamed of himself; generally with a blackened eye or two, if not with a broken nose, and looking very seedy in the way of apparel, as the chances are that he has sold or exchanged the tidy suit in which he went on shore, for some 'long-shore toggery, the better to enable him to prolong that delightful drunk of his. It was quite enough to have such scenes as these repeated once in three or four months.

When I had put my ship in a tolerable state of defence, and given a little practice at the guns, to my crew, I turned her head toward her cruising ground. It so happened that this was not very far off. Following Porter's example in the Pacific,—I mean the first Porter, the father of the present Admiral in the Federal Navy,—I resolved to strike a blow at the enemy's whale-fishery, off the Azores. There is a curious and beautiful problem—that of Providence feeding the whale —connected with this fishery, which I doubt not will interest the reader, as it did the writer of these pages, when it first came under his notice. It is because of that problem, that the Azores are a whaling station. The food which attracts the whale to these islands is not produced in their vicinity, but is carried thither by the currents—the currents of the ocean performing the same functions for the finny tribe, that the atmosphere does for the plants. The fishes of the sea, in their kingdom beneath the waters, have thus their highways and byways, as well as the animals upon the land, and are always to be found congregated where their great food-bearers, the currents, make their deposits. Animalculæ, infusoria, small fishes, minute crustacea, and shell-fish found on the algæ, or floating sea-weed, sea-nettles, and other food, are produced in the more calm latitudes, where the waters are comparatively still, taken up by the currents, and transported to the more congenial feeding-grounds of the whales, and other fishes.

Much of this food is produced in the tepid waters of the sea, into which, it is well known, some descriptions of whales can-

not enter. The equatorial belt of waters surrounding the
earth, between the tropics, whose temperature is generally 80°
of Fahrenheit, is as a sea of fire to the "right" whale. It
would be as certain death for this species of whale to attempt
to cross these waters, as for a human being to plunge into a
burning lake. The proof of this is that the "right" whale of
the northern hemisphere is never found in the southern hemisphere, or *e converso*. It is a separate and distinct species of
fish. See how beneficent, therefore, the arrangement is, by
which the food for these monsters of the deep is transported
from the tepid waters, into which they cannot enter in pursuit
of it, to the cooler waters in which they delight to gambol.
The Gulf Stream is the great food-carrier for the extra-tropical
whales of the northern hemisphere. An intelligent sea-captain, writing to Superintendent Maury of the National Observatory, some years before the war, informed him, that in the
Gulf Stream, off the coast of Florida, he fell in with "such a
school of young sea-nettles, as had never before been heard
of." The sea was literally covered with them for many square
leagues. He likened them, in appearance, to acorns floating on
the water, but they were so thick as completely to cover the
sea. He was bound to England, and was five or six days in
sailing through them. In about sixty days afterward, on his
return voyage, he fell in with the same school off the Azores,
and here he was three or four days in passing them again. He
recognized them as the same, for he had never before seen any
quite like them; and on both occasions he frequently hauled
up buckets full, and examined them. In their adventurous
voyage of sixty days, during which they must have been
tossed about in several gales of wind, these little marine animals had grown considerably, and already the whales had begun to devour them; for the school was now so much diminished in size, that the captain was enabled to sail through it,
in three or four days, instead of the five or six which it had
formerly taken him. We see, thus, that the fishes of the sea
have their seed-time and harvest; that the same beneficent
hand that decks the lilies of the field in garments more superb
than those of Solomon, and feeds the young raven, seeds down
the great equatorial belt of waters for the fishes; and that

when the harvest-time has come, he sends in his reapers and
gleaners, the currents, which bind up the sheaves, and bear
them off three thousand miles, to those denizens of the great
deep, which, perhaps, but for this beautiful and beneficent arrangement, would die of inanition.

The whaling season ends at the Azores about the first of
October, when the first winter gales begin to blow, and the
food becomes scarce. The whales then migrate to other feeding-grounds, and the adventurous whaler follows them. As
we were now, in the first days of September, on board the *Alabama*, the reader will see, that we had but a few weeks left, in
which to accomplish our purpose of striking a blow at the
enemy's whale fishery. In the afternoon of September 4th,
the weather being fine and clear, we made Pico and Fayal,
and reducing sail to topsails, lay off and on during the night.
The next day, the weather being cloudy, and the wind light
from the eastward, we made our first prize, without the excitement of a chase. A ship having been discovered, lying to, with
her foretopsail to the mast, we made sail for her, hoisting the
United States colors, and approached her within boarding distance, that is to say, within a few hundred yards, without her
moving tack or sheet.. She had shown the United States colors in return, as we approached, and proved to be a whaler,
with a huge whale, which she had recently struck, made fast
alongside, and partially hoisted out of the water by her yard
tackles. The surprise was perfect and complete, although
eleven days had elapsed since the *Alabama* had been commissioned at a neighboring island, less than a hundred miles off.

The captured ship proved to be the *Ocmulgee*, of Edgartown,
Massachusetts, whose master was a genuine specimen of the
Yankee whaling skipper; long and lean, and as elastic, apparently, as the whalebone he dealt in. Nothing could exceed
the blank stare of astonishment, that sat on his face, as the
change of flags took place on board the *Alabama*. He had
been engaged, up to the last moment, with his men, securing
the rich spoil alongside. The whale was a fine "sperm," and
was a "big strike," and had already been denuded of much of
its blubber when we got alongside. He naturally concluded,
he said, when he saw the United States colors at our peak, that

we were one of the new gunboats sent out by Mr. Welles to protect the whale fishery. It was indeed remarkable, that no protection should have been given to these men, by their Government. Unlike the ships of commerce, the whalers are obliged to congregate within small well-known spaces of ocean, and remain there for weeks at a time, whilst the whaling season lasts. It was the most obvious thing in the world, that these vessels, thus clustered together, should attract the attention of the Confederate cruisers, and be struck at. There are not more than half a dozen principal whaling stations on the entire globe, and a ship, of size and force, at each, would have been sufficient protection. But the whalers, like the commerce of the United States generally, were abandoned to their fate. Mr. Welles did not seem capable of learning by experience even; for the *Shenandoah* repeated the successes of the *Alabama*, in the North Pacific, toward the close of the war. There were Federal steam gunboats, and an old sailing hulk cruising about in the China seas, but no one seemed to think of the whalers, until Waddel carried dismay and consternation among them.

It took us some time to remove the crew of the *Ocmulgee*, consisting of thirty-seven persons, to the *Alabama*. We also got on board from her some beef and pork, and small stores, and by the time we had done this, it was nine o'clock at night; too late to think of burning her, as a bonfire, by night, would flush the remainder of the game, which I knew to be in the vicinity; and I had now become too old a hunter to commit such an indiscretion. With a little management and caution, I might hope to uncover the birds, no faster than I could bag them. And so, hoisting a light at the peak of the prize, I permitted her to remain anchored to the whale, and we lay by her until the next morning, when we burned her; the smoke of the conflagration being, no doubt, mistaken by vessels at a distance, for that of some passing steamer.

To those curious in such matters, I may state that a large sperm whale will yield twenty-five barrels of oil from the head alone. The oil is found in its liquid state, and is baled out with buckets, from a hole cut in the top of the head. What can be the uses in the animal economy to which this immense quantity of oil in the head of the fish is applied? They are probably twofold. First, it may have some connection with the sustenance of the animal, in seasons of scarcity of food, and secondly, and more obviously, it appears to be a provision of nature, designed on the same principle on which birds are supplied with air-cells in their bones. The whale, though a very intelligent fish, and with an affection for its "calf," almost human, has but a small brain, the great cavity of its skull being filled as described. As the specific gravity of oil is considerably less than that of water, we can be at no loss to conjecture why the monster has so bountiful a supply, nor why it is that it carries the supply in its head. As is well known, the whale is a warm-blooded mammal, as much so as the cow that roams our pastures, and cannot live by breathing the water alone. Instead of the gill arrangement of other fishes, which enables them to extract from the water sufficient air to vitalize the blood, it has the lungs of the mammal, and needs to breathe the atmosphere. The oil in the head, acting on the principle of the cork, enables it to ascend very rapidly, from great depths in the ocean, when it requires to breathe, or "blow." See how beautiful this oil arrangement is, too, in another aspect. It enables the monster, when it requires rest, to lay its head on the softest kind of a pillow, an ocean wave, and sleep as unconcernedly as the child does upon the bosom of its mother.

On the day after the capture of the *Ocmulgee*, we chased and overhauled a French ship, bound to Marseilles. After speaking this ship, and telling her that we were a United States cruiser, we bore away north, half west, and in a couple of hours made the island of Flores, the westernmost of the Azores, and a favorite island to be sighted by the whalers, for the correction of their chronometers. Approaching it just at nightfall, we shortened sail, and lay off and on during the night. This island is an exceedingly picturesque object. It rises like a huge mountain from the depths of the sea, with the bluest and deepest of water all around it. It is rock-bound, and there is scarcely any part of it, where a ship might not haul alongside of the rocks, and make fast to the shore. It rises to the height of a thousand feet and more, and is covered with a luxuriant vegetation, the substratum of rock being overlaid with a generous soil. The climate is genial for three-fourths of the year, but almost a perpetual gale howls over it in winter. At a distance, the island appeared like an unbroken mountain, but as we approached it, many beautiful valleys, and gaps in the mountain presented themselves, with the neat white farmhouses of the lonely dwellers peeping out from beneath the dense foliage. It was indeed a beautiful scene to look upon, and such was the air of perfect repose and peace that pervaded it, that a ship of war seemed out of place, approaching its quiet shores.

The next day, Sunday, dawned beautiful and bright, and the *Alabama* having approached this semi-tropical island, sufficiently near to inhale the fragrance of its shrubs and flowers, mustered her crew for the first time. The reader has now been sufficiently long with us to know, that when we speak of "muster" on board a ship of war, we do not mean simply the calling of the roll, but a ceremony of dress and inspection. With clean, white decks, with the brass and iron work glittering like so many mirrors in the sun, and with the sails neatly trimmed, and the Confederate States flag at our peak, we spread our awnings and read the Articles of War to the crew. A great change had taken place in the appearance of the men, since I made that stump speech to them which has been described Their parti-colored garments had been cast aside, and they were all neatly arrayed in duck frocks and trousers, well-polished shoes, and straw hats. There was a visible improvement in their health, too. They had been long enough out of Liverpool to recover from the effects of their debauches, and regain their accustomed stamina. This was the first reading of the Articles of War to them, and it was curious to observe the attention with which they listened to the reading, occasionally eying each other, as they were struck by particular portions of them. These Articles, which were copied from similar Articles, for the "better government of the Navy of the United States," were quite severe in their denunciations of crime. The penalty of death frequently occurred in them, and they placed the power of executing this penalty in the hands of the captain and a court-martial.

Jack had already had a little foretaste of discipline, in the two weeks he had been on board; the first lieutenant having brought several of them to the "mast," whence they had been sent into confinement by me, for longer or shorter intervals, according to the grade of their offences; and he now began more distinctly to perceive that he had gotten on board a *ship of war*, instead of the *privateer* he had supposed the *Alabama* to be, and that he would have to toe a pretty straight mark. It is with a disorderly crew, as with other things, the first blows are the most effective. I had around me a large staff of excellent officers, who always wore their side arms, and pistols, when on duty, and from this time onward we never had any trouble about keeping the most desperate and turbulent characters in subjection. My code was like that of the Medes and Persians—it was never relaxed. The moment a man offended, he was seized and confined in irons, and, if the offence was a grave one, a court-martial was sitting on his case in less than twenty-four hours. The willing and obedient were treated with humanity and kindness; the turbulent were jerked down, with a strong hand, and made submissive to discipline. I was as rigid with the officers as with the crew, though, of course, in a different way, and, both officers and men soon learning what was required of them, everything went on, on board the *Alabama*, after the first few weeks, as smoothly, and with as little jarring as if she had been a well-constructed and well-oiled machine.

CHAPTER XXXIII.

CAPTURE OF THE STARLIGHT, OCEAN ROVER, ALERT, WEATHER-GAUGE — A RACE BY NIGHT — CAPTURE OF THE ALTAMAHA, VIRGINIA, AND ELIJA DUNBAR — A ROUGH SEA, TOILING BOATS, AND A PICTURESQUE BURNING OF A SHIP IN A GALE.

WE were running in, while the muster described in the last chapter was going on, for the little town, or, rather, sea-side village of Lagens, on the south side of the island of Flores, and, having approached the beach quite near, we hove the ship to, and hauling alongside, from the stern, where they had been towing, the whale-boats of the captured ship, which we had brought away from the prize for this purpose, we paroled our prisoners, and, putting them in possession of their boats, shoved them off for the shore. I had two motives in thus landing my prisoners in their own boats, or, to speak more properly, in the boats which had once belonged to them. It saved me the trouble of landing them myself; and, as the boats were valuable, and I permitted the prisoners to put in them as many provisions as they desired, and as much other plunder as they could pick up about the decks of their ships — excepting always such articles as we needed on board the *Alabama* — the sale of their boats and cargoes to the islanders gave them the means of subsistence, until they could communicate with their consul in the neighboring island of Fayal.

We had scarcely gotten through with the operation of landing our prisoners, before the cry of "sail ho!" came to us from the mast-head; and we made sail in chase of a schooner which was approaching the island, hoisting the English colors to throw the stranger off his guard. As the two vessels were sailing toward each other, they approached very rapidly, and in the course of an hour we were within a mile of each other. Still the schooner did not show any colors. The reason was quite plain; she was American in every feature, and could show us no other colors than such as would subject her to capture, in case we should prove to be her enemy, of which she seemed to be suspicious. Indeed, the gallant little craft, with every stitch of canvas set, sails well hoisted, and sheets a little eased, was now edging off a little from us, and endeavoring to gain the shelter of the well-known marine league, the land being distant only about five miles. Perceiving her object, and seeing that I had only a couple of miles to spare, I kept my own ship off, the better to throw myself across the stranger's path, changed my colors, and fired a blank cartridge to heave her to. But she neither hove to, nor showed colors, being evidently intent upon giving me a race. Although I already had the little craft under my guns, I humored her for a few minutes, just to show her that I could beat her in a fair trial of speed, and when I had proved this, by gaining rapidly upon her, I sent a round shot from one of the bow guns between her masts, a few feet only over the heads of her people. If the reader has heard a 32-pounder whistle, in such close proximity, he knows very well what it says, to wit, that there must be no more trifling. And so the captain of the schooner understood it, for in a moment afterward we could see the graceful little craft luffing up in the wind, brailing up her foresail, and hauling her jib sheet to windward. The welcome stars and stripes fluttered soon afterward from her peak. The master being brought on board with his papers, the prize proved to be the schooner *Starlight*, of Boston, from Fayal, bound to Boston by the way of Flores, for which island she had some passengers, several ladies among the number.

The crew consisted of seven persons—all good Yankee sailors. Having heard, by this time, full accounts of the shameful treatment of my paymaster of the *Sumter*, which has been described, in a former chapter, I resolved to practise a little retaliation upon the enemy, and ordered the crew of the *Starlight* put in irons. I pursued this practice, painful as it was, for the next seven or eight captures, putting the masters and mates of the ships, as well as the crews, in irons. The masters would frequently remonstrate with me, claiming that it was an indignity put upon them; and so it was, but I replied to them, that their countrymen had put a similar indignity upon an officer and a gentleman, who had worn the uniform of the navies of both our countries. By the time that the capture of the *Starlight* had been completed, the sun was near his setting, and it was too late to land the passengers. I therefore sent a prize crew on board the captured ship, directing the prize-master to lie by me during the night, and giving him especial charge to inform the passengers that they should be safely landed in the morning, and, in the meantime, to quiet the fears of the ladies, who had been much alarmed by the chase and the firing, we hoisted a light at the peak of the *Alabama*, and lay to, all night, in nearly a calm sea. There were some dark clouds hanging over the island, but they had apparently gone there to roost, as no wind came from them. Among the papers captured on board the *Starlight* were a couple of despatches from the Federal Consul at Fayal, to the Sewards—father and son —in which there was the usual amount of stale nonsense about "rebel privateers," and "pirates."

The weather proved fine, the next morning, and standing in, within a stone's throw of the little town of Santa Cruz, we landed both passengers and prisoners, putting the latter, as usual, under *parole*. In the meantime, the Governor of the island, and a number of the dignitaries came off to visit us. They were a robust, farmer-looking people, giving evidence, in their persons, of the healthfulness of the island, and were very polite, franking to us the ports of the island, and informing us that supplies were cheap, and abundant. Their visit was evidently one of curiosity, and we treated his Excellency with all due ceremony, notwithstanding the smallness of his dominions. We talked to him, however, of bullocks, and sheep, fish and turtles, yams and oranges, rather than of the war between the States, and the laws of nations. Bartelli made the eyes of the party dance with flowing goblets of champagne, and when I thought they had remained long enough, I bowed them out of the cabin, with a cigar all round, and sent them on shore, with rather favorable impressions, I do not doubt, of the "pirate."

Hauling off, now, from the island, and running seaward for a space, we chased and overhauled a Portuguese whaling brig. Seeing by her boats and other indications that she was a whaler, I thought, at first, that I had a prize, and was quite disappointed when she showed me the Portuguese colors. Not being willing to trust to the verity of the flag, I sent a boat on board of her, and invited the master to visit me with his papers, which he did. The master was himself a Portuguese, and I found his papers to be genuine. Thanking him for his visit, I dismissed him in a very few minutes. I had no right to command him to come on board of me—he being a neutral, it was my business to go on board of him, if I desired to examine his papers, but he waived ceremony, and it was for this that I had thanked him. I may as well remark here, in passing, that this was the only foreign whaling-ship that I ever overhauled; the business of whaling having become almost exclusively an American monopoly—the monopoly not being derived from any sovereign grant, but resulting from the superior skill, energy, industry, courage, and perseverance of the Yankee whaler, who is, perhaps, the best specimen of a sailor, the world over.

Later in the same afternoon, we chased a large ship, looming up almost like a frigate, in the northwest, with which we came up about sunset. We had showed her the American colors, and she approached us without the least suspicion that she was running into the arms of an enemy; the master crediting good old Mr. Welles, as the master of the *Ocmulgee* had done, with sending a flashy-looking Yankee gunboat, to look out for his whalebone and oil. This large ship proved to be, upon the master being brought on board with his papers, the *Ocean Rover*, of New Bedford, Massachusetts. She had been out three years and four months, cruising in various parts of the world, had sent home one or two cargoes of oil, and was now returning, herself, with another cargo, of eleven hundred barrels. The master, though anxious to see his wife, and dandle on his knee the babies that were no longer babies, with true Yankee thrift thought he would just take the Azores in his way home, and make another "strike," or two, to fill up his empty casks. The consequence was, as the reader has seen, a little disappointment.

I really felt for the honest fellow, but when I came to reflect, for a moment, upon the diabolical acts of his countrymen of New England, who were out-heroding Herod, in carrying on against us a vindictive war, filled with hate and vengeance, the milk of human kindness which had begun to well up in my heart disappeared, and I had no longer any spare sympathies to dispose of.

It being near night when the capture was made, I directed the prize to be hove to, in charge of a prize crew until morning. In the meantime, however, the master, who had heard from some of my men, that I had permitted the master of the *Ocmul-gee*, and his crew, to land in their own boats, came to me, and requested permission to land in the same manner. We were four or five miles from the land, and I suggested to him, that it was some distance to pull. "Oh! that is nothing," said he, "we whalers sometimes chase a whale, on the broad sea, until our ships are hull-down, and think nothing of it. It will relieve you of us the sooner, and be of some service to us besides." Seeing that the sea was smooth, and that there was really no risk to be run, for a Yankee whale-boat might be made, with a little management, to ride out an ordinary gale of wind, I consented, and the delighted master returned to his ship, to make the necessary preparations. I gave him the usual permission to take what provisions he needed, the whaling gear belonging to his boats, and the personal effects of himself and men. He worked like a beaver, for not more than a couple of hours had elapsed, before he was again alongside of the *Alabama*, with all his six boats, with six men in each, ready to start for the shore. I could not but be amused when I looked over the side into these boats, at the amount of plunder that the rapacious fellow had packed in them. They were literally loaded down, with all sorts of traps, from the seamen's chests and bedding, to the tabby cat and parrot. Nor had the "main chance" been overlooked, for all the "cabin stores" had been secured, and sundry barrels of beef and pork, besides. I said to him, "Captain, your boats appear to me, to be rather deeply laden; are you not afraid to trust them?" "Oh! no," he replied; "they are as buoyant as ducks, and we shall not ship a drop of water." After a detention of a few minutes, during which my clerk was putting the crew under *parole*, I gave the master leave to depart.

The boats, shoving off from the side, one by one, and falling into line, struck out for the shore. That night-landing of this whaler's crew was a beautiful spectacle. I stood on the horse-block, watching it, my mind busy with many thoughts. The moon was shining brightly, though there were some passing clouds sailing lazily in the upper air, that fleckered the sea. Flores, which was sending off to us, even at this distance, her perfumes of shrub and flower, lay sleeping in the moonlight, with a few fleecy, white clouds wound around the mountain-top, like a turban. The rocky islets that rise like so many shafts out of the sea, devoid of all vegetation, and at different distances from the shore, looked weird and unearthly, like sheeted ghosts. The boats moving swiftly and mysteriously toward the shore, might have been mistaken, when they had gotten a little distance from us, for Venetian gondolas, with their peaked bows and sterns, especially when we heard coming over the sea, a song, sung by a powerful and musical voice, and chorussed by all the boats. Those merry fellows were thus making light of misfortune, and proving that the sailor, after all, is the true philosopher. The echo of that night-song lingered long in my memory, but I little dreamed, as I stood on the deck of the *Alabama*, and witnessed the scene I have described, that four years afterward, it would be quoted against me as a violation of the laws of war! And yet so it was. It was alleged by the malice of my defamers, who never have, and never can forgive me for the destruction of their property, that miles away at sea, in rough and inclement weather, I *compelled* my prisoners to depart for the shore, in leaky and unsound boats, at the hazard of their lives, designing and desiring to drown them! And this was all the thanks I received for setting some of these fellows up as nabobs, among the islanders. Why, the master of the *Ocean Rover*, with his six boats, and their cargoes, was richer than the Governor, when he landed in Flores; where the simple islanders are content with a few head of cattle, a cast-net, and a canoe.

The *Alabama* had now two prizes in company, with which she lay off and on the island during the night, and she was destined to secure another before morning. I had turned in, and was sleeping soundly, when about midnight, an officer came below to inform me that there was another large ship close on board of us. I was dressed and on deck in a few minutes. The stranger was plainly visible, being not more than a mile distant. She was heading for the island. I wore ship, as quietly as possible, and followed her, but she had, in the meantime, drawn some distance ahead, and an exciting chase now ensued. We were both close-hauled, on the starboard tack, and the stranger, seeing that he was pursued, put every rag of sail on his ship that he could spread. I could but admire her, with her square yards and white canvas, every sheet home, and every leach taut. For the first half hour, it was hard to tell which ship had the heels of the other, but at the end of that time, we began to head-reach the chase very perceptibly, though the latter rather "eat us out of the wind," or, to speak more conformably with the vocabulary of the land, went to windward of us. This did not matter much, however, as when we should be abreast of her, we would be near enough to reach her with a shot. After a chase of about four hours, day broke, when we hoisted the English ensign. This was a polite invitation to the chase, to show her colors, but she declined to do so. We now felt sure that she was an enemy, and a prize, and as we were still gaining on her, it was only a matter of an hour or two, when she would fall into our hands. Our polite invitation to the chase, to show her colors, not succeeding, we became a little more emphatic, and fired a blank cartridge. Still she was obstinate. She was steering for Flores, and probably, like the *Starlight*, had her eye on the marine league. Having approached her, in another half hour, within good round-shot range, I resolved to treat her as I had treated the *Starlight*, and threw a 32-pounder near enough to her stern to give the captain a shower-bath. Shower-baths are very efficacious, in many cases, and we found it so in this, for in a moment more, we could see the stars and stripes ascending to the stranger's peak, and that he had started his tacks and sheets, and was in the act of hauling up his courses. This done, the main-yard was swung aback, and the prize had surrendered herself a prisoner.

Bartelli now came to tell me, that my bath was ready, and descending to the cabin, I bathed, and dressed for breakfast, whilst the boarding-officer was boarding the prize. She proved to be the *Alert*, of, and from New London, and bound, by the way of the Azores, and Cape de Verde Islands, to the Indian Ocean. She was only sixteen days from port, with files of late newspapers; and besides her own ample outfit for a large crew, and a long voyage, she had on board supplies for the group known as the Navigators' Islands, in the South Indian Ocean, where among icebergs and storms, the Yankees had a whaling and sealing station. This capture proved to be a very opportune one, as we were in want of just such a lot of clothing, for the men, as we found on board the prize; and the choice beef, and pork, nicely put up ship-bread, boxes of soap, and tobacco, and numerous other articles of seaman's supplies did not come amiss. We had been particularly short of a supply of tobacco, this being a costly article in England, and I could see Jack's eye brighten, as he rolled aft, and piled up on the quarter-deck, sundry heavy oaken boxes of good "Virginia twist." That night the pipes seemed to have wonderfully increased in number, on board the *Alabama*, and the song and the jest derived new inspiration from the fragrance of the weed. We paroled the officers and crew of the *Alert*, and sent them ashore, in their own boats, as we had done the others.

I had now three prizes on my hands, viz.: the *Starlight*, the *Ocean Rover*, and the *Alert*, with a prize crew on board of each, and as I could make no better use of them than to destroy them, thanks to the unfriendly conduct of neutrals, so often referred to, it became necessary to think of burning them. They were lying at distances, ranging from half a mile to three miles from the *Alabama*, and were fired within a short time of each other, so that we had three funeral pyres burning around us at the same moment. The other whalers at a distance must have thought that there were a good many steamers passing Flores, that day. It was still early in the afternoon, and there was more work before us ere night set in. I had scarcely gotten my prize crews on board, and my boats run up, before another sail was discovered standing in for the island. We immediately gave chase, or rather, to speak more correctly, proceeded to meet the stranger, who was standing in our direction. The ships approached each other very rapidly, and we soon discovered the new sail to be a large schooner, of unmistakable Yankee build and rig. We hoisted the United States colors, and she responded soon afterward with the stars and stripes. She came on quite unsuspiciously, as the two last prizes had done, until she arrived near enough to see that the three mysterious cones of smoke, at which she had probably been wondering for some time past, proceeded from three ships on fire. Coupling this unusual spectacle with the approach toward her of a rakish-looking barkentine, she at once smelt rather a large rat, and wheeled suddenly in flight. But it was too late. We were already within three miles of her, and a pursuit of half an hour brought her within effective range of our bow-chaser. We now changed colors, and fired a blank cartridge. This was sufficient. She saved us the expenditure of a shot, and hove to, without further ado. Upon being boarded, she proved to be the *Weathergauge*, a whaler of Provincetown, Massachusetts, six weeks from the land of the Puritan, with other files of newspapers, though not so late as those captured on board the *Alert*.

In running over these files, it was wonderful to observe the glibness with which these Massachusetts brethren of ours now talked of treason, and of rebels, and traitors, at no greater distance, in point of time, than forty-five years, from the Hartford Convention; to say nothing of certain little idiosyncrasies of theirs, that were developed during the annexation of Texas. There were some "Sunday" papers among the rest, and all the pious parsons and deacons in the land were overflowing with patriotism, and hurling death and damnation from their pulpits, against those who had dared to strike at the "Lord's anointed," the sainted Abraham Lincoln. But as the papers contained little or no war news, we had no time to bestow upon the crotchets of the Yankee brain, and they were promptly consigned to the waste-paper basket. Another sail being discovered, whilst we were receiving the surrender of the *Weathergauge*, we hastily threw a prize crew on board this latter vessel, directing the prize-master to "hold on to the island of Corvo," during the ensuing night, which was now falling, until we

should return, and started off in pursuit of the newly discovered sail.

Chasing a sail is very much like pursuing a coy maiden,
the very coyness sharpening the pursuit. The chase, in the
present instance, seemed determined to run away from us; and
as she was fast, and we were as determined to overhaul her as
she was to run away, she led us a beautiful night-dance over
the merry waters. The moon rose bright, soon after the chase
commenced, and, striking upon the canvas of the fleeing vessel, lighted it up as though it had been a snow-bank. The
American vessels are distinguished, above all others, for the
whiteness of their canvas; being clothed, for the most part, in
the fibre of our cotton-fields. The cut of the sails, and the
taper of the spars of the chase looked American, and then the
ship was cracking on every stitch of canvas that would draw,
in the effort to escape — she must surely be American, we
thought. And so we "looked on her, to lust after her," and
gave our little ship the benefit of all our skill in seamanship.
The speed of the two ships was so nearly matched, that, for
the first hour or two, it was impossible to say whether we had
gained on her an inch. We were both running dead before
the wind, and this was not the *Alabama's* most favorable sail-
ing-point. With her tall lower masts, and large fore-and-aft
sails, she was better on a wind, or with the wind abeam. The
chase was leading us away from our cruising-ground, and I
should have abandoned it, if I had not had my pride of ship
a little interested. It would never do for the *Alabama* to be
beaten in the beginning of her cruise, and that, too, by a merchantman; and so we threw out all our "light kites" to the
wind, and gave her the studding-sails "alow and aloft." To
make a long story short, we chased this ship nearly all night,
and only came up with her a little before dawn; and when
we did come up with her, she proved to be a Dane! She was
the bark *Overman*, from Bankok, in Siam, bound to Hamburg.
There had been no occasion, whatever, for this neutral ship to
flee, and the long chase which she had given me was evidently
the result of a little spleen; and so, to revenge myself, in a good-
natured way, I insisted upon all my belligerent rights. Though
satisfied from her reply to my hail, that she was what she pro-

claimed herself to be, I compelled her to heave to, which involved the necessity of taking in all that beautiful white canvas, with which she had decoyed me so many miles away from my cruising-ground, and sent a boat on board of her to examine her papers. She thus lost more time than if she had shortened sail earlier in the chase, to permit me to come up with her.

It was late next day before I rejoined the *Weathergauge* off Corvo, and I felt, as I was retracing my steps, pretty much as Music or Rover may be supposed to feel, as he is limping back to his kennel, after a run in pursuit of a fox that has escaped him. Bartelli failed to call me at the usual hour, that morning, and I need not say that I made a late breakfast. We now landed the crew of the *Weathergauge*, in their own boats, with the usual store of provisions, and traps, and burned her. Two days elapsed now without a capture, during which we overhauled but one ship, a Portuguese bark homeward bound. Having beaten the "cover" of which Flores was the centre, pretty effectually, I now stretched away to the north-west, and ran the island out of sight, intending to skirt it, at the distance of forty or fifty miles. On the third day, the welcome cry of "sail ho!" again rang from the masthead, and making sail in the direction indicated by the look-out, we soon discovered that the chase was a whaler. Resorting to the usual *ruse* of the enemy's flag, the stranger did not attempt to escape, and in an hour or two more, we were alongside of the American whaling brig *Altamaha*, from New Bedford, five months out. The *Altamaha* had had but little success, and was comparatively empty. She did not make so beautiful a bonfire, therefore, as the other whalers had done.

In the afternoon, we overhauled a Spanish ship. Our position, to-day, was latitude 40° 34′ N., and longitude 35° 24′ 15″ W. The barometer stood at 30.3 inches, and the thermometer at 75°; from which the reader will see that the weather was fine and pleasant. It was now the middle of September, however, and a change might be looked for at any moment. On the night after capturing the *Altamaha*, we had another night-chase, with more success, however, than the last. It was my habit, when there was no "game up," to turn in

early, usually at nine o'clock, to enable my *physique* to withstand the frequent drafts upon its energies. I was already in
a sound sleep, when about half-past eleven, an old quartermaster came below, and giving my cot a gentle shake, said: "There
has a large ship just passed to windward of us, on the opposite tack, sir." I sprang out of bed at once, and throwing on
a few clothes, was on deck almost as soon as the quartermaster.
I immediately wore ship, and gave chase. My ship was under
topsails, and it took us some little time to make sail. By this
time the chase was from two and a half to three miles distant,
but quite visible to the naked eye, in the bright moonlight.
We were both close-hauled on the starboard tack, the chase
about three points on the weather bow. The stranger, who
was probably keeping a better look-out than is usual with
merchant-ships, in consequence of the war, had discovered our
movement, and knew he was pursued, as we could see him setting his royals and flying jib, which had been furled. The
Alabama was now at her best point of sailing. The sailors
used to say, when we drew aft the sheets of those immense
trysails of hers, and got the fore-tack close aboard, that she
was putting on her seven-league boots. She did, indeed, then
seem

> "To walk the waters like a thing of life,"

and there were few sailing ships that could run away from her.

We gained from the start upon the chase, and in a couple
of hours, were on his weather-quarter, having both head-
reached, and gone to windward of him. He was now no more
than about a mile distant, and I fired the accustomed blank
cartridge to heave him to. The sound of the gun broke upon
the stillness of the night, with startling effect, but the chase
did not stir tack or sheet in obedience to it. She was evidently
resolved to try conclusions with me a little farther. Finding that I had the advantage of him, on a wind, he kept off a
little, and eased his sheets, and we could see, with our night-
glasses, that he was rigging out his studding-sail booms preparatory to setting the sails upon them. We kept off in turn,
bringing the wind a little forward of the beam, and such good
use did the *Alabama* make of her seven-league boots, that

before the stranger could get even his foretopmast studding-sail set, we had him within good point-blank range of a 32-pounder. The moon was shining very poetically, and the chase was very pretty, but it was rather "after hours," and so I I resolved to shift the scenes, cut short the drama an act or two, and bring it to a close. I now fired a second gun, though still unshotted, and the smoke had hardly blown away before we could see the stranger hauling up his courses, and bringing his ship to the wind, as much as to say, "I see you have the heels of me, and there is no use in trying any longer." I gave the boarding-officer orders, in case the ship should prove to be a prize, of which I had but little doubt, to show me a light as soon as he should get on board of her. The oars of his boat had scarcely ceased to resound, before I saw the welcome light ascending to the stranger's peak, and knew that another of the enemy's ships had fallen into my power. It was now nearly daylight, and I went below and finished the nap which had been so unceremoniously broken in upon. I may as well observe here, that I scarcely ever disturbed the regular repose of the officers and crew during these night operations. Everything was done by the watch on deck, and "all hands" were never called except on emergencies.

When I came on deck the next morning, there was a fine large ship lying under my lee, awaiting my orders. She proved to be the *Benjamin Tucker*, of New Bedford, eight months out, with three hundred and forty barrels of oil. We received from her an additional supply of tobacco, and other small stores. As early as ten o'clock, the crew of the *Tucker*, numbering thirty persons, were on board the *Alabama*, and the ship was on fire. The remainder of this day, and the next, passed without incident, except the incidents of wind, and weather, which have so often been recorded. We improved the leisure, by exercising the men at the guns, and caulking the decks, which were again beginning to let water enough through them, to inconvenience the men in their hammocks below. Just as the sun was setting, on the evening of the second day, we caught a glimpse from the mast-head of the island of Flores, distant about forty miles.

The next morning dawned bright and clear, with a smooth

sea, and summer clouds sailing lazily overhead, giving us just
breeze enough to save us from the *ennui* of a calm. As soon
as the morning mists lifted themselves from the surface of the
waters, a schooner appeared in sight, at no great distance. We
had approached each other unwittingly during the night. We
immediately gave chase, hoisting the United States colors, for
the schooner was evidently Yankee. She did not attempt to
escape, and when, as early as half-past seven A. M., we came
near enough to fire a gun, and change colors, she hove to, and
surrendered. She was the whaling-schooner *Courser*, of Provincetown, Massachusetts. Her master was a gallant young
fellow, and a fine specimen of a seaman, and if I could have separated him, in any way, from the "Universal Yankee Nation,"
I should have been pleased to spare his pretty little craft from
the flames; but the thing was impossible. There were too
many white-cravatted, long-haired fellows, bawling from the
New-England pulpits, and too many house-burners and pilferers
inundating our Southern land, to permit me to be generous, and
so I steeled my heart, as I had done on a former occasion, and
executed the laws of war.

Having now the crews of the three last ships captured, on
board, amounting to about seventy, who were not only beginning, on account of their number, and the limited accommodations of the *Alabama*, to be uncomfortable themselves, but were
inconveniencing my own people, and hindering more or less
the routine of the ship, I resolved to run back to Flores, and
land them. I had eight whale-boats in tow, which I had brought
away from the burning ships, for the purpose of landing these
prisoners, and, no doubt, the islanders, as they saw my well-
known ship returning, with such a string of boats, congratulated
themselves upon the prospect of other good bargains with the
Yankees. The traffic must now have been considerable in this
little island ; such was the avalanche of boats, harpoons, cordage,
whales' teeth, whalebones, beef, pork, tobacco, soap, and jack-
knives that I had thrown on shore. When we had reached sufficiently near, I shoved all the boats off at once, laden with my
seventy prisoners, and there was quite a regatta under the lee
of Flores that afternoon, the boats of each ship striving to beat
the others to the shore. The fellows seemed to be so well

pleased, that I believe, with a little coaxing, they would have been willing to give three cheers for the *Alabama*.

We had some sport ourselves, after the prisoners had departed; for we converted the *Courser* into a target, before setting fire to her, and gave the crew a little practice at her, with the battery. They did pretty well for green hands, but nothing to boast of. They were now becoming somewhat familiar with the gun exercise, and in the evolutions that are usually taught sailors at general quarters. Not only my excellent first lieutenant, but all the officers of the divisions, took great pains with them, and their progress was quite satisfactory.

We again stood away to the northward and westward, under easy sail, during the night, and the next day, the weather being still fine, and the breeze moderate from the south-west, in latitude about 40°, and longitude 33°, we chased a large ship which tried her heels with us — to no purpose, however — as we overhauled her in about three hours and a half. It was another American whaling ship, the *Virginia*, only twenty days out, from New Bedford. She brought us another batch of late newspapers, and being fitted out, like the *Alert*, for a long cruise, we got on board some more supplies from her. The master of this ship expressed great surprise at the speed of the *Alabama*, under sail. His own ship, he said, was fast, but he had stood "no chance" with the *Alabama*. It was like a rabbit attempting to run away from a greyhound. We burned the *Virginia*, when we had gotten our supplies on board, and despoiled her of such cordage, and spare sails as we needed, and stood away to the north-west again. The torch having been applied to her rather late in the afternoon, the burning wreck was still visible some time after nightfall.

The next morning the weather had changed considerably. It was cloudy, and rather angry-looking, and the wind was fresh and increasing. We overhauled a French brig, during the day, and after detaining her no longer than was necessary to examine her papers, permitted her to depart. We had barely turned away from the Frenchman, when a bark was announced from the mast-head. We immediately gave chase. We had to wear ship for this purpose, and the bark, which seemed to have descried us, quite as soon as we had descried

her, observing the evolution, made all sail at once. in flight.
Here was another chase, and under different circumstances from
any of those that had preceded it. It was blowing half a gale
of wind, and it remained to be proved whether the *Alabama*
was as much to be dreaded in rough weather as in smooth.
Many smooth-water sailers lose their quality of speed entirely,
when the seas begin to buffet them. I had the wind of the
chase, and was thus enabled to run down upon her, with a
flowing sheet. I held on to my topgallant sails, though the
masts buckled, and bent as though the sticks would go over
the side. The chase did the same. It was soon quite evident
that my gallant little ship was entirely at home in the roughest
weather. She seemed, like a trained racer, to enjoy the sport,
and though she would tremble, now and then, as she leaped
from sea to sea, it was the tremor of excitement, not of weakness. We gained so rapidly upon the chase, that in three
hours from the time the race commenced, we had her within
the range of our guns. By way of a change, I had chased this
ship under English colors, but she obstinately refused to show
any colors herself, until she was compelled, by the loud-
mouthed command of a gun. She then ran up that "flaunting
lie," the "old flag," and clewed up her topgallant sails, and
hauled up her courses, and submitted to her fate, with such
resignation as she might.

I now not only took in my topgallant sails, and hauled up
my courses, but furled the latter, and took a single reef in my
topsails, so fresh was the wind blowing. Indeed it was so
rough, that I hesitated a moment about launching my boats;
but there was evidently a gale brewing, and if I did not take
possession of my prize, she would in all probability escape
during the darkness and tempest of the ensuing night. I had
a set of gallant, and skilful young officers around me, who
would dare anything I told them to dare, and some capital
seamen, and with the assistance I could give them, by manœuvring the ship, I thought the thing could be managed; and so
I ordered two of the best boats to be launched, and manned.
We were lying to, to windward of the prize, and the boats had
nothing to do, of course, but to pull before the wind and sea
to reach her. I directed the boarding-officers to bring off noth-

ing whatever, from the prize, in the way of property, except
her chronometer, and her flag, and told them when they should
have gotten the prisoners on board and were ready to return,
that I would run down to leeward of the prize to receive them.
They would thus, still, only have to pull before the wind, and
the sea, to regain their ship. The prize was to be fired just
before leaving her. This was all accomplished successfully;
but the reader may well conceive my anxiety, as I watched
those frail, tempest-tossed boats, as they were returning to me,
with their human freight; now thrown high on the top of
some angry wave, that dashed its foam and spray over them,
as though it would swamp them, for daring thus to beard it,
and now settling entirely out of sight in the trough of the sea.
When they pulled under the lee of the *Alabama*, and we threw
them a rope, I was greatly relieved. This was the only ship
I ever burned, before examining her papers. But as she was a
whaler, and so could have no neutral cargo on board, the risk
to be run was not very great. She proved to be the *Elisha
Dunbar* of New Bedford, twenty-four days out.

This burning ship was a beautiful spectacle, the scene being
wild and picturesque beyond description. The black clouds
were mustering their forces in fearful array. Already the entire heavens had been overcast. The thunder began to roll,
and crash, and the lightning to leap from cloud to cloud in a
thousand eccentric lines. The sea was in a tumult of rage;
the winds howled, and floods of rain descended. Amid this
turmoil of the elements, the *Dunbar*, all in flames, and with
disordered gear and unfurled canvas, lay rolling and tossing
upon the sea. Now an ignited sail would fly away from a
yard, and scud off before the gale; and now the yard itself, released from the control of its braces, would swing about wildly,
as in the madness of despair, and then drop into the sea. Finally
the masts went by the board, and then the hull rocked to and
fro for a while, until it was filled with water, and the fire
nearly quenched, when it settled to the bottom of the great
deep, a victim to the passions of man, and the fury of the elements.

CHAPTER XXXIV.

THE YANKEE COLONY IN THE ISLAND OF FLORES—
WHAT THE CAPTAINS OF THE VIRGINIA AND ELISHA
DUNBAR SAID OF THE ALABAMA, WHEN THEY GOT
BACK TO THE LAND OF THE "SAINTS"—THE WHAL-
ING SEASON AT THE AZORES AT AN END—THE ALA-
BAMA CHANGES HER CRUISING GROUND—WHAT SHE
SAW AND DID.

THE reader has seen how rapidly we had been peopling the little island of Flores. I had thrown ashore there, nearly as many Yankee sailors as there were original inhabitants. I should now have gone back with the crews of two more ships, but for the bad weather. Jack, suddenly released from the labors and confinement of his ship, must have run riot in this verdant little paradise, where the law was too weak to restrain him. With his swagger, devil-may-care air, and propensity for fun and frolic, when he has a drop in his eye, the simple inhabitants must have been a good deal puzzled to fix the *genus* of the bird that had so suddenly dropped down upon them. The history of my colony would, no doubt, be highly interesting; and I trust that some future traveller will disinter it from the archives of the island, for the benefit of mankind. The police reports would be of especial interest. In due time the Federal Consul at Fayal chartered a vessel, and removed the colony back to the New England States.

The gale which was described in the last chapter, did not prove to be very violent, though it blew sufficiently fresh to reduce the *Alabama* to close-reefed topsails, with the bonnets off her trysails. It was but the forerunner of a series of gales, occurring about the period of the equinox. The bad weather

had the effect to put an end to the whaling season, a little in
advance of the regular time.   From the 19th to the 23d of
September, we were constantly under reefed sails, and the
wind being from the northward, we drifted as far south as the
34th degree of latitude.   We were now in a comparatively
unfrequented part of the ocean, and had not seen a sail since
the capture of the *Elisha Dunbar*.   During the prevalence of
this bad weather, our prisoners necessarily suffered some inconvenience, and were obliged to submit to some discomforts.
I need not say that these were greatly magnified by the Northern press.   The masters of the captured ships took this mode
of revenging themselves upon me.   The captains of the last
two ships captured, made long complaints against the *Alabama*,
when they got back to New England, and I will here give
them the benefit of their own stories, that the reader may see
what they amount to.   It is the master of the *Virginia* who
speaks first — a Captain Tilton.   He says:—

"I went on the quarter-deck, with my son, when they ordered
me into the lee waist, with my crew, and all of us were put in
irons, with the exception of the two boys, and the cook and steward.   I asked if I was to be put in irons?   The reply of Captain
Semmes was, that his purser had been put in irons, and had his
head shaved by us, and that he meant to retaliate.   We were put
in the lee waist, with an old sail over us, and a few planks to lie
upon.   The steamer was cruising to the west, and the next day,
they took the *Elisha Dunbar*, her crew receiving the same treatment as ourselves.   The steamer's guns being kept run out, the
side ports could not be shut, and when the sea was a little rough,
or the vessel rolled, the water was continually coming in on both
sides, and washing across the deck where we were, so that our
feet and clothing were wet all the time, either from the water below, or the rain above.   We were obliged to sleep in the place
where we were, and often waked up in the night nearly under
water.   Our fare consisted of beef and pork, rice, beans, tea, and
coffee, and bread.   Only one of my irons was allowed to be taken
off at a time, and we had to wash in salt water.   We kept on deck
all the time, night and day, and a guard was placed over us."

The above statement is substantially correct, with the exception that the prisoners were not drenched with sea-water,
or with the rain, all the time, as is pretended.   It is quite true
that they were compelled to live, and sleep on deck.   We had
nowhere else to put them.   My berth-deck was filled with my

own crew, and it was not possible to berth prisoners there, without turning my own men out of their hammocks. To remedy this difficulty, we spread a tent, made of spare sails, and which was quite tight, in the lee waist, and laid gratings upon the deck, to keep the men and their bedding as dry as possible. Ordinarily they were very comfortable, but sometimes, during the prevalence of gales, they were, no doubt, a little disturbed in their slumbers by the water, as Captain Tilton says. But I discharged them all in good physical condition, and this is the best evidence I could give, that they were well cared for. It was certainly a hardship that Captain Tilton should have nothing better to eat than my own crew, and should be obliged, like them, to wash in salt water, but he was waited upon by his own cook and steward, and the reader can see from his own bill of fare, that he was in no danger of starving. He was, as he says, ordered off the quarter-deck. That is a place sacred to the officers of the ship, where even their own crew are not permitted to come, except on duty, and much less a prisoner. He explains, himself, as I had previously explained to the reader, how he came to be put in irons. The "good book" says that we must have "an eye for an eye, and a tooth for a tooth." The enemy had put one of my officers in irons, and I had followed the rule of the "good book." Now let us hear from Captain Gifford, of the *Dunbar*. This witness says:—

"On the morning of the 18th of September, in latitude 39° 50', longitude 35° 20', with the wind from the south-west, and the bark heading south-east, saw a steamer on our port-quarter, standing to the north-west. Soon after, found she had altered her course, and was steering for the bark. We soon made all sail to get out of her reach, and were going ten knots at the time ; but the steamer, gaining on us, under canvas alone, soon came up with us, and fired a gun under our stern, with the St. George's cross flying at the time. Our colors were set, when she displayed the Confederate flag. Being near us, we hove to, and a boat, with armed officers and crew, came alongside, and upon coming on board, stated to me that my vessel was a prize to the Confederate steamer *Alabama*, Captain Semmes. I was then ordered on board the steamer with my papers, and the crew to follow me with a bag of clothing each. On getting on board, the captain claimed me as a prize, and said that my vessel would be burned. Not having any clothes with me, he allowed me to return for a small trunk of clothes ;—the officer on board asked me what I was coming back for, and tried to prevent me from coming on board. I told him I came after a few clothes, which I took, and returned to the steamer. It ·blowing very hard at the time, and very squally, nothing but the chronometer, sextant, charts, &c., were taken, when the vessel was set fire to, and burnt; there were sixty-five barrels of sperm oil on deck, taken on the passage, which were consumed. We were all put in irons, and received the same treatment that Captain Tilton's officers and crew did, who had been taken the day before. While on board, we understood that the steamer would cruise off the Grand Banks, for a few weeks, to destroy the large American ships, to and from the Channel ports. They had knowledge of two ships being loaded with arms for the United States, and were in hopes to capture them. They were particularly anxious to fall in with the clipper-ship *Dreadnought*, and destroy her, as she was celebrated for speed; and they were confident of their ability to capture, or run away from any vessel in the United States. The steamer being in the track of outward and homeward-bound vessels, and more or less being in sight, every day, she will make great havoc among them."

Captain Gifford does not seem to have anything to complain of, in particular, except that the sailors had to put their clothes in bags, and that his trunk was "small;" but both he and his sailors got their clothing, which was more than some of our women and children, in the South, did, when the gallant Sherman, and the gallant Wilson, and the gallant Stoneman, and a host of other gallant fellows, were making their "grand marches," and "raids" in the South, merely for the love of "grand moral ideas." The terrible drenchings, that Captain Tilton got, did not seem to have made the same impression upon Captain Gifford.

Few of the masters, whose ships I burned, ever told the whole truth, when they got back among their countrymen. Some of them forgot, entirely, to mention how they had implored me to save their ships from destruction, professing to be the best of *Democrats*, and deprecating the war which their countrymen were making upon us! How they had come to sea, bringing their New England cousins with them, to get rid of the draft, and how abhorrent to them the sainted Abraham was. "Why, Captain," they would say, "it is hard that I should have my ship burned; I have voted the *Democratic* ticket all my life; I was a *Breckinridge* man in the last Presidential contest; and as for the 'nigger,' if we except a few ancient spinsters, who pet the darkey, on the same principle that they pet a lap-dog, having nothing else to pet, and a few of our deacons and 'church-members,' who have never been out of New England—all of whom are honest people enough in their way—and some cunning political rascals, who expect to rise into fame and fortune on the negro's back, we, New England people, care nothing about him." "That may be all very true," I would reply; "but, unfortunately, the 'political rascals,' of whom you speak, have been strong enough to get up this war, and you are in the same boat with the 'political rascals,' whatever may be your individual opinions. Every whale you strike will put money into the Federal treasury, and strengthen the hands of your people to carry on the war. I am afraid I must burn your ship." "But, Captain, can't we arrange the matter in some way? I will give you a ransom-bond, which my owners and myself will regard as a debt of honor." (By the way, I have some of these debts of honor in my possession, now, which I will sell cheap.) And so they would continue to remonstrate with me, until I cut short the conversation, by ordering the torch applied to their ships. They would then revenge themselves in the manner I have mentioned; and historians of the Boynton class would record their testimony as truth, and thus Yankee history would be made.

The whaling season at the Azores being at an end, as remarked, I resolved to change my cruising-ground, and stretch over to the Banks of Newfoundland, and the coast of the United States, in quest (as some of my young officers, who had served in the China seas, playfully remarked) of the great American junk-fleet. In China, the expression "junk-fleet" means, more particularly, the grain-ships, that swarm all the seas and rivers in that populous empire, in the autumn, carrying their rich cargoes of grain to market. It was now the beginning of October. There was no cotton crop available, with which to freight the ships of our loving Northern brethren, and conduct their exchanges. They were forced to rely upon the grain crop of the great Northwest; the "political rascals" having been cunning enough to wheedle these natural allies of ours into this New England war. They needed gold abroad, with which to pay for arms, and military supplies of various kinds, shiploads of which were, every day, passing into New York and Boston, in violation of those English neutrality laws, which, as we have seen, Mr. Seward and Mr. Adams had been so persistently contending should be enforced against ourselves. Western New York, Ohio, Indiana, Illinois, Michigan, Minnesota, and Iowa had gathered in the rich harvests from their teeming grain-fields; and it was this grain, laden in Yankee ships, which it was my object now to strike at.

The change from one cruising-ground to another, during which no vessels were sighted, afforded my crew a much-needed relaxation of a few days, for they had been much fagged and worn during the last month, by a succession of captures. That which had been but a pleasurable excitement, in the beginning, soon became a wearing and exhausting labor, and they were glad to be relieved, for a time, from the chasing and burning of ships, hard service in boats during all kinds of weather, and the wet jackets and sleepless nights, which had sometimes been the consequences of these. I will avail myself of this comparative calm, in the moral atmosphere on board the *Alabama*, to introduce the reader, more particularly, to our interior life. Thus far, he has only seen the ship of war, in her outward garb, engaged in her vocation. I propose to give him a sight of my military family, and show him how my children played as well as worked; how I governed them, and with what toys I amused them.

From the very beginning of our captures, an order had been issued, that no sailor should lay his hand on any article of property, to appropriate it to his own use, unless by permission of an officer; and especially that no spirituous liquors should be brought on board the *Alabama*. It was made the duty of every boarding-officer, upon getting on board a prize, to demand possession of the keys of the liquor-lockers, and either to cause the liquor to be destroyed, or thrown overboard. To the rigid enforcement of this rule, I attribute much of the good order which prevailed on board my ship. It was enforced against the officers, as well the men, and no officer's mess was allowed to supply itself with liquor, by purchase, or otherwise, unless by my consent; and I never gave this consent to the midshipmen's mess. We burned, on one occasion, a ship, whose entire cargo consisted of French brandies, and champagne, and other wines, without allowing a bottle of it to be brought on board. But whilst I used these precautions, I caused a regular allowance of "grog" to be served out to the crew, twice in each day. I was quite willing that Jack should drink, but I undertook to be the judge of how much he should drink.

Such articles of clothing and supplies as were captured, were turned over to the paymaster, to be credited to the Government, and duly issued and charged to the crew, as if they had been purchased in the market. In spite of all these precautions, however, a sailor would now and then be brought on board from a prize, drunk, would manage to smuggle liquor to his comrades, and would be found arrayed in all sorts of strange garbs, from whaler's boots, and red flannel shirts and comforters, to long-tailed coats and beaver hats. Notwithstanding the discipline of the ship, the gravity of the crew would sometimes give way to merriment, as one of these fellows, thus ludicruously apparelled, would have to be hoisted or lifted on board, being too comfortably drunk to attend to his own locomotion. Each offender knew that he would have to walk straight into the "Brig," upon being thus detected in the violation of these orders, and that punishment would speedily follow the offence; and yet I found it one of the most difficult parts of my duty, to convince some of these free-and-easy fellows, who had mistaken the *Alabama*, when they signed the articles off Terceira, (after that stump speech before referred to,) for what Mr. Seward and Mr. Adams insisted she was, a "privateer," that everything was captured in the name of the Confederate States, and that nothing belonged to them personally. The California-bound ships frequently had on board boxes and bales of fine clothing, boots, shoes, and hats, but not a garment was allowed to be brought on board except such as the paymaster might need for issue. It seemed hard to consign all these tempting articles to the flames, without permitting the sailors to help themselves, but if such license had been permitted, disorder and demoralization would have been the consequence.

I had no chaplain on board, but Sunday was always kept as

a day of abstinence from labor, when the exigencies of war and weather would permit, and it was my uniform practice on this day, to have the ship thoroughly cleansed, in every part, for inspection — particularly the sleeping apartments, and the engine-room — and to require the officers and seamen to appear on the quarter-deck for muster; the former in their appropriate uniforms, and the latter in clean duck frocks and trousers, or other clothing adapted to the latitude and climate. The reader has already been present at several of these musters. The boys of the ship, of whom I had quite a number on board, were placed under the special charge of the master-at-arms — a subordinate officer, with police-powers, in charge of the berth-deck — whose duty it was to inspect them, in every morning watch, with reference to personal cleanliness; turning down the collars, and rolling up the trousers of the youngsters, to see that they had duly performed their ablutions. These boys had been taken from the stews, and haunts of vice about Liverpool, and were as great a set of scamps as any disciplinarian could desire to "lick into shape," but it is astonishing what a reformation soap and water and the master-at-arms effected in them, in a short time. Many of them became very respectable young fellows, for which they were indebted almost entirely to the free use of soap and water.

As a hygienic precaution, when we were cruising in warm latitudes, where the dews were heavy, the whole crew was required to appear, every evening, at sunset muster, in blue flannel shirts and trousers. They could then sleep in the dews, without the fear of colds or rheumatisms. We were always supplied with the best of provisions, for, being at war with a provision-producing people, almost every ship we captured afforded us a greater or less supply; and all the water that was drank on board the *Alabama* was condensed by the engine from the vapor of sea-water. The consequence of all this care was highly gratifying to me, as, in the three years I was afloat, I did not lose a man by disease, in either of my ships! When it is recollected that I cruised in all parts of the world, now fencing out the cold, and battling with the storms of the North Atlantic and South Indian Oceans, and now being fried, and baked, and stewed within the tropics, and on the equator, and that, besides my own crews, some two thousand of the enemy's sailors passed through my hands, first and last, as prisoners, this is a remarkable statement to be able to make. My excellent surgeon, Dr. Galt, and, after him, Dr. Llewellyn, ably seconded me by their skill and experience.

On week days we mustered the crew at their quarters twice a day—at nine A. M., and at sunset, and when the weather was suitable, one division, or about one fourth of the crew, was exercised, either at the battery, or with small arms. This not only gave them efficiency in the use of their weapons, but kept them employed—the constant employment of my men being a fundamental article of my philosophy. I found the old adage, that "Idleness is the parent of vice," as true upon the sea as upon the land. My crew were never so happy as when they had plenty to do, and but little to think about. Indeed, as to the thinking, I allowed them to do very little of that. Whenever I found I had a sea-lawyer among them, I got rid of him as soon as possible—giving him a chance to desert. I reserved the *quids*, and *quos*, and *pros* and *cons*, exclusively for myself.

But though I took good care to see that my men had plenty of employment, it was not all work with them. They had their pastimes and pleasures, as well as labors. After the duties of the day were over, they would generally assemble on the forecastle, and, with violin, and tambourine—and I always kept them supplied with these and other musical instruments—they would extemporize a ball-room, by moving the shot-racks, coils of rope, and other impediments, out of the way, and, with handkerchiefs tied around the waists of some of them, to indicate who were to be the ladies of the party, they would get up a dance with all due form and ceremony; the ladies, in particular, endeavoring to imitate all the airs and graces of the sex—the only drawback being a little hoarseness of the voice, and now and then the use of an expletive, which would escape them when something went wrong in the dance, and they forgot they had the aprons on. The favorite dancing-tunes were those of Wapping and Wide Water Street, and when I speak of the airs and graces, I must be understood to

mean those rather demonstrative airs and graces, of which
Poll and Peggy would be likely to be mistresses of. On these
occasions, the discipline of the ship was wont to be purposely
relaxed, and roars of laughter, and other evidences of the rapid
flight of the jocund hours, at other times entirely inadmissible,
would come resounding aft on the quarter-deck.

Sometimes the recreation of the dance would be varied, and
songs and story-telling would be the amusements of the evening. The sea is a wide net, which catches all kinds of fish,
and in a man-of-war's crew a great many odd characters are
always to be found. Broken-down gentlemen, who have spent
all the money they have been able to raise, upon their own
credit, or that of their friends; defaulting clerks and cashiers;
actors who have been playing to empty houses; third-class
musicians and poëts, are all not unfrequently found in the
same ship's company. These gentlemen play a very unimportant *role* in seamanship, but they take a high rank among
the crew, when fun and frolic, and not seamanship, are the
order of the day — or rather night. In the *Alabama*, we had
a capital Falstaff, though Jack's capacious pouch was not
often with "fat capon lined;" and as for "sherry-sack," if he
now and then got a good glass of "red-eye" instead, he was
quite content. We had several Hals, who had defied their
harsh old papas, and given them the slip, to keep Falstaff
company; and as for *raconteurs*, we had them by the score.
Some of these latter were equal to the Italian *lazzaroni*, and
could extemporize yarns by the hour; and there is nothing of
which a sailor is half so fond as a yarn.

It was my custom, on these occasions, to go forward on the
bridge — a light structure spanning the deck, near amidships
— which, in the twilight hours, was a sort of lounging-place for
the officers, and smoke my single cigar, and listen to whatever
might be going on, almost as much amused as the sailors themselves. So rigid is the discipline of a ship of war, that the
captain is necessarily much isolated from his officers. He
messes alone, walks the quarter-deck alone, and rarely, during
the hours of duty, exchanges, even with his first lieutenant,
or officer of the deck, other conversation than such as relates
to the ship, or the service she is upon. I felt exceedingly the

irksomeness of my position, and was always glad of an opportunity to escape from it.   On the "bridge," I could lay aside the "captain," gather my young officers around me, and indulge in some of the pleasures of social intercourse; taking care to tighten the reins, gently, again, the next morning. When song was the order of the evening, after the more ambitious of the *amateurs* had delivered themselves of their *solos* and *cantatas*, the entertainment generally wound up with *Dixie*, when the whole ship would be in an uproar of enthusiasm, sometimes as many as a hundred voices joining in the chorus; the unenthusiastic Englishman, the stolid Dutchman, the mercurial Frenchman, the grave Spaniard, and even the serious Malayan, all joining in the inspiring refrain,—

" We'll live and die in Dixie! "

and astonishing old Neptune by the fervor and novelty of their music.

Eight o'clock was the hour at which the night-watches were set, when, of course, all merriment came to an end.   When the officer of the deck reported this hour to the captain, and was told by the latter, to "make it so," he put the trumpet to his mouth, and sang out in a loud voice, "Strike the bell eight — call the watch!"   In an instant, the most profound silence fell upon the late uproarious scene.   The witches did not disappear more magically, in that famous revel of Tam O'Shanter, when Tam sang out, "Weel dune, Cutty Sark!" than the sailors dispersed at this ominous voice of authority.   The violinist was arrested with half-drawn bow; the *raconteur* suddenly ceased his yarn in the most interesting part of his story, and even the inspiring chorus of " Dixie " died a premature death, upon the lips of the singers.   The shrill call of the boatswain's whistle, followed by his hoarse voice, calling "All the starboard watch!" or "All the port watch!" as the case might be, would now be heard, and pretty soon, the watch, which was off duty, would "tumble" below to their hammocks, and the midshipman would be seen coming forward from the quarterdeck, with lantern and watch-bill in hand, to muster the watch whose turn it was to be on deck.   The most profound stillness now reigned on board during the remainder of the night, only broken by the necessary orders and movements, in making or taking in sail, or it may be, by the whistling of the gale, and the surging of the sea, or the cry of the look-outs at their posts, every half hour.

To return now to our cruise. We are passing, the reader will recollect, from the Azores to the Banks of Newfoundland. On the 1st of October, the following record is found upon my journal: "The gale moderated during the last night, but the weather, to-day, has been thick and rainy, with the wind from the north-west, and a confused, rough sea. No observation for latitude. The barometer, which had gone down to 29.8 is rising, and stands at nine P. M. at 29.9. The ship being about two hundred miles only, from the Banks of Newfoundland, we are trying the temperature of the air and water every hour. At nine P. M. we found the temperature of the former to be 63°, and of the latter 70°, indicating that we have passed into the Gulf Stream." The thick, rainy weather is almost as unerring a sign of the presence of this stream as the thermometer.

The stream into which we have now passed is, literally, an immense salt-water river in the sea. Coming out of the Gulf of Mexico, it has brought the temperature of the tropics, all the way to the Banks of Newfoundland, in the latitude of 50° north, and it has run this distance between banks, or walls of cold water, on either side, parting with very little of its warmth, by the way. When it is recollected that this salt-water river in the sea is about three thousand times larger than the Mississippi River, that is to say, that it brings out of the Gulf of Mexico, three thousand times as much water, as that river empties into it, and that all this great body of water is carried up into the hyperborean regions of Newfoundland, at a temperature, even in mid-winter, ranging from 73 to 78 degrees, it will be seen at once what a powerful weather-breeder it must be. Accordingly, no port of the world is more stormy than the Gulf Stream, off the north-eastern coast of the United States, and the Banks of Newfoundland. Such is the quantity of heat brought daily by this stream, and placed in juxtaposition with the rigors of a Northern winter, that it is estimated, that if it were suddenly stricken from it, it would be sufficient to make the column of superincumbent atmosphere hotter than melted iron! With such an element of atmospheric disturbance, it is not wonderful that the most terrific gales, that rage on the ocean, are wont to sweep over the surface of this stream.

Indeed, this stream not only generates hurricanes of its own, it seems to attract to it such as are engendered in the most distant parts of our hemisphere; for hurricanes known to have originated near Cape St. Roque, in Brazil, have made their way straight for the Gulf Stream, and followed it, in its course, for a thousand miles and more, spreading shipwreck and disaster, broadcast, in their track. The violence of these gales is inconceivable by those who have not witnessed them. The great hurricane of 1780 originated to the eastward of the island of Barbadoes, and made straight for the Gulf Stream. As it passed over the West India Islands, trees were uprooted, and the bark literally blown from them. The very bottom and depths of the sea, in the vicinity of some of the islands, were uncovered, and rocks torn up, and new channels formed. The waves rose to such a height, that forts, and castles, removed, as it was thought, far out of the reach of the water, were washed away, and the storm, taking hold of their heavy artillery, played with it, as with so many straws, throwing it to considerable distances. Houses were razed, and ships wrecked, and the bodies of men and beasts were lifted up into the air and dashed to pieces in the storm. Still, the European-bound ships defy all the bad weather, so prevalent in this stream, on account of the easterly current which accelerates their passage, at the rate of from two, to three miles, per hour. The stream, therefore, has been literally bearded by commerce, and has become one of its principal highways. It is because it is a highway of commerce that the *Alabama* now finds herself in it. Nor was she long in it, before the travellers on the highway began to come along.

Early on the morning of the 3d of October, two sail were simultaneously reported by the look-out at the mast-head — one right ahead, and the other on the lee-bow. As both the ships were standing in our direction, there was no necessity for a chase. We had nothing to do but await their approach. As

their hulls were lifted above the horizon, we could see that
they were fine, large ships, with a profusion of tapering spars
and white canvas. We at once pronounced them American;
and so, after a little, they proved to be. They were, in fact,
the *avant courriers* of the "junk fleet," for which we had
come to look. The wind was light, and they came on, with
all their sails set, from truck to rail. We, on our part, put
on an air of perfect indifference. We made no change in
our sail, and it was not necessary to alter our course, as the
strangers would pass sufficiently near us, unless they altered
their own courses, which they did not seem inclined to do.
They apparently had no suspicion of our real character. We
did not hoist any colors, until the vessels were nearly abreast
of us, and only a few hundred yards distant, when, suddenly
wheeling, we fired a gun, and hoisted the Confederate flag.
The capture of these two ships must have been a perfect surprise to them, judging by the confusion that was visible on
board. There was a running about the decks, and an evident
indecision for a few moments, as to what was best to be done;
but it did not take the masters long to take an intelligent view
of the "situation." There was nothing to be done, but surrender; and this they did, by hoisting their colors, and heaving to their ships.

We now shortened sail, and laying the maintopsail to the
mast, lowered a couple of quarter boats, and boarded the
prizes. One of them proved to be the *Brilliant*, from New York,
for London, laden with flour and grain; and the other, the
Emily Farnum, from New York, for Liverpool, with a similar
cargo. The cargo of the *Farnum* being properly documented
as neutral property, I released her on ransom-bond, and converting her into a cartel, sent on board of her all my prisoners,
of whom I had fifty or sixty on board the *Alabama*, besides
those just captured in the *Brilliant*. The latter ship was
burned, and her destruction must have disappointed a good
many holders of bills of exchange, drawn against her cargo,
as this was large and valuable. The owners of the ship have
since put in a claim, in that little bill, which Mr. Seward has
pressed with so little effect hitherto against the British Government, for indemnity for the "depredations of the *Alabama*,"

for the ship alone, and the freight-moneys which they lost by her destruction, to the amount of $93,000. The cargo was probably even more valuable than the ship.

I made a positive stipulation with the *Farnum*, upon releasing her, that she should continue her voyage to Liverpool, and not put back into any American port; the master pledging me his word that he would comply with it. My object was, of course, to prevent him from giving news of me to the enemy. He had no sooner passed out of sight, however, steering his course for Liverpool, than he dodged and put into Boston, and reported me. This being nothing more than a clever "Yankee trick," of course there was no harm done the master's honor.

I was much moved by the entreaties of the master of the *Brilliant* to spare his ship. He was a hard-working seaman, who owned a one third interest in her. He had built her, and was attached to her, and she represented all his worldly goods. But I was forced again to steel my heart. He was, like the other masters who had remonstrated with me, in the same boat with the "political rascals," who had egged on the war; and I told him he must look to those rascals for redress. The ship made a brilliant bonfire, lighting up the Gulf Stream, for many miles around. Having been set on fire near night, and the wind falling to nearly a calm, we remained in sight of the burning wreck nearly all night.

Among the many slanders against me, to which the Northern press gave currency during the war, it was stated, that I decoyed ships into my power, by setting fire to my prizes at night, and remaining by them in ambuscade. Of course, when seamen discover a ship on fire at sea they rush, with all their manly sympathies aroused, to the rescue of their comrades, who are supposed to be in danger; but if they should find, it was said, that they were waylaid, and captured, none would go to the rescue in future, and thus many seamen would perish. It can scarcely be necessary for me to say, that I never purposely lay by a burning ship, by night, or by day, longer than *to see her well on fire*. The substantial answer to the slander is, that I never captured a ship, under the circumstances stated.

For the next few days we had fine, clear weather, and chased and overhauled a number of neutral ships, most of them out of

New York, and bound for Europe, laden with grain. The English, French, Prussian, Hamburg, Oldenham, and other flags were fast monopolizing the enemy's carrying trade, and enjoying a rich harvest. These were not the sort of "junks" that we were in quest of, but they compensated us, somewhat, for the time and labor lost in chasing and boarding them, by supplying us with late newspapers of the enemy, and giving us valuable information concerning the progress of the war.

On the afternoon of the 7th of October, the weather being fine, and the breeze light, we chased and captured the American bark, *Wave Crest,* from New York, bound for Cardiff, in Wales, with flour and grain. In the language of the enemy, we "plundered her," that is, we received on board from her, such articles as we needed, and after having made use of her for a while, as a target, at which to practise the men at the battery, we burned her.

Filing away, we again made sail to the north-west. We were now, in about latitude 41°, and longitude 54°, and were working our way, under easy sail, toward the coasts of the United States. Just before nightfall, on the same afternoon, another sail was cried from aloft, and we made all sail in pursuit, immediately, anxious to draw sufficiently near the chase before dark, to prevent losing sight of her. By this time, the wind, which had been very light all day, had freshened to a stiff breeze, and the chase, soon perceiving our object, spread a cloud of canvas, with studding-sails "alow and aloft," in the effort to escape. She had seen the fire of the burning *Wave Crest,* and knew full well the doom that awaited her, if she were overtaken. As night threw her mantle over the scene, the moon, nearly at the full, rose with unusual splendor and lighted up the sea for the chase; and a beautiful, picturesque chase it was. Although it lasted several hours, our anxiety as to the result was relieved, in a very short time, for we could see, from the first, that we gained upon the fleeing ship, although her master practised every stratagem known to the skilful seaman. As soon as we approached sufficiently near to get a good view of her through our excellent night-glasses, which, in the bright moonlight, brought out all her features almost as distinctly as if we had been viewing them by the rays of the sun, we dis-

covered that she was one of those light, and graceful hermaphrodite brigs, that is, a rig between the brig and the schooner,
so peculiarly American. Her sails were beautifully cut, well
hoisted, and the clews well spread; her masts were long and
tapering, and her yards more square than usual. There was
just sea enough on, to give her, now and then, a gentle motion,
as she rose upon a wave, and scudded forward with renewed
impulse. Her sails looked not unlike so many silver wings, in
the weird moonlight, and with a little effort of the imagination,
it would not have been difficult to think of her as some immense water-fowl, which had been scared from its roost and
flown seaward for safety.

I sat astride of the hammock-cloth on the weather-quarter,
and watched the beautiful apparition during the whole chase,
only taking off my eye, now and then, to give some order to
the officer of the deck, or to cast it admiringly upon the buckling and bending masts and spars of my own beautiful ship, as
she sped forward, with all the animation of a living thing, in
pursuit. The poor little, affrighted fawn ahead of us, how its
heart must have gone pit-a-pat, as it cast its timid eyes behind
it, and saw its terrible pursuer looming up larger, and larger,
and coming nearer and nearer! Still there might be some
hope. The pursuing vessel might be some peaceful merchant-
ship, bound on the same errand of commerce with herself, and
only trying heels with her, in sport, over these dancing waves,
and by this bright moonlight. Alas! the hope was short-lived;
for presently, in the stillness of near midnight, a flash was seen,
followed by the sound of a booming gun, and there could no
longer be any doubt, that the pursuer was a ship of war, and
most likely a Confederate. Halliards and tacks, and sheets
were let fly on board the brigantine, and as soon as her seamen could gather in the folds of the flapping sails, and haul
up clew-garnets, her helm was put down, and she rounded
gracefully to the now whistling wind, with fore-topsail aback.
So rapidly had this been done, and so close was the *Alabama*
upon the chase, that we had just time to sheer clear of her by
a little trick of the helm. Our own sail was now shortened,
and the boarding-officer dispatched on board the prize.

She proved to be the *Dunkirk*, from New York, with a cargo

of grain for Lisbon. There being no evidence of neutral ownership of the cargo, among the papers, she was burned, as soon as her crew could be transferred to the *Alabama*. We made two novel captures on board this ship — one was a deserter from the *Sumter*, a worthless sailor out of one of the Northern States, whom we afterward discharged from the Confederate Naval service, in disgrace, instead of hanging him, as we might have done under our Articles of War; and the other a number of very neatly put up *tracts* in the Portuguese language; our Northern brethren dealing in a little piety as well as trade. These tracts had been issued by that pious corporation, the "American Tract Society," of New York, whose fine fat offices are filled with sleek, well-fed parsons, of the Boynton stripe, whose business it is to prey upon the credulity of kind-hearted American women, and make a pretence of converting the heathen! On the cover of these tracts was printed the following directions, as to how the doses were to be taken. "Portuguese tracts, from the 'American Tract Society,' for distribution among Portuguese passengers, and to give, upon the coast, to visitors from the shore, &c. When in port, please keep conspicuously on the cabin-table, for all comers to read: but be very careful not to take any ashore, as the laws do not allow it." A pen had been run through the last injunction, as though the propagandists of "grand moral ideas" had become a little bolder since the war, and were determined to thrust their piety down the throats of the Portuguese, whether they would or not. If there should be any attempt now, on the part of poor old Portugal, to seize the unlawful distributor of the tracts, a gunboat or two would set the matter right. A little farther on, on the same cover, was the following instruction: "As may be convenient, please report, (by letter if necessary,) anything of interest which may occur, in connection with the distribution; also take any orders for Bibles, and forward to John S. Pierson, Marine Agent, New York Bible Society, No. 7 Beekman Street."

CHAPTER XXXV.

THOUGH the month of October is remarkable for its fine
weather, along the American coast, yet here in the Gulf
Stream, we had a constant succession of changes, the wind
going regularly around the compass every two or three days,
and thick, rainy weather predominating. We were now, besides, experiencing a south-easterly current of about two knots
per hour, and as we were bound to the north-west, and frequently had the wind, as well as the current ahead, we made but
slow progress. On the second day after capturing the *Dunkirk*, the familiar cry of "sail ho!" again came ringing from the
mast-head, and pretty soon a large ship loomed up above the
horizon. We gave chase, and, just before sunset, came up
with a fine packet-ship, whose deck, we could see, was crowded
with passengers. This was a somewhat unusual spectacle — a
sailing ship filled with passengers for Europe, during the
month of October. Since the introduction of the steam-packet,
but few passengers, except emigrants, take passage in a sailing
ship, and the current of emigration sets the other way.

Upon being boarded, the ship proved to be the *Tonawanda*,
of, and from Philadelphia, bound to Liverpool. Some of the
passengers were foreigners, fleeing from the tyranny, and outrages of person and property, which had overtaken them, under the reign of the Puritan, in the "land of the free, and the
home of the brave," and others were patriotic Puritans themselves running away from the "City of Brotherly Love," to
escape the draft. We captured the *Tonawanda*, and the question immediately presented itself what should we do with her?

There being no claim, by any neutral, for the cargo, both ship and cargo were good prize of war, but unfortunately we could not burn the ship, without encumbering ourselves with the passengers; and thirty of the sixty of these were women and children! The men we might have disposed of, without much inconvenience, but it was not possible to convert the *Alabama* into a nursery, and set the stewards to serving pap to the babies. Although I made it a rule never to bond a ship if I could burn her, I released the *Tonawanda* on bond, though there was no legal impediment to her being burned. I kept her cruising in company with me, however, for a day or two, hoping that I might fall in with some other ship of the enemy, that might be less valuable, or might have a neutral cargo on board, to which I could transfer the passengers, and thus be enabled to burn her. But here, again, her owners were in luck, for the finest, and most valuable ships, with cargoes entirely uncovered, would persist in crossing my path.

On the second day after the capture of the *Tonawanda*—that ship being still in our company, with a prize crew on board—the weather inclining to be overcast, and the breeze light—a ship was reported, at early daylight, on our weather-quarter. It was another heavy ship of the "junk fleet," and as we were lying right across her path, we had nothing to do but await her approach. She came along under a cloud of canvas, though, as the wind was light, it took her some three or four hours to come up with us. To disarm her of suspicion, I hoisted the American colors, and caused my prize to do the same. She naturally concluded that the two ships were "visiting," which ships sometimes do at sea, when the wind is light, and there is not much time lost by the operation, and came on without so much as shifting her helm, or stirring tack or sheet. When she had approached sufficiently near, I invited her, too, to visit me; my card of invitation being a blank cartridge, and a change of flags. She hove to at once, and, upon being boarded, proved to be the ship *Manchester* from New York, bound to Liverpool. I now threw the *Manchester's* crew, together with the crews of the *Wave Crest*, and *Dunkirk*, on board the *Tonawanda*, as being the less valuable ship of the two, and permitted the latter to depart; but

before doing so, I took from on board of her, one of her passengers. This was a likely negro lad of about seventeen years
of age — a slave until he was twenty-one, under the laws of
Delaware. This little State, all of whose sympathies were
with us, had been ridden over, rough-shod, by the Vandals
north of her, as Maryland afterward was, and was arrayed on
the side of the enemy. I was obliged, therefore, to treat her as
such. The slave was on his way to Europe, in company with
his master. He came necessarily under the laws of war, and
I brought him on board the *Alabama*, where we were in
want of good servants, and sent him to wait on the ward-room
mess.

The boy was a little alarmed at first, but, when he saw
kindly faces beaming upon him, and heard from his new masters, and the servants of the mess, some words of encouragement, he became reassured, and, in the course of a few days,
was not only at home, but congratulated himself on the exchange he had made. He became, more especially, the servant of Dr. Galt, and there at once arose, between the Virginia
gentleman and the slave boy, that sympathy of master and
servant, which our ruder people of the North find it so impossible to comprehend. Faithful service, respect, and attachment followed protection and kind treatment, and the slave
was as happy as the day was long. David soon became to
Galt what Bartelli was to me — indispensable — and the former
was really as free as the latter, except only in the circumstance
that he could not change masters. I caused his name to be
entered on the books of the ship, as one of the crew, and
allowed him the pay of his grade. In short, no difference was
made between him and the white waiters of the mess. His
condition was in every respect bettered; though, I doubt not,
a howl went up over his capture, as soon as it became known
to the pseudo-philanthropists of the North, who know as little
about the negro and his nature, as they do about the people of
the South.

It was pleasant to regard the affection which this boy conceived for Galt, and the pride he took in serving him. As he
brought the doctor's camp-stool for him to the "bridge,"
placed it in the cosiest corner he could find, and ran off to

bring him a light for his cigar, his eyes would dilate, and his "ivories" shine. Dave served us during the whole cruise. He went on shore in all parts of the world, knew that the moment he touched the shore he was at liberty to depart, if he pleased, and was tampered with by sundry Yankee Consuls, but always came back to us. He seemed to have the instinct of deciding between his friends and his enemies.

The following correspondence took place between the Liverpool Chamber of Commerce, and Earl Russell, the British Foreign Secretary, on the occasion of the two last captures: —

To the Rt. Hon. Earl Russell, etc., etc. :—

My Lord:— I have been requested by the Council of this Chamber to inform you that they have had brought before them the facts of the destruction at sea, in one case, and of seizure and release under ransom-bond in another case, of British property on board Federal vessels, (the *Manchester* and the *Tonawanda*,) by an armed cruiser sailing under the Confederate flag, the particulars of which have been already laid before your Lordship. As the question is one of serious importance to the commerce of this country, the Council wish me most respectfully to solicit the favor of your Lordship's acquainting them, for the information of the mercantile community, what, in the opinion of her Majesty's Government, is the position of the owners of such property, in these and other similar cases. Submitting this question with every respect to your Lordship, I have the honor to be, my Lord, your most obedient humble servant,

THOMAS CHILTON,
President Chamber of Commerce.

LIVERPOOL, 8th Nov., 1862.

To Thomas Chilton, Esq., Chamber of Commerce, Liverpool.

Sir:— I am directed by Earl Russell to acknowledge the receipt of your letter of the 8th inst., calling attention to the recent proceedings of the armed vessel *Alabama*, with regard to British property on board the Federal vessels *Manchester* and *Tonawanda*, and requesting the opinion of her Majesty's Government with regard to the position of the owners of such property in those and other similar cases which may arise ; and I am to request that you will inform the Council of the Chamber of Commerce that the matter is under the consideration of her Majesty's Government.

I am, sir, your most obedient, humble servant,

E. HAMMOND.

FOREIGN OFFICE, Nov. 7th, 1862.

After the usual period of gestation, Earl Russell informed his questioners, that British owners of property, on board of

Federal ships, alleged to have been wrongfully captured by Confederate cruisers, were in the same position as any other neutral owners shipping in enemy's bottoms during a war; they must look for redress to the country of the captor. But these British owners did what was more sensible — they withdrew, in due time, their freights from the enemy's ships; and British and other neutral ships soon became the carriers of the American trade. It is claimed in the above correspondence, that there was British property destroyed on board the *Manchester*. If so, it was the fault of the British owner, in failing to document his property properly, for there was no certificate or other paper found on board that ship, claiming that any part of the cargo belonged to neutrals.

The *Manchester* brought us a batch of late New York papers, and I was much obliged to the editors of the New York "Herald," for valuable information. I learned from them where all the enemy's gunboats were, and what they were doing; which, of course, enabled me to take better care of the *Alabama*, than I should otherwise have been enabled to do. The Americans effected many reforms in the art of war during our late struggle. Perhaps this was the only war in which the newspapers ever explained, beforehand, all the movements of armies, and fleets, to the enemy.

The reader will observe, that I received my mails quite regularly, now, from the United States. They were sometimes daily, and rarely less frequent than tri-weekly. I appointed my excellent clerk, Mr. Breedlove Smith, whom I am glad to have this opportunity of introducing to the reader, postmaster, and he delivered the mail regularly to the officers and crew — that is to say, the newspaper and periodical mail — the letters I considered as addressed to myself personally. They might give valuable information of the objects and designs of the enemy, and throw some light upon the true ownership of cargoes, falsely documented. I therefore took the liberty, which the laws of war gave me, of breaking the seals. There were some curious developments made in some of these letters, nor were they all written on business. Sometimes, as I would break a seal, a photograph would tumble out, and the first few lines of the letter would inform me of a tender pas-

sion that was raging in the heart of the writer. These epis-
tles, photographs, and all, were always pitched, with a pshaw!
into the waste-paper basket, and were soon afterward consigned
by Bartelli to the sea. So that the fair writers—and some of
the writers were fair if I might judge by their portraits—
may rest satisfied that their secrets are safe. My young officers became so accustomed to their morning's newspaper, as
they sat down to the breakfast-table, that if it was not forth-
coming, they would wonder "what the d—l *Alabama* had been
about, the past night, that she had not gotten hold of a mail?"

For two or three days after capturing the *Manchester*, we fell
in with nothing but neutral vessels. When the nationality of
these was distinctly marked, as generally it was, we forbore to
chase them. The weather began now to give unmistakable
signs, of a general disturbance of the atmospheric machine.
On the 15th of October, we captured our next ship. It was
blowing half a gale of wind, with a thick atmosphere, and
rain-squalls. We were lying to, under topsails, when she was
reported. As in the case of the *Manchester*, we had only to await
her approach, for we were still in the beaten track of these lone
travellers upon the sea. She came along quite fast, before the
gale, and when within reach, we hove her to, with the accustomed gun. She proved, upon being boarded, to be the bark
Lamplighter, of Boston, from New York, for Gibraltar, with a
cargo of tobacco. There was no attempt to cover the cargo, and
when we had removed the crew to the *Alabama*, we burned her.

From the frequent mention which has been made of "uncovered cargoes," the reader will see how careless the enemy's
merchants were, and how little they dreamed of disaster.
They had not yet heard of the *Alabama*, except only that she
had escaped from Liverpool, as the "290." They looked upon
her, yet, as a mere myth, which it was not necessary to take
any precautions against. But the reader will see how soon
their course will change, and in what demand British Consular certificates, vouching for the neutrality of good American
cargoes, will be, in the good city of Gotham, toward which, the
Alabama is slowly working her way.

We captured the *Lamplighter* early in the day, and it was
well for us she came along when she did. If she had delayed

her arrival a few hours, we should probably not have been able to board her, so much had the gale increased, and the sea risen.   For the next few days, as the reader will speedily see, we had as much as we could do to take care of ourselves, without thinking of the enemy, or his ships.   We had a fearful gale to encounter.   As this gale was a cyclone, and the first really severe gale that the *Alabama* had met with, it is worthy of a brief description.   We begin, in our generation, to have some definite knowledge of the atmospheric laws.   To our ancestors, of only a generation or two back, these laws were almost a sealed book.   It is now well ascertained, that all the great hurricanes which sweep over the seas, are cyclones; that is, circular gales, revolving around an axis, or vortex, at the same time that they are travelling in a given direction.   These gales all have their origin in warm latitudes, or, as has been prettily said, by an officer of the Dutch Navy writing on the subject, they "prefer to place their feet in warm water."   They do not, however, confine themselves to the places of their origin, but, passing out of the tropics, sweep over large tracts of extra-tropical seas. These circular gales are the great regulators, or balance-wheels, as it were, of the atmospheric machine.   They arise in seasons of atmospheric disturbance, and seem necessary to the restoration of the atmospheric equilibrium.

In the East Indian and China seas, the cyclone is called a typhoon.   It prevails there with even more destructive effect than in the western hemisphere.   It takes its origin during the change of the monsoons.   Monsoons are periodical winds, which blow one half of the year from one direction — the north-east for example — and then change, and blow the other half of the year, from the opposite direction, the south-west. When these monsoons are changing, there is great disturbance in the atmospheric equilibrium.   A battle of the winds, as it were, takes place; the out-going wind struggling for existence, and the in-coming wind endeavoring to throttle it, and take its place.   Calms, whirlwinds, water-spouts, and heavy and drenching rains set in; the black, wild-looking clouds, sometimes rent and torn, sweeping with their heavy burdens of vapor over the very surface of the sea.   Now, the out-going,

or dying monsoon will recede, for days together, its enemy,
the in-coming monsoon, greedily advancing to occupy the
space left vacant. The retreating wind will then rally, regain
its courage, and drive back, at least for a part of the way, the
pursuing wind. In this way, the two will alternate for weeks,
each watching the other as warily, as if they were opposing
armies. It is during these struggles, when the atmosphere is
unhinged, as it were, that the typhoon makes its awful appearance. Every reader is familiar with the phenomenon of the
miniature whirlwind, which he has so often seen sweep along
a street or road, for a short distance, and then disappear ; the
want of local equilibrium in the atmosphere, which gave rise
to it, having been restored.

These little whirlwinds generally occur at street-corners, or
at cross-roads, and are produced by the meeting of two winds.
When these winds meet, the stronger will bend the weaker,
and a whirl will ensue. The two winds still coming on, the
whirl will be increased, and thus a whirlwind is formed, which
immediately begins to travel — not at random, of course, but
in the direction of least pressure. The meeting of two currents of water, which form a whirlpool, may be used as
another illustration. It is just so, that the typhoon is formed.
It steps in as a great conservator of the peace, to put an end
to the atmospherical strife which has been going on, and to
restore harmony to nature. It is a terrible scourge whilst it
lasts ; the whole heavens seem to be in disorder, and that which
was only a partial battle between outposts of the aërial armies,
has now become a general engagement. The great whirl
sweeps over a thousand miles or more, and when it has ceased,
nature smiles again ; the old monsoon has given up the ghost,
and the new monsoon has taken its place. All will be peace
now until the next change — the storms that will occur in the
interval, being more or less local. We have monsoons in the
western hemisphere, as well as in the eastern, though they are
much more partial, both in space and duration.

The cyclones which sweep over the North Atlantic are gen-
erated, as has been remarked, to the eastward of the West India
Islands — somewhere between them and the coast of Brazil.
They occur in August, September, and October — sometimes,

indeed, as early as the latter part of July. In these months, the sun has drawn after him, into the northern hemisphere, the south-east trade-winds of the South Atlantic. These trade-winds are now struggling with the north-east trade-winds, which prevail in these seas, for three fourths of the year, for the mastery. We have, thus, another monsoon struggle going on; and the consequence of this struggle is the cyclone. The reader may recollect the appearances of the weather, noted by me, some chapters back, when we were in these seas, in the *Sumter*, in July and August, of 1861; to wit, the calms, light, baffling winds, water-spouts, and heavy rains.

If the reader will pay a little attention to the diagram on page 473, it will assist him, materially, in comprehending the nature of the storm into which the *Alabama* had now entered. The outer circle represents the extent of the storm; the inner circle, the centre or vortex; the arrows along the inner edge of the outer circle represent the direction, or gyration of the wind, and the dotted line represents the course travelled by the storm. The figures marked, 1, 2, and 3, represent the position of the *Alabama*, in the different stages of the storm, as it passed over her; the arrow-heads on the figures representing the head of the ship.

If the reader, being in the northern hemisphere, will turn his face toward the sun, at his rising, and watch his course for a short time, he will observe that this course is from left to right. As the course of the arrows in the figure is from right to left, the reader observes that the gyration of the wind, in the storm, is *against the course of the sun*. This is an invariable law in both hemispheres; but, in the southern hemisphere, the reader will not fail to remark, that the gyration of the wind is in the opposite direction from its gyration in the northern hemisphere, for the reason, that, to an observer in the southern hemisphere the sun appears to be moving, not from left to right, but from right to left. Whilst, therefore, the storm, in the northern hemisphere, gyrates from right to left, in the southern hemisphere, it gyrates from left to right; both gyrations being *against the course of the sun*.

This is a curious phenomenon, which has, thus far, puzzled all the philosophers. It is a double puzzle; first, why the storm should gyrate always in the same direction, and secondly, why this gyration should be different in the two hemispheres. The law seems to be so subtle, as utterly to elude investigation. There is a curious phenomenon, in the vegetable world, which seems to obey this law of storms, and which I do not recollect ever to have seen alluded to by any writer. It may be well known to horticulturists, for aught that I know, but it attracted my attention, in my own garden, for the first time, since the war. It is, that all creeping vines, and tendrils, when they wind themselves around a pole, invariably wind themselves from right to left, or *against the course of the sun!* I was first struck with the fact, by watching, from day to day, the tender unfolding of the Lima bean — each little creeper, as it came forth, feeling, as with the instinct of animal life, for the pole, and then *invariably* bending around it, in the direction mentioned. I have a long avenue of these plants, numbering several hundred poles, and upon examining them all, I invariably found the same result. I tried the experiment with some of these little creepers, of endeavoring to compel them to embrace the pole from left to right, or *with the course of the sun*, but in vain. In the afternoon I would gather blades of grass, and tie some of the tendrils to the poles, in a way to force them to disobey the law, but when I went to inspect them, the following morning, I would invariably find, that the obedient little plants *had turned back*, and taken the accustomed track! What is the subtle influence which produces this wonderful result? May it not be the same law which rides on the whirlwind, and directs the storm?

The cyclone, of which I am writing, must have travelled a couple of thousand miles, before it reached the *Alabama*. Its approach had been heralded, as the reader has seen, by several days of bad weather; and, on the morning of the gale, which was on the 16th of October, the barometer — that faithful sentinel of the seaman — began to settle very rapidly. We had been under short sail before, but we now took the close reefs in the topsails, which tied them down to about one third of their original size, got up, and bent the main storm-staysail, which was made of the stoutest No. 1 canvas, and scarcely larger than a pocket-handkerchief, swung in the quarter-boats,

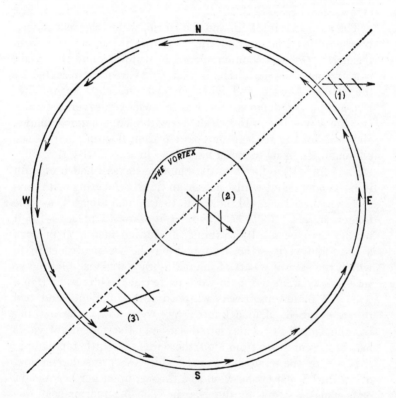

Diagram of the Cyclone experienced by the *Alabama* on the 16th of
October, 1862.

and passed additional lashings around them; and, in short, made all the requisite preparations for the battle with the elements which awaited us. If the reader will cast his eye upon the diagram, at *Alabama*, No. 1, he will see that the ship has her head to the eastward, that her yards are braced up on the starboard tack, and that she took the wind, as indicated by the arrows, from S. to S. S. E.

The ship is lying still, and the storm, which the reader sees, by the dotted line, is travelling to the north-east, is approaching her. She was soon enveloped in its folds; and the winds, running around the circle, in that mad career represented by the arrows, howled, and whistled, and screeched around her like a thousand demons. She was thrown over, several streaks, and the waves began to assault her with sledge-hammer blows, and occasionally to leap on board of her, flooding her decks, and compelling us to stand knee-deep in water. By this time, we had furled the fore-topsail; the fore-staysail had been split into ribbons; and whilst I was anxiously debating with myself, whether I should hold on to the main-topsail, a little longer, or start its sheets, and let it blow to pieces—for it would have been folly to think of sending men aloft in such a gale, to furl it—the iron bolt on the weather-quarter, to which the standing part of the main-brace was made fast, gave way; away went the main-yard, parted at the slings, and, in a trice, the main-topsail was whipped into fragments, and tied into a hundred curious knots. We were now under nothing but the small storm-staysail, described; the topgallant yards had been sent down from aloft, there was very little top-hamper exposed to the wind, and yet the ship was pressed over and over, until I feared she would be thrown upon her beam-ends, or her masts swept by the board. The lee-quarter-boat was wrenched from the davits, and dashed in pieces; and, as the sea would strike the ship, forward or aft, she would tremble in every fibre, as if she had been a living thing, in fear of momentary dissolution.

But she behaved nobly, and I breathed easier after the first half hour of the storm. All hands were, of course, on deck, with the hatches battened down, and there was but little left for us to do, but to watch the course of the storm, and to ease the ship, all it was possible to ease her, with the helm. Life-lines had been rove, fore and aft the decks, by my careful first lieutenant, to prevent the crew from being washed overboard, and it was almost as much as each man could do, to look out for his own personal safety.

The storm raged thus violently for two hours, the barometer settling all the while, until it reached 28.64. It then fell suddenly calm. Landsmen have heard of an "ominous" calm, but this calm seemed to us almost like the fiat of death. We knew, at once, that we were in the terrible vortex of a cyclone, from which so few mariners have ever escaped to tell the tale! Nothing else could account for the suddenness of the calm, coupled with the lowness of the barometer. We knew that when the vortex should pass, the gale would be renewed, as suddenly as it had ceased, and with increased fury, and that the frail little *Alabama*—for indeed she looked frail and small, now, amid the giant seas that were rising in a confused mass around her, and threatening, every moment, to topple on board of her, with an avalanche of water that would bury her a hundred fathoms deep—might be dashed in a thousand pieces in an instant. I pulled out my watch, and noted the time of the occurrence of the calm, and causing one of the cabin-doors to be unclosed, I sent an officer below to look at the barometer. He reported the height already mentioned—28.64. If the reader will cast his eye upon the diagram again—at figure No. 2—he will see where we were at this moment. The *Alabama's* head now lies to the south-east—she having "come up" gradually to the wind, as it hauled—and she is in the south-eastern hemisphere of the vortex. The scene was the most remarkable I had ever witnessed. The ship, which had been pressed over, only a moment before, by the fury of the gale as described, had now righted, and the heavy storm staysail, which, notwithstanding its diminutive size, had required two stout tackles to confine it to the deck, was now, for want of wind to keep it steady, jerking these tackles about as though it would snap them in pieces, as the ship rolled to and fro! The aspect of the heavens was appalling. The clouds were writhing and twisting, like so many huge serpents engaged in combat, and hung so low, in the thin air of the vortex, as almost to touch our mast-heads. The best description I can give of the sea, is that of a number of huge watery cones—for the waves seemed now in the diminished pressure of the atmosphere in the vortex to *jut up into the sky,* and assume a conical shape—that were dancing an infernal reel, played by some necromancer. They were not running in any given direction, there being no longer any wind to drive them, but were jostling each other, like drunken men in a crowd, and threatening, every moment, to topple, one upon the other.

With watch in hand I noticed the passage of the vortex. It was just thirty minutes in passing. The gale had left us, with the wind from the south-west; the ship, the moment she emerged from the vortex, took the wind from the north-west. We could see it coming upon the waters. The disorderly seas were now no longer jostling each other; the infernal reel had ended; the cones had lowered their late rebellious heads, as they felt the renewed pressure of the atmosphere, and were being driven, like so many obedient slaves, before the raging blast. The tops of the waves were literally cut off by the force of the wind, and dashed hundreds of yards, in blinding spray. The wind now struck us " butt and foremost," throwing the ship over in an instant, as before, and threatening to jerk the little storm-sail from its bolt-ropes. It was impossible to raise one's head above the rail, and difficult to breathe for a few seconds. We could do nothing but cower under the weather bulwarks, and hold on to the belaying pins, or whatever other objects presented themselves, to prevent being dashed to leeward, or swept overboard. The gale raged, now, precisely as long as it had done before we entered the vortex —two hours—showing how accurately Nature had drawn her circle.

At the end of this time, the *Alabama* found herself in position No. 3. The reader will observe that she is still on the starboard tack, and that from east, she has brought her head around to nearly west. The storm is upon the point of passing away from her. I now again sent an officer below, to inspect the barometer, and he reported 29.70; the instrument having risen a little more than an inch in two hours! This, alone, is evidence of the violence of the storm. During the

KELLY, PIET & CO., ENGRAVERS.

LITH. BY A.HOEN & CO. BALTⁿ

The Alabama in a cyclone, in the Gulf Stream, on the 16ᵗʰ October, 1862.

whole course of the storm, a good deal of rain had fallen.   It
is the rain which adds such fury to the wind.   These storms
come to us, as has been said, from the tropics, and the winds,
by which they are engendered, are highly charged with vapor.
In the course of taking up this vapor from the sea, the winds
take up, along with it, a large quantity of latent heat,
or heat whose presence is not indicated by the thermometer.
As the raging cyclone is moving onward in its path, the winds
begin to part with their burden — it begins to rain.   The
moment the vapor is condensed into rain, the latent heat,
which was taken up with the vapor, is liberated, and the consequence is, the formation of a furnace in the sky, as it were,
overhanging the raging storm, and travelling along with it.
The more rain there falls, the more latent heat there escapes;
the more latent heat there escapes, the hotter the furnace
becomes; and the hotter the furnace, the more furiously the
wind races around the circle, and rushes into the upper air to
fill the vacuum, and restore the equilibrium .

In four hours and a half, from the commencement of the
gale, the *Alabama* was left rolling, and tumbling about in the
confused sea, which the gale had left behind it, with scarcely
wind enough to fill the sails, which, by this time, we had
gotten upon her, to keep her steady.   Little more remains to
be said of the cyclone.   If the reader will take a last look at the
diagram, he will see how it is, that the wind, which appears to
him to change, has not changed in reality.   The wind, from
first to the last, is travelling around the circle, changing not
at all.   It is the passage of the circle over the ship — or over
the observer upon the land — which causes it apparently to
change.   The *Alabama* lay still during the whole gale, not
changing her position, perhaps, half a mile.   As the circle
touched her, she took the wind from S. to S. S. E., and when it
had passed over her, she had the wind at north-west.   In the
intermediate time, the wind had *apparently* hauled first to one,
and then to the other, of all the intermediate points of the compass, and yet it had not changed a hair's breadth.

The weather did not become fine, for several days after the
gale.   On the following night, it again became thick and
cloudy, and the wind blew very fresh from the south-west.

The sea, though it had somewhat subsided, was still very rough, and the night was so dark, that the officer of the deck could not see half the length of the ship in any direction. The south-west wind was a fair wind from the enemy's ports, to Europe, and we kept a very bright look-out, to prevent ourselves from being run over, by some heavy ship of commerce, hurrying, with lightning speed, before wind and sea.

CHAPTER XXXVI.

THE PHYSIOGNOMY OF SHIPS—CAPTURE OF THE LA-
FAYETTE—DECREE OF THE ADMIRALTY COURT ON
BOARD THE ALABAMA IN HER CASE, AND IN THAT
OF THE LAURETTA—THE CRITICISMS OF THE NEW
YORK PRESS—FARTHER PROOF OF THE ROTARY
NATURE OF THE WIND—THE LAURETTA CAPTURED
—THE CRENSHAW CAPTURED—THE NEW YORK
CHAMBER OF COMMERCE CRIES ALOUD IN PAIN—
CAPTURE OF THE BARON DE CASTINE, AND THE
LEVI STARBUCK—CAPTURE OF THE T. B. WALES—
LADY PRISONERS.

THE day after the gale recorded in the last chapter, we set
all hands at work repairing damages—the carpenters
fishing, and the boatswain and his gang refitting the broken
main-yard; the gunners putting their battery in order, the sailmaker repairing sails, and the old signal-quartermaster "breaking out" his signal-lockers, which had been invaded by the
sea-water, and airing his flags. The latter was enabled, by this
time, to make quite a display of Yankee flags, from his signal-
halliards—the *Alabama* having captured seventeen ships in
six weeks. As the Yankee ships now began to wear, out of
pure patriotism, (though they were out of the war, and profitably chasing the honest penny,) the biggest sort of "flaunting
lies," there were several bagsful of these flags.

We began now to overhaul sails again. From the 16th to the
20th of October, we chased and boarded nine, all of which were
neutral! We were, in fact, in an American sea—the Gulf
Stream being the thoroughfare of American and West Indian
commerce to Europe—and yet the American flag was begin-

ning to disappear from it. Such of the Federal ships as could not obtain employment from the Government, as transports, or be sold under neutral flags, were beginning to rot at the wharves of the once thrifty sea-ports of the Great Republic. Our "nautical enterprise" was beginning to tell on the enemy, and if we had had the ability to imitate Massachusetts, in the war of the first revolution, in the way of putting forth armed cruisers, to prey upon the enemy's commerce, the said enemy would not have had so much as a rope-yarn upon the sea, in the course of twelve months. But at the time of which I am writing, the *Alabama* and the *Florida* were the only two Confederate ocean cruisers afloat.

On the 21st of October, we observed in latitude 39° 35', and longitude 63° 26', and on that day, we made our first capture since the gale. We were lying to, as usual, when a large ship was descried, in the north-west, running in our direction. Though the wind was very fresh, she had her royals and fore-topmast studding-sails set, and was, in consequence, running before the wind, with great speed. I shook the reefs out of my own topsails, and prepared to set the topgallant-sails if it should be necessary, and filled away, and moved toward the path of the stranger as she approached, with the English colors at my peak. The fine, large ship, as she ran down to us, presented a beautiful picture—all the more beautiful because we knew her to be Yankee, although she had not yet shown her colors.

We had become now very expert in detecting the nationalities of ships. I had with me a master's mate—Evans—who had a peculiar talent in this respect. He had been a pilot out of Savannah, and had sailed in the *Savannah*, privateer, at the beginning of the war. He escaped the harsh treatment, and trial for piracy, which, as the reader may recollect, were the fate of the prisoners captured in that little vessel, by being absent in a prize at the time of her capture. He afterward joined me at Liverpool. Whenever I had any doubt about the nationality of a ship, I always sent for Mr. Evans, and putting my telescope in his hand, I would say to him, " Look at that ship," pointing in the given direction, "and tell me to what nation she belongs." A glance of a minute or two was all he required. Lowering his glass at the end of this time, he would say to me, "She is a Yankee, sir," or, "She is not a Yankee," as the case might be; and if she was not a Yankee, he would say, "I think she is English," or French, or Dutch, or whatever other nation to which he supposed her to belong. He sometimes failed, of course, in assigning their proper nationality to neutrals, but his judgment seemed to amount to an instinct, with regard to the question, Yankee, or no Yankee. When he pronounced a ship a Yankee, I was always certain of her. I never knew him to fail, in this particular, but once, and that can scarcely be said to have been a failure. He once mistook a St. John's, New Brunswick-built ship, for an enemy; and the ships built in the British Colonies, on the Yankee border, are such counterparts of American ships, that it is very difficult to distinguish one from the other.

The ship which was now running down for us was, as I have said, a picture, with her masts yielding and swaying to a cloud of sail, her tapering poles shooting skyward, even above her royals, and her well-turned, *flaring* bows — the latter a distinctive feature of New York-built ships. She came on, rolling gracefully to the sea, and with the largest kind of a "bone in her mouth." She must have suspected something, from our very equivocal attitude in such weather, and in such a place; but she made no change in her course, and was soon under our guns. A blank cartridge brought her to the wind. If the scene was beautiful before, it was still more so now. If she had been a ship of war, full of men, and with hands stationed at sheets, halliards, and braces, she could not have shortened sail much more rapidly, or have rounded more promptly and gracefully to the wind, with her main topsail aback. Her cloud of canvas seemed to shrivel and disappear, as though it had been a scroll rolled up by an invisible hand. It is true, nothing had been furled, and her light sails were all flying in the wind, confined to the yards only by their clew-lines, but the ship lay as snugly and conveniently for boarding, as I could desire. I frequently had occasion, during my cruises, to admire the seamanship of my enemies. The Yankee is certainly a remarkable specimen of the *genus homo.* He is at once a duck, and a chicken, and takes to the water,

or the land, with equal facility. Providence has certainly designed him for some useful purpose. He is ambitious, restless,
scheming, energetic, and has no inconvenient moral nature to
restrain him from the pursuit of his interests, be the path to
these never so crooked. In the development of material
wealth he is unsurpassed, and perhaps this is his mission on
this new continent of ours. But he is like the beaver, he
works from instinct, and is so avid of gain, that he has *no time
to enjoy the wealth he produces.* Some malicious demon seems
to be goading him on, in spite of himself, to continuous and
exhausting exertion, which consigns him to the tomb before
his time, leaving a "pile" of untouched wealth behind him.

The prize, upon being boarded, proved to be the *Lafayette*,
from New York, laden with grain, chiefly for Irish ports. We
learned from newspapers captured on board of her, that news
of our capture of the *Brilliant* and *Emily Farnum* off the
Banks of Newfoundland, had reached the United States, and,
as was to be expected, I found, when I came to examine the
papers of the *Lafayette*, plenty of certificates to cover her cargo.
In fact, from this time onward, I rarely got hold of an enemy's
ship, whose cargo was not certificated all over — oaths for this
purpose being apparently as cheap, as the much-derided custom-house oaths, that every ship-master is expected to take,
without the least regard to the state of the facts. Upon examination of these certificates, I pronounced them fraudulent, and
burned the ship.

As the burning of this vessel, with her cargo nicely "covered," as the shippers had hoped, with British Consular seals
and certificates, seemed to warm up the Northern press, and
cause it to hurl fresh denunciations of "piracy" against me,
I will detain the reader, a moment, from the thread of my narrative, to look a little into the facts. The reader has already
been told that I held a regular prize-court on board the *Sumter*. I did the same thing on board the *Alabama*, never condemning a ship or cargo, when there was any claim of neutral
property, without the most careful, and thorough examination
of her papers, and giving to the testimony the best efforts of
my judgment. I had every motive not to offend neutrals.
We were hoping for an early recognition of our independence,

by the principal powers of the earth, and were covetous of the good-will of them all. I had, besides, the most positive instructions from Mr. Mallory, our Secretary of the Navy, to pay the utmost attention and respect to neutral rights.

Referring to the records of "The Confederate States Admiralty Court, held on board the Confederate States steamer *Alabama*, on the High Seas," I find the following decree entered, in the case of the *Lafayette*.

"*In re* LAFAYETTE.

"The ship being under the enemy's flag and register, is condemned. With reference to the cargo, there are certificates, prepared in due form, and sworn to before the British Consul, that it was purchased, and shipped, on neutral account. These *ex parte* statements are precisely such as every unscrupulous merchant would prepare, to deceive his enemy, and save his property from capture. There are two shipping-houses in the case; that of Craig & Nicoll, and that of Montgomery Bros. Messrs. Craig & Nicoll say, that the grain shipped by them, belongs to Messrs. Shaw & Finlay, and to Messrs. Hamilton, Megault & Thompson, all of Belfast, in Ireland, to which port the ship is bound, but the grain is not consigned to them, and they could not demand possession of it, under the bill of lading. It is, on the contrary, consigned *to the order* of the shippers; thus leaving the possession, and control of the property, in the hands of the shippers. Farther: The shippers, instead of sending this grain to the pretended owners, in a *general* ship, on freight, consigned to them, they paying freight, as usual, have chartered the whole ship, and stipulated, themselves, for the payment of all the freights. If this property had been, *bona fide*, the property of the parties in Belfast, named in the depositions, it would undoubtedly have gone consigned to them, in a bill of lading, authorizing them to demand possession of it, and the agreement with the ship would have been, that the consignees and owners of the property should pay the freight, upon delivery. But even if this property were purchased, as pretended, by Messrs. Craig & Nicoll, for the parties named, still, their not consigning it to them, and delivering them the proper bill of lading, passing the possession, left the property in the possession, and under the dominion of Craig & Nicoll, and as such liable to capture. See 3 *Phillimore on International Law*, 610, 612, to the effect, that if the goods are going on account of the shipper, *or subject to his order or control*, they are good prize. They cannot even be sold, and transferred to a neutral, *in transitu*. They must abide by their condition, *at the time of the sailing of the ship*.

"The property attempted to be covered by the Messrs. Montgomery Bros., is shipped by Montgomery Bros., of New York, and consigned to Montgomery Bros., in Belfast. Here the consignment is all right. The possession of the property has legally passed to the Belfast house. But when there are two houses of trade doing business as partners, and one of them resides in the enemy's country, the other house, though resident in a neutral country, becomes also enemy, *quoad* the trade of the house in the enemy's country, and its share in any property belonging to the joint concern is subject to capture, equally with the share of the house in the enemy's country. To this point, see 3 *Phillimore*, 605. Cargo condemned."

This is the whole case of the *Lafayette*. As this case was coupled, in the criticisms in the Yankee papers to which I have alluded, and which the reader will see presently, with the case of the *Lauretta*, not yet captured, I will anticipate the capture of this ship by a few days, that the reader may have the facts also in her case.

" *In re* LAURETTA.

" The ship being under the enemy's colors and register, is condemned. There are two shippers of the cargo, the house of Chamberlain, Phelps & Co., and Mr. H. J. Burden — all the shippers resident, and doing business in the city of New York. Chamberlain, Phelps & Co., ship 1424 barrels of flour, and a lot of pipe staves, to be delivered at Gibraltar, *or* Messina, *to their own order*, and 225 kegs of nails to be delivered at Messina, to Mariano Costarelli. The bill of lading for the flour and staves has the following indorsement, sworn to before a notary: 'State, City, and County of New York: Louis Contencin, being duly sworn, says, that he is clerk wlth Chamberlain, Phelps & Co., and that part of the merchandise in the within bill of lading is the property of the subjects of the King of Italy.' This certificate is void for uncertainty. It does not separate the property in the bill of lading, and say which of it belongs to the 'subjects of the King of Italy,' and which to the enemy. For aught that appears, 'the subjects' alluded to may own no more than a single pipe-staff apiece. Indeed, they can own nothing, as it does not appear *what* they own. Further: If the property was identified in the certificate, the 'subjects of the King of Italy' are not. No man — for there is none named — could claim the property under this certificate. It is, therefore, void, for this reason. See 3 *Phillimore*, 596.

But the flour and staves are consigned *to the order of the shippers*, and this, alone, would be sufficient to condemn them, even if the articles had been identified, and the proper owners pointed out in the certificate. The *possession of the property at the time of the sailing of the ship, must be divested out of the enemy-shipper.* See 3 *Phillimore*, 610, 612, cited in the case of the *Lafayette*.

The contingent destination of this property, is another pregnant circumstance. It shows that it was intended *for a market*, and not for any particular neutral owner. It was to be delivered at Gibraltar *or* Messina, as the shippers might determine, after the sailing of the ship — probably upon advices received by steamer. So much for the claim of Chamberlain, Phelps & Co.

"The property shipped by H. J. Burden, consists of 998 barrels of flour, and 290 boxes of herring, and is consigned to Charles R. Blandy, Esq., at Funchal, Madeira. The shipper makes the following affidavit before the British Consul, in New York: 'That all and singular, the goods specified in the annexed bill of lading, were shipped by H. J. Burden, in the bark *Lauretta*, for, and on account of, H. J. Burden, subject of her Britannic Majesty.' Mr. Burden may be a very good subject of her Britannic Majesty, but he describes himself as of 42 Beaver Street, New York City, and seems to lose sight of the fact, that his domicile in an enemy's country, for the purposes of trade, makes him, *quoad* that trade, an enemy. Cargo condemned."

The reader is now in a condition to understand the following criticism, from that very elegant sheet, the New York "Commercial Advertiser," and to appreciate the justice and courtesy with which I was treated by the press of New York, generally.

"THE ALABAMA.

"BRITISH AND ITALIAN PROPERTY DESTROYED — PORTUGAL ALSO INVOLVED.

" *The English Authorities Acting.— Important Facts.—* Some important facts have just been developed in relation to the operations of the rebel privateer *Alabama*, and the present and prospective action of the British and other foreign Governments, whose citizens have lost property by the piracies of her commander. The depredations of the vessel involve the rights of no less than three European governments — England, Italy, and Portugal — and are likely to become a subject of special interest to all maritime nations.

"Already the capture and burning of the ship *Lafayette*, which contained an English cargo, has been the occasion of a correspondence between the British Consul at this port, Mr. Archibald, and Rear-Admiral Milne, commanding the British squadron on the American coast; and it is stated (but we cannot vouch for the truth of the statement) that the Admiral has dispatched three war-vessels in pursuit of the pirate. The Consul has also, we understand, communicated the facts of the case to the British Government and Her Majesty's Minister at Washington. What action will be taken by the British Government, remains to be seen.

"The *Lafayette* sailed from this port with a cargo of grain for Belfast, Ireland. The grain was owned *by two English firms of this city*, and the facts were properly certified on the bills of lading under the British national seal. The *Lafayette* was, however, **a** Boston vessel, and was commanded by Captain Saunders. The facts of the burning have been published.

"But another case (that of the bark *Lauretta*) is about to be submitted for the consideration of the British authorities, as well as those of Italy and Portugal. The facts establish a clear case of piracy. The *Lauretta*, which had on board a cargo consisting principally of flour and staves, was burned by Semmes on the 28th of October. She was bound from this port for the island of Madeira and the port of Messina, in Italy. Nearly a thousand barrels of flour and also a large number of staves were shipped by Mr. H. J. Burden, a British subject residing in this city, to a relative in Funchal, Madeira. The bill of lading bore the British seal affixed by the Consul, to whom the shipper was personally known. The other part of the cargo was shipped by Chamberlain, Phelps & Co., to the order of parties in Messina, and this property was also covered by the Italian Consular certificates.

"The Portuguese Consul at this port also sent a package under seal, to the authorities at Madeira, besides giving a right to enter the port and sending an open bill of lading.

"Captain Wells' account of the manner in which Semmes disposed of these documents, and which he has verified under oath, is not only interesting, but gives an excellent idea of the piratical intentions of the commander of the *Alabama.*

"The papers of the bark were, at the command of Semmes, taken by Captain Wells on board the *Alabama.* There was no American cargo, and therefore no American papers, except those of the vessel. These, of course, were not inquired into. Semmes took first the packet which bore the Portuguese seal, and with an air which showed that he did not regard it as of the slightest consequence, ripped it open, and threw it upon the floor, with the remark that 'he did not care a d—n for the Portuguese.' The Italian bill of lading was treated in a similar manner, except that he considered it unworthy even of a remark.

"Taking up the British bill of lading and looking at the seal, Semmes called upon Captain Wells, with an oath, to explain. It was evidently the only one of the three he thought it worth his while to respect.

"'Who is this Burden?' he inquired sneeringly. 'Have you ever seen him?'

"'I am not acquainted with him; but I have seen him once, when he came on board my vessel,' replied Captain Wells.

"'Is he an Englishman — does he look like an Englishman?'

"'Yes,' rejoined the captain.

"'I'll tell you what,' exclaimed the pirate, 'this is a d—d pretty business — it's a d—d Yankee hash, and I'll settle it,'— whereupon he proceeded to rob the vessel of whatever he wanted, including Captain Wells' property to a considerable amount; put the crew in irons; removed them to the *Alabama;* and concluded by burning the vessel.

"These facts will at once be brought before the British Consul. The preliminary steps have been taken. The facts will also be furnished the Portuguese Consul, who announces his intention of placing them before his Government; and besides whatever action the Italian Consul here may choose to take, the parties in Messina, to whom the property lost on the *Lauretta* was consigned, will of course do what they can to maintain their own rights. The case is likely to attract more attention than all the previous outrages of the *Alabama*, inasmuch as property rights of the subjects of other nations are involved, and the real character of Semmes and his crew becomes manifest.

"Some interesting facts are given by Captain Wells in regard to the *Alabama*, to which, however, we can only make a brief allusion. The officers of the privateer are principally Southern men, but the crew are nearly all English and Irish. They claim that they were shipped by stratagem; that they were told the vessel was going to Nassau, and now they are promised shares in captured property — not only the property taken, but that which is burned, of which Semmes says he keeps an accurate account. The bills are to be paid by the 'Confederate Government,' which Semmes, who enforces discipline only by terrorism, declares will soon achieve its independence. The men suppose they are gaining fortunes — though some of them protest against the cheat which has been practised upon them."

The above is a fair specimen of the average intelligence of Yankee newspapers, on any subject outside of the dirty pool of politics, in which they habitually dabble. I was not *quite* sure when I burned the *Lafayette*, that her cargo belonged to the shippers, British merchants resident in New York. The shippers swore that it did not belong to them, but to other parties resident in Ireland, on whose account they had shipped it. I *thought* they swore falsely, but, as I have said, I was not quite certain. The "Advertiser" sets the matter at rest. It says that I was right. And it claims, with the most charming simplicity, that I was guilty of an act of piracy, in capturing and destroying the property of neutral merchants, *domiciled in the enemy's country, and assisting him to conduct his trade!* The reader now sees what estimate to put upon all the other balderdash of the article. I presume, the only thing Admiral Milne, and the British Minister at Washington did, was to wonder at the stupidity of the New York "Commercial Advertiser." It is scarcely necessary to say, that Captain Wells of the *Lauretta*, took a "custom-house" oath, when he swore to the account which the "Advertiser" gives of his interview

with me, when I burned his ship.   It was a business operation
with these Yankees to abuse me, and they performed it in a
business-like manner — with oaths and affidavits.

Having captured the *Lafayette* at nightfall, it was as late as
ten P. M. before we got through with the business of "robbing"
her — robbing her, in spite of all those nicely contrived certificates, and British consular seals — when we set her on fire.
In a few hours, she was a mere beacon-light, upon the sea,
marking, as so many other fine ships had marked, the track
of the "pirate."   Though I have given the reader already a
pretty large dose of the meteorology of the Gulf Stream, in
which we are still cruising, I cannot forbear to call his attention to other proofs of the rotary character of the winds which
prevail along this hot-water river in the sea.   From the 2d to
the 22d of October, a period of twenty days, the wind had
gone *nine* times entirely around the compass, with the regularity of clock-work.   With the exception of the cyclone of
the 16th, we had had no regular gale of wind; though the
wind frequently blew very fresh, with the barometer sometimes as low as 29.60.   These rotary winds were circles of
greater or less diameter, obeying the laws of storms, and travelling along in the direction of the current, or about north-east.
There was an interval of only a few hours between them, the
barometer rising regularly as one circle or whirl departed, and
falling as the next approached.   I was much struck with the
exceeding regularity of the recurrence of this phenomenon.
The received impression is, that it is only the great gales,
which we call cyclones, or hurricanes, that gyrate.   From my
observations in the Gulf Stream — and I lay in it, continuously,
for something like a month, changing place, in all this time,
but a few hundred miles — gyration is the normal condition of
the winds in this stream — that even the most gentle winds,
when undisturbed by local causes — the proximity of the land,
for instance — are gyrating winds, winding around, and around
their respective vortices, *against the motion of the sun*, as we
have seen the tendril of the vine to wind around the pole to
which it clings.

On the third day after capturing the *Lafayette*, having chased
and overhauled, in the meantime, a number of neutrals, we descried

a large schooner, evidently American, bound to the southward, and eastward. We gave chase at once, but as the schooner was to windward of us, a considerable distance, the chase promised to be long, without the aid of steam, and this, for reasons already explained, I was averse to using, though we kept, at all times, banked fires in the furnaces, and warm water in the boilers. The stranger hugged his wind very closely, this being always the best point of sailing with schooners; but this was also the best point of sailing with the *Alabama*. The reader has seen, that she always put on her seven-league boots, when she had a chance of drawing aft the sheets of those immense trysails of hers. We gained perceptibly, but the wind was falling light, and it was to be feared night would overtake us, before we could bring the chase within reach of our guns. She was still good four miles to windward of us, when I resolved to try the effect of a solid shot from my rifled pivot, on the forecastle. Elevating the gun some ten degrees, we let fly the bolt. It threw up the water in a beautiful jet, within less than half a mile of her! It was enough. The schooner came to the wind, with the Federal colors at her masthead, and awaited our approach. Upon being boarded, she proved to be the *Crenshaw*, three days out from New York, and bound for Glasgow, in Scotland.

The *Crenshaw* was grain-laden, though rather small for a member of the "junk fleet," and there was the usual number of certificates, and British consular seals on board of her, vouching, upon good Yankee oaths, that her cargo was neutral. It was amusing to see how these merchants clung to the British seal, and appealed to the British power, when their grain sacks were in danger. But it was all to no purpose. I would have respected scrupulously any *bona fide* neutral ownership of property, but I knew all these certificates to be fraudulent. Fraudulent as the transactions were, however, some of the shippers might have imposed upon me, if they had only known how to prepare their vouchers. But they were such bunglers, that they committed the most glaring mistakes. The New York merchant is a pretty sharp fellow, in the matter of shaving paper, getting up false invoices, and "doing" the custom-house; but the laws of nations, which had had little connection, heretofore, with the debit and credit side of his ledger, rather muddled his brain. The *Crenshaw's* certificates were precisely like so many others I had, by this time, overhauled. They simply stated, that the cargo belonged to "subjects of her Britannic Majesty," without naming them. To quote the certificates literally, they were in these terms: "The goods specified, in the annexed bills of lading, were shipped on board the schooner *Crenshaw,* for, and on account of subjects of her Britannic Majesty, and the said goods are wholly, and *bona fide*, the property of British subjects." And when I came to look at the bills of lading, I found that the property was consigned *to the order of the shippers*. Here was evidently another of those "Yankee hashes," spoken of by the New York "Commercial Advertiser;" or, if it was not a Yankee hash, it was an English hash, gotten up by some "subjects of her Britannic Majesty," who were *resident merchants in the enemy's country* — whose property the aforesaid "Advertiser" so innocently thought was not subject to capture. For aught that appeared from the certificates, the "subjects" were all resident in New York. And so we did the usual amount of "plundering" on board the *Crenshaw*, and then consigned her to the flames.

From papers captured on board this vessel, we learned that the New York Chamber of Commerce — whose leading spirit seemed to be a Mr. Low, one or two of whose ships, if I mistake not, I had burned — was in a glow of indignation. Its resolutions were exceedingly eloquent. This Chamber of Commerce was a sort of debating society, which by no means confined itself to mere commerce, as its name would seem to imply, but undertook to regulate the affairs of the Yankee nation, generally, and its members had consequently become orators. The words "privateer," "pirate," "robbery," and "plunder," and other blood-and-thunder expressions, ran through their resolutions in beautiful profusion. These resolutions were sent to Mr. Seward, and that renowned statesman sat down, forthwith, and wrote a volume of despatches to Mr. Adams, in London, about the naughty things that the "British Pirate" was doing in American waters. The *Alabama*, said he, was burning everything, right and left, even *British* property; would the Lion stand it?

Another set of resolutions was sent to Mr. Welles, the Fede

ral Secretary of the Navy, and that old gentleman put all the telegraph wires in motion, leading to the different sea-port towns; and the wires put in motion a number of gunboats which were to hurry off to the banks of Newfoundland and capture the *Alabama*. Whilst these gunboats were going from New York to cruise among the cod-fishermen and icebergs, the *Alabama* was jogging along, under easy sail, toward New York. *We* kept ourselves, all the time, in the track of commerce; what track the gunboats, — some of which only mounted a couple of guns, and would have been very shy of falling in with the *Alabama*, — took, to look for us, we never knew, as we did not see any of them.

On the day after capturing the *Crenshaw*, we observed in latitude 39° 47', and longitude 68° 06'. Being near the edge of St. George's Bank, off the coast of New England, we sounded with eighty-five fathoms of line, but got no bottom. Here another gale of wind overtook us; the barometer descending as low as 29.33, at the height of the gale. On the next day, the 28th of October, the weather being still rough, we captured the bark *Lauretta*, of which the veracious Captain Wells was master, and of which the reader has already had some account. The *Lauretta* was skirting St. George's Bank, on her way to Madeira and the Mediterranean, and literally ran into our arms. We had no other trouble than to heave her to, with a gun, as she approached, and send a boat on board, and take possession of her; transferring her crew to the *Alabama*, with as much dispatch as possible, and "robbing" Captain Wells, as he states—by which he means, probably, that we deprived him of his chronometer and nautical instruments; for the mere personal effects of a prisoner, as the reader has already been informed, were never disturbed. We burned the ship.

On the next day, the weather being thick and rainy, and the *Alabama* being about two hundred miles from New York, we chased and captured the brig *Baron de Castine*, from Bangor, in Maine, and bound, with a load of lumber, to Cardenas, in the island of Cuba. This vessel being old, and of little value, I released her on ransom-bond, and sent her into New York, with my prisoners, of whom I had now a large number

on board. I charged the master of this ship, to give my special
thanks to Mr. Low, of the New York Chamber of Commerce,
for the complimentary resolutions he had had passed, in regard
to the *Alabama*. The more the enemy abused me, the more I
felt complimented, for it is "the galled jade only that winces."
There must have been a merry mess in the cabin of the *Baron*
that night, as there were the masters and mates of three burned
ships. New York was "all agog" when the *Baron* arrived,
and there was other racing and chasing after the "pirate," as
I afterward learned.

The engineer having now reported to me, that we had no
more than about four days of fuel on board, I resolved to
withdraw from the American coast, run down into the West
Indies, to meet my coal ship, and renew my supply. Being
uncertain, in the commencement of my career, as to the reception I should meet with, in neutral ports, and fearing that I
might have difficulty in procuring coal in the market, I had
arranged, with my ever-attentive co-laborer, Captain Bullock,
when we parted off Terceira, to have a supply-ship sent out to
me, from time to time, as I should indicate to him the rendezvous. The island of Martinique was to be the first rendezvous,
and it was thither accordingly that we were now bound. This
resolution was taken on the 30th of October, and shaping our
course, and making sail accordingly, we soon crossed the southern edge of the Gulf Stream, and were in a comparatively
desert track of the ocean. Our sinews were once more relaxed, and we had a few days of the *dolce far niente*. The
weather became fine, as we proceeded southward, and the
sailors, throwing aside their woollen garments, were arrayed
again in their duck frocks and trousers. Our mornings were
spent in putting the ship in order, preparatory to going into
port, and in exercising the crew at the battery, and the evenings were given up to amusement. Great inroads had been
made, by the continuous bad weather of the Gulf Stream, on
both duty and pleasure. Sometimes a week or ten days would
elapse, during which it would not be possible to cast loose a
heavy gun, for exercise; and evening after evening passed in
drenching rain and storm, when not so much as a note on the
violin was heard or even a song. The men were, however,

cheerful and obedient, were as much excited as ever by the chase and the capture, and were fast becoming a well-disciplined crew. If there was any of that discontent, spoken of by Captain Wells, it was not visible to the eyes of the officers. Our numbers had been considerably increased, by recruits from the enemy's ships, and we now had men enough to man all our guns, which added considerably to our sense of security. The young officers had gained much experience in the handling of their ship, and I began in consequence to sleep more soundly in my cot, at night, when the weather was dark and stormy.

On the 2d of November, when we were scarcely expecting it, we captured another of the enemy's ships. She was descried from the mast-head, about half-past eight in the morning, and we immediately gave chase. It was Sunday, and the muster-hour coming on, we mustered the crew, and read the Articles of War in the midst of the chase. We came up with the stranger about noon, with the United States colors at our peak, and upon firing a gun, the fugitive hoisted the same colors, and hove to. She proved to be the *Levi Starbuck*, a whaler, out of New Bedford, and bound on a voyage of thirty months, to the Pacific Ocean. Here was another store-ship for us, with plenty of provisions, slops, and small stores. Getting on board from her such articles as we stood in need of, and removing the crew, we burned her about nightfall.

Her New Bedford papers were only four days old, with the latest news from the "seat of war." The two armies were watching each other on the Potomac, and additional gun-boats had been sent "in pursuit of the *Alabama*." In the meantime, the *Alabama* was approaching another track of commerce, across which she intended to run, on her way to Martinique —the track of the homeward-bound East India ships of the enemy.

Toward midnight of the 7th of November, we descried a schooner, standing to the southward, to which we gave chase. She had heels, as well as the *Alabama*, and when day dawned she was still some distance from us, though we had gained on her considerably. But fortune came to her rescue, for very soon, a large ship, looming up on the horizon like a frigate,

came in sight, steering to the north-west. She was under all
sail, with studding-sails, and sky-scrapers set, and Evans,
having been sent for, pronounced her "Yankee." The small
craft was probably Yankee, too, but we were like a maiden
choosing between lovers—we could not have both—and so
we took the biggest prize, as maidens often do in a similar
conjuncture. The large ship was standing in our direction,
and we had nothing to do, but await her approach. When
she came sufficiently near to distinguish our colors, we showed
her the stars and stripes, which she was apparently very glad
to see, for she began, of her own accord, to shorten sail, as she
neared us, evidently with the intention of speaking us, and
getting, it might be, a welcome newspaper from "home." The
stars and stripes were, by this time, flying from her own peak.
She was terribly astonished, as her master afterward confessed,
when the jaunty little gun-boat, which he had eyed with so
much pleasure, believing her to be as good a Yankee as himself, fired a gun, and hauling down "hate's polluted rag,"
hoisted, in its stead, the banner of the Southern Republic.

The stranger had not much more to do, in order to surrender
himself a prisoner. His studding-sails had already been hauled
down, and he now hauled up his courses, and backed his main-
yard. We were once more in gentle airs, and a smooth sea; and
in a few minutes, the boarding-officer was alongside of him.
She proved to be as we had expected, an East India trader.
She was the *T. B. Wales*, of Boston, from Calcutta, for Boston,
with a cargo consisting chiefly of jute, linseed, and saltpetre.
Of the latter, she had 1700 bags, sufficient to supply our pious
Boston brethren, who were fighting for nothing but "grand
moral ideas," with a considerable quantity of powder. But for
the *Wales* meeting with the *Alabama*, it would, probably, have
gone into some of the same Yankee mills, which, just before
the war broke out, had supplied the Confederate States under
the contracts which, as the reader has seen, I had made with
them. The jute, which she had on board, was intended as a
substitute for cotton, in some of the coarser fabrics; the Boston
people being somewhat pressed, at the period, for the Southern
staple.

The captain of the *Wales*, though a Northern man, had **very** few of the ear-marks of the Yankee skipper about him. He was devoid of the raw-bone angularity which characterizes most of them, and spoke very good English, through his mouth, instead of his nose. His pronunciation and grammar were both good—quite an unusual circumstance among his class. He had been five months on his voyage, and, of course, had not heard of any such craft as the *Alabama.* He had quite a domestic establishment on board his ship, as, besides his own wife, who had accompanied him on the voyage, there was an ex-United States Consul, with his wife and three small daughters, returning with him, as passengers, to the New England States.

There was no attempt to cover the cargo of the *Wales,* and I was glad to find, that it was consigned to, and probably owned by, the obnoxious house of the Barings, in Boston, whose ship, the *Neapolitan,* I had burned, in the Strait of Gibraltar. This British house had rendered itself exceedingly active, during the war, in the Federal interest, importing large quantities of arms, and otherwise aiding the enemy; and I took especial pleasure, therefore, in applying the torch to its property. It was one of the New York "Commercial Advertiser's" pets—being a *neutral house, domiciled in an enemy's country, for the purposes of trade.* I have not heard what Admiral Milne and the British Minister at Washington did, when they heard of the burning of the *Wales,* or whether the "Advertiser" invoked, anew, the protection of the British lion. A few hours sufficed to transfer the crew and passengers of the East-Indiaman to the *Alabama,* and to get on board from her, some spars of which we were in want. It was found, upon measurement, that her main-yard was almost of the precise dimensions of that of the *Alabama,* and as ours had been carried away in the cyclone of the 16th of October, and had only been fished for temporary use, we got down the yard from the *Wales,* and brought it on board.

We treated the ladies—our first prisoners of the sex—with all due consideration, of course; but I was forced to restrict them in the matter of baggage and furniture, for the want of room. I permitted them to bring on board their entire wardrobes, of course, without permitting it to be examined, but was forced to consign to the flames some fancy chairs and other articles of East India workmanship, which they seemed to prize very highly. I dare say they thought hard of it, at the time, though, I doubt not, they have long since forgiven me. Both ladies were gentle. The Consul's wife was an Englishwoman, the daughter of a general in the British army, serving in the *Mauritius*, where her husband had met and married her. She was refined and educated, of course, and her three little daughters were very beautiful children. Mr. George H. Fairchild — for such was her husband's name — though a New-Englander, was, apparently, an unbigoted gentleman, and observed all the gentlemanly proprieties, during his stay on board my ship.

When I was arrested, after the war, by the Administration of President Johnson, in violation of the contract which the Government had made with me, at my surrender, and threatened with a trial, by one of those Military Commissions which have disgraced American civilization, on the trumpea-up charge, among others, of cruelty to prisoners, Mr. Fairchild was kind enough to write to me, in prison, and tender himself as a witness in my behalf. In the then state of New England feeling, with all the passions, and especially those of malignity, and hate, running riot through the land, it required moral courage to do this; and I take this opportunity of thanking a New England man, for obeying the instincts of a Christian and a gentleman..

It took us some time to despoil the *Wales* of such of her spars and rigging as we wanted, and it was near nightfall when we applied the torch to her. We had scarcely turned away from the burning prize, when another sail was discovered, in the fading twilight, but the darkness soon shutting her out from view, it was useless to attempt to chase. The *Wales* was one of the most useful of my captures. She not only served as a sort of ship-yard, in enabling me to repair the damages I had suffered in the Gulf Stream, but I received eight recruits from her, all of whom were fine, able-bodied seamen. My crew now numbered 110 men — 120 being my full complement. I bestowed the ladies, with their husbands, upon the ward-room mess, consigning them to the care of my gallant friend, Kell.

Some of the lieutenants were turned out of their state-rooms, for their accommodation, but being carpet knights, as well as knights of the lance, they submitted to the discomfort with becoming grace.

My *ménage* began now to assume quite a domestic air. I had previously captured another interesting prisoner, who was still on board — not having been released on parole. This prisoner was a charming little canary-bird, which had been brought on board from a whaler, in its neat gilded cage. Bartelli had the wonderful art, too, of supplying me with flowers — brought from the shore when this was practicable, and when not practicable, raised in his own tiny pots. When I would turn over in my cot, in the morning, for another nap, in that dim consciousness which precedes awakening, I would listen, in dreamy mood, to the sweet notes of the canary, the pattering of the tiny feet of the children and their gleeful voices over my head; inhaling, the while, the scent of the geranium, or the jessamine, and forget all about war's alarms. "Home, Sweet Home," with all its charms, would cluster around my imagination, and as my slumber deepened, putting reason to rest, and giving free wing to fancy, I would be clasping again the long-absent dear ones to my heart. Bartelli's shake of my cot, and his announcement that it was "seven bells"—half-past seven, which was my hour for rising — would often be a rude dispeller of such fancies, whilst the Fairchilds were on board.

CHAPTER XXXVII.

WE captured the *Wales*, as described in the last chapter,
on the 8th of November. On the 10th of the same
month, we observed in latitude 25°. We were approaching the
calm-belt of Cancer. There are three of these calm-belts on
the surface of the earth, and the phenomena which they present
to the eye of the seaman are very beautiful. A ship coming
out of New York, for instance, and bound south, will first
encounter the calm-belt which the *Alabama* is now approaching — that of Cancer. She will lose the wind which has brought
her to the "belt," and meet with light airs, and calms, accompanied, frequently, by showers of rain. She will probably be
several days in passing through this region of the "doldrums,"
as the sailors expressively call it, continually bracing her yards,
to catch the "cats-paws" that come, now from one, and now
from another point of the compass; and making no more than
twenty, or thirty miles per day. As she draws near the southern edge of the belt, she will receive the first light breathings
of the north-east trade-wind. These will increase, as she proceeds farther and farther south, and she will, ere long, find
herself with bellying canvas, in a settled "trade." She will
now run with this wind, blowing with wonderful steadiness and
regularity, until she begins to near the equator. The wind
will now die away again, and the ship will enter the second of
these belts — that of equatorial calms. Wending her way
slowly and toilsomely through these, as she did through those

of Cancer, she will emerge next into the south-east trade-wind, which she will probably find somewhat stronger than the north-east trade.   This wind will hurry her forward to the tropic of Capricorn, in the vicinity of which she will find her third and last calm-belt.

These three calm-belts enclose, the reader will have observed, two systems of trade-winds.   To understand something of these winds, and the calms which enclose them, a brief reference to the atmospheric machine in which we "live, and breathe, and have our being" will be necessary.   A philosopher of the East has thus glowingly described some of the beauties of this machine: "It is," says he, "a spherical shell, which surrounds our planet, to a depth which is unknown to us, by reason of its growing tenuity, as it is released from the pressure of its own superincumbent mass.   Its surface cannot be nearer to us than fifty, and can scarcely be more remote than five hundred miles.   It surrounds us on all sides, yet we see it not; it presses on us with a load of fifteen pounds on every square inch of surface of our bodies, or from seventy to one hundred tons on us, in all, and yet we do not so much as feel its weight.   Softer than the softest down — more impalpable than the finest gossamer — it leaves the cobweb undisturbed, and scarcely stirs the lightest flower that feeds on the dew it supplies; yet it bears the fleets of nations on its wings around the world, and crushes the most refractory substances with its weight.   When in motion, its force is sufficient to level the most stately forests, and stable buildings with the earth — to raise the waters of the ocean into ridges like mountains, and dash the strongest ship to pieces like toys.

"It warms and cools, by turns, the earth, and the living creatures that inhabit it.   It draws up vapors from the sea and land, retains them dissolved in itself, or suspended in cisterns of clouds, and throws them down again, as rain or dew when they are required.   It bends the rays of the sun from their path, to give us the twilight of evening, and of dawn; it disperses, and refracts their various tints, to beautify the approach and the retreat of the orb of day.   But for the atmosphere, sunshine would burst on us, and fail us at once, and at once remove us from midnight darkness to the blaze of noon.   We should have no twilight to soften, and beautify the landscape; no clouds to shade us from the scorching heat, but the bald earth, as it revolved on its axis, would turn its tanned and weakened front to the full and unmitigated rays of the lord of day.

"It affords the gas which vivifies, and warms our frames, and receives into itself that which has been polluted by use, and thrown off as noxious. It feeds the flame of life, exactly as it does that of the fire. It is in both cases consumed, and affords the food of consumption,— in both cases it becomes combined with charcoal, which requires it for combustion, and is removed by it, when this is over."

The first law of nature may be said to be *vis inertiæ*, and the atmosphere thus beautifully described, following this law, would be motionless, if there were not causes, outside of itself, to put it in motion. The atmosphere in motion is *wind*, with which the sailor has so much to do, and it behooves him to understand, not only the causes which produce it, but the laws which control it. " Whence cometh the wind, and whither goeth it?" It comes from heat, and as the sun is the father of heat, he is the father of the winds. Let us suppose the earth, and atmosphere both to be created, but not yet the sun. The atmosphere, being of equal temperature throughout the earth, would be in equilibrium. It could not move in any direction, and there would not be the slightest breeze to fan the brow. Now let us suppose the sun to be called into existence, and to begin to dart forth his rays. If he heated the earth, and the atmosphere in all parts alike, whilst there would be a swelling of the atmosphere into greater bulk, there would still be no motion which we could call wind. But the earth being placed in an elliptical orbit, and made to revolve around the sun, with its axis inclined to the plane in which it revolves, now approaching, and now receding from the sun, and now having the sun in one hemisphere, and now in another, the atmosphere is not only heated differently, in different parts of the earth, but at different seasons of the year; and thus the winds are engendered.

Let us imagine this heating process to be going on for the first time. How we should be astonished? The atmosphere having hitherto had no motion, in our experience, we should have conceived it as immovable as the hills, and would be quite as much astonished to see it putting itself in motion, as to see the hills running away from us. But in what direction is the atmosphere now moving? Evidently from the north, and south poles toward the equator, because we know that the intertropical portions of the earth are more heated, than the extratropical portions.

Thus far, we have not given the earth any diurnal motion around its axis. Let us give it this motion. It is revolving now from west to east, at the rate of fifteen miles in a minute. If the atmosphere had been perfectly still when this motion was given to the earth, as we have supposed it to have been before the creation of the sun, the consequence would be a breeze directly from the east, blowing with different degrees of strength, as it was nearer to, or further from the equator. For it is obviously the same thing whether the atmosphere stands still, and the earth revolves, or whether the earth stands still, and the atmosphere moves. In either case we have a wind.

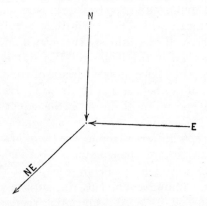

But the atmosphere was not still, when we gave the diurnal motion to the earth. There was already a breeze blowing, as we have seen, from the north, and south poles toward the equator. We have thus generated two winds — a north wind and an east wind. But these two winds cannot blow in the same place at the same time; and the result will be a wind compounded of the two. Thus in the northern hemisphere we shall have a north-east wind, and in the southern hemi-sphere we shall have a south east-wind.

These are the two trade-winds, enclosed by the three calm-belts which have been described to the reader. The three arrows on the preceding page will illustrate the manner in which the north-east trade-wind is formed by the north wind and the east wind, which our theory puts in motion.

Why it is that the trade-winds do not extend all the way from the poles to the equator, but take their rise in about the thirtieth parallel of latitude, north and south, we do not know. The theory would seem to demand that they should spring up at the poles, and blow continuously to the equator; in which case we should have but two systems of winds covering the entire surface of the earth. This non-conformity of the winds of the extra-tropical regions to our theory, does not destroy it, however, but brings into the meteorological problem other and beautiful features. Having put the winds in motion, our next business is to follow them, and see what "circuits" they travel. The quantity of atmosphere carried to the equator by the north-east and south-east trade-winds, must find its way back whence it came, in some mode or other; otherwise, we should soon have all the atmosphere drawn away from the poles, and piled up at the equator. We can easily conceive this, if we liken the atmosphere to fleeces of wool, and suppose an invisible hand to be constantly drawing away the fleeces from the poles, and piling them up at the equator. But how to get it back is the difficulty. It cannot go back on the sur-face of the earth, within the tropics, for there is a constant sur-face current here toward the equator. There is but one other way, of course, in which it can go back, and that is, as an upper current, running counter to the surface current. We may assume, indeed, we *must* assume, that there are two upper currents of air, setting out from the equator, and travelling, one of them to the 30th degree of north latitude, and the other to the 30th degree of south latitude.

What becomes of these two upper currents, when they reach these parallels of latitude, is not quite so certain; but there is good reason for believing that they now descend, become surface currents, and continue their journey on to the

poles.   It is further supposed that, when they reach the poles,
they "whirl about" them, ascend, become upper currents
again, and start back to the 30th parallel; and that, when they
have returned to this parallel, they descend, become a surface
current again—in other words, the trade-wind—and proceed
to the equator as before.

But there is another, and more beautiful problem still, connected with these winds.   It is their crossing each other at
the equator, of which the proofs are so abundant, that there
can be but little doubt concerning it.   And yet the proposition,

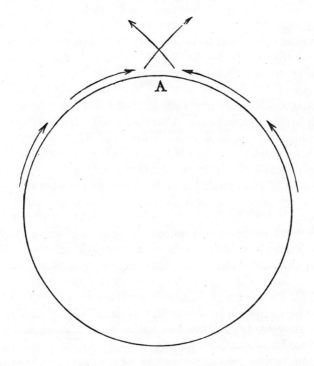

looked at apart from the proofs, is a very startling one.   One
would think that when the two winds met at the equator,
there would be a general intermingling, and confounding of
particles, and that when they ascended to form the upper currents, of which I have spoken, the northern particle would be

as likely to turn back to the north, as to cross the equator and go south. The preceding figure will illustrate the crossing. Let A represent the equator, the arrows near the surface of the circle the two trade-winds, and the two cross arrows, two particles of wind in the act of crossing. The difficulty is to conceive how these particles should cross, without mixing with each other, and losing their identity; or why they should not turn back, as well as continue their course. What law of nature is it, that makes the particles of atmosphere which have come from the north pole, so separate and distinct from those which have come from the south pole, as to prevent the two from fusing, and becoming one? Is it because the two particles, as they have gyrated around their respective poles, have received a repulsive polarity? Whatever may be the reason, there can be no doubt, as remarked, that they do actually cross. One strong proof of their crossing is, that we cannot conceive, otherwise, how the great atmospheric machine could perform its office of distributing rain over the earth in due proportions. The reader will recollect that there is from a fourth, to a third, more land than water, in the northern hemisphere, and that there is from a fourth to a third more water than land in the southern hemisphere. The consequence of this unequal distribution of land and water in the two hemispheres is, that the northern hemisphere requires more rain than the southern, in the proportion in which it has more land to be rained upon. Now it is these mysterious trade-winds, of which we have been speaking, that are the water-carriers of the two hemispheres. These winds, on their way to the equator, generally reach the 30th parallel as dry winds. These dry winds, sweeping over the tropical seas, take up, in the shape of vapor, the water with which, in due time, they are to fertilize the fields of the farmer, and make the rose blossom. The quantity which they take up is in proportion to the sea-surface, or evaporating surface, they have respectively passed over. Now, if we will examine the jars of these water-carriers, when they reach the equator, we shall find that the northern jars are not nearly so full as the southern jars; the reason being, that the northern winds have passed over less evaporating surface.

Now, if the two systems of winds, with their jars thus filled, were to turn back to their respective hemispheres, and pour down upon them their water, in the shape of rain, the consequence would be, as the reader sees, that we should have less rain in the northern hemisphere, than they would have in the southern hemisphere; whereas, we require more, having more land to be watered. The atmospheric machine would thus be at fault. But the all-wise and beneficent ruler of the universe, makes nothing faulty. We know from the evidence of that silent witness, the rain-gauge, that more water falls in the northern hemisphere, than in the southern; in other words, that the more heavily laden of those jars which we examined, a moment ago, at the equator, have come to us, instead of returning to the south; the less heavily laden jars going south. The crossing of the winds thus satisfies our theory, and nothing else can; which is, of course, the most conclusive of all proofs.

But we have other proofs. For a number of years past, as the East India ships would be returning home from their voyages, they would report a curious phenomenon to have befallen them, as they passed the parallel of the Cape de Verde. This was the falling, or rather silting down upon their decks and rigging, of a brick-dust or cinnamon-colored powder. This dust, which when rubbed between the thumb and forefinger would be impalpable, would sometimes nearly cover the entire deck and rigging. The ships would be hundreds of miles away from the land, and where could this dust come from? The fact puzzled the philosophers, but having been reported so often, it ceased to attract attention. Still it was a fact, and was laid away carefully in the archives of philosophy for future use. Years passed away, and the great traveller and philosopher, Humboldt, arose to instruct and delight mankind. He travelled extensively in South America; and, among other places, visited the lower valley of the Orinoco. He happened there in the dry season, and gives a graphic account of the wild and weird spectacle of desolation which met his eye in that season of universal drought.

All annual vegetation lay dead and desiccated on the immense pampas or plains. The earth was cracked open, gaping, as it were, for rain. The wild cattle were roaming about in herds, bellowing for their accustomed food and water; many of them perishing. Even the insect world, so numerous and vivacious in all southern climates, had perished. Their tiny little organisms lay in heaps, fast disintegrating, and being reduced to powder, by the scorching and baking rays of a perpendicular sun, between which and the parched earth, not so much as a speck of cloud appeared. The philosopher examined a number of these little organisms with his microscope. They were peculiar to the region in which he found them, and he was struck with the fact. There was another phenomenon which he observed. A number of little whirlwinds were playing their pranks about the arid waste, sporting, as it were, with dead nature. These little whirlwinds, as they travelled hither and thither, would draw up into their vortices, and toss high into the upper air, the impalpable dust that lay everywhere, and which was composed, in great measure, of the decomposed and decomposing organisms of which I have spoken. The atmosphere, at times, when filled with this dust, would assume a yellowish, or pale straw-colored hue.

The reader probably, by this time, sees my design of connecting the dusty remains, described by Humboldt, with the rain dust reported by the mariners to have fallen on the decks and rigging of their ships, in the neighborhood of the Cape de Verde islands. But the "rain-dust" was of brick-dust, or cinnamon color, when collected by the masters of the ships, as specimens and the heavens, when filled with the dust thrown up by the whirlwinds, as described by Humboldt, appeared to him to be of a straw color. Here is a discrepancy to be reconciled, and we must call in the aid of another philosopher, Captain M. F. Maury, late Superintendent of the National Observatory, at Washington, before alluded to in these pages, and to whom I am indebted for many of the facts here quoted. Captain Maury was struck with this discrepancy, and in reconciling it with the theory here discussed, makes the following statement: "In the search for spider lines, for the diaphragms of my telescopes, I procured the finest, and best threads from a cocoon of a mud-red color; but the threads of this cocoon, as seen singly in the diaphragm, were of a golden color; there would seem, therefore, no difficulty in reconciling the difference between the colors of the rain-dust, when viewed in little piles by the microscopist, and when seen attenuated and floating in the wind by the regular traveller."

There remains but another link in the chain of evidence, to render it complete. It remains to be shown how the whirl-wind dust, of the valley of the lower Orinoco, can be identified with the rain-dust of the Cape de Verde. Ehrenberg, a German philosopher, has done this, in our day. Some specimens of the rain-dust having been sent him by ship-captains, he brought them under his microscope, as Humboldt had done the whirlwind-dust, and to his great astonishment, and delight, he found it to be the same. These facts correspond entirely with our theory of the crossing of the trade-winds at the equator. The reader has been with us near the mouth of the Orinoco. This great river disembogues near the island of Trinidad, which we visited in the *Sumter*, in about the latitude of 9° N. The vernal equinox is the dry season here, and at this season, the north-east trade-wind is quite fresh. Running counter to this wind, in the upper atmosphere, there is, according to our theory, a strong south-west wind blowing. Now, if the reader will inspect a map, he will find that a south-west wind, starting from the mouth of the Orinoco, will blow over the Cape de Verde islands. The rest is plain. The whirl-wind-dust is tossed high enough into the upper atmosphere, to be taken in charge by the counter south-west wind, is carried to the Cape de Verde, and there silted down upon the decks and rigging of the passing ships, as gently as so many snow-flakes, becoming the rain-dust which so long puzzled the philosophers!

We have reasoned, hitherto, on the supposition, that the three calm-belts, one of which the *Alabama* is now passing, and the two systems of trade-winds which they enclose, are stationary within certain limits. But this is not so; the whole system of belts and winds is moved north and south, as the sun passes now into one hemisphere, and now into another. The calm-belt of Cancer is not always in the latitude of 30° N.; nor is the calm-belt of the equator always at the equator. The reader will recollect that we observed, on board the *Ala-*

bama, on the 10th of November, in latitude 25° N., and that we were only just then entering the calm-belt of Cancer. The reason is, that the sun, on that day, was in the southern hemisphere, well advanced toward his extreme limit in that hemisphere, and that he had dragged, as it were, the whole system of belts and winds after him. The figures below will make this idea plain. Let the broad, dark lines in the circles represent the system of belts and winds, all in one; and in circle A let the sun be in the northern hemisphere, and in circle B let him be in the southern.

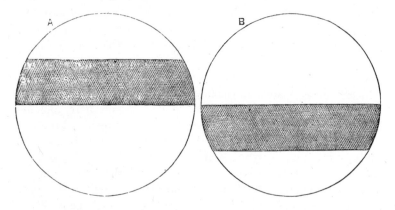

The reader will see, how the sun, having hitched this system of belts and winds to his chariot wheels, as it were, has drawn it after him. The distances north and south, to which they have been drawn, are exaggerated in the figures, but this is only for the purpose of better illustration. The reader will see, from this diagram, how much farther South the *Alabama* will have to run, in November, to catch the north-east trade-wind, than she would have had to run in May. We may now return to our ship, and our cruise, and when I shall mention the trade-winds and the calm-belts, hereafter, the reader will not, I hope, regret the time I have consumed in refreshing his memory on so interesting a subject. We spoke several English vessels after burning the *Wales,* and a couple of them, bound to Demerara, kept company with us through the calm-belt. We sent a boat on board one of them, from New York, but she had neither news nor newspapers. At length, when we had reached the parallel of about 20°, we began to receive the first gentle breathings of the trade-wind. Our light sails aloft began first to "belly out," and then a topsail would fill for a moment, until the ship rising on the gentle undulations of the sea, and falling again, would flap the wind out of it. The zephyr—for, as yet, it was nothing more—visibly gained strength, however, from hour to hour, and on the 16th of November, I find the following record in my journal: "Beautiful, clear weather, with a moderate trade-wind, from about east by south, and the well-known fleecy trade-clouds sailing leisurely over our heads."

It is Sunday, and muster-day, and the *Alabama* has once more been put in perfect order. She has had a coat of paint, inside and out, her masts have been freshly scraped, and her rigging re-rattled, and tarred down. Her guns are glistening in the new coat of "composition" which the gunner and his mates have put upon them; her engine-room is all aglow with burnished brass and steel; her decks are white and sweet, and her awnings are spread. The muster is over, the men are lying listlessly about the decks, and our lady passengers are comfortably seated on the quarter-deck, with several of the young officers around them, and with the children playing at their feet. Such was the contrast which the *Alabama* presented, on that quiet Sabbath day, with her former self only a few weeks back, when we had been rolling and tumbling in the Gulf Stream, with crippled yards, torn sails, and her now bright sides seamed and defaced with iron-rust from her corroding chains.

We were soon ready to go into port—our first port since leaving Terceira. Men and officers were all desirous of a little relaxation, and were pretty soon on the look-out for land. On the next day, at two P. M., we made the island of Dominica—the same Dominica that lay so fast asleep in the gentle moonlight, on the night that the little *Sumter* ran so close along it, like a startled deer, after her escape from the *Iroquois*. We were returning to our old cruising-ground, after an interval of just one year, in a finer and faster ship, and we cared very little now about the *Iroquois*, and vessels of her class. Having doubled the north-east end of Dominica, during the night, at four o'clock, the next morning, we lowered the propeller, put the ship under steam, and ran down for the island of Martinique. We passed close enough to the harbor of St. Pierre, where we had been so long blockaded, to look into it, and see that there were no men-of-war of the enemy anchored there, and, continuing our course, ran into the anchorage of Fort de France, and dropped our anchor at about ten A. M.

Rear-Admiral Condé was still Governor, and I sent a lieutenant, immediately, to call on him, and report our arrival. He received me kindly, notwithstanding the little sharp-shooting that had passed between us, in the way of official correspondence — and franked the ports of the island to me as before. I had long since forgiven him, for the want of independence and energy he had displayed, in not preventing the Yankee skipper from making signals to the *Iroquois* on the night of my escape, as the said signals, as the reader has seen, had redounded to my benefit, instead of Palmer's. In an hour or two, we had landed our prisoners; the ladies and their husbands taking a very civil leave of us. In the course of the afternoon, our decks were crowded with curious Frenchmen, come off to look at the "pirate" ship, of which they had heard so much, through Mr. Seward's interesting volumes of "English Composition," called "State Papers," and the villification and abuse of the Northern press. They were evidently a little puzzled at finding in the *Alabama* a rather stylish-looking ship of war, with polite young officers to receive them, at the gangway, and show them round the ship, instead of the disorderly privateer, or pirate, they had expected to find. I could see some of these gentlemen eying me with curiosity, and with evident disappointment depicted in their countenances, as my young officers would point me out to them. They had come on board to see a Captain Kidd, or Blue Beard, at the least, and had found only a common mortal, in no wise distinguished from the officers by whom he was surrounded, except, perhaps, that his gray coat was a little more faded, and his moustache a little more the color of his coat.

The ship was surrounded with bum-boats, laden with fruits, and other supplies for the sailors, and a brisk traffic was going on, alongside, and in the port gangway, in pipes, and tobacco,

orchata, and orange-water; and, as we found as night began to
set in, in something a little stronger. We had no marine guard
on board the *Alabama*, and there was, consequently, no sentinel
at the gangway in the daytime. We were necessarily obliged
to rely upon the master-at-arms, and the quartermasters, for
examining all boats that came alongside, to see that no liquor
was smuggled into the ship. These petty officers were old
sailors like the rest, and I have rarely seen a sailor who could
be relied upon, for any purpose of police, where his brother
sailor was concerned.

Whilst I was below, a little after sunset, taking a cup of tea,
and enjoying some of the delicious fruit which Bartelli had
provided for me, I heard some confusion of voices, and a tramp-
ing of feet on the deck over my head, and soon afterward, the
first lieutenant came into my cabin to tell me, that there was
considerable disorder in the ship. I repaired on deck immediately, and saw at a glance that the crew was almost in a state
of mutiny. It was evidently a drunken mutiny, however, and
not very alarming. An officer had gone forward to quell some
disturbance on the forecastle, when one of the sailors had thrown
a belaying-pin at him, and others had abused him, and threatened him with personal violence. Some of the men, when directed to assist in seizing and confining their more disorderly
comrades, had refused; and as I reached the deck, there was a
surly, and sulky crowd of half-drunken sailors gathered near
the foremast, using mutinous language, and defying the authorities of the ship. I immediately ordered the first lieutenant to
"beat to quarters." The drum and fife were gotten up, and such
was the effect of previous discipline upon the crew, that the
moment they heard the well-known beat, and the shrill tones
of the fife, they "fell in," mechanically, at their guns—some
of them so drunk, that their efforts to appear sober were quite
ludicrous.

This was what I had reckoned upon. At quarters, the officers
always appeared armed, as if they were going into battle.
There were very few arms about the deck, upon which the
sailors could lay their hands—the cutlasses and pistols being
kept locked up, in the arms-chests. Of course, I now had it
all my own way—thirty armed officers being more than a

match for 110 men armed with nothing but sheath-knifes and belaying-pins. I began now to quell the mutiny; or rather it was already quelled, and I began to bring Jack back to his senses. In company with my first lieutenant and aide-de-camp, I passed along the platoons of men as they stood at their guns, and stopping wherever I observed a drunken man, I ordered his comrades to arrest him. This was immediately done, without demur in any instance, and the culprit was ironed. In this way I got as many as twenty disorderly fellows. These drunken men, the moment the attempt was made to arrest them, began to show fight, and to be abusive in their language. They were, however, soon overpowered, and rendered harmless. In this way I passed forward and aft, two or three times, eying the men as I passed, to be certain that I had gotten hold of all the rioters.

When I had done this, I directed the mutineers to be taken to the gangway, and calling two or three of the most active of the quartermasters, I made them provide themselves with draw-buckets, and commencing with the most noisy and drunken of the culprits, I ordered them to dash buckets of water over them in quick succession. The punishment was so evidently novel to the recipients, that they were at first disposed to deride it. With drunken gravity they would laugh and swear by turns, and tell the "bloody quartermasters" to "come on with their water, *they* were not afraid of it." But I was quite sure of my remedy, for I had tried it before; and as the drunken fellows would call for more water, in contempt and derision, I gratified them, and caused bucketsful to be dashed on them with such rapidity, that pretty soon they found it difficult to catch their breath, in the intervals between the showers. The more they would struggle and gasp for breath, the more rapidly the buckets would be emptied upon them.

The effect was almost electric. The maudlin fellows, somewhat sobered by the repeated shocks of the cold water, began now to swear less vociferously. In fact, they had no voice to swear with, for it was as much as they could do, to breathe. They no longer "bloodied" the quartermasters, or called for more water. Being reduced thus to silence, and still the water descending upon them as rapidly as ever, with half-sobered brain, and frames shivering with the cold, they would now become seriously alarmed. Did the captain mean to drown them? Was this the way he designed to punish them for mutiny, instead of hanging them at the yard-arm? They now turned to me, and begged me, for God's sake, to spare them. If I would only let them go this time, I should never have cause to complain of them again. I held off a little while, as if inexorable to their prayers and entreaties, the better to impress upon them the lesson I was teaching them, and then ordered them to be released. When their irons were taken off, they were sober enough to go below to their hammocks, without another word, and "turn in" like good boys! It took me some time to get through with this operation, for I had the delinquents—about a dozen of the most noisy—soused one at a time. The officers and crew were all this while—some two hours—standing at their guns, at quarters, and I could, now and then, overhear quite an audible titter from some of the sober men, as the drunken ones who were undergoing the shower-bath would now defy my authority, and now beg for mercy. When, at last, I had finished, I turned to my first lieutenant, and told him to "beat the retreat."

And this was the way, reader, in which I quelled my first, and only mutiny on board the *Alabama*. It became a saying afterward, among the sailors, that "Old Beeswax was h—ll upon watering a fellow's grog."

CHAPTER XXXVIII.

THE ALABAMA AT MARTINIQUE—IS BLOCKADED BY THE
ENEMY'S STEAMER, SAN JACINTO—HOW SHE ESCAPED
THE "OLD WAGON"—THE ISLAND OF BLANQUILLA,
THE NEW RENDEZVOUS—COALING SHIP—A YANKEE
SKIPPER—HOW THE OFFICERS AND MEN AMUSED
THEMSELVES—THE CAPTURE OF THE PARKER COOKE,
UNION, AND STEAMER ARIEL.

I FOUND here at her anchors, as I had expected, my coal-
ship, the *Agrippina*. She had been lying here eight days.
Her master, an old Scotchman, who, like most old sailors, was
fond of his grog, had been quite indiscreet, as I soon learned,
in talking about his ship, and her movements. Instead of pretending to have come in for water or repairs, or to hunt a
market, or for something of the kind, he had frequently, when
"half seas-over," in the coffee-houses on shore, boasted of his
connection with the *Alabama*, and told his brother tars that
that ship might be daily looked for. Eight days were a sufficient space of time for these conversations to be repeated, in
the neighboring islands; and as I knew that the enemy had
several cruisers in the West Indies, I was only surprised that
some one of them had not looked in upon the *Agrippina*
before. It would not do for me to think of coaling in Martinique under the circumstances, and so I ordered my coal-
ship to get under way forthwith, and proceed to a new rendezvous—a small island on the Spanish Main, where, in due
time, we will rejoin her. I had the satisfaction of seeing her
get a good offing before nightfall, and knew that she was safe.

It was well that I took this precaution, for on the very next
morning, before I had turned out, an officer came below to inform me that an enemy's ship-of-war had appeared off the har-

bor! Dressing myself, and going on deck, sure enough, there was one of the enemy's large steamships, lying close within the mouth of the harbor, with one of the brightest and largest of "old flags" flying from her peak. She did not anchor, lest she should come under the twenty-four hours' rule; but pretty soon lowered a boat, and communicated with the authorities on shore. It soon transpired that she was the famous *San Jacinto*, a name which has become inseparably connected in the American memory, with one of the greatest humiliations ever put upon the Great Republic. Wilkes, and Seward, and the *San Jacinto* have achieved fame. They began by attempting to make a little war-capital out of John Bull, and ended by singing, as we have seen, the "seven penitential psalms;" or, at least, as many of these psalms as could be sung in "*seven days*," *short metre being used*. I could not help thinking, as I looked at the old ship, of Mr. Seward's elaborate despatch to Lord Russell, set to the tune of "Old Hundred," and of the screams of Miss Slidell, as she had been gallantly charged by the American marines, commanded, for the occasion, by an officer bearing the proud old name of Fairfax, and born in the State of Virginia!

We paid no sort of attention to the arrival of this old wagon of a ship. She was too heavy for me to think of engaging, as she threw more than two pounds of metal to my one — her battery consisting of fourteen eleven-inch guns — and her crew was more than twice as numerous as my own; but we had the speed of her, and could, of course, go to sea whenever we pleased. I was glad, however, that I had gotten the *Agrippina* safely out of her way, as she might otherwise have been indefinitely blockaded. We remained quietly at our anchors during the day; such of the officers visiting the shore as desired, and the stewards of the messes being all busy in laying in a supply of fruits and other refreshments. We were, in the meantime, quite amused at the warlike preparations that were going on on board the *San Jacinto*. The captain of that ship, whose name, I believe, was Ronckendorff, made the most elaborate preparations for battle. We could see his men aloft, busily engaged in slinging yards, stoppering topsail sheets, getting up preventer braces, and making such other preparations, as the *Victory* or *Royal Sovereign* might have made on the eve of Trafalgar.

Poor Ronckendorff, what a disappointment awaited him! the *Alabama* was going to sea that very night. There was a Yankee merchant-ship in the harbor, and just at nightfall, a boat pulled out from her to the *San Jacinto*, to post her, probably, as to the channels and outlets, and to put her in possession of the rumors afloat. The fates were much more propitious as to weather, than they had been to the little *Sumter*, when she eluded the *Iroquois*. The night set in dark and rainy. We ran up our boats, lighted our fires, and when the steam was ready, got under way, as we would have done on any ordinary occasion, except only that there were no lights permitted to be seen about the ship, and that the guns were loaded and cast loose, and the crew at quarters. In the afternoon, a French naval officer had come on board, kindly bringing me a chart of the harbor, from which it appeared that I could run out in almost any direction I might choose. I chose the most southern route, and giving my ship a full head of steam, we passed out, without so much as getting a glimpse of the *San Jacinto!* The next news that we received from the "States," informed us that the *San Jacinto* was perfectly innocent of our escape until the next morning revealed to her our vacant place in the harbor. Her commander was even then incredulous, and remained cruising off the harbor for a day or two longer, until he could satisfy himself that I had not hauled my ship up into some cunning nook, or inlet, and hid her away out of sight!

The next afternoon I had joined my coal-ship, and we ran in to our anchorage, together, in the little, barren island of Blanquilla, off the coast of Venezuela, where we came to about nightfall. This was one of those little coral islands that skirt the South American coast, not yet fully adapted to the habitation of man. It was occasionally visited by a passing fisherman, or turtler, and a few goat-herds, from the main-land, had come over to pasture some goats on the coarse grass. As we ran in to this anchorage, which I remembered well from having visited it once in a ship of war of the old service, I was surprised to see a Yankee whaling schooner at anchor. She was lying very close in with the beach, on which she had a tent pitched, and some boilers in operation, trying out the oil from a whale which she had recently struck. The master of this little vessel, seeing us running down the island, under the United States colors, came off, in one of his boats, to pilot us in, and was apparently quite pleased to find himself on board one of his own gun-boats. He told us all he had heard about the *Alabama*, and went into ecstasies over our fine battery, and the marvellous accounts of our speed, which some of the young men gave him, and declared that we were the very ship to "give the pirate Semmes fits."

A terrible collapse awaited him. When I had let go my anchor, I sent for him, and told him who we were. That we were no less than the terrible *Alabama* herself. He stood aghast for a moment. An awful vision seemed to confront him. His little schooner, and his oil, and the various little 'ventures which he had on board, with which to trade with the natives along the coast, and turn that "honest penny," which has so many charms in the eyes of his countrymen, were all gone up the spout! And then he stood in the presence of the man whose ship he had characterized as a "pirate," and whom he had told to his face, he was no better than a freebooter. But I played the magnanimous. I told the skipper not to be alarmed; that he was perfectly safe on board the *Alabama*, and that out of respect for Venezuela, within whose maritime jurisdiction we were, I should not even burn his ship. I should detain him, however, as a prisoner, for a few days, I added, to prevent his carrying news of me to the enemy, until I was ready myself to depart. He gladly assented to these terms, and was frequently afterward on board the ship during our stay.

We lay five days at the little island of Blanquilla, coaling ship, and getting ready for another cruise. We broke out our hold for the first time, and cleansed and whitewashed it. We hoisted out our boats, and rigged them for sailing; and in the afternoons, after the excessive heats had moderated a little, sailing and fishing parties were formed, and the officers had some very pleasant little picnics on shore. Fish were abundant, and on occasion of these picnics, a fine red-fish, weighing twenty pounds and more, would sometimes be found cut up, and in the frying-pan, almost before it had ceased floundering. The crew were sent on shore, "on liberty," in quarter watches, taking their rifles and ammunition, and fish-spears, and fishing-lines along with them. The water was as clear as crystal, and there being some beautiful bathing-places along the beach, bathing became a favorite amusement. Although this coast abounds in sharks of large size, they are not found to be dangerous, when there is a number of bathers enjoying the sport together. The shark is a great coward, and rarely attacks a man, unless it can surprise him.

My gig was a fine boat, fitted with a lug sail, and I used frequently to stretch off long distances from the land in her, enjoying her fine sailing qualities, in the fresh sea-breeze that would be blowing, the greater part of the day. At other times I would coast the island along for miles, now putting into one little cove, and now into another, sometimes fishing, and at others hunting sea-shells, and exploring the wonders of the coral banks. Pelican, gulls, plover, and sand-snipe were abundant, and my boat's crew, when we would land, and haul our boat up for a stroll, would sometimes make capital shots. Indeed, we generally returned on board laden with fish, game, and marine curiosities, of various kinds,—prominent among which would be specimens of the little coral insect, and its curious manufactures. Miniature limestone-trees, with their pointed branches, shrubs, fans, and a hundred other imitations of the flora of the upper world would be fished up from beneath the sparkling waters, live their day of wonder, and when they had faded and lost their beauty, be thrown overboard again.

We found here flocks of the flamingo—a large bird of the crane species, with long legs and bill, for wading and feeding in the shallow lagoons which surround the island. Its plumage is of the most delicate pink, inclining to scarlet, and when the tall birds are drawn up in line, upon a sand beach, where there is some mirage, or refraction, they look not unlike a regiment of red-coated soldiers. They are quite shy, but we carried some of them on board, out of the rich plumage of which Bartelli made me some fans. Officers and men, both of whom had been long confined on board ship—it being now three months since the *Alabama* was commissioned—visibly improved in health whilst we lay at Blanquilla. The reader may recollect that we captured in the brig *Dunkirk*, a deserter from the *Sumter*. We had tried him by court-martial before reaching Martinique, and sentenced him to serve out his term, under certain penalties. At Martinique, we found him a chief spirit among the mutineers, whose grog I had "watered" as described in the last chapter. Another court now sat upon his case, and in obedience to its sentence, the fellow was turned upon the beach at Blanquilla, with "bag and hammock." This worthy citizen of the Great Republic joined the Yankee whaling schooner, and went into more congenial company and pursuits.

Having finished our coaling, and made the other preparations necessary for sea, I dispatched my coal-ship, which had still another supply of coal left, to another rendezvous — the Arcas islands, in the Gulf of Mexico, and gave the Yankee schooner leave to depart, telling the master to make a free sheet of it, and not let me catch him on the high seas, as it might not be so well for him a second time. He took me at my word, had all the sail on his little craft in the twinkling of an eye, and I question whether he stopped this side of Nantucket.

My object, in running into the Gulf of Mexico, was to strike a blow at Banks' expedition, which was then fitting out for the invasion of Texas. This gentleman, who had been a prominent Massachusetts politician, but who had no sort of military talent, had risen to the surface with other scum, amid the bubbling and boiling of the Yankee caldron, and was appointed by "Honest Abe" to subjugate Texas. Banks had mounted a stud-horse, on Boston Common, on militia-review days, before the war, and had had himself lithographed, stud-horse, cocked-hat, feathers, and all, and these were credentials not to be despised. I had learned from captured Northern papers, that he was fitting out at Boston and New York, a large expedition, to consist of not less than 30,000 men. A large proportion of this army was to consist of cavalry and light artillery. To transport such an army, a large number of transport-ships would be required. The expedition was to rendezvous at Galveston, which the enemy had captured from us, not a great while before.

As there were but twelve feet of water on the Galveston bar, very few of these transport-ships would be able to enter the harbor; the great mass of them, numbering, perhaps, a hundred and more, would be obliged to anchor, pell-mell, in the open sea. Much disorder, and confusion would necessarily attend the landing of so many troops, encumbered by horses, artillery, baggage-wagons, and stores. My design was to surprise this fleet by a night-attack, and if possible destroy it, or at least greatly cripple it. The Northern press, in accordance with its usual habit, of blabbing everything, had informed me of the probable time of the sailing of the expedition, and I designed so to time my own movements, as to arrive simultaneously with the stud-horse and the major-general, or at least a day or two afterward.

It was to be presumed, of course, that some of the enemy's gun-boats would accompany the expedition, but I hoped to be able to fall so unexpectedly upon their convoy, as to find them off their guard. There was no Confederate cruiser in the Gulf, and I learned from the enemy's own papers, that the *Alabama* was *well on her way to the coast of Brazil and the East Indies*. The surprise would probably be complete, in the dead of night, and when the said gun-boats of the enemy would be sleeping in comparative security, with but little, if any steam in their boilers. Half an hour would suffice for my purpose of setting fire to the fleet, and it would take the gun-boats half an hour to get up steam, and their anchors, and pursue me.

It was with this object in view, that we were now getting under way from the island of Blanquilla. But the Banks' expedition would not arrive off Galveston, probably, before about the 10th of January, and as we were now only in the latter days of November, I had several weeks on my hands, before it would become necessary for me to proceed to my new rendezvous. I resolved to devote this interval to the waylaying of a California treasure-steamer, as a million or so of dollars in gold, deposited in Europe, would materially aid me, in my operations upon the sea. I could purchase several more *Alabamas*, to develop the "nautical enterprise" of our people, and assist me to scourge the enemy's commerce.

There were two routes by which the California steamers

returned from Aspinwall — one by the east end of Cuba, and the other by the west end. I chose the former for my ambuscade, as being probably the most used. To reach my new cruising-ground, I put my ship under sail, and made a detour by the way of the islands of Porto Rico and St. Domingo, passing through the Mona Passage, through which much of the West India commerce of the enemy passed, with the hope of picking up something by the way. We left our anchorage at Blanquilla on the 26th of November, and made the island of Porto Rico on the morning of the 29th. We coasted along the south side of this island, with a gentle breeze and smooth sea, sufficiently near to enjoy its fine, bold scenery, passing only a couple of sail during the day — one a large French steamer, bound to the eastward, and the other an English bark. We showed them the United States colors. The bark saluted the " old flag," by striking her colors to it, but the " old flag " did not return the salute, as it was hoisted at the wrong peak. The Englishman must have thought his Yankee friend rather discourteous.

We entered the Mona Passage, lying between St. Domingo and Porto Rico, after nightfall, but the moon was shining sufficiently bright to enable us to get hold of the small islands of Mona and Desecho, and thus grope our way in safety. The currents in this strait being somewhat uncertain, the navigation is treacherous when the weather is dark. Early on the next morning, we were off the Bay of Samana, and were running with a flowing sheet along the coast of St. Domingo. I had approached the Mona Passage with much caution, fully expecting to find so important a thoroughfare guarded by the enemy, but there was nothing in the shape of a ship of war to be seen. The enemy was too busy blockading the Southern coasts to pay much attention to his commerce. In the course of the morning, we boarded a Spanish schooner, from Boston, bound for the old city of St. Domingo, from which we received a batch of late newspapers, giving us still further accounts, among other things, of the preparation of the Banks' expedition, about which all New England seemed, just then, to be agog.

The great Massachusetts leader had been given *carte blanche*, and he was making the best possible use of it. He was fitting himself out very splendidly, but his great expedition resembled rather one of Cyrus' or Xerxes', than one of Xenophon's. The Boston papers dilated upon the splendid bands of music, the superb tents, the school-marms, and the relays of stud-horses that were to accompany the hero of Boston Common. But the best feature of the expedition was the activity and thrift which had suddenly sprung up in all the markets of New England, in consequence. The looms, the spindles and the shoemakers' awls were in awful activity. In short, every man or boy who could whittle a stick, whittled it, and sold it to the Government. The whalemen in New Bedford, Nantucket, and Martha's Vineyard were in especial glee. They were selling all their whaling ships, which were too old, or too rotten for further service, to the Government, for transports, at enormous prices. Many a bluff old whaler that had rode out a gale under the lee of an iceberg at the Navigators' Islands, or "scraped her keel on Coromandel's coast," forty years before, was patched and caulked and covered over with pitch and paint, and sold to an ignorant, if not corrupt, army quartermaster, for as good as "bran new." No wonder that the war was popular in New England. There was not only negro in it, but there was money in it also.

Filling away from the Spanish schooner, which we requested to report us, in St. Domingo, as the United States steamer *Iroquois*, we continued our course down the island. It was Sunday, and the day was fine. The crew was dressed, as usual, for muster, and what with the ship in her gala-dress of awnings, and glitter of "bright-work," the island, the sea, and the weather, a more beautiful picture could not well have been presented to the beholder. In the distance were the blue, and hazy hills, so fraught with the memories of Columbus, and the earlier Spanish explorers. Nearer to, was the old town of Isabella, the first ever built in the New World by civilized men, and nearer still was the bluff, steep, rock-bound coast, against which the most indigo of seas was breaking in the purest and whitest of foam. The sailors had thrown themselves upon the deck in groups, each group having its reader, who was reading aloud to attentive listeners the latest war-news, as gleaned from the papers we had received from the

Spanish schooner; and the officers, through whose hands the said newspapers had already passed, were smoking and chatting, now of Columbus, and now of the war.   Presently the shrill cry of "sail ho!" came ringing from aloft; and the scene on board the *Alabama* shifted almost as magically as it does in a theatre.   Every man sprang to his feet, without waiting for an order; the newspapers were stuck away in cracks and crannies; the helm was shifted, to bring the ship's head around to the proper point for chasing, and studding-sails, and kites were given simultaneously to the wind.

When we began to raise the spars and sails of the chase above the sea, from the deck, there was a general exclamation of "Yankee!"   The tapering royal and sky-sail masts, with the snowiest of canvas, told the tale, as they had told it so often before.   A run of a few hours more brought us up with the American bark *Parker Cooke*, of, and from Boston, bound to Aux Cayes, on the south side of the island of St. Domingo. If the *Cooke* had been chartered, and sent out for our especial benefit, the capture could not have been more opportune.   The *Alabama's* commissariat was beginning to run a little low, and here was the *Cooke* provision-laden.   We had found, by experience in the *Sumter*, that our Boston friends put up the very best of crackers, and ship-bread, and sent excellent butter, and cheese, salted beef and pork, and dried fruits to the West India markets; nor were we disappointed on the present occasion.   Both ships were now hove to, under short sail, within convenient boating distance, and the rest of the day was consumed in transporting provisions from the prize.   It was sunset before we concluded our labors, and at the twilight hour, when the sea-breeze was dying away, and all nature was sinking to repose, we applied the torch to the *Cooke*.

As we filled away, and made sail, I could not but moralize on the spectacle.   Sixty years before, the negro had cut the throat of the white man, ravished his wife and daughters, and burned his dwelling in the island of St. Domingo, now in sight. The white man, in another country, was now inciting the negro to the perpetration of the same crimes against another white man, whom he had called brother.   The white man who was thus inciting the negro, was the Puritan of New England, whose burning ship was lighting up the shores of St. Domingo! That Puritan, only a generation before, had entered into a solemn league and covenant, to restore to the Southern man his fugitive slave, if he should escape into his territory. This was the way in which he was keeping his plighted faith! Does any one wonder that the *Alabama* burned New England ships?

We began now to receive some "returns" of the effect of our late captures upon Northern commerce. The papers captured on board the *Cooke* were full of lamentations. Our pious brethren did not confine themselves to the forms set down by Jeremiah, however, but hissed their execrations through teeth grinding with rage. I will not treat my readers to any of these specimens of the art Philippic, but will confine myself to a few business excerpts instead, taken indiscriminately from the New York and Boston papers.

Boston crieth aloud.

"ADVANCES ON MARINE INSURANCE.— In consequence of the destruction caused at sea by the privateer steamer *Alabama*, the officers of the insurance companies of Boston have fixed the present war rates on different voyages as follows: — To the north of Europe, 4@5 per cent. ; Mediterranean, 5@6 ; India, 4½ ; Gulf ports, 4 ; California gold steamers, 4 ; West India risks, 5 ; coastwise, ½@1½. These rates are liable to be altered according to the necessary requirements of the times, consequent upon the unusual hazards to which commerce is now exposed."

New York responds to the cry of Boston.

"The damaging effect of the *Alabama's* raid on our shipping upon the maritime interests of this port were as conspicuous to-day as yesterday. It was next to impossible for the owner of an American ship to procure freight unless he consented to make a bogus sale of his ship."

"Freights to Great Britain are rather more active, under favorable foreign advices for breadstuffs, but rates by American vessels depressed ; foreign bottoms most in favor, but even these now find it difficult to employ themselves profitably. To Liverpool, flour is 9d@2s."

I heard again from the New York Chamber of Commerce, by the *Cooke*. My friend, Low, was still lamenting over his lost ships. Like Rachael weeping for her children, he refused to be comforted because they were not. Another grand *pow-*

wow had been called, and another set of resolutions passed. SCENE: *A luxuriously furnished suite of apartments, with well-padded arm-chairs, and big ink-stands; a table; on the walls, several pictures of burning ships, with the "pirate ship" in the distance; of John Bull running off with the "carrying-trade," and Jonathan screaming after him; and of Mr. Low tearing his hair.* Enter the *dramatis personæ.* Low loquitur: —

"Mr. A. Low read a very long preamble and resolution expressive of the feelings of the American public in regard to the shelter afforded to the *Alabama* by British authorities. He also read a letter from our Consul at Liverpool, Mr. Dudley, in which that functionary sets forth the efforts he made to direct the attention of the British authorities to the *Alabama*, and concludes by asserting that there are now four large vessels fitting out at Liverpool to follow the piratical example of the *Alabama*—three of iron and one of wood. Nine vessels are preparing to run the blockade.

"Mr. Low explained at some length the object and scope of his proposed resolution. He declared that American ships could no longer get cargoes, in consequence of the depredations of the *Alabama.*

"Hon. F. A. Conkling spoke in behalf of granting letters-of-marque. He saw no other alternative between this and a complete paralyzation of our commerce. He read extracts from Cogswell's 'Maritime History,' showing the effectiveness of privateers in our previous wars.

"C. H. Marshall spoke in favor of the adoption of Mr. Low's preamble and resolution.

"Mr. Maury stated that he had received a letter from Liverpool, saying that the new pirate ships building for the Confederates are vastly more formidable than the *Alabama.*

"The preamble and resolutions set forth at length the evil consequences likely to ensue from a repetition of such piratical acts as the fitting out of more vessels like the *Alabama*, in the ports of Great Britain; that information has been received of other vessels having sailed to prey upon the commerce of the United States; that the English Government does not interfere to put a stop to the aggressions of the pirate, though British goods have been destroyed; that the *Alabama* is continually supplied from Great Britain with coal and ammunition, by which she is enabled to pursue her piratical courses against American commerce, the consequence being to raise the premium upon American vessels and their cargoes, and to depress the rates of freight upon American ships, and to transfer our carrying-trade to the ships of other nations. Therefore the Chamber is led to the following conclusions:

"1st. That through the active instrumentality of the subjects of Great Britain, the so-called Confederate States are furnished with ships, men, arms, and ammunition, with which to war upon the commerce of the United States;

"2d. That without such foreign aid the States in revolt against the Government of the United States would be powerless to effect any injury to our commerce on the high seas.

"3d. That this war upon American commerce carried on by ships built and manned in Great Britain, is not rebuked by the British press generally; is not discouraged by the public sentiment of a once friendly nation claiming to be governed by high and honorable principles, and is not effectively and thoroughly arrested by the stronger arm of the British Government.

"4th. That as a result of the foregoing acts and conclusions, the merchants of the United States are subject in a certain degree to the evils that would attend a state of war with Great Britain, and are compelled to witness the carrying-trade of their country transferred from their own vessels to British bottoms, under all the sanctions and advantages of peace and neutrality to the latter — while the source of this great peril, threatening to drive American commerce from the ocean, is of British origin.

"Now, therefore, resolved, that a Committee of ten be appointed to take into consideration the foregoing, and to report, at a special meeting to be called for the purpose, what action it becomes this Chamber to take in the premises."

How astonishing it is, that these gentlemen when they were denouncing Great Britain for supplying the Confederates with men and munitions of war, did not think of the supplies they were themselves drawing from the same source. I have before referred to a speech of Mr. Laird, the builder of the *Alabama*, in the British House of Commons. I now refer to another passage of the same speech, as a sufficient answer to Mr. Low's complaints: —

"If a ship without guns and without arms, [he is alluding to the *Alabama* when she left the Mersey,] is a dangerous article, surely rifled guns and ammunition of all sorts are equally — (cheers) — and even more dangerous. (Cheers.) I have referred to the bills of entry in the Custom-houses of London and Liverpool, and I find there have been vast shipments of implements of war to the Northern States, through the celebrated houses of Baring & Co. — (loud cheers and laughter), — Brown, Shipley & Co., of Liverpool, and a variety of other names, which I need not more particularly mention, but whose Northern tendencies are well known to this House. (Hear! hear!) If the member for Rochdale, or the honorable member for Branchford wishes to ascertain the extent to which the Northern States of America have had supplies of arms from this country, they have only to go to a gentleman who, I am sure, will be ready to afford them every information, and much more readily than he would to me, or to any one else calling upon him — the American Consul in Liverpool.   Before that gentleman, the manifest of every ship is laid, he has to give an American pass to each vessel; he is, consequently, able to tell the exact number of rifles which have been shipped from this country for the United States — information, I doubt not, which would be very generally desired by this House.   (Loud cries of 'hear!')   I have obtained from the official custom-house returns, some details of the sundries exported from the United Kingdom to the Northern States of America, from the 1st of May, 1861, to the 31st of December, 1862. There were — Muskets, 41,500 — (hear! hear!) — rifles, 341,000 — (cheers) — gun-flints, 26,500—percussion-caps, 49,982,000 — (cheers and laughter)— and swords, 2250.   The best information I could obtain, leads me to believe that from one third to a half may be added to these numbers for items which have been shipped to the Northern States as hardware. (Hear! hear!)   I have very good reason for saying that a vessel of 2000 tons was chartered six weeks ago, for the express purpose of taking out a cargo of "hardware" to the United States. (Cheers.) The exportation has not ceased yet.   From the 1st of January to the 17th of March, 1863, the customs bills of entry show that 23,870 gun-barrels, 30,802 rifles, and 3,105,800 percussion-caps were shipped to the United States. (Hear! hear!)   So that if the Southern States have got two ships unarmed, unfit for any purpose of warfare — for they procured their armaments somewhere else — the Northern States have been well supplied from this country, through the agency of some most influential persons. (Hear! hear!)"

"The American Consul in Liverpool," alluded to in the above extract, is the same gentleman — Dudley — who was assisting Mr. Low to denounce Great Britain for supplying the Confederate States!

The *Parker Cooke* made a beautiful bonfire, lighting up the sea and land for leagues; and as the wind continued light, it was near midnight before we had run it below the horizon. Before morning we gave chase to another sail, but at daylight, by which time we were within a couple of miles of her, she showed us the Spanish colors.   We chased, and overhauled soon afterward a Dutch galliot, and later in the day, a Spanish bark.   The land was still in sight on our port beam, and toward nightfall, we passed Cape François.

Between midnight and dawn, on this same night, we had quite an alarm.   A large ship-of-war came suddenly upon us, in the darkness!   Like ourselves, she was running down the coast, but she was under both steam and sail, having her studding-sails set on both sides, whereas the *Alabama* was entirely without steam, with her propeller triced up. If the stranger had been an enemy, we should have been almost entirely at her mercy. The reader may imagine, therefore, how anxious I was for the next few minutes. She soon dispelled my fears, however, for she passed rapidly on, at no greater distance from us, than a hundred yards, her lights lighting up the countenances of my men, as they stood at their guns — for by this time I had gotten them to their quarters — quite distinctly. She did not take the least notice of us, or swerve a hair's-breadth from her course. I knew, from this, she could not be an enemy, and told my first lieutenant, even before she had well passed us, that he might let his men leave their guns. She was, probably, a Spanish steam-frigate, on her way to the island of Cuba.

On the evening of the 2d of December, we passed the little island of Tortuga, so famous in the history of the buccaneers and pirates who once infested these waters, and on the next day, found ourselves in the passage between St. Domingo and Cuba. There were many sails passing in different directions, all of which we overhauled, but they proved to be neutral. Here was another important thoroughfare of the enemy's commerce entirely unguarded. There was not only no ship-of-war of the enemy to be seen, but none of the neutrals that I had spoken, had fallen in with any. We had, therefore, a clear sea before us, for carrying out our design of waylaying a California steamer. In the afternoon, we stretched over to the east end of Cuba, and took our station in "watch and wait."

On the same night, we chased and overhauled a French bark. The sea was smooth, and a bright moon shining. The chase paid no attention to our blank cartridge, though we were close on board of her, and stood a shot before she would come to the wind. As we threw this purposely between her masts, and pretty close over the heads of her people, she came to the conclusion that it would not be safe to trifle longer, and rounded to and backed her main yard. When asked by the boarding-officer, why he did not heave to, at the first signal, the master replied naively that he was a Frenchman, and at war with nobody! Philosophical Frenchman!

We had accurate time-tables of the arrivals and departures of the California steamers, in the files of the New York papers, that we had captured, and by these tables, the homeward-bound steamer would not be due for a few days yet. We spent this interval in lying off and on the east end of Cuba, under easy sail, chasing more or less during the day, but without success, all the vessels overhauled being neutrals, and closing in with Cape Maize during the night, and holding on to its very brilliant light until morning. The weather was clear, and the moon near her full, so that I had almost as good a view of the passage by night as by day.

On the 5th of December, a prize ran into our arms, without the necessity of a chase. It was a Baltimore schooner called the *Union,* old, and of little value. She had, besides, a neutral cargo, properly documented, for a small town called Port Maria, on the north side of Jamaica. I transferred the prisoners of the *Cooke* to her, and released her on ransom-bond. My original orders were not to capture Maryland vessels, but that good old State had long since ceased to occupy the category in which our Congress, and the Executive had placed her. She was now ranged under the enemy's flag, and I could make no discrimination in her favor.

On the next day the California steamer was due, and a very bright lookout was kept; a number of the young officers volunteering their services for the occasion. In the transparent atmosphere of this delightful climate, we could see to great distances. The west end of St. Domingo, about Cape Tiburon, was visible, though distant ninety miles. But not so much as a smoke was seen during the entire day, and the sun went down upon disappointed hopes. The next day was Sunday, and the holy-stones had been busy over my head during all the morning watch, putting the decks in order for muster. I had turned out, and dressed, and swept the entire horizon with my telescope, without seeing anything to encourage me. The crew had breakfasted, and the word, "All hands clean yourselves, in white frocks and trousers, for muster!" had been growled out by the boatswain, and echoed by his mates. The decks were encumbered with clothes-bags, and Jack was arraying himself as directed. I had gone down to my own breakfast, and was enjoying one of Bartelli's cups of good coffee, hopeless for that day of my California steamer, and my million of dollars in gold. Suddenly the prolonged cry of "S-a-i-l h-o! " came ringing, in a clear musical voice, from aloft; the look-out having at length descried a steamer, and being anxious to impart the intelligence in as emphatic a manner as possible, to the startled listeners on the deck below. The "Where-away?" of the officer of the deck, shouted through his trumpet, followed, and in a moment more came the rejoinder, "Broad on the port bow, sir!" "What does she look like?" again inquired the officer of the deck. "She is a large steamer, brig-rigged, sir!" was the reply. An officer now came below to announce to me what I had already heard.

Here was a steamer at last, but unfortunately she was not in the right direction, being in the north-west instead of the south-east — the latter being the direction in which the California steamer should appear. All was excitement now on deck. The engineers and firemen were set at work, in great haste, to get up their steam. The sailors were hurried with their "cleaning," and the bags stowed away. "All hands work ship!" being called, the first lieutenant took the trumpet, and furled the sails, making a "snug roll-up of it," so that they might hold as little wind as possible, and lowered the propeller. In twenty minutes we were ready for the chase, with every thing snug "alow and aloft," and with the steam hissing from the gauge-cocks. The strange steamer came up very rapidly, and we scrutinized her anxiously to see whether she was a ship of war, or a packet-ship. She showed too much hull out of the water to be a ship of war, and yet we could not be sure, as the enemy had commissioned a great many packet-steamers, and put heavy armaments on board of them. When she was within three or four miles of us, we showed her the United States colors, and she responded in a few minutes, by hoisting the same. Like ourselves, she had her sails furled, and was carrying a very large "bone in her mouth" under steam alone.

We could now see that she was fast, and from the absence of guns at her sides, a packet-ship. I now put my ship in motion, with a view to lay her across the stranger's path, as though I would speak her. But I missed doing this by about a couple of ship's lengths, the stranger passing just ahead of me. A beautiful spectacle presented itself as I passed under the stern of that monster steamship. The weather was charming, there being a bright, clear sky, with only a few fleecy trade-clouds passing. There was just enough of the balmiest and gentlest of winds, to ruffle, without roughening the surface of the sea. The islands of Cuba, St. Domingo, and Jamaica— the two latter, in the blue and hazy distance, and the former robed in the gorgeous green known only to the tropics—were in sight. The great packet-steamer had all her awnings set, and under these awnings, on the upper deck, was a crowd of passengers, male and female. Mixed with the male passengers were several officers in uniform, and on the forward deck, there were groups of soldiers to be seen. This crowd presented a charming picture, especially the ladies, most of whom were gayly dressed, with the streamers from their bonnets, their veils, and their waste ribbons flirting with the morning breeze. We were sufficiently close to see the expression of their countenances. Many of them were viewing us with opera glasses, evidently admiring the beautiful proportions, fine trim, and general comeliness of one of their own gun-boats —for the reader will recollect, we were wearing still the United States flag.

As I passed the wake of the steamer, I wheeled in pursuit, fired a blank cartridge, and hauling down the Federal, threw the Confederate flag to the breeze. It was amusing to witness the panic which ensued. If that old buccaneer, Blue Beard, himself, had appeared, the consternation could not have been greater. The ladies screamed—one of those delightful, dramatic screams, half fear, half acting, which can only ascend from female voices—and scampered off the deck in a trice; the men running after them, and making quite as good, if not better time. The effect of my gun, and change of flags on the steamer herself, seemed to be scarcely less electric. She had no intention, whatever, of obeying my command to halt. On the contrary, I could see from the increased impetus with which she sprang forward, and the dense volumes of black smoke that now came rushing, and whirling from her smoke-stack, that she was making every possible effort to escape. She had gotten a little the start of me, as I was wheeling to pursue her, and might be now, some three or four hundred yards distant.

The reader has been on the race-course, and seen two fleet horses, with necks and tails straightened, and running about "neck and neck." This will give him a pretty good idea of the race which is now going on. We had not stretched a mile, when it became quite evident that the stranger had the heels of me, and that, if I would capture her, I must resort to force. I ordered my "persuader," as the sailors called my rifled bow-gun, to be cleared away, and sent orders to the officer, to take aim at the fugitive's foremast, being careful to throw his shot high enough above the deck not to take life. When the gun was ready to be fired, I yawed the ship a little, though the effect of this was to lose ground, to enable the officer the better, to take his aim. A flash, a curl of white smoke, and a flying off of large pieces of timber from the steamer's mast, were simultaneous occurrences. It was sufficient. The mast had not been cut quite away, but enough had been done to satisfy the master of the steamer that he was entirely within our power, and that prudence would be the better part of valor. In a moment after, we could see a perceptible diminution in the motion of the "walking-beam," and pretty soon the great wheels of the steamer ceased to revolve, and she lay motionless on the water.

We "slowed down" our own engine, and began to blow off steam at once, and ranging up alongside of the prize, sent a boat on board of her. It was thus we captured the steamer *Ariel*, instead of going to muster, on Sunday, the 7th of December, 1862. But Fortune, after all, had played us a scurvy trick. The *Ariel* was indeed a California steamer, but instead of being a homeward-bound steamer, with a million of dollars in gold, in her safe, I had captured an outward-bound steamer, with five hundred women and children on board! This was an elephant I had not bargained for, and I was seriously embarrassed to know what to do with it. I could not take her into any neutral port, even for landing the passengers, as this was forbidden, by those unfriendly orders in council I have more than once spoken of, and I had no room for the passengers on board the *Alabama*. The most that I could hope to do, was to capture some less valuable prize, within the next few days, turn the passengers of the *Ariel* on board of her, and destroy the steamer. Our capture, however, was not without useful results. The officers and soldiers mentioned as being on board of her, were a battalion of marines, going out to the Pacific, to supply the enemy's ships of war on that station. There were also some naval officers on board, for the same purpose. These were all *paroled*, and deprived of their arms. The rank and file numbered 140.

When my boarding-officer returned, he reported to me that there was a great state of alarm among the passengers on board. They had been reading the accounts which a malicious, and mendacious Northern press had been giving of us, and took us to be no better than the "plunderers," and "robbers" we had been represented to be. The women, in particular, he said, were, many of them, in hysterics, and apprehensive of the worst consequences. I had very little sympathy for the terrors of the males, but the tear of a woman has always unmanned me. And as I knew something of the weakness of the sex, as well as its fears, I resorted to the following stratagem to calm the dear creatures. I sent for my handsomest young lieutenant—and I had some very handsome young fellows on board the *Alabama*—and when he had come to me, I told him to go below, and array himself in his newest and handsomest uniform, buckle on the best sword there was in the ward-room, ask of Bartelli the loan of my brightest sword-knot, and come up to me for his orders. Sailors are rapid dressers, and in a few minutes my lieutenant was again by my side, looking as bewitching as I could possibly desire. I gave him my own boat, a beautiful gig, that had been newly painted, and which my coxswain, who was a bit of a sea-dandy, had furnished with scarlet cushions, and fancy yoke and steering ropes, and directed him to go· on board the *Ariel*, and coax the ladies out of their hysterics. "Oh! I'll be sure to do that, sir," said he, with a charming air of coxcombry, "I never knew a fair creature who could resist me more than fifteen minutes." As he shoved off from the side, in my beautiful little cockle-shell of a boat, with its fine-looking, lithe and active oarsmen, bending with the strength of athletes to their ashen blades, I could but pause a moment, myself, in admiration of the picture.

A few strokes of his oars put him alongside of the steamer, and asking to be shown to the ladies' cabin, he entered the scene of dismay and confusion. So many were the signs of distress, and so numerous the wailers, that he was abashed, for a moment, as he afterward told me, with all his assurance. But summoning courage, he spoke to them about as follows:—
"Ladies! The Captain of the *Alabama* has heard of your distress, and sent me on board to calm your fears, by assuring you, that you have fallen into the hands of Southern gentlemen, under whose protection you are entirely safe. We are by no means the ruffians and outlaws, that we have been represented by your people, and you have nothing whatever to fear." The sobs ceased as he proceeded, but they eyed him askance for the first few minutes. As he advanced in their midst, however, they took a second, and more favorable glance at him. A second glance begat a third, more favorable still, and when he entered into conversation with some of the ladies nearest him—picking out the youngest and prettiest, as the rogue admitted—he found no reluctance on their part to answer him. In short, he was fast becoming a favorite. The ice being once broken, a perfect avalanche of loveliness soon surrounded him, the eyes of the fair creatures looking all the brighter for the tears that had recently dimmed them.

Presently a young lady, stepping up to him, took hold of one of the bright buttons that were glittering on the breast of his coat, and asked him if he would not permit her to cut it off, as a memento of her adventure with the *Alabama*. He assented. A pair of scissors was produced, and away went the button! This emboldened another lady to make the same request, and away went another button; and so the process went on, until when I got my handsome lieutenant back, he was like a plucked peacock—he had scarcely a button to his coat! There were no more Hebes drowned in tears, on board the *Ariel*.

But what struck my young officer as very singular was the deportment of the male passengers. Some of these seemed to be overhauling their trunks in a great hurry, as though there were valuables in them, which they were anxious to secrete. Their watches, too, had disappeared from some of their vest-pockets. "I verily believe," said he, as he was giving me an account of the manner in which he performed his mission, "that these fellows think we are no better than the Northern thieves, who are burning dwelling-houses, and robbing our women and children in the South!"

I take pleasure in contrasting, in these memoirs, the conduct of my officers and crew, during the late war, in the uniform respect which they paid to the laws of war, and the dictates of humanity, with that of some of the generals and colonels of the Federal Army, who debased our common nature, and disgraced the uniforms they wore by the brutality and pil-ferings I have described. There were 500 passengers on board the *Ariel*. It is fair to presume, that each passenger had with him a purse, of from three to five hundred dollars. Under the laws of war, all this money would have been good prize. But not one dollar of it was touched, or indeed so much as a passenger's baggage examined.

I carried out my intention, already expressed, of keeping the *Ariel* in company with me, for two or three days, hoping that I might capture some less valuable ship, into which to turn her passengers, that I might destroy her. I was very anxious to destroy this ship, as she belonged to a Mr. Vanderbilt, of New York, an old steamboat captain, who had amassed a large fortune, in trade, and was a bitter enemy of the South. Lucrative contracts during the war had greatly enhanced his gains, and he had ambitiously made a present of one of his steamers to the Federal Government, to be called after him, to pursue "rebel pirates."

Failing to overhaul another ship of the enemy in the few days that I had at my disposal, I released the *Ariel*, on ransom-bond, and sent her, and her large number of passengers, on their way rejoicing. I found Captain Jones of the *Ariel* a clever and well-informed gentleman, and I believe he gave a very fair account of the capture of his ship when he reached New York. He pledged me that Vanderbilt's ransom-bond, which he signed as his agent, would be regarded as a debt of honor. The bond is for sale; cheap, to any one desiring to redeem Mr. Vanderbilt's honor

CHAPTER XXXIX.

THE ALABAMA IS DISABLED, AND STOPS TO REPAIR HER MACHINERY—PROCEEDS TO HER NEW RENDEZVOUS, THE ARCAS ISLANDS, AND THENCE TO GALVESTON—COMBAT WITH THE UNITED STATES STEAMER HATTERAS.

THE *Alabama* was disabled for two or three days, soon after the events recorded in the last chapter, by an accident which occurred to her engine—the giving way of one of the valve castings. I was, in consequence, obliged to withdraw from the tracks of commerce, and lie as *perdue* as possible, until the damage could be repaired. For this purpose, I ran close in with the land, on the north side of the island of Jamaica, where, with the exception of an occasional fishing-boat, and a passing coasting sloop, nothing was to be seen. Mr. Freeman, my chief engineer, was a capital machinist, and a man of great fertility of resource, and he went to work at once to remedy the mishap. Nothing but the puffing of the bellows, the clinking of the hammer on the anvil, and the rasping of files was heard now for forty-eight hours. At the end of this time, the engine was again in order for service. But we should have no occasion to use it for some days yet.

It was now the 12th of December, and it was time for us to begin to think of running into the Gulf of Mexico, in pursuit of General Banks. Accordingly we put the ship under sail, and ran along down the island of Jamaica to the west end. Hence we stretched over into that other track of the California steamers, returning to the United States by the west end of Cuba; intending to follow this track as far as Cape San Antonio, hoping that we might stumble upon something by the way. The California steamer was not now my principal object, however, but only an incident to my Mexican Gulf scheme. I did not design to waste time upon her. Whilst pursuing our way leisurely along this track, we experienced a most singular series of bad weather. We took an old-fashioned norther, which lasted us three days, and blew us well down into the Gulf of Honduras. Here we became the sport of a variety of currents—setting generally to the westward, but sometimes in a contrary direction. We sighted some of the islands lying parallel with the coast, but being anxious to get forward, did not touch at any of them As we drew out of the Gulf of Honduras, we again crossed the track of the California steamers, but fortune continued adverse, and none came along. A delay of a week or two here might enable me to pick up one of these treasure steamers, but this would interfere with my designs against Banks, as before remarked, and I forbore.

On the 20th of December we made the Mexican province of Yucatan, and, just before nightfall, got hold of Cape Catoche. My land fall was a very happy one, though, owing to the bad weather, I had had no "observation" for thirty-six hours. I sounded soon after dark, in twenty-eight fathoms of water, and being quite sure of my position, ran into the Yucatan passage, by the lead, the night being too dark to permit us to discern anything. The coast is clean, and the soundings regular, and I felt my way around the Cape without the least difficulty, finding myself, the next morning, in the Gulf of Mexico, running off to the westward with a free wind. The water was of a chalky whiteness, a little tinged with green, resembling the water on the Bahama Banks, and we ran along in a depth of twenty fathoms, the entire day, scarcely varying a foot. I had accomplished my object, thus far, with perfect success. I had not sighted a sail since leaving the west end of Jamaica, which could report me, and had entered the Gulf of Mexico, by night, unseen of any human eye, on the land or the sea. On the day after entering the Gulf, we did pass a solitary sail—a large steamer—steering in the direction of Havana, but she was hull down, and could make nothing of us. She may have been an enemy, but was probably a French ship of war, or transport, from Vera Cruz; the French expedition that culminated in the death of the unfortunate Maximilian having landed in Mexico about a year before, and there being much passing of steamships between France and Vera Cruz.

On the 22d of December, night overtaking us, within about twenty miles of the Arcas, we anchored in twenty fathoms of water, in the open sea. The Yucatan coast is like that of West Florida, and the Guianas, before described. It is a continuous harbor, a ship being able to hold on to her anchors in the heaviest gale. Getting under way the next morning, we continued on our course, and pretty soon made a bark standing in the same direction with ourselves. It was our old friend, the *Agrippina*, with her bluff bows, and stump top-gallant masts. She had been all this time making her way hither from Blanquilla — a period of nearly four weeks; the incorrigible old Scotch captain having stopped, on his way, to refresh his crew, and do a little private trading. However, he was in good time, and so, letting him off with a gentle reprimand, we ran in to the Arcas together, and anchored at about five o'clock in the afternoon.

We remained at these little islands a week, coaling ship, and refitting and repainting. We could not have been more thoroughly out of the world if we had been in the midst of the great African desert. A Robinson Crusoe here might have had it all to himself; and to give color to the illusion, we found on one of the islands a deserted hut, built of old boards and pieces of wreck, with an iron pot or two, and some pieces of sail-cloth lying about. An old dug-out, warped and cracked by the sun, lay hauled up near the hut, and a turtle-net, in pretty good repair, was found, stowed away in one corner of Crusoe's abode. But what had become of the hermit who once inhabited these desolate little coral islands, over which the wild sea-bird now flew, and screamed, in undivided dominion? An humble grave, on the head-board of which had been rudely carved with a knife, a name, and a date, told the brief and mournful story. A companion had probably laid the hermit away and departed. A more fitting burial-place for a sailor could not well be conceived; for here the elements with which he was wont to battle had full sweep, and his requiem was sung, without ceasing, by the booming wave, that shook and rocked him in his winding-sheet of sand, when the storm raged.

The islands are three in number, lying in a triangle. They are surrounded by deep water, and it is probably not a great many years since the little stone-mason of the sea, the coralline insect, first brought them to the surface, for the only vegetation as yet on any of them is a carpet of sea-kale, on the largest of them, and a stunted bush or two. In the basin, in the centre of the triangle, the *Alabama* is anchored, and so pellucid is the water, that not only her anchor, which lies in seven fathoms, is visible, from stock to fluke, but all the wonders of the coral world, before described, lie open to inspection; with the turtle groping about amid the sea-fern, the little fishes feeding, or sporting, and madrepore and sponges lying about in profusion. Bartelli drew up from this submarine forest, one of the largest of the latter, and having cured it in the sun, and rendered it sweet by frequent ablution, transferred it to my bath-room. The naturalist would have revelled at the Arcas, in viewing the debris of sea-shells, and coral, and the remains of stranded fish, that lay strewn along the beach; and in watching the habits of the gannet, man-of-war bird, and a great variety of the sea-gull, all of which were laying, and incubating. As the keel of one of our boats would grate upon the sand, clouds of these birds would fly up, and circle around our heads, screaming in their various and discordant notes at our intrusion. Beneath our feet, the whole surface of the islands was covered with eggs, or with young birds, in various stages of growth. Here, as at Blanquilla, all our boats were hoisted out, and rigged for sailing; and fishing, and turtling parties were sent out to supply the crew, and in the evening sailing and swimming matches, and target-shooting took place. This was only the by-play, however, whilst the main work of the drama was going forward, viz., the coaling, and preparation of the *Alabama* for her dash at the enemy.

Our upper deck had again become open, and required re-caulking; and some patching and refitting was necessary to be done to the sails. As we wanted our heels to be as clean as possible, we careened the ship, and gave her copper a good scrubbing below the water-line, where it had become a little foul. Having taken all the coal out of the *Agrippina*, we ballasted her with the coral rock, which we found lying abundantly at our hands, watered her from the *Alabama*, and gave her her sailing orders for Liverpool. She was to report to Captain Bullock, for another cargo of coal, to be delivered at another rendezvous, of the locality of which the reader will be informed in due time. During the week that we lay at the Arcas, there had evidently been several gales of wind at work around us, though none of them had touched us. On two or three occasions, when the wind was quite light, and the sky clear overhead, a heavy sea was observed to be breaking on the northern shores of the islands. There is no doubt that on these occasions there were "northers" prevailing along the Mexican coast. I was led hence to infer, that these terrible gales do not extend, as a general rule, a great distance seaward from that coast. We were very little more than a hundred miles from Vera Cruz, which is in the track of these terrible storms, and yet we had only felt the pulsations of them, as it were; the huge breakers on the Arcas beating time, in a still atmosphere, to the storm which was raging at Vera Cruz. It was seventeen days from the time we doubled Cape Catoche, until we left the Arcas. During all this time, we were off the coast of Yucatan, the season was near mid-winter, and yet we had not had a norther. Along the Mexican coast from Tampico to Vera Cruz, at this season of the year, the usual interval between these gales, is from three to five days.

As has been mentioned to the reader, the Banks' expedition was expected to rendezvous at Galveston, on the 10th of January. On the 5th of that month we got under way from the Arcas, giving ourselves five days in which to make the distance, under sail. Our secret was still perfectly safe, as only a single sail had passed us, whilst we lay at anchor, and she at too great a distance to be able to report us. We had an abundant supply of coal on board, the ship was in excellent trim, and as the sailors used to say of her, at this period, could be made to do everything but "talk." My crew were well drilled, my powder was in good condition, and as to the rest, I trusted to luck, and to the "creek's not being too high." The weather

continued fine throughout our run, and on the 11th at noon—
having been delayed a day by a calm—we observed in latitude 28° 51' 45'', and longitude 94° 55', being just thirty miles
from Galveston. I now laid my ship's head for the Galveston
light-house, and stood in, intending to get a distant sight of
the Banks' fleet before nightfall, and then haul off, and await
the approach of night, before I ran in, and made the assault.

I instructed the man at the mast-head, to keep a very bright
look-out, and told him what to look out for, viz., an immense
fleet anchored off a light-house. The wind was light, and the
afternoon was pretty well spent before there was any sign from
the mast-head. The look-out at length cried, "Land ho! sail ho!"
in quick succession, and I already began to make sure of my
game. But the look-out, upon being questioned, said he did not
see any fleet of transports, but only five steamers which looked
like ships of war. Here was a damper! What could have become
of Banks, and his great expedition, and what was this squadron
of steam ships-of-war doing here? Presently a shell, thrown
by one of the steamers, was seen to burst over the city. "Ah,
ha!" exclaimed I, to the officer of the deck who was standing
by me, "there has been a change of programme here. The
enemy would not be firing into his own people, and we must
have recaptured Galveston, since our last advices." "So it
would seem," replied the officer. And so it turned out. In
the interval between our leaving the West Indies, and arriving
off Galveston, this city had been retaken by General Magruder,
assisted by a gallant seaman of the merchant service, Captain
Leon Smith. Smith, with a couple of small river steamers,
protected by cotton bags, and having a number of sharp-
shooters on board, assaulted and captured, or drove to sea the
enemy's entire fleet, consisting of several heavily armed steamships.

The recapture of this place from the enemy changed the
destination of the Banks' expedition. It rendezvoused at New
Orleans, whence General Banks, afterward, attempted the invasion of Texas by the valley of the Red River. He was here
met by General Dick Taylor, who, with a much inferior force,
demolished him, giving him such a scare, that it was with difficulty Porter could stop him at Alexandria, to assist him in the

defence of his fleet, until he could extricate it from the shallows of the river where it was aground. The hero of Boston Common had not had such a scare since Stonewall Jackson had chased him through Winchester, Virginia.

What was best to be done in this changed condition of affairs? I certainly had not come all the way into the Gulf of Mexico, to fight five ships of war, the least of which was probably my equal. And yet, how could I very well run away, in the face of the promises I had given my crew? for I had told them at the Arcas islands, that they were, if the fates proved propitious, to have some sport off Galveston. Whilst I was pondering the difficulty, the enemy himself, happily, came to my relief; for pretty soon the look-out again called from aloft, and said, "One of the steamers, sir, is coming out in chase of us." The *Alabama* had given chase pretty often, but this was the first time she had been chased. It was just the thing I wanted, however, for I at once conceived the design of drawing this single ship of the enemy far enough away from the remainder of her fleet, to enable me to decide a battle with her before her consorts could come to her relief.

The *Alabama* was still under sail, though, of course, being so near the enemy, the water was warm in her boilers, and in a condition to give us steam in ten minutes. To carry out my design of decoying the enemy, I now wore ship, as though I were fleeing from his pursuit. This, no doubt, encouraged him, though, as it would seem, the captain of the pursuing ship pretty soon began to smell a rat, as the reader will see presently by his report of the engagement. I now lowered my propeller, still holding on to my sails, however, and gave the ship a small head of steam, to prevent the stranger from overhauling me too rapidly. We were still too close to the fleet, to think of engaging him. I thus decoyed him on, little by little, now turning my propeller over slowly, and now stopping it altogether. In the meantime night set in, before we could get a distinct view of our pursuer. She was evidently a large steamer, but we knew from her build and rig, that she belonged neither to the class of old steam frigates, or that of the new sloops, and we were quite willing to try our strength with any of the other classes.

At length, when I judged that I had drawn the stranger out about twenty miles from his fleet, I furled my sails, beat to quarters, prepared my ship for action, and wheeled to meet him. The two ships now approached each other, very rapidly. As we came within speaking distance, we simultaneously stopped our engines, the ships being about one hundred yards apart. The enemy was the first to hail. "What ship is that?" cried he. "This is her Britannic Majesty's steamer *Petrel,*" we replied. We now hailed in turn, and demanded to know who he was. The reply not coming to us very distinctly, we repeated our question, when we heard the words, "This is the United States ship——" the name of the ship being lost to us. But we had heard enough. All we wanted to know was, that the stranger was a United States ship, and therefore our enemy. A pause now ensued—a rather awkward pause, as the reader may suppose. Presently, the stranger hailed again, and said, "If you please, I will send a boat on board of you." His object was, of course, to verify or discredit the answer we had given him, that we were one of her Britannic Majesty's cruisers. We replied, "Certainly, we shall be happy to receive your boat;" and we heard a boatswain's mate call away a boat, and could hear the creaking of the tackles, as she was lowered into the water.

Things were now come to a crisis, and it being useless to delay our engagement with the enemy any longer, I turned to my first lieutenant, and said, "I suppose you are all ready for action?" "We are," he replied; "the men are eager to begin, and are only waiting for the word." I then said to him, "Tell the enemy who we are, for we must not strike him in disguise, and when you have done so, give him the broadside." Kell now sang out, in his powerful, clarion voice, through his trumpet, "This is the Confederate States steamer *Alabama!*" and turning to the crew, who were all standing at their guns—the gunners with their sights on the enemy, and lock-strings in hand—gave the order, fire! Away went the broadside in an instant, our little ship feeling, perceptibly, the recoil of her guns. The night was clear. There was no moon, but sufficient star-light to enable the two ships to see each other quite distinctly, at the distance of half a mile, or more, and a state of the atmosphere highly favorable to the conduct of sound. The wind, besides, was blowing in the direction of the enemy's fleet. As a matter of course, our guns awakened the echoes of the coast, far and near, announcing very distinctly to the Federal Admiral — Bell, a Southern man, who had gone over to the enemy — that the ship which he had sent out to chase the strange sail, had a fight on her hands. He immediately, as we afterward learned, got under way, with the *Brooklyn*, his flag-ship, and two others of his steamers, and came out to the rescue.

Our broadside was returned instantly; the enemy, like ourselves, having been on his guard, with his men standing at their guns. The two ships, when the action commenced, had swerved in such a way, that they were now heading in the same direction — the *Alabama* fighting her starboard-broadside, and her antagonist her port-broadside. Each ship, as she delivered her broadside, put herself under steam, and the action became a running fight, in parallel lines, or nearly so, the ships now nearing, and now separating a little from each other. My men handled their pieces with great spirit and commendable coolness, and the action was sharp and exciting while it lasted; which, however, was not very long, for in just *thirteen minutes* after firing the first gun, the enemy hoisted a light, and fired an off-gun, as a signal that he had been beaten. We at once withheld our fire, and such a cheer went up from the brazen throats of my fellows, as must have astonished even a Texan, if he had heard it. We now steamed up quite close to the beaten steamer, and asked her captain, formally, if he had surrendered. He replied that he had. I then inquired if he was in want of assistance, to which he responded promptly that he was, that his ship was sinking rapidly, and that he needed all our boats. There appeared to be much confusion on board the enemy's ship; officers and crew seemed to be apprehensive that we would permit them to drown, and several voices cried aloud to us for assistance, at the same time. When the captain of the beaten ship came on board to surrender his sword to me, I learned that I had been engaged with the United States steamer *Hatteras*, Captain Blake. I will now let Captain Blake tell his own story. The following is his official report to the Secretary of the Federal Navy: —

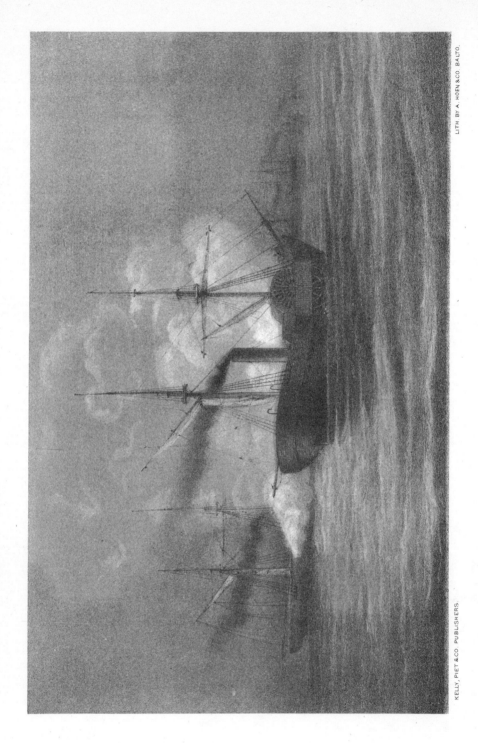

The Combat between the Alabama and the Hatteras, off Galveston, on the 11th of January, 1863.

United States' Consulate, }
Kingston, Jamaica, Jan. 21, 1863. }

Sir:—It is my painful duty to inform the Department of the destruction of the United States steamer *Hatteras*, recently under my command, by the rebel steamer *Alabama*, on the night of the 11th inst., off the coast of Texas. The circumstances of the disaster are as follows:—

Upon the afternoon of the 11th inst., at half-past two o'clock, while at anchor in company with the fleet under Commodore Bell, off Galveston, Texas, I was ordered by signal from the United States flag-ship *Brooklyn*, to chase a sail to the southward and eastward. I got under way immediately, and steamed with all speed in the direction indicated. After some time the strange sail could be seen from the *Hatteras*, and was ascertained to be a steamer, which fact I communicated to the flag-ship by signal. I continued the chase and rapidly gained upon the suspicious vessel. Knowing the slow rate of speed of the *Hatteras*, I at once suspected that deception was being practised, and hence ordered the ship to be cleared for action, with everything in readiness for a determined attack and a vigorous defence.

When within about four miles of the vessel, I observed that she had ceased to steam, and was lying broadside and awaiting us. It was nearly seven o'clock, and quite dark; but, notwithstanding the obscurity of the night, I felt assured, from the general character of the vessel and her manœuvres, that I should soon encounter the rebel steamer *Alabama*. Being able to work but four guns on the side of the *Hatteras*—two short 32-pounders, one 30-pounder rifled Parrott gun, and one 20-pounder rifled gun—I concluded to close with her, that my guns might be effective, if necessary.

I came within easy speaking range—about seventy-five yards—and upon asking, "What steamer is that?" received the answer, "Her Britannic Majesty's ship *Vixen*." I replied that I would send a boat aboard, and immediately gave the order. In the meantime, the vessels were changing positions, the stranger endeavoring to gain a desirable position for a raking fire. Almost simultaneously with the piping away of the boat, the strange craft again replied, "We are the Confederate steamer *Alabama*," which was accompanied with a broadside. I, at the same moment, returned the fire. Being well aware of the many vulnerable points of the *Hatteras*, I hoped, by closing with the *Alabama*, to be able to board her, and thus rid the seas of the piratical craft. I steamed directly for the *Alabama*, but she was enabled by her great speed, and the foulness of the bottom of the *Hatteras*, and, consequently, her diminished speed, to thwart my attempt when I had gained a distance of but thirty yards from her. At this range, musket and pistol shots were exchanged. The firing continued with great vigor on both sides. At length a shell entered amidships in the hold, setting fire to it, and, at the same instant—as I can hardly divide the time—a shell passed through the sick bay, exploding in an adjoining compartment, also producing fire.   Another entered the cylinder, filling the engine-room and deck with steam, and depriving me of my power to manœuvre the vessel, or to work the pumps, upon which the reduction of the fire depended.

With the vessel on fire in two places, and beyond human power, a hopeless wreck upon the waters, with her walking-beam shot away, and her engine rendered useless, I still maintained an active fire, with the double hope of disabling the *Alabama* and attracting the attention of the fleet off Galveston, which was only twenty-eight miles distant.

It was soon reported to me that the shells had entered the *Hatteras* at the water-line, tearing off entire sheets of iron, and that the water was rushing in, utterly defying every attempt to remedy the evil, and that she was rapidly sinking.   Learning the melancholy truth, and observing that the *Alabama* was on my port bow, entirely beyond the range of my guns, doubtless preparing for a raking fire of the deck, I felt I had no right to sacrifice uselessly, and without any desirable result, the lives of all under my command.

To prevent the blowing up of the *Hatteras* from the fire, which was making much progress, I ordered the magazine to be flooded, and afterward a lee gun was fired.   The *Alabama* then asked if assistance was desired, to which an affirmative answer was given.

The *Hatteras* was then going down, and in order to save the lives of my officers and men, I caused the armament on the port side to be thrown overboard.   Had I not done so, I am confident the vessel would have gone down with many brave hearts and valuable lives.   After considerable delay, caused by the report that a steamer was seen coming from Galveston, the *Alabama* sent us assistance, and I have the pleasure of informing the Department that every living being was conveyed safely from the *Hatteras* to the *Alabama*.

Two minutes after leaving the *Hatteras* she went down, bow first, with her pennant at the mast-head, with all her muskets and stores of every description, the enemy not being able, owing to her rapid sinking, to obtain a single weapon.

The battery upon the *Alabama* brought into action against the *Hatteras* numbered seven guns, consisting of four long 32-pounders, one 100-pounder, one 68-pounder, and one 24-pounder rifled gun. The great superiority of the *Alabama*, with her powerful battery and her machinery under the water-line, must be at once recognized by the Department, who are familiar with the construction of the *Hatteras*, and her total unfitness for a conflict with a regular built vessel of war.

The distance between the *Hatteras* and the *Alabama* during the action varied from twenty-five to one hundred yards.   Nearly fifty shots were fired from the *Hatteras*, and I presume a greater number from the *Alabama*.

I desire to refer to the efficient and active manner in which Acting Master Porter, executive officer, performed his duty.   The conduct of Assistant Surgeon Edward S. Matthews, both during the action and afterward, in attending to the wounded, demands my unqualified commendation. I would also bring to the favorable notice of the Department Acting Master's Mate McGrath, temporarily performing duty as gunner. Owing to the darkness of the night, and the peculiar construction of the *Hatteras*, I am only able to refer to the conduct of those officers who came under my especial attention; but from the character of the contest, and the amount of damage done to the *Alabama*, I have personally no reason to believe that any officer failed in his duty.

To the men of the *Hatteras* I cannot give too much praise. Their enthusiasm and bravery was of the highest order.

I enclose the report of Assistant Surgeon E. S. Matthews, by which you will observe that five men were wounded and two killed. The missing, it is hoped, reached the fleet at Galveston.

I shall communicate to the Department, in a separate report, the movements of myself and my command, from the time of our transfer to the *Alabama* until the departure of the earliest mail from this place to the United States.

I am, very respectfully, your obedient servant,

H. C. BLAKE,
Lieutenant Commanding.

Hon. GIDEON WELLES,
Secretary of the Navy, Washington.

Setting aside all the discourteous stuff and nonsense about "a *rebel* steamer," and a "piratical craft," of which Captain Blake, who had been bred in the old service, should have been ashamed, especially after enjoying the hospitalities of my cabin for a couple of weeks, the above is a pretty fair report of the engagement. I am a little puzzled, however, by the Captain's statement, that he could use but four guns on a side. We certainly understood from all the officers and men of the *Hatteras*, at the time, that she carried eight guns; six in broadside, and two pivots, just like the *Alabama*,—the only difference between the two ships being, that the *Alabama's* pivot guns were the heaviest.

There is another remark in the report that is quite new to me. I am informed, for the first time, that Captain Blake desired to board me. I cannot, of course, know what his intentions were, but I saw no evidence of such an intention, in the handling of his ship; and Captain Blake must himself have known that, in the terribly demoralized condition of his crew, when they found that they had really fallen in with the

Alabama, he could not have depended upon a single boarder. What Captain Blake means by saying that his ship went down, with her pennant flying, I am at a loss, as every seaman must be, to understand. Did he not surrender his ship to me? And if so, what business had his pennant, any more than his ensign, to be flying? But this, I suppose, was a little clap-trap, like his expressions, "rebel," and "pirate," thrown in to suit the Yankee taste of the day. Indeed, nothing was more lamentable to me, during the whole war, than to observe how readily the officers of the old Navy, many of whom belonged to the gentle families of the land, and all of whom had been bred in a school of honor, took to the slang expressions of the day, and fell, pell-mell, into the ranks of the vulgar and fanatical rabble that was hounding on the war.

The officers of the Confederate States Navy, to say the least, were as much entitled to be regarded as fighting for a principle as themselves, and one would have thought that there would have been a chivalrous rivalry between the two services, as to which should show the other the most courtesy. This was the case, a thousand years ago, between the Christian and the Saracen. Did it result from their forms of government, and must democrats necessarily be vulgarians? Must the howling Demos devour everything gentle in the land, and reduce us all to the common level of the pot-house politician, and compel us to use his slang? Radicalism seemed to be now, just what it had been in the great French Revolution, a sort of mad-dog virus; every one who was inoculated with it, becoming rabid. The bitten dog howled incessantly with rage, and underwent a total transformation of nature. But our figure does not fit the case exactly. There was more method in this madness, than in that of the canine animal, for the human dog howled as much to please his master, as from rage. The size of the sop which he was to receive depended, in a great measure, upon the vigor of his howling.

But to return to the *Alabama* and the *Hatteras.* As soon as the action was over, and I had seen the latter sink, I caused all lights to be extinguished on board my ship, and shaped my course again for the passage of Yucatan. In the meantime, the enemy's boat, which had been lowered for the purpose of boarding me, pulled in vigorously for the shore, as soon as it saw the action commence, and landed safely; and Admiral Bell, with his three steamers, passed on either side of the scene of action—the steamers having been scattered in the pursuit, to cover as much space as possible, and thus increase their chances of falling in with me. They did not find the *Alabama*, or indeed anything else during the night, but as one of the steamers was returning to her anchorage off Galveston, the next morning, in the dejected mood of a baffled scout, she fell in with the sunken *Hatteras*, the tops of whose royal masts were just above water, and from the main of which, the pennant—the *night* pennant, for the action was fought at night—spoken of by Captain Blake, was observed to be flying. It told the only tale of the sunken ship which her consort had to take back to the Admiral. The missing boat turned up soon afterward, however, and the mystery was then solved. There was now as hurried a saddling of steeds for the pursuit as there had been in the chase of the young Lochinvar, and with as little effect, for by the time the steeds were given the spur, the *Alabama* was distant a hundred miles or more.

There was very little said by the enemy, about this engagement, between the *Alabama* and the *Hatteras*, as was usual with him when he met with a disaster; and what was said was all false. My own ship was represented to be a monster of speed and strength, and the *Hatteras*, on the other hand, to be a tug, or river steamer, or some such craft, with two or three small guns at the most. The facts are as follows: The *Hatteras* was a larger ship than the *Alabama*, by one hundred tons. Her armament, as reported to us by her own people, was as follows: Four 32-pounders; two Parrot 30-pounder rifles; one 20-pounder rifle; and one 12-pounder howitzer—making a total of eight guns. The armament of the *Alabama* was as follows: Six 32-pounders; one 8-inch shell gun; one Blakeley rifle of 100 pounds—total, eight guns. There was, besides, a little toy-rifle—a 9-pounder—on the quarter-deck of the *Alabama*, which had been captured from a merchant-ship, and which, I believe, was fired once during the action. The crew of the *Hatteras* was 108 strong; that of the *Alabama* 110. There was thus, as the reader sees, a considerable disparity between the two ships, in the weight of their pivot-guns, and the *Alabama* ought to have won the fight; and she did win it, in *thirteen minutes*—taking care, too, though she sank her enemy at night, to see that none of his men were drowned —a fact which I shall have occasion to contrast, by-and-by, with another sinking. The only casualty we had on board the *Alabama* was one man wounded. The damages to our hull were so slight, that there was not a shot-hole which it was necessary to plug, to enable us to continue our cruise; nor was there a rope to be spliced. Blake behaved like a man of courage, and made the best fight he could, ill supported as he was by the "volunteer" officers by whom he was surrounded, but he fell into disgrace with the Demos, and had but little opportunity shown him during the remainder of the war, to retrieve his disaster.

CHAPTER XL.

THE little by-play, in the Gulf of Mexico, related in the
last chapter, being over, I determined to make the best
of my way to the island of Jamaica, there land my prisoners,
on *parole*, patch up the two or three shot-holes the enemy had
made above the water-line, re-coal, and proceed on my eastern
cruise, against the enemy's commerce, as originally contemplated. We had a long passage to Jamaica, as we took a succession of southerly gales, that greatly retarded our speed.
My first intention was to make the whole run under steam, but
after struggling against these gales for three or four days, I
found my fuel diminishing so rapidly, that it became prudent
to let the fires go down, and put the ship under sail. This
delay was very vexatious, as our little ship was greatly inconvenienced by the number of prisoners we had on board.

Friday, the 16th of January, is noted on my journal as follows:—The gale continued all day, moderating toward night.
The sky is overcast with a dull canopy of leaden clouds, the
sun barely showing himself to us, for a moment at a time,
through an occasional rift, during the entire day. Observing the
water to be discolored, at one P. M. we sounded on the Yucatan Bank. The soundings on this bank being an excellent
guide, I continued to run along the edge of it until eleven P.
M., when we passed off it, into the deep waters of the Yucatan
Passage. We now put the ship under steam again, and aiding

the steam by reefed trysails, we battled with an adverse sea and current during the rest of the night. We found the current setting into the passage, to be as much as two and a half knots per hour, which was greater than I had ever known it before.

I may take this occasion to remind the reader, that the old theory of Dr. Franklin and others, was, that the Gulf Stream, which flows out of the Gulf of Mexico, between the north coast of Cuba, and the Florida Reefs and Keys, flows *into* the Gulf, through the channel between the west end of Cuba, and the coast of Yucatan, in which the *Alabama* now was. But the effectual disproof of this theory is, that we know positively, from the strength of the current, and its volume, or cross section, in the two passages, that more than twice the quantity of water flows out of the Gulf of Mexico, than flows into it through this passage. Upon Dr. Franklin's theory, the Gulf of Mexico in a very short time would become dry ground. Nor can the Mississippi River, which is the only stream worth noticing, in this connection, that flows into the Gulf of Mexico, come to his relief, as we have seen that that river only empties into the Gulf of Mexico, about *one three thousandth* part as much water, as the Gulf Stream takes out. We must resort, of necessity, to an under-current from the north, passing into the Gulf of Mexico, under the Gulf Stream, rising to the surface when heated, and thus swelling the volume of the outflowing water. I refer my readers, curious in this matter, to the work of ·Captain Maury, entitled the "Physical Geography of the Sea." It is full of profound philosophy, on the subjects of which it treats, and is written in so pleasing a style, and is so strewn with flowers, as to make the reader forget that he is travelling the thorny paths of science.

The 18th of January was Sunday, and we were obliged to intermit the usual Sunday muster, on account the of bad weather, which continued without intermission — the wind still blowing a gale, and the passing clouds deluging us with rain. Two days afterward, viz., on the 20th, we made the west end of the island of Jamaica, a little after midnight, and as we crawled under the lee of the coast, we broke, for the first time, the force of the wind with which we had been so long struggling.

We had been thus nine days making the passage from Galveston to the west end of Jamaica, and were the greater part of another day, in coasting the island up to Port Royal. We had shown first one, and then another neutral flag to several neutral ships that we had passed, but the enemy's flag was nowhere to be seen. Giving chase to a bark, whilst we were still in the Gulf of Mexico, we were quite amazed, as we came up with her, to find that she was our old consort, the *Agrippina!* This bluff-bowed old Scotch ship had been all the time since she left us at the Arcas Islands—eight days—battling with adverse winds, and was still only a couple of hundred miles or so advanced on her voyage.

We made the Plum Point lighthouse, at half-past four P. M., and were off the mouth of the harbor of Port Royal just as the evening began to deepen into twilight. We hoisted the French flag, and firing a gun, and making the usual signal for a pilot, one came promptly on board of us. Day was fading into night so fast, that we had scarcely light enough left to enable us to grope our way through the tortuous and narrow channel, and it was quite dark when our anchor was let go. Of course, we did not permit the pilot to anchor us *as a Frenchman,* and when we told him that it was the *Alabama* he was taking in, he did not appear at all surprised, but remarked very coolly, "I knew all the while that you were no Frenchman." I felt much relieved, when at length I heard the plunge of the anchor into the water, followed by the rattling of the chain-cable through the hawse-hole. On the high seas, with the enemy all the time in full chase of me, constant vigilance was required to guard against surprise; and my battle with the elements was almost as constant, as that with the enemy. When I reached the friendly shelter, therefore, of a neutral port, belonging to such of the powers of the earth as were strong enough to prevent themselves from being kicked by the enemy, my over-taxed nervous system relaxed in a moment, and I enjoyed the luxury of a little gentlemanly idleness. Kell was of wonderful assistance to me, in this respect. I always left the ship in his hands, with the utmost confidence, and my confidence was never misplaced. He was, as the reader has seen, an excellent disciplinarian, and being, besides, a thorough master of his profession, I had in him all that I could desire.

We were boarded by a lieutenant from the English flag-ship, immediately upon anchoring, and the news spread like wild-fire through all Port Royal, that the *Alabama* had arrived, with the officers and crew of a Federal gunboat which she had sunk in battle, on board as prisoners.   Night as it was, we were soon swarmed with visitors, come off to welcome us to the port, and tender their congratulations.   The next morning I called on Commodore Dunlap, who commanded a squadron of Admiral Milne's fleet, and was the commanding naval officer present. This was the first English port I had entered, since the *Alabama* had been commissioned, and no question, whatever, as to the antecedents of my ship was raised.   I had, in fact, brought in pretty substantial credentials, that I was a ship of war — 130 of the officers and men of one of the enemy's sunken ships. Great Britain had had the good sense not to listen to the frantic appeals, either of Mr. Seward or Minister Adams, both of whom claimed, as the reader has seen, that it was her duty to stultify herself, and ignore the commission of my ship. Nor did Commodore Dunlap say anything to me of my destruction of British property, or of the three ships of war, which that adept in international law, the "Commercial Advertiser," of New York, had asserted Admiral Milne had sent after me.   These questions, indeed, had all been authoritatively settled, I found, by Earl Russell, the British Foreign Secretary, by the following letter to the Liverpool Chamber of Commerce, which had applied to him for information.   It is copied from the New York "World":

"Sir: I am directed by Earl Russell to reply to your letters of the 6th inst., respecting the destruction by the Confederate steamer *Alabama* of British property embarked in American vessels and burned by that steamer.   Earl Russell desires me to state to you that British property on board a vessel belonging to one of the belligerents must be subject to all the risks and contingencies of war, so far as the capture of the vessel is concerned.   The owners of any British property, not being contraband of war, on board a Federal vessel captured and destroyed by a Confederate vessel of war, may claim in a Confederate Prize Court compensation for the destruction of such property."

The "World" said lachrymosely of the above, that "it was but one of a crowd of eloquent indications which constantly multiply upon us to prove that Earl Russell, like Mr. Gladstone, whatever his sympathies may be, really regards the 'nation of Jefferson Davis' as substantially created, and looks upon recognition as simply a question of time."

I forwarded, through Commodore Dunlap, an official report of my arrival to the Governor of the island, with a request to be permitted to land my prisoners, and put some slight repairs upon my ship; both of which requests were promptly granted. Governor Eyre was then in authority. He behaved with great spirit and firmness, afterward, in nipping in the bud a widespread negro insurrection, which had for its object, the massacre of the whites and the plunder of their property. A few negroes were killed by the troops, and I have been sorry to learn since, that his Excellency has been much harassed, in consequence, by both English and American fanatics. The English squadron at anchor consisted of the *Jason*, the *Challenger*, and *Greyhound*. The most cordial relations were at once established between the officers of all these ships, and those of the *Alabama*. Indeed, many of them were our old acquaintances.

An English friend having come on board, to invite me to pass a few days with him, in the mountains, while my ship was being prepared for sea, I accepted his invitation, and turning over all the unfinished business of the ship to Kell, we pulled up to Kingston in my gig. Here I found my friend's carriage in waiting, and entering it, we were soon whirled out of the limits of the dusty city, into the most charming of tropical scenery. Except landing, occasionally, for a few hours at a time, at the desert little islands I had visited in the Caribbean Sea, and the Gulf of Mexico, I had not had a holiday on shore, since leaving the *Mersey*, on my way to commission the *Alabama*, five months before. I needed a little rest, and recreation, to restore my wasted energies, and I found both with my excellent friend, Mr. Fyfe.

For the first ten miles, we rode over a beautiful macadamized road, or rather avenue, lined with the gigantic cactus, growing frequently to the height of twenty and thirty feet, and several specimens of the palm; chief among which was the cocoanut-tree, shooting its trunk with the straightness of an arrow to a great height, and waving gracefully in the breeze, its superb, feather-like foliage. The way was lined with many picturesque country houses, each surrounded by its extensive and well-kept grounds, on which were growing crops, chiefly of fruits and vegetables, but interspersed occasionally with a field of Indian corn, or sugar-cane. Hedge-rows and shade-trees adorned the front yards, and protected the residences from the sun, giving them an air of seclusion, coolness, and quiet that was very inviting. We occasionally obtained glimpses of beautiful valleys, on the right hand, and on the left, in which fairy cottages were nestled. The scenery was continually changing, as the road wound along, now skirting the base of abrupt hills, now running over a stream, and now plunging into the recesses of a wood, with the trees arching overhead, like the groined work of a cathedral.

At the end of our ten miles of carriage-drive, we found ourselves at the foot of the mountains. Here we alighted at a large hostelry, which was a sort of combination of the inn, caravansary, and country store, and after some refreshment, mounted saddle-horses which we found in waiting. The roads soon became mere bridle-paths. As we ascended the slopes of the mountains, we changed rapidly the character of the vegetation; every hundred feet of elevation being equivalent to a change of a degree or more of latitude, and bringing us in the presence of new forest-trees and new plants, until we dismounted on the lawn of my friend, the immediate surroundings of which were all English; the cedar, and other well-known trees and shrubs of the temperate latitudes, supplanting the tropical vegetation we had left in the *tierra caliente* below us. The air, too, was so delightfully changed, from the sultry heats of the coast, that we found a fire lighted of the dry and fragrant branches of the cedar-tree, quite pleasant as the night set in.

The reader may imagine how magical the change was, from the cramped quarters, and other *desagremens* of a small ship, to the ample halls, and elegant leisure of an English home, perched on the mountain-side, and overlooking a perfect wilderness of tropical vegetation. The sea was in plain sight to the eastward of us, and Kingston and Port Royal lay, as it were, at our feet. With the aid of a fine telescope which my friend had mounted in his piazza, I could distinguish my own ship from the other vessels in the harbor, though they all appeared as diminutive as so many sea-gulls, nestling upon the water.   I need not say how soundly I slept that night, far away from war's alarms, fanned by the gentlest of sea-breezes, in the sweetest of sheets, and lullabied by the distant breaker, as it stranded itself at regular intervals upon the beach.

I was awakened the next morning by the merry songs of a hundred birds, that came appropriately blended with the perfume of the flowers that clustered around my windows; and I have seldom looked upon a more beautiful picture, than when I threw back the blinds, and caught a view of the landscape, rejoicing in the morning's sun, with all its wealth of tropical fruits and flowers, and the sea—the glorious sea—glittering like a mirror in the distance.   Nothing can be more charming than the interior of an English household, when the ice has been broken and you have fairly gained admission into the interior of the temple.   The successful entertainment of a guest is one of those *artless* arts, of which the English gentleman, above all others, is master; and the art consists in putting the guest so entirely at ease, as to make him feel at home in the first half-hour.   With a library, servants, and horses at your command, you are literally left to take care of yourself —meeting the family in the parlors and sitting-rooms, as much, or as little as you please.

From Flamstead, which was the name of the country-seat of my friend, we rode over to Bloxburg, the country-seat of his brother, where some ladies from the neighborhood did me the honor to make me a visit; and from Bloxburg we made several other agreeable visits to neighboring plantations.   I was in an entirely new world—those mountains of Jamaica—and was charmed with everything I saw.   All was nature; and nature presented herself in her most lovely aspect, whether we viewed the sky overhead, the sea at our feet, or the broken and picturesque country around us.   Time flew rapidly, and what with delightful rides, and lunches, and evening parties, where music, and the bright eyes of fair women beguiled the senses, I should have been in danger of forgetting the war, and the *Alabama*, if Kell had not sent me a courier, on the third or fourth day, informing me that he was nearly ready for sea.

I descended at once from the empyrean in which I had been wandering, took a hasty leave of my friends, and in company with Mr. Fyfe, rode back to the coast. We took a new route back, and re-entered Kingston through a different suburb — stopping to lunch with one of Mr. Fyfe's friends, an English merchant, at his magnificent country-house. But, alas! much of the magnificence of the Kingston of former years is passing away. I had known it in its palmiest days, having visited it when a midshipman in the old service, before the happy slave had been converted into the wretched freedman. It was then a busy mart of commerce, and the placid waters of its unrivalled harbor were alive with shipping bearing the flags of all nations, come in quest of her great staples, sugar, coffee, cocoa, gensing, &c. Now, a general air of dilapidation and poverty hangs over the scene. A straggling ship or two only are seen in the harbor; the merchants have become shopkeepers, and the sleek, well-fed negro has become an idler and a vagrant, with scarce rags enough to hide his nakedness. My host, in the few days I remained with him, gave me much valuable information concerning the negro, since his emancipation, which I will not detain the reader to repeat. I may say in a few words, however, that the substance of this information was, that there has been no increase, either in numbers, intelligence, or morals among them; and that, too, under circumstances, all of which were favorable to the negro. He was the pet of the government for years after his emancipation, and English fanatics have devoted their lives to his regeneration, but all without success. He is, to-day, with a few exceptions about the towns, the same savage that he is in his native Dahomey. An English parliament had declared that he was the political equal of the white man — that is, of the colonial white man, for England takes the best of care, that the imperial legislature is never tainted by his presence — and I found him a generation afterward, far below his former level of slave.

I found my gig in waiting for me at the wharf in Kingston, and taking leave of my friend, with many thanks for his hospitality, I pulled on board of my ship about sunset. And here, what a scene of confusion met me, and what reports Kell had to make of how my fellows had been "cutting up!" The paymaster had been drunk ever since he landed, neglecting his duty, and behaving in a most disreputable manner. He was "hail fellow, well met" with all the common sailors, and seemed to have an especial fancy for the sailors of the enemy. Kell had suspended his functions; and had sent on shore, and had him brought off under arrest. He had become partially sobered, and I at once ordered him to pack up his clothing, and be off. He was landed, bag and baggage, in half an hour, and in due time, as the reader has already seen, he married a negro wife, went over to England with her, swindled her out of all her property, and turned Yankee, going over to Minister Adams, and becoming one of his right-hand men, when there was any hard swearing wanted in the British courts against the Confederates.

This little matter disposed of, we turned our attention to the crew. They had had a run on shore, and Kell was just gathering them together again. The ship's cutters, as well as the shore-boats, were constantly coming alongside with small squads, all of them drunk, some in one stage of drunkenness, and some in another. Liquor was acting upon them like the laughing gas; some were singing jolly, good-humored songs, whilst others were giving the war-whoop, and insisting on a fight. They were seized, ironed and passed below to the care of the master-at-arms, as fast as they came on board.

A couple of them, not liking the appearance of things on board, jumped into a dug-out alongside, and seizing the paddles from the negroes, shoved off in great haste, and put out for the shore. It was night, and there was a bright moon lighting up the bay. A cutter was manned as speedily as possible, and sent in pursuit of the fugitives. Jack had grog and Moll ahead of him, and irons and a court-martial behind him, and he paddled like a good fellow. He had gotten a good start before the cutter was well under way, but still, the cutter, with her long sweeping oars, was rather too much for the dug-out, especially as there were five oars to two paddles. She gained, and gained, coming nearer and nearer, when presently the officer of the cutter heard one of the sailors in the dug-out say to the other, "I 'll tell you what it is, Bill, there 's too much cargo in this here d—d craft, and I 'm going to lighten ship a little," and at the same instant, he saw the two men lay in their paddles, seize one of the negroes, and pitch him head foremost overboard! They then seized their paddles again, and away darted the dug-out with renewed speed.

Port Royal Bay is a large sheet of water, and is, besides, as every reader of Marryatt's incomparable tales knows, full of ravenous sharks. It would not do, of course, for the cutter to permit the negro either to drown or to be eaten by the sharks, and so, as she came up with him, sputtering and floundering for his life, she was obliged to "back of all," and take him in. The sailor who grabbed at him first, missed him, and the boat shot ahead of him, which rendered it necessary for her to turn and pull back a short distance before she could rescue him. This done, he was flung into the bottom of the cutter, and the pursuit renewed. By this time the dug-out had gotten even a better start than she had had at first, and the two fugitive sailors, encouraged by the prospect of escape, were paddling more vigorously than ever. Fast flew the dug-out, but faster flew the cutter. Both parties now had their blood up, and a more beautiful and exciting moonlight race has not often been seen. We had watched it from the *Alabama*, until in the gloaming of the night, it had passed out of sight. We had seen the first manœuvre of the halting, and pulling back of the cutter, but did not know what to make of it. The cutter began now to come up again with the chase. She had no musket on board, or in imitation of the *Alabama*, she might have "hove the chase to," with a blank cartridge, or a ball. When she had gotten within a few yards of her, a second time, in went the paddles again, and overboard went the other negro! and away went the dug-out! A similar delay on the part of the cutter ensued as before, and a similar advantage was gained by the dug-out.

But all things come to an end, and so did this race. The cutter finally captured the dug-out, and brought back Tom Bowse and Bill Bower to their admiring shipmates on board the *Alabama*. This was the only violation of neutrality I was guilty of, in Port Royal—chasing, and capturing a neutral craft, in neutral waters. My excuse was, the same that Wilkes made—she had contraband on board. I do not know whether Commodore Dunlap ever heard of it; but if he had complained,

I should have set-off the rescuing of two of her Majesty's colored subjects from drowning, against the recapture of my own men. The fact is, the towns-people, themselves, were responsible for all these disorders. They had made heroes of all my fellows, and plied them with an unconscionable number of drinks. Every sea-port town has its sailor quarter, and this in the good old town of Kingston was a constant scene of revelry, by day as well as by night, during the stay of the *Alabama's* liberty men on shore. There was no end to the "breakdowns," and "double-shuffles," which had been given in their honor, by the beaux and belles of Water Street. Besides my own crew, there were always more or less English man-of-war sailors on shore, on liberty from the different ships, and upwards of a hundred had been landed from the *Hatteras*. It was quite remarkable that in these merry-makings, and debaucheries, the Confederate sailors and the Yankee sailors harmonized capitally together. They might frequently be seen arm and arm in the streets, or hob-nobbing together — the Confederate sailor generally paying the score, as the Yankee sailor's strong box had gone down with his ship, and his paymaster was rather short of cash. They sailed as amicably together, up and down the contradance, and hailed each other to "heave to," when it was time to "freshen the nip," as though the *Alabama* and *Hatteras* had never been yard-arm and yard-arm, throwing broadsides into each other. In short, my men behaved capitally toward their late enemies. There was no unmanly exultation over their victory. The most that could be seen was an air of patronage very delicately put on, as though they would say, "Well, you know we whipped you, but then you did the best you could, and there's an end of it."

Among the amusing things that had occurred during my absence in the Jamaica mountains, was a flare-up, which Captain Blake, my prisoner, had had with the British Commodore.

The steamer *Greyhound* had a band of music on board, and as one of the young lieutenants was an old acquaintance of several of my officers, whom he had met at Nassau, he ordered the band on the evening after our arrival, and whilst Captain Blake was still on board the *Alabama*, to play "Dixie;" which, I may remark, by the way, had become a very popular **air** everywhere, as much on account of the air itself, perhaps, as because of its association with a weak and gallant people struggling for the right of self-government.   Captain Blake chose to construe this little compliment to the *Alabama*, as an insult to Yankeedom, and made a formal protest to the British Commodore, in behalf of himself, and the "old flag."   Commodore Dunlap must have smiled, when he read Blake's epistle. He was certainly a man of humor, for he hit upon the following mode of settling the grave international dispute.   He ordered the offending *Greyhound*, when she should get up her band, on the following evening, first to play "Dixie," and then "Yankee Doodle."

When the evening, which was to salve the Yankee honor, arrived, great was the expectation of every one in the squadron.   The band on board the *Jason*, flag-ship, led off by playing "God save the Queen," that glorious national anthem, which electrifies the Englishman, as the Marseilles' hymn does the Frenchman, the world over.   The *Challenger's* band followed and played a fine opera air.   The evening was still and fine, and the poops of all the ships were filled with officers.   It then came the *Greyhound's* turn.   She first played something unusually solemn, then "Dixie," with slowness, sweetness, and pathos, and when the chorus

"In Dixie's land, I'll take my stand,
I'll live, and die in Dixie!"

had died away on the soft evening air, such an infernal din, of drums, and fifes, and cymbals, and wind instruments, each after its fashion, going it strong upon

"Yankee Doodle Dandy!"

arose, as to defy all description!   The effect was electric; the officers had to hold their sides to preserve their dignity, and — Captain Blake was avenged.   There could be no protest made against this time-honored rogue's march.   It was the favorite tune of the b'hoys, and there the matter had to end.   I have never learned whether Mr. Seward ever called Lord Palmerston to an account about it, in any one of his "Essays on English Composition."

CHAPTER XLI.

DEPARTURE FROM JAMAICA — CAPTURE OF THE GOLDEN
RULE — COASTING THE ISLAND OF HAYTI — CAPTURE
OF THE CHASTELAINE — THE OLD CITY OF ST. DO-
MINGO, AND ITS REMINISCENCES — THE DOMINICAN
CONVENT, AND THE PALACE OF DIEGO COLUMBUS —
THE CAPTURE OF THE PALMETTO, THE OLIVE JANE,
AND THE GOLDEN EAGLE — HOW THE ROADS ARE
BLAZED OUT UPON THE SEA — CAPTAIN MAURY.

ON the 25th of January, 1863, or just five days after our
arrival at Jamaica, we had completed all our preparations
for sea, and at half-past eight P. M. steamed out of the harbor of
Port Royal, bound to the coast of Brazil, and thence to the Cape
of Good Hope. We had made many friends during our short
stay, and mutual regrets were expressed at departure. My gallant young officers had not been idle, whilst I had been visiting
the mountains. Many little missives, put up in the tiniest and
prettiest of envelopes, were discovered among the mail, as our
last mail-bag was prepared for the shore, and as a good deal of
damage may be done in five days, there were probably some
heart-beatings among the fair islanders, as those P. P. Cs. were
perused. There is no lover so susceptible, or so devoted, or
whose heart is so capacious, as that of the young seaman. His
very life upon the sea is a poem, and his habitual absence from
the sex prepares him to see loveliness in every female form.

Though it was night when we emerged from the harbor, and
when we ought to have met with the blandest and gentlest of
land breezes, laden with the perfume of shrub and flower, we
passed at once into a heavy head sea, with a stiff north-easter
blowing. With yards pointed to the wind, and a laboring engine, we steamed along past Point Mayrant light, off which, the

reader may recollect, we discharged the *Ariel,* some weeks
before, and the morning's light found us in the passage be
tween Jamaica and St. Domingo.   The sun rose brightly, the
wind moderated, and the day proved to be very fine.

My first duty, after the usual morning's muster at quarters,
was to hold a court of general sessions, for the discharge of
my vagabonds, many of whom, the reader will recollect, were
still in irons; and a beautiful-looking set of fellows they were,
when their irons were removed, and they were brought on
deck for this purpose.   They were now all sober, but the
effects of their late debauches were visible upon the persons
of all of them.   Soiled clothing, blackened eyes, and broken
noses, frowsy, uncombed hair, and matted and disordered
beard, with reddened eyes that looked as if sleep had long
been a stranger to them — these were the principal features.
Poor Jack! how much he is to be pitied!   Cut loose early
from the gentle restraints of home, and brought into contact
with every description of social vice, at an age when it is so
difficult to resist temptation, what wonder is it, that we find
him a grown-up child of nature, subject to no other restraint
than such as the discipline of his ship imposes upon him?

" When wine is in, wit is out," was the proverb I always
acted upon, on occasions similar to the present; that is to say,
when the " wine " had any business to be " in."   I expected,
as a matter of course, when I sent my sailors on shore, " on
liberty," that the result was to be a frolic, and I was always
lenient to the mere concomitants of a frolic; but I never permitted them to abuse or maltreat the inhabitants, or perpetrate
any malicious mischief.   But if they got drunk on board, in
violation of the discipline of the ship, or, in other words, if
the wine had no business to be " in," I considered that the wit
had no business to be " out."   And so I listened to their penitential excuses, one by one, and restored them to duty, retaining one or two of the greatest culprits for trial by court-martial,
as an example to the rest.   Having disposed of the other cases,
I turned to Tom Bowse and Bill Bower, the heroes of the
moonlight-chase, and said to them, " And so you are a pretty
set of fellows; you not only tried to desert your ship and flag,
but you endeavored to commit murder, in your attempt to

escape!" "Murder!" replied Bowse, with a start of horror, that I could see was entirely honest, "we never thought of such a thing, sir; them Jamaica niggers, they take to the water as natural as South-Sea Islanders, and there's no such thing as drowning them, sir." "That was it, your honor," now put in Bowse; "it was only a bit of a joke, you see, sir, played upon the officer of the cutter. We knew he'd stop to pick 'em up, and so give us the weathergauge of him." "That may do very well for the murder," I now rejoined, "but what about the desertion?" "Nary-a-bit of it, your honor," again replied Bowse; "we only meant to have another bit of a frolic, and come back all in good time, before the ship sailed." "Just so," added Bower; "the fact is, your honor, we were hardly responsible for what we did that night; for we had a small drop aboard, and then the moon was so bright, and Moll Riggs she had sent us such a kind message!" The moonlight and Moll clinched the argument, and turning to the master-at-arms, with an ill-suppressed smile, I directed him to turn the prisoners loose.

I had scarcely gotten through with this jail-delivery, before the cry of "sail ho!" rang out upon the clear morning air, from the mast-head. There was no necessity to alter our course, for the sail was nearly ahead. In an hour more, a very pretty, newly-painted bark, with her sails flapping idly in the calm which was now prevailing, arose to view from the deck. She had the usual Yankee ear-marks, tapering masts and cotton sails, and we felt sure of another prize. We showed her the United States colors as we approached, and a very bright "old flag" soon afterward ascended to her peak, drooping despondently for want of wind to blow it out. The cat did not torture the mouse long, for we soon changed flags, and gave the master of the doomed ship the same satisfaction that Jacob Faithful received, when he found his missing son's shirt in the maw of the shark—the satisfaction of being put out of doubt, and knowing that his ship would be burned. The prize proved, upon being boarded, to be the *Golden Rule*, from New York, for Aspinwall. She belonged to the Atlantic and Pacific Steamship Company, and was filled with an assorted cargo—having on board, among other things, masts, and a complete set of rigging for the United States brig *Bainbridge,* which had recently had everything swept by the board, in a gale at Aspinwall.

Judging from the bills of lading found on board, some small portions of the cargo appeared to be neutral, but there being no sworn evidence to vouch for the fact, in the way of Consular, or other certificates, I applied the well-known rule of prize law to the case, viz., that everything found on board an enemy's ship is presumed to belong to the enemy, until the contrary is shown by proper evidence; and at about six P. M. applied the torch. The islands of St. Domingo and Jamaica were both sufficiently near for their inhabitants to witness the splendid bonfire, which lighted up the heavens far and near, soon after dark. A looker-on upon that conflagration would have seen a beautiful picture, for besides the burning ship, there were the two islands mentioned, sleeping in the dreamy moonlight, on the calm bosom of a tropical sea, and the rakish-looking "British Pirate" steaming in for the land, with every spar, and line of cordage brought out in bold relief, by the bright flame—nay, with the very "pirates" themselves visible, handling the boxes, and bales of merchandise, which they had "robbed" from this innocent Yankee, whose countrymen at home were engaged in the Christain occupation of burning our houses and desolating our fields.

One of the pleasant recollections connected with the picture, was that I had tied up for a while longer, one of the enemy's gun-brigs, for want of an outfit. It must have been some months before the Bainbridge put to sea. There was another good act performed. Lots of patent medicines, with which the enemy was about inundating the South American coast, for the benefit of the livers of their fellow-democrats, were consigned to the flames. The reader had an opportunity to observe, when we captured the *Dunkirk,* how zealously our pious brethren of the North were looking out for the religion, and morals of the Portuguese, *in a sly way.* He now sees what a regard they have for the health of the atrabilious South Americans. Both operations *paid,* of course, and whether it was a tract, or a pill that was sold, could make but little difference to the manufacturers of the merchandise.

We steamed along the coast, at a distance of seven or eight miles, the remainder of that night without further adventure; and the next morning dawned clear, with a slight change of programme as to weather. There were clouds hurrying past us, wetting our jackets, now, and then, without interrupting the sunshine, and a stiff northeaster blowing. This was a head-wind, and we labored against it all day, with diminished speed. At three P. M. we made the remarkable island, or rather, mountain of rock, called in the beautiful Spanish, Alta Vela, or Tall Sail, from its resemblance to a ship under sail, at a distance. It rises, at a distance of ten or twelve miles from the main island of St. Domingo, with almost perpendicular sides, to the height of several hundred feet, and affords a foothold for no living creature, but the sea-gull, the gannet, and other water-fowl. Soon after nightfall, we boarded a Spanish brig from Montevideo, bound for Havana; and at eleven P. M., Alta Vela bearing north, and being distant from us, about five miles, we hove to, with a shot, another sail, that was running down the coast. She was a rakish-looking hermaphrodite brig, and in the bright moonlight looked Yankee. The report of our heavy gun, reverberated by a hundred echoes from Alta Vela, had a magical effect upon the little craft. Flying like a sea-gull before a gale only a moment before, she became, in an instant, like the same sea-gull with its wings folded, and riding upon the wave, without other motion than such as the wave gave it. Ranging within a convenient distance, we lowered, and sent a boat on board of her. She proved to be American, as we had suspected. She was the *Chastelaine* of Boston, last from the island of Guadeloupe, whither she had been to deliver a cargo of staves, and was now on her way to Cienfuegos, in the island of Cuba, in quest of sugar and rum for the Boston folks. We applied the torch to her, lighting up the sea-girt walls of Alta Vela with the unusual spectacle of a burning ship, and disturbing the slumber of the sea-gulls and gannets for the balance of the night.

The next morning found us still steaming to the eastward, along the Haytian coast. Having now the crews of two ships on board, as prisoners, I hauled in closer to the coast, with the intention of running into the old town of St. Domingo, and landing them. We got sight of this old city early in the afternoon, and at about four P. M. ran in and anchored. The anchorage is an open roadstead, formed by the *debouchement* of the picturesque little river Ozama, which seems to have burst through the rocky barrier of the coast, to find its way to the sea. We found but two vessels anchored here—one of them being a New York brig, recently put under English colors. She had a "bran-new" English ensign flying. Admiral Milne having failed to respond to the frantic cries of the New York "Commercial Advertiser," to protect the Yankee flag, the Yankee ship-owners, with many loathings and contortions, were at last forced to gulp the English flag. There was no other way of coaxing England to protect them. Being in a neutral port, I had no opportunity, of course, of testing the verity of this "cross of St. George," as the Yankees were fond of calling the hated emblem of England—hated, but hugged at the same time, for the protection which it gave ship and cargo.

It will be recollected that, at the time of my visit, Spain had repossessed herself of the eastern, or Dominican end of the island of St. Domingo; and a Spanish naval commander now came on board to visit me. I had no difficulty in arranging with him for the landing of my prisoners. I sent them to the guard-ship, and he sent them thence to the shore. This done, and arrangements being made for some fresh provisions and other refreshments, to be sent off to the crew in the morning, I landed for a stroll, on this most classical of all American soil.

The old city of St. Domingo! How many recollections does it not call up! It was a large and flourishing city a hundred years before that pestiferous little craft, called the *Mayflower*, brought over the cockatrice's egg that hatched out the Puritan. It was mentioned, incidentally, as the reader may remember, whilst we were running down the north side of the island, on our way to catch Mr. Vanderbilt's California steamer, that the little town of Isabella, on that side of the island, was the first city founded in the New World; and that the new settlement was soon broken up, and transferred to the city of St. Domingo. The latter city grew apace, and flourished, and was, for many years, the chief seat of the Spanish empire in the

New World. It is, to-day, in its ruins, the most interesting city in all the Americas. Columbus himself lived here, and hither his remains were brought from Spain, and reposed for many years, until they were transferred to Cuba, with great pomp and ceremony. The names of Las Casas, Diego Columbus, the son and successor of the admiral, Oviedo, Hernando Cortez, and a host of others, are bound up in its history. The latter, the renowned conqueror of Mexico, was for several years a notary in an adjoining province.

We have not much time to spare, reader, as the *Alabama* will be on the wing, again, with the morning's light, but I cannot forbear pointing out to you two of the principal ruins of this famous old city. One of them is the Dominican Convent, and the other the *Palacio*, or residence of Diego Columbus. The old city being named in honor of St. Dominic, great pains were evidently bestowed upon the church and convent that were to bear his name; and so substantially was the former built, that it stands entire, and is still used as a place of worship, after the lapse of three hundred and fifty years. The altars are all standing, though faded and worm-eaten, and see! there is a lamp still burning before the altar of the Holy Eucharist. That lamp was lighted in the days of Columbus, and has been burning continuously ever since! Observe these marble slabs over which we are walking. The entire floor is paved with them. They are the tombstones of the dead, that were distinguished in their day, but who have long since been forgotten. Here is a date of 1532, on one of them. It is much defaced and worn by the footsteps of the generations that have passed over it, but we can see by the mitre and crozier, that have been sculptured on it, in *bas-relief*, that the remains of a bishop lie beneath. His name? We cannot make it out. The record of a bishop, carved upon the enduring marble, and placed upon the floor of his own cathedral, has been lost. What a sermon is here in this stone! Raise your eyes now from the floor, and cast them on the wall opposite. In that niche, in the great cathedral wall, sang the choir of ancient days. These vaulted roofs have resounded with music from the lips of many generations of beauties, that have faded like the butterfly of the field, leaving no more trace of their

names and lineage than that little wanderer of an hour. There
stands the silent organ, whose last note was sounded a century
or more ago, with its gilding all tarnished, its stately carving
tumbled down and lying in debris at its feet, and the bat and
the spider building their nests in the cylinders that once mim-
icked the thunder, and sent thrills of devotion through the
hearts of the multitude. There are remains of frescoes on the
walls, but the damp and the mildew, in this humid climate,
have so effectually performed their office, that the bright
colors have disappeared, and only a dim outline of their design
is visible.

Let us step over from the cathedral, to the conventual portion of the massive block. The walls, as you see, are extensive, and are standing, in a sufficient state of preservation, to
enable us to trace out the ground-plan, and reconstruct, in
imagination, the ancient edifice. Its design is that of a hollow
square, after the fashion prevalent in Spain. On all four sides
of the square are arrayed the cells of the monks, the colon-
nades in front of which are still standing. In the centre of
the square, occupying the space, which, in a private house,
would have been appropriated to a *jet d'eau,* and flowers in
vases, is an oblong hall, connected at either end with the main
building. This was the refectory of the ancient establishment.
What scenes does not the very sight of this refectory present
to the imagination? We see the table spread, with its naked
board, humble service, and still more humble food; we hear
the dinner-signal sound; and we see long lines of bearded and
hooded monks, with crosses and beads pendent from their
girdles, enter, and seat themselves to partake of the wonted
refreshment. We hear the subdued hum of many voices—
the quiet joke, and half-suppressed merriment. There, at the
head of the board, sits the venerable abbot, whilst the chaplain
reads his Latin text, from his stand, during the repast. Let
now the years begin to roll by. We shall miss, first one
familiar face from the humble board, and then another, until
finally they all disappear, being carried away, one by one, to
their silent tombs! The abbots repose beneath those marble
slabs in the cathedral that we so lately wandered over, with
lightened footfall, and subdued breath; but the brothers are

carried to the common burial-ground of the order, in the out-skirts of the town. New generations enter, occupy the same seats, go through the same routine of convent life, and in turn disappear, to give place to newer comers still; and thus is ever swollen the holocaust of the mighty dead! "What is man, O Lord! that thou shouldst be mindful of him?"

> "The dead — the honored dead are here —
>   For whom, behind the sable bier,
>   Through many a long-forgotten year,
>   Forgotten crowds have come,
>   With solemn step and falling tear,
>   Bearing their brethren home.
>
> "Beneath these boughs, athwart this grass,
>   I see a dark and moving mass,
>   Like Banquo's shades across the glass,
>   By wizard hands displayed;
>   Stand back, and let these hearses pass,
>   Along the trampled glade."

The Convent of St. Dominic being situated in the southern part of the old city, in the angle formed by the river Ozama, and the sea, observe what a delightful sea-breeze meets us, as we emerge from the ruined refectory. Let us pause a while, to lift our hats, from our heated brows, and refresh ourselves, while we listen to the unceasing roar of the surf, as it beats against the rocky cliff below, and throws its spray half-way to our feet. What a charming view we have of the sea, as it lies in its blue expanse, dotted here and there with a sail; and of the coasts of the island east and west of us — those blackened, rock-bound shores that seem hoary with age, and so much in unison with the train of thought we have been pursuing.

There are but three crafts anchored in the roadstead, where formerly fleets used to lie. Of two of these, we have already spoken. The third is the *Alabama*. There is a little current setting out of the river, and she lies, in consequence, broadside to the sea, which is setting in to the beach. She is rolling gently to this sea, displaying every now and then, bright streaks of the copper on her bottom. She is full of men, and a strange flag is flying from her peak — not only strange to the dead generations of whom we have been speaking, but new even to our own times and history. It is the flag of a nation which has just risen above the horizon, and is but repeating the history of the world. The oppressed has struggled against the oppressor since time began. The struggle is going on still. It will go on forever, for the nature of man will always be the same. The cockatrice's egg has been hatched, and swarms of the Puritan have come forth to overrun the fair fields of the South that they may possess them; just as the wild Germans overran the plains of Italy centuries before.

But away with such thoughts for the present. We came on shore to get rid of them. They madden the brain, and quicken the pulse. The little craft, with the strange flag, has borne her captain hither, on a pilgrimage to the shrine of the great discoverer, whose history may be written in a single couplet.

> "A Castilla, y Leon
> Nuevo Mundo, dio Colon."

On her way hither, her keel has crossed the very track of the three little vessels from Palos—two of them mere open caravels—that first ventured across the vast Atlantic; and now her commander is standing where the great admiral himself once stood—on the very theatre of his early glory. And alas! for Spain, on the theatre of his shame, or rather of her shame, too; for there stands the fortress still, in which are exhibited to the curious spectator the rings in the solid masonry of the wall, to which Columbus was chained!

A short walk will take us to the ruins of the palace of Diego Columbus. We must ascend the river a few hundred yards. Here it is, a little below the port of the present day. When built it stood alone, and we may remember that the townspeople complained of it, on this account—saying that it was intended as a fortress, to keep them in subjection. It is now surrounded, as you see, by the ruins of many houses. If you have read Oviedo's description of it, you are disappointed in its appearance; for that historian tells us, that "no man in Spain had a house to compare with it." Its form is that of two quadrangles connected by a colonnade, but it, by no means, comes up to the modern idea of a palace. The roof has entirely disappeared, and the quadrangles are mere shells filled with the accumulating debris of centuries, amid which

large forest-trees have taken root and are flourishing. It was
built of solid and substantial blocks of stone, and in any other
country but the tropics, would have scarcely shown signs of
age in three centuries. But here the fierce rays of a perpendicular sun, the torrents of rain in the wet season, and the
occasional hurricanes and earthquakes, that desolate and destroy everything in their path, soon beat down the stanchest
buildings — the very blocks of granite being disintegrated, by
the alternate rain and sunshine, and crumbling away beneath
their influence. It is situated on a rising ground, commanding a fine view of the sea, and the surrounding country. It
is surrounded by walls and battlements, but the most imposing
feature about it, must have been the approach to it from the
city — the visitor passing through a wide avenue of shade-
trees, and gaining admission to it by a majestic flight of stone
steps. The shade-trees have disappeared, and the stone steps
have been removed to be worked up into other buildings.

We have called this house, the palace of Diego Columbus,
but it must have been constructed either by his father, the
admiral, or his uncle Bartholomew, the *Adelantado*, as we read
that when Diego came out, after his father's death, to assume
the viceroyalty, he found it ready built at his hand. Its
blackened walls and dirt-filled saloons, now in the midst of a
squalid purlieu of the modern city, must have witnessed many
a scene of revelry in its day, as Oviedo tells us, that when the
young admiral was restored to the honors and command of
his father, he brought out to his new government, with him,
some of the most elegant young women of Spain, as a sort of
maids of honor to his own beautiful young wife — the mar-
riage portions of all of whom he undertook to provide. And
that in due time these young women were all happily bestowed upon gallant knights and wealthy planters.

There, now, reader, we have taken a stroll through the
classical old city of St. Domingo — a piece of good fortune,
which falls to the lot of very few. Its romantic history seems
to have been forgotten; it has fallen into the hands of a mongrel race of blacks and whites, and is rarely visited for any
other purpose than that of trade. The negro and the mulatto
in this oldest of American cities are thought rather more of

than the white man, and the Yankee skipper finds in it, a con
genial mart, in which to vend his cheese and his codfish, and
distribute his tracts—political and moral—and put forth his
patent medicines!

We did not get under way, the next morning, until eight
o'clock, as the supplies from the butchers and fruiterers could
not be gotten on board at an earlier hour.   Bartelli came off
from the market, loaded as usual, bringing with him a bunch of
wild pigeons, very similar to those found in our forests, and some
excellent cigars.   The flavor of the latter is not quite equal to
those of the Havana, but they are mild and pleasant smokers.
He brought off, also, a specimen of the Haytian paper money,
worth five cents on the dollar.   Like the American greenback,
it is the offshoot of revolution and political corruption.

As eight o'clock struck, turning out of the ship the motley
crowd of negroes and mulattoes who had come off to trade
with the sailors, we tripped our anchor, and turning the ship's
head again to the eastward, gave her the steam.   The day was
fine, and the sea smooth, and we had a picturesque run along
the Haytian coast, for the rest of the day.   The coast is generally clean, what few dangers there are being all visible.
The only sails sighted were fishing-boats and small coasters
laden with farm produce, running down to St. Domingo for a
market.   At times a number of these were in sight, and the
effect was very pleasing.   The coasts of Hayti abound in fish,
and as there is a succession of fruits all the year round, it is
the paradise of the negro.   A canoe and a fishing-line, or cast-
net, and a few plantain and mango-trees supply his table; and
two or three times a year, he cuts a mahogany log, and floats
it down the little mountain streams, to the coast, where he sells
it for paper money enough to buy him a few yards of cotton
cloth, or calico.   *Voila tout!*

We entered the Mona Passage at half-past eight P. M.   It
was unguarded as before.   During the night, we let our steam
go down, to give the engineer an opportunity of screwing up
the cylinder-head.   Under way again before daylight.   The
weather continued fine, and we began again to fall in with
sails.   They were all neutral, however.   We spoke a Spanish
schooner, among the rest, and gave her the longitude.   As

soon as we had well cleared the passage, we banked fires, and lowering the propeller, put the ship under sail. On Sunday, February 1st, we had our first muster since leaving Jamaica. We had been out now a week, and in that time I had gotten my crew straightened up again. The rum had been pretty well worked out of them; most of the black rings around the eyes had disappeared, and beards had been trimmed, and heads combed. The court-martial which had been trying the few culprits, that had been retained for trial, had gotten through its labors, and been dissolved, and Jack, as he answered to his name, and walked around the capstan, was "himself again," in all the glory of white "ducks," polished shoes, straw hats, and streaming ribbons. No more than two or three desertions had occurred, out of the whole crew, and this was very gratifying.

The next day, we had an alarm of fire on board. It was near twelve o'clock. I happened to be standing on the horse-block, at the time, observing the sun for latitude, when suddenly I heard a confusion of voices below, and simultaneously the officer of the deck, with evident alarm depicted in his countenance, came running to me, and said, "The ship is on fire, sir!" This is an alarm that always startles the seaman. The "fire-bell in the night" is sufficiently alarming to the landsman, but the cry of fire at sea imports a matter of life and death—especially in a ship of war, whose boats are always insufficient to carry off her crew, and whose magazine and shell-rooms are filled with powder, and the loaded missiles of death. The fire-bell on board a ship of war, whose crew is always organized as a fire company, points out the duty of every officer and man in such an emergency. The first thing to be done is to "beat to quarters," and accordingly I gave this order to the officer; but before the drummer could brace his drum for the operation, it was announced that all danger had disappeared. When we had a little leisure to look into the facts, it appeared, that the alarm had arisen from the carelessness of the "captain of the hold," who, in violation of the orders of the ship, had taken a naked light below with him, into the spirit-room, to pump off the grog by. The candle had ignited some of the escaping gas, but the flame was suppressed almost immediately. The captain of the hold, who is a petty officer, paid the penalty of his disobedience, by being dismissed from his office; and in half an hour, the thing was forgotten.

Since leaving the Mona Passage, we had been steering about N. N. W., or as near north as the trade-wind would permit us. We expected, as a matter of course, to meet with the usual calms, as we came up with the Tropic of Cancer, but the north-east trade, instead of dying away, as we had expected, hauled to the south-east, and shot us across the calm-belt, with a fine breeze all the way. We carried this wind to the twenty-seventh parallel, when we took, with scarcely any intermission, a fresh north-wester. This does not often happen in the experience of the navigator, as the reader has seen, when he has before been crossing the calm-belts with us.

On the 3d of February, we made our first capture since leaving St. Domingo. It was the schooner *Palmetto*, bound from New York to St. John's, in the island of Porto Rico. We gave chase to her, soon after breakfast, and came up with her about half-past one P. M. It was a fair trial of heels, with a fine breeze and a smooth sea; both vessels being on a wind; and it was beautiful to see how the *Alabama* performed her task, working up into the wind's eye, and overhauling her enemy, with the ease of a trained courser coming up with a saddle-nag. There was no attempt to cover the cargo of the *Palmetto*. The enemy merchants seemed to have come to the conclusion, that it was no longer of any use to prepare bogus certificates, and that they might as well let their cargoes run the chances of war, without them. Upon examination of the papers of the schooner, it appeared that the cargo was shipped by the Spanish house of Harques & Maseras, domiciled, and doing business in New York, to Vincent Brothers, in San Juan, Porto Rico, on joint account; the shippers owning one third, and the consignee two thirds. The case came, therefore, under the rule applied in a former case, viz., that when partners reside, some in a belligerent, and some in a neutral country, the property of all of them, which has any connection with the house in the belligerent country, is liable to confiscation. (3 *Phillimore*, 605, and 1 *Robinson*, 1, 14, 19. Also, *The Susa, ib.* 255.) Getting on board from the *Palmetto*, such articles of provisions—and she was chiefly provision-laden—as we needed, we applied the torch to her about sunset, and filled away, and made sail.

The next afternoon we sighted a sail on our weather-bow, close hauled, like ourselves, and continued to gain upon her, until night shut her out from view, when we discontinued the chase. We were satisfied from her appearance, that she was neutral, or we should, probably, have expended a little steam upon her. At night the weather set in thick, and the wind blew so fresh from the north-east, that we took a single reef in the topsails. This bad weather continued for the next two or three days, reducing us, a part of the time, to close reefs. The reader is probably aware, that a ship bound from the West Indies to the coast of Brazil, is compelled to run up into the "variables," and make sufficient easting, to enable her to weather Cape St. Roque. This is what the *Alabama* is now doing—working her way to the eastward, on the parallel of about 30°. We observed on the 20th of February, in latitude 28° 32′; the longitude being 45° 05′.

The next day, the weather being very fine, with the wind light from the southward and eastward, a sail was descried from aloft, and soon afterward another, and another, until four were seen. We gave chase to the first sail announced; standing to the eastward, in pursuit of her, for an hour or two, but she being a long distance ahead, and to windward, and the chase being likely, in consequence, to be long, and to draw us away from the other three sail, besides, we abandoned it, and gave chase to two of the latter. These were fine, tall ships, under a cloud of canvas, steering, one to the eastward, and the other to the westward. Being quite sure that they were Americans, and the wind falling light, we got up steam for the chase. Coming up with the eastward-bound ship, we hove her to, but not until we had thrown a couple of shot at her, in succession—the latter whizzing over the master's head on the quarter-deck. She was evidently endeavoring to draw us after her, as far to the eastward as possible, to give her consort, with whom she had spoken, and who was running, as the reader has seen, to the westward, an opportunity to escape. Throwing a boat's crew hastily on board of her, and directing the prize-master to follow us, we now wheeled in pursuit of the other fugitive. The latter was, by this time, fifteen miles distant — being hull down — and was running before the wind with studding sails, "alow and aloft." Fortunately for the *Alabama*, as before remarked, the wind was light, or the chase might have put darkness between us, before we came up with her. As it was, it was three P. M. before we overhauled her, and we had run our other prize nearly out of sight. She was less obstinate than her consort, and shortened sail, and hove to, at the first gun, hoisting the United States colors at her peak. She proved to be the bark *Olive Jane*, of New York, from Bordeaux, bound to New York, with an assorted cargo of French wines, and brandies, canned meats, fruits, and other delicacies. There was no attempt to cover the cargo. There were a great many shippers. Some few of these had consigned their goods to their own order, but most of the consignments were to New York houses. It is possible that some of the consignments, "to order," really belonged to French owners, but if so, I was relieved from the necessity of making the investigation, by the carelessness of the owners themselves, who had taken no pains to protect their property, by proper documentary evidence of its neutral character. In the absence of sworn proof, as before remarked, the rule of law is imperative, that all property found on board of an enemy's ship, is presumed to belong to the enemy. I acted upon this presumption, and set fire to the *Olive Jane*. What a splendid libation was here to old Neptune! I did not permit so much as a bottle of brandy, or a basket of champagne to be brought on board the *Alabama*, though, I doubt not, the throats of some of my vagabonds, who had so recently cooled off, from the big frolic they had had in Jamaica, were as dry as powder-horns. There were the richest of olives, and *patés de fois gras*, going to tickle the palates of the New York shoddyites, and other *nouveau-riche* plebeians, destroyed in that terrible conflagration. I should have permitted Bartelli, and the other stewards to have a short run among these delicacies, but for the wine and the brandy. A Fouché could not have prevented the boats' crews from smuggling some of it on board, and then I might have had another Martinique grog-watering on my hands.

Amid the crackling of flames, the bursting of brandy casks, the shrivelling of sails, as they were touched by the fire, and the tumbling of the lighter spars of the *Olive Jane* from aloft, we turned our head to the eastward again, and rejoined our first prize, coming up with her just as the shades of evening were closing in. I had now a little leisure to look into *her* character. She, like the *Olive Jane*, had shown me the "old flag," and that, of course, had set at rest all doubts as to the nationality of the ship. There was as little doubt, as soon appeared, about the cargo. The ship was the *Golden Eagle*, and I had overhauled her near the termination of a long voyage. She had sailed from San Francisco, in ballast, for Howland's Island, in the Pacific; a guano island of which some adventurous Yankees had taken possession. There she had taken in a cargo of guano, for Cork and a market; the guano being owned by, and consigned to the order of the American Guano Company. This ship had buffeted the gales of the frozen latitudes of Cape Horn, threaded her pathway among its icebergs, been parched with the heats of the tropic, and drenched with the rains of the equator, to fall into the hands of her enemy, only a few hundred miles from her port. But such is the fortune of war. It seemed a pity, too, to destroy so large a cargo of a fertilizer, that would else have made fields stagger under a wealth of grain. But those fields would be the fields of the enemy; or if it did not fertilize his fields, its sale would pour a stream of gold into his coffers; and it was my business upon the high seas, to cut off, or dry up this stream of gold. The torch followed the examination of the papers. The reader may, perhaps, by this time have remarked, how fond the Yankees had become of the qualifying adjective, "golden," as a prefix to the names of their ships. I had burned the *Golden Rocket*, the *Golden Rule*, and the *Golden Eagle*.

We were now in latitude 30°, and longitude 40°, and if the curious reader will refer to a map, or chart of the North Atlantic Ocean, he will see that we are on the charmed "crossing," leading to the coast of Brazil. By "crossing" is meant the point at which the ship's course crosses a given parallel of latitude. We must not, for instance, cross the thirtieth parallel, going southward, until we have reached a certain meridian

—say that of 40° W. If we do, the north-east trade-wind will pinch us, and perhaps prevent us from weathering Cape St. Roque.

And when we reach the equator, there is another crossing recommended to the mariner, as being most appropriate to his purpose. Thus it is, that the roads upon the sea have been blazed out, as it were — the blazes not being exactly cut upon the forest-trees, but upon parallels and meridians. The chief blazer of these roads, is an American, of whom all Americans should be proud — Captain Maury, before mentioned in these pages. He has so effectually performed his task, in his "Wind and Current Charts," that there is little left to be desired. The most unscientific and practical navigator, may, by the aid of these charts, find the road he is in quest of. Maury has been, in an eminent degree, the benefactor of the very men who became most abusive of him, when they found that he, like other Southern statesmen — for he is a statesman as well as sailor — was obliged to preserve his self-respect, by spitting upon the "old flag." He has saved every Yankee ship, by shortening her route, on every distant voyage she makes, thousands of dollars. The greedy ship-owners pocket the dollars, and abuse the philosopher.*

---

* "Now let us make a calculation of the annual saving to the commerce of the United States, effected by these charts, and sailing directions. According to Mr. Maury, the average freight from the United States to Rio Janeiro, is 17.7 cents per ton, per day ; to Australia, 20 cents ; to California, 20 cents. The mean of this is a little over 19 cents per ton, per day ; but to be within the mark, we will take it at 15 cents, and include all the ports of South America, China, and the East Indies. The 'Sailing Directions' have shortened the passage to California, thirty days ; to Australia, twenty days ; and to Rio Janeiro, ten days. The mean of this is twenty, but we will take it at fifteen, and also include the above-named ports of South America, China, and the East Indies. We estimate the tonnage of the United States, engaged in trade with these places, at 1,000,000 tons per annum. With these data, we see that there has been effected, a saving for each one of those tons, of 15 cents per day, for a period of fifteen days, which will give an aggregate of $2,250,000 saved per annum. This is on the outward voyage alone, and the tonnage trading with all other parts of the world is also left out of the calculation. Take these into consideration, and also the fact that there is a vast amount of foreign tonnage, trading between those places and the United States, and it will be seen that the annual sum saved will swell to an enormous amount."—*Hunt's Merchants' Magazine, May*, 1854.

CHAPTER XLII.

THE "CROSSING" OF THE THIRTIETH PARALLEL — THE TOLL-GATE UPON THE SEA — HOW THE TRAVELLERS PASS ALONG THE HIGHWAY — CAPTURE OF THE WASHINGTON; THE JOHN A. PARKS; THE BATHIAH THAYER; THE PUNJAUB; THE MORNING STAR; THE KINGFISHER; THE CHARLES HILL; AND THE NORA — CROSSES THE EQUATOR — CAPTURE OF THE LOUISA HATCH — ARRIVAL AT FERNANDO DE NORONHA.

REACHING the blazed road, of which I spoke in the last chapter, I shortened sail, at the crossing mentioned, that I might waylay such of the passengers as chanced to be enemies. There were a great many ships passing, both ways, on this road, some going to the Pacific, or the Far East, and others returning from those distant points; but they were nearly all neutral. The American ships, having, by this time, become thoroughly alarmed, especially since they learned that neither English sealing-wax, nor Admiral Milne could save them, had dodged the highways, as skulkers and thieves are wont to do, and taken to the open fields and by-ways for safety. On the day after the capture of the *Olive Jane* and *Golden Eagle*, the weather being cloudy and rainy, and the wind light, four more sail were seen — all European bound. At eight A. M. we showed the United States colors to one of them, which proved to be a French bark. It now became calm, and we were compelled to get up steam, to overhaul the rest. They lay long distances apart, and we were several hours in passing from one to the other. They were all Englishmen, with various histories and destinations, one of them — a fine frigate-built ship — being a Melbourne and Liverpool packet. We received a paper from her, printed at the anti-podes, but there was not much in it, besides the proceedings of the Australian Parliament, news from the gold-diggings, and the price of wool; in neither of which subjects were we much interested.

On the next day but a solitary passenger came over the road. It was late at night when she made her appearance—there being a bright moon and a brisk breeze. We made sail in chase, and the chase, taking the alarm, gave us a very pretty run for a few hours. We overhauled her, however, at length, and fired the usual blank cartridge, to heave her to. She was an hermaphrodite brig, and might be, for aught we could see, in the uncertain light, American. The gun had no effect. We waited a few minutes for a response, but none coming, we fired again—sending a shot whizzing, this time, over the little craft. Still no response. We were now only a few hundred yards distant. What could the fellow mean? All was as silent on board the chase as death, and not a tack or sheet had been started. We ran now almost on board of her, and hailing her, commanded her to heave to. Great confusion followed. We could hear voices speaking in a foreign tongue, and presently a disorderly array of sails whipping and flapping in the wind, and of yards swinging to and fro, presented itself. At last the little craft managed to come to the wind, and make a halt. She proved to be a Portuguese brig, and the crew had been so alarmed, at being chased and fired at, by night, as to lose all presence of mind, and become incapable of any action what-ever, until they were somewhat reassured, by the near pres-ence of our ship and the sound of our voices. She was bound from Pernambuco to Lisbon, with a cargo of hides and sugar. It was, indeed, something like a ghost-chase, to see the *Ala-bama* coming, in the dead of night after the little craft, with her seven-league boots on, and those awful trysails of hers spread out in the moonlight like so many winding-sheets.

On the day after this adventure, a Dutch bark and an Eng-lish brig came along; and on the same night, we boarded the English four-master, the *Sarah Sands*, from the East Indies for Falmouth. At daylight, the next morning, the look-out at the mast-head began to cry sails, until he reported as many as seven in sight at one time. They were all European bound, and were jogging along, in company, following Maury's blazes, like so many passengers on a highway. The *Alabama* stood like a toll-gate before them, and though we could not take toll of them, as they were all neutral, we made each traveller show us his passport, as he came up. One obstinate fellow — a Hamburger — refused to show us his colors, until he was commanded to do so by a gun. I made it a practice to punish these unmannerly fellows, for their want of civility. On the present occasion, the Hamburger was detained a considerable time, whilst I exercised, at my leisure, my belligerent right of *viséing* his papers. When his travelling companions were some miles ahead of him, I told the surly fellow to pick up his hat and be off.

On the next day, being still in latitude 30°, and longitude 40°, or at the "crossing," an English and an American ship came along. The Englishman saluted us civilly as he passed. He was from the East Indies, laden with silks and wines. But the American, seeing that we were under short sail — though the weather was fine — resting by the wayside, as it were, and remembering that there was a little unpleasantness between the North and South, fought rather shy of us, and endeavored to get out of the way of possible harm. She was a fine, large ship, and the moment she showed an intention not to pass through the toll-gate, we made sail in pursuit. She had heels, but they were not quite as clean as the *Alabama's*, and we came up with her, in the course of two or three hours; she having approached pretty close, before she smelt the rat. She was obstinate, and compelled me to wet the people on her poop, by the spray of a shot, before she would acknowledge that she was beaten. The shower-bath made a stir among the bystanders; there was a running hither and thither, a letting go of sheets and halliards, and pretty soon the main-yard swung aback, and the stars and stripes were seen ascending to the stranger's peak. When the boarding-officer brought the master of the captured ship on board, with his papers, she proved to be the ship *Washington*, of New York, from the Chincha Islands, bound to Antwerp, with a cargo of guano, laden on account of the Peruvian government, and consigned to its agent at Antwerp, for sale. Being unable to destroy the ship, because of the neutral ownership of her cargo, I released her on ransom-bond, sent my prisoners on board of her to be landed, and permitted her to depart. This capture was made on the 27th of February. On the 28th we overhauled two English ships, from the East Indies, homeward bound, and a French ship, from Batavia, for Nantes. The weather continued very fine, and we had had a uniformly high barometer, ever since we had reached the "crossing."

The morning of the 1st of March dawned charmingly, with a very light breeze. The night had been rather dark, and we had been lying-to under topsails. In the darkness of the night, an enemy's ship had approached us unawares. She had been following the blazes, without seeing the toll-gate, and the revelations made by the morning's light, must have startled her; for she found herself within half a mile of an exceedingly saucy-looking gunboat, lying in wait for somebody, or something. It was nearly calm, and she could not help herself if she would. On the other hand, the gunboat was delighted to see a tall ship, whose masts tapered like a lady's fingers, arrayed in the whitest of petticoats — to carry out our figure — and which, from the course she was steering, was evidently just out from Yankee-land, with that mail on board, which we had been anxiously looking for, for several days past. We were in the midst of the scrubbing and cleaning of the morning watch, and to effect the capture, it was not even necessary to lay aside a holy-stone, or a scrubbing-brush. A gun and a Confederate flag, were all that was required to bring the tall ship to a halt, and remove her doubts, if she had had any. She was the *John A. Parks*, of Hallowell, Maine.

The cargo of the *Parks* consisted of white pine lumber which she had taken on board at New York, and she was bound to Montevideo, or Buenos Ayres, as the consignee might elect. There was an affidavit found among her papers, made by one Snyder, before a Mr. Edwards Pierrepont, who appears to have been acting as British Consul, claiming that the cargo was shipped on account of a London house. The real facts of the case, however, as gathered from the correspondence, and the testimony of the master, were, that one Davidson, a lumber dealer in New York had chartered the ship, and shipped the lumber, in the usual course of his business, to the parties in Montevideo; that he had paid most of the freight, in advance, and insured himself against the *war risk*, both upon the cargo and the freight. The manner in which this case was "put up," in the papers, was an improvement upon some others I had examined. The New York merchants were evidently becoming expert in the preparation of bogus certificates. It was no longer merely stated that the property belonged to "neutral owners," but the owners themselves were named. In short, the certificate found on board the *Parks* was in due form, but unfortunately for the parties who contrived the clever little plot, the master forgot to throw overboard his letter-bag, and among the letters found in that bag, was one written by Davidson, giving instructions to the consignees, in which the following expressions occur: "The cargo of the *John A. Parks*, I shall have certified to, by the British Consul, as the property of British subjects. You will find it a very good cargo, and should command the highest prices." By the time that I had finished the examination of the case, Bartelli announced breakfast, and I invited my Hallowell friend to take a cup of coffee with me, telling him, at the same time, that I should burn his ship. As well as I recollect, he declined the coffee, but I am quite certain that the ship was burned. The carpenter of the *Alabama* was thrown into ecstasies by this capture. All the other departments of the ship had been kept well supplied, except his own. The paymaster, who was also commissary, the boatswain, the sailmaker, had all been "plundering" the enemy quite extensively, but no "boards" had come along, until now, for the poor carpenter. Here they were at last, however, and if I had not put some restraint upon my zealous officer of the adze and chisel, I believe he would have converted the *Alabama* into a lumberman.

We received from the *Parks*, sure enough, the mail we had been waiting for. There must have been a barrel-full, and more of newspapers and periodicals, going to the *Montevideans* and *Buenos Ayreans*—many of them in the best of Spanish, and all explaining the "great moral ideas," on which the Southern people were being robbed of their property, and having their throats cut. We gleaned one gratifying piece of intelligence, however, from these papers. "The Pirate *Florida*" had put to sea from Mobile, to assist the "British Pirate," in plundering, and burning the "innocent merchant-ships of the United States, pursuing their peaceful commerce," as Mr. Charles Francis Adams, so often, and so *naively* expressed it to Earl Russell. Whilst the *Parks* was still burning, an English bark passed through the toll-gate, the captain of which was prevailed upon, to take the master of the burning ship, his wife, and two nephews, to London. We were glad, on the poor lady's account, that she was so soon relieved from the discomforts of a small and crowded ship.

The next traveller that came along was the *Bethiah Thayer*, of Rockland, Maine, last from the Chincha Islands, with a cargo of guano for the Peruvian Government. The cargo being properly documented, I put the ship under ransom-bond, and permitted her to pass. It was Sunday; the *Bethiah* was dressed in a new suit of cotton canvas, and looked quite demure and saint-like, while her papers were being examined. I have no doubt if I had questioned her master, that he would have been found to have voted for Breckinridge.

I now resolved to fill away, stand down toward the equator, and hold myself stationary, for a few days, at the "crossing" of that famous great circle. I was far enough to the eastward, to make a free wind of the north-east trade, and we jogged along under topsails, making sail only when it became necessary to chase. We lost our fine weather almost immediately upon leaving the "crossing," and took a series of moderate gales — sometimes, however, reducing us to close reefs — which lasted us for a week or ten days, or until we began to approach the rains and calms of the equator. We met a number of sails on the road, and now and then chased one, but they all proved to be neutral. On the night of the 15th of March, at a few minutes before midnight, the weather being thick and murky, the look-out at the cat-head suddenly cried "sail ho! close aboard;" and in a few minutes a large ship passed us on the opposite tack, within speaking distance. We hailed, but she passed on like a goblin ship, without giving us any reply. She had all sails set, there was no one stirring on board of her, and the only light that was visible, was the one which twinkled in the binnacle. We wore ship with all expedition, shook the reefs out of the topsails, and made sail in pursuit. It took us some minutes to accomplish this, and by the time we were well under way, the stranger was nearly out of sight. Both ships were on a wind, however, and this, as the reader has seen, was the *Alabama's* best point of sailing. Our night-glasses soon began to tell the usual tale. We were overhauling the chase; and at a quarter past three, or a little before dawn, we were near enough to heave her to, with a gun. She proved to be the *Punjaub*, of Boston, from Calcutta for London. Her cargo consisted chiefly of jute and linseed, and was properly certificated as English property. The goods were, besides, of foreign growth, and were going from one English port to another. I released her on ransom-bond, and sent on board of her the prisoners from the last ship burned.

Soon after daylight, we gave chase to another sail in the E. S. E., with which we came up about eight A. M. She was an English ship, from the Mauritius, for Cork. She confirmed our suspicion, that the Yankee ships were avoiding, as a general rule, the beaten tracks, having spoken one of them on the "line," bound to the coast of Brazil, which had travelled as far east as the twenty-third meridian; or about four hundred miles out of her way. We were still standing to the southward, and on the 21st of March we were very near the sun, for while he was crossing the equator, we were in latitude 2° 47' N.; our longitude being 26° W. On that day, the weather is thus recorded in my journal: "Cloudy, with squalls of rain, and the wind shifting, indicating that we have lost the 'trades.' It is pleasant to hear the thunder roll, for the first time in several months, sounding like the voice of an old friend; and the crew seem to enjoy a ducking from the heavy showers — rain having been a rare visitor of late." And on the next day, the following is the record: "Rains, and calms all day; the officers and crew alike, are paddling about the deck in bare feet, and enjoying the pelting of the rain, like young ducks. Three neutrals, in company, bound like ourselves, across the 'line.' They look, at a distance, with their drooping sails flapping idly in the calm, as disconsolate as wet barn-yard fowls at home, on a rainy day."

On the 23d of March, the weather being still as described, and very little change having taken place in our position, we made two more captures; the first, the *Morning Star* of Boston, from Calcutta for London, and the second the whaling schooner *Kingfisher*, of Fairhaven, Massachusetts. The cargo of the *Morning Star* being in the same category as that of the *Punjaub*, we released her also, on ransom-bond. The *Kingfisher* we burned. This adventurous little whaler had a crew of twenty-three persons, all of whom were Portuguese, except the master, and mate, and one or two boat-steerers. We set fire to her just at nightfall, and the conflagration presented a weird-like spectacle on the "line," amid the rumbling of thunder, the shifting, but ever black scenery, of the nimbi, or rain clouds, and the pouring and dashing of torrents of rain. Sometimes the flames would cower beneath a drenching shower, as though they had been subdued, but in a moment afterward, they would shoot up, mast-head high, as brightly and ravenously as before. The oil in her hold kept her burning on the surface of the still sea, until a late hour at night.

On the next day, we boarded, as usual, a number of neutral ships, of different nationalities, some going south, and some going north. We were at the "crossing" of the equator, "blazed" by Maury, and with the main topsail at the mast, were reviewing, as it were, the commerce of the world. We were never out of sight of ships. They were passing, by ones, and twos, and threes, in constant succession, wreathed in rain and mist, and presenting frequently the idea of a funeral procession. The honest traders were all there, except the most honest of them all — the Yankees — and they were a little afraid of the police. Still we managed to catch a rogue now and then.

On the second day after burning the *Kingfisher*, we made two more captures. Late in the afternoon of that day, we descried two large ships approaching us, in company. They came along lovingly, arm-in-arm, as it were, as though in the light airs and calms that were prevailing, they had been having a friendly chat, or one of the masters had been dining on board of the other. They were evidently American ships, and had most likely been having a cosy talk about the war.

The "sainted" Abraham's Emancipation Proclamation was the favorite topic of the day, as we had learned from the mail-bags of the *Parks*, and perchance they had been discussing that; or perhaps the skippers were congratulating themselves upon having escaped the *Alabama;* they probably supposing her to be at the other toll-gate still. Whatever may have been the subject of their discourse, they evidently pricked up their ears, as soon as they saw the *Alabama,* stripped like a gentleman who was taking it coolly, with nothing but her topsails set, and lying across their path. They separated gradually; and quietly, and by stealth, a few more studding-sails were sent up aloft.

It was time now for the *Alabama* to move. Her main yard was swung to the full, sailors might have been seen running up aloft, like so many squirrels, who thought they saw "nuts" ahead, and pretty soon, upon a given signal the top-gallant sails and royals might have been seen fluttering in the breeze, for a moment, and then extending themselves to their respective yard-arms. A whistle or two from the boatswain and his mates, and the trysail sheets are drawn aft, and the *Alabama* has on those seven-league boots which the reader has seen her draw on so often before. A stride or two, and the thing is done. First, the *Charles Hill,* of Boston, shortens sail, and runs up the "old flag," and then the *Nora,* of the same pious city, follows her example. They were both laden with salt, and both from Liverpool. The *Hill* was bound to Montevideo, or Buenos Ayres, and there was no attempt to cover her cargo. The *Nora* was bound to Calcutta, under a charter-party with one W. N. de Mattos. In the bill of lading, the cargo was consigned to order, and on the back of the instrument was the following indorsement: "I hereby certify, that the salt shipped on board the *Nora,* is the property of W. N. de Mattos, of London, and that the said W. N. de Mattos is a British subject, and was so at the time of the shipment." This certificate was signed by one H. E. Folk, and at the bottom of the certificate were the words, "R. C. Gardner, Mayor"—presumed to mean the Mayor of Liverpool.

Here was a more awkward attempt to cover a cargo than any of my Yankee friends of New York or Boston had ever made.

There was very little doubt that the salt was English-owned, but the certificate, I have recited, did not amount even to an *ex parte* affidavit, it not being sworn to.   As a matter of course, I was bound to presume the property to be enemy, it being found, unprotected by any legal evidence, in an enemy's ship. The *Hill* and the *Nora* were, therefore, both consigned to the flames, after we had gotten on board from them such articles as we stood in need of.   We received from the two ships between thirty and forty tons of coal, or about two days' steaming. It took us nearly all the following day to transport it in our small boats, and we did not set fire to the ships until five in the afternoon.   We received, also, half a dozen recruits from them.   I had now quite as many men as I wanted.

Among the papers of the *Hill* was found the following brief letter of instructions from her owner to her master.   It is dated from the good city of Boston, and was written while the ship was lying at that other good city, Philadelphia.   It is addressed to Captain F. Percival, and goes on to say : —

"DEAR SIR : — I have received your several letters from Philadelphia.   As a rebel privateer has burned several American ships, it may be as well if you can have your bills of lading indorsed as English property, and have your cargo certified to by the British Consul."

Such nice little missives as these, written from one city of "grand moral ideas," to another city, whose ideas were no less grand or moral, quietly instructing ship-masters to commit perjury, were of great assistance to me, when, in the classical words of the New York "Commercial Advertiser," I had a "Yankee hash" to deal with.

On the 29th of March we crossed the equator.   The event is thus recorded in my journal: "Crossed the equator at five P. M. in the midst of a dense rain-squall, with lowering, black clouds, and the wind from the south-west.   We were in chase of a sail at the time, but lost her in the gloom.   It rained all night, with light airs and calms.   We have experienced a southeasterly current, setting at the rate of a knot and a half the hour, for the last twenty-four-hours."   We made our crossing a little farther to the eastward than usual — 26° — on purpose to counteract the Yankee dodge spoken of a little while back. We now encountered a variety of currents, some setting to the south-east as just mentioned, others to the east, others to the south, until finally we fell in with the great equatorial current setting to the westward.

The study of the phenomena of the currents, is one of the most interesting that can engage the attention of the marine philosopher. We have already had occasion to explain the circulation of the atmosphere—how the wind "cometh and goeth," not at random, but in obedience to certain well-defined natural laws. The circulation of the sea is no less regular than that of the atmosphere, and has equally important offices to perform. If the sea were a stagnant mass of waters, some portions of the earth which now enjoy temperate climates, and teem with millions of population in the enjoyment of an abundant fauna and flora, would be almost uninhabitable because of the extreme cold. Some portions of the sea would dry up, and become beds of salt, and others again would, from the superabundance of precipitation, become fresh, or nearly so. In short, there would be a general disturbance of the harmonies of creation. To obviate this, and to put the sea in motion, various agencies have been set at work by the great Architect; chief among which is the unequal distribution of heat over the earth's surface. We have already called the sun the Father of the Winds; he is equally the father of the currents. The warm water of the equator is constantly flowing off to the poles, and the cold water of the poles flowing back, as undercurrents, to the equator. This flow is not directly north, or directly south, but by a variety of tortuous channels. The different depths of the ocean, the obstructions of islands, and continents, clouds and sunshine, and a great many other agencies, combine to give this tortuosity and seeming irregularity to the currents.

Let us take an example. The *Alabama* has just experienced a south-east current in a locality where the current sets, as a general rule, to the westward. How are we to account for this? It may be due to a variety of causes, all working in harmony, however, with the general design. In the first place, it may be a counter-current going to fill the place left vacant by some other current; for, as a matter of course, when a given quantity of water flows away from a place, the same quantity must flow back to it. Or it may be a principal, and not an accessory current, set in motion, say by heat. Let us see how easily this may be accomplished. Suppose a dense canopy of clouds to overshadow some considerable space of the sea, for a day, or it may be, for a few hours only. Whilst the rays of the sun are shut out from this space, they are pouring down their heat with tropical fervor, say to the south of this cloud-bank. Under the cloud-bank the water is cooling, beyond the bank it is being heated Under the bank evaporation has ceased almost altogether, beyond the bank it is going on at the rate of about an inch in twenty-four hours. Here are powerful agencies at work, changing both the temperature, and specific gravity of the waters.

Waters to be at rest must have the same temperature and specific gravity. These waters therefore cannot remain at rest, and a current is the consequence. To-morrow, perhaps, the process will be reversed, the cloud and the sunshine changing places, and the current flowing in a contrary direction. These are local disturbances of the system of oceanic circulation — little venous derangements, as it were, the great arterial system not being materially affected by them.

There are other exceedingly beautiful agencies at work, on a smaller scale, to disturb the oceanic equilibrium, and set the waters in motion. It has puzzled philosophers to account for the saltness of the sea. Whatever may be its cause, it plays a very important part in giving vitality to its circulation. If sea-water were fresh, evaporation would not produce any change in its specific gravity. One element of motion, therefore, would be wanted. But being salt, and the salts not being taken up by the thirsty air, in the process of evaporation, every rain-drop that is withdrawn from it, helps to put the currents in motion.

But these are surface operations; let us dive beneath the surface, and witness some of the wonders that are going on in the depths below. We have before shown the reader, the coralline insect, that wonderful little stone-mason of the sea, which, in the hands of Providence, is the architect of islands and continents. The sea-water is the quarry from which this little toiler extracts his tiny blocks of masonry. If the water were fresh, it would not hold the materials in solution, which he needs for his work. But being salt, it has just the materials which he needs.

But how does he affect the currents? the reader will ask. As follows: Every particle of solid matter that he extracts from the sea-water—and he must have limestone to build those islands and continents of which he is the architect—alters its specific gravity. The little globule of water, from which he has just taken the block of stone that would be scarcely visible under a powerful microscope, has become lighter than the surrounding globules, and ascends to the surface. In obedience to the law which we have mentioned, that as much water must flow back to a place, as flows away from it, a globule of water from the surface now descends to take the place of that which has arisen; descends to the little stonemason, that he may rob it, in turn, of the block of stone that it contains. The globules of water thus become the hod-carriers for these little stone-masons, working away, in countless myriads, at the bottom of the sea.

But what becomes of this lighter globule of water, which has arisen to the surface, because it has been deprived of its solid matter? It must flow away somewhere in search of the salts it has lost, for if it remain stationary, in course of time, the sea in its neighborhood will all be deprived of its salts, and there will be no more globules to descend to the little stonemason. But when the globule starts to flow off, a current is established.

The reader may recollect that when we were at the Azores, breaking up that Yankee whaling station, we spoke of the currents, in connection with the whales, and other fishes; how, like "reapers and gleaners," they bore to them the food which was prepared for them in other latitudes. The reader sees, now, how the currents build the coral bank. Every sea-shell, as it secretes the solid matter for its edifice, helps on the movement set on foot by the coral insect.

On the 3d of April, we observed in latitude 2° 11′ S.; our longitude being 26° 02′. The weather was still thick and rainy, and we had fitful gusts of wind, and calms by turns.

During the morning watch, the dense clouds lifted for a while, and showed us a fine, tall ship, steering, like ourselves, to the southward. We immediately made sail in chase. The wind was blowing quite fresh from the south-west, at the time, and we gained very rapidly upon the stranger. At twelve o'clock the wind died away, and the heavy rains being renewed, she was entirely shut out from view. We continued the chase all day; now being sure of her, and now being baffled by the ever-shifting clouds, and changing wind and weather. At length, at five P. M., it being no longer safe to trust to contingencies, as night would set in, in another hour, I sent a whale-boat to board, and halt her, although she was still two miles distant. The boarding was successfully accomplished, and just before dark, we could see the stranger's head turned in our direction. We knew from this circumstance that she was a prize, and hoisting a light, as night set in, to guide the boarding-officer, in an hour or two more she was alongside of us.

The prize proved to be the *Louisa Hatch*, of Rockland, Maine, from Cardiff, with a cargo of the best Welsh coal, for Point-de-Galle, in the island of Ceylon. The bill of lading required the cargo to be delivered to the "*Messageries Imperiales*," steamship company, and there was a certificate on the back of the bill of lading to the effect that the coal belonged to that company, but the certificate was not sworn to by the subscriber. This was tantamount to no evidence at all, and I condemned both ship and cargo as prize of war. Here was quite a windfall — a thousand tons of coal, near the coast of Brazil, where it was worth $17 per ton. But what was I to do with the prize? It would be an interminable job to attempt to supply myself from her, by means of my boats, and hauling the two ships alongside of each other, at sea, was not to be thought of. I was bound to the island of Fernando de Noronha, that being the second rendezvous which I had assigned to my old Scotch collier, the *Agrippina*, and I resolved to take the *Hatch* in, with me, to abide contingencies. If the *Agrippina* should arrive in due time, I could burn the *Hatch*; if not, the *Hatch* would supply her place.

This being determined upon, I sent a prize crew on board the captured ship, and directed the prize-master to keep company with me. We overhauled an English bark, the next day, bound from Lisbon to Rio Janeiro, from which we received some late Portuguese newspapers, of no particular interest; and on the day afterward, we chased what we took certainly to be a Yankee whaling schooner, but which we found, upon coming up with her, to be a Portuguese. The schooner was a capital imitation of the "down East" fore-and-after, but upon being boarded, she not only proved to be foreign built, but her master and crew were all Portuguese, nearly as black as negroes, with a regular set of Portuguese papers. What added considerably to the cheat was, that the little craft had heels, and I was some two or three hours in coming up with her.

The weather was so thick for the next two or three days, that it was necessary to keep the prize very close to me, to prevent losing sight of her. At night I showed her a light from my peak, and we jogged along within speaking distance of each other. Having had no observation for fixing the position of my ship, during the prevalence of this thick weather, and the direction and velocity of the currents being somewhat uncertain, I was quite anxious lest I should drift past the island I was in quest of, and fall upon some of the foul ground lying between it and the coast of Brazil. On the 9th of April, the sun showed himself for an hour or two, near noon, and I got latitude and longitude, and found that we were in the great equatorial current, as I had supposed, setting us about S. W. by W. at the rate of a knot and a half per hour. I now got up steam, and taking the prize in tow, for it was nearly calm, with but a few cats'-paws playing upon the water, made the best of my way toward Fernando de Noronha.

At daylight, the next morning, we made the famous peak, some forty miles distant, and at half-past two P. M. we came to anchor in thirteen fathoms water. The prize, having been cast off as we ran in, anchored near us. The *Agrippina* had not arrived; nor did I ever see her afterward. Captain Bullock had duly dispatched her, but the worthless old Scotch master made it a point not to find me, and having sold his coal in some port or other, I have forgotten where, returned to England with a cock-and-a-bull story, to account for his failure. The fact is, the old fellow had become alarmed lest he should fall into the hands of the Yankees. It was fortunate that I had not burned the *Louisa Hatch*.

CHAPTER XLIII.

FERNANDO DE NORONHA lies not a great way from
Cape St. Roque in Brazil. It forms the western end of a
chain of volcanic islands and deep-sea soundings that extend
some distance along the equator. Earthquakes have been frequently experienced by ships when passing along this chain,
and the charts point out a number of supposed dangers here-
about. Many of these dangers have no real existence, but still
the prudent mariner gives them a wide berth, when sailing
past the localities assigned them. The island of Fernando de
Noronha is evidently of volcanic origin. Its whole appearance indicates that it was thrown from the depths of the sea,
by nature, when in one of her most fearful paroxysms. Its
abrupt and rugged sides of solid rock, rent and torn, and
blackened by the torrents, rise almost perpendicularly from
the waters to the height of several hundred feet.

The famous peak before spoken of, and which the mariner
at sea descries long before the body of the island becomes visible, is a queer freak of nature. It looks as though the giants
had been playing at church-steeples, and had upraised this
immense shaft of granite to mark one of nature's cathedrals.
The illusion is almost perfect. When "land ho!" is first cried
by the look-out at the mast-head, and the glass is applied in

the given direction, the observer is startled at the resemblance. Nor is his surprise diminished, as his ship approaches nearer, and the body of the island begins to make its appearance above the water; for there is the roof of the massive cathedral, to which the steeple belongs! The peak is a mass of solid granite, shot by the earthquake through the solid crust of the mountain, and is almost symmetrical enough to have been shaped by human hands. We lay nearly two weeks at Fernando de Noronha, and I was never tired of gazing upon this wonderful evidence of the power of volcanic forces.

The winds, the rains, and the sunshine have, in the course of ages, disintegrated enough of the surface of this rocky island, to form a rich soil, which is covered with a profusion of tropical vegetation, including forest-trees of considerable size; and a number of small farms, with neat farm-houses, add to the picturesqueness of the scene. Fruits and vegetables, the Indian corn, and the sugar-cane, flourish in great perfection, and a few ponies and horned cattle have been introduced from the main land. Swine, goats, and domestic fowls abound. Fernando de Noronha stands as a great sign-board, as it were, on the principal commercial thoroughfare of the world. Almost all the ships that cross the line, from Europe and America, to the East Indies and Pacific Ocean, and *vice versa*, sight it, for the purpose of taking a new departure from it. The dwellers on its lonely hills look out upon a constant stream of commerce, but they are like prisoners looking out from their prison-windows upon a scene of which they are not a part. A ship rarely ever touches at the island. There is nothing to invite communication. It is too insignificant for traffic, and has no good harbor where a ship could repair damages or refit. It is, besides, a penal colony of Brazil, to which it belongs. It is under the government of an officer of the Brazilian Army, who has a battalion of troops under him, and hither are sent from Rio Janeiro, and the other cities of the empire, all the noted criminals who are condemned to long terms of imprisonment. Very few of the prisoners are kept in close confinement. The island itself is prison enough, and there are no possible means of escape from it. The prisoners are, therefore, permitted to run at large, and mitigate the horrors of their lot by manual labor on the farms, or engage in the mechanic arts.

Our arrival was announced in due form to the Governor, and the paymaster had, besides, at my suggestion, addressed him a letter on the subject of supplies. In the meantime, we hauled the *Louisa Hatch* alongside, and commenced coaling. The next morning a couple of gentlemen visited me, on the part of the Governor, to arrange personally with the paymaster, the matter of supplies, and to welcome me to the island. No objection was made to our bringing in the *Hatch*, or to our receiving coal from her. The state of my diplomatic relations with the Governor was thus so satisfactory, that I invited his ambassadors into the cabin, and summoned Bartelli to provide champagne. A popping of corks, and a mutual clinking of glasses ensued, and when we had resumed conversation and lighted cigars, one of the gentlemen diplomats informed me, in the most easy and *san souciant* manner possible, that he was one of the convicts of the island! He had been sentenced for six years, he said, but had nearly served his term out. He was a German, and spoke very good English. Several of my officers were present, and there was, of course, a casting of glances from one to the other. But Bartelli, who was still standing a few paces in the rear, with a fresh bottle of uncorked champagne in his hand, seemed to be most shocked. My faithful steward felt the honors and dignity of my station much more than I did myself, and it was amusing to see the smile of derision and contempt, with which he wheeled round, and replaced the uncorked bottle in the champagne basket.

The next day, accompanied by my paymaster — by the way, I have forgotten to mention that I had appointed Dr. Galt, my esteemed surgeon, paymaster, at the time I made a present of my former paymaster to Mr. Adams, as related; and that I had promoted Dr. Llewellyn to be surgeon — I made a visit to the Governor at his palace. He had kindly sent horses for us to the beach, and we had a pleasant ride of about a mile, before we reached his headquarters. It was about eleven A. M., when we alighted, and were escorted by an aide-de-camp to his presence. The Governor was a thin, spare man, rather under the medium height, and of sprightly manners and conversation. His complexion, like that of most Brazilians, was about that of a side of tanned sole-leather. His rank was that of a major in the Brazilian Army He received us very cordially. We found him at breakfast with his family and some guests, and he insisted that we should be seated at the breakfast-table, and partake of a second breakfast, though we endeavored to decline. The meal was quite substantial, consisting of a variety of roast meats, as well as fruits and vegetables.

As soon as I could find a little time to look around me, I discovered that her ladyship, the governess, was a very sprightly and not uncomely mulatto, and that her two little children, who were brought to me with all due ceremony, to be praised, and have their heads patted, had rather kinky, or, perhaps, I should say curly, hair. But I was a man of the world, and was not at all dismayed by this discovery; especially when I observed that my *vis-a-vis* — one of the guests — was a beautiful blonde, of sweet seventeen, with a complexion like a lily, tinted with the least bit of rose, and with eyes so melting and lovely, that they looked as though they might have belonged to one of the houris, of whom that old reprobate Mahomet used to dream. To set off her charms still further, she was arrayed in a robe of the purest white, with a wreath of flowers in her flaxen hair. She was a German, and was seated next to her father, a man of about sixty, who, as the Governor afterward informed me, was one of his chief criminals.

The Governor seeing me start a little as he gave me this information, made haste to explain, that his guest was not of the *canaille*, or common class of rogues, but a gentleman, who, in a moment of weakness, had signed another gentleman's name to a check for a considerable amount, which he had been clever enough to have cashed. "He is only a forger, then!" said I to the Governor. "That is all," replied he; "he is a very clever old gentleman, and, as you see, he has a very pretty daughter." There was certainly no gainsaying the latter proposition. The chaplain of the penal colony — which numbered about one thousand convicts, the entire population of the island being about two thousand — a portly and dignified priest, was also at the breakfast-table, and my paymaster and myself spent a very pleasant half-hour around this social board, at which were represented so many of the types of mankind, and so different moral elements.

From the breakfast-table, we retired to a withdrawing-room, which was pretty well filled when we entered, showing that his Excellency had done me the honor to get some guests together to greet me. The paymaster and myself were personally presented to most of these distinguished gentlemen — some military men, some civilians. Among others, was present the ambassador of the day previous, who had given such a shock to Bartelli's nerves, as to render him incapable of doing that which he loved above all other things to do — draw a champagne cork for the Captain's guests, whom he regarded, after a certain fashion, as his own. The Governor had evidently been select in his society, for most of these gentlemen were not only well dressed, but well-mannered, and some of them were even distinguished in appearance. They were mostly homicides and forgers, and seemed rather to pride themselves upon the distinction which they had attained in their *professions*. There was one young fellow present, upon whom all seemed to look with admiration. He was a dashing young German, who had evidently driven fast horses, and kept the best of company. He wore an elaborately embroidered shirt-bosom, on which glittered a diamond brooch of great brilliancy, and there were chains hung about his neck, and signet and other rings on his fingers. This fellow was such a master of the pen, that he could cheat any man out of his signature, after having seen him write but once. To give us an example of his skill, he sketched, whilst we were talking to him, the *Alabama*, and her surroundings, as they appeared from the window of the saloon in which we were sitting, so perfectly, with pen and ink, as to create a murmur of applause among the bystanders. This charming young gentleman had "done" the Bank of Rio Janeiro out of a very large sum, which was the cause of his being the guest of the Governor.

Wine and cigars were brought in, and as we chatted, and smoked with these fellows, the paymaster, and I were highly amused — amused at our own situation, and by the variety of characters by whom we were surrounded. The levée being at an end, the Governor ordered horses, and, accompanied by an orderly, we rode over his dominions. It was in the midst of the rainy season, and the island was almost constantly wreathed in mists and rain, but as these rains continue for months, no one thinks of housing himself on account of them.

We passed within a stone's throw of the Peak, and were more struck than ever, with the grandeur of its proportions and the symmetry of its form. The island is broken and picturesque, as all volcanic countries are, and in the midst of the rains, it was one mass of rank vegetation, it being as much as the farmers could do to keep a few patches of cultivation free from the encroaching weeds and jungle. We had not been in the saddle more than twenty minutes, when a heavily laden, vaporous cloud swept over us, and drenched us to the skin. But I found that this was not to interfere, in the least, with our ride. Its only effect was, to induce the Governor to call a temporary halt, at a Manioc factory, in which he was interested, and whistle up a boy, who brought each of us a very small glass filled with the villanous *aguadiente* of the country. The Governor tossed his off at a single gulp, and not to be discourteous, we made wry faces, and disposed of as much of ours as we could.

We passed through tangled forests, the trees of which were all new to us, and through dells and ravines, in which the living, and the decaying vegetation seemed to be struggling for the mastery, and emerged in a beautiful cocoanut plantation, on the south end of the island, which lay only a few feet above the sea-level. I was now at the end of the Governor's dominions—an hour's ride had brought me from the sea, on one side of them, to the sea, on the other, and there was nothing more to be seen. Other showers coming on, we entered a tiny country house of the Governor's, and had some grapes, figs, and melons brought in to us by the major domo. The green cocoanut was brought to us among other delicacies, to be eaten with spoons. We were quite amused at the manner in which these nuts were gathered. The major domo called a boy, and tying his legs together, just above the ankles, so that the ankles were about six inches apart, set him down at the foot of a tree. These trees, as the reader knows, grow to a great height, are perfectly cylindrical, and have not an excrescence of any kind from root to top; and yet the boy, by the aid of the bandage described, wriggled himself to the top of one of the tallest, with the agility of a squirrel.

There being at length a pause in the rains, the sun even peeping through an occasional rift in the ragged and watery clouds, we remounted, and rode back. The tiny mountain paths had,. many of them, by this time become rills and torrents, and our horses were frequently knee-deep in water. The paymaster and I pulled on board at five P. M., without having suffered any inconvenience, either from the rains, or the Governor's *aguadiente;* nor did our morals suffer materially by what we had seen and heard in the island of Fernando de Noronha. The next morning the Governor's wife sent me a fat turkey for dinner, accompanied by the most charming of bouquets. This was evidently my reward for patting the little curly heads of her children. My diplomacy from this time onward was all right. I did not hear a word from the Governor, or any one in authority, about neutral rights, or the violation of neutral jurisdictions. Brazil had, I knew, followed the lead of the European powers, in excluding prizes from her ports, and I had fully expected to receive some remonstrance against my bringing in the *Louisa Hatch,* but Madame was too strong for the Governor, and, as the reader has seen, I received fat turkeys, and bouquets, instead of remonstrances. The anchorage being nothing but an open roadstead, we soon found it too rough to permit a ship to lie alongside of us, and so were obliged to haul the *Hatch* off to her anchors, and continue our coaling with boats. This was rather a tedious process, and it was not until the 15th of April, or five days after our arrival, that we were coaled.

We had not once thought of a prize, since we came in. Our whole attention had been given to coaling ship, and refitting for another cruise, refreshing the crew, and attending to the ladies at the Government House. But the ubiquitous Yankee would turn up in spite of us. Just as we had gotten our last boat-load of coal on board, two ships appeared off the harbor, and were seen to heave to, and lower boats. We soon made them out to be whalers, and knew them to be American, though they had not as yet hoisted any colors. The boats pulled in apace, and soon entered the harbor. They contained the masters of the two whalers, who had come in to barter a little whale oil for supplies. The *Alabama* was lying, without any colors hoisted, as was her wont while she remained at this island, and, of course, the *Louisa Hatch,* her prize, had none set. The boats pulled in quite unsuspiciously, and observing that the *Hatch* was an American-built ship, went alongside of her. The prize-master, who was taking it easily, in his shirt-sleeves, and so had no uniform on which could betray him, went to the gangway and threw them a rope. The two masters declined to come on board, as they were in a hurry, they said, but remained some time in conversation — the prize-master, who was an Englishman, endeavoring to play Yankee, the best he could. He repeatedly invited them to come on board, but they declined. They wanted to know what steamer "that was," pointing to the *Alabama.* They were told that it was a Brazilian packet-steamer, come over to the colony to bring some convicts. "What are *you* doing here," they now inquired. "We sprang a pretty bad leak, in a late gale, and have come in to see if we can repair damages." Presently there was a simultaneous start, on the part of both the boat's crews, and the words "starn, all!" being bawled, rather than spoken, both boats backed out, in "double quick," and put off, with the most vigorous strokes of their oars, for the shore, like men who were pulling for their lives. The prize-master, a little astonished at this sudden movement, looked around him to see what could have caused it. The cause was soon apparent. A small Confederate flag — a boat's ensign — had been thrown by the coxswain of one of the boats on the spanker-boom to dry, and while the conversation was going on, a puff of wind had blown out the folds, and disclosed the little tell-tale to the gaze of the astonished whalers. It was not precisely a Gorgon's head; they did not turn to stone, but perhaps there was some of the tallest pulling done, that day, at Fernando de Noronha, that was ever done by a Yankee boat's crew.

In the meantime, the "Brazilian packet-steamer" having gotten up steam, was moving quietly out of the harbor, to look after the ships outside. They were still lying to, and fortunately for me, they were four or five miles off; outside of the charmed marine league. There was an outlying shoal or two, in the direction in which they were, and this was the reason, probably, why they had not ventured nearer. It did not take us long to come up with them. We fired the usual gun as we approached, and as there was no occasion for *ruse*, we showed them our own flag. They saw in a moment that their fate was sealed, and did not attempt to stir, but hoisted the United States colors, and patiently waited to be taken possession of. The first we came up with, was the bark *Lafayette*, of New Bedford. There were no papers to be examined — the mate, in the absence of the captain, having thrown them overboard, as we approached — and we gave her a short shrift. She was burning brightly, in less than an hour. We now ranged up alongside of the other, which proved to be the hermaphrodite brig, *Kate Cory*, of Westport. Instead of burning the *Cory*, I took her in tow, and stood back to the anchorage with her, it being my intention to convert her into a cartel, and dispatch her to the United States, with my prisoners, who were now quite as numerous as my crew, there being 110 of them. By seven P. M., we had again anchored in our old berth; the burning ship outside lighting us into the roadstead, and throwing a bright glare over much of the island. A number of ships that passed Fernando de Noronha that night, must have been astonished at this illumination of the lonely mile-post. The sea was smooth, and the ship was still burning, the next morning, though by this time she had drifted so far, that there was nothing visible except a column of smoke. I afterward changed my determination of converting the *Cory* into a cartel. A small Brazilian schooner having come into the anchorage, offered to take all my prisoners to Pernambuco, if I would provision them, and give her, besides, a few barrels of pork and flour for her trouble. This I at once consented to do, and the Governor having no objection, the arrangement was forthwith made. I was thus enabled to burn the *Cory*, and to put the enemy, to the expense of sending his released prisoners to the United States. I burned the *Louisa Hatch* along with the *Cory*, having no farther use for her; taking the pains to send them both beyond the marine league, that I might pay due respect to the jurisdiction of Brazil.

And now we were ready for sea again, though I remained a few days longer at my anchors, hoping that the *Agrippina* might arrive. She was past due, but I had not yet given up all hope of her.

We were now getting well along into the latter part of April, and a great change was taking place in the weather. It had been raining, as the reader has observed, ever since we reached the vicinity of the equator. The rains were now becoming less frequent, from day to day, and we had the showers agreeably alternated with sunshine. The rainy season was passing away, and the dry season was about to set in. I watched this phenomenon with great interest—all the more narrowly, because I had nothing to do, but look out for the weather, and the *Agrippina;* except, indeed, to attend to the refreshment, and recreation of my crew, and send Bartelli on shore, occasionally, with messages to the ladies at the Government House. The reader, who has now been a passenger with us for some time, has watched the trade-winds, as he has crossed the tropics, and has fanned himself and panted for breath, when we have been working our tedious way through the calm-belts. He has seen how this system of trade-winds and calm-belts wanders up and down the earth, from north to south, and south to north, drawn hither and thither by the sun. But we have had no conversation, as yet, about the Equatorial Cloud Ring. He has been, for the last three weeks, under this very Cloud Ring, but has probably failed to remark it. He has only seen that the flood-gates of the heavens have been raised, and witnessed the descending torrents, and the roll of the thunder, and the play of the lightning, without stopping to ask himself the reason.

Let us pause a moment, and look into this beautiful phenomenon of the Equatorial Cloud Ring, before we flit away to other seas, and are absorbed by new phenomena. The north-east and south-east trade-winds, meeting near the equator, produce the Cloud Ring. Let us suppose the *Alabama* back at the crossing of the 30th parallel, where, as the reader will recollect, we established the toll-gate. She had, whilst there, a high barometer. Starting thence on her way to the equator, as soon as she enters the north-east trade, she finds that her barometer settles a little—perhaps a tenth of an inch on an average. The reader has seen, that we had, whilst passing through this region, a series of half gales, and bad weather; but this was an exceptional state of the atmospheric phe-

nomena. The normal condition of the weather is that of a
clear sky, with passing trade-clouds, white and fleecy, and
with moderate breezes. If the reader has watched his barometer narrowly, he has observed a very remarkable phenomenon,
which is not known to prevail outside of the trade-wind belts—
an atmospheric tide. The atmosphere ebbs and flows as regularly as the sea. This atmospheric tide is due, no doubt, to
the same cause that produces the aqueous tides—the attrac-
tion of the moon. It occurs twice in twenty-four hours, just
like the aqueous tides, and there is no other cause to which
we can attribute it.

The needle has a like semi-diurnal—indeed, hourly varia-
tion—showing the normal, electrical condition of the atmosphere. The atmospherical, tidal wave, as it ebbs and flows,
seems to carry the needle backward and forward with it.
The average barometer being but a very little under thirty,
there is an agreeable elasticity in the atmosphere, and officers,
and crew are generally in fine spirits. The sailors enjoy their
evening dances, and story-tellings, and when the night-watches
are set, sleep with impunity about the decks—guarded, however, by those woollen garments, of which I spoke, when describing our routine life. But observe, now, what a change
will take place, as we approach the equator. We are approaching not only the calm-belt, which has been before described, but the Cloud Ring, for the latter is the concomitant
of the former. The winds die away, the muttering of thunder
is heard, and a pall of black clouds, along which dart frequent
streaks of lightning, is seen hanging on the verge of the
horizon, ahead of the ship. As she advances, fanned along
by puffs of wind from various quarters, she loses sight of the
sun altogether, and enters beneath the belt of clouds, where
she is at once deluged with rain. She is at once in the equatorial calm-belt, and under the Equatorial Cloud Ring.

The north-east and south-east trade-winds,· as they came
sweeping along, charged to saturation with the vapors which
they have licked up from a torrid sea, have ascended as they
met, and when they have reached the proper dew-point, or
point of the wet-bulb of the thermometer, precipitation has
commenced. The barometer falls another tenth of an inch, or

so, all elasticity departs from the atmosphere, and officers and crew lose their cheerfulness. They feel all the lassitude and weariness of men in a perpetual vapor-bath. The sailor no longer mounts the ratlines, as if he had cork in his heels, but climbs up sluggishly and slothfully, devoid of his usual pride to be foremost. In other words, though not absolutely sick, he is "under the weather." The rays of the sun being perpetually excluded, the thermometer stands lower under the Cloud Ring, than on either side of it. At least this is the normal condition. Sometimes, however, the most oppressive heats occur. They are local, and of short duration. These local heats are occasioned as follows: When a cooler stratum of the upper air sweeps down nearer the earth than usual, bringing with it the dew-point, condensation takes place so near the surface, that the rain-drops have not time to cool, at the same time that an immense quantity of latent heat has been liberated in the act of condensation. At other times, when the dew-point is far removed from the earth, the latent heat is not only thrown off at a greater distance from us, but the rain-drops cool in their descent, and greatly reduce the temperature.

The Cloud Ring is being perpetually formed, and is perpetually passing away. Fresh volumes of air, charged as described, are constantly rushing in from the north and from the south, and as constantly ascending, parting with a portion of their water, and continuing their journey to the poles, in obedience to the laws providing for the equal distribution of rain to the two hemispheres, before explained. The Cloud Ring encircles the entire earth, and if it could be viewed by an eye at a distance from our planet, would appear like a well-defined black mark drawn around an artificial globe. Its width is considerable, being from three to six degrees.

It remains to speak of the offices which this remarkable ring performs. It is an important cog-wheel in the great atmospherical machine, for the distribution of water over the earth; but, besides its functions in the general system, it has local duties to perform. These are the hovering by turns over certain portions of the earth, giving them an alternation of rain and sunshine. In short, it causes the rainy, and dry seasons,

ın certain parallels, north and south, within the limits assigned
to it. The ancients were of the opinion that the equatorial
regions of the earth were a continuous, burning desert, devoid
of vegetation, and of course uninhabitable; and perhaps this
opinion would not be very far wrong, but for the arrangement
of which I am about to speak. The Cloud Ring is a part of the
system of calm-belts, and trade-winds. It overhangs the equatorial calm-belt, as has been stated, and it travels north and
south with it. It travels over as much as twenty degrees of
latitude—from about 5° S. to 15° N., carrying, as before remarked, rain to the regions over which it hovers, and letting
in the sunshine upon those regions it has left. If the reader
will inspect a map, he will find that it extends as far into our
hemisphere, as the island of Martinique, in the West Indies.
Fernando de Noronha, where we are now lying in the *Alabama*,
is near its southern limit, being in the latitude of about 4° S.

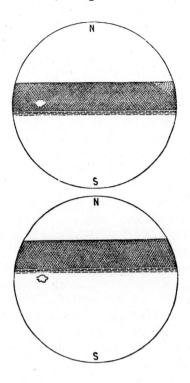

The reader has seen that the rainy season was still prevailing, when we arrived at this island, on the 10th of April; and that it had begun to pass away, while we still lay there—the rain and the sunshine playing at "April showers." The preceding diagram will explain how the Cloud Ring travels:—

Figure 1 represents the island of Fernando de Noronha still under the Cloud Ring. It is early in April, and only about three weeks have elapsed since the sun crossed the equator on his way back to the northern hemisphere. When he was in the southern hemisphere, he had drawn the ring so far south, as to cover the island. His rays had been shut out from it, and it was constantly raining. The little island would have been drowned out, if this state of things had continued; but it was not so ordered by the great Architect.

Suppose now a month to elapse. It is early in May, and behold! the sun has travelled sufficiently far north, to draw the Cloud Ring from over the island, and leave it in sunshine, as represented in figure 2. Thus the island is neither parched by perpetual heat, nor drowned by perpetual rains, but its climate is delightfully tempered by an alternation of each, and it has become a fit abode for men and animals.

As we have seen in a former chapter, a benign Providence has set the trade-winds in motion, that they might become the water-carriers of the earth, ordering them, for this purpose, to cross the equator, each into the hemisphere of the other. We now see that he has woven, with those same winds, a shield, impenetrable to the sun's rays, which he holds in his hand, as it were, first over one parched region of the earth, and then over another—the shield dropping "fatness" all the while!

CHAPTER XLIV.

THE ALABAMA LEAVES FERNANDO DE NORONHA FOR A
CRUISE ON THE COAST OF BRAZIL — ENTERS THE
GREAT HIGHWAY AND BEGINS TO OVERHAUL THE
TRAVELLERS — CAPTURE OF THE WHALER NYE; OF
THE DORCAS PRINCE; OF THE UNION JACK; OF THE
SEA LARK — A REVEREND CONSUL TAKEN PRISONER
— ALABAMA GOES INTO BAHIA — WHAT OCCURRED
THERE — ARRIVAL OF THE GEORGIA — ALABAMA PRO-
CEEDS TO SEA AGAIN — CAPTURES THE FOLLOWING
SHIPS: THE GILDERSLIEVE; THE JUSTINA; THE JA-
BEZ SNOW; THE AMAZONIAN, AND THE TALISMAN.

THE 22d of April having arrived, we gave up all further
hopes of the *Agrippina*, and went to sea. As we passed
out of the roadstead, we cut adrift the four whale-boats which
we had brought in from the captured whalers, rather than
destroy them. They would be valuable to the islanders, who
had treated us kindly, and it was amusing to see the struggle
which took place for the possession of them. The good people
seemed to have some anticipation of what was to take place,
and all the boatmen of the island had assembled to contest the
prizes, in every description of craft that would float, from the
dug-out to the tidy cutter. The boatmen stripped themselves
like athletes for the fray, and as whale-boat after boat was cut
adrift, there was a pulling and splashing, a paddling and a
screaming that defy all description; the victors waving their
hats, and shouting their victory and their good-bye to us, in
the same breath.

We steamed due east from the island some forty miles, when
we let our steam go down, raised the propeller, and put the

ship under sail. The *Alabama*, with full coal-bunkers and a refreshed crew, was again in pursuit of the enemy's commerce. I had at last accomplished my cherished design — which had been frustrated in the *Sumter* — of a cruise on the coast of Brazil. In my stanch and fleet little ship, I was in a condition to defy both winds and currents. On the day after leaving Fernando de Noronha, I observed in latitude 5° 45′ S., and had thus run entirely from under the Cloud Ring. We were met by a bright sky, and the first gentle breathings of the south-east trade. This change in the weather had an electric effect upon my people. Cheerfulness returned to their countenances, and elasticity to their step. It took us some time to dry and ventilate the ship, the rigging being filled, for a day or two, with wet pea-jackets and mattresses, and the decks strewed with mouldy boots and shoes.

Before we had been twenty-four hours at sea, the usual bugle-note was sounded from the mast-head, and the *Alabama* had pricked up her ears in chase. It was another unfortunate whaler. The fates seemed to have a grudge against these New England fishermen, and would persist in throwing them in my way, although I was not on a whaling-ground. This was the sixteenth I had captured — a greater number than had been captured from the English by Commodore David Porter, in his famous cruise in the Pacific, in the frigate *Essex*, during the war of 1812. The prize proved to be the bark *Nye*, of New Bedford. This bluff old whaler was returning home from a cruise of thirty-one months in the far-off Pacific, during which her crew had become almost as much Sandwich Islanders, as Americans in appearance, with their garments so saturated with oil that they would have been quite valuable to the soap-boiler. She had sent "home" one or two cargoes of oil, and had now on board 425 barrels more. It seemed a pity to break in upon the *menage* of these old salts, who had weathered so many gales, and chased the whale through so many latitudes, but there was no alternative. The New England wolf was still howling for Southern blood, and the least return we could make for the howl, was to spill a little "*ile*." Everything about the *Nye* being greased to saturation, she made a splendid conflagration.

The next day the wind freshened, and we might now be said to be in the well-pronounced south-east trades. Indeed, it blew so fresh at nightfall, that we took the single reefs in the top-sails. We were jogging along leisurely on the great Brazilian highway, waiting for the passengers, rather than hunting them up. Presently another came along—a fine, taunt ship, that represented the boxes and bales of merchandise, rather than harpoons and whale-oil. We gave chase under the enemy's colors, but the chase was coy and shy, and refused to show colors in return, until she was commanded to do so by a gun. The stars and stripes, which now fluttered to the breeze, suffi-ciently explained her reluctance. Upon being boarded she proved to be the *Dorcas Prince*, of New York, bound for Shanghai. Her cargo consisted chiefly of coal. She had been fourty-four days out, an unusually long passage, and what was quite wonderful for an American ship, she had no documents on board from the college, either of the political or religious propaganda, and only three or four old newspapers. When we learned she was from New York, we had been in hopes of capturing a mail. We burned her as soon as we could trans-fer her crew, there being no claim of neutral cargo found among her papers. Her master had his wife on board, which resulted, as usual, in sending one of my young lieutenants into the "country."

Reducing sail again, we jogged along as before, but for the next few days we overhauled nothing but neutrals. A St. John's, New Brunswick, ship, brought us the mail we had ex-pected to receive by the *Dorcas Prince*, but it contained noth-ing of interest. On the 3d of May, the weather being fine, though interrupted occasionally by a rain-squall, we gave chase, about eleven A. M., to a clipper-ship, with square yards, white canvas, and long mast-heads—and the reader must be enough of an expert, by this time, to know what these mean. In an hour and a half of fine sailing, we came near enough to the chase, to make her show the Federal colors, and heave to. She proved to be the *Union Jack*, of Boston, bound for Shang-hai. Whilst we had been pursuing the *Union Jack*, another "suspicious" sail hove in sight, and as soon as we could throw a prize-crew on board of the former, we started off in pursuit of the latter.   This second sail proved also to be a prize, being the *Sea Lark*, of New York, bound for San Francisco.   Here were two prizes, in as many hours.

There was no attempt to cover the cargo of the *Sea Lark*, and the only attempt that was made in the case of the *Union Jack*, was made by one Allen Hay, who was anxious to save five cases of crackers, and ten barrels of butter from capture. In this case, a Mr. Thomas W. Lillie, made oath before the British Consul in New York, that the said articles were shipped "for and on account of subjects of her Britannic Majesty." The reader has seen me burn several other ships, with similar certificates, the reasons for which burnings were assigned at the time.   I will not stop, therefore, to discuss this.   In due time both ships were consigned to the flames.   I was sorry to find three more women, and two small children on board of the *Union Jack*.   That ship was, in fact, about to expatriate herself for several years, after the fashion of many of the Yankee ships in the Chinese coasting-trade, and the master was taking his family out to domicile it somewhere in China. There were several male passengers also on board this ship, among them an ex-New-England parson, the Rev. Franklin Wright, who was going out as Consul to Foo Chow.   The Rev. Mr. Wright had been editor of a religious paper for some years, in one of the New England villages, and probably owed his promotion to the good services he had rendered in hurrying on the war.   He had Puritan written all over his lugubrious countenance, and looked so solemn, that one wondered how he came to exchange the clergyman's garb for the garb of Belial.   But so it was; Franklin was actually going out to India, in quest of the dollars.   We deprived him of his Consular seal and commission, though we did not molest his private papers, and of sundry very pretty Consular flags, that had been carefully prepared for him by Mr. Seward, *fils*, at the State Department, in Washington.   I am pained to see, by that "little bill" of Mr. Seward, *père*, against the British Government, for "depredations of the *Alabama*," before referred to, that the Rev. Mr. Wright puts his damages down at $10,015. I had no idea that a New England parson carried so much plunder about with him.

We received large mails from these two last ships, and had our "moral ideas" considerably expanded, for the next few days, by the perusal of Yankee newspapers. We found among other interesting items, a vivid synopsis of the war news, in a speech of Governor Wright, of Indiana, who, if I mistake not, had been chargé to Berlin, where he had been in the habit of holding conventicles and prayer-meetings. The Governor is addressing a meeting of the "truly loil" at Philadelphia, and among other things, said:—

"The stars and stripes now wave over half the slave grounds. I believe in less than thirty days we will open the Mississippi and take Charleston. [Loud applause.] Leave Virginia alone, that can't sprout a black-eyed pea. [Laughter.] Scripture teaches us that no people can live long where there is no grass. The question then is only, whether they can live thirty or sixty days."

Thus, amid the laughter and jeers of an unwashed rabble, did an ex-Governor, and ex-U. S. Minister, gloat over the prospect of *starving* an entire people, women and children included. Did we need other incitement on board the *Alabama*, to apply a well-lighted torch to the enemy's ships?

There were copious extracts from the English papers found in this mail, and I trust the reader will excuse me, while I give a portion of a speech made to his constituents, by a member of the British Parliament, who was also a member of the cabinet. The speaker is Mr. Milner Gibson, President of the Board of Trade. A great war, which covered a continent with the fire and smoke of battle, was raging between a people, who were the near kinsmen of the speaker. Battles were being fought daily, that dwarfed all the battles that had gone before them. Feats of brilliant courage were being performed, on both sides, that should have made the blood of the speaker course more rapidly through his veins, and stir to their depths the feelings of humanity and brotherhood. Under such circumstances, what think you, reader, was the subject of Mr. Gibson's discourse? It was bacon and eggs! Listen: —

"Now," continues Mr. Gibson, "these large importations of foreign wheat and flour, and other provisions, into this country, must, to some extent, have tended to mitigate the distress, and have enabled many to provide for the wants of others out of their own surplus means. But supposing that the Government of this country had been induced, as they were urged frequently, to involve themselves in interference in the affairs of the United States; supposing, by some rash and precipitate recognition of those who are conducting hostilities against the United States — called the Confederate States of America—we had brought ourselves into collision with the United States, where would have been this flour, and ham, and bacon, and eggs? I suppose, if we had been compelled to take up arms against the United States, by any unfortunate policy, blockading would have been resorted to, and we should have been obliged to establish a blockade of the coast of America, for the very purpose of keeping out of this country all this wheat, flour, and eggs which have gone to mitigate the distress of the cotton industry in the present alarming state of affairs. We have from the commencement carried out the doctrine of non-intervention. We have endeavored to preserve a strict neutrality between the two contending parties. It was impossible to avoid recognizing the belligerent rights of the South at the outset of the contest, because it was a contest of such magnitude, and the insurgents, as they were called, were so numerous and so powerful, that it would have been impossible to recognize them in any other capacity but as persons entitled to bear arms; and if we had not done so, and if their armed vessels found on the seas were treated as pirates, it must be obvious to every one that this would have been an unparalleled course of action. We were compelled to recognize the belligerent rights of the South, but there has been no desire on the part of the Government to favor either the one side or the other. My earnest desire is to preserve strict neutrality; and, whatever may be my individual feelings — for we must have our sympathies on the one side or the other—whatever may be my feelings as a member of Parliament and the executive administration, I believe it to be for the interest of England that this neutrality should be observed."

Poor old John Bull! What a descent have we here, from the Plantagenets to Mr. Milner Gibson? From Cœur de Leon, "striking for the right," to Mr. Milner Gibson, of the *Board of Trade*, advising his countrymen to smother all their more noble and generous impulses, that they might continue to fry cheap bacon and eggs!

We had been working our way, for the last few days, toward Bahia, in Brazil, and being now pretty well crowded with prisoners, having no less than the crews of four captured ships on board, I resolved to run in and land them. We anchored about five P. M., on the 11th of May. Bahia is the

second city, in size and commercial importance, in the Brazilian empire. We found a large number of ships at anchor
in the harbor, but no Yankees among them. The only man-
of-war present was a Portuguese. We were struck with the
spaciousness of the bay, and the beauty of the city as we approached. The latter crowns a crescent-shaped eminence, and
its white houses peep cosily from beneath forest-trees, of the
richest and greenest foliage. The business part of the city
lies at the foot of the crescent, near the water's edge. It, too,
looks picturesque, with its quays, and shipping, and tugs, and
wherries. But, as is the case with most Portuguese towns—
for the Brazilians are only a better class of Portuguese—the
illusion of beauty is dispelled, as soon as you enter its narrow
and crooked streets, and get sight of its swarthy population,
the chief features of which are *sombreros* and garlic. We were
boarded by the health-officer just at dark, and admitted to
pratique.

The next morning, the weather set in gloomy and rainy.
The requisite permission having been obtained, we landed our
prisoners, there being upward of a hundred of them. Parson
Wright here took the back track, I believe. Whether, after
stating his grievances at the State Department in Washington,
he renewed his commission, and proceeded, in some more fortunate Yankee ship to Foo Chow, or went back to his religious
paper, and his exhortations against the Southern heathen, I
have never learned. The reverend gentleman forgot his Christian charity, and did not come to say "good-bye," when he
landed, though we had treated him with all due consideration.

I had now another little diplomatic matter on my hands. I
had scarcely risen from the breakfast-table, on the morning
after my arrival, when an aide-de-camp of the Governor, or
rather President of the Department, came off to see me on official business. He brought on board with him a copy of the
"Diario de Bahia," a newspaper very respectable for its size and
typography, containing an article, which I was requested to
read, and answer in writing. This I promised to do, and the
messenger departed. I found, upon glancing over the article,
which filled a couple of columns, that it was a Yankee production done into very good Portuguese—the joint work,

probably, of the Yankee Consul at Pernambuco, where the article had originated — for it had been copied into the Bahia paper — and the President of that province. It was written after the style of a proclamation, was signed by the President, and strangely enough addressed to myself — supposed to be still at Fernando de Noronha, with the *Alabama*. After charging me with sundry violations of the neutrality of Brazil, it ordered me to depart the island, within twenty-four hours.

Instead of sending a ship of war, to examine into the facts, and enforce his order, if necessary, the President had been satisfied to send this paper bullet after me. It reminded me very much of the "stink-pots," which the Chinese are in the habit of throwing at their enemies, and I could not restrain a smile, as I called upon Bartelli to produce my writing materials. The aide-de-camp who had brought me the paper, had brought off a message, along with it, from the President, to the effect that he desired I would hold no communication with the shore, until I had answered the article; which was tantamount to informing me, that he was somewhat in doubt whether he would permit me to communicate at all or not. I really wanted nothing — though I afterward took in a few boat-loads of coal, merely to show the President that I was disposed to be civil — and this consideration, along with the fact, that I had the heaviest guns in the harbor, induced me to be rather careless, I am afraid, in the choice of phraseology, as I penned my despatch. I simply charged that the whole proclamation was a budget of lies, and claimed that I had been insulted by the Government of Brazil, by the lies having been put into an official shape by it, without first communicating with me.

The Brazilians are a very polite people, and my reply was "perfectly satisfactory." Jack went on shore, and had his frolic, and the *Alabama* remained a week in the port, enjoying the hospitalities of the numerous English, and other foreign residents. Among other entertainments, we had a splendid ball given us by Mr. Ogilvie, a British merchant, at which much of the foreign and native beauty was present. Mr. Ogilvie's tasteful residence overlooked the bay from the top of the crescent I have described; his grounds, redolent of the perfumes of tropical flowers, were brilliantly illuminated, and a

fine band of music charmed not only the revellers, but the numerous ships in the Bay.   Several Brazilian dignitaries and
foreign Consuls were present.   I took all my young gentlemen
on shore with me, who could be spared from the ship, and they
did their "devoirs" as only gallant knights can, and carried on
board with them, in the "wee sma'" hours of the morning,
several tiny kid gloves and scarfs, as mementos to accompany
them on their cruises—every villain of them swearing to return at some future day.   So it is always with the sailor.   As
before remarked, his very life is a poem, and his heart is capacious enough to take in the whole sex.

On the morning after this brilliant entertainment, an officer
came below to inform me that a strange steamer of war had
entered during the night, which, as yet, had shown no colors.
I directed our own colors to be shown to the stranger—for
the regular hour of hoisting them had not yet arrived—and
the reader may judge of our delight, when we saw the Confederate States flag thrown to the breeze in reply, by the new-
comer.   It was the *Georgia*, Commander Lewis F. Maury, on
a cruise, like ourselves, against the enemy's commerce.   She
had come in to meet her coal-ship, the *Castor*, which had been
ordered to rendezvous here.   We had now other troubles with
the authorities.   The President, seeing another Confederate
steamer arrive, became nervous, lest he should be compromised in some way, and be called to account by the Emperor.
The little gad-fly of a Yankee Consul was, besides, constantly
buzzing around him.   He declined to permit the *Georgia* to
receive coal from her transport, though he was forced to admit
that the transport had the right to land it, and that, when
landed, the *Georgia* might receive it on board, like any other
coal.   Still it must be landed.   The gad-fly had buzzed in his
ear, that there was a "cat in the meal tub;" the *Castor* having,
as he alleged, some guns and ammunition covered up in her
coal!   His Excellency then wanted to see my commission —
the gad-fly having buzzed "pirate! pirate!"   To add to the
complication, news now came in that the *Florida* also had arrived at Pernambuco!   Diablo! what was to be done?   An
aide-de-camp now came off with a letter from his Excellency,
telling me, that I had already tarried too long in the port of

Bahia, and that he desired me to be off. I wrote him word that I was not ready, and sent another batch of liberty men on shore. Presently another missive came. His Excellency had learned from the gad-fly, that I had enlisted one of my late prisoners, after setting him on shore, which, as he said, was a grave breach of the laws of nations. I replied that I had not only not enlisted one of my late prisoners, after setting him on shore, but that, my crew being full, I had *refused to enlist a good many of my late prisoners*, who had applied to me before being set on shore, which was the literal fact. I mention these occurrences to show what a troublesome little insect I found the gad-fly in Brazil.

We had a few days of very pleasant intercourse with the *Georgia*. Maury had been my shipmate in the old service, and two of my old *Sumter* lieutenants, Chapman and Evans, were serving on board of her. In company with her officers, we made a railroad excursion into the interior, upon the invitation of the English company which owned the road. A splendid collation was prepared in one of the cars, decorated and furnished for the occasion, and a variety of choice wines broke down the barrier between strangers, and drew men of the same blood closer together.

At length, when I was entirely ready for sea, I delighted the President one evening, by sending him word that I should go to sea the next morning. The *Georgia* was nearly through coaling, and would follow me in a day or two. The poor President of the province of Bahia! The Yankees treated him, afterward, as they do everybody else with whom they have to do. They first endeavored to use him, and then kicked him. The *Florida* coming into Bahia, a few months afterward, as related in a former page, a Federal ship of war violated the neutrality of the port, by seizing her, and carrying her off; and the Yankee nation, rather than make the amends which all the world decided it was bound to make, by delivering back the captured ship to Brazil, ordered her to be sunk by *accident* in Hampton Roads! The "*trick*" was eminently Yankee, and I presume could not possibly have been practised in any other civilized nation of the earth.

Whilst the *Alabama* is heaving up her anchor, I deem **it** proper to say a word or two, about emigration to Brazil; a subject which has been a good deal canvassed by our people. Brazil is an immense Empire, and has almost all the known climates and soils of the world. Nature has bestowed upon her her choicest gifts, and there is perhaps no more delightful country to reside in than Brazil. But men live for society, as well as for climate and soil. The effete Portuguese race has been ingrafted upon a stupid, stolid, Indian stock, in that country. The freed negro is, besides, the equal of the white man, and as there seems to be no repugnance, on the part of the white race — so called — to mix with the black race, and with the Indian, amalgamation will go on in that country, until a mongrel set of curs will cover the whole land. This might be a suitable field enough for the New England school-ma'am, and carpet-bagger, but no Southern gentleman should think of mixing his blood or casting his lot with such a race of people.

Sail ho! was shouted from the mast-head of the *Alabama*, on the afternoon of the 25th of May, a few days after she had put to sea from Bahia. We had regained the track of commerce, and were again looking out for our friends. We immediately gave chase, and had scarcely gotten the canvas on the ship, before the look-out announced a second sail, in the same direction. The wind was fresh, there was a heavy sea on, and the *Alabama* darted forward, making her eleven, and twelve knots. As we began to raise the fugitives above the horizon from the deck, it was plain to see, that they were both American. We overhauled them rapidly, making them show their colors, and heaving them to, with the accustomed guns. By the time we had gotten up with them, the sun had set, and it was blowing half a gale of wind. Our boats had a rough job before them, but they undertook it with a will. The first ship boarded was the *Gilderslieve*, and the second, the *Justina*. The former was a New York ship, last from London, with a cargo of coal, purporting to be shipped for the service of the "Peninsular, and Oriental Steam Navigation Company," but there was no certificate of neutral ownership on board. Ship and cargo were therefore condemned. The *Justina* was a Baltimore ship, with some neutral property, not amounting to a full cargo, on board. I converted her into a cartel, and throwing the prisoners from the *Gilderslieve* on board of her, released her on ransom-bond. I then burned the *Gilderslieve.* The sea was so rough, and the boating so difficult, that it was eleven P. M. before the torch could be applied to the doomed ship. We lay to during the remainder of the night, under reefed topsails.

The next day the weather moderated somewhat, though the wind still continued fresh from about S. S. E. At about half-past eight P. M., the night being quite light, we gave chase to an exceedingly rakish-looking ship, whose canvas showed white under the rays of the moon, and which was carrying a press of sail. We, too, crowded sail, and for a long time it was doubtful which ship was the faster. The *Alabama* seemed to have found her match at last. Our pride was aroused, and we put our best foot foremost. We saw all the sheets snugly home, the sails well hoisted, and properly trimmed, and put the most skilful seamen at the wheel. Little by little we began to crawl upon the chase, but hour after hour passed, and still we were almost as far astern as ever. Midnight came, and the watch was relieved, and still the fugitive was beyond our grasp. Four A. M. arrived, and the old watch came back on deck again, only to wonder that the chase still continued. At last the day dawned and still the ship, with the square yards, and white canvas, was four or five miles ahead of us. We had been all night in chase of a single ship—a thing which had never happened to us before. When daylight appeared, I went below, and turned in, handing the chase over to the first lieutenant. At half-past seven—my usual time for rising—I heard the report of a gun, and pretty soon afterward an officer came below to say, that the chase proved to be a Dutchman! I must have looked a little sour at the breakfast-table, that morning, as Bartelli was evidently a little nervous and fidgety.

Forty-eight hours after this night-chase, we had another, though with better success, as a prize rewarded me for my loss of rest. The chase commenced about two A. M., and it was half-past seven A. M., before we were near enough to heave the fugitive to, with a gun. She proved to be the *Jabez Snow,* of

Buckport, Maine, last from Cardiff, with a cargo of coal, for Montevideo. On the back of the bill of lading was the following certificate: "We certify that the cargo of coals per *Jabez Snow*, for which this is the bill of lading, is the *bona fide* property of Messrs. Wilson, Helt, Lane & Co., and that the same are British subjects, and merchants, and also that the coals are for their own use." This certificate was signed by "John Powell & Sons," but unfortunately for the owners of the "coals" was not sworn to, and was therefore of no more validity as evidence, than the bill of lading itself. Having gotten on board from the prize, a quantity of provisions, and cordage, of both of which we were in need, we consigned her to the flames. We found on board this ship, from the sober "State of Maine," a woman who passed under the *sobriquet* of "chamber-maid." These shameless Yankee skippers make a common practice of converting their ships into brothels, and taking their mistresses to sea with them. For decency's sake, I was obliged to turn the junior lieutenant out of his state-room for her accommodation.

There were some letters found on board the *Snow* not intended for our eyes, inasmuch as they informed us of the damage we were doing the Yankee commerce. Here is one of them from the owner to the master. It is dated Boston, November 25th, 1862. "We hope you may arrive safely, and in good season, but we think you will find business rather flat at Liverpool, as American ships especially are under a cloud, owing to dangers from pirates, more politely styled privateers, which our kind friends in England are so willing should slip out of their ports, to prey on our commerce." Our torches always grew brighter as we read such effusions of joint stupidity and malice.

Here is another wail from Buckport, Maine, under date of January 16th, 1863. It instructs the master as to the best mode of employing his ship. "In the first place, it will not do to come this way with the ship; as New York business for ships is flat enough—a large fleet in that port, and nothing for them to do, that will pay expenses, and more arriving daily."

And another from the same place. "I hope you will be as prudent and economical as possible in managing your ship matters, as your owners want all the money they can get hold of, to aid in putting down this terrible rebellion of ours. The progress our war is making, I shall leave for you to gather from the papers, for it makes me sick to think of it, much more to talk about it." No doubt—the ships were being laid up, and no freights were coming in. We knew very well, on board the *Alabama*, the use to which all the "money the ship-owners could get hold of" was being put. It was to purchase "gold bonds" at half price, and push on the war. Hence our diligence in scouring the seas, and applying the torch. Whenever we heard a Yankee howl go up over a burned ship, we knew that there were fewer dollars left, with which to hire the *canaille* of Europe to throttle liberty on the American continent.

We captured the *Jabez Snow*, on the 29th of May. On the 2d of June, being in latitude 15° 01′, and longitude 34° 56′ at half-past three A. M., or just before daylight, we passed a large ship on the opposite tack. We were under topsails only, standing leisurely across the great highway. We immediately wore ship, and gave chase, crowding all sail. When day dawned, the fugitive was some six or seven miles ahead of us, and as the chase was likely to be long, I fired a gun, and hoisted the Confederate colors, to intimate to the stranger, that I would like him to be polite, and save me. the trouble of catching him, by heaving to. Pretty soon, I fired a second gun—blank cartridge—with the same intent. But the stranger had faith in his heels, and instead of heaving to, threw out a few more kites to the balmy morning breeze. But it was of no use. Both ships were on a wind, and the *Alabama* could, in consequence, use her monster trysails. My large double glasses—themselves captured from a Yankee ship, the captain of which had probably bought them to look out for the "pirate"—soon told the tale. We were gaining, but not very rapidly. Still anxious to save time, when we had approached within about four miles of the stranger, we cleared away our pivot rifle, and let him have a bolt. We did not quite reach him, but these rifle-bolts make such an ugly whizzing, and hissing, and humming as they pass along, that their commands are not often disobeyed. The stranger clewed up, and backed his main yard, and hoisted the Federal colors. We were alongside of him about half-past eleven A. M.—the chase having lasted eight hours.

The prize proved to be the bark *Amazonian* of Boston, from New York, with an assorted cargo, for Montevideo. There was an attempt to cover two of the consignments of this ship, in favor of French citizens, but the "hash" being evidently Yankee, the certificates were disregarded. The prisoners, and such "plunder" as we desired, being brought on board the *Alabama*, the ship was consigned to the flames. The following letter from a merchant in New York, to his correspondent in Buenos Ayres, was found among a very large commercial and literary mail—the literature being from the college of the Republican Propaganda—on board the *Amazonian*. "When you ship in American vessels, it would be well to have the British Consul's certificate of English property attached to bill of lading and invoice, as in the event of falling in with the numerous privateers, it would save both cargo and vessel in all probability. An American ship recently fallen in with, was released by the *Alabama*, on account of British Consul's certificate, showing greater part of cargo to be English property. If you ship in a neutral vessel, we save five per cent. war insurance."

On the day after capturing the *Amazonian*, we boarded an English brig, and I made an arrangement with the master to take my prisoners—forty-one in number—to Rio Janeiro, whither he was bound. The consideration was, twice as many provisions as the prisoners could consume, and a chronometer. The master had been afraid of offending Earl Russell, until the chronometer was named to him, when his scruples were at once removed. Virtuous Briton! thou wert near akin to the Yankee.

On the following night, a little before daylight, whilst we were lying to, with the main-topsail to the mast, a large, tall ship suddenly loomed up in close proximity to us, and as suddenly passed away into the gloom, gliding past us like a ghost. We filled away and made chase on the instant, and being still within gun-shot, fired a blank cartridge. The chase at once hove to, and we ranged up, just as day was breaking, alongside of the clipper-ship *Talisman*, from New York, with an assorted cargo, for Shanghai. There was no claim of neutral cargo among her papers, and as soon as we could remove the crew, and some necessary articles, we consigned her also, to that torch which Yankee malice had kept burning so brightly in our hands.

The rebellion of the Taepings was still going on in China, and we found a nice little "speculation" in-connection with it, embarked on board the *Talisman.* The speculators had put on board four very pretty rifled 12-pounder brass guns, and steam boilers and machinery for a gun-boat; the design being to build, and equip one of this class of vessels in the East, and take part in the Chinese war. I am afraid I spoiled a "good thing." With a Yankee Mandarin on board, and a good supply of opium, and tracts, what a smashing business this little cruiser might have done? We took a couple of these brass pieces on board the *Alabama,* and in due time, sent them afloat after the Yankee commerce, as the reader will see.

The next vessel that we overhauled was a "converted" ship — that is, a Yankee turned into an Englishman. I desired very much to burn her, but was prevented by the regularity of her papers and the circumstances surrounding her. She was a Maine-built ship, but had evidently been *bona fide* transferred, as her master and crew were all Englishmen, and she was then on a voyage from London to Calcutta. She received on board from us, a couple of the passengers — an Irishman and his wife — captured on board of the *Talisman,* who were anxious to go to Calcutta. For the next two or three days, we had a series of blows, amounting almost to gales of wind. We had arrived off the Abrolhos Shoals — a sort of Brazilian Cape Hatteras, for bad weather. On the 9th and 10th of June, we were reduced to close reefs; and, which was remarkable, we had a high barometer all the time. We had, for some days, experienced a northerly current. The whole coast of Brazil is coral-bound, and it is, for this reason, very dangerous. The coral shoals rise abruptly, from great depths, and are some-times found in very small patches, with deep water all around them. Many of these patches have been missed by the surveyor, and are not laid down on any charts, in consequence. Hence it behooves the prudent mariner, to give the banks that fringe the coasts of Brazil, a pretty wide berth.

CHAPTER XLV.

WE captured our last ship off the Abrolhos, as related in
the last chapter. We have since worked our way as
far south, as latitude 22° 38′, and it is the middle of June —
equivalent in the southern hemisphere, to the middle of December, in the northern. Hence the blows, and other bad
weather we are beginning to meet with. On the 16th of June,
we overhauled two more American ships, under English colors.
One of these was the *Azzapadi* of Port Louis, in the Mauritius.
She was formerly the *Joseph Hale*, and was built at Portland,
Maine. Having put into Port Louis, in distress, she had been
sold for the benefit of "whom it might concern," and purchased by English parties, two years before. The other was
the *Queen of Beauty*, formerly the *Challenger*. Under her new
colors and nationality, she was now running as a packet between London, and Melbourne in Australia. These were both
bona fide transfers, and were evidence of the straits to which
Yankee commerce was being put. Many more ships disappeared from under the "flaunting lie" by sale, than by capture,
their owners not being able to employ them.

The day after we overhauled these ships, we boarded a Bremen bark, from Buenos Ayres, for New York, with hides and tal-

low, on Yankee account. The correspondents of the New York merchants were taking the advice of the latter, and shipping in neutral bottoms to avoid paying the premium on the war risk.

On the 20th of June, we observed in latitude 25° 48', and found the weather so cool, as to compel us to put on our thick coats. On that day we made another capture. It was the *Conrad*, of Philadelphia, from Buenos Ayres, for New York, with part of a cargo of wool. There were certificates found on board claiming the property as British, but as there were abundant circumstances in the *res gestæ*, pointing to American ownership, I disregarded the certificates, and condemned both ship and cargo as good prize. The *Conrad* being a tidy little bark, of about three hundred and fifty tons, with good sailing qualities, I resolved to commission her as a cruiser. Three or four officers, and ten or a dozen men would be a sufficient crew for her, and this small number I could spare from the *Alabama*, without putting myself to material inconvenience. Never, perhaps, was a ship of war fitted out so promptly before. The *Conrad* was a commissioned ship, with armament, crew, and provisions on board, flying her pennant, and with sailing orders signed, sealed, and delivered, before sunset on the day of her capture. I sent Acting-Lieutenant Low on board to command her, and gave him Midshipman George T. Sinclair, as his first lieutenant; and promoted a couple of active and intelligent young seamen, as master's mates, to serve with Mr. Sinclair, as watch officers. Her armament consisted of the two 12-pounder brass rifled guns, which we had captured from the Yankee mandarin, who was going out, as the reader has seen, on board of the *Talisman*, to join the Taepings; twenty rifles, and half a dozen revolvers. I called the new cruiser, the *Tuscaloosa*, after the pretty little town of that name, on the Black Warrior River in the State of Alabama. It was meet that a child of the *Alabama* should be named after one of the towns of the State. The baptismal ceremony was not very elaborate. When all was ready—it being now about five P. M.—at a concerted signal, the *Tuscaloosa* ran up the Confederate colors, and the crew of the *Alabama* leaped into the rigging; and taking off their hats, gave three hearty cheers! The cheers were answered by the small crew of the newly commissioned ship, and the ceremony was over. Captain Low had now only to fill away, and make sail, on his cruise. Our first meeting was to be at the Cape of Good Hope. My bantling was thus born upon the high seas, in the South Atlantic Ocean, and no power could gainsay the legitimacy of its birth. As the reader will see, England was afterward compelled to acknowledge it, though an ill-informed cabinet minister — the Duke of Newcastle — at first objected to it.

On the same evening that we parted with the *Tuscaloosa*, we boarded the English bark, *Mary Kendall*, from Cardiff for Point de Galle, but which having met with heavy weather, and sprung a leak, was putting back to Rio Janeiro for repairs. At the request of her master I sent my surgeon on board to visit a seaman who had been badly injured by a fall. As we were within a few days' sail of Rio, I prevailed upon the master of this ship to receive my prisoners on board, to be landed. There were thirty-one of them, and among the rest, a woman from the *Conrad*, who claimed to be a passenger.

The time had now arrived for me to stretch over to the Cape of Good Hope. I had been three months near the equator, and on the coast of Brazil, and it was about time that some of Mr. Welles' ships of war, in pursuance of the tactics of that slow old gentleman, should be making their appearance on the coast in pursuit of me. I was more than ever astonished at the culpable neglect or want of sagacity of the head of the Federal Navy Department, when I arrived on the coast of Brazil, and found no Federal ship of war there. Ever since I had left the island of Jamaica, early in January, I had been working my way, gradually, to my present cruising ground. My ship had been constantly reported, and any one of his clerks could have plotted my track, from these reports, so as to show him, past all peradventure, where I was bound. But even independently of any positive evidence, he might have been sure, that sooner or later I would make my way to that great thoroughfare.

As has been frequently remarked in the course of these pages, the sea has its highways and byways, as well as the land. Every seaman, now, knows where these highways are, and when he is about to make a voyage, can plot his track in advance. None of these highways are better defined, or per-

haps so well defined, as the great public road that leads along
the coast of Brazil.   All the commerce of Europe and America, bound to the Far East or the Far West, takes this road.   The
reader has seen a constant stream of ships passing the toll-gate
we established at the crossing of the thirtieth parallel, north,
all bound in this direction.   And he has seen how this stream
sweeps along by the island of Fernando de Noronha, on its
way to the great highway on the coast of Brazil.   The road
thus far is wide—the ships having a large discretion.   But
when the road has crossed the equator, and struck into the
region of the south-east trades, its limits become much circum-
scribed.   It is as much as a ship can do now, to stretch by the
coast of Brazil without tacking.   The south-east trades push
her so close down upon the coast, that it is touch and go
with her.   The road, in consequence, becomes very narrow.
The more narrow the road, the more the stream of ships is
condensed.   A cruiser, under easy sail, stretching backward
and forward *across* this road, must necessarily get sight of
nearly everything that passes.   If Mr. Welles had stationed a
heavier and faster ship than the *Alabama*—and he had a
number of both heavier and faster ships—at the crossing of
the 30th parallel; another at or near the equator, a little to
the eastward of Fernando de Noronha, and a third off Bahia,
he must have driven me off, or greatly crippled me in my
movements.   A few more ships in the other chief highways,
and his commerce would have been pretty well protected.
But the old gentleman does not seem once to have thought of
so simple a policy as *stationing* a ship anywhere.

   The reader who has followed the *Alabama* in her career
thus far, has seen how many vital points he left unguarded.
His plan seemed to be, first to wait until he heard of the *Alabama* being somewhere, and then to send off a number of
cruisers, post-haste, in pursuit of her, as though he expected
her to stand still, and wait for her pursuers!   This method of
his left the game entirely in my own hands.   My safety depended upon a simple calculation of times and distances.   For
instance, when I arrived off the coast of Brazil, I would take
up my pencil, and make some such an estimate as this : I discharged my prisoners from the first ship captured, on such a

day. It will take these prisoners a certain number of days to reach a given port. It will take a certain other number of days, for the news of the capture to travel thence to Washington. And it will take a certain other number still, for a ship of war of the enemy to reach the coast of Brazil. Just before this aggregate of days elapses, I haul aft my trysail sheets, and stretch over to the Cape of Good Hope. I find no enemy's ship of war awaiting me here. I go to work on the stream of commerce doubling the Cape. And by the time, I think, that the ships which have arrived on the coast of Brazil in pursuit of me, have heard of my being at the Cape, and started in fresh chase; I quietly stretch back to the coast of Brazil, and go to work as before. *Voila tout!* The reader will have occasion to remark, by the time we get through with our cruises, how well this system worked for me; as he will have observed, that I did not fall in with a single enemy's cruiser at sea, at any time during my whole career!

We had, some days since, crossed the tropic of Capricorn, and entered the "variables" of the southern hemisphere; and having reached the forks of the great Brazilian highway, that is to say, the point at which the stream of commerce separates into two principal branches, one passing around Cape Horn, and the other around the Cape of Good Hope, we had taken the left-hand fork. We had not proceeded far on this road, however, before we found upon examination of our bread-room, that the weevil, that pestilent little destroyer of bread-stuffs in southern climates, had rendered almost our entire supply of bread useless! It was impossible to proceed on a voyage of such length, as that to the Cape of Good Hope, in such a dilemma, and I put back for Rio Janeiro, to obtain a fresh supply; *unless I could capture it by the way.* We were now in latitude 28° 01', and longitude 28° 29', or about 825 miles from Rio; some little distance to travel to a baker's shop. We were saved this journey, however, as the reader will presently see, by a Yankee ship which came very considerately to our relief.

For the next few days, the weather was boisterous and unpleasant — wind generally from the north-west, with a south-easterly current. Ships were frequently in sight, but they all proved to be neutral. On the 30th of June, the weather moderated, and became fine for a few days. On the 1st of July, after overhauling as many as eleven neutral ships, we gave chase, at eleven P. M., to a twelfth sail looming up on the horizon. She looked American, and had heels, and the chase continued all night. As the day dawned, a fine, tall ship, with taper spars, and white canvas, was only a few miles ahead of us. A blank cartridge brought the United States colors to her peak, but still she kept on. She was as yet three miles distant, and probably had some hope of escape. At all events, her captain had pluck, and held on to his canvas until the last moment. It was not until we had approached him near enough to send a shot whizzing across his bow, that he consented to clew up, and heave to. She proved to be the *Anna F. Schmidt*, of Maine, from Boston, for San Francisco, with a valuable cargo of assorted merchandise; much of it consisting of ready-made clothing, hats, boots, and shoes. Here was a haul for the paymaster! But unfortunately for Jack, the coats were too fine, and the tails too long. The trousers and undergarments were all right, however, and of these we got a large supply on board. The *Schmidt* had on board, too, the very article of bread, and in the proper quantity, that we were in want of. We received on board from her thirty days' supply, put up in the nicest kind of air-tight casks. Crockery, china-ware, glass, lamps, clocks, sewing-machines, patent medicines, clothes-pins, and the latest invention for killing bed-bugs, completed her cargo. No Englishman or Frenchman could possibly own such a cargo, and there was, consequently, no attempt among the papers to protect it. It took us nearly the entire day to do the requisite amount of "robbing" on board the *Schmidt*, and the torch was not applied to her until near nightfall. We then wheeled about, and took the fork of the road again, for the Cape of Good Hope.

Whilst we were yet busy with the prize, another American ship passed us, but she proved, upon being boarded, to have been sold, by her patriotic Yankee owners, to an Englishman, and was now profitably engaged in assisting the other ships of John Bull in taking away from the enemy his carrying-trade. I examined the papers and surroundings of all these ships, with great care, being anxious, if possible, to find a peg on which I might hang a doubt large enough to enable me to burn them. But, thus far, all the transfers had been *bona fide.* In the present instance, the papers were evidently genuine, and there was a Scotch master and English crew on board. At about nine P. M., on the same evening, the *Schmidt* being in flames, and the *Alabama* in the act of making sail from her, a large, taunt ship, with exceedingly square yards, passed us at rapid speed, under a cloud of canvas, from rail to truck, and from her course seemed to be bound either to Europe or the United States. She had paid no attention to the burning ship, but flew past it as though she were anxious to get out of harm's way as soon as possible. I conceived thence the idea, that she must be one of the enemy's large clipper-ships, from "round the Horn," and immediately gave chase, adding, in my eagerness to seize so valuable a prize, steam to sail. It was blowing half a gale of wind, but the phantom ship, for such she looked by moonlight, was carrying her royals and top-gallant studding-sails. This confirmed my suspicion, for surely, I thought, no ship would risk carrying away her spars, under such a press of sail, unless she were endeavoring to escape from an enemy. By the time we were well under way in pursuit, the stranger was about three miles ahead of us. I fired a gun to command him to halt. In a moment or two, to my astonishment, the sound of a gun from the stranger came booming back over the waters in response. I now felt quite sure that I had gotten hold of a New York and California clipper-ship. She had fired a gun to make me believe, probably, that she was a ship of war, and thus induce me to desist from the pursuit. But a ship of war would not carry such a press of sail, or appear to be in such a hurry to get out of the way—unless, indeed, she were an enemy's ship of inferior force; and the size of the fugitive, in the present instance, forbade such a supposition. So I sent orders below to the engineer, to stir up his fires, and put the *Alabama* at the top of her speed. My crew had all become so much excited by the chase, some of the sailors thinking we had scared up the Flying Dutchman, who was known to cruise in these seas, and others expecting a fight, that the watch had forgotten to go below to their hammocks. About midnight we overhauled the stranger near enough to speak her. She loomed up terribly large as we approached. She was painted black, with a white streak around her waist, man-of-war fashion, and we could count, with the aid of our night-glasses, five guns of a side frowning through her ports. "What ship is that?" now thundered my first lieutenant through his trumpet. "This is her Britannic Majesty's ship, *Diomede!*" came back in reply very quietly. "What ship is that?" now asked the *Diomede*. "This is the Confederate States steamer *Alabama*." "I suspected as much," said the officer, "when I saw you making sail, by the light of the burning ship." A little friendly chat now ensued, when we sheared off, and permitted her Britannic Majesty's frigate to proceed, without insisting upon an examination of "*her papers;*" and the sailors slunk below, one by one, to their hammocks, disappointed that they had neither caught the Flying Dutchman, a California clipper, or a fight.

The next day, and for several days, the weather proved fine. We were running to the eastward on the average parallel of about 30°, with the wind from N. N. E. to the N. W. Saturday, *July 4th*, 1863, is thus recorded in my journal:—"This is 'Independence day' in the 'old concern;' a holiday, which I feel half inclined to throw overboard, because it was established in such bad company, and because we have to fight the battle of independence over again, against a greater tyranny than before. Still, old feelings are strong, and it will not hurt Jack to give him an extra glass of grog."

The morning of the 6th proved cloudy and squally, and we had some showers of rain, though the barometer kept steadily up. At thirty minutes past midnight, an officer came below to inform me, that there was a large sail in sight, not a great way off. I sent word to the officer of the deck to chase, and repaired on deck pretty soon myself. In about three hours, we had approached the chase sufficiently near, to heave her to, with a shot, she having previously disregarded two blank cartridges. She proved to be another prize, the ship *Express*, of Boston, from Callao, for Antwerp, with a cargo of guano from the Chincha Islands. This cargo probably belonged to the Peruvian Government, for the guano of the Chincha Islands is a government monopoly, but our Peruvian friends had been

unfortunate in their attempts to cover it.   It had been shipped
by Messrs. Sescau, Valdeavellano & Co., and consigned to J.
Sescau & Co., at Antwerp.   On the back of the bill of lading
was the following indorsement:—"Nous soussigné, Chargé
d'Affairs, et Consul General de France, a Lima, certifions que
la chargement de mille soixante deuze tonneaux, de register, de
Huano, specifié au présent connaissement, est propriéte neutre.
Fait a Lima, le 27 Janvier, 1863."   This certificate was no
better than so much waste paper, for two reasons.   First, it
was not sworn to, and secondly, it simply averred the property
to be neutral, without stating who the owners were.   I was
sorry to burn so much property belonging, in all probability,
to Peru, but I could make no distinction between that government and an individual.   I had the right to burn the enemy's
ship, and if a neutral government chose to put its property on
board of her, it was its duty to document it according to the
laws of war, or abide the consequences of the neglect.   The
certificate would not have secured individual property, and I
could not permit it to screen that of a government, which was
presumed to know the law better than an individual.   As the
case stood, I was bound to presume that the property, being in
an enemy's bottom, was enemy's.   The torch followed this
decision.

The *Express* had had a long and boisterous passage around
Cape Horn, and gave signs of being much weather-beaten—
some of her spars and sails were gone, and her sides were
defaced with iron rust.   The master had his wife on board, a
gentle English woman, with her servant-maid, or rather humble companion, and it seemed quite hard that these two females,
after having braved the dangers of Cape Horn, should be carried off to brave other dangers at the Cape of Good Hope.

We were now in mid-winter, July 15th, when the storms
run riot over these two prominent head-lands of our globe.
We were fast changing our skies as we proceeded southward.
Many of the northern constellations had been buried beneath
the horizon, to rise no more, until we should recross the equa-
tor, and other new and brilliant ones had risen in their places.
We had not seen the familiar "North Star" for months.   The
Southern Cross had arisen to attract our gaze to the opposite

pole instead. The mysterious Magellan clouds hovered over the same pole, by day, and caused the mariner to dream of far-off worlds. They were even visible on very bright nights. The reader will perhaps remember the meteorological phenomena which we met with in the Gulf Stream—how regularly the winds went around the compass, from left to right, or with the course of the sun, obeying the laws of storms. Similar phenomena are occurring to us now. The winds are still going round with the sun, but they no longer go from left to right, but from right to left; for this is now the motion of the sun. Instead of watching the winds haul from north-east to east; from east to south-east; from south-east to south, as we were wont to do in the northern hemisphere, we now watch them haul from north-east to north; from north to north-west; and from north-west to west. And when we get on shore, in the gardens, and vineyards, at the Cape of Good Hope, we shall see the tendrils of the vine, and the creeping plants, twining around their respective supports, in the opposite direction, from left to right, instead of from right to left, as the reader has seen them do in the writer's garden in Alabama.

After capturing the *Express*, we passed into one of the by-ways of the sea. The fork of the road which we had been hitherto pursuing, now bore off to the south-east—the India-bound ships running well to the southward of the Cape. We turned out of the road to the left, and drew in nearer to the coast of Africa. With the exception of an occasional African trader, or a chance whaler, we were entirely out of the track of commerce. In the space of seven or eight hundred miles, we sighted but a single ship.

As we drew down toward the Cape, that singular bird, the Cape pigeon came to visit us. It is of about the size of a small sea-gull, and not unlike it in appearance. Like the petrel, it is a storm-bird, and seems to delight in the commotion of the elements. It is quite gentle, wheeling around the ship, and uttering, from time to time, its cheerful scream, or rather whistle. A peculiarity of this bird is, that it is entirely unknown in the northern hemisphere; from which it would appear, that, like the "right" whale, it is incapable of enduring the tropical heats. It would probably be death to it, to attempt to cross the equator.

On the 28th of July, we observed in latitude 33° 46′, and longitude 17° 31′, and the next day, at about nine A. M., we made Daffen Island, with its remarkable breaker, lying a short distance to the northward of the Cape of Good Hope. Instead of running into Cape Town, I deemed it more prudent to go first to Saldanha Bay, and reconnoitre. There might be enemy's ships of war off the Cape, and if so, I desired to get news of them, before they should hear of my being in these seas. As we were running in for the bay, we overhauled a small coasting schooner, the master of which volunteered to take us in to the anchorage; and early in the afternoon, we came to, in five and three quarter fathoms of water, in a cosy little nook of the bay, sheltered from all winds. There was no Yankee man-of-war at the Cape, nor had there been any there for some months! Mr. Welles was asleep, the coast was all clear, and I could renew my "depredations" upon the enemy's commerce whenever I pleased.

There is no finer sheet of land-locked water in the world than Saldanha Bay. Its anchorage is bold, and clean, and spacious enough to accommodate the largest fleets. It is within a few hours' sail of the cape, which is the halfway mile-post, as it were, between the extreme east, and the extreme west, and yet commerce, with a strange caprice, has established its relay-house at Cape Town, whose anchorage is open to all the winter gales, from which a ship is in constant danger of being wrecked. We did not find so much as a coaster at anchor, in this splendid harbor. The country around was wild and picturesque in appearance; the substratum being of solid rock, and nature having played some strange freaks, when chaos was being reduced to order. Rocky precipices and palisades meet the beholder at every turn, and immense boulders of granite lie scattered on the coast and over the hills, as if giants had been amusing themselves at a game of marbles. A few farm-houses are in sight from the ship, surrounded by patches of cultivation, but all the rest of the landscape is a semi-barren waste of straggling rocks, and coarse grass. The country improves, however, a short distance back from the coast, and the grazing becomes fine. Beef cattle are numerous, and of fair size, and the sheep flourishes in great perfection — wool being one of the staple products of the colony. The cereals are also produced, and, as every one knows, the Cape has long been famous for its delicate wines.

My first care was to send the paymaster on shore, to contract for supplying the crew with fresh provisions, during our stay, and my next to inform the Governor at the Cape of my arrival. As I turned into my cot that night, with a still ship, in a land-locked harbor, with no strange sails, or storms to disturb my repose, I felt like a weary traveller, who had laid down, for the time, a heavy burden. The morning after our arrival — the 30th of July — was bright and beautiful, and I landed early to get sights for my chronometers. It was the first time I had ever set foot on the continent of Africa, and I looked forth, from the eminence on which I stood, upon a wild, desolate, and yet picturesque scene. The ocean was slumbering in the distance, huge rocky precipices were around me, the newly risen sun was scattering the mists from the hills, and the only signs of life save the *Alabama* at my feet, and the ox-team of a boer which was creeping along the beach, were the screams of the sea-fowl, as they whirled around me, and, from time to time, made plunges into the still waters in quest of their prey. A profusion of wild flowers bloomed in little parterres among the rocks, and among others, I plucked the geranium, in several varieties. This was evidently its native home.

Returning on board at the usual breakfast hour, I found that Bartelli had made excellent use of his time. There was a hut or two on the beach, to which a market-boat had been sent from the ship, to bring off the fresh beef and vegetables for the crew, which the paymaster had contracted for on the previous evening. Bartelli had accompanied it, and the result was a venison steak, cut fresh from a spring-bok that a hunter had just brought in, simmering in his chafing dish. There were some fine pan-fish on the table, too; for my first lieutenant, ever mindful of the comfort of his people, had sent a party on shore with the seine, which had had fine success, and reported the bay full of fish. Jack, after having been nearly three months on a diet of salted beef and pork, was once more in clover, and my young officers were greatly excited by the reports that came off to them from the shore, of the variety and abundance of game, in the neighborhood. Besides the curlew, snipe, and plover, that were to be found on the beach, and in the salt marshes adjacent, the quail, pheasant, deer in several varieties, and even the ostrich, the lion, and the tiger, awaited them, if they should think proper to go a little distance inland. The small islands in the bay abounded in rabbits, which might be chased and knocked on the head with sticks. Hunting-parties were soon organized, and there was a great cleaning and burnishing of fowling-pieces, and adjusting and filling of powder-flasks and shot-pouches going on.

But all was not to be pleasure; there was duty to be thought of as well. The *Alabama* required considerable overhauling after her late cruise, both in her machinery, and hull, and rigging. Among other things, it was quite necessary that she should be re-caulked, inside and out, and re-painted. There were working-parties organized, therefore, as well as hunting and fishing-parties. We soon found, too, that we had the duties of hospitality to attend to. The fame of the "British Pirate" had preceded her. Every ship which had touched at the Cape, had had more or less to say of the *Alabama*. Mr. Seward and Mr. Adams, Lord Russell and the "London Times" had made her famous, and the people manifested great curiosity to see her. We were, in a measure, too, among our own kinsmen. The Cape of Good Hope, as all the world knows, had been a Dutch colony, and was now inhabited by a mixed population of Dutch and English. The African had met the usual fate of the savage, when he comes in contact with civilized man. He had been thrust aside, and was only to be seen as a straggler and stranger in his native land.

From far and near, the country-people flocked in to see us, in every description of vehicle, from the tidy spring-wagon, with its pair of sleek ponies, to the ox-cart. The vehicles, containing mostly women and children, were preceded or followed by men on horseback, by twos and threes, and sometimes by the dozen. The men brought along with them their shot-guns and rifles, thus converting their journey into a hunting-party, as well as one of curiosity. Those from a distance came provided with tents and camp-equipage. Almost every one had some present of game or curiosity to offer, as he came on board. One would bring me a wild-peacock for dinner, which he had shot on the wayside; another a brace of pheasants; others ostrich-eggs fresh from the nest, plumes of ostrich-feathers, spikes from the head of the spring-bok three and four feet in length, &c. We showed them around the ship — the young boers lifting our hundred-pound rifle-shot, and looking over the sights of our guns, and the young women looking at the moustaches of my young officers.

The Saldanha settlement is almost exclusively Dutch, notwithstanding it has been fifty years and more in possession of the English. Dutch is the language universally spoken; all the newspapers are published in that melodious tongue, and the "young idea" is being taught to "shoot" in it. One young man among our visitors, though he was twenty-three years of age, and lived within twenty miles of the sea, told me he had never been on board of a ship before. He became very much excited, and went into ecstasies at everything he saw, particularly at the size and weight of the guns, which seemed to transcend all his philosophy — the largest gun which he had hitherto seen, being his own rifle, with which he was in the habit of bringing down the ostrich or the tiger. The climate seemed to be well suited to these descendants of the Hollanders. The men were athletic and well-proportioned, and the young women chubby, and blooming with the blended tints of the lily and the rose — the rose rather preponderating. The beauty of these lasses — and some of them were quite pretty — was due entirely to mother Nature, as their large and somewhat rough hands, and awkward courtesies showed that they were rather more familiar with milking the cows and churning the butter, than with the airs and graces of the saloon.

We remained a week in Saldanha Bay, during the whole of which, we had exceedingly fine weather; the wind generally prevailing from the south-east, and the sky being clear, with now and then a film of gray clouds. This was quite remarkable for the first days of August — this month being equivalent, at the "stormy Cape," to the month of February, in the northern hemisphere. The natives told us that so gentle a winter had not been known for years before. The temperature was delightful. Although we were in the latitude of about 34° — say the equivalent latitude to that of south-western Virginia — we did not feel the want of fires. Indeed, the grasses were green, and vegetation seemed to have been scarcely suspended. The graziers had no need to feed their cattle.

A schooner came in while we lay here, bringing us some letters from merchants at Cape Town, welcoming us to the colony, and offering to supply us with coal, or whatever else we might need. I had left orders both at Fernando de Noronha, and Bahia, for the *Agrippina*, if she should arrive at either of those places, after my departure, to make the best of her way to Saldanha Bay, and await me there. She should have preceded me several weeks. She was not here — the old Scotchman, as before remarked, having played me false.

When Kell had put his ship in order, he took a little recreation himself, and in company with one or two of his messmates went off into the interior, on an ostrich hunt. Horses and dogs, and hunters awaited them, at the country-seat of the gentleman who had invited them to partake of this peculiarly African sport. They had a grand hunt, and put up several fine birds, at which some of the party — Kell among the number, got shots — but they did not bring any "plumes" on board; at least of their own capturing. The devilish birds, as big as horses, and running twice as fast, as some of the young officers described them, refused to "heave to," they said, though they had sent sundry whistlers around their heads, in the shape of buck-shot.

A sad accident occurred to one of our young hunters before we left the bay. One afternoon, just at sunset, I was shocked to receive the intelligence that one of the cutters had returned alongside, with a dead officer in it. Third Assistant Engineer Cummings was the unfortunate officer. He had been hunting with a party of his messmates. They had all returned with well-filled game-bags to the boat, at sunset, and Cummings was in the act of stepping into her, when the cock of his gun striking against the gunwale, a whole load of buck-shot passed through his chest in the region of the heart, and he fell dead, in an instant, upon the sands. The body was lifted tenderly into the boat, and taken on board, and prepared by careful and affectionate hands for interment on the morrow. This young gentleman had been very popular, with both officers and crew, and his sudden death cast a gloom over the ship. All amusements were suspended, and men walked about with softened foot-fall, as though fearing to disturb the slumbers of the dead. Arrangements were made for interring him in the grave-yard of a neighboring farmer, and the next morning, the colors of the ship were half-masted, and all the boats — each with its colors also at half-mast — formed in line, and as many of the officers and crew as could be spared from duty, followed the deceased to his last resting-place. There were six boats in the procession, and as they pulled in for the shore, with the well-known funeral stroke and drooping flags, the spectacle was one to sadden the heart. A young life had been suddenly cut short in a far distant land. A subscription was taken up to place a proper tomb over his remains, and the curious visitor to Saldanha Bay may read on a simple, but enduring marble slab, this mournful little episode in the history of the cruise of the *Alabama*.

CHAPTER XLVI.

THE CONNECTING THREAD OF THE HISTORY OF THE WAR
TAKEN UP — A BRIEF REVIEW OF THE EVENTS OF THE
TWELVE MONTHS DURING WHICH THE ALABAMA HAD
BEEN COMMISSIONED — ALABAMA ARRIVES AT CAPE
TOWN — CAPTURE OF THE SEA BRIDE — EXCITEMENT
THEREUPON — CORRESPONDENCE BETWEEN THE AMER-
ICAN CONSUL AND THE GOVERNOR ON THE SUBJECT OF
THE CAPTURE.

THE *Alabama* has been commissioned, now, one year. In accordance with my plan of connecting my cruises with a thread—a mere thread—of the history of the war, it will be necessary to retrace our steps, and take up that thread at the point at which it was broken—August, 1862. At that date, as the reader will recollect, the splendid army of McClellan had been overwhelmed with defeat, and driven in disorder, from before Richmond, and the fortunes of the Confederacy had greatly brightened in consequence. Lee followed up this movement with the invasion of Maryland; not for the purpose of fighting battles, but to free the people of that Southern State from the military despotism which had been fastened upon them by the enemy, and enable them, if they thought proper, to join their fortunes with those of the Confederacy. But he penetrated only that portion of the State in which the people had always been but lukewarm Southerners, and an indifferent, if not cold, reception awaited him. The result might have been different if he could have made his way into the city of Baltimore, and the more Southern parts of the State. There the enemy was as cordially detested, as in any part of the Confederacy. The Federal Government had, by this time, gotten firm military possession of the State, through the treason of Governor Bradford, Mayor Swann, and others, and nothing short of driving out the enemy from the city of Baltimore, and occupying it by our troops, could enable the people of that true and patriotic city to move in defence of their liberties, and save their State from the desecration that awaited her.

Harper's Ferry was captured by a portion of Lee's forces; the battle of Sharpsburg was fought (17th September, 1862) without decisive results, and Lee recrossed his army into Virginia.

In the West, Corinth was evacuated by General Beauregard, who was threatened with being flanked, by an enemy of superior force.

Memphis was captured soon afterward, by a Federal fleet, which dispersed the few Confederate gunboats that offered it a feeble resistance.

The fall of Fort Pillow and Memphis opened the way for the enemy, as far down the Mississippi as Vicksburg. Here Farragut's and Porter's fleets—the former from below, the latter from above—united in a joint attack upon the place, but Van Dorn beat them off.

The Confederates made an attempt to dislodge the enemy from Baton Rouge, the capital of Louisiana, about forty miles below the mouth of the Red River, but failed. The expedition was to be a joint naval and military one, but the naval portion of it failed by an unfortunate accident. Breckinridge, with less than 3000 men, fought a gallant action against a superior force, and drove the enemy into the town, but for want of the naval assistance promised could not dislodge him. We now occupied Port Hudson below Baton Rouge, and the enemy evacuated Baton Rouge in consequence. We thus held the Mississippi River between Port Hudson and Vicksburg, a distance of more than 200 miles.

General Bragg now made a campaign into Kentucky, which State he occupied for several weeks, but was obliged finally to evacuate, by overwhelming forces of the enemy. During this campaign, the battles of Richmond and Perryville were fought. Bragg gathered immense supplies during his march, killed, wounded, or captured 25,000 of the enemy's troops, and returned with a well-clothed, well-equipped, more numerous, and better disciplined army than he had at the beginning of the campaign. The effect of this campaign was to relieve North Alabama and Middle Tennessee of the presence of the enemy for some months.

In September, 1862, Van Dorn attacked Rosencrans at Corinth, but was obliged to withdraw after a gallant and bloody fight. He retreated in good order.

After Lee's retreat into Virginia, from his march into Maryland, which has been alluded to, McClellan remained inactive for some time, and the Northern people becoming dissatisfied, clamored for a change of commanders. Burnside was appointed to supersede him — a man, in every way unfit for the command of a large army. With an army of 150,000 men, this man of straw crossed the Rappahannock, and attacked Lee at Fredericksburg, in obedience to the howl of the Northern Demos, of "On to Richmond!" A perfect slaughter of his troops ensued. As far as can be learned, this man did not cross the river at all himself, but sent his troops to assault works in front which none but a madman would have thought of attempting — especially with a river in his rear. It is only necessary to state the result. Federal loss in killed, 1152; wounded, 7000. Confederate loss in killed and wounded, 1800. During a storm of wind and rain, the beaten army regained the shelter of its camps on the opposite side of the river. Burnside was now thrown overboard by the Northern Demos, as McClellan had been before him.

As the old year died, and the new year came in, the battle of Murfreesborough, in Middle Tennessee, was fought between Bragg and Rosencrans, which was bloody on both sides, and indecisive. Bragg retired from Murfreesborough, but was not molested by the enemy during his retreat. The year 1862 may be said, upon the whole, to have resulted brilliantly for the Confederate arms. We had fought drawn battles, and had made some retrograde movements, but, on the other hand, we had gained splendid victories, made triumphant marches into the enemy's territory, and even threatened his capital. The nations of the earth were looking upon us with admiration, and we had every reason to feel encouraged.

One of the first events of the year 1863, was the dispersion of the enemy's blockading fleet, off Charleston, by Commodore Ingraham, with two small iron-clads, the *Chicora* and the *Palmetto State*. This gallant South Carolinian, in his flag-ship, the *Chicora*, first attacked the *Mercedita*, Captain Stellwagen. Having run into this vessel, and fired one or two shots at her, she cried for quarter, and surrendered, believing herself to be in a sinking condition. In a few minutes, the *Mercedita* sent a boat alongside the *Chicora*, with her first lieutenant, who, by authority of his captain, surrendered the ship, and assented to the *paroling* of the officers and crew. The two little iron-clads then went in pursuit of the enemy's other ships, and succeeded in getting a shot at one or two of them, but they were all too fast for them, and betaking themselves to their heels, soon put themselves out of harm's way. In a short time there was not a blockader to be seen!

Judge of the surprise of Commodore Ingraham, when, upon his return, he found that his prize, the *Mercedita*, which he had left at anchor, under *parole*, had cleared out. Captain Stellwagen, and every officer and man on board the *Mercedita*, had solemnly promised *on honor* — for this is the nature of a parole — that they would do no act of war until exchanged. From the moment they made that promise, they were *hors du combat*. They were prisoners at large, on board the ship which they had surrendered to the enemy. And yet, when that enemy turned his back — relying upon the *parole* which they had given him — they got up their anchor, and steamed off to Port Royal, and reported to their Admiral — Dupont! Did Dupont send her back to Ingraham? No. He reported the facts to Mr. Secretary Welles. And what did Mr. Secretary Welles do? He kept possession of the ship at the sacrifice of the honor of the Department over which he presided. And what think you, reader, was the excuse? It is a curiosity. Admiral Dupont reported the case thus to Mr. Welles:—" * * * Unable to use his [Stellwagen's] guns, and being at the mercy of the enemy, which was lying alongside, on his starboard quarter, all further resistance was deemed hopeless by Captain Stellwagen, and he surrendered. The crew and officers were paroled, *though nothing was said about the ship;* the executive officer, Lieutenant-Commander Abbot, having gone on board the enemy's ship, and made the arrangements." Mr. Welles, thus prompted by Admiral Dupont, adopted the exceedingly brilliant idea, that as *nothing had been said about the ship* — that is, as the *ship* had not been paroled, she might, like every other unparoled prisoner, walk off with herself, and make her escape! But to say nothing of the odd idea of paroling a ship, these honorable casuists overlooked the small circumstance that the ship could not make her escape without the assistance of the paroled officers; and it was an act of war for paroled officers to get under way, and carry off from her anchors, a prize-ship of the enemy. It was a theft, and breach of honor besides.

A few days after Ingraham's raid, Galveston was recaptured by the Confederates, as already described when speaking of the victory of the *Alabama* over the *Hatteras*.

Sherman made an attempt upon Vicksburg, and failed. Admiral Dupont, with a large and well appointed fleet of ironclads, attacked Charleston, and was beaten back — one of his ships being sunk, and others seriously damaged. On the Potomac, Hooker had been sent by the many-headed monster to relieve Burnside, which was but the substitution of one dunderhead for another. But Hooker had the *sobriquet* of "fighting Joe," and this tickled the monster. "With the most splendid army on the planet," as characterized by the hyperbolous Joe himself, he crossed the Rappahannock, *on his way to Richmond.* Lee had no more than about one third of Hooker's force, with which to oppose him. Three battles ensued — at the Wilderness, Chancellorsville, and Salem Church, which resulted in the defeat and rout of "fighting Joe," and his rapid retreat to the north bank of the Rappahannock. But these victories cost us the life of Stonewall Jackson, the Cœur de Leon of the Southern Confederacy. His body has been given to the worms, but his exploits equal, if they do not excel, those of Napoleon in his first Italian campaign, and will fire the youth of America as long as our language lives, and history continues to be read.

A third attempt was made upon Vicksburg; this time by General Grant, with a large army that insured success. With this army, and a fleet of gunboats, he laid siege to Pemberton. On the 4th of July Pemberton surrendered. This was a terrible blow to us. It not only lost us an army, but cut the Confederacy in two, by giving the enemy the command of the Mississippi River. Port Hudson followed. As a partial set-off to these disasters, General Dick Taylor captured Brasher City, a very important base which the enemy had established for operations in Louisiana and Texas. Nearly five million dollars' worth of stores fell into Taylor's hands.

After the defeat of Hooker, Lee determined upon another move across the enemy's border. Hooker followed, keeping himself between Lee and Washington, supposing the latter to be the object of Lee's movement. But Lee moved by the Shenandoah Valley, upon Gettysburg in Pennsylvania. Hooker now resigned the command, for which he found himself unfitted, and Meade was sent to relieve him. The latter marched forthwith upon Gettysburg, cautiously disposing his troops, meanwhile, so as to cover both Baltimore and Washington. The greatest battle of the war was fought here during the first three days of July. Both parties were whipped, and on the 4th of July, when Pemberton was surrendering Vicksburg to Grant, Lee was preparing to withdraw from Gettysburg for the purpose of recrossing the Potomac. If the battle had been fought in Virginia, Meade would have been preparing, in like manner, to cross the same river, but to a different side. Lee withdrew without serious molestation, Meade being too badly crippled, to do more than follow him at a limping gait. The disproportion of numbers in this battle was greatly in favor of Meade, and he had, besides, the advantage of acting on the defensive, in an intrenched position.

Vicksburg and Gettysburg mark an era in the war. The Confederates, from this time, began to show signs of weakness. In consequence of the great disparity of numbers, we had been compelled, at an early day in the war, to draw upon our whole fighting population. The Northern hive was still swarming, and apparently as numerous as ever. All Europe was, besides, open to the North as a recruiting station, and we have seen, in the course of these pages, how unscrupulously and fraudulently the Federal agents availed themselves of this advantage. We were being hard pressed, too, for *material*, for the enemy was maintaining a rigid blockade of our ports, and was, besides, with a barbarity unknown in civilized war, laying waste our plantations and corn-fields. We need no better evidence of the shock which had been given to public confidence in the South, by those two disasters, than the simple fact, that our currency depreciated almost immediately a thousand per cent.! Later in the summer, another attempt was made upon Charleston, which was repulsed as the others had been. Dupont, after his failure, had been thrown overboard, and Admiral Foote ordered to succeed him; but Foote dying before he could assume command, Dahlgren was substituted. This gentleman had, from a very early period in his career, directed his attention to ordnance, and turned to account the experiments of Colonel Paixan with shell-guns and shell-firing. He had much improved upon the old-fashioned naval ordnance, in vogue before the advent of steamships, and for these labors of his in the foundries and work-shops, he had been made an Admiral. He was now sent to aid General Gilmore, an engineer of some reputation, to carry out the favorite Boston idea of razing Charleston to the ground, as the original hot-bed of secession. They made a lodgment on Morris Island, but failed, as Dupont had done, against the other works. We have thus strung, as it were, upon our thread of the war, the more important military events that occurred during the first year of the cruise of the *Alabama*. We will now return to that ship. We left her at Saldanha Bay, near the Cape of Good Hope.

On the morning of the 5th of August, the weather being fine, and the wind light from the south, we got under way for Table Bay. As we were steaming along the coast, we fell in with our consort, the *Tuscaloosa*, on her way to join us, at Saldanha Bay, in accordance with her instructions. She had been delayed by light winds and calms. She reported the capture of the enemy's ship *Santee*, from the East Indies, laden with rice, on British account, and bound for Falmouth, in England. She had released her on ransom-bond. The *Tuscaloosa* being in want of supplies, I directed her to proceed to Simon Town, in Simon's Bay, to the eastward of the Cape, and there refit, and provide herself with whatever might be necessary. A little after mid-day, as we were hauling in for

Cape Town, "sail ho!" was cried from aloft; and when we had raised the sail from the deck, we could see quite distinctly that the jaunty, newly painted craft, with the taper spars, and white canvas, was an American bark, bound, like ourselves, into Table Bay. As before remarked, the wind was light, and the bark was not making much headway. This was fortunate, for if there had been a brisk breeze blowing, she must have run within the charmed marine league, before we could have overhauled her.

Hoisting the English colors, we gave the *Alabama* all steam in chase, and came near enough to heave the stranger to, when she was still five or six miles from the land. She proved to be the *Sea-Bride*, of Boston, from New York, and bound, with an assorted cargo of provisions and notions, on a trading voyage along the eastern coast of Africa. I threw a prize crew on board of her, and as I could not take her into port with me, I directed the officer to stand off and on until further orders— repairing to Saldanha Bay, by the 15th of the month, in case he should be blown off by a gale. The capture of this ship caused great excitement at Cape Town, it having been made within full view of the whole population. The editor of a daily newspaper published at the Cape—the "Argus"—witnessed it, and we will let him describe it. The following is an extract from that paper, of the date of the 6th of August, 1863 :—

"Yesterday, at almost noon, a steamer from the northward was made down from the signal-post, on Lion's Hill. The Governor had, on the previous day, received a letter from Captain Semmes, informing his Excellency that the gallant captain had put his ship into Saldanha Bay for repairs. This letter had been made public in the morning, and had caused no little excitement. Cape Town, that has been more than dull—that has been dismal for months, thinking and talking of nothing but bankruptcies—bankruptcies fraudulent, and bankruptcies unavoidable—was now all astir, full of life and motion. The stoop of the Commercial Exchange was crowded with merchants, knots of citizens were collected at the corner of every street; business was almost, if not entirely suspended.

"All that could be gleaned, in addition to the information of Captain Semmes' letter to the Governor, a copy of which was sent to the United States Consul, immediately it was received, was that the schooner *Atlas* had just returned from Malagas Island, where she had been with water and vegetables for men collecting guano there. Captain Boyce, the master of the *Atlas*, reported that he had himself actually seen the *Alabama ;* a boat from the steamer had boarded his vessel, and he had been on board of her. His report of Captain Semmes corroborated that given by every one else. He said the Captain was most courteous and gentlemanly. He asked Captain Boyce to land thirty prisoners for him, in Table Bay, with which request Captain Boyce was unable to comply. Captain Semmes said that the *Florida* was also a short distance off the Cape, and that the *Alabama*, when she had completed her repairs, and was cleaned and painted, would pay Table Bay a visit. He expected to be there, he said, very nearly as soon as the *Atlas*. Shortly after the *Atlas* arrived, a boat brought up some of the prisoners from Saldanha Bay, and among them one of the crew of the *Alabama*, who said he had left the ship. All these waited on the United States Consul, but were unable to give much information, beyond what we had already received.

"The news that the *Alabama* was coming into Table Bay, and would probably arrive about four o'clock this afternoon, added to the excitement. About noon, a steamer from the north-west was made down by the signal-man on the hill. Could this be the *Alabama ?* or was it the *Hydaspes*, from India, or the *Lady Jocelyn* from England? All three were now hourly expected, and the city was in doubt. Just after one, it was made down '*Confederate steamer Alabama from the north-west, and Federal bark from the south-east.*' Here was to be a capture by the celebrated Confederate craft, close to the entrance of Table Bay. The inhabitants rushed off to get a sight. Crowds of people ran up the Lion's Hill, and to the Kloof Road. All the cabs were chartered — every one of them ; there was no cavilling about fares ; the cabs were taken, and no questions asked, but orders were given to drive as hard as possible.

"The bark coming in from the south-east, and, as the signal-man made down, five miles off ; the steamer coming in from the north-west, eight miles off, led us to think that the kloof road was the best place for a full view. To that place we directed our Jehu to drive furiously. We did the first mile in a short time ; but the kloof-hill for the next two and a half miles is up-hill work. The horse jibbed, so we pushed on, on foot, as fast as possible, and left the cab to come on. When we reached the summit, we could only make out a steamer on the horizon, from eighteen to twenty miles off. This could not be the *Alabama*, unless she was making off to sea again. There was no bark. As soon as our cab reached the crown of the hill, we set off at a break-neck pace, down the hill, on past the Round-house, till we came near Brighton, and as we reached the corner, there lay the *Alabama* within fifty yards of the unfortunate Yankee. As the Yankee came around from the south-east, and about five miles from the Bay, the steamer came down upon her. The Yankee was evidently taken by surprise. The *Alabama* fired a gun, and brought her to.

"When first we got sight of the *Alabama*, it was difficult to make out what she was doing; the bark's head had been put about, and the *Alabama* lay off quite immovable, as if she were taking a sight of the 'varmint.' The weather was beautifully calm and clear, and the sea was as smooth and transparent as a sheet of glass. The bark was making her way slowly from the steamer, with every bit of her canvas spread. The *Alabama*, with her steam off, appeared to be letting the bark get clear off. What could this mean? No one understood. It must be the *Alabama*. 'There,' said the spectators, 'is the Confederate flag at her peak; it must be a Federal bark, too, for there are the stars and stripes of the States flying at her main.' What could the *Alabama* mean lying there—

> 'As idly as a painted ship
> Upon a painted ocean.'

What it meant was soon seen. Like a cat, watching and playing with a victimized mouse, Captain Semmes permitted his prize to draw off a few yards, and then he up steam again, and pounced upon her. She first sailed round the Yankee from stem to stern, and stern to stem again. The way that fine, saucy, rakish craft was handled was worth riding a hundred miles to see. She went round the bark like a toy, making a complete circle, and leaving an even margin of water between herself and her prize, of not more than twenty yards. From the hill it appeared as if there was no water at all between the two vessels. This done, she sent a boat with a prize crew off, took possession in the name of the Confederate States, and sent the bark off to sea.

"The *Alabama* then made for the port. We came round the Kloof to visit Captain Semmes on board. As we came, we found the heights overlooking Table Bay covered with people; the road to Green Point lined with cabs. The windows of the villas at the bottom of the hill were all thrown up, and ladies waved their handkerchiefs, and one and all joined in the general enthusiasm; over the quarries, along the Malay burying-ground, the Gallows Hill, and the beach, there were masses of people—nothing but a sea of heads as far as the eye could reach. Along Strand Street, and Alderley Street, the roofs of all the houses, from which Table Bay is overlooked, were made available as standing-places for the people who could not get boats to go off to her. The central, the north, the south, and the coaling jetties were all crowded. At the central jetty it was almost impossible to force one's way through to get a boat. However, all in good time, we did get a boat, and went off, in the midst of dingies, cargo-boats, gigs, and wherries, all as full as they could hold. Nearly all the city was upon the bay; the rowing clubs in uniform, with favored members of their respective clubs on board. The crews feathered their oars in double-quick time, and their pulling, our 'stroke' declared, was a 'caution, and no mistake.' * * * On getting alongside the *Alabama*, we found about a dozen boats before us, and we had not been on board five minutes before she was surrounded by nearly every boat in Table

Bay, and as boat after boat arrived, three hearty cheers were given for Captain Semmes and his gallant privateer. This, upon the part of a neutral people, is, perchance, wrong; but we are not arguing a case — we are recording facts. They did cheer, and cheer with a will, too. It was not, perhaps, taking the view of either side, Federal or Confederate, but in admiration of the skill, pluck, and daring of the *Alabama*, her captain, and her crew, who afford a general theme of admiration for the world all over.

"Visitors were received by the officers of the ship most courteously, and without distinction, and the officers conversed freely and unreservedly of their exploits. There was nothing like brag in their manner of answering questions put to them. They are as fine and gentlemanly a set of fellows as ever we saw; most of them young men. The ship has been so frequently described, that most people know what she is like, as we do who have seen her. We should have known her to be the *Alabama*, if we had boarded her in the midst of the ocean, with no one to introduce us to each other. Her guns alone are worth going off to see, and everything about her speaks highly of the seamanship and discipline of her commander and his officers. She had a very large crew, fine, lithe-looking fellows, the very picture of English man-of-war's men."

The editor of the "Argus" has not overdrawn the picture when he says, that nearly all Cape Town was afloat, on the evening of the arrival of the *Alabama*. The deck of the ship was so crowded, that it was almost impossible to stir in any direction. Nor was this simply a vulgar crowd, come off to satisfy mere curiosity. It seemed to be a generous outpouring of the better classes. Gentlemen and ladies of distinction pressed into my cabin, to tender me a cordial greeting. Whatever may have been the cause, their imaginations and their hearts seemed both to have been touched. I could not but be gratified at such a demonstration on the part of an entire people. The inhabitants of the Cape colony seemed to resemble our own people in their excitability, and in the warmth with which they expressed their feelings, more than the phlegmatic English people, of whom they are a part. This resemblance became still more apparent, when I had the leisure to notice the tone, and temper of their press, the marshalling of political parties, and the speeches of their public men. The colony, with its own legislature, charged with the care of its own local concerns, was almost a republic. It enjoyed all the freedom of a republic, without its evils. The check upon the franchise, and the appointment of the Executive by the Crown, so tempered the republican elements, that license was checked, without liberty being restrained.

Bartelli, my faithful steward, was in his element during the continuance of this great levée on board the *Alabama*.   He had dressed himself with scrupulous care, and posting himself at my cabin-door, with the air of a chamberlain to a king, he refused admission to all comers, until they had first presented him with a card, and been duly announced.   Pressing some of the ward-room boys into his service, he served refreshments to his numerous guests, in a style that did my *menage* infinite credit.   Fair women brought off bouquets with them, which they presented with a charming grace, and my cabin was soon garlanded with flowers.   Some of these were *immortelles* peculiar to the Cape of Good Hope, and for months afterward, they retained their places around the large mirror that adorned the after-part of my cabin, with their colors almost as bright as ever.   During my entire stay, my table was loaded with flowers, and the most luscious grapes, and other fruits, sent off to me every morning, by the ladies of the Cape, sometimes with, and sometimes without, a name.   Something has been said before about the capacity of the heart of a sailor.   My own was carried by storm on the present occasion.   I simply surrendered at discretion, and whilst Kell was explaining the virtues of his guns to his male visitors, and answering the many questions that were put to him about our cruises and captures, I found it as much as I could do, to write autographs, and answer the pretty little perfumed billets that came off to me.   Dear ladies of the Cape of Good Hope! these scenes are still fresh in my memory, and I make you but a feeble return for all your kindness, in endeavoring to impress them upon these pages, that they may endure "yet a little while."   I have always found the instincts of women to be right, and I felt more gratified at this spontaneous outpouring of the sympathies of the sex, for our cause, than if all the male creatures of the earth had approved it, in cold and formal words.

I found, at the Cape of Good Hope, the stereotyped American Consul ; half diplomat, half demagogue.   Here is a letter which the ignorant fellow wrote to the Governor, whilst I was still at Saldanha Bay : —

"SIR: From reliable information received by me, and which you are also doubtless in possession of, a war-steamer called the *Alabama*, is now in Saldanha Bay, being painted, discharging prisoners of war, &c. The vessel in question was built in England, to prey upon the commerce of the United States, and escaped therefrom while on her trial-trip, forfeiting bonds of £20,000 (!) which the British Government exacted under the Foreign Enlistment Act. Now, as your Government has a treaty of amity and commerce with the United States, and has not recognized the persons in revolt against the United States as a government at all, the vessel alluded to should be at once seized, and sent to England, whence she clandestinely escaped. Assuming that the British Government was sincere in exacting the bonds, you have, doubtless, been instructed to send her home to England, where she belongs. But if, from some oversight, you have not received such instructions, and you decline the responsibility of making the seizure, I would most respectfully protest against the vessel remaining in any port of the Colony, another day. She has been at Saldanha Bay four days already, and a week previously on the coast, and has forfeited all right to remain an hour longer, by this breach of neutrality. Painting a ship [especially with Yankee paint] does not come under the head of "necessary repairs," and is no proof that she is unseaworthy ; and to allow her to visit other ports, after she has set the Queen's proclamation of neutrality at defiance, would not be regarded as in accordance with the spirit and purpose of that document."

This letter, in its loose statement of facts, and in its lucid exposition of the laws of nations, would have done credit to Mr. Seward himself, the head of the department to which this ambitious little Consul belonged. Instead of a week, the *Alabama* had been less than a day on the coast, before she ran into Saldanha Bay ; and, if she had chosen, she might have cruised on the coast during the rest of the war, in entire conformity with the Queen's proclamation, and the laws of nations. But the richest part of the letter is that wherein the Consul tells the Governor, that inasmuch as the Confederate States had not been acknowledged as a nation, they had no right to commission a ship of war! It is astonishing how dull the Federal officials, generally, were on this point. The Consul knew that Great Britain had acknowledged us to be in possession of belligerent rights, and that the only rights I was pretending to exercise, in the *Alabama*, were those of a belligerent. But the Consul was not to blame. He was only a Consul, and could not be supposed to know better. Mr. Seward's despatches on the subject of the

Alabama had so muddled the brains of his subordinates, that they could never make head or tail of the subject.

The following was the reply of the Governor, through the Colonial Secretary: —

"I am directed by the Governor, to acknowledge the receipt of your letter of yesterday's date, relative to the *Alabama*. His Excellency has no instructions, neither has he any authority, to seize, or detain that vessel; and he desires me to acquaint you, that he has received a letter from the Commander, dated the 1st instant, stating that repairs were in progress, and as soon as they were completed he intended to go to sea. He further announces his intention of respecting the neutrality of the British Government. The course which Captain Semmes here proposes to take, is, in the Governor's opinion, in conformity with the instructions he has himself received, relative to ships of war and privateers, belonging to the United States, and the States calling themselves the Confederate States of America, visiting British ports. The reports received from Saldanha Bay induce the Governor to believe, that the vessel will leave that harbor, as soon as her repairs are completed; but he will immediately, on receiving intelligence to the contrary, take the necessary steps for enforcing the observance of the rules laid down by her Majesty's Government."

Another correspondence now sprang up between the Consul and the Governor in relation to the capture of the *Sea-Bride*. The Consul wrote to the Governor, as follows: —

"The Confederate steamer *Alabama* has just captured an American bark off Green Point, or about four miles from the nearest land — Robben Island. I witnessed the capture with my own eyes, as did hundreds of others at the same time. This occurrence at the entrance of Table Bay, and clearly in British waters, is an insult to England, and a grievous injury to a friendly power, the United States."

This remark about the honor of England will remind the reader of the article I quoted some pages back, from the New York "Commercial Advertiser," to the same effect. How wonderfully alive these fellows were to English honor, when Yankee ships were in danger! But as the Consul admits, upon the testimony of his "own eyes," that the capture was made *four* miles from the nearest land, the reader will, perhaps, be curious to see how he brings it within British waters. The marine league is the limit of jurisdiction, and the writers on international law say that that limit was probably adopted, because a cannon-shot could not be thrown farther than three miles from the shore. It may have been the cannon-shot which suggested the league, but it was the league, and not the cannot-shot, which was the limit. Now the Consul argued that the Yankees had invented some "big guns," which would throw a shot a long way beyond the league—ergo, the Yankee guns had changed the Laws of Nations.

But the Consul wrote his letter in too great a hurry. He had not yet seen the master of the captured ship. This clever Yankee, backed by several of his crew equally clever, made a much better case for him; for they swore, in a batch of affidavits before the Consul himself, and in spite of the Consul's "own eyes," that the ship had been captured within *two miles and a half* of Robben Island! Imprudent Consul, to have thus gone off half cocked! This discovery of new testimony was communicated to the Governor, as follows: "I beg now to enclose for your Excellency's perusal, the affidavit of Captain Charles F. White, of the *Sea-Bride*, protesting against the capture of the said bark in British waters. The bearings taken by him at the time of capture, conclusively show that she was in neutral waters, being about two and a half miles from Robben Island. This statement is doubtless more satisfactory than the testimony of persons, who measured the distance by the eye." Doubtless, if the bearings had been correct; but unfortunately for Captain White, there were too many other witnesses, who were under no temptation to falsify the truth. A fine ship, and a lucrative trading voyage along the eastern coast of Africa were to be the reward of his testimony; the simple telling of the truth the reward of the other witnesses. The usual consequences followed. The interested witness perjured himself, and was disbelieved. I remained entirely neutral in the matter, volunteered no testimony, and only responded to such questions as were asked me—not under oath —by the authorities. The following was the case made in rebuttal of this "Yankee hash":—

STATEMENT OF JOSEPH HOPSON.

Joseph Hopson, keeper of the Green Point Light-house, states:—

"I was on the look-out on Wednesday afternoon, when the *Alabama* and *Sea-Bride* were coming in. When I first saw them, the steamer was coming round the north-west of Robben Island, and the bark bore from her about five miles W. N. W. The bark was coming in under all sail, with a good breeze, and she took nothing in, when the gun was fired. I believe two guns were fired, but the gun I mean was the last, and the steamer then crossed the stern of the bark, and hauled up to her on the starboard side. He steamed ahead gently, and shortly afterward I saw the bark put round, with her head to the westward, and a boat put off from the steamer and boarded her. Both vessels were then good five miles off the mainland, and quite five, if not six, from the north-west point of Robben Island."

STATEMENT OF W. S. FIELD, COLLECTOR OF THE CUSTOMS.

"I was present at the old light-house, on Green Point, on Wednesday afternoon at two P. M., and saw the *Alabama* capture the American bark *Sea-Bride*, and I agree with the above statement, as far as the position of the vessels, and their distance from shore are concerned. I may also remark that I called the attention of Colonel Bisset and the lighthouse keeper, Hopson, to the distance of the vessels at the time of the capture, as it was probable we should be called upon to give our evidence respecting the affair, and we took a note of the time it occurred."

STATEMENT OF JOHN ROE.

"I was, yesterday, the 5th day of August, 1863, returning from a whale chase in Hunt's Bay, when I first saw the bark *Sea-Bride* standing from the westward, on to the land. I came on to Table Bay, and when off Camp's Bay, I saw the smoke of the *Alabama*, some distance from the westward of Robben Island. When I reached the Green Point lighthouse, the steamer was standing up toward the bark, which was about five miles and a half to the westward of Green Point, and about four and a half from the western point of Robben Island. This was their position—being near each other — when the gun was fired."

STATEMENT OF THE SIGNAL-MAN AT THE LION'S RUMP TELEGRAPH STATION.

"On Wednesday last, the 5th day of August, 1863, I sighted the bark *Sea-Bride*, about seven o'clock in the morning, about fifteen or twenty miles off the land, standing into Table Bay from the south-west. There was a light breeze blowing from the north-west, which continued until mid-day. About mid-day I sighted the *Alabama*, screw-steamer, standing from due north, toward Table Bay, intending, as it appeared to me, to take the passage between Robben Island, and the Blueberg Beach. She was then between fifteen and eighteen miles off the land. After sighting the steamer, I hoisted the demand for the bark, when she hoisted the American flag, which I reported to the port-office, the bark being then about eight miles off the land, from Irville Point. No sooner had the bark hoisted the American flag, than the steamer turned sharp round in the direction of, and toward the bark. The steamer appeared at that time to be about twelve miles off the land, from Irville Point, and about four or five miles outside of Robben Island, and about seven miles from the bark. The steamer then came up to, and alongside of the bark, when the latter was good four miles off the land, at or near the old lighthouse, and .five miles off the island. The steamer, after firing a gun, stopped the farther progress of the bark, several boats were sent to her, and after that the bark stood out to sea again, and the *Alabama* steamed into Table Bay."

At the time of the capture, her Majesty's steamship *Valorous* was lying in Table Bay, and the Governor, in addition to the above testimony, charged Captain Forsyth, her commander, also, to investigate the subject, and report to him. The following is Captain Forsyth's report: —

HER MAJESTY'S SHIP VALOROUS, August 6, 1863.

In compliance with the request conveyed to me by your Excellency, I have the honor to report that I have obtained from Captain Semmes, a statement of the position of the Confederate States steamer *Alabama*, and the American bark *Sea-Bride*, when the latter was captured, yesterday afternoon. Captain Semmes asserts, that at the time of his capturing the *Sea-Bride*, Green Point lighthouse bore from the *Alabama*, south-east, about six or six and a half miles. [The Yankee master said that it bore south, by east.] This statement is borne out by the evidence of Captain Wilson, Port-Captain of Table Bay, who has assured me, that at the time of the *Sea-Bride* being captured, he was off Green Point, in the port-boat, and that only the top of the *Alabama's* hull was visible. I am of opinion, if Captain Wilson could only see that portion of the hull of the *Alabama*, she must have been about the distance from shore, which is stated by Captain Semmes, and I have, therefore, come to the conclusion, that the bark *Sea-Bride* was beyond the limits assigned, when she was captured by the *Alabama*.

The Governor, after having thus patiently investigated the case, directed his Secretary to inform the Consul of the result in the following letter: —

" With reference to the correspondence that has passed, relative to the capture, by the Confederate States steamer *Alabama*, of the bark *Sea-Bride*, I am directed by the Governor to acquaint you, that, on the best information he has been enabled to procure, he has come to the conclusion, that the capture cannot be held to be illegal, or in violation of the neutrality of the British Government, by reason of the distance from the land at which it took place."

The Consul was foiled; but he was a man of courage, and resolved to strike another blow for the *Sea-Bride*. He next charged that the prize-master had brought her within the marine league *after her capture*. He made this charge upon the strength of another affidavit — that ready resource of the enemy when in difficulty. Enclosing this affidavit to the Governor, he wrote as follows: —

" From the affidavit of the first officer, it appears that the alleged prize was brought within one mile and a half of Green Point lighthouse, yesterday, at one o'clock A. M. Now, as the vessel was, at the time, in charge of a prize-crew, it was a violation of neutrality, as much as if the capture had been made at the same distance from the land."

And he required that the ship should be seized.

Without stopping to inquire into the truth of the fact stated, the Governor directed his Secretary to reply, that —

" His Excellency is not prepared to admit that the fact of a vessel having been brought, by the prize-crew, within one and a half mile of the Green Point lighthouse 'was a violation of the neutrality, as much as if the capture had taken place at the same distance from the land,' although both the belligerents are prohibited from bringing their prizes into British ports. The Governor does not feel warranted in taking steps for the removal of the prize-crew from the *Sea-Bride* "

CHAPTER XLVII.

A GALE AT CAPE TOWN — ALABAMA GETS UNDER WAY
FOR SIMON'S TOWN — CAPTURE OF THE MARTHA WEN-
ZELL — THE TUSCALOOSA; HER STATUS AS SHIP OF
WAR CONSIDERED — THE TUSCALOOSA PROCEEDS TO
SEA — THE ALABAMA FOLLOWS HER — THEY, WITH
THE SEA-BRIDE, RENDEZVOUS AT ANGRA PEQUENA.

HAVING brushed away Mr. Seward's gadfly, as described
in the last chapter, we may turn our attention again to
the *Alabama*. On the 7th of August, we took one of the gales
so common at the Cape, in the winter season. Dense banks of
black clouds hove up in the north-west, soon overspreading
the whole heavens, and the wind came out whistling from that
quarter. The reader must bear in mind, that when he crossed
into the southern hemisphere he reversed the points of the
compass, so far as wind and weather are concerned, and that
the north-wester, at the Cape of Good Hope, answers to our
south-easter, on the American coast — bringing with it thick,
rainy weather. There was a number of ships in the harbor,
and the gale drove in upon them without the least protection.
These ships, forewarned by the usual signs, had all struck
their upper masts, sent down their yards, and let go second
anchors, and veered to long scopes. We did the same in the
Alabama.

It was a sublime spectacle to look abroad upon the bay in
the height of the gale. The elements seemed to be literally
at war, a low scud rushing to the shore, and climbing, as if
pursued by demons, up and over the Lion's Rump and Table
Mountain. Huge waves were rolling in upon the struggling
shipping, trying its ground-tackle to its utmost tension; the
jetties and landings were covered with spray; and Cape

Town, though only a mile off, looked like a spectre town, as viewed through the spray and driving scud. And what added much to the interest of the scene, was the daring and skill of the watermen. These men, in substantial launches, under close-reefed sails, and with spare anchors and cables on board, for the use of any ships that might be in distress for want of sufficient ground-tackle, were darting hither and thither, like so many spirits of the storm. They seemed to be sporting with the dashing and blinding waves and the fury of the gale, in very wantonness, as though they would defy the elements. The ships at anchor were all fortunate enough to hold on; but a luckless Bremen brig, outside, which had ventured too near the land, was wrecked, during the night, on Green Point. Fortunately, no lives were lost.

The gale lasted about twenty-four hours; and when it had sufficiently abated, we communicated with the shore, and got off such supplies as we needed; it being my intention to run round to Simon's Town, on the opposite side of the Cape, where there is shelter from these gales, for the purpose of completing my repairs. On the 9th, the weather had again become fine. The wind had gone round to south-east, the fair-weather quarter, and the Devil had spread his table-cloth on Table Mountain. Every one has heard of this famous table-cloth at the Cape of Good Hope. It is a fleecy, white cloud, which hangs perpetually over Table Mountain during fine weather. The south-east winds, as they climb the steep ascent, bring with them more or less moisture. This moisture is sufficiently cooled as it passes over the "table"—a level space on the top of the mountain—to become condensed into a white vapor, very similar to that which escapes from a steam-pipe. When the wind shifts, and the storm begins to gather, the table-cloth disappears.

At nine o'clock, on this morning, we got under way, and steamed out of the harbor, on our way to Simon's Town. The day was charmingly fine. The atmosphere was soft and transparent, and the sun bright, bringing out all the beauties of the bold promontories and the deep-water bays that indent the coast. We were now really doubling the Cape of Good Hope. As we approached the famous headland, with its lighthouse perched several hundred feet above the bold and blackened rocks, our imaginations busy with the past, endeavoring to depict the frail Portuguese bark, which had first dared its stormy waters, the cry of "sail ho!" resounded most musically from the mast-head. Imagination took flight at once, at the sound of this practical cry. It recalled us from our dream of John of Portugal, to one Abraham Lincoln and his surroundings. Here was not the poetical bark, of four centuries ago, that had at last found its way to those "Indies," which Columbus so long sought for in vain, but a Yankee ship laden with rice; for an hour's steaming brought us alongside of the *Martha Wenzell*, of Boston, from Akyab for Falmouth in England. The *Wenzell* had better luck than the *Sea-Bride*, for she had clearly entered the mouth of False Bay, and though seven or eight miles yet from the land, was within a line drawn from point to point of the Bay. Being thus within British jurisdiction, I astonished the master by releasing, instead of burning his ship. He looked so dumfounded when I announced to him this decision, that if I had been a Yankee, he would, no doubt, have suspected me of some Yankee trick. He gathered his slow ideas together, by degrees, however, and was profuse in his thanks. I told him he had none to give me, for I was only too sorry not to be able to burn him.

We now hauled in for the coast, and taking a pilot, as we approached the harbor, anchored at two P. M. in Simon's Bay. This is the naval station of the colony, and we found here the frigate *Narcissus*, wearing the flag of Rear Admiral Sir Baldwin Walker, the commander-in-chief of the British naval forces at the Cape. We were visited immediately upon anchoring by a lieutenant from the flag-ship. The *Tuscaloosa* had preceded me, as the reader has seen, a few days, and we found her still here, not having quite completed her preparations for sea. The gadfly, I found, had been buzzing around her, too, but her difficulties were all ended. As the correspondence is short, I will give it to the reader. The Federal Consul wrote to the Governor, as follows: —

"An armed vessel named the *Tuscaloosa*, claiming to act under the authority of the so-called Confederate States, entered Simon's Bay, on Saturday, the 8th instant. That vessel was formerly owned by citizens of the United States, and while engaged in lawful commerce [as if lawful commerce was not a subject of capture, during war] was captured as a prize by the *Alabama*. She was subsequently fitted out with arms, by the *Alabama*, to prey upon the commerce of the United States, and now, without having been condemned as a prize, by any Admiralty Court of any recognized government, she is permitted to enter a neutral port, in violation of the Queen's proclamation, with her original cargo on board. Against this proceeding, I, hereby, most emphatically protest, and I claim that the vessel ought to be given up to her lawful owners."

It is quite true that the *Tuscaloosa* had not been condemned by a prize court of the Confederacy, but it was equally true that the Sovereign Power of the Confederacy, acting through its authorized agent, had commissioned her as a ship of war, which was the most solemn condemnation of the prize, that the Sovereign could give. It was equally true, that no nation has the right to inquire into the *antecedents* of the ships of war of another nation. But these were points beyond the comprehension of the gadfly. The following was the answer of the Governor. The Colonial Secretary writes :—

"I am directed by the Governor to acknowledge the receipt of your letter of this date, and to acquaint you, that it was not until late last evening, that his Excellency received from the Naval Commander-in-Chief, information, that the condition of the *Tuscaloosa* was such as, as his Excellency is advised, to entitle her to be regarded as a vessel of war. The Governor is not aware, nor do you refer him to the provisions of the International Law, by which captured vessels, as soon as they enter our neutral ports, revert to their original owners, and are forfeited by their captors. But his Excellency believes, that the claims of contending parties to vessels captured can only be determined, in the first instance, by the courts of the captor's country."

We remained five days at Simon's Town. We did not need coal, but we had some caulking of the bends, and replacing of copper about the water-line to do, and some slight repairs to put upon our engine. Whilst these preparations for sea were going on, we had some very pleasant intercourse with the officers of the station and the citizens on shore. Besides the *Narcissus*, flag-ship, there were one or two other British ships of war at anchor. There were some officers stationed at the navy-yard, and there was a Chinese gunboat, the *Kwan-Tung*, with an English commander and crew, which had put into the harbor, on her way to the east. Simon's Town was thus quite gay. The Governor, Sir Philip Wodehouse, also came over from Cape Town during our stay. Lunches on board the different ships, excursions on board the *Kwan-Tung*, and dinner-parties were the order of the day. As I have before remarked, the English naval officers discarded all the ridiculous nonsense about our not being "recognized," and extended to us official, as well as private civilities.

The Admiral was kind enough to give me a dinner-party, at which the Governor, and his lady, and the principal officers of his squadron were present. I found the ladies of the Admiral's family exceedingly agreeable. They were living in a picturesque cottage, near the sea-shore, and solaced themselves for their temporary banishment from "dear old England," by making their home as English as possible. They had surrounded themselves by fine lawns and shrubbery and flowers, and Mrs. Walker, and one of the bewitching young ladies were kind enough to show me over their extensive and well-cultivated garden, in which they took much interest. Horseback riding, picnics to the country, and balls on board the ships were the principal amusements of the young people. Whilst my officers and myself were thus relaxing ourselves, my sailors were also making the most of their time. Kell had told them off, by quarter watches, and sent them on "liberty." Each batch was mustered, and inspected as it was sent on shore, and pretty soon we had the old Jamaica scenes over again. Most of them went over to Cape Town, in the stage-coach that was running between the two places, and put that lively commercial town "in stays." The sailor quarter was a continuous scene of revelry for several days. The townspeople humored and spoiled them. They all overstayed their time, and we only got them back by twos and threes. It was of no use to muster, and inspect them now. The tidy, new suits, in which they had gone on shore, were torn and draggled, and old-drunks were upon nearly all of them.

The *Tuscaloosa* went to sea at daylight on the 14th, and we followed her in the *Alabama* the next day. The former was to proceed to Saldanha Bay, and thence take the *Sea-Bride* with her to one of the uninhabited harbors, some distance to the northward, and the *Alabama* was to follow her thither, after a cruise of a few days off the Cape.   The object of these movements will be explained in due time.   I now threw myself into that perpetual stream of commerce, that comes setting around the Cape of Good Hope from the East Indies.   From daylight until dark, ships are constantly in sight from the lighthouse on the Cape.   The road is about twenty miles wide — no more.   We kept our station in this road, day in and day out for ten days, during which we chased and overhauled a great number of ships, but there was not a Yankee among them!   It was winter-time, we were off the "stormy Cape," and we had the weather suited to the season and the locality.   Storms and fogs and calms followed in succession — the storm being the normal meteorological condition. As we would be lying to, in this track, under reefed sails, in a dark and stormy night, our very hair would sometimes be made to stand on end, by the apparition of a huge ship rushing past us at lightning speed, before the howling gale, at no more than a few ships' lengths from us.   A collision would have crushed us as if we had been an egg-shell.

At length, when I supposed the *Tuscaloosa* and the *Sea-Bride* had reached their destination, I filled away and followed them.   As we were making this passage, it was reported to me that our fresh-water condenser had given out.   Here was a predicament!   The water was condensed once a week, and we had no more than about one week's supply on hand.   The joints of the piping had worked loose, and the machine had become nearly useless.   It was now still more necessary to make a harbor, where we might get access to water, and see what could be done in the way of repairs.   We worked our way along the African coast somewhat tediously, frequently encountering head-winds and adverse currents.   On the morning of the 28th of August, we sighted the land, after having been delayed by a dense fog for twenty-four hours, and in the course of the afternoon we ran into the Bay of Angra Pequeña, and anchored.   This was our point of rendezvous.   I found the *Tuscaloosa* and the *Sea-Bride* both at anchor.   I had at last found a port into which I could take a prize! I was now, in short, among the Hottentots; no civilized nation claiming jurisdiction over the waters in which I was anchored.

When at Cape Town, an English merchant had visited me, and made overtures for the purchase of the *Sea-Bride* and her cargo. He was willing to run the risk of non-condemnation by a prize-court, and I could put him in possession of the prize, he said, at some inlet on the coast of Africa, without the jurisdiction of any civilized power. I made the sale to him. He was to repair to the given rendezvous in his own vessel, and I found him here, according to his agreement, with the stipulated price — about one third the value of the ship and cargo — in good English sovereigns, which, upon being counted, were turned over to the paymaster, for the military chest. The purchaser was then put in possession of the prize. I had made an arrangement with other parties for the sale of the wool still remaining on board the *Tuscaloosa*. This wool was to be landed at Angra Pequeña, also, the purchaser agreeing to ship it to Europe, and credit the Confederate States with two thirds of the proceeds. The reader will see how easy it would have been for me, to make available many of my prizes in this way, but the great objection to the scheme, was the loss of time which it involved, and the risks I ran of not getting back my prize crews. If I had undertaken, whenever I captured a prize, to follow her to some out-of-the-way port, and spend some days there, in negotiating for her sale, and getting back my prize crew, I should not have accomplished half the work I did. The great object now was to destroy, as speedily as possible, the enemy's commerce, and to this I devoted all my energies. I did not, therefore, repeat the experiment of the *Sea-Bride*.

I could not have chosen a better spot for my present purpose. At Angra Pequeña I was entirely out of the world. It was not visited at all, except by some straggling coaster in quest of shelter in bad weather. There was, indeed, no other inducement to visit it. It was in a desert part of Africa. The region was rainless, and there was not so much as a shrub, or even a blade of grass to be seen. The harbor was rock-bound, and for miles inland the country was a waste of burning sand.

The harbor did not even afford fresh water, and we were obliged to supply ourselves from the vessel of my English friend, until our condenser could be repaired.   The whole country was a waste, in which there was no life visible away from the coast.   On the coast itself, there were the usual sea-birds — the gannet and the sea-gull — and fish in abundance. We hauled the seine, and caught a fine mess for the crews of all the ships.   Three or four naked, emaciated Hottentots, having seen the ships from a distance, had made their way to the harbor, and came begging us for food.   They remained during our stay, and had their emptiness filled.   Some thirty or forty miles from the coast, they said, vegetation began to appear, and there were villages and cattle.

I ordered Lieutenant Low, the commander of the *Tuscaloosa*, as soon as he should land his cargo, to ballast his ship with the rock which abounded on every hand, and proceed on a cruise to the coast of Brazil.   Sufficient time had now elapsed, I thought, for the ships of war of the enemy, which had been sent to that coast, in pursuit of me, to be coming in the direction of the Cape of Good Hope.   Lieutenant Low would, therefore, in all probability, have a clear field before him. Having nothing further to detain me in the *Alabama*, I got under way, on my return to Simon's Town, intending to fill up with coal, and proceed thence to the East Indies, in compliance with the suggestion of Mr. Secretary Mallory.   The *Tuscaloosa*, after cruising the requisite time on the coast of Brazil, was to return to the Cape to meet me, on my own return from the East Indies.

When I reached the highway off the Cape again, I held myself there for several days, cruising off and on, and sighting the land occasionally, to see if perchance I could pick up an American ship.   But we had no better success than before. The wary masters of these ships, if there were any passing, gave the Cape a wide berth, and sought their way home, by the most unfrequented paths, illustrating the old adage, that "the farthest way round is the shortest way home."   Impatient of further delay, without results, on Wednesday, the 16th of September, I got up steam, and ran into Simon's Bay.   I learned, upon anchoring, that the United States steamer *Van-*

derbilt, late the flag-ship of Admiral Wilkes, and now under the command of Captain Baldwin, had left the anchorage, only the Friday before, and gone herself to cruise off the Cape, in the hope of falling in with the *Alabama*. She had taken her station, as it would appear, a little to the eastward of me, off Cape Agulhas and Point Danger. On the day the *Vanderbilt* went to sea, viz., Friday, the 11th of September, it happened that the *Alabama* was a little further off the land than usual, which accounts for the two ships missing each other. The following is the record on my journal, for that day: "Weather very fine, wind light from the south-west. At half-past six, showed the English colors to an English bark, after a short chase." On the following Sunday, we were in plain sight of Table Mountain. The two ships were thus cruising almost in sight of each other's smoke.

The *Vanderbilt* visited both Cape Town, and Simon's Town, and lay several days at each. I did not object that she had been "painting ship," and should have been sent to sea earlier. The more time Baldwin spent in port, the better I liked it. Indeed, it always puzzled me, that the gadflies should insist upon my being sent to sea so promptly, when nearly every day that the *Alabama* was at sea, cost them a ship.

I had scarcely come to anchor, before Captain Bickford, of the *Narcissus*, came on board of me, on the part of the Admiral, to have an "explanation." The gadfly had continued its buzzing, I found, during my late absence from the Cape. A short distance to the northward of the Cape of Good Hope, in the direction of Angra Pequeña, there is an island called Ichaboe, a dependency of the Cape colony. It had been represented to the Admiral, by the Consul, that the transactions which have been related as taking place at Angra Pequeña, had taken place at this island, in violation of British neutrality. In what the evidence consisted I did not learn, but the Consul, in his distress and extremity, had probably had recourse to some more Yankee affidavits. It was this charge which Captain Bickford had come on board to ask an explanation of. The following letter from Sir Baldwin Walker, to the Secretary of the Admiralty in London, will show how easily I brushed off the gadfly, for the second time: —

"With reference to my letters, dated respectively the 19th' and 31st ult., relative to the Confederate States ship-of-war *Alabama*, and the prizes captured by her, I beg to enclose, for their lordships information, the copy of a statement forwarded to me by the Collector of Customs at Cape Town, wherein it is represented, that the *Tuscaloosa* and *Sea-Bride* had visited Ichaboe, which is a dependency of this colony. Since the receipt of the above-mentioned document, the *Alabama* arrived at this anchorage, (the 16th instant,) and when Captain Semmes waited on me, I acquainted him with the report, requesting he would inform me if it was true. I was glad to learn from him that it was not so. He frankly explained that the prize *Sea-Bride*, in the first place, had put into Saldanha Bay, through stress of weather, and on being joined there, by the *Tuscaloosa*, both vessels proceeded to Angra Pequeña, on the west coast of Africa, where he subsequently joined them in the *Alabama*, and there sold the *Sea-Bride* and her cargo, to an English subject who resides at Cape Town. The *Tuscaloosa* had landed some wool at Angra Pequeña, and received ballast, but he states, is still in commission as a tender. It will, therefore, be seen, how erroneous is the accompanying report. I have no reason to doubt Captain Semmes' explanation ; and he seems to be fully alive to the instructions of her Majesty's Government, and appears to be most anxious not to commit any breach of neutrality. The *Alabama* has returned to this port for coal, some provisions, and to repair her condensing apparatus. From conversation with Captain Semmes, I find he has been off this Cape for the last five days, and as the *Vanderbilt* left this, on the night of the 11th inst., it is surprising they did not meet each other."

The *Vanderbilt*, I found, had exhausted the supply of coal at Simon's Town, having taken in as much as eight or nine hundred tons. Commodore Vanderbilt, as he is called, had certainly presented a mammoth coal-consumer to the Federal Government, if nothing else. I was obliged, in consequence, to order coal for the *Alabama*, around from Cape Town. And as the operation of coaling and making the necessary repairs would detain me several days, and as I was, besides, bound on a long voyage, I yielded to the petitions of my crew, and permitted them to go on liberty again. The officers of the station were as courteous to us as before, and I renewed my very pleasant intercourse with the Admiral's family. The owner of the famous Constantia vineyard, lying between Simon's Town and Cape Town, sent me a pressing invitation to come and spend a few days with him, but I was too busy to accept his hospitality. He afterward sent me a cask of his world-renowned wine. This cask of wine, after making the voyage to India, was offered as a libation to the god of war. It went down in the *Alabama* off Cherbourg. We had another very pleasant dinner at the Admiral's—the guests being composed, this time, exclusively of naval officers. After our return to the drawing-room, the ladies made their appearance, and gave us some delightful music. These were some of the oases in the desert of my life upon the ocean.

In the course of five or six days, by the exercise of great diligence, we were again ready for sea. But unfortunately all my crew were not yet on board. My rascals had behaved worse than usual, on this last visit to Cape Town. Some of them had been jugged by the authorities for offences against the peace, and others had yielded to the seductions of the ever vigilant Federal Consul, and been quartered upon his bounty. The Consul had made a haul. They would be capital fellows for "affidavits" against the *Alabama*. I need not say that they were of the cosmopolitan sailor class, none of them being citizens of the Southern States. I offered large rewards for the apprehension and delivery to me of these fellows; but the police were afraid to act—probably forbidden by their superiors, in deference to their supposed duty under the neutrality laws. That was a very one-sided neutrality, however, which permitted the Federal Consul to convert his quarters into a hostile camp, for the seduction of my sailors, and denied me access to the police for redress. My agent at Cape Town, having made every exertion in his power to secure the return of as many of my men as possible, finally telegraphed me, on the evening of the 24th of September, that it was useless to wait any longer. As many as fourteen had deserted; enough to cripple my crew, and that, too, with an enemy's ship of superior force on the coast.

What was to be done? Luckily there was a remedy at hand. A sailor-landlord, one of those Shylocks who coin Jack's flesh and blood into gold, hearing of the distress of the *Alabama*, came off to tell me that all his boarders, eleven in number, had volunteered to supply the place of my deserters. This seemed like a fair exchange. It was but "swapping horses," as the "sainted Abraham" would have said, if he had been in my place—only I was giving a little "bout"—fourteen well-fed, well-clothed fellows, for eleven ragged, whiskey-filled vagabonds. It was a "swap" in another sense, too, as, ten to one, all these eleven fellows were deserters from other ships that had touched at this "relay house" of the sea. There was only one little difficulty in the way of my shipping these men. There was my good friend, her Majesty, the Queen —I must not be ungallant to her, and violate her neutrality laws. What monstrous sophists we are, when interest prompts us? I reasoned out this case to my entire satisfaction. I said to myself, My sailors have gone on shore in her Majesty's dominions, and refuse to come back to me. When I apply to her Majesty's police, they tell me that so sacred is the soil of England, no man must be coerced to do what he does n't want to do. Good! I reply that a ship of war is a part of the territory to which she belongs, and that if some of the subjects of the Queen should think proper to come into my territory, and refuse to go back, I may surely apply the same principle, and refuse to compel them.

When I had come to this conclusion, I turned to the landlord, and said: "And so you have some *gentlemen* boarding at your house, who desire to take passage with me?" The landlord smiled, and nodded assent. I continued: "You know I cannot ship any seamen in her Majesty's ports, but I see no reason why I should not take passengers to sea with me, if they desire to go." "Certainly, your honor—they can work their passage, you know." "I suppose you'll charge something for bringing these gentlemen on board?" "Some'at, your honor." Here the landlord pulled out a greasy memorandum, and began to read. "Bill Bunting, board and lodging, ten shillings—drinks, one pound ten. Tom Bowline, board and lodging, six shillings—Tom only *landed* yesterday from a Dutch ship —drinks, twelve shillings." "Hold!" said I; "never mind the board and lodging and drinks—go to the paymaster,"—and turning to Kell, I told him to give the paymaster the necessary instructions,—"and he will pay you your *fares* for bringing the passengers on board." The "passengers" were already alongside, and being sent down to the surgeon, were examined, and passed as sound and able-bodied men.

It was now nine o'clock at night. It had been blowing a
gale of wind, all day, from the south-east; but it was a fair-
weather gale, if I may use the solecism; the sky being clear,
and the barometer high. These are notable peculiarities of
the south-east gales at the Cape of Good Hope. The sky is
always clear, and the gale begins and ends with a high barometer. I was very anxious to get to sea. A report had come
in, only a day or two before, that the *Vanderbilt* was still cruising off Cape Agulhas, and I was apprehensive that she might
get news of me, and blockade me. This might detain me several days, or until I could get a dark night — and the moon
was now near her full — in which to run the blockade. I need
not remark that the *Vanderbilt* had greatly the speed of me,
and threw twice my weight of metal. The wind having partially lulled, we got up steam, and at about half-past eleven,
we moved out from our anchors. The lull had only been temporary, for we had scarcely cleared the little islands that give
a partial protection to the harbor from these south-east winds,
when the gale came whistling and howling as before. The wind
and sea were both nearly ahead, and the *Alabama* was now put
upon her metal, under steam, as she had been so often before, under sail. False Bay is an immense sheet of water, of a horse-shoe
shape, and we had to steam some twenty miles before we could
weather the Cape of Good Hope, under our lee. We drove
her against this heavy gale at the rate of five knots per hour.

This struggle of the little ship with the elements was a thing
to be remembered. The moon, as before remarked, was near
her full, shedding a flood of light upon the scene. The Bay
was whitened with foam, as the waters were lashed into fury
by the storm. Around the curve of the "horse-shoe" arose
broken, bald, rocky mountains, on the crests of which were
piled fleecy, white clouds, blinking in the moonlight, like banks
of snow. These clouds were perfectly motionless. It appeared
as if the D—l had spread a great many "table-cloths" around
False Bay, that night; or, rather, a more appropriate figure
would be, that he had touched the mountains with the stillness
of death, and wreathed them with winding-sheets. The scene
was wild and weird beyond description. It was a picture for
the eye of a poet or painter to dwell upon. Nor was the im-

agination less touched, when, from time to time, the revolving light upon the grim old Cape — that Cape which had so long divided the Eastern from the Western world — threw its full blaze upon the deck of the struggling ship. Overhead, the sky was perfectly clear, there being not so much as a speck of a cloud to be seen — and this in the midst of a howling gale of wind! At three A. M. we cleared the Cape, and keeping the ship off a few points, gave her the trysails, with the bonnets off. She bounded over the seas like a stag-hound unleashed. I had been up all night, and now went below to snatch some brief repose. before the toils of another day should begin.

CHAPTER XLVIII.

THE ALABAMA ON THE INDIAN OCEAN — THE PASSEN-
GERS QUESTIONED, AND CONTRACTED WITH — THE
AGULHAS CURRENT — THE "BRAVE WEST WINDS" —
A THEORY — THE ISLANDS OF ST. PETER AND ST.
PAUL — THE TROPIC OF CAPRICORN — THE SOUTH-EAST
TRADES AND THE MONSOONS — THE ALABAMA ARRIVES
OFF THE STRAIT OF SUNDA, AND BURNS ONE OF THE
SHIPS OF THE ENEMY — RUNS IN AND ANCHORS UNDER
THE ISLAND OF SUMATRA.

WHEN Bartelli awakened me, at the usual hour of "seven
bells" — half-past seven A. M., — on the morning after
the events described in the last chapter, the *Alabama* was well
launched upon the Indian Ocean. She had run the Cape of
Good Hope out of sight, and was still hieing off before the
gale, though this had moderated considerably as she had run
off the coast. We were now about to make a long voyage,
tedious to the unphilosophical mariner, but full of interest to
one who has an eye open to the wonders and beauties of
nature. My first duty, upon going on deck, was to put the
ship under sail, and let the steam go down; and my second, to
have an interview with the "passengers," who had come on
board, overnight. We were now on the high seas, and might,
with all due respect to Queen Victoria, put them under contract.
If the reader recollects Falstaff's description of his ragged battalion, he will have a pretty good idea of the *personnel* I had
before me. These subjects of the Queen stood in all they possessed. None of them had brought any baggage on board with
them. Ragged blue and red flannel shirts, tarred trousers, and
a mixture of felt hats and Scotch caps, composed their wardrobe.
Their persons had passed muster of the surgeon, it is true, but it

was plain that it would require a deal of washing and scrubbing and wholesome feeding, and a long abstinence from "drinks," to render them fit for use. Upon questioning them, I found that each had his cock-and-a-bull story to tell, of how he was "left" by this ship, or by that, without any fault of his own, and how he had been tricked by his landlord. I turned them over to the first lieutenant, and paymaster, and they were soon incorporated with the crew. I hold that her Majesty owes me some "boot," for the "swap" I made with her, on that remarkable moonlight night when I left the Cape. At all events, I never heard that she complained of it.

I was grieved to find that our most serious loss among the deserters, was our Irish fiddler. This fellow had been remarkably diligent, in his vocation, and had fiddled the crew over half the world. It was a pity to lose him, now that we were going over the other half. When the evening's amusements began, Michael Mahoney's vacant camp-stool cast a gloom over the ship. There was no one who could make his violin "talk" like himself, and it was a long time before his place was supplied. Poor Michael! we felt convinced he had not been untrue to us—it was only a "dhrop" too much of the "crayture" he had taken.

For the first few days after leaving the Cape, we ran off due south, it being my intention to seek the fortieth parallel of south latitude, and run my easting down on that parallel. As icebergs have been known to make their appearance near the Cape in the spring of the year, I ordered the temperature of the air and water to be taken every hour during the night, to aid me in detecting their presence. We did not discover any icebergs, but the thermometer helped to reveal to me some of the secrets of the deep, in this part of the ocean. Much to my surprise, I found myself in a sort of Gulf Stream; the temperature of the water being from three to five degrees higher, than that of the air. My celestial observations for fixing the position of the ship, informed me at the same time that I was experiencing a south-easterly current; the current bending more and more toward the east, as I proceeded south, until in the parallel of 40°, it ran due east. The rate of this current was from thirty to fifty miles per day. This was undoubtedly a branch of the great Agulhas current.

If the reader will inspect a map, he will find that the North Indian Ocean is bounded wholly by tropical countries—Hindostan, Beloochistan, and Arabia to the Red Sea, and across that sea, by Azan and Zanguebar. The waters in this great bight of the ocean are intensely heated by the fervor of an Indian and African sun, and flow off in quest of cooler regions through the Mozambique Channel. Passing thence over the Agulhas Bank, which lies a short distance to the eastward of the Cape of Good Hope, they reach that Cape, as the Agulhas current. Here it divides into two main prongs or branches; one prong pursuing a westerly course, and joining in with the great equatorial current, which, the reader recollects, we encountered off Fernando de Noronha, and the other bending sharply to the south-east, and forming the Gulf Stream of the South Indian Ocean, in which the *Alabama* is at present. What it is, that gives this latter prong its sudden deflection to the southward is not well understood. Probably it is influenced, to some extent, by the southerly current, running at the rate of about a knot an hour along the west coast of Africa, and debouching at the Cape of Good Hope. Here it strikes the Agulhas current at right angles, and hence possibly the deflection of a part of that current.

But if there be a current constantly setting from the Cape of Good Hope to the south-east, how is it that the iceberg finds its way to the neighborhood of that Cape, from the south polar regions? There is but one way to account for it. There must be a counter undercurrent. These bergs, setting deep in the water, are forced by this counter-current against the surface current. This phenomenon has frequently been witnessed in the Arctic seas. Captain Duncan, of the English whaler *Dundee*, in describing one of his voyages to Davis' Strait, thus speaks of a similar drift of icebergs:—"It was awful to behold the immense icebergs working their way to the north-east from us, and not one drop of water to be seen; they were working themselves right through the middle of the ice." Here was an undercurrent of such force as to carry a mountain of ice, ripping and crashing through a field of solid ice. Lieutenant De Haven, who made a voyage in search of Sir John Franklin, describes a similar phenomenon as follows: — "The iceberg, as before observed, came up very near to the stern of our ship; the intermediate space, between the berg and the vessel, was filled with heavy masses of ice, which, though they had been previously broken by the immense weight of the berg, were again formed into a compact body by its pressure. The berg was drifting at the rate of about four knots, and by its force on the mass of ice, was pushing the ship before it, as it appeared, to inevitable destruction." And again, on the next day, he writes: — "The iceberg still in sight, but drifting away fast to the north-east." Here was another undercurrent, driving a monster iceberg through a field of broken ice at the rate of four knots per hour!

When we had travelled in the *Alabama* some distance to the eastward, on the 39th and 40th parallels, the current made another curve — this time to the north-east. If the reader will again refer to a map, he will find that the Agulhas current, as it came along through the Mozambique Channel and by the Cape of Good Hope, was a south-westerly current. It being now a north-easterly current, he observes that it is running back whence it came, in an ellipse! We have seen, in a former part of this work, that the Gulf Stream of the North Atlantic performs a circuit around the coasts of the United States, Newfoundland, the British Islands, the coasts of Spain and Portugal, the African coast, and so on, into the equatorial current, and thence back again to the Gulf of Mexico. From my observation of currents in various parts of the world, my impression is, that the circle or ellipse is their normal law. There are, of course, offshoots from one circle, or ellipse, to another, and thus a general intermingling of the waters of the earth is going on — but the normal rule for the guidance of the water, as of the wind, is the curve.

As we approached the 40th parallel of latitude, my attention was again forcibly drawn to the phenomena of the winds. The "Brave West Winds" — as the sailors call them — those remarkable polar trade-winds, now began to prevail with wonderful regularity. On the 30th of September, we observed in latitude 39° 12′, and longitude 31° 59′. The following is the entry on my journal for that day: — "Rough weather, with the wind fresh from the N. N. W. with passing rain-squalls. Sea turbulent. Barometer 29.47; thermometer, air 55°, water 58; distance run in the last twenty-four hours, 221 miles. Weather looking better at noon. The water has resumed its usual deep-sea hue. [We had been running over an extensive tract of soundings, the water being of that pea-green tint indicating a depth of from sixty to seventy-five fathoms.] In high southern latitudes, in the Indian Ocean, the storm-fiend seems to hold high carnival all the year round. He is constantly racing round the globe, from west to east, howling over the waste of waters in his mad career. Like Sisyphus, his labors are never ended. He not only does not rest himself, but he allows old Ocean none, constantly lashing him into rage. He scatters the icebergs hither and thither to the great terror of the mariner, and converts the moisture of the clouds into the blinding snow-flake or the pelting hail. As we are driven, on dark nights, before these furious winds, we have only to imitate the Cape Horn navigator — 'tie all fast, and let her rip,' iceberg or no iceberg. When a ship is running at a speed of twelve or fourteen knots, in such thick weather that the look-out at the cat-head can scarcely see his own nose, neither sharp eyes, nor water thermometers are of much use."

These winds continued to blow from day to day, hurrying us forward with great speed. There being a clear sweep of the sea for several thousand miles, unobstructed by continent or island, the waves rose into long, sweeping swells, much more huge and majestic than one meets with in any other ocean. As our little craft, scudding before a gale, would be overtaken by one of these monster billows, she would be caught up by its crest, like a cock-boat, and darted half-way down the declivity that lay before her, at a speed that would cause the sailor to hold his breath. Any swerve to the right, or the left, that would cause the ship to "broach to," or come broadside to the wind and sea, would have been fatal. These "brave west winds," though thus fraught with danger, are a great boon to commerce. The reader has seen how the currents in this part of the ocean travel in an ellipse. We have here an ellipse of the winds. The *Alabama* is hurrying to the Far East, before a continuous, or almost continuous north-west gale. If she were a few hundred miles to the northward of her present position, she might be hurrying, though not quite with equal speed, before the south-east trades, to the Far West. We have thus two parallel winds blowing all the year round in opposite directions, and only a few hundred miles apart.

Storms are now admitted by all seamen to be gyratory, as we have seen. When I was cruising in the Gulf Stream, I ventured to enlarge this theory, as the reader may recollect, and suggested that rotation was the normal condition of all extra-tropical winds on the ocean, where there was nothing to obstruct them — of the moderate wind, as well as of the gale. I had a striking confirmation of this theory in the "brave west winds." These winds went regularly around the compass, in uniform periods; the periods occupying about three days. We would take them at about N. N. W., and in the course of the "period" they would go entirely around the compass, and come back to the same point; there being an interval of calm of a few hours. The following diagram will illustrate this rotary motion.

Let Figure 1, on the opposite page, represent a circular wind — the wind gyrating in the direction of the arrows, and the circle travelling at the same time, along the dotted lines from west to east. If the northern segment of this circular wind passes over the ship, the upper dotted line from A to A^2, will represent her position during its passage. At A, where the ship first takes the wind, she will have it from about north-west; and at A^2, where she is about to lose it, she will have it from about south-west. The ship is supposed to remain stationary, whilst the circle is passing over her. Now, this is precisely the manner in which we found all these winds to haul in the *Alabama*. We would have the wind from the north-west to the south-west, hauling gradually from one point to the other, and blowing freshly for the greater part of three days. It would then become light, and, in the course of a few hours, go round to the south, to the south-east, to the east, and then settle in the north-west, as before.

Figure 2 represents two of these circular winds — and the reader must recollect that there is a constant series of them — one following the other so closely as to overlap it. Now, if the reader will cast his eye upon the letter C, near the upper

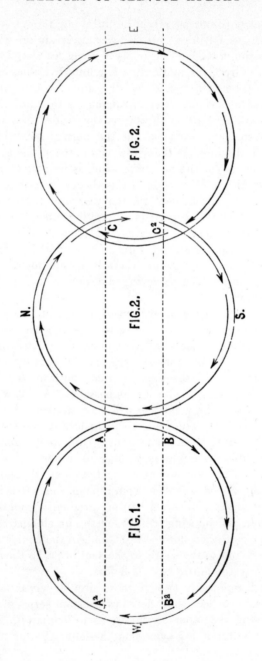

dotted line, in the overlapped space, he will observe why it is, that there is always a short interval of calm before the northwest wind sets in, the second time. The wind within that space is blowing, or rather should blow, according to the theory, two opposite ways at once — from the N. N. W., and the S. S. E. The consequence is, necessarily, a calm. It is thus seen that the theory, that these "brave west winds" are a series of circular winds, harmonizes entirely with the facts observed by us. The lower dotted line is merely intended to show in what direction the wind would haul, if the southern segment, instead of the northern, passed over the ship. In that case, the ship would take the wind, from about N. N. E., as at B, and lose it at south-east, as at B². In the region of the "brave west winds," it would seem that the northern segment always passes over that belt of the ocean. The received theory of these south polar-winds, is not such as I have assumed. Former writers have not supposed them to be circular winds at all. They suppose them to pass over the southeast trade-winds, as an upper current, and when they have reached the proper parallel, to descend, become surface-winds, and blow home, as straight winds, to the pole. But I found a difficulty in reconciling this theory with the periodical veering of the wind entirely around the compass, as above described. If these were straight winds, blowing contrary to the trades, why should they not blow steadily like the trades? But if we drop the straight-wind theory, and take up the circular hypothesis, all the phenomena observed by us will be in conformity with the latter. The periodical hauling of the wind will be accounted for, and if we suppose that the northern half of the circle invariably passes over the ship, in the passage-parallels, we shall see how it is that the wind is blowing nearly all the time from the westward. To account for the fact that the northern half of the circle invariably passes over these parallels, we have only to suppose the circle to be of sufficient diameter to extend to, or near the pole.

Here is the figure. It extends from the parallel of 40°, to the pole; it is therefore fifty degrees, or three thousand miles, in diameter. Half-way from its northern to its southern edge, would be the 65th parallel. Along this parallel, represented

by the dotted line, which passes through the centre of the circle, the vortex, V, or calm spot, would travel. There should

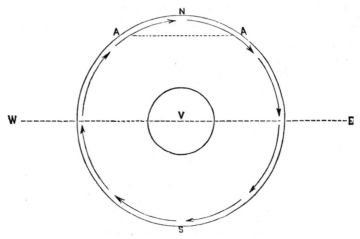

be calms, therefore, about the 65th parallel. In the southern
half of the circle, or that portion of it between the vortex and
the pole, easterly winds should prevail. Navigators between
the parallels of 65° and 75°, speak of calms as the normal
meteorological condition. All nature seems frozen to death,
the winds included. Unfortunately, we have no reliable data
for the parallels beyond, and do not know, therefore, whether
easterly winds are the prevalent winds or not. It is probable,
as we approached the pole, that we should find another calm.
The winds, [see the arrows,] as they come hurrying along the
circle, from its northern segment, bring with them an impetus
toward the east, derived from the diurnal motion of the earth,
on its axis. As these winds approach the pole, this velocity
increases, in consequence of the diminishing diameter of the
parallels. To illustrate. If a particle of air on the equator,
having a velocity eastward of fifteen miles per hour — and
this is the rate of the revolution of the earth on its axis —
should be suddenly transported to a point, distant five miles
from the pole, it would have sufficient velocity to carry it
entirely around the pole in one hour. Here we have two forces
acting in opposition to each other — the impetus of the wind
toward the east, given to it by the diurnal motion of the earth,

and an impetus *from* the east, given to it by whatever causes are hurrying it around the circle. These two forces necessarily neutralize each other, and a calm is the consequence. It is in this calm region near the poles, that the winds probably ascend, to take their flight back to the equator, in obedience to that beautiful arrangement for watering the earth, which I described some pages back.

There remains but one other fact to be reconciled with our theory. It has been seen that consecutive circles of wind passed over the *Alabama*, in periods of three days each. Did this time correspond with the known rate of travel of the circles? Almost precisely. Referring again to the last diagram, it will be remembered that the *Alabama* was near the northern edge of the circle. Let A A represent her position at the beginning and end of each wind. The chord of the segment, represented by the dotted line, is about 1500 miles in length. The circles travel at the rate of about 20 miles per hour. Multiply the number of hours — 72 — in three days, by 20, and we shall have 1440 miles. It is not pretended, of course, that these figures are strictly accurate, but they are sufficiently so to show, at least, that there is no discordance between the fact and the theory.

Soon after leaving the Cape of Good Hope, the storm-birds began to gather around us in considerable numbers—the Cape pigeon, the albatross, and occasionally the tiny petrel, so abundant in the North Atlantic. These birds seemed to be quite companionable, falling in company with the ship, and travelling with her for miles at a time. On the occasion of one of the short calms described, we caught an albatross, with hook and line, which measured ten feet across the wings. The monster bird was very fat, and it was quite a lift to get it inboard. Though very active on the wing, and rising with great facility from the water, in which it sometimes alights, it lay quite helpless when placed upon the deck. It did not seem to be much alarmed at the strangeness of its position, but looked at us with the quiet dignity and wisdom of an owl, as though it would interrogate us as to what we were doing in its dominions. These birds live in the midst of the great Indian Ocean, thousands of miles away from any land—only making periodical visits to some of the desert islands; or, it may be, to the Antarctic Continent, to incubate and rear their young.

I have described at some length the nature of the great circles of wind which form the normal meteorological condition of the region of ocean through which we were passing. This normal condition was sometimes interfered with by the passage of cyclones of smaller diameter — a circle within a circle; both circles, however, obeying the same laws. We took one of these cyclones on the 5th of October. I do not design to repeat, here, the description of a cyclone, and only refer to that which we now encountered, for the purpose of showing that the *Alabama ran a race with it, and was not very badly beaten.* This race is thus described in my journal: "Morning dull, cloudy, and cool. The wind hauled, last night, to north, and is blowing a fresh breeze at noon. Barometer, 30.14. Thermometer, air 54°, water 60°. Current during the last twenty-four hours, thirty miles east. The weather continued to thicken in the afternoon, and the wind to increase, with a falling barometer, indicating the approach of a gale. At nine P. M., the squalls becoming heavy, we furled the top-gallant sails and foresail, close-reefed the topsails, and took the bonnets off the trysails. Under this reduced sail we continued to scud the ship all night — the barometer still falling, the wind increasing, and a heavy sea getting up. We had entered the north-eastern edge of a cyclone. The next morning the wind was still north by west, having hauled only a single point in twelve hours; showing that we had been running, neck and neck, with the gale.

If the reader will recollect that, in these circular gales, the change of the wind is due to the passage of the circle over the ship, he will have no difficulty in conceiving that, if the ship travels as fast as the circle, and in the same direction, the wind will not change at all. Now, as the wind had changed but a single point in twelve hours, it is evident that the *Alabama* had been travelling nearly as fast as the circular gale. The race continued all the next day — the wind not varying half a point, and the barometer settling by scarcely perceptible degrees. Toward night, however, the barometer began to settle quite rapidly, and the wind increased, and began to haul to the westward. The gale had acquired accelerated speed, and was now evidently passing ahead of us quite rapidly ; for by half-past four A. M. the wind was at west, having hauled nearly a quadrant in twelve hours. At this point we had the lowest barometer, 29.65. The centre of the storm was then just abreast of us, bearing about south, and distant perhaps a hundred miles. At five A. M., or in half an hour afterward, the wind shifted suddenly from W. to W. S. W., showing that the vortex had passed us, and that the *Alabama* was at last beaten! The wind being still somewhat fresher than I desired, I hove the ship to, on the port tack, to allow the gale to draw farther ahead of me. After lying to three hours, the barometer continuing to rise, and the wind to moderate, we filled away, and shaking out some of the reefs, continued on our course.

On the 12th of October, we passed the remarkable islets of St. Peter and St. Paul, a sort of half-way mile posts between the Cape of Good Hope and the Strait of Sunda. These islets are the tops of rocky mountains, shooting up from great depths in the sea. They are in the midst of a dreary waste of waters, having no other land within a thousand miles and more, of them. They are composed of solid granite, without vegetation, and inhabited only by the wild birds of the ocean. I cannot imagine a more fitting station for a meteorologist. He would be in the midst of constant tempests, and might study the laws of his science, without interruption from neighboring isle or continent. There being an indifferent anchorage under the lee of St. Paul, we scanned the island narrowly with our glasses, as we passed, not knowing but we might find some adventurous Yankee whaler, or seal-catcher, trying out blubber, or knocking a seal on the head. These islands are frequently sighted by India-bound ships, and it was my intention to cruise a few days in their vicinity, but the bad weather hurried me on.

We took another gale, on the night after leaving them, and had some damage done to our head-rail and one of our quarter-boats. The scene was a sublime one to look upon. The seas — those long swells before described — were literally running mountains high, the wind was howling with more than usual fury, and a dense snow-storm was pelting us from the blackest and most angry-looking of clouds. I was now in longitude 83° E., and bore away more to the northward. Although the thermometer had not settled below 50°, we felt the cold quite piercingly — our clothing being constantly saturated with moisture. On the 14th of October, we had the first tolerably fine day we had experienced for the last two weeks, and we availed ourselves of it, to uncover the hatches and ventilate the ship, getting up from below, and airing the damp bedding and mildewed clothing. The constant straining of the ship, in the numerous gales she had encountered, had opened the seams in her bends, and all our state-rooms were leaking more or less, keeping our beds and clothing damp. On the next day, another gale overtook us, in which we lay to ten hours, to permit it, as we had done the gale we ran the race with, to pass ahead of us.

And thus it was, that we ran down our easting, in the region of the "brave west winds," with every variety of bad weather, of the description of which, the reader must, by this time, be pretty well tired. On the 17th of October, I was nearly *antipodal* with my home in Alabama. By the way, has the reader ever remarked that land is scarcely ever antipodal with land? Let him take a globe, and he will be struck with the fact, that land and water have been almost invariably arranged opposite to each other. May not this arrangement have something to do with the currents, and the water-carriers, the winds?

On the morning of the 21st of October, at about five o'clock, we crossed the tropic of Capricorn, on the 100th meridian of east longitude. We still held on to our west winds, though they had now become light. We took the trade-wind from about S. S. E. almost immediately after crossing the tropic. We thus had the good fortune, a second time, to cross the tropic without finding a calm-belt; the two counter-winds blowing almost side by side with each other. We had been twenty-four days and three quarters from the Cape of Good Hope, and in that time had run, under sail alone — occasionally lying to, in bad weather — 4410 miles; the average run, per day, being 178 miles. We had brought the easterly current with us, too, all the way. It had set us twenty miles to the north-east, on the day we reached the tropic. In all this lengthened run, we had sighted only two or three sails. One of these was a steamer, which we overhauled, and boarded, but which proved to be English. For nineteen days we did not see a sail; and still we were on the great highway to India. There must have been numerous travellers on this highway, before and behind us, but each was bowling along at a rapid, and nearly equal pace, before the "brave west winds," enveloped in his own circle, and shut out from the view of his neighbor by the mantle of black rain-clouds in which he was wrapped. Our mysterious friends, the Cape-pigeons, disappeared, as we approached the tropics.

We now ran rapidly through the south-east trades, with fine weather, until we reached the 12th parallel of south latitude, when we passed suddenly into the monsoon region. The monsoons were undergoing a change. The east monsoon was dying out, and the west monsoon was about to take its place. The struggle between the outgoing, and the incoming wind would occupy several weeks, and during all this time I might expect sudden shifts and squalls of wind and rain, with densely overcast skies, and much thunder and lightning. My intention was to make for the Strait of Sunda, that well-known passage into, and out of the China seas, between the islands of Java and Sumatra, cruise off it some days, and then run into the China seas. On the evening of the 26th we spoke an English bark, just out of the Strait, which informed us that the United States steamer *Wyoming* was cruising in the Strait, in company with a three-masted schooner, which she had fitted up as a tender, and that she anchored nearly every evening under the island of Krakatoa. Two days afterward, we boarded a Dutch ship, from Batavia to Amsterdam, which informed us, that a boat from the *Wyoming* had boarded her, off the town of Anger in the Strait. There seemed, therefore, to be little doubt, that if we attempted the Strait, we should find an enemy barring our passage.

As we drew near the Strait, we began to fall in with ships in considerable numbers. On the 31st of October, no less than six were cried from aloft, at the same time, all standing to the south-west, showing that they were just out of the famous passage. The wind being light and baffling, we got up steam, and chased and boarded four of them—three English, and one Dutch. By this time, the others were out of sight—reported, by those we had overhauled, to be neutral—and the night was setting in dark and rainy. The Dutch ship, like the last one we had boarded, was from Batavia, and corroborated the report of the presence of the *Wyoming* in these waters. She had left her at Batavia, which is a short distance only from the Strait of Sunda. The weather had now become exceedingly oppressive. Notwithstanding the almost constant rains, the heat was intense. On the morning of the 6th of November, we boarded an English ship, from Foo Chow for London, which informed us, that an American ship, called the *Winged Racer*, had come out of the Strait, in company with her. In the afternoon, two ships having been cried from aloft, we got up steam, and chased, hoping that one of them might prove to be the American ship reported. They were both English; but whilst we were chasing these two English ships, a third ship hove in sight, farther to windward, to which we gave chase in turn.

This last ship was to be our first prize in East-Indian waters. A gun brought the welcome stars and stripes to her peak, and upon being boarded, she proved to be the bark *Amanda*, of Boston, from Manilla bound to Queenstown for orders. The *Amanda* was a fine, rakish-looking ship, and had a cargo of hemp, and sugar. She was under charter-party to proceed first to Queenstown, and thence to the United States, for a market, if it should be deemed advisable. On the face of each of the three bills of lading found among her papers, was the following certificate from the British Consul at Manilla:—"I hereby certify that Messrs. Ker & Co., the shippers of the merchandise specified in this bill of lading, are British subjects established in Manilla, and that according to invoices produced, the said merchandise is shipped by order, and for account of Messrs. Holliday, Fox & Co., British subjects, of London, in Great Britain." As nobody swore to anything, before the Consul, his certificate was valueless to protect the property, and the ship and cargo were both condemned. The night set in very dark and squally, whilst we were yet alongside of this ship. We got on board from her some articles of provisions, and some sails and cordage to replace the wear and tear of the late gales we had passed through, and made a brilliant bonfire of her at about ten P. M. The conflagration lighted up the sea for many miles around, and threw its grim and ominous glare to the very mouth of the Strait.

The next day we ran in and anchored under Flat Point, on the north side of the Strait, in seventeen fathoms water, about a mile from the coast of Sumatra. My object was to procure some fruits and vegetables for my crew, who had been now a long time on salt diet.

CHAPTER XLIX.

THE ALABAMA PASSES THROUGH THE STRAIT OF SUNDA,
SEEING NOTHING OF THE WYOMING — BURNS THE
WINGED RACER JUST INSIDE THE STRAIT — THE
MALAY BOATMEN AND THEIR ALARM — ALABAMA
MAKES FOR THE GASPAR STRAIT, AND BURNS THE CON-
TEST, AFTER AN EXCITING CHASE — PASSES THROUGH
THE CARIMATA PASSAGE — DISCHARGES HER PRISON-
ERS INTO AN ENGLISH SHIP — MINIATURE SEA-SER-
PENTS — THE CURRENTS — PULO CONDORE — ARRIVAL
AT SINGAPORE

SOON after anchoring as described in the last chapter, we
had a false alarm. It was reported that a bark some distance off had suddenly taken in all sail, and turned her head
in our direction, as though she were a steamer coming in chase.
Orders were given to get up steam, to be ready for any emergency, but countermanded in a few minutes, when upon a partial lifting of the rain-clouds, it was ascertained that the strange
sail was a merchant-ship and had only taken in her top-gallant
sails to a squall, and clewed down her topsails, to reef. She
was indeed coming in our direction, but it was only to take
shelter for the night. She was a Dutch bark from Batavia,
for the west coast of Sumatra.

The next morning, we got under way, at an early hour, to
pass through the Strait of Sunda into the China Sea. We
hove up our anchor in the midst of a heavy rain-squall, but
the weather cleared as the day advanced, and a fresh and
favorable wind soon sprang up. We ran along by Keyser
Island, and at half-past ten lowered the propeller and put the
ship under steam. Under both steam and sail we made rapid
headway. We passed between the high and picturesque islands

of Beezee and Soubooko, the channel being only about a mile in width.   Groves of cocoanut-trees grew near the beach on the former island, among which were some straw-thatched huts.   From these huts, the natives, entirely naked, except a breech-cloth around the loins, flocked out in great numbers to see the ship pass.   Ships do not often take this narrow channel, and the spectacle was, no doubt, novel to them.   They made no demonstration, but gazed at us in silence as we flew rapidly past them.   We ran through the Strait proper of Sunda, between one and two o'clock in the afternoon, passing to the westward of the island called Thwart-the-Way, and close to the Stroom Rock, lying with its blackened and jagged surface but a few feet above the water.   This course carried us in full view of the little town and garrison of Anjer, but we saw nothing of the *Wyoming*.   We found the Strait of Sunda as unguarded by the enemy, as we had found the other highways of commerce along which we had passed.

Just where the Strait debouches into the China Sea, we descried, in the midst of a rain-squall, to which we were both obliged to clew up our top-gallant sails, a tall clipper ship, evidently American.   She loomed up through the passing shower like a frigate.   We at once gave chase, and in a very few minutes hove the stranger to with a gun.   It was the *Winged Racer*, which our English friend told us had passed out of the Strait some days before in his company.   She had lingered behind for some reason, and as a consequence had fallen into the power of her enemy, with no friendly gun from the *Wyoming* to protect her.   The *Winged Racer* was a perfect beauty —one of those New York ships of superb model, with taunt, graceful masts, and square yards, known as "clippers."   She was from Manilla, bound for New York, with a cargo consisting chiefly of sugar, hides, and jute.   There was no claim of neutral property, and condemnation followed the capture as a matter of course.   We anchored her near North Island, and came to, ourselves, for the convenience of "robbing" her.   She had sundry provisions on board—particularly sugar and coffee— of which we stood in need.   She had, besides, a large supply of Manilla tobacco, and my sailors' pipes were beginning to want replenishing.   It took us a greater part of the night—for night had set in by the time the two ships were well anchored—to transport to the *Alabama* such things as were needed. In the meantime, the master of the captured ship, who had his family on board, requested me to permit him and his crew to depart in his own boats. The portion of the Javan sea in which we were anchored was a mere lake, the waters being shallow, and studded every few miles with islands. He proposed to make his way to Batavia, and report to his Consul for further assistance. I granted his request, made him a present of all his boats, and told him to pack into them as much plunder as he chose. About one o'clock he was ready, and his little fleet of boats departed. The prisoners from the *Amanda* took passage with him.

Whilst these things were going on, a number of Malay bumboatmen had collected around us, with their stores of fruits, and vegetables, and live stock. These boatmen, like the Chinese, live on the water, and make a business of supplying ships that pass through the Strait. The stewards of the different messes had all been busy trading with them, and there was a great squalling of chickens, and squealing of pigs going on. An amusing scene was now to occur. The boatmen had no suspicion that the *Alabama* had captured the *Winged Racer*, and was about to destroy her. They were lying on their oars, or holding on to lines from the two ships, with the most perfect *insouciance*. Presently a flame leaped up on board the *Winged Racer*, and in a few minutes enveloped her. Terror at once took possession of the Malay boatmen, and such a cutting of lines, and shouting, and vigorous pulling were perhaps never before witnessed in the Strait of Sunda. These boats had informed us that the *Wyoming* was at Anger only two days before, when they left.

It was now about two o'clock A. M., and the *Alabama* getting up her anchor, steamed out into the China Sea, by the light of the burning ship. We had thus lighted a bonfire at either end of the renowned old Strait of Sunda. After having thus advertised our presence in this passage, it was useless to remain in it longer. Ships approaching it would take the alarm, and seek some other outlet into the Indian Ocean. Most of the ships coming down the China Sea, with a view of passing out at the

Strait of Sunda, come through the Gaspar Strait.   I resolved now to steam in the direction of this latter strait, and forestall such as might happen to be on their way.   By daylight we had steamed the coast of Sumatra and Java out of sight, and soon afterward we made the little island called the North Watcher, looking, indeed, as its name implied, like a lone sentinel posted on the wayside.   We had lost the beautiful blue waters of the Indian Ocean, with its almost unfathomable depths, and entered upon a sea whose waters were of a whitish green, with an average depth of no more than about twenty fathoms.   Finding that I should be up with Gaspar Strait, sometime during the night, if I continued under steam, and preferring to delay my arrival until daylight the next morning, I let my steam go down, and put my ship under sail, to take it more leisurely.

We were about to lift the propeller out of the water, when the cry of " sail ho ! " came from the vigilant look-out at the mast-head.   We at once discontinued the operation, not knowing but we might have occasion to use steam.   As the stranger was standing in our direction, we soon raised her from the deck, and as my glass developed, first one, and then another of her features, it was evident that here was another clipper-ship at hand.   She had the well-known tall, raking masts, square yards, and white canvas.   She was on a wind, with everything set, from courses to skysails, and was ploughing her way through the gently ruffled sea, with the rapidity, and at the same time, the grace of the swan.   We made her a point or two on our lee bow, and not to excite her suspicion we kept away for her, so gradually, that she could scarcely perceive the alteration in our course.   We hoisted at the same time the United States colors.   When we were within about four miles of the chase, she responded by showing us the same colors. Feeling now quite sure of her, we fired a gun, hauled down the enemy's flag, and threw our own to the breeze.   (We were now wearing that splendid white flag, with its cross and stars, which was so great an improvement upon the old one.)   So far from obeying the command of our gun, the gallant ship kept off a point or two — probably her best point of sailing — gave herself top-gallant and topmast studding-sails, and away she went!

I had been a little premature in my eagerness to clutch so beautiful a prize. She was not as yet under my guns, and it was soon evident that she would give me trouble before I could overhaul her. The breeze was tolerably fresh, but not stiff. We made sail at once in chase. Our steam had been permitted to go down, as the reader has seen; and as yet we had not much more than enough to turn over the propeller. The chase was evidently gaining on us. It was some fifteen or twenty minutes before the engineer had a head of steam on. We now gave the ship all steam, and trimmed the sails to the best possible advantage. Still the fugitive ship retained her distance from us, if she did not increase it. It was the first time the *Alabama* had appeared dull. She was under both sail and steam, and yet here was a ship threatening to run away from her. She must surely be out of trim. I tried, therefore, the effect of getting my crew aft on the quarter-deck, and shifting aft some of the forward guns. This helped us visibly, and the ship sprang forward with increased speed. We were now at least holding our own, but it was impossible to say, as yet, whether we were gaining an inch. If the breeze had freshened, the chase would have run away from us beyond all question. I watched the signs of the weather anxiously. It was between nine and ten o'clock A. M. Fortunately, as the sun gained power, and drove away the mists of the morning, the breeze began to decline! Now came the triumph of steam. When we had come within long range, I threw the spray over the quarter-deck of the chase, with a rifle-shot from my bow-chaser. Still she kept on, and it was not until all hope was evidently lost, that the proud clipper-ship, which had been beaten rather by the failure of the wind, than the speed of the *Alabama*, shortened sail and hove to.

When the captain was brought on board, I congratulated him on the skilful handling of his ship, and expressed my admiration of her fine qualities. He told me that she was one of the most famous clipper-ships out of New York. She was the *Contest*, from Yokohama, in Japan, bound to New York. She was light, and in fine sailing trim, having only a partial cargo on board. There being no attempt to cover the cargo, consisting mostly of light Japanese goods, lacker-ware, and curiosities, I condemned both ship and cargo. I was sorry to be obliged to burn this beautiful ship, and regretted much that I had not an armament for her, that I might commission her as a cruiser. Both ships now anchored in the open sea, with no land visible, in fourteen fathoms of water, whilst the crew was being removed from the prize, and the necessary preparations made for burning her. It was after nightfall before these were all completed, and the torch applied. We hove up our anchor, and made sail by the light of the burning ship. Having now burned a ship off Gaspar Strait, I turned my ship's head to the eastward, with the intention of taking the Carimata Strait.

My coal was running so short, by this time, that I was obliged to dispense with the use of steam, except on emergencies, and work my way from point to point wholly under sail. Fortune favored me however, for I passed through the Carimata Strait in the short space of five days against the northwest monsoon, which was a head-wind. Ships have been known to be thirty days making this passage. I generally anchored at night, on account of the currents, and the exceeding difficulty of the navigation — shoals besetting the navigator on every hand in this shallow sea. We began now to fall in with some of the curiosities of the China Sea. Salt-water serpents made their appearance, playing around the ship, and cutting up their antics. These snakes are from three to five feet long, and when ships anchor at night, have been known to crawl up the cables, and make their way on deck through the hawse-holes, greatly to the annoyance of the sailors who chance to be sleeping on deck. They are not known to be poisonous. Never having been in the China seas before, I was quite amused at the gambols of these minature sea-serpents. Seeing an old sailor stopping up the hawse-holes, with swabs, one evening after we had anchored, I asked him what he was about. "I 'm stopping out the snakes, y'r honor," he replied. "What," said I, "do they come on deck?" "Oh! yes, y'r honor; when I was in the ship *Flying Cloud*, we killed forty of them on deck in one morning watch."

Naked Malays frequently paddled off to us, when we anchored near their villages, with fowls, and eggs, and fruits, and vegetables, which they desired to exchange for rice and ship-bread. In frail piraguas, these amphibious bipeds will make long voyages from island to island. They seem to be a sort of wandering Arabs of the sea, and, as a rule, are a great set of villains, not hesitating to take a hand at piracy when opportunity offers. So intricate are some of the archipelagos which they inhabit, that it is next to impossible to track them to their hiding-places. These nomads, upon whom no civiliza tion seems to make any impression, will probably long remain the pests of the China seas, in spite of the steamship.

Emerging from the Carimata passage, we stood over to the west end of the island of Souriton, where we anchored at four P. M., on the 18th of November. Here we lay several days, and for the convenience of overhauling passing ships, without the necessity of getting under way, we hoisted out, and rigged our launch, a fine cutter-built boat, and provisioning and wa-tering her for a couple of days at a time, sent her out cruising; directing her, however, to keep herself within sight of the ship. A number of sails were overhauled, but they all proved to be neutral — mostly English and Dutch. I was much struck with the progress the Dutch were making in these seas. Hol-land, having sunk to a fourth or fifth rate power in Europe, is building up quite an empire in the East. The island of Java is a little kingdom in itself, and the boers, with the aid of the natives, whom they seem to govern with great success are fast bringing its fertile lands into cultivation. Batavia, Sou-rabia, and other towns are rising rapidly into importance. The Dutch are overrunning the fine island of Sumatra, too. They have established military stations over the greater part of it, and are gradually bringing the native chiefs under subjection. They occupy the spice islands, and are extending their domin-ion thence to the northward. In short, Great Britain must look to her laurels in the China seas, if she would not divide them with Holland.

In the meantime, the inquiry naturally presents itself, Where is the Yankee? that he is permitting all this rich harvest of colonization and trade in the East to pass away from him. It was at one time thought that he would contest the palm of enterprise with England herself, but this dream has long since been dispelled. Even before the war, his trade began to dwindle. During the war it went down to zero, and since the war it has not revived. Is he too busy with his internal dissensions and politics? Is the miserable faction which has ruled the country for the last seven years determined to destroy all its prosperity, foreign as well as domestic?

While lying at Souriton, we boarded the British ship *Avalanche*, two days from Singapore, with newspapers from America just forty days old! Here was a proof of the British enterprise of which we have just been speaking. The Atlantic, the Mediterranean, the Red Sea, the Indian Ocean, and a part of the China Sea, are traversed by British steam and sail, and the *Alabama* shakes out the folds of a newspaper from the land of her enemy, at an out-of-the-way island in the China Sea, just forty days old! The *Avalanche* kindly consenting, we sent by her our prisoners to Batavia. We now got under way, and stood over to the west coast of Borneo, where we cruised for a few days, working our way gradually to the northward; it being my intention as soon as I should take the north-east monsoon, which prevails at this season in the China Sea, to the northward of the equator, to stretch over to the coast of Cochin China, and hold myself for a short time in the track of the ships coming down from Canton and Shanghai. I was greatly tempted as I passed Sarawak, in the island of Borneo, to run in and visit my friend Rajah Brooke, whose career in the East has been so remarkable a one. Cruising in these seas, years ago, when he was a young man, in his own yacht, a jaunty little armed schooner of about 200 tons, he happened in at Sarawak. The natives, taking a fancy to him and his tiny man-of-war, insisted upon electing him their Rajah, or Governor. He assented, got a foothold in the island. grew in favor, increased his dominions, and was, at the period of our visit to the coast, one of the most powerful Rajahs in Borneo. Since my return from the China seas, the Rajah has died, full of years and full of honors, bequeathing his government to a blood relation. It would be difficult for even a Yankee to beat that!

Upon reaching this coast, we struck a remarkable northerly current. It ran at the rate of two knots per hour, its general set being about north-east. The weather falling calm, we were several days within its influence. When it had drifted us as far to the northward as I desired to go, I was obliged to let go a kedge in fifty fathoms water to prevent further drift. The current now swept by us at so rapid a rate, that we were compelled to lash two deep sea leads together, each weighing forty-five pounds, to keep our drift-lead on the bottom. Here was another of those elliptical currents spoken of a few pages back. If the reader will look at a map of the China Sea, he will observe that the north-east monsoon, as it comes sweeping down that sea, in the winter months, blows parallel with the coasts of China and Cochin China. This wind drives a current before it to the south-west. This current, as it strikes the peninsula of Malacca, is deflected to the eastward toward the coast of Sumatra. Impinging upon this coast, it is again deflected and driven off in the direction of the island of Borneo. This island in turn gives it a northern direction, and the consequence is, that the south-westerly current which came sweeping down the western side of the China Sea, is now going up on the eastern side of the same sea, as a north-easterly current. We lay five days at our kedge, during a calm that lasted all that time. The monsoons were changing; the west monsoon was setting in in the East Indian archipelago, and the north-eastern monsoon in the China Sea. Hence the calms, and rains, and sudden gusts of wind, now from one quarter, and now from another, which we had experienced. At the end of these five days of calm, we took the north-east monsoon, from about N. N. E., and, getting up our kedge, we made our way over to the coast of Cochin China, in accordance with the intention already expressed.

There is no navigation, perhaps, in the world, so trying to the vigilance and nerves of the mariner as that of the China seas. It is a coral sea, and filled with dangers in almost every direction, especially in its eastern portion, from the Philippine Islands down to the Strait of Sunda. The industrious little stone-mason, which we have before so often referred to, has laid the foundation of a new empire, at the bottom of the China Sea, and is fast making his way to the surface. He has already dotted the sea with ten thousand islands, in its eastern portion, and is silently and mysteriously piling up his tiny blocks of stone, one upon another, in the central and western portions. He is working very irregularly, having large gangs of hands employed here, and very few there, and is running up his structures in very fantastic shapes, some in solid blocks, with even surfaces, some as pyramids, and some as cones. The tops of the pyramids and cones are sometimes as sharp as needles, and pierce a ship's bottom as readily as a needle would a lady's finger. It is impossible to survey such a sea with accuracy. A surveying vessel might drop a lead on almost every square foot of bottom, and yet miss some of these mere needle-points. A ship, with the best of modern charts, may be threading this labyrinth, as she thinks, quite securely, and suddenly find herself impaled upon one of these dangers.

To add to the perplexity of the navigator, days sometimes elapse, especially when the monsoons are changing, during which it is impossible to get an observation for fixing the position of his ship; and during these days of incessant darkness, and drenching rains, he is hurried about by currents, he knows not whither. And then, perhaps, the typhoon comes along — that terrible cyclone of the China seas — at the very moment, it may be, when he is, by reason of the causes mentioned, uncertain of his position, and compels him to scud his ship at hazard, among shoals and breakers! I lost many nights of rest when in these seas, and felt much relieved when the time came for me to turn my back upon them. The wind freshened as we drew out from the coast of Borneo, and by the time we had reached the track of the westward-bound ships, we found the monsoon blowing a whole topsail-breeze. We struck, at the same time, the south-westerly current described, and what with the wind and the current, we found it as much as we could do to hold our own, and prevent ourselves from being drifted to leeward. It soon became apparent that it would be useless to attempt operations here, unless assisted by steam. Every chase would probably carry us miles to leeward, whence it would be impossible, under sail alone, to regain our position. Still, we held ourselves a day or two in the track, in accordance with my previous determination, overhauling several ships, none of which, however, proved to be enemy.

At the end of this short cruise, we made sail for the island of Condore, or, as it is called on the charts of the China Sea, Pulo Condore, the word "pulo" being the Chinese term for island. My intention was to run into this small island, which has a snug harbor, sheltered from the monsoon, do some necessary repairs with my own mechanics, refit and repaint, and then run down to Singapore, and fill up with coal. My future course would be guided by contingencies. We made Pulo Condore early in the afternoon of the second of December, and passing to the northward of the "White Rock," bore up, and ran along the western side of the island until nightfall, when we anchored under the lee of a small, rocky island, near the mouth of the harbor. The scenery was bold, picturesque, and impressive. All was novelty; the shallow sea, the whistling monsoon, and the little islands rising so abruptly from the sea, that a goat could scarcely clamber up their sides. The richest vegetation covered these islands from the sea-level to their summits. Occasionally a break or gap in the mountain — for Pulo Condore rises to the height of a mountain — disclosed charming ravines, opening out into luxuriant plains, where were grazing the wild cattle of the country — the bison, or small-humped buffalo of the East.

At daylight the next morning, upon looking into the harbor with our glasses, we were surprised to see a small vessel at anchor, wearing the French flag; and pretty soon afterward we were boarded by a French boat; Pulo Condore — lying off the coast of Cochin China — having recently become a French colony. The island had been taken possession of by France two years before. The vessel was a ship of war, keeping watch and ward over the lonely waters. This was a surprise. I had expected to find the island in the hands of the Malay nomads who infest these seas, and to have converted it into Confederate territory, as I had done Angra Pequeña, on the west coast of Africa — at least during my stay. And so when I had invited the French officer, who was himself the commander of the little craft, into my cabin, I remarked to him, "You have spoiled a pet project of mine." "How so?" said he. I then explained to him how, in imitation of my friend Brooke, I had intended to play Rajah for a few weeks, in Pulo

Condore. He laug..ed heartily, and said, "*Serà tout le même chose, Monsieur. Vous portez plus de cannons que moi, et vous serez Rajah, pendant votre séjour.*" I did carry a few more guns than my French friend, for his little man-of-war was only a craft of the country, of less than a hundred tons burden, armed with one small carronade. His crew consisted of about twenty men.

I found him as good as his word, with reference to my play-ing Rajah, for he did not so much as mention to me, once, any rule limiting the stay of belligerents in French waters. We now got under way, and stood in to the anchorage, the French officer kindly consenting to show me the way in; though there was but little need, as the harbor was quite free from obstruc-tions, except such as were plainly visible. The water in this cosy little harbor was as smooth as a mill-pond, notwithstand-ing occasional gusts of the monsoon swept down the moun-tain sides. There were mountains on two sides of us, both to the north and south. The harbor was, in fact, formed by two mountainous islands, both passing under the name of Condore; there being only a boat-passage separating them on the east.

This was our first real resting-place, since leaving the Cape of Good Hope, and both officers and men enjoyed the relaxa-tion. The island was full of game, the bay full of fish, and the bathing very fine. We felt quite secure, too, against the approach of an enemy. The only enemy's steamer in these seas was the *Wyoming*, for which we regarded ourselves as quite a match. We had, besides, taken the precaution, upon anchoring, to lay out a spring, by which we could, in the course of a few minutes, present our broadside to the nar-row entrance of the harbor, and thus rake anything that might attempt the passage. The Governor of the island now came on board to visit us. He had his headquarters at a small Malay village on the east coast, where, by the aid of a ser-geant's guard, he ruled his subjects with despotic sway. He brought me on board a present of a pig, and generously offered to share with me a potato-patch near the ship. What more could a monarch do? This was an exceedingly clever young Frenchman — Monsieur Bizot — he was an ensign in the French

Navy, about twenty-two years of age, and a graduate of the
French naval school. The commander of his flag-ship—the
small country craft already described—was a midshipman.
These two young men had entire control of the government of
the island, civil and military.

Kell having set his mechanics at work in the various departments, to effect the necessary repairs on the ship, I relaxed the
reins of discipline, as much as possible, that, by boat-sailing,
fishing, and hunting excursions, my people might recruit from
the ill effects of their long confinement on ship-board, and the
storms and bad weather they had experienced. The north-
east monsoon having now fairly set in, the weather had become
fine. The heat was very great, it is true, but it was much tempered by the winds. During the two weeks that we remained
in the island, almost every part of it was explored by my adventurous hunters—even the very mountain tops—and marvellous were the reports of their adventures which they brought
on board. Some small specimens of deer were found; the
bison—the bull of which is very savage, not hesitating to assault the hunter, under favorable circumstances—abounded on
the small savannas; monkeys travelled about in troops; parrots,
and other birds of beautiful plumage, wheeled over our heads
in flocks—in short, the whole island seemed teeming with life.
The natives told us that there were many large, and some poisonous serpents in the jungles, but fortunately none of my
people were injured by them.

We found here the famous vampyre of the East. Several
specimens were shot, and brought on board. Some of these
monster bats measure from five to six feet from tip to tip of
wing. The head resembles that of a wolf. It has long and
sharp incisor-teeth and tusks, and would be a dangerous animal to attack an unarmed man. The reptile tribe flourishes in
perfection. A lizard, measuring five feet ten inches in length,
was brought on board by one of the hunters. Nature runs
riot in every direction, and the vegetable world is as curious
as the animal. The engineer coming on board, one day, from
one of his excursions, pulled out his cigar case, and offered
me a very tempting Havana cigar. Imagine my surprise when
I found it a piece of wood! It had been plucked fresh from

the tree. The size, shape, and color—a rich brown—were all perfect. It was not a capsule or a seed-pod, but a solid piece of wood, with the ordinary woody fibre, and full of sap. I put it away carefully among my curiosities, but after a few days it shrivelled, and lost its beauty.

The apes did not appear to be afraid of the gun—probably because they were not accustomed to be shot at. They would cluster around a hunting-party, and grin and chatter like so many old negroes, one sometimes sees on the coast of Africa. One of the midshipmen having shot one, described the death of the old gentleman to me, and said that he felt almost as if he had killed his old "uncle" on his father's plantation. The wounded creature—whatever it may be, man or animal—threw its arms over the wound, and moaned as plaintively and intelligibly as if it had been gifted with the power of speech, and were upbraiding its slayer. During our stay I made the acquaintance—through my opera-glass—of several of these lampoons upon human nature. A gang of apes, old and young, came down to the beach regularly every morning, to look at the ship. The old men and women would seat themselves in rows, and gaze at us, sometimes for an hour, without changing their places or attitudes—seeming to be absorbed in wonder. I became quite familiar with some of their countenances. The young people did not appear to be so strongly impressed. They would walk about the beach in twos and threes—making love, most likely, and settling future family arrangements. The children, meanwhile, would be romping around the old people, screaming and barking in very delight. If a boat approached them, the old people would give a peculiar whistle, when the younger members of the tribe would betake themselves at once to the cover of the adjoining jungle.

A hunting party, landing here one morning, shot one of these old apes. The rest scampered off, and were seen no more that day. The next morning, upon turning my opera-glass upon the beach, I saw the monkeys as usual, but they were broken into squads, and moving about in some disorder, instead of being seated as usual. I could plainly see some of them at work. Some appeared to be digging in the sand, and others to be bringing twigs and leaves of trees, and such of the debris of the forest as they could gather conveniently. It was my usual hour for landing, to get sights for my chronometers. As the boat approached, the whole party disappeared. I had the curiosity to walk to the spot, to see what these semi-human beings had been doing. They had been burying their dead comrade, and had not quite finished covering up the body, when they had been disturbed! The deceased seemed to have been popular, for a large concourse had come to attend his funeral. The natives told us, that this burial of the monkeys was a common practice. They believe in monkey doctors, too, for they told us that when they have come upon sick monkeys in the woods, they have frequently found some demure old fellows looking very wise, with their fingers on their noses sitting at their bed-sides. The ladies may be curious to know, from the same good authority, how the monkeys of Pulo Condore treat their women. As among the Salt Lake saints, polygamy prevails, and there are sometimes as many as a dozen females "sealed" to one old patriarch—especially if he be broad across the shoulders, and have sharp teeth. The young lady monkeys are required to form matrimonial connections during the third or fourth season of their belledom; that is to say, the parent monkeys will permit their daughters to sally out and return home as often as they please, after they have "come out," until three or four moons have elapsed. After that time they are expected to betake themselves to their own separate trees for lodging.

I was frequently startled, whilst we lay at Pulo Condore, at hearing what appeared to be the whistle of a locomotive—rather shrill, it may be, but very much resembling it. It proceeded from an enormous locust.

Pulo Condore lies in the route of the French mail-steamer, between Singapore and Saigon, the latter the capital of the French possessions in Cochin China, and the Governor receiving a large mail while we were here, was kind enough to send us some late papers from Paris and Havre. Every two or three days, too, he sent us fresh beef, fowls, and fruits. On the Sunday evening after our arrival, he, and his paymaster repeated their visit to us, and brought in the same boat with themselves, a bullock—a fine fat bison! In a country comparatively wild, and where supplies were so difficult to be obtained, these presents were greatly enhanced in value. Poor Monsieur Bizot! we all regretted to learn, upon our return to Europe, that this promising young officer, so full of talent, life, energy, hope, had fallen a victim to a malarial fever.

Kell performed quite a feat at Pulo Condore in the way of ship-carpentry. Our copper having fallen off, some distance below the water-line, he constructed a coffer or caisson, that fitted the side of the ship so nicely, when sunk to the required depth, that he had only to pump it out, with our fire-engine and suction-hose, to enable his mechanics to descend into a dry box and effect the necessary repairs. We found our ship so much out of order, that it required two weeks to get her ready for sea. At the end of this time, we took an affectionate leave of our French friends, and getting under way, under sail, we again threw ourselves into the monsoon, and south-west current, and turned our head in the direction of Singapore. We crossed the Gulf of Siam under easy sail, that we might have the benefit of any chance capture, that might present itself. There was a number of vessels hurrying on before the brisk monsoon, but no Yankee among them. The Yankee flag had already become a stranger in the China Sea. On the evening of the 19th of December, we ran in, and anchored under Pulo Aor, in twenty fathoms water, within half a mile of the village, on the south-west end of the island. The island is high, and broken —its forests being composed almost entirely of the cocoanut— and is inhabited by the same class of Malay nomads already described. Their houses were picturesquely scattered among the trees, and several large boats were hauled up near them, on the beach, ready for any enterprise that might offer, in their line. The head man came off to visit me, and some piraguas with fowls and fruits came alongside, to trade with the sailors.

These islanders appeared to be a merry set of fellows, for during nearly the whole night, we could hear the sound of tom-toms, and other musical instruments, as though they were engaged in the mysteries of the dance. Some very pretty specimens of young women, naked to the middle, came off in their light piraguas, handling the paddle equally with the men, and appearing quite as much at home on the water. The next day being Sunday, and the weather not being very propitious for our run to Singapore, it being thick and murky, we remained over at our anchors, at this island, mustering the crew, and inspecting the ship as usual. After muster, some of the officers visited the shore, and were hospitably received by the natives. They saw no evidences of the cultivation of the soil, or of any other kind of labor. Nature supplied the inhabitants, spontaneously, with a regular succession of fruits all the year round, and as for clothing, they needed none, so near the equator. The sea gave them fish; and the domestic fowl, which seemed to take care of itself, and the goat which browsed without care also on the mountain-side, secured them against the caprice of the elements. Their *physique* was well developed, and life seemed to be with them a continual holiday. Who shall say that the civilized man is a greater philosopher, than the savage of the China seas?

On the next morning, at a very early hour—just as the cocks on shore were crowing for early daylight—we hove up our anchor, and giving the ship both steam and sail, shaped our course for Singapore. Soon after getting under way, we fell in company with an English steamer running also in our direction. The navigation, as one approaches the Strait of Malacca, on which Singapore is situated, is very difficult, there being some ugly shoals by the wayside; and the weather coming on thick, and heavy rains setting in, we were obliged to anchor in the mouth of the Strait for several hours. The weather now lifting, and the clouds breaking away, we got under way, again, and taking a Malay pilot soon afterward, we ran into Singapore, and anchored, at about five P. M. The harbor was filled with shipping, but there was no United States ship of war among the number. The reader has seen that the *Wyoming* was at Anger in the Strait of Sunda, only two days before we burned the *Winged Racer*. She must have heard of that event soon after its occurrence, and also of our burning the *Contest* near Gaspar Strait. The English ship *Avalanche* had, besides, carried news to Batavia, that we were off Sorouton, still higher up the China Sea. The *Wyoming*, if she had any intention of seeking a fight with us, was thus entirely deceived by our movements. These indicated that we were bound to Canton and Shanghai, and thither, probably, she had gone. She must have passed within sight of Pulo Condore, while we were scraping down our masts, tarring our rigging, and watching the funeral of the dead monkey described; and about the time she was ready to run into Hongkong, in the upper part of the China Sea, we had run into Singapore, and anchored in the lower part.

CHAPTER L.

THE ALABAMA AT SINGAPORE — PANIC AMONG THE EN-
EMY'S SHIPPING IN THE CHINA SEA — THE MULTITUDE
FLOCK TO SEE THE ALABAMA — CURIOUS RUMOR CON-
CERNING HER — AUTHOR RIDES TO THE COUNTRY, AND
SPENDS A NIGHT — THE CHINESE IN POSSESSION OF ALL
THE BUSINESS OF THE PLACE — ALABAMA LEAVES SIN-
GAPORE — CAPTURE OF THE MARTABAN, ALIAS TEXAN
STAR — ALABAMA TOUCHES AT MALACCA — CAPTURE
OF THE HIGHLANDER AND SONORA — ALABAMA ONCE
MORE IN THE INDIAN OCEAN.

IT turned out as I had conjectured in the last chapter. The
Wyoming had been at Singapore on the 1st of December.
She had gone thence to the Rhio Strait, where a Dutch settlement had given her a ball, which she had reciprocated. Whilst
these Yankee and Dutch rejoicings were going on, the *Alabama*
was crossing the China Sea, from Borneo to Pulo Condore.
All traces of the *Wyoming* had since been lost. She had
doubtless filled with coal at Rhio, and gone northward. We
had thus a clear sea before us.

A very gratifying spectacle met our eyes at Singapore.
There were twenty-two American ships there—large India-
men—almost all of which were dismantled and laid up! The
burning of our first ship in these seas, the *Amanda*, off the
Strait of Sunda, had sent a thrill of terror through all the
Yankee shipping, far and near, and it had hastened to port, to
get out of harm's way. We had recent news here from all
parts of the China seas, by vessels passing constantly through
the Strait of Malacca, and touching at Singapore for orders or
refreshments. There were two American ships laid up in Bankok, in Siam; one or two at Canton; two or three at Shang-

hai; one at the Phillippine Islands; and one or two more in
Japanese waters.   These, besides the twenty-two ships laid up
in Singapore, comprised all of the enemy's once numerous
Chinese fleet!   No ship could get a freight, and the commerce
of the enemy was as dead, for the time being, as if every ship
belonging to him had been destroyed.   We had here the key
to the mystery, that the *Alabama* had encountered no American ship, in the China Sea, since she had burned the *Contest*.
The birds had all taken to cover, and there was no such thing
as flushing them.   This state of things decided my future
course.   I had, at first, thought of running up the China Sea,
as far as Shanghai, but if there were no more than half a
dozen of the enemy's ships to be found in that part of the sea,
and these had all fled to neutral ports for protection, *cui bono?*
It would be far better to return to the western hemisphere,
where the enemy still had some commerce left.   Indeed, my
best chance of picking up these very ships, that were now anchored under my guns in Singapore, and disconsolate for want
of something to do, would be to waylay them on their homeward voyages.   They would not venture out in a close sea like
that of China, so long as I remained in it.   After I should
have departed, and they had recovered somewhat from their
panic, they might pick up partial cargoes, at reduced rates, and
once more spread their wings for flight.

I had another powerful motive influencing me.   My ship was
getting very much out of repair.   The hard usage to which
she had been subjected since she had been commissioned
had very much impaired her strength, and so constantly had
she been under way, that the attrition of the water had worn
the copper on her bottom so thin that it was daily loosening
and dropping off in sheets.   Her speed had, in consequence,
been much diminished.   The fire in her furnaces, like that of
the fire-worshipping Persian, had never been permitted to go
out, except for a few hours at rare intervals, to enable the engineer to clink his bars, and remove the incrustations of salt
from the bottoms of his boilers.   This constant action of fire
and salt had nearly destroyed them.   I resolved, therefore, to
turn my ship's head westward from Singapore, run up into the
Bay of Bengal, along the coast of Hindostan to Bombay,

through the Seychelle Islands to the mouth of the Red Sea, thence to the Comoro Islands; from these latter to the Strait of Madagascar, and from the latter Strait to the Cape of Good Hope—thus varying my route back to the Cape.

We were received with great cordiality by the people of Singapore, and, as at the Cape of Good Hope, much curiosity was manifested to see the ship. After she had hauled alongside of the coaling wharf, crowds gathered to look curiously upon her, and compare her appearance with what they had read of her. These crowds were themselves a curiosity to look upon, formed, as they were, of all the nations of the earth, from the remote East and the remote West. Singapore being a free port, and a great centre of trade, there is always a large fleet of shipping anchored in its waters, and its streets and other marts of commerce are constantly thronged with a promiscuous multitude. The canal—there being one leading to the rear of the town—is filled with country boats from the surrounding coasts, laden with the products of the different countries from which they come. There is the pepper-boat from Sumatra, and the coaster of larger size laden with tin-ore; the spice-boats from the spice islands; boats with tin-ore, hides, and mats from Borneo; boats from Siam, with gums, hides, and cotton; boats from different parts of the Malay peninsula, with canes, gutta-percha, and India-rubber. In the bay are ships from all parts of the East—from China, with silks and teas; from Japan, with lacker-ware, raw silk, and curious manufactures of iron, steel, and paper; from the Phil-lippine Islands, with sugar, hides, tobacco, and spices. Inter-mixed with these are the European and American ships, with the products of their various countries. As a consequence, all the races and all the religions of the world were represented in the throngs that crowded the coaling jetty, to look upon the *Alabama*, wearing the new flag of a new nation, mysterious for its very distance from them. We were to their eastern eyes a curious people of the antipodes.

The physical aspect of the throng was no less curious than its moral. There was the Malay, the Chinese, the Japanese, the Siamese, the Hindoo, the Persian, the wild Tartar, the Bor-nese, the Sumatran, the Javanese, and even the New Zealander

—all dressed, or undressed, as the case might be, in the garb of their respective tribes and countries. Some of the most notable objects among the crowd, were jet-black Africans, with the amplest of petticoat trousers gathered at the knee, sandalled feet, and turbaned heads — the more shining the jet of the complexion, the whiter the turban. The crowd, so far from diminishing, increased daily, so that it was at times difficult to pass into and out of the ship; and it was some time before we could learn what had excited all this curiosity among those simple inhabitants of the isles and continents. Some of these wonder-mongers actually believèd, that we kept chained in the hold of the *Alabama*, several negro giants — they had heard something about the negro and slavery having something to do with the war — whom we armed with immense weapons and let loose, in time of battle, as they were wont to do their elephants! They waited patiently for hours, under their paper umbrellas, hoping to catch a sight of these monsters.

Singapore, which was a fishing village half a century ago, contains a hundred thousand inhabitants, and under the free-port system has become, as before remarked, a great centre of trade. It concentrates nearly all the trade of the southern portion of the China Sea. There are no duties on exports or imports; and the only tonnage due paid by the shipping, is three cents per ton, register, as a lighthouse tax. The currency is dollars and cents; Spanish, Mexican, Peruvian, and Bolivian dollars are current. Great Britain, with an infinite forecaste, not only girdles the seas with her ships, but the land with her trading stations. In her colonization and commerce consists her power. Lop off these, and she would become as insignificant as Holland. And so beneficent is her rule, that she binds her colonies to her with hooks of steel. A senseless party in that country has advocated the liberation of all her colonies. No policy could be more suicidal. Colonization is as much of a necessity for Great Britain as it was for the Grecian States and for Rome, when they became overcrowded with population. Probably, in the order of nature, colonies, as they reach maturity, may be expected to go off to themselves, but for each colony which thus puts on the *toga virilis*, Great Britain should establish another, if she would preserve her empire, and her importance with the nations of the earth.

The most notable feature about Singapore is its Chinese population. I consider these people, in many respects, the most wonderful people of the earth. They are essentially a people of the arts, and of trade, and in the changing aspect of the world must become much more important than they have hitherto been. It is little more than half a century since Napoleon twitted the English people with being a nation of "shop-keepers." So rapid have been the changes since, that other nations besides Great Britain are beginning to covet the designation as one of honor. Even military France, the very country which bestowed the epithet in scorn, is herself becoming a nation of mechanics and shop-keepers. Industrial Congresses, and Palaces of Industry attract more attention, in that once martial country, than military reviews, and the marching and countermarching of troops on the Campus Martius. An Emperor of France has bestowed the cordon of the Legion of Honor on a Yankee piano-maker! These are some of the signs of the times in which we live. And they are signs which the wise statesman will not ignore. A nation chooses wisely and well, which prefers the pursuits of peace to those of war; and that nation is to be envied, which is better constituted by the nature of its people for peaceful, than for warlike pursuits. This is eminently the case with the Chinese. Nature has kindly cast them in a mould, gentle and pacific. They are human, and have, therefore, had their wars, but compared with the western nations, their wars have been few. The Taeping rebellion of our day, which has lasted so long, had its origin in the brigandage of an idle and leprous soldiery, who sought to live at ease, at the expense of the honest producer.

It is only lately that we have been able to obtain an interior view of these people. A few years back, and China was a sealed book to us. Our merchants were confined to certain "factories" outside of the walls of Canton, and we were permitted to trade at no other points. But since we have gotten a glimpse of these wonderful people, we have been astonished at the extraordinary productiveness and vitality of Chinese commerce. We have been amazed whilst we have looked upon the wonderful stir and hum and bustle of so immense a hive of human beings, all living and prospering by the mechanic arts and commerce. The Chinaman is born to industry, as naturally as the negro is to sloth. He is the cheapest producer on the face of the earth, because his habits are simple and frugal. The proof of this is, that no western nation can sell its goods in the Chinese market. We are all compelled to purchase whatever we want from them, for cash. When we can work cheaper than the Chinese, we may hope to exchange our manufactured goods with them, but not until then.

Singapore is a miniature Canton, and the visitor, as he passes through its streets, has an excellent opportunity of comparing the industry of the Chinese with that of other nations. As a free port, Singapore is open to immigration from all parts of the earth, on equal terms. There are no jealous laws, guilds, or monopolies, to shackle the limbs, or dampen the energy or enterprise of any one. Free competition is the presiding genius of the place. The climate is healthy—the English call it the Madeira of the East—and the European artisan can labor in it as well as the East Indian or the Chinese. All nations flock hither to trade, as has already been remarked. Now what is the result? Almost all the business of every description is in the hands of the Chinese. Large Chinese houses monopolize the trade, and the Chinese artisan and day-laborer have driven out all others. Ninety thousand of the one hundred thousand of the population are Chinese.

Now that the exclusiveness of China has been broken in upon, and emigration permitted, what a destiny awaits such a people in the workshops and fields of the western world! Already they are filling up the States on the Pacific coast, and silently, but surely, possessing themselves of all the avenues of industry in those States, thrusting aside the more expensive European and American laborers. They will cross the Rocky Mountains, and effect, in course of time, a similar revolution in the Western and Southern States. In the latter States their success will be most triumphant; for in these States, where the negro is the chief laborer, the competition will be between frugality, forecast, and industry on the one hand, and wastefulness, indifference to the future, and laziness on the other. The negro must, of necessity, disappear in such a conflict. Cheap labor must and will drive out dear labor. This law is as inexorable as any other of Nature's laws. This is the probable fate, which the Puritan has prepared for his friend the negro, on the American continent. Our system of slavery might have saved his race from destruction — nothing else can.

The Governor of Singapore was a colonel in the British army. He had a small garrison of troops — no more, I believe, than a couple of companies — to police this large population. I sent an officer, as usual, to call on him and acquaint him with my wants and intention as to time of stay. Mr. Beaver, of the firm of Cumming, Beaver & Co., a clever English merchant, came on board, and offered to facilitate us all in his power, in the way of procuring supplies. I accepted his kind offer, and put him in communication with the paymaster, and the next day rode out, and dined, and spent a night with him at his country-seat. He lived in luxurious style, as do most European merchants in the East. The drive out took us through the principal streets of the city, which I found to be laid out and built with great taste — the edifices having a semi-English, semi-Oriental air. The houses of the better classes were surrounded by lawns and flower-gardens, and cool verandahs invited to repose. Mr. Beaver's grounds were extensive, and well kept, scarcely so much as a stray leaf being visible on his well mown lawns. His household — the lady was absent in England — was a pattern of neatness and comfort. His bath-rooms, bed-rooms, library, and billiard-room — all showed signs of superintendence and care, there being an air of cleanliness and neatness throughout, which one rarely ever sees in a bachelor establishment. His servants were all Chinese, and males. Chi-hi, and Hu-chin, and the rest of them, ploughed his fields, mowed his hay, stabled his horses, cooked his dinners, waited on his guests, washed his linen, made his beds, and marked his game of billiards; and all at a ridiculously low rate of hire. If there had been a baby to be nursed, it would have been all the same.

On my return to the city, next day, I lunched, by invitation, at the officers' mess. English porter, ale, and cheese, cold meats, and a variety of wines were on the table. An English officer carries his habits all over the world with him, without stopping to consider climates. No wonder that so many of them return from the east with disordered hepatic arrangements.

When I returned to the ship, in the evening, I found that Kell and Galt had made such good use of their time, that everything was on board, and we should be ready for sea on the morrow. Our coaling had occupied us but ten hours — so admirable are the arrangements of the P. and O. Steamship Company, at whose wharf we had coaled. A pilot was engaged, and all the preparations made for an early start. There was nothing more to be done except to arrange a little settlement between the Queen and myself, similar to the one which had taken place at the Cape of Good Hope. As we were obliged to lie alongside of the wharf, for the convenience of coaling, it had been found impossible, in the great press and throng of the people who were still anxious to get a sight of my black giants, to prevent the sailors from having grog smuggled to them. When an old salt once gets a taste of the forbidden nectar, he is gone — he has no more power of resistance than a child. The consequence on the present occasion was, that a number of my fellows "left" on a frolic. We tracked most of them up, during the night, and arrested them — without asking any aid of the police, this time — and brought them on board. One of the boozy fellows dived under the wharf, and played mud-turtle for some time, but we finally fished him out. When we came to call the roll, there were half a dozen still missing. A number of applications had been made to us by sailors who wanted to enlist, but we had hitherto resisted them all. We were full, and desired no more. Now, however, the case was altered, and the applications being renewed after the deserters had run off — for sailors are a sort of Freemasons, and soon learn what is going on among their craft — we permitted half a dozen picked fellows to come on board, to be shipped as soon as we should get out into the Strait.

The next morning, bright and early, the *Alabama* was under way, steaming through the Strait of Malacca. At half-past eleven A. M., "sail ho!" was cried from the mast, and about one P. M., we came up with an exceedingly American-looking ship, which, upon being hove to by a gun, hoisted the English colors. Lowering a boat, I sent Master's Mate Fullam, one of the most intelligent of my boarding-officers, and who was himself an Englishman, on board to examine her papers. These were all in due form — were undoubtedly genuine, and had been signed by the proper custom-house officers. The register purported that the stranger was the British ship *Martaban*, belonging to parties in Maulmain, a rice port in India. Manifest and clearance corresponded with the register; the ship being laden with rice, and having cleared for Singapore — of which port, as the reader sees, she was within a few hours' sail. Thus far, all seemed regular and honest enough, but the ship was American — having been formerly known as the *Texan Star* — and her transfer to British owners, if made at all, had been made within the last ten days, after the arrival of the *Alabama* in these seas had become known at Maulmain. Mr. Fullam, regarding these circumstances as at least suspicious, requested the master of the ship to go on board the *Alabama* with him, that I might have an opportunity of inspecting his papers in person. This the master declined to do. I could not, of course, compel an English master to come on board of me, and so I was obliged to go on board of him — and I may state, by the way, that this was the only ship I ever boarded personally during all my cruises.

I could not but admire the beautiful, "*bran new*" English flag, as I pulled on board, but, as before remarked, every line of the ship was American — her long, graceful hull, with flaring bow, and rounded stern, taunt masts with sky-sail poles, and square yards for spreading the largest possible quantity of canvas. Passing up the side, I stepped upon deck. Here everything was, if possible, still more American, even to the black, greasy cook, who, with his uncovered woolly head, naked breast, and uprolled sleeves in the broiling sun, was peeling his Irish potatoes for his codfish. I have before remarked upon the national features of ships. These features are as well marked in the interior organism, as in the exterior. The master received me at the gangway, and, after I had paused to take a glance at things on deck, I proceeded with him into his cabin, where his papers were to be examined. His mates were standing about the companion-way, anxious, of course, to know the fate of their ship. If I had had any doubts

before, the unmistakable persons of these men would have removed them. In the person of the master, the long, lean,
angular-featured, hide-bound, weather-tanned Yankee skipper
stood before me. Puritan, *May-Flower*, Plymouth Rock, were
all written upon the well-known features. No amount of
English custom-house paper, or sealing-wax could, by any
possibility, convert him into that rotund, florid, jocund Briton
who personates the English shipmaster. His speech was even
more national—taking New England to be the Yankee *nation*
—than his person; and when he opened his mouth, a mere
novice might have sworn that he was from the "State of
Maine"—there, or thereabouts. When he told me that I
"hadn't-ought-to" burn his ship, he pronounced the shibboleth
which condemned her to the flames.

The shrift was a short one. When the papers were produced, I found among them no bill of sale or other evidence
of the transfer of the property—the register of an English
ship, as every seaman knows, not being such evidence. His
crew list, which had been very neatly prepared, was a mute
but powerful witness against him. It was written, throughout,
signatures and all, in the same hand—the signatures all being
as like as two peas. After glancing at the papers, and making
these mental observations as I went along, I asked the master
a few questions. As well as I recollect, he was from Hallowell, Maine. His ship had been two years in the East Indies,
trading from port to port; and, as before remarked, had only
been transferred within a few days. The freshly painted assumed name on her stern was scarcely dry. The master had
sat with comparative composure during this examination, and
questioning, evidently relying with great confidence upon his
English flag and papers; but when I turned to him, and told
him that I should burn his ship, he sprang from his chair, and
said with excited manner and voice—"You dare not do it,
sir; that flag—suiting the action to the word, and pointing
with his long, bony finger up the companion-way to the flag
flying from his peak—won't stand it!" "Keep cool, captain,"
I replied, "the weather is warm, and as for the flag, I shall
not ask it whether it will stand it or not—the flag that *ought*
to be at your peak, will have to stand it, though" In half

an hour, or as soon as the crew could pack their duds, and be transferred to the *Alabama*, the *Texan Star*—alias the *Marta-ban*—was in flames; the beautiful, new English ensign being marked with the day, and latitude and longitude of the capture, and stowed away carefully by the old signal-quartermaster, in the bag containing his Yankee flags.

The cargo was *bona fide* English property, and if the owner of it, instead of combining with the master of the ship to perpetrate a fraud upon my belligerent rights, had contented himself with putting it on board under the American flag, properly documented as British property, he might have saved it, and along with it, the ship; as, in that case, I should have been obliged to bond her. But when I had stripped off the disguise, and the ship stood forth as American, unfortunately for the owner of the cargo, no document could be presented to show that it was English; for the very attempt to document it would have exposed the fraud. Unfortunate Englishman! He had lost sight of the "copy" he had been used to transcribe at school—"Honesty is the best policy."

It was still early in the afternoon when we resumed our course, and gave the ship steam. After a few hours had elapsed, and Captain Pike—for this was the name of the master of the captured ship—had realized that his ship was no more, I sent for him, into my cabin, and directing my clerk to produce writing materials, we proceeded to take his formal deposition; preliminary to which, my clerk administered to him the usual oath. I felt pretty sure now of getting at the truth, for I had resorted to a little arrangement for this purpose quite common in the courts of law—I had *released* the interest of the witness. As soon, therefore, as the witness was put upon the stand, I said to him:—"Now, captain, when you and I had that little conversation in your cabin, you had hopes of saving your ship, and, moreover, what you said to me was not under oath. You were, perhaps, only practising a pardonable *ruse de guerre.* But now the case is altered. Your ship being destroyed, you have no longer any possible interest in misstating the truth. You are, besides, under oath. Be frank; was, or was not, the transfer of your ship a *bona fide* transaction?" After a moment's reflection he replied:—

"I will be frank with you, captain. It was not a *bona fide* transaction. I was alarmed when I heard of your arrival in the East Indies, and I resorted to a sham sale in the hope of saving my ship." Upon this answer being recorded. the court adjourned.

At a late hour in the night, the moon shining quite brightly, we ran in past some islands, and anchored off the little town of Malacca—formerly a Portuguese settlement, but now, like Singapore, in the possession of the English. My object was to land my prisoners, and at early dawn we dispatched them for the shore, with a note to the military commander asking the requisite permission. It was Christmas-day, and as the sun rose, we could see many signs of festive preparation on shore. The little town, with its white houses peeping out of a wilderness of green, was a pretty picture as it was lighted up by the rays of the rising sun. Back of the town, on an isolated hill, stood the lighthouse, whose friendly beacon had guided us into our anchorage over night, and near by was the barrack, from whose flag-staff floated, besides the proud old flag of our fatherland, a number of gay streamers. Our ship in the offing, and our boats in the harbor, created quite a stir in this quiet Malay-English town; and forthwith a couple of boats filled with officers and citizens—ladies included—came off to visit us. It was still very early, and the excitement of the morning's row, and the novelty of the presence of the *Alabama* seemed greatly to excite our new friends. The males grasped our hands as though they had been our brothers, and the ladies smiled their sweetest smiles —and no one knows how sweet these can be, better than the sailor who has been a long time upon salt water, looking upon nothing but whiskers and mustachios. They were very pressing that we should remain a day, and partake of their Christmas dinner with them. But we excused ourselves, telling them that war knows no holidays. They left us after a short visit, and at half-past nine A. M., our boats having returned, we were again under steam. Bartelli was seen lugging a basketful of fine Malacca oranges into the cabin, soon after the return of our boats—a gift from some of our lady friends who had visited us.

I have observed by Mr. Seward's "little bill," before referred to, that Pike, having been foiled in that game of flags which he had attempted to play with me, has put in his claim, along with other disconsolate Yankees, for the destruction of his ship. When *will* naughty England pay that little bill?

After a good day's run — during which we overhauled an English bark, from Singapore, for Madras — we anchored at night-fall near Parceelar Hill, in twenty-five fathoms of water. The only Christmas kept by the *Alabama* was the usual "splicing of the main-brace" by the crew. We were under way again, the next morning at six o'clock; the weather was clear, with a few passing clouds, and the look-out had not been long at the mast-head before he cried "sail ho!" twice, in quick suggestion. Upon being questioned, he reported two large ships at anchor, that looked "sort o' Yankee." We soon began to raise these ships from the deck, and when we got a good view of them through our powerful glasses, we were of the same·opinion with the look-out. They were evidently Yankee. As they were at anchor, and helpless — waiting for a fair wind with which to run out of the Strait — we had nothing to gain by a concealment of our character, and showed them at once the Confederate flag. That flag — beautiful though it was — must have been a terrible wet blanket upon the schemes of these two Yankee skippers. It struck them dumb, for they refused to show me any bunting in return. I captured them both, with the "flaunting lie" stowed away snugly in their cabins. They were monster ships, both of them, being eleven or twelve hundred tons burden. In their innocence — supposing the *Alabama* had gone up the China Sea — they had ventured, whilst lying at Singapore, to take charter-parties for cargoes of rice to be laden at Akyab, for Europe; and were now on their way to Akyab in ballast. They had left Singapore several days before our arrival there, and had been delayed by head-winds.

Both were Massachusetts ships — one the *Sonora* of New-buryport, and the other, the *Highlander* of Boston. The master of one of these ships, when he was brought on board, came up to me good-humoredly on the quarter-deck, and offering me his hand, which I accepted, said: "Well, Captain Semmes,

I have been expecting every day for the last three years, to fall in with you, and here I am at last!" I told him I was glad he had found me after so long a search. "Search!" said he; "it is some such search as the Devil may be supposed to make after holy water. The fact is," continued he, "I have had constant visions of the *Alabama*, by night and by day; she has been chasing me in my sleep, and riding me like a night-mare, and now that it is all over, I feel quite relieved." I permitted the masters and crews of both these ships to hoist out, and provision their own boats, and depart in them for Singapore. The ships when overhauled were lying just inside of the light-ship, at the western entrance of the Strait of Malacca, and it was only pleasant lake or river sailing to Singapore. Having fired the ships, we steamed out past the light-ship, and were once more in the Indian Ocean. We found on board one of the prizes a copy of the Singapore "Times," of the 9th of December, 1863, from which I give the following extract. At the date of the paper, we were at Pulo Condore, and the Yankee ships were still flocking into Singapore:—

" From our to-day's shipping-list it will be seen that there are no fewer than seventeen American merchantmen at present in our harbor, and that they include some of the largest ships at present riding there. Their gross tonnage may be roughly set down at 12,000 tons. Some of these have been lying here now for upward of three months, and most of them for at least half that period. And all this, at a time when there is no dulness in the freight market; but, on the contrary, an active demand for tonnage to all parts of the world. It is, indeed, to us, a home picture — the only one we trust to have for many years to come — of the wide-spread evils of war in these modern days. But it is a picture quite unique in its nature; for the nation to which these seventeen fine ships belong has a Navy perhaps second only to that of Great Britain, and the enemy with which she has to cope, is but a schism from herself, possessed of no port that is not blockaded, and owning not more than five or six vessels no the high seas; and yet there is no apathy and nothing to blame on the part of the United States Navy. The tactics with which the Federals have to combat are without precedent, and the means to enable them successfully to do so have not yet been devised."

CHAPTER LI.

ALABAMA CROSSES THE BAY OF BENGAL — THE PIL-
GRIMS ! O MECCA AND THE BLACK GIANTS — BURNING
OF THI. EMMA JANE — THE TOWN OF AUJENGA, AND
THE HINDOOS — THE GREAT DESERTS OF CENTRAL
ASIA, AND THE COTTON CROP OF HINDOSTAN — ALA-
BAMA CROSSES THE ARABIAN SEA — THE ANIMALCULÆ
OF THE SEA — THE COMORO ISLANDS — JOHANNA AND
ITS ARAB POPULATION — THE YANKEE WHALERS AT JO-
HANNA — ALABAMA PASSES THROUGH THE MOZAMBIQUE
CHANNEL, AND ARRIVES AT THE CAPE OF GOOD HOPE.

ON the afternoon after leaving the Strait of Malacca, we
overhauled another American ship under neutral colors
—the Bremen ship *Ottone*. The transfer had been made at
Bremen, in the previous May; the papers were genuine, and
the master and crew all Dutchmen, there being no Yankee on
board. The change of property, in this case, having every
appearance of being *bona fide*, I permitted the ship to pass on
her voyage, which was to Rangoon for rice. For the next few
days we coasted the island of Sumatra — taking a final leave
of the North end of that island on the last day of the year
1863. A court-martial had been in session several days, settling accounts with the runaways at Singapore, whom we had
arrested and brought back. Having sentenced the prisoners,
and gotten through with its labors, it was dissolved on this
last day of the old year, that we might turn over a new leaf.

Clearing the Sumatra coast, we stretched across to the Bay
of Bengal, toward Ceylon, overhauling a number of neutral
ships by the way. Among others, we boarded a large English
ship which had a novel lot of passengers on board. She was

from Singapore, bound for Jiddah on the Red Sea, and was filled with the faithful followers of Mohammed, on a pilgrimage to Mecca — Jiddah being the nearest seaport to that renowned shrine. My boarding-officer was greeted with great cordiality by these devotees, who exchanged salaams with him, in the most reverential manner, and entered into conversation with him. They wanted to know, they said, about those black giants we had on board the *Alabama,* and whether we fed them on live Yankees, as they had heard. The boarding-officer, who was a bit of a wag, told them that we had made the experiment, but that the Yankee skippers were so lean and tough, that the giants refused to eat them. Whereupon there was a general grunt, and as near an approach to a smile as a Mohammedan ever makes. They then said that they "had heard that we were in favor of a plurality of wives." They had heard of Brigham Young and Salt Lake. The officer said, "Yes, we had a few; three or four dozen a piece." They now insisted upon his smoking with them, and plied him with other questions, to which they received equally satisfactory answers; and when he got up to depart, they crowded around him at the gangway, and salaamed him over the side, more reverentially than ever. I have no doubt that when these passengers arrived at Mecca, and discussed learnedly the American war, half the pilgrims at that revered shrine became good Confederates.

Having doubled the island of Ceylon, and hauled up on the coast of Malabar, we captured on the 14th of January, the *Emma Jane,* of Bath, Maine, from Bombay, bound to Amherst. Having removed from her such articles of provisions as we required, and transferred her crew to the *Alabama,* we burned her. She was in ballast, seeking a cargo, and there was, therefore, no claim of neutral property. The master had his wife on board. Being not a great distance from the land, we ran in for the purpose of discharging our prisoners; and descried the Ghaut mountains the next day. Coasting along a short distance to the eastward, we made the small Hindoo-Portuguese town of Anjenga, where we came to anchor at about four P. M. The town lies on the open coast, having a roadstead, but no harbor. We ran in and anchored without a pilot. We were soon surrounded by native boats — large canoes capable of carrying considerable burdens—filled with Portuguese, and Hindoos, and a mixture of both. Though the dominion of Portugal, on the Malabar coast, has long since departed, there are many mementos of that once enterprising people still to be found. Her churches and fortifications are still standing, the blood of her people is still left—in most cases mixed—and her language, somewhat corrupted, is still spoken. There was no Englishman at Anjenga—the resident magistrate being a Portuguese. He sent his son off to visit us, and make arrangements for landing our prisoners. Later in the afternoon, I sent a lieutenant to call on him. The boat being delayed until some time in the night, and a firing of musketry being heard, I feared that my lieutenant had gotten into some difficulty with the natives, and dispatched Kell, with an armed boat to his assistance. It proved to be a false alarm. It was a feast day, the magistrate had gone to church,—which caused the delay of the officer—and the firing was a *feu de joie.*

The next morning we sent the prisoners on shore. They were to proceed by inland navigation—parallel with the coast, through a series of lagoons and canals—to Cochin, a sea-port town about sixty miles distant, where they would find Englishmen and English shipping. I was to provision them, and the Resident Magistrate would send them forward free of expense. The prisoners landed in presence of half the town, who had flocked down to the beach to see the sight. As our boats approached the shore, on which there was quite a surf breaking, a number of native boats came out to receive and land the prisoners. These boats were managed with great dexterity, and passed in and out through the roaring surf, without the least accident. This matter of business accomplished, the natives came off to visit us, in considerable numbers, both men and women. They were a fine, well-formed, rather athletic people, nearly as black as the negro, but with straight hair and prominent features. Very few of them wore any other dress than a cloth about the loins. They were sprightly and chatty, and ran about the decks as pleased as children, inspecting the guns, and other novelties. Some of the young women had very regular and pleasing features. The best description I can give of them is to request the reader to imagine some belle of his acquaintance to be divested of those garments which would be useless to her in Anjenga — latitude 8° — and instead of charming him with the lily and the rose, to be shining in lustrous jet.

Having received on board some fresh provisions for the crew, and gotten rid of our lady and gentlemen visitors, we got under way and stood out to sea, and were still in sight of the Ghaut Mountains when the sun went down. These mountains will be lost to our view to-morrow; but before they disappear, I have a word to say concerning them, and the fertile country of Hindostan, in which they are situated; for nature elaborates here one of her most beautiful and useful of meteorological problems. British India is the most formidable competitor of the Confederate States for the production of cotton, for the supply of the spindles and looms of the world. The problem to which I wish to call the reader's attention may be stated thus:—*The Great Deserts of Central Africa produce the cotton crop of Hindostan.* I have before had frequent occasion to speak of the monsoons of the East — those periodical winds that blow for one half of the year from one point of the compass, and then change, and blow the other half of the year from the opposite point. It is these monsoons that work out the problem we have in hand; and it is the Great Deserts alluded to that produce the monsoons.

On the succeeding page will be found a diagram, which will assist us in the conception of this beautiful operation of nature. It consists of an outline sketch of so much of Asia and the Indian Ocean as are material to our purpose. The Great Deserts, the Himalayas and the Ghauts, are marked on the sketch. Let the dotted line at the bottom of the sketch represent the equator, and the arrows the direction of the winds. Hindostan being in the northern tropic, the north-east monsoon or trade-wind, represented by the arrow A, would prevail there all the year round, but for the local causes of which I am about to speak. The reader will observe that this wind, coming from a high northern latitude, passes almost entirely over *land* before it reaches Hindostan. It is, therefore, a dry wind. It is rendered even more dry, by its passage over the Himalaya range of mountains which wring from it what little moisture

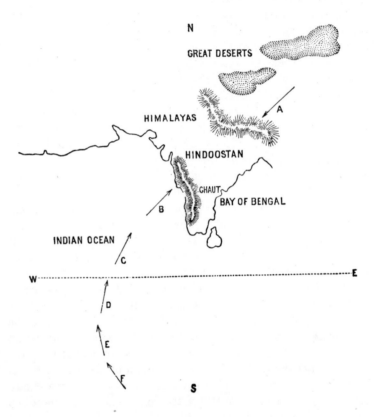

it may have evaporated from the lakes and rivers over which it has passed. When it reaches the extensive plains between the Himalayas and Ghauts, which are the great cotton region of Hindostan, it has not a drop of water with which to nourish vegetation; and if it were to prevail all the year round, those plains would speedily become parched and waste deserts.

Let us see, now, how this catastrophe is avoided. When the sun is in the southern hemisphere, that is, during the winter season, the north-east monsoon prevails in Hindostan. When he is in the northern hemisphere, the south-west monsoon, which is the rainy monsoon, or crop monsoon, prevails. This change of monsoons is produced as follows: Soon after the sun crosses the equator into the northern hemisphere, he begins to pour down his fierce rays upon Hindostan, and, passing farther and farther to the north, in the latter part of April, or the beginning of May, he is nearly perpendicularly over the Great Deserts marked in the sketch. These deserts are interminable wastes of sand, in which there is not so much as a blade of grass to be found. They absorb heat very rapidly, and in a short time become like so many fiery furnaces. The air above them rarefies and ascends, a comparative vacuum of great extent is formed, and a great change begins now to take place in the atmospheric phenomena. This vacuum being in the rear of the arrow A, or the north-east monsoon blowing over Hindostan, first slackens the force of this wind—drawing it back, as it were. It becomes weaker and weaker, as the furnaces become hotter and hotter. Calms ensue, and after a long struggle, the wind is finally turned back, and the south-west monsoon has set in.

If the reader will cast his eye on the series of arrows, B, C, D, E, and F, he will see how this gradual change is effected. I say gradual, for it is not effected *per saltum*, but occupies several weeks. The arrow F represents the south-east trade-wind, blowing toward the equator. As this wind nears the equator, it begins to feel the influence of the deserts spoken of. The calm which I have described as beginning at the arrow A, is gradually extended to the equator. As the south-east wind approaches that great circle, it finds nothing to oppose its passage. Pretty soon, it not only finds nothing to oppose its passage, but something to invite it over; for the calm begins now to give place to an indraught toward the Great Deserts. The south-east wind, thus encouraged, changes its course, first to the north, and then to the north-east, and blows stronger and stronger as the season advances, and the heat accumulates over the deserts ; until at last the south-east trade-wind of the southern hemisphere has become the south-west monsoon of the northern hemisphere !   This monsoon prevails from about the 1st of May to the 1st of November, when the sun has again passed into the southern hemisphere, and withdrawn his heat from the great deserts.   The normal condition of things being thus restored, the vanquished north-east trade-wind regains its courage, and, chasing back the south-west monsoon, resumes its sway.

If the reader will again cast his eye upon the sketch, he will see that the south-west winds which are now blowing over Hindostan, instead of being dry winds, must be heavily laden with moisture.   They have had a clean sweep from the tropic of Capricorn, with no land intervening between them and the coast of Hindostan.   They have followed the sun in his course, and under the influence of his perpendicular rays have lapped up the waters like a thirsty wolf.   The evaporation in these seas is enormous.   It has been stated, on the authority of the Secretary of the Geographical Society of Bombay, that it has been found in the Bay of Bengal to exceed an inch daily. From having too little water during the winter months in Hindostan, we are now, in the summer months, in danger of having too much.   The young cotton crop will be drowned out.   What is to prevent it ?   Here we have another beautiful provision at hand.   The reader has observed the Ghaut Mountains stretching along parallel with the west coast of Hindostan.   These mountains protect the plains from inundation. They have, therefore, equally important functions to perform with the deserts.   The south-west monsoon blows square across these mountains.   As the heavily laden wind begins to ascend the first slopes, it commences to deposit its moisture. Incessant rains set in, and immense quantities of water fall before the winds have passed the mountains.   The precipitation has been known to be as great as twelve or thirteen inches in a single day !   The winds, thus deprived of their excess of water are now in a proper condition to fertilize, without drowning the immense plains that lie between the Ghauts and the Himalayas — which, as before remarked, is the cotton region of India. It is thus that the *Great Deserts of Central Asia produce the cotton crop of Hindostan.* To the ignorant Tartar who ventures across the margins of these deserts, all seems dreary, desolate, and death-like, and he is at a loss to conceive for what purpose they were created. Clothe these deserts with verdure, and intersperse them with rivers and mountains, and forthwith the fertile plains of Hindostan would become a great desert, and its two hundred millions of inhabitants perish.

We captured on board the last prize a batch of Bombay newspapers — large " dailies," edited with ability, and filled with news from all parts of the world. It is the press, more than anything else, that indicates the growth and prosperity of a country. One only needed to look at the long columns of these immense dailies, filled with advertisements, to realize the fact that Bombay was a bee-hive, containing its three hundred thousand inhabitants. We were, indeed, in the midst of a great empire, of which, in the western world, we read, it is true, but of which we have no just conception until we visit it. The British empire in India, stretching from the Persian Gulf to the Strait of Malacca, is a creation which does honor to our race and language. I had coasted nearly its whole extent, and everywhere I found evidences of contentment, thrift, and prosperity. A constant stream of British shipping was passing to and fro, developing its immense commerce, and pouring its untold millions into the British exchequer. Powerful and swift steamships bring the home mails to three or four prominent points along the coast, as Aden, Ceylon, Singapore, Hong Kong, and from these points other steamers spread it broadcast over the empire. Railroads are pushed in every direction, there being as many as three thousand miles in operation, and the navigation of the coast districts of Hindostan has been carried, by means of a series of lagoons and canals, from Cape Comorin, hundreds of miles to the northward. These railroads and canals have opened up new fields of industry, and have been of especial service in developing that pet idea of England, the production of cotton.

Up to the breaking out of our war, the cultivation of this valuable staple in India was a mere experiment. It is now an assured success. Those great fields lying between the Ghauts and the Himalayas of which we have been speaking, are being brought into connection with the sea-board, by lines of easy and cheap transportation. They have been found equal to our Southern plantations in the production of the article, and labor is a hundred per cent. cheaper, at least, than with us. Here are all the elements of cheap production. Our Yankee brethren have talked a good deal of what they "conquered" in the war, and have been quarrelling ever since over the fruits of their victory. Here is one of their conquests which no one can doubt — the transfer of the cotton supply of the world, from these Southern States to British India. The time is not far distant when Yankee spindles and looms will be spinning and weaving India cotton for the supply of their own people.

The moral conquest of India, by the British people, is even more remarkable and more admirable than its physical conquest. Since their last Indian war, the whole country, from one end of it to the other, has settled down in the most profound peace. Nor is this the peace of despotism, for in comparison with the extent of territory, and the two hundred millions of people to be governed, the number of troops is ridiculously small. The conquest is one of arts and civilization, and not of arms. The railroad, the canal, the ship, the printing press, and above all, a paternal and beneficent government, have worked out the wonderful problem of the submission of teeming millions to the few. It is the conquest of race and of intellect. The docile Hindoo, not devoid of letters himself, has realized the fact that a superior people has come to settle in his country, to still domestic broils, strip former despots of their ill-gotten and much-abused power, and to rule him with humanity and justice. The torch of civilization has shone in dark places, dispelled many prejudices, and brought to light and broken up many hideous practices. Schools and colleges have sprung up everywhere, and the natural taste of the native population for letters has been cultivated. In the very newspapers which we are reviewing are to be found long dissertations and criticisms, by Hindoo scholars, on various matters of morals, science, and literature.

A government whose foundations are thus laid will be durable. In Australia, New Zealand, and other colonies, where the white population, in the course of a few years, will greatly preponderate over the native, mere adolescence will bring about independence. But India will never become adolescent in this sense. She will remain indefinitely a prosperous ward in chancery — the guardian and the ward living amicably together, and each sharing the prosperity of the other.

On the day after leaving the Malabar coast, we spoke a Portuguese bark, from Rio Janeiro bound to Goa, a short distance to the northward of us. This was the only Portuguese we met in these seas, of which they were, at one period of their history, entire masters. Vasco de Gama had made the seas classic by his adventures, and his countrymen, following in his track, had studded the coast with towns, of which Goa was one of the most ancient and important. As between the Hindoo and the Portuguese, the latter would probably long have maintained his ascendency, but there came along that superior race — that white race which has never submitted to any admixture of its blood — of which we have just been speaking, and nature, with her unvarying laws, had done the rest. The Portuguese gave place to the Englishman, as naturally as the African, and afterward the Hindoo, had given place to the Portuguese.

Passing through the chain of islands which extends parallel with the Malabar coast for some distance, we stretched across the Arabian Sea in the direction of the east coast of Africa. We were now in the height of the season of the north-east monsoon, which was a fair wind for us, and the weather was as delightful as I have ever experienced it in any part of the globe — not even excepting our own Gulf of Mexico, and coasts of Alabama, and Florida, in the summer season. For twelve successive days, we did not have occasion to lower a studding sail, day or night! We had a constant series of clear skies, and gentle breezes. The nights were serene, and transparent, and the sunsets were magnificent beyond description. The trade wind is, *par excellence*, the wind of beautiful sunsets.

Bright, gauzy clouds, float along lazily before it, and sometimes the most charming cumuli are piled up on the western
horizon while the sun is going down.   Stately cathedrals, with
their domes and spires complete, may be traced by the eye of
fancy, and the most gorgeous of golden, violet, orange, purple,
green, and other hues, light up now a colonnade, now a dome,
and now a spire of the aërial edifice.   And then came on the
twilight, with its gray and purple blended, and with the twilight, the sounds of merriment on board the *Alabama*—for we
had found a successor for Michael Mahoney, the Irish fiddler, and
the usual evening dances were being held.   We had been now
some time at sea, since leaving Singapore; the "jail had been
delivered," the proper punishments administered, and Jack,
having forgotten both his offences, and their punishment, had
again become a "good boy," and was as full of fun as ever.

We had some fine fishing while passing through the Arabian
Sea.   The dolphin came around us in schools, and a number
of them were struck with the "grains," and caught with lines
—the bait being a piece of red flannel rag.   And some of the
seamen resorted to an ingenious device for entrapping the
flying fish by night.   A net being spread, with out-riggers, under the bow of the ship, and a light being held just above it,
the fish, as they would rise in coveys—being flushed from time
to time by the noise of the ship through the water—would
rush at the light, and striking against the bow of the ship,
tumble into the net beneath.   Bartelli, on several mornings,
spread my breakfast-table with them.

On the 29th of January, we observed in latitude 2° 43' north,
and longitude 51° east; and on the following evening passed
through a remarkable patch of the sea.   At about eight P. M.,
there being no moon, but the sky being clear, and the stars
shining brightly, we suddenly passed from the deep blue water
in which we had been sailing, into a patch of water so white
that it startled me; so much did it appear like a shoal.   To
look over the ship's side, one would have sworn that she was
in no more than five or six fathoms of water.   The officer of
the deck became evidently alarmed, and reported the fact to
me, though I myself had observed it.   There was no shoal
laid down, within several hundred miles of our position, on

the chart, and yet here was so manifestly one, that I shortened sail—we were running seven or eight knots per hour at the time, with a fresh breeze—hove the ship to, and got a cast of the deep-sea lead. The line ran out, and out, until a hundred fathoms had been taken by the lead, and still we found no bottom. We now checked the line, and hauling in the lead, made sail again. My fears thus quieted, I observed the phenomenon more at leisure. The patch was extensive. We were several hours in running through it. Around the horizon there was a subdued glare, or flush, as though there were a distant illumination going on, whilst overhead there was a lurid, dark sky, in which the stars paled. The whole face of nature seemed changed, and with but little stretch of the imagination, the *Alabama* might have been conceived to be a phantom ship, lighted up by the sickly and unearthly glare of a phantom sea, and gliding on under the pale stars one knew not whither.

Upon drawing a bucket of this water, it appeared to be full of minute luminous particles; the particles being instinct with life, and darting, and playing about in every direction; but upon a deck-lantern being brought, and held over the bucket, the little animals would all disappear, and nothing but a bucket full of *grayish* water would be left. Here was an area of twenty miles square, in which Nature, who delights in life, was holding one of her starlight revels, with her myriads upon myriads of living creatures, each rejoicing in the life given it by its Creator, and dying almost as soon as born. The sun would rise on the morrow, over a sea as blue as usual, with only some motes in the pelluced waters glinting back his rays; and this twenty miles square of life would be no longer distinguishable from the surrounding waters.

We crossed the equator on the 30th of January. The winds had now become light, and frequent calms ensued, though the bright weather continued. On the 9th of February we made the Comoro islands, that lie not a great way from the coast of Africa, and, getting up steam, ran in, and anchored at Johanna. This island is the most frequented of the group; ships bound to and from the East Indies, by the way of the Mozambique channel, frequently stopping here for refreshments. All these islands are volcanic in origin. They are of small extent, rise abruptly out of the sea, with deep water around them, and are mountainous. They are not claimed by any European nation; nor do any of the chiefs on the neighboring coast of Africa attempt to exercise jurisdiction over them. They are inhabited by a mixed race of Arabs, Africans, and East Indians, and each has its separate government, which is always a government of force, and is frequently overthrown by revolutions. Johanna, at the time we visited it, was under the rule of an Arab, who styled himself, the "Sultan Abdallah." From the circumstance that English ships frequently stop here, most of the inhabitants who live on the sea-coast speak a little English, and we were surprised, when we anchored, to find ourselves quite well known. The name of our ship was familiar to the dusky inhabitants, and they were evidently much delighted at our arrival. The "Sultan" did not come on board — he was busy, he said, putting up a sugar-mill — but he sent his Minister of Foreign Affairs, and Commander-in-Chief of his Army to see me; and with these, Galt, my paymaster, had no difficulty in contracting for the regular supply of bullocks and vegetables, to be sent off to us during our stay.

I had come in solely for the purpose of refreshing my crew, and for this purpose we remained a week. During this time we became quite friendly with the Johannese — receiving frequent visits from them, and visiting them at their houses in return. We were quite surprised at the intelligence and civilization which characterized them. They nearly all read and write, and the better classes set up some pretensions to literature. They are Mohammedans in faith, and I found some of their priests, who were fond of visiting me, sprightly, well informed, and liberal men, acknowledging both Moses and Christ to have been prophets, and entertaining a respect for the Christian religion; doubtless the result of their intercourse with the English.

I visited the houses of some of my friends with the hope of getting a glimpse at their domestic life, but was disappointed. They received me with all cordiality and respect, but the females of their families were carefully kept out of sight. A female slave would fan me, and hand me my coffee and sher-

bet, but that was all. Their slavery appeared to be of a miti-
gated form, the slaves being on easy and even familiar terms
with their masters. The houries who fanned me could have
been bought for twenty dollars each. The price of a slave
fresh from the coast, is not more than half that sum.

I gave my sailors a run on shore, but this sort of " liberty "
was awful hard work for Jack. There was no such thing
as a glass of grog to be found in the whole town, and as for a
fiddle, and Sal for a partner — all of which would have been a
matter of course in *civilized* countries — there were no such
luxuries to be thought of. They found it a difficult matter to
get through with the day, and were all down at the beach long
before sunset — the hour appointed for their coming off —
waiting for the approach of the welcome boat. I told Kell to
let them go on shore as often as they pleased, but no one made
a second application.

On the 15th of February, having received on board a supply of half a dozen live bullocks, and some fruits and vegetables, we got under way, and again turned our head to the south-
west. The winds were light, but we were much assisted by
the currents; for we were now approaching the Mozambique
Channel, and the south-west current, of which I spoke when
we left the Cape of Good Hope for our run before the "brave
west winds," to the eastward, was hurrying us forward, sometimes at the rate of forty or fifty miles a day. As we progressed, the wind freshened, and by the time we had entered
the narrowest part of the channel between Madagascar and the
African coast, which lies in about 15° south latitude, we lost
the fine weather and clear skies, which we had brought all the
way across the Arabian Sea. We now took several gales of
wind. Rain-squalls were of frequent occurrence. As we approached the south-west end of Madagascar, which lies just
without the Tropic of Capricorn, we encountered one of the
most sublime storms of thunder and lightning I ever witnessed.
It occurred at night. Black rain-clouds mustered from every
quarter of the compass, and the heavens were soon so densely
and darkly overcast, that it was impossible to see across the
ship's deck. Sometimes the most terrific squalls of wind ac
company these storms, and we furled most of the sails, and

awaited in silence the *denouement*. The thunder rolled and
crashed, as if the skies were falling in pieces; and the lightning — sheet lightning, streaked lightning, forked lightning —
kept the firmament almost constantly ablaze. And the rain!
I thought I had seen it rain before, but for an hour, Madagascar beat the Ghaut Mountains. It came down almost literally
by the bucketfull. Almost a continual stream of lightning
ran down our conductors, and hissed as it leaped into the sea.
There was not much wind, but all the other meteorological elements were there in perfection. Madagascar is, perhaps, above
all other countries, the bantling and the plaything of the
storm, and thunder and lightning. Its plains, heated to nearly
furnace-heat, by a tropical sun, its ranges of lofty mountains,
the currents that sweep along its coasts, and its proximity to
equatorial Africa, all point it out as being in a region fertile of
meteorological phenomena. Cyclones of small diameter are
of frequent occurrence in the Mozambique Channel. They
travel usually from south-east to north-west, or straight across
the channel. We took one of these short gales, which lasted
us the greater part of a day.

Leaving the channel, and pursuing our way toward the Cape
of Good Hope, we sounded on the Agulhas Bank on the 7th
of March — our latitude being 35° 10′, and longitude 24° 08′.
This bank is sometimes the scene of terrible conflicts of the
elements in the winter season. Stout ships are literally
swamped here, by the huge, wall-like seas; and the frames of
others so much shaken and loosened in every knee and joint,
as to render them unseaworthy. The cause of these terrible,
short, racking seas, is the meeting of the winds and currents.
Whilst the awful, wintry gale is howling from the west and
north-west, the Mozambique, or Agulhas current, as it is now
called, is setting in its teeth, sometimes at the rate of two or
three knots per hour. A struggle ensues between the billows
lashed into fury by the winds, and the angry current which is
opposing them. The ground-swell contributes to the turmoil
of the elements, and the stoutest mariner sometimes stands
appalled at the spectacle of seas with nearly perpendicular
walls, battering his ship like so many battering-rams, and
threatening her with instant destruction. Hence the name of
the "stormy cape," applied to the Cape of Good Hope.

Arriving on our old cruising ground off the pitch of the Cape, we held ourselves here a few days, overhauling the various ships that passed. But American commerce, which, as the reader has seen, had fled this beaten track before we left for the East Indies, had not returned to it. The few ships of the enemy that passed, still gave the Cape a wide berth, and winged their flight homeward over the by-ways, instead of the highways of the ocean. We found the coast clear again of the enemy's cruisers. That huge old coal-box, the *Vanderbilt*, having thought it useless to pursue us farther, had turned back, and was now probably doing a more profitable business, by picking up bockade-runners on the American coast. This operation *paid*—the captain might grow rich upon it. Chasing the *Alabama* did not. Finding that it was useless for us to cruise longer off the Cape, we ran into Cape Town, and came to anchor at half-past four, on the afternoon of the 20th of March. We had gone to sea from Simon's Town, on our way to the East Indies, on the 24th of the preceding September,— our cruise had thus lasted within a day or two of six months.

CHAPTER LII.

ALABAMA AGAIN IN CAPE TOWN — THE SEIZURE OF THE
TUSCALOOSA, AND THE DISCUSSION WHICH GREW OUT OF
IT — CORRESPONDENCE BETWEEN THE AUTHOR AND
ADMIRAL WALKER — FINAL ACTION OF THE HOME GOV-
ERNMENT, AND RELEASE OF THE TUSCALOOSA.

AFTER our long absence in the East Indies, we felt like
returning home when we ran into Table Bay. Familiar
faces greeted us, and the same welcome was extended to us as
upon our first visit. An unpleasant surprise awaited me, however, in the course the British Government had recently pursued in regard to my tender, the *Tuscaloosa*. The reader will
recollect, that I had dispatched this vessel from Angra Pequeña, back to the coast of Brazil, to make a cruise on that
coast. Having made her cruise, she returned to Simon's Town,
in the latter part of December, in want of repairs and supplies.
Much to the astonishment of her commander, she was seized,
a few days afterward, by Admiral Sir Baldwin Walker, under
orders from the Home Government. Since I had left the Cape,
a correspondence had ensued between the Governor, Sir Philip
Wodehouse, and the Secretary for the Colonies, the Duke of
Newcastle; the latter disapproving of the conduct of the former, in the matter of the reception of the *Tuscaloosa*. It was
insisted by the Duke, that inasmuch as the *Tuscaloosa* was an
uncondemned prize, she was not entitled to be regarded as a
ship of war; but that, on the contrary, having been brought
into British waters, in violation of the Queen's orders of neutrality, she should have been detained, and handed over to her
original owners. Under these instructions, the *Tuscaloosa* was
seized upon her return to the Cape. This correspondence between the Governor and the Duke had not yet been made pub-

lic, and it was supposed that the seizure had been made by order of Lord John Russell. Under this impression I sat down, and addressed the following letter to Sir Balwin Walker, the Admiral, on the subject: —

CONFEDERATE STATES STEAMER ALABAMA, ⎱
TABLE BAY, March 22, 1864.   ⎰

SIR: — I was surprised to learn, upon my arrival at this port, of the detention, by your order, of the Confederate States bark *Tuscaloosa*, a tender to this ship. I take it for granted that you detained her by order of the Home Government, as no other supposition is consistent with my knowledge of the candor of your character — the *Tuscaloosa* having been formerly received by you as a regularly commissioned tender, and no new facts appearing in the case to change your decision. Under these circumstances, I shall not demand of you the restoration of that vessel, with which demand you would not have the power to comply, but will content myself with putting this, my protest, on record, for the future consideration of our respective Governments. Earl Russell, in reaching the decision which he has communicated to you, must surely have misapprehended the facts; for if he had correctly understood them, he could not have been capable of so grossly misapplying the law. The facts are briefly these: *First,* The *Tuscaloosa* was formerly the enemy's ship *Conrad,* lawfully captured by me on the high seas, in my recognized character of a belligerent. *2dly,* She was duly commissioned by me, as a tender to the Confederate States steamer *Alabama,* then, as now, under my command. *3dly,* In this character she entered British waters, was received with the courtesy and hospitality due to a ship of war of a friendly power, and was permitted to repair and refit, and depart on a cruise.

These were the facts up to the time of Earl Russell's issuing to you the order in the premises. Let us consider them for a moment, and see if they afford his lordship any ground for the extraordinary conclusion at which he has arrived. My right to capture, and the legality of the capture, will not be denied. Nor will you deny, in your experience as a naval officer, my right to commission this, or any other ship lawfully in my possession, as a tender to my principal ship. British Admirals do this every day, on distant stations; and the tender, from the time of her being put in commission, wears a pennant, and is entitled to all the immunities and privileges of a ship of war, the right of capturing enemy's ships included. Numerous decisions are to be found in your own prize law to this effect. In other words, this is one of the recognized modes of commissioning a ship of war, which has grown out of the convenience of the thing, and become a sort of naval common law of the sea, as indisputable as the written law itself. The only difference between the commission of such a ship, and that of a ship commissioned by the sovereign authority at home is, that the word "tender" appears in the former commission, and not in the latter.

The *Tuscaloosa* having, then, been commissioned by me, in accordance with the recognized practice of all civilized nations that have a marine, can any other government than my own look into her antecedents? Clearly not. The only thing which can be looked at, upon her entering a foreign port, is her commission. If this be issued by competent authority, you cannot proceed a step further. The ship then becomes a part of the territory of the country to which she belongs, and you can exercise no more jurisdiction over her, than over that territory. The self-respect, and the independence of nations require this; for it would be a monstrous doctrine, to admit, that one nation may inquire into the title by which another nation holds her ships of war. And there can be no difference, in this respect, between tenders, and ships originally commissioned. The flag and the pennant fly over them both, and they are both withdrawn from the local jurisdiction by competent commissions. On principle you might as well have undertaken to inquire into the antecedents of the *Alabama* as of the *Tuscaloosa*. Indeed, you had a better reason for inquiring into the antecedents of the former, than of the latter; it having been alleged that the former escaped from England in violation of your Foreign Enlistment Act. Mr. Adams, the United States Minister at London, did, in fact, set up this pretension, and demand that the *Alabama* should be seized in the first British port into which she should enter; but Earl Russell, in pointed contradiction of his recent conduct in the case of the *Tuscaloosa*, gave him the proper legal reply, viz.: that the *Alabama* being now a ship of war, he was estopped from looking into her antecedents.

A simple illustration will suffice to show you how untenable your position is in this matter. If the *Tuscaloosa's* commission be admitted to have been issued by competent authority, and in due form — and I do not understand this to be denied — she is as much a ship of war as the *Narcissus*, your flag-ship. Suppose you should visit a French port, under circumstances similar to those under which the *Tuscaloosa* visited Simon's Town, and the French Government should threaten you with seizure, unless you satisfied it as to the antecedents of your ship, what would you think of the pretension? Suppose your late war with Russia was still progressing — France being neutral — and your ship had been captured from the Russians, and commissioned by your Government, without having first been condemned by a prize court, would this make any difference? You see that it would not. The pretension would be an insult to your Government. And in what does the supposed proceeding differ from the one in hand? In both it is a pretension on the part of a foreign power, to look into the antecedents of a ship of war — neither more nor less in the one case than in the other.

I will even put the case stronger. If I had seized a ship belonging to a power with which my Government was at peace, and commissioned her, you could not undertake to inquire into the fact. You would have no right to know, but that I had the orders of my Government for the seizure. In short, you would have no right to inquire into the matter at all. My ship being regularly commissioned, I am responsible to my Government for my acts, and that Government, in the case supposed, would be responsible to the friendly power whose ship had been seized, and not to you. Nay, the case may be put stronger still. The Federal States have captured a number of British vessels, in the act of attempting to run the blockade of the ports of the Confederate States. Suppose the Federal States had commissioned one of these ships, without her having been first condemned by a prize-court, and she had afterward come into British waters, could you have seized her, even though you might know her capture to have been wrongful? Certainly not. It would be a matter which you could inquire into in another form, but not in this. The ship would have become a ship of war, exempt from your jurisdiction, and you could not touch her. If this reasoning be correct—and with all due submission to his lordship, I think it is sustained by the plainest principles of the International Code—it follows that the condemnation of a prize in a prize-court, is not the only mode of changing the character of a captured ship. When the sovereign of the captor puts his commission on board such a ship, this is a condemnation in its most solemn form; and is notice to all the world.

Further, as to this question of adjudication. Your letter to Lieutenant Low, the late commander of the *Tuscaloosa*, assumes that as that ship was not condemned, she was the property of the enemy from whom she had been taken. On what ground can you undertake to make this decision? Condemnation is intended for the benefit of neutrals, and to quiet the titles of purchasers, but is never necessary as against the enemy. He has, and can have no rights in a prize-court at all. He cannot appear there, either in person or by attorney. He is divested of his property by *force*, and not by any legal process. The *possession* of his property by his enemy, is all that is required as against him. What right, then, has the British Government to step in between me and my right of possession—waiving, for the present, the question of the commission, and supposing the *Tuscaloosa* to be nothing more than a prize-ship? Does the fact of my prize being in British waters, in violation of the Queen's proclamation, give it this right? Clearly not; for we are speaking now of rights under the laws of nations, and a mere municipal order cannot abrogate these. The prize may be ordered out of the port, but my possession is as firm in port, as out.

There is but a single class of cases that I am aware of, in which a neutral power can undertake to adjudicate a prize-case, and that is, where it is alleged that the capture has been made in neutral waters, in violation of the neutral jurisdiction. In that case a neutral Court of Admiralty may, in case the prize be afterward brought *infra presidia* of the neutral country, inquire into the facts, and may even restore the prize to the enemy, if it should appear that the neutral jurisdiction has been violated. But this restoration of the property to the enemy depends upon an entirely different principle. The right of capture does not exist within the marine league. There was, therefore, no capture ; and there having been no capture, as a matter of course, the property belongs to the enemy, and must be restored to him. To show the irrefragable nature of my possession, permit me to quote to your Excellency, one of your own authorities. On page forty-two of the first volume of "Phillimore on International Law," you will find the following passage : — "In 1654 a treaty was entered into between England and Portugal, by which, among other things, both countries mutually bound themselves not to suffer the ships and goods of the other, taken by enemies and carried into the ports of the other, to be conveyed away from the original owners or proprietors." Here two powers bound themselves, by treaty, to do what the British Government is now attempting to do ; that is, to interpose between the captor and his prize, undo his possession, and hand the prize back to its original owners. Great Britain said to Portugal, "I will not permit your enemies to bring any ships they may capture from you, into my ports, and if they do, I will restore them to you." In 1798, in a case before Lord Stowell, that great admiralty judge had occasion to comment on this treaty, and used the following language in relation to it : — "Now I have no scruple in saying, that this is an article incapable of being carried into literal execution, according to the modern understanding of the laws of nations ; for no neutral country can intervene to wrest from a belligerent prizes *lawfully taken.* This is, perhaps, the strongest instance that could be cited of what civilians call the *consuetudo obrogatoria.*" The *cus om*, in the law of nations, *abrogated* even a treaty, in that case. The prize being once *lawfully made*, an English Court of Admiralty could not intervene to wrest it from the captor, even though commanded so to do by a treaty. Will Lord Russell undertake, in face of this decision, and of his own mere motion, without even the formality of process from an Admiralty Court, to wrest my prize from me, and hand it over to the enemy ? My Government cannot fail, I think, to view this matter in the light in which I have placed it ; and it is deeply to be regretted, that a weaker people, struggling against a stronger for very existence, should have so much cause to complain of the unfriendly disposition of a Government, from which, if it represents truly the generous instincts of Englishmen, we had the right to expect, at least, a manly disposition to do us justice.

Governor Wodehouse was, from the first, very clearly of the opinion that the *Tuscaloosa* was entitled to be considered and treated as a ship of war, and in his correspondence with the Duke of Newcastle, before referred to, he maintained this opinion with great force and clearness. He was, besides, fortified by the opinion of the Attorney-General of the Colony.

The seizure of the *Tuscaloosa* made some stir among the politicians in England. The subject was brought to the notice of the House of Commons, and information asked for. The Cabinet took it up, and were obliged to reverse the decision of the Duke of Newcastle. On the 4th of March, 1864, the Duke wrote to Governor Wodehouse as follows: "I have received your despatches of the 11th and 19th of January, reporting the circumstances connected with the seizure of the Confederate prize-vessel *Tuscaloosa*, under the joint authority of the naval commander-in-chief and yourself. I have to instruct you to restore the *Tuscaloosa* to the lieutenant of the Confederate States, who lately commanded her, or if he should have left the Cape, then to retain her until she can be handed over to some person who may have authority from Captain Semmes, of the *Alabama*, or from the Government of the Confederate States, to receive her."

The London "Times," of the 8th of March, 1864, in reporting the proceedings of the House of Commons for the preceding day, contained the following paragraph:—

"*The Tuscaloosa.*—Mr. Peacocke asked on what grounds the *Tuscaloosa* had been seized at the Cape of Good Hope. Lord Palmerston said, that it was in conformity with the instructions received, that the authorities at the Cape of Good Hope had seized this vessel, but on representations that had been made to the Government, and on full consideration of the case, it had been determined that there had been no proper ground for the seizure of the vessel, and its release had been ordered."

The order to restore the *Tuscaloosa* did not reach the Cape until after both Lieutenant Low and myself had left, and the war drew so speedily to a close, that possession of her was never resumed. At the close of the war, she fell, along with other Confederate property, into the hands of the Federals. Besides embalming the beautiful name "*Tuscaloosa*" in history, this prize-ship settled the law point I had been so long contesting with Mr. Seward and Mr. Adams, to wit: that "one nation cannot inquire into the antecedents of the ships of war of another nation;" and consequently that when the *Alabama* escaped from British waters and was commissioned, neither the United States nor Great Britain could object to her *status* as a ship of war.

CHAPTER LIII.

THE ALABAMA AT THE CAPE OF GOOD HOPE — LEAVES ON HER RETURN TO EUROPE — CAPTURE OF THE ROCKINGHAM AND OF THE TYCOON — CROSSES THE EQUATOR INTO THE NORTHERN HEMISPHERE, AND ARRIVES AND ANCHORS AT CHERBOURG ON THE 11TH OF JUNE, 1864 — THE COMBAT BETWEEN THE ALABAMA AND THE KEARSARGE.

WE entered Table Bay on the 20th of March, and on the next day we had the usual equinoctial gale. The wind was from the south-east, and blew very heavily for twenty-four hours. We let go a second anchor, and veered to ninety fathoms on the riding-chain. The usual phenomena accompanied this south-east gale, viz., a clear sky and a high barometer. The D—l kept his table-cloth spread on the top of the mountain during the whole of the gale, and it was wonderful to watch the unvarying size and shape of this fleecy cloud, every particle of which was being changed from moment to moment. Some boats visited us, notwithstanding the gale, and brought us off some of the delightful grapes and figs of the Cape. We were in the midst of the fruit season. Our old friend, Mr. William Anderson, of the firm of Anderson, Saxon & Co., who had acted as our agent, on the occasion of our former visit, so much to our satisfaction, also came off to arrange for further supplies. There was no occasion any longer for him to draw upon our public chest, the proceeds of the merchandise shipped by him to Europe, on our account, being sufficient to pay all bills.

The gale having moderated the next day, lighters came alongside, and we began coaling, and receiving such supplies of provisions as we needed. Visitors again thronged on board, and the energies and address of Bartelli were freshly taxed. For a phlegmatic, impassible people, the English are, perhaps, the greatest sight-seekers in the world; and the Cape of Good Hope, being, as before remarked, a relay station on the principal highway of travel, is always filled with new-comers. Military and naval officers, governors, judges, super-intendents of boards of trade, attorney-generals, all on their way to their missions in the Far East, came to see the *Alabama*. Though we were sometimes incommoded by the crowd, in the midst of our coaling and provisioning ship, scraping masts and tarring down rigging, we received everybody politely, and answered patiently their curious questions. When we were here last, we had had occasion to notice an American bark called the *Urania*, a trader between Boston and the Cape, which took every opportunity to display a very large and very bright "old flag," during our stay. The *Urania* had made a voyage to Boston and back, during our absence, and now came in, tricked out so finely in her "bran-new" English flag that we hardly knew her!

In three days we were ready for sea. On the morning of the 25th, we got up steam, and moved out of Table Bay for the last time, amidst lusty cheers, and the waving of handkerchiefs from the fleet of boats by which we were surrounded. As we were going out, it so happened that a Yankee steamer was coming in. The *Quang Tung*, a fast steamer, recently built for the China trade, and now on her way to the Flowery Land, not dreaming that the *Alabama* was at the Cape, had made Table Mountain that morning, and now came steaming into the harbor. Both ships being within the marine league, we could not touch her, which was a sore trial, for the *Quang Tung* was a beauty, and passed so close under our guns, that the Confederate and United States flags nearly touched each other; the crews of the two ships looking on in silence. Half an hour more, and the capture of the *Sea-Bride* would have been repeated, to the gratification of our many friends at the Cape. Reaching the offing, we permitted our fires to go down, and put the ship, as usual, under sail. My intention now was, to make the best of my way to England or France, for the purpose of docking, and thoroughly overhauling and repairing my ship, in accordance with my previously expressed design.

I had been so much occupied with business and visitors, at the Cape, that I had not even had time to read the newspapers. But my friends had brought me off a bountiful supply for sea, and I now had a little leisure to look at them. The news was not encouraging. Our people were being harder and harder pressed by the enemy, and post after post within our territory was being occupied by him. The signs of weakness, on our part, which I mentioned as becoming, for the first time, painfully apparent, after the battle of Gettysburg, and the surrender of Vicksburg, were multiplying. The blockade of the coast, by reason of the constantly increasing fleets of the enemy, was becoming more and more stringent. Our finances were rapidly deteriorating, and a general demoralization, in consequence, seemed to be spreading among our people. From the whole review of the "situation," I was very apprehensive that the cruises of the *Alabama* were drawing to a close. As for ourselves, we were doing the best we could, with our limited means, to harass and cripple the enemy's commerce, that important sinew of war; but the enemy seemed resolved to let his commerce go, rather than forego his purpose of subjugating us; rendering it up a willing sacrifice on the profane altar of his fanaticism, and the devilish passions which had been engendered by the war. Probably, if the alternative had been presented to him, in the beginning of the war, " Will you lose your commerce, or permit the Southern States to go free ? " he would have chosen the latter. But he seemed, in the earlier stages of the war, to have had no thought of losing his commerce; and when it became apparent that this misfortune would befall him, he was, as before remarked, too deeply engaged in the contest to heed it.

Among the speeches that met my eye, in the English papers, was another from my friend, Mr. Milner Gibson, President of the Board of Trade — him of the "ham and eggs," whom I quoted some chapters back. Mr. Gibson had risen above ham and eggs, this time, and was talking about English and American shipping. As President of the Board of Trade, he was good authority, and I was glad to learn from him, the extent to which, in conjunction with other Confederate cruisers, I had damaged the enemy's commerce. His speech was delivered at

Ashton-under-Lyne, on the 20th of January, 1864, and among other things he said:—

"The number of British ships entering in, and clearing out with cargoes in the United Kingdom, has increased in the present year to an amount of something like fourteen million of tons and upward, against seven million tons of foreign shipping; thus showing, that with a great increase altogether, British shipping has kept gradually in advance of foreign shipping in the trade with the United Kingdom. But it would not be fair to take credit for this improvement in shipping, as due to any policy in this country. I am afraid that some of it is due to the transference of the carrying-trade from American ships to British ships. And why this transference from American ships to British ships? No doubt, partially in consequence of the war that prevails in America, there may not be the same power in manning and fitting out merchant vessels. But I am afraid there is something more than that. There is the fear among the American merchant shipping of attacks by certain armed vessels that are careering over the ocean, and that are burning and destroying all United States merchant ships that they find upon the high seas. The fear, therefore, of destruction by these cruisers, has caused a large transfer of American carrying to British ships. Now the decrease in the employment of American shipping is very great in the trade between England and the United States. It is something like 46 or 47 per cent. I mention these facts to show you that it is right that the attention of this great commercial nation should be seriously turned to those laws which govern the action of belligerents upon the high seas—(hear! hear!)—for if some two or three armed steamers, which a country with no pretensions to a navy, can easily send upon the ocean, armed with one or two guns, can almost clear the seas of the merchant shipping of a particular nation, what might happen to this country, with her extensive commerce over the seas, if she went to war with some nation that availed herself of the use of similar descriptions of vessels. (Hear! hear!)"

Though the subject was done up in a new form, it was still "ham and eggs"—British interests—as the reader sees. Mr. Milner Gibson was not over-stating the damage we had done the enemy. He was unfriendly to us, and therefore inclined to under-state it. According to his statistics, we had destroyed, or driven for protection under the English flag, in round numbers, one half of the enemy's ships engaged in the English trade. We did even greater damage to the enemy's trade with other powers. We broke up almost entirely his trade with Brazil, and the other South American States, greatly crippled his Pacific trade, and as for his East India trade, it is only necessary to refer the reader to the spectacle presented at Singapore, to show him what had become of that.

I threw my ship, now, into the "fair way," leading from the Cape of Good Hope, to the equatorial crossing, east of our old trysting-place, Fernando de Noronha; shortening sail, from time to time, and see-sawing across the highway, to give any Yankee ships that might be travelling it, the opportunity to come up with me. I held myself in check, a day or two, in the vicinity of St. Helena, experiencing all the vicissitudes of weather, so feelingly complained of by the "Great Captive" on that barren rock. Leaving St. Helena, we jogged along leisurely under topsails, the stream of commerce flowing past us, but there being no Yankee ships in the stream.

> "Howl, ye ships of Tarshish,
> For your strength is laid waste."

On the 22d of April, having reached the track of the homeward-bound Pacific ships of the enemy, we descried an unlucky Yankee, to whom we immediately gave chase. The chase continued the whole night, the moon shining brightly, the breeze being gentle, and the sea smooth. The Yankee worked like a good fellow to get away, piling clouds of canvas upon his ship, and handling her with the usual skill, but it was of no use. When the day dawned we were within a couple of miles of him. It was the old spectacle of the panting, breathless fawn, and the inexorable stag-hound. A gun brought his colors to the peak, and his main-yard to the mast. The prize proved to be the ship *Rockingham*, from Callao, bound to Cork for orders. Her cargo consisted of guano from the Chincha Islands, and there was an attempt to protect it It was shipped by the "Guano Consignment Company of Great Britain." Among the papers was a certificate, of which the following is the purport: One Joseph A. Danino, who signs for Danino & Moscosa, certifies that the guano belongs to the Peruvian Government; and Her Britannic Majesty's Consul at Lima, certifies that the said Joseph A. Danino appeared before him, and "voluntarily declared, that the foregoing signature is of his own handwriting, and also, that the cargo above mentioned is truly and verily the property of the Peruvian Government." This was about equal to some of the Yankee attempts, that have been noticed, to cover cargoes. With the most perfect unconcern for the laws of nations, no one swore to anything. Mr. Danino certified, and the Consul certified that Mr. Danino had certified. *Voila tout!* We transferred to the *Alabama* such stores and provisions as we could make room for, and the weather being fine, we made a target of the prize, firing some shot and shell into her with good effect; and at five P. M. we burned her, and filled away on our course.

A few days afterward—on the 27th of April—being in latitude 11° 16′ S. and longitude 32° 07′ W., the weather being fine, and the wind light from the south-east, we descried, at three P. M., a large ship standing directly for us. Neither ship changed tack or sheet until we were within speaking distance. Nor had we shown the stranger any colors. We now hailed, and ordered him to heave to, whilst we should send aboard of him, hoisting our colors at the same time. We had previously seen the Yankee colors in the hands of one of his seamen, ready to be hoisted. The whole thing was done so quietly, that one would have thought it was two friends meeting. The prize proved to be the *Tycoon*, from New York, for San Francisco. She had the usual valuable and assorted cargo. There was no claim of neutral property among the papers. The ship being only thirty-six days from New York, we received from her a batch of late newspapers; and a portion of her cargo consisting of clothing, the paymaster was enabled to replenish his store-rooms with every variety of wearing apparel. We applied the torch to her soon after nightfall.

On the 2d of May, we recrossed the equator into the northern hemisphere, took the north-east trade-wind, after the usual interval of calm, and the usual amount of thunder, lightning, and rain, and with it, ran up to our old toll-gate, at the crossing of the 30th parallel, where, as the reader will recollect, we halted, on our outward passage, and *viséd* the passports of so many travellers. The poor old *Alabama* was not now what she had been then. She was like the wearied fox-hound, limping back after a long chase, foot-sore, and longing for quiet and repose. Her commander, like herself, was well-nigh worn down. Vigils by night and by day, the storm and the drenching rain, the frequent and rapid change of climate, now freezing, now melting or broiling, and the constant excitement of the chase and capture, had laid, in the three years of war he had been afloat, a load of a dozen years on his shoulders. The shadows of a sorrowful future, too, began to rest upon his spirit. The last batch of newspapers captured were full of disasters. Might it not be, that, after all our trials and sacrifices, the cause for which we were struggling would be lost? Might not our federal system of government be destroyed, and State independence become a phrase of the past; the glorious fabric of our American liberty sinking, as so many others had done before it, under a new invasion of Brennuses and Attilas? The thought was hard to bear.

We passed through our old cruising-ground, the Azores, sighting several of the islands which called up reminiscences of the christening of our ship, and of the sturdy blows she had struck at the enemy's whaling fleet, in the first days of her career. Thence we stretched over to the coasts of Spain and Portugal, and thence to the British Channel, making the Lizard on the 10th of June, and being fortunate enough to get a channel pilot on board, just as night was setting in, with a thick south-wester brewing. By eleven P. M., we were up with the "Start" light, and at ten the next morning, we made Cape La Hague, on the coast of France. We were now boarded by a French pilot, and at thirty minutes past noon, we let go our anchor in the port of Cherbourg.

This was to be the *Alabama's* last port. She had run her career, her record had been made up, and in a few days more, she would lay her bones beneath the waters of the British Channel, and be a thing of the past. I had brought back with me all my officers, except the paymaster, whom I had discharged at the island of Jamaica, as related in a former chapter, and the young engineer, who had been accidentally killed at Saldanha Bay. Many changes had taken place, of course, among my crew, as is always the case with sailors, but still a large proportion of my old men had come back with me. These were faithful and true, and took more than an ordinary interest in their ship and their flag. There were harmony and mutual confidence between officers and men. Our discipline had been rigid, but mercy had always tempered justice, and the sailors understood and appreciated this. I had been successful with the health of my men beyond precedent. In my two ships, the *Sumter* and *Alabama,* I had had, first and last, say five hundred men under my command. The ships were small and crowded. As many as two thousand prisoners were confined, for longer or shorter periods, on board the two ships; and yet, out of the total of twenty-five hundred men, *I had not lost a single man by disease.* I had skilful and attentive surgeons, I gave them *carte blanche* with regard to medicines and diet, and my first lieutenant understood it to be an important part of his duty to husband the strength of his men. The means which were resorted to by all these officers, for preserving the health of the crew, have been detailed. The reader has seen, not only how their clothing was changed as we changed our latitude, but how it was changed every evening, when we were in warm climates. He has seen how sedulously we guarded against intemperance, at the same time that we gave the sailor his regular allowance of grog. And last, though by no means least, he has seen how we endeavored to promote a cheerful and hilarious spirit among them, being present at, and encouraging them in their diversions.

Immediately upon anchoring, I sent an officer to call on the Port Admiral, and ask leave to land my prisoners from the two last ships captured. This was readily granted, and the next day I went on shore to see him myself, in relation to docking and repairing my ship. My arrival had, of course, been telegraphed to Paris, and indeed, by this time, had been spread all over Europe. The Admiral regretted that I had not gone into Havre, or some other commercial port, where I would have found private docks. Cherbourg being exclusively a naval station, the docks all belonged to the Government, and the Government would have preferred not to dock and repair a belligerent ship. No positive objection was made, however, and the matter was laid over, until the Emperor could be communicated with. The Emperor was then at Biarritz, a small watering-place on the south coast, and would not be back in Paris for several days. It was my intention, if I had been admitted promptly into dock, to give my crew a leave of absence for a couple of months. They would have been discharged, and dispersed, in the first twenty-four hours after my arrival, but for this temporary absence of the Emperor. The combat, therefore, which ensued, may be said to be due to the Emperor's accidental absence from Paris.

When the *Alabama* arrived in Cherbourg, the enemy's steamer *Kearsarge* was lying at Flushing. On the 14th of June, or three days after our arrival, she steamed into the harbor of Cherbourg, sent a boat on shore to communicate with the authorities, and, without anchoring, steamed out again, and took her station off the breakwater. We had heard, a day or two before, of the expected arrival of this ship, and it was generally understood among my crew that I intended to engage her. Her appearance, therefore, produced no little excitement on board. The object which the *Kearsarge* had in view, in communicating with the authorities, was to request that the prisoners I had sent on shore might be delivered up to her. To this I objected, on the ground, that it would augment her crew, which she had no right to do, in neutral waters, and especially in the face of her enemy. Captain Winslow's request was refused, and the prisoners were not permitted to go on board of him. I now addressed a note to Mr. Bonfils, our agent, requesting him to inform Captain Winslow, through the United States Consul, that if he would wait until I could receive some coal on board — my supply having been nearly exhausted, by my late cruising — I would come out and give him battle. This message was duly conveyed, and the defiance was understood to have been accepted.

We commenced coaling ship immediately, and making other preparations for battle; as sending down all useless yards and top-hamper, examining the gun equipments, and overhauling the magazine and shell-rooms. My crew seemed not only willing, but anxious for the combat, and I had every confidence in their steadiness and drill; but they labored under one serious disadvantage. They had had but very limited opportunities of actual practice at target-firing, with shot and shell. The reason is obvious. I had no means of replenishing either shot or shell, and was obliged, therefore, to husband the store

I had on hand, for actual conflict. The stories that ran the round of the Federal papers at the time, that my crew was composed mainly of trained gunners from the British practice-ship *Excellent*, were entirely without foundation. I had on board some half dozen British seamen, who had served in ships of war in former years, but they were in no respect superior to the rest of the crew. As for the two ships, though the enemy was superior to me, both in size, stanchness of construction, and armament, they were of force so nearly equal, that I cannot be charged with rashness in having offered battle. The *Kearsarge* mounted seven guns:—two eleven-inch Dahlgrens, four 32-pounders, and a rifled 28-pounder. The *Alabama* mounted eight:—one eight-inch, one rifled 100-pounder, and six 32-pounders. Though the *Alabama* carried one gun more than her antagonist, it is seen that the battery of the latter enabled her to throw more metal at a broadside—there being a difference of three inches in the bore of the shell-guns of the two ships.

Still the disparity was not so great, but that I might hope to beat my enemy in a fair fight. But he did not show me a fair fight, for, as it afterward turned out, his ship was iron-clad. It was the same thing, as if two men were to go out to fight a duel, and one of them, unknown to the other, were to put a shirt of mail under his outer garment. The days of chivalry being past, perhaps it would be unfair to charge Captain Winslow with deceit in withholding from me the fact that he meant to wear armor in the fight. He may have reasoned that it was my duty to find it out for myself. Besides, if he had disclosed this fact to me, and so prevented the engagement, the Federal Secretary of the Navy would have cut his head off to a certainty. A man who could permit a ship of war, which had surrendered, to be run off with, by her crew, *after they had been paroled*—see the case of the *Mercedita* described in a former chapter—and who could contrive, or connive at the sinking of the *Florida*, to prevent the making of a reparation of honor to Brazil, would not be likely to be very complacent toward an officer who showed any signs of *weakness* on the score of *honor* or *honesty*. Judging from the tone of the Yankee press, too, when it came afterward to describe the engagement, Winslow seemed to have gauged his countrymen correctly, when he came to the conclusion that it would not do to reveal his secret to me. So far from having any condemnation to offer, the press, that chivalrous exponent of the opinions of a chivalrous people, was rather pleased at the "Yankee trick." It was characteristic, "cute," "smart."

"Appleton's Encyclopedia of the War," much more liberal and fair than some of its congeners, thus speaks of Winslow's device:— "Availing himself of an ingenious expedient for the protection of his machinery, first adopted by Admiral Farragut, in running past the rebel forts on the Mississippi in 1862, Captain Winslow had hung all his spare anchor cable over the midship section of the *Kearsarge*, on either side; and in order to make the addition less unsightly, the chains were boxed over with inch deal boards, forming a sort of case, which stood out at right-angles to the side of the vessel." One sees a twinge of honesty in this paragraph. The boxing stood out at right-angles to the side of the ship, and therefore the *Alabama ought to have seen it*. But unfortunately for the *Alabama*, the right-angles were not there. The forward and after ends of the "boxing," went off at so fine a point, in accordance with the lines of the ship, that the telescope failed to detect the cheat. Besides, when a ship is preparing for a fight, she does not care much about *show*. It is a fight, and not a review that she has on hand. Hence, we have another twinge, when the paragraphist remarks that the boxing was resorted to, to make the armor appear "*less unsightly!*" And, then, what about the necessity for *protecting the machinery at all?* The machinery of all the enemy's new sloops was below the water-line. Was the *Kearsarge* an exception? The plain fact is, without any varnish, the *Kearsarge*, though as effectually protected as if she had been armored with the best of iron plates, was to all appearance a wooden ship of war. But, to admit this, would spoil the *éclat* of the victory, and hence the effort to explain away the cheat, as far as possible.

In the way of crew, the *Kearsarge* had 162, all told—the *Alabama*, 149. I had communicated my intention to fight this battle to Flag-Officer Barron, my senior officer in Paris, a few days before, and that officer had generously left the matter to my own discretion. I completed my preparations on Saturday evening, the 18th of June, and notified the Port-Admiral of my intention to go out on the following morning. The next day dawned beautiful and bright. The cloudy, murky weather of some days past had cleared off, and a bright sun, a gentle breeze, and a smooth sea, were to be the concomitants of the battle. Whilst I was still in my cot, the Admiral sent an officer off to say to me that the iron-clad frigate *Couronne* would accompany me a part of the way out, to see that the neutrality of French waters was not violated. My crew had turned in early, and gotten a good night's rest, and I permitted them to get their breakfasts comfortably — not turning them to until nine o'clock — before any movement was made toward getting under way, beyond lighting the fires in the furnaces. I ought to mention that Midshipman Sinclair, the son of Captain Terry Sinclair, of the Confederate Navy, whom I had sent with Low, as his first lieutenant in the *Tuscaloosa*, being in Paris when we arrived, had come down on the eve of the engagement — accompanied by his father — and endeavored to rejoin me, but was prevented by the French authorities. It is opportune also to state, that in view of possible contingencies, I had directed Galt, my acting paymaster, to send on shore for safe-keeping, the funds of the ship, and complete pay-rolls of the crew, showing the state of the account of each officer and man.

The day being Sunday, and the weather fine, a large concourse of people — many having come all the way from Paris — collected on the heights above the town, in the upper stories of such of the houses as commanded a view of the sea, and on the walls and fortifications of the harbor. Several French luggers employed as pilot-boats went out, and also an English steam-yacht, called the *Deerhound*. Everything being in readiness between nine and ten o'clock, we got under way, and proceeded to sea, through the western entrance of the harbor; the *Couronne* following us. As we emerged from behind the mole, we discovered the *Kearsarge* at a distance of between six and seven miles from the land. She had been apprised of our intention of coming out that morning, and was awaiting us. The *Couronne* anchored a short distance outside of the harbor.

We were three quarters of an hour in running out to the *Kearsarge*, during which time we had gotten our people to quarters, cast loose the battery, and made all the other necessary preparations for battle. The yards had been previously slung in chains, stoppers prepared for the rigging, and preventer braces rove. It only remained to open the magazine and shell-rooms, sand down the decks, and fill the requisite number of tubs with water. The crew had been particularly neat in their dress on that morning, and the officers were all in the uniforms appropriate to their rank. As we were approaching the enemy's ship, I caused the crew to be sent aft, within convenient reach of my voice, and mounting a gun-carriage, delivered them the following brief address. I had not spoken to them in this formal way since I had addressed them on the memorable occasion of commissioning the ship.

"OFFICERS AND SEAMEN OF THE ALABAMA!—You have, at length, another opportunity of meeting the enemy—the first that has been presented to you, since you sank the *Hatteras!* In the meantime, you have been all over the world, and it is not too much to say, that you have destroyed, and driven for protection under neutral flags, one half of the enemy's commerce, which, at the beginning of the war, covered every sea. This is an achievement of which you may well be proud; and a grateful country will not be unmindful of it. The name of your ship has become a household word wherever civilization extends. Shall that name be tarnished by defeat? The thing is impossible! Remember that you are in the English Channel, the theatre of so much of the naval glory of our race, and that the eyes of all Europe are at this moment, upon you. The flag that floats over you is that of a young Republic, who bids defiance to her enemies, whenever, and wherever found. Show the world that you know how to uphold it! Go to your quarters."

The utmost silence prevailed during the delivery of this address, broken only once, in an enthusiastic outburst of *Never! never!* when I asked my sailors if they would permit the name of their ship to be tarnished by defeat. My official report of the engagement, addressed to Flag-Officer Barron, in Paris, will describe what now took place.   It was written at Southampton, England, two days after the battle.

SOUTHAMPTON, June 21, 1864.

SIR:—I have the honor to inform you, that, in accordance with my intention as previously announced to you, I steamed out of the harbor of Cherbourg between nine and ten o'clock on the morning of the 19th of June, for the purpose of engaging the enemy's steamer *Kearsarge*, which had been lying off, and on the port, for several days previously.   After clearing the harbor, we descried the enemy, with his head off shore, at the distance of about seven miles. We were three quarters of an hour in coming up with him.   I had previously pivotted my guns to starboard, and made all preparations for engaging the enemy on that side.   When within about a mile and a quarter of the enemy, he suddenly wheeled, and, bringing his head in shore, presented his starboard battery to me.   By this time, we were distant about one mile from each other, when I opened on him with solid shot, to which he replied in a few minutes, and the action became active on both sides.   The enemy now pressed his ship under a full head of steam, and to prevent our passing each other too speedily, and to keep our respective broadsides bearing, it became necessary to fight in a circle; the two ships steaming around a common centre, and preserving a distance from each other of from three quarters to half a mile.   When we got within good shell range, we opened upon him with shell.   Some ten or fifteen minutes after the commencement of the action, our spanker-gaff was shot away, and our ensign came down by the run.   This was immediately replaced by another at the mizzen-masthead.   The firing now became very hot, and the enemy's shot, and shell soon began to tell upon our hull, knocking down, killing, and disabling a number of men, at the same time, in different parts of the ship.   Perceiving that our shell, though apparently exploding against the enemy's sides, were doing him but little damage, I returned to solid-shot firing, and from this time onward alternated with shot, and shell.

After the lapse of about one hour and ten minutes, our ship was ascertained to be in a sinking condition, the enemy's shell having exploded in our side, and between decks, opening large apertures through which the water rushed with great rapidity.   For some few minutes I had hopes of being able to reach the French coast, for which purpose I gave the ship all steam, and set such of the fore-and-aft sails as were available.   The ship filled so rapidly, however, that before we had made much progress, the fires were extinguished in the furnaces, and we were evidently on the point of sinking.   I now hauled down my colors, to prevent the further destruction of life, and dispatched a boat to inform the enemy of our condition.   Although we were now but 400 yards from each other, the enemy fired upon me five times after my colors had been struck.   It is charitable to suppose that a ship of war of a Christian nation could not have done this, intentionally. We now directed all our exertions toward saving the wounded, and such of the boys of the ship as were unable to swim. These were dispatched in my quarter-boats, the only boats remaining to me; the waist-boats having been torn to pieces. Some twenty minutes after my furnace-fires had been extinguished, and when the ship was on the point of settling, every man, in obedience to a previous order which had been given the crew, jumped overboard, and endeavored to save himself. There was no appearance of any boat coming to me from the enemy, until after my ship went down. Fortunately, however, the steam-yacht *Deerhound*, owned by a gentleman of Lancashire, England —Mr. John Lancaster—who was himself on board, steamed up in the midst of my drowning men, and rescued a number of both officers and men from the water. I was fortunate enough myself thus to escape to the shelter of the neutral flag, together with about forty others, all told. About this time, the *Kearsarge* sent one, and then, tardily, another boat. Accompanying, you will find lists of the killed and wounded, and of those who were picked up by the *Deerhound;* the remainder, there is reason to hope, were picked up by the enemy, and by a couple of French pilot boats, which were also fortunately near the scene of action. At the end of the engagement, it was discovered by those of our officers who went alongside of the enemy's ship, with the wounded, that her mid-ship section, on both sides, was thoroughly iron-coated; this having been done with chains, constructed for the purpose, placed perpendicularly, from the rail to the water's edge, the whole covered over by a thin outer planking, which gave no indication of the armor beneath. This planking had been ripped off, in every direction, by our shot and shell, the chain broken, and indented in many places, and forced partly into the ship's side. She was effectually guarded, however, in this section, from penetration. The enemy was much damaged, in other parts, but to what extent it is now impossible to say. It is believed he is badly crippled. My officers and men behaved steadily and gallantly, and though they have lost their ship, they have not lost honor. Where all behaved so well, it would be invidious to particularize, but I cannot deny myself the pleasure of saying that Mr. Kell, my first lieutenant, deserves great credit for the fine condition in which the ship went into action, with regard to her battery, magazine and shell-rooms, and that he rendered me great assistance, by his coolness, and judgment, as the fight proceeded. The enemy was heavier than myself, both in ship, battery, and crew; but I did not know until the action was over, that she was also iron-clad. Our total loss in killed and wounded, is 30, to wit: 9 killed, and 21 wounded.

It was afterward ascertained, that as many as ten were drowned. As stated in the above despatch, I had the satisfaction of saving all my wounded men. Every one of them was passed carefully into a boat, and sent off to the enemy's ship, before the final plunge into the sea was made by the unhurt portion of the crew. Here is the proper place to drop a tear over the fate of a brave officer. My surgeon, D. H. Llewellyn, of Wiltshire, England, a grandson of Lord ·Herbert, lost his life by drowning. It was his privilege to accompany the wounded men, in the boats, to the *Kearsarge*, but he did not do so. He remained and took his chance of escape, with the rest of his brethren in arms, and perished almost in sight of his home, after an absence of two years from the dear ones who were to mourn his loss. With reference to the drowning of my men, I desire to present a contrast to the reader. I sank the *Hatteras* off Galveston, in a *night* engagement. When the enemy appealed to me for assistance, telling me that his ship was sinking, I sent him all my boats, and saved every officer and man, numbering more than a hundred persons. The *Alabama* was sunk in *open daylight*—the enemy's ship being only 400 yards distant—and ten of my men were permitted to drown. Indeed, but for the friendly interposition of the *Deerhound*, there is no doubt that a great many more would have perished.

Captain Winslow has stated, in his despatch to his Government, that he desired to board the *Alabama*. He preserved a most respectful distance from her, even after he saw that she was crippled. He had greatly the speed of me, and could have laid me alongside, at any moment, but, so far from doing so, he was shy of me even after the engagement had ended. In a letter to the Secretary of the Federal Navy, published by Mr. Adams, in London, a few days after the engagement, he says:—"I have the honor to report that, toward the close of the action between the *Alabama* and this vessel, all available sail was made on the former, for the purpose of regaining Cherbourg. When the object was apparent, the *Kearsarge* was steered across the bow of the *Alabama*, for a raking fire, but before reaching this point, the *Alabama* struck. Uncertain whether Captain Semmes was not making some *ruse*, the *Kearsarge* was stopped." This is probably the explanation of the whole of Captain Winslow's strange conduct at the time. He was afraid to approach us because of some *ruse* that we might be practising upon him. Before he could recover from his bewilderment, and make up his mind that we were really beaten, my ship went down. I acquit him, therefore, entirely, of any intention of permitting my men to drown, or even of gross negligence, which would be almost as criminal. It was his *judgment* which was entirely at fault. I had known, and sailed with him, in the old service, and knew him *then* to be a humane and Christian gentleman. What the war may have made of him, it is impossible to say. It has turned a great deal of the milk of human kindness to gall and wormwood.

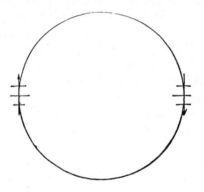

CHAPTER LIV.

OTHER INCIDENTS OF THE BATTLE BETWEEN THE ALA-
BAMA AND THE KEARSARGE — THE RESCUE OF OFFI-
CERS AND SEAMEN BY THE ENGLISH STEAM-YACHT
DEERHOUND — THE UNITED STATES GOVERNMENT DE-
MANDS THAT THEY BE GIVEN UP — BRITISH GOVERN-
MENT REFUSES COMPLIANCE — THE RESCUED PERSONS
NOT PRISONERS — THE INCONSISTENCY OF THE FEDERAL
SECRETARY OF THE NAVY.

NOTWITHSTANDING my enemy went out chivalrously
armored, to encounter a ship whose wooden sides were
entirely without protection, I should have beaten him in the
first thirty minutes of the engagement, but for the defect of
my ammunition, which had been two years on board, and become much deteriorated by cruising in a variety of climates.
I had directed my men to fire low, telling them that it was
better to fire too low than too high, as the *ricochet* in the former case — the water being smooth — would remedy the defect
of their aim, whereas it was of no importance to cripple the
masts and spars of a steamer. By Captain Winslow's own account, the *Kearsarge* was struck twenty-eight times; but his
ship being armored, of course, my shot and shell, except in so
far as fragments of the latter may have damaged his spars and
rigging, fell harmless into the sea. The *Alabama* was not mortally wounded, as the reader has seen, until after the *Kearsarge*
had been firing at her *an hour and ten minutes.* In the mean
time, in spite of the armor of the *Kearsarge*, I had *mortally
wounded* that ship in the first thirty minutes of the engagement. I say, "mortally wounded her," because the wound
would have proved mortal, but for the defect of my ammunition above spoken of. I lodged a rifled percussion shell near

her stern post—*where there were no chains*—which failed to
explode because of the defect of the cap.˙ If the cap had
performed its duty, and exploded the shell, I should have been
called upon to save Captain Winslow's crew from drowning,
instead of his being called upon to save mine.   On so slight
an incident—the defect of a percussion-cap—did the battle
hinge.   The enemy were very proud of this shell.   *It was the
only trophy they ever got of the Alabama!*   We fought her until
she would no longer swim, and then we gave her to the waves.
This shell, thus imbedded in the hull of the ship, was carefully
cut out, along with some of the timber, and sent to the Navy
Department in Washington, to be exhibited to admiring Yankees.   It should call up the blush of shame to the cheek of
every Northern man who looks upon it.   It should remind
him of his ship going into action with *concealed* armor; it
should remind him that his ship fired into a beaten antagonist
five times, after her colors had been struck and when she was
sinking; and it should remind him of the drowning of helpless men, struggling in the water for their lives!

Perhaps this latter spectacle was something for a Yankee to
gloat upon.   The *Alabama* had been a scourge and a terror to
them for two years.   She had destroyed their *property!*   *Yankee* property!   Curse upon the "pirates," let them drown!   At
least this was the sentiment uttered by that humane and Christian gentleman, to whom I have before had occasion to allude
in these pages—Mr. William H. Seward—one of the chief
Vandals, who found themselves in the possession and control of
the once glorious "Government of the States," during the war.
This gentleman, in one of his despatches to Mr. Adams,
prompting him as to what he should say to the English Government, on the subject of the rescue of my men by the *Deerhound*, remarks: "I have to observe, upon these remarks of
Earl Russell, that it was the right of the *Kearsarge that the
pirates should drown*, unless saved by humane exertions of the
officers and crew of that vessel, or by their own efforts, *without
the aid of the Deerhound.*   The men were either already actually
prisoners, or they were desperately pursued by the *Kearsarge.*
If they had *perished* [by being permitted to be drowned, in
cold blood after the action], the *Kearsarge would have had the*

advantage of a lawful destruction of so many enemies; if they had been recovered by the *Kearsarge,* with or without the aid of the *Deerhound,* then the voluntary surrender of those persons would have been perfected, and they would have been prisoners. In neither case would they have remained hostile Confederates."

No one who is not a seaman can realize the blow which falls upon the heart of a commander, upon the sinking of his ship. It is not merely the loss of a battle — it is the overwhelming of his household, as it were, in a great catastrophe. The *Alabama* had not only been my battle-field, but my home, in which I had lived two long years, and in which I had experienced many vicissitudes of pain and pleasure, sickness and health. My officers and crew formed a great military family, every face of which was familiar to me; and when I looked upon my gory deck, toward the close of the action, and saw so many manly forms stretched upon it, with the glazed eye of death, or agonizing with terrible wounds, I felt as a father feels who has lost his children — his children who had followed him to the uttermost ends of the earth, in sunshine and storm, and been always true to him.

A remarkable spectacle presented itself on the deck of the sinking ship, after the firing had ceased, and the boats containing the wounded had been shoved off. Under the order, which had been given, "Every man save himself who can!" all occupations had been suspended, and all discipline relaxed. One man was then as good as another. The *Kearsarge* stood sullenly at a distance, making no motion, that we could see, to send us a boat. The *Deerhound* and the French pilot-boats were also at a considerable distance. Meantime, the water was rushing and roaring into the ship's side, through her ghastly death-wound, and she was visibly settling — lower and lower. There was no panic, no confusion, among the men. Each stood, waiting his doom, with the most perfect calmness. The respect and affection manifested for their officers was touching in the extreme. Several gathered around me, and seemed anxious for my safety. One tendered me this little office of kindness, and another, that. Kell was near me, and my faithful steward, Bartelli, also, was at my side. Poor Bartelli! he could not swim a stroke — which I did not know at the time, or I should have saved him in the boats — and yet he was calm and cheerful; seeming to think that no harm could befall him, so long as he was at my side. He asked me if there were not some papers I wanted, in the cabin. I told him there were, and sent him to bring them. He had to wade to my state-room to get them. He brought me the two small packages I had indicated; and, with tears in his eyes, told me how the cabin had been shattered by the enemy's shot — our fine painting of the *Alabama*, in particular, being destroyed. Poor fellow! he was drowned in ten minutes afterward.

Two of the members of my boat's crew being around me, when the papers were brought, insisted that I should give them to them to take care of. They were good swimmers, they said, and would be sure to preserve them for me. I gave each a package — put up tightly between small slats — and they thrust them in the bosoms of their shirts. One of them then helped me off with my coat, which was too well laden with buttons, to think of retaining, and I sat down whilst the other pulled off my boots. Kell stripped himself in like manner. The men with the papers were both saved. One swam to a French pilot-boat, and the other to the *Deerhound*. I got both packages of papers. The seaman who landed on the French coast sought out Captain Sinclair, who was still at Cherbourg, and delivered them to him. A writer in the London "Times" thus describes how I got the other package: "When the men came on board the *Deerhound*, they had nothing on but their drawers and shirts, having been stripped to fight; and one of them, with a sailor's devotedness, insisted on seeing his Captain, who was then lying in Mr. Lancaster's cabin, in a very exhausted state, as he had been intrusted by Captain Semmes with the ship's papers, and to no one else would he give them up. The men were all very anxious about their Captain, and were rejoiced to find that he had been saved. They appeared to be a set of first-rate fellows, and to act well together, in perfect union, under the most trying circumstances."

The ship settled by the stern, and as the taffarel was about to be submerged, Kell and myself threw ourselves into the sea, and swam out far enough from the sinking ship to avoid

KELLY, PIET & CO. PUBLISHERS.

The Combat between the Alabama and the Kearsage, off Cherbourg, on the 19th of June, 1864.

LITH. BY A. HOEN & CO. BALTO.

being drawn down into the vortex of waters. We then turned to get a last look at her, and see her go down. Just before she disappeared, her main-topmast, which had been wounded, went by the board; and, like a living thing in agony, she threw her bow high out of the water, and then descended rapidly, stern foremost, to her last resting-place. A noble Roman once stabbed his daughter, rather than she should be polluted by the foul embrace of a tyrant. It was with a similar feeling that Kell and I saw the *Alabama* go down. We had buried her as we had christened her, and she was safe from the polluting touch of the hated Yankee!

Great rejoicing was had in Yankeedom, when it was known that the *Alabama* had been beaten. Shouts of triumph rent the air, and bonfires lighted every hill. But along with the rejoicing there went up a howl of disappointed rage, that I had escaped being made a prisoner. The splendid victory of their iron-clad over a wooden ship was shorn of half its brilliancy. Mr. Seward was in a furor of excitement; and as for poor Mr. Adams, he lost his head entirely. He even conceived the brilliant idea of demanding that I should be delivered up to him by the British Government. Two days after the action, he wrote to his chief from London as follows: —

"The popular excitement attending the action between the *Alabama* and the *Kearsarge* has been considerable. I transmit a copy of the "Times," of this morning, containing a report made to Mr. Mason, by Captain Semmes. It is evidently intended for this meridian. The more I reflect upon the conduct of the *Deerhound*, the more grave do the questions to be raised with this Government appear to be. I do not feel it my duty to assume the responsibility of demanding, without instructions, the surrender of the prisoners. Neither have I yet obtained directly from Captain Winslow, any authentic evidence of the facts attending the conflict. I have some reason to suspect, that the subject has already been under the consideration of the authorities here."

Mr. Seward and Mr. Adams were both eminently civilians. The heads of both of them were muddled, the moment they stepped from the Forum to the Campus Martius. Mr. Adams was now busy preparing another humiliation for the great American statesman. Some men learn wisdom by experience, and others do not. Mr. Adams seems to have been of the latter class. He had made a great many *demands* about the *Alabama*, which had been refused, and was now about to make another which was more absurd even than those that had gone before. The "instructions" coming from Mr. Seward in due time, the demand was made, and here is the reply of Lord Russell : —

" Secondly,"—[his lordship had been considering another point, which Mr. Adams had introduced into his despatch, not material to the present question,]—"I have to state, that it appears to her Majesty's Government, that the commander of the private British yacht, the *Deerhound*, in saving from drowning some of the officers and crew of the *Alabama*, after that vessel had sunk, performed a praiseworthy act of humanity, to which, moreover, he had been exhorted by the officer commanding the *Kearsarge*, to which vessel the *Deerhound* had, in the first instance, gone, in order to offer to the *Kearsarge* any assistance which, after her action with the *Alabama*, she might stand in need of; and it appears further, to her Majesty's Government, that, under all the circumstances of the case, Mr. Lancaster was not under any obligation to deliver to the captain of the *Kearsarge* the officers and men whom he had rescued from the waves. But however that may be, with regard to the demand made by you, by instructions from your Government, that those officers and men should now be delivered up to the Government of the United States, as being escaped prisoners of war, her Majesty's Government would beg to observe, that there is no obligation by international law, which can bind the government of a neutral State, to deliver up to a belligerent prisoners of war, who may have escaped from the power of such belligerent, and may have taken refuge within the territory of such neutral. Therefore, even if her Majesty's Government had any power, by law, to comply with the above-mentioned demand, her Majesty's Government could not do . so, without being guilty of a violation of the duties of hospitality. In point of fact, however, her Majesty's Government have no lawful power to arrest, and deliver up the persons in question. They have been guilty of no offence against the laws of England, and they have committed no act, which would bring them within the provisions of a treaty between Great Britain and the United States, for the mutual surrender of offenders, and her Majesty's Government are, therefore, entirely without any legal means by which, even if they wished to do so, they could comply with your above-mentioned demand."

This reasoning is unanswerable, and adds to the many humiliations the Federal Government received from England during the war in connection with the *Alabama*, through the bungling of its diplomatists. The *Deerhound*, a neutral vessel, was not only under no obligation, in fact, to deliver up the prisoners she had rescued from the water, but she could not, lawfully, have put herself under such obligation. The prisoners had rights in the premises as well as the *Deerhound*. The moment they reached the deck of the neutral ship, *by whatever means*, they were entitled to the protection of the neutral flag, and any attempt on the part of the neutral master, whether by agreement with the opposite belligerent or not, to hand them over to the latter, would have been an exercise of force by him, and tantamount to an act of hostility against the prisoners. It would have been our right and our duty to resist any such attempt; and we would assuredly have done so if it had been made. It will be observed that Lord Russell does not discuss the question whether we were prisoners. It was not necessary to his argument; for even admitting that we were prisoners, hospitality forbade him to deliver us up.

But we were not prisoners. A person, to become a prisoner, must be brought within the power of his captor. There must be a manucaption, a possession, if even for a moment. I never was at any time, during the engagement, or after, in the power of the enemy. I had struck my flag, it is true, but that did not make me a prisoner. It was merely an *offer* of surrender. It was equivalent to saying to my enemy, "I am beaten, if you will take possession of me, I will not resist." Suppose my ship had not been fatally injured, and a sudden gale had sprung up, and prevented the enemy from completing his capture, by taking possession of her, and I had escaped with her, will it be pretended that she was his prize? There have been numerous instances of this kind in naval history, and no one has ever supposed that a ship under such circumstances would be a prize, or that any person on board of her would be a prisoner. Nor can the *cause* which prevents the captor from taking possession of his prize, make any difference. If from *any* cause, he is unable to take possession, he loses her. If she takes fire, and burns up, or sinks, she is equally lost to him, and if any one escapes from the burning or sinking ship to the shore, can it be pretended that he is a prisoner? And is there any difference between escaping to the shore, and to a neutral flag? The folly of the thing is too apparent for argument, and yet the question was pressed seriously upon the British Government; and the head of Mr. Gideon Welles, the Secretary of the Federal Navy, was, for a long time, addled on the subject. I question, indeed, whether the head of the old gentleman has recovered from the shock it received, to this day. He afterward had me arrested, as the reader will see in due time, and conveyed to Washington a prisoner, and did all in his power to have me tried by a military commission, *in time of peace,* because I did not insist upon Mr. Lancaster's delivering me up to Captain Winslow! Will any one believe that this is the same Mr. Welles who approved of Captain Stellwagen's running off with the *Mercedita,* after he had been *paroled?*

But here is another little incident in point, which, perhaps, Mr. Welles had forgotten when he ordered my arrest. It arose out of Buchanan's gallant fight with the enemy's fleet in Hampton Roads, before alluded to in these pages. I will let the Admiral relate it, in his own words. He is writing to Mr. Mallory, the Secretary of the Navy, and after having described the ramming and sinking of the *Cumberland,* proceeds: —

" Having sunk the *Cumberland,* I turned our attention to the *Congress.* We were some time in getting our proper position, in consequence of the shoalness of the water, and the great difficulty of manœuvring the ship, when in or near the mud. To succeed in my object, I was obliged to run the ship a short distance above the batteries on James River, in order to wind her. During all this time her keel was in the mud; of course she moved but slowly. Thus we were subjected twice to the heavy guns of all the batteries, in passing up and down the river, but it could not be avoided. We silenced several of the batteries, and did much injury on the shore. A large transport steamer, alongside of the wharf, was blown up, one schooner sunk, and another captured and sent to Norfolk. The loss of life on shore we have no means of ascertaining. While the *Virginia* was thus engaged in getting her position for attacking the *Congress,* the prisoners state it was believed on board that ship, we had hauled off; the men left their guns, and gave three cheers. They were sadly undeceived, for, a few minutes after, we opened upon her again, she having run on shore, in shoal water. The carnage, havoc, and dismay, caused by our fire, compelled them to haul down their colors, and hoist a white flag at their gaff, and half-mast another at the main. The crew instantly *took to their boats and landed.* Our fire immediately ceased, and a signal was made for the *Beaufort* to come within hail.   I then ordered Lieutenant-Commanding Parker to take possession of the *Congress*, secure the officers as prisoners, allow the men to land, and burn the ship.   He ran alongside, received her flag and surrender from Commander William Smith, and Lieutenant Pendergrast, with the side-arms of these officers.   They delivered themselves as prisoners of war, on board the *Beaufort*, and afterward were permitted, *at their own request*, to return to the *Congress*, to assist in removing the wounded to the *Beaufort*.   *They never returned*, and I submit to the decision of the Department, whether they are not our prisoners?"

Aye, these *paroled* gentlemen escaped, and Mr. Welles *forgot* to send them back.   There was some excuse for Mr. Seward and Mr. Adams making the blunder they did, of supposing that the rescued officers and men of the *Alabama* were prisoners to the *Kearsarge*, but there was none whatever for Mr. Welles. He was the head of the enemy's Navy Department, and it was his business to know better; and if he did not know better, himself, he should have called to his assistance some of the clever naval men around him.   Nay, if he had taken down from its shelf almost any naval history in the library of his department, he could have set himself right in half an hour. James' "English Naval History" is full of precedents, where ships which have struck their flags, have afterward escaped —the enemy failing to take possession of them—and no question has been raised as to the propriety of their conduct.   So many contingencies occur in naval battles, that it has become a sort of common law of the sea, that a ship is never a prize, or the persons on board of her prisoners, *until she has actually been taken possession of by the enemy.*   A few of these cases will doubtless interest the reader, especially as they have an interest of their own, independently of their application.

THE REVOLUTIONNAIRE AND THE AUDACIOUS.

Lord Hood fought his famous action with the French fleet in 1794. In that action, the French ship *Revolutionnaire* struck her colors to the English ship *Audacious*, but the latter failing to take possession of her, she escaped.   The following is the historian's relation of the facts:—

"The *Audacious*, having placed herself on the *Revolutionnaire's* lee quarter, poured in a heavy fire, and, until recalled by signal, the *Russell*, who was at some distance to leeward, also fired on her. The *Audacious* and *Revolutionnaire* now became so closely engaged, and the latter so disabled in her masts and rigging, that it was with difficulty the former could prevent her huge opponent from falling on board of her.   Toward ten P. M., the *Revolutionnaire*, having, besides the loss of her mizzen-mast, had her fore and main yards, and main-topsail yard shot away, dropped across the hawse of the *Audacious;* but the latter quickly extricating herself, and the French ship, with her fore-topsail full, but owing to the sheets being shot away, still flying, directed her course to leeward The men forward, in the *Audacious*, declared that the *Revolutionnaire* struck her colors, just as she got clear of them, and the ship's company cheered in consequence.   The people of the *Russell* declared, also, that the *Revolutionnaire*, as she passed under their stern, had no colors hoisted.   That the latter was a beaten ship, may be inferred from her having returned but three shots to the last broadside of the *Audacious;* moreover, her loss in killed and wounded, if the French accounts are to be believed, amounted to nearly 400 men.   Still *the Revolutionnaire became no prize to the British;* owing partly to the disabled state of the *Audacious*, but chiefly because the *Thunderer*, on approaching the latter, and being hailed to take possession of the French ship, made sail after her own fleet." 1 *James*, 132, 133.

It is observable in the above extract, that the historian does not complain that the French ship escaped; does not deny her right to do so, but remarks, as a matter of course, that she did not become a prize, *because she was not taken possession of*.

THE ACHILLE AND THE BRUNSWICK.

In the same action, the French ship *Achille*, struck to the British ship *Brunswick*, and *not being taken possession of*, endeavored to escape.   The relation of this engagement is as follows : —

"At eleven A. M., a ship was discovered through the smoke, bearing down on the *Brunswick's* larboard quarter, having her gangways and rigging crowded with men, as if with the intention of releasing the *Vengeur*, [a prize made by the *Brunswick*,] by boarding the *Brunswick*.   Instantly the men stationed at the five aftermost lower-deck guns, on the starboard side, were turned over on the larboard side; and to each of the latter guns, already loaded with a single 32-pounder, was added a double-headed shot.   Presently, the *Achille*, for that was the ship, advanced to within musket-shot; when five or six rounds from the *Brunswick's* after-guns, on each deck, brought down by the board the former's only remaining mast, the foremast. The wreck of this mast, falling where the wreck of the main and mizzen-masts already lay, on the starboard side, prevented the *Achille* from making the slightest resistance; and, after a few unreturned broadsides from the *Brunswick*, the French ship struck her colors. It was, however, wholly out of the *Brunswick's* power *to take possession*, and the *Achille* very soon rehoisted her colors, and setting her sprit-sail endeavored to escape."

The escape, however, was prevented by the appearance of a new ship upon the scene, the *Ramilles*. This ship, after dispatching an antagonist with which she had been engaged, perceiving the attempt of the *Achille*, made sail in pursuit, and coming up with her, took possession of her, and thus, for the first time, made her a *prize*. 1 *James*, 162-4.

THE BELLONA AND THE MILLBROOK.

In the year 1800, the French ship *Bellona* struck to the British ship *Millbrook*, and afterward escaped. The following is the account of the engagement. The battle having continued some little time, the historian proceeds: —

"The carronades of the *Millbrook* were seemingly fired with as much precision, as quickness; for the *Bellona*, from broadsides, fell to single guns, and showed by her sails and rigging, how much she had been cut up by the schooner's shot. At about ten A. M., the ship's colors came down, and Lieutenant Smith used immediate endeavors to take possession of her. Not having a rope wherewith to hoist out a boat, he launched one over the gunwale, but having been pierced with shot in various directions, the boat soon filled with water. About this time, the *Millbrook*, having had two of her guns disabled, her masts, yards, sails, and rigging shot through, and all her sweeps shot to pieces, lay quite unmanageable, with her broadside to the *Bellona's* stern. In a little while, a light breeze sprung up, and the *Bellona* hoisted all the canvas she could, and sought safety in flight." 3 *James*, 57.

THE SAN JOSÉ AND THE GRASSHOPPER.

In 1807, off the coast of Spain, the Spanish brig *San José* struck to the British brig *Grasshopper*— having first run on shore—when the greater part of her crew escaped *before she could be taken possession of.* The affair is thus related: —

"At about half an hour after noon, having got within range, the *Grasshopper* opened a heavy fire of round and grape upon the brig.

A running fight was maintained — about fifteen minutes of its close — until two P. M., when the latter, which was the Spanish brig-of-war *San José*, of ten 24-pounder carronades, and two long sixes, commanded by Lieutenant Don Antonio de Torres, ran on shore under Cape Negrete, and struck her colors. The greater part of her crew, which, upon leaving Carthagena, on the preceding evening, numbered 99 men, then swam on shore, and effected their escape." 4 *James*, 374.

THE VAR AND THE BELLE POULE.

In 1809, in the Gulf of Velona, the French ship-of-war *Var*, struck to the British frigate *Belle Poule*, but *before she could be taken possession of*, the officers, and a greater part of the crew escaped. The action is described as follows: —

"On the 15th, at daybreak, the *Var* was discovered moored with cables to the fortress of Velona, mounting fourteen long 18 and 24-pounders, and upon an eminence above the ship, and apparently commanding the whole anchorage, was another strong fort. A breeze at length favoring, the *Belle Poule*, at one P. M., anchored in a position to take, or destroy the *Var*, and, at the same time, to keep in check the formidable force, prepared, apparently, to defend the French ship. The *Belle Poule* immediately opened upon the latter an animated and well-directed fire, and, as the forts made no efforts to protect her, the *Var* discharged a few random shots, that hurt no one, and then hauled down her colors. *Before she could be taken possession of*, her officers, and a greater part of her crew escaped to the shore." 5 *James*, 154.

THE VIRGINIA AND THE CONGRESS.

In the year 1862, one Gideon Welles being Secretary of the Federal Navy, Admiral Buchanan, of the Confederate States Navy, in the engagement in Hampton Roads, already referred to, for another purpose, sunk the frigate *Congress*, and, *before she could be taken possession of, the crew took to their boats and escaped.* Buchanan did not claim that the crew of the *Congress*, that had thus escaped, were his prisoners; he only claimed that Commander Smith, and Lieutenant Pendergrast were his prisoners, *he having taken possession of them*, and they having escaped, in violation of the *special parole*, under which he had permitted them to return to their ship.·

It thus appears, that, so far from its being the exception, it is the rule, in naval combats, for both ship and officers, and crew, to escape, after surrender, if possible. The enemy may prevent it by force, if he can, but if the escape be successful, it is a valid escape. I have thus far been considering the case, as though it were an escape with, or from a ship, which had not been fatally injured, and on board which the officers and crew might have remained, if they had thought proper. If the escape be proper in such a case as this, how much more must it be proper when, as was the case with the *Alabama*, the officers and crew of the ship are compelled to throw themselves into the sea, and struggle for their lives? Take my own individual case. The Federal Government complained of me because I threw my sword into the sea, which, as the Federal Secretary of the Navy said, no longer belonged to me. But what was I to do with it? Where was Mr. Welles' officer, that he did not come to demand it? It had been tendered to him, and *would* have belonged to him, if he had had the ability, or the inclination to come and take it. But he did not come. I did not betake myself to a boat, and seek refuge in flight. I waited for him, or *his* boat, on the deck of my sinking ship, until the sea was ready to engulf me. I was ready and willing to complete the surrender which had been tendered, but as far as was then apparent, the enemy intended to permit me to drown. Was I, under these circumstances, to plunge into the water with my sword in my hand and endeavor to swim to the *Kearsarge?* Was it not more natural, that I should hurl it into the depths of the ocean in defiance, and in hatred of the Yankee and his accursed flag? When my ship went down, I was a waif upon the waters. Battles and swords, and all other things, except the attempt to save life, were at an end. I ceased from that moment to be the enemy of any brave man. A true sailor, and above all, one who had been bred to arms, when he found that he could not himself save me, as his prisoner, should have been glad to have me escape from him, with life, whether by my own exertions, or those of a neutral. I believe this was the feeling, which, at that moment, was in the heart of Captain Winslow. It was reserved for William H. Seward to utter the atrocious sentiment which has been recorded against him, in these pages. Mr. Seward is now an old man, and he has the satisfaction of reflecting that he is responsible for more of the woes which have fallen upon the American people, than any other citizen of the once proud republic. He has worked, from first to last, for self, and he has met with the usual reward of the selfish — the contempt and neglect of all parties. He has need to utter the prayer of Cardinal Wolsey, and to add thereto, "Forgive, O Lord! him who never did forgive."

With the permission of the reader, I will make another brief reference to Naval History, to show how gallant men regard the saving of life, from such disasters during battle, as befell the *Alabama;* how, in other words, they cease to be the enemies of disarmed men, struggling against the elements for their lives.

DESTRUCTION OF L'ORIENT AT THE BATTLE OF THE NILE.

At the battle of the Nile, fought by Lord Nelson, in 1798, with Admiral Brueyes, the flag-ship of the French fleet, *L'Orient,* took fire and blew up, after having surrendered. Admiral Ganteaume, the third in command of the fleet, was on board the ill-fated ship, and being blown into the water by the explosion of the magazine, was picked up by one of his boats and conveyed to a French brig of war, in which he escaped to Alexandria. This escape, after surrender, was regarded as valid by Lord Nelson. The disaster is thus described by the historian. After giving the position of the French fleet, at anchor in the Bay of Aboukir, and describing the mode of attack by the English fleet, the narrator proceeds : —

" It was at nine P. M., or a few minutes after, that the *Swiftsure's* people discovered a fire on board of the *Orient,* and which, as it increased, presently bore the appearance of being in the ship's mizzen chains. It was, in fact, on the poop-deck, and in the admiral's cabin, and its cause we shall hereafter endeavor to explain. As many of the *Swiftsure's* guns as could be brought to bear were quickly directed to the inflamed spot, with, as was soon evident, dreadful precision. After spreading along the decks, and ascending the rigging with terrific and uncontrollable rapidity, the flames reached the fatal spot, and at about ten P. M., the *Orient* blew up with a most tremendous explosion."

The historian then describes the terrible night-scene that followed; how it put an end, for the time, to the action, and the efforts which were made by the English boats to save life. We have only to do, however, with Admiral Ganteaume. This gentleman describes his escape as follows : —

"It was by an accident, [he is writing to the Minister of Marine,] which I cannot yet comprehend, that I escaped from the midst of the flames of the *Orient*, and was taken into a yawl, lying under the ship's counter.   Not being able to reach the vessel of General Villeneuve, [the second in command,] I made for Alexandria.   At the beginning of the action, Admiral Brueyes, all the superior officers, the first commissary, and about twenty pilots, and masters of transports, were on the poop of the *Orient*, employed in serving musketry.   After the action had lasted about an hour, the admiral was wounded in the body, and in the hand; he then came down from the poop, and a short time after was killed on the quarter-deck.   The English having utterly destroyed our van, suffered their ships to drift forward, still ranging along our line, and taking their different stations around us.   One, however, which attacked, and nearly touched us, on the starboard side, being totally dismasted, ceased her fire, and cut her cable to get out of reach of our guns; but obliged to defend ourselves against two others, who were furiously thundering upon us on the larboard quarter, and on the starboard bow, we were again compelled to heave in our cable.   The 36 and 24-pounders were still firing briskly, when some flames, accompanied with an explosion, appeared on the after-part of the quarter-deck," &c.

Admiral Ganteaume does not mention the striking of the colors of this ship, and the fact has been disputed.   But Lord Nelson believed that she had struck, and that is all we need for our purpose, which is to show that, with the belief of this fact, he did not pretend to regard Admiral Ganteaume as a prisoner.   In 2 Clarke's "Life of Lord Nelson," p. 135, occurs the following passage:—

"In a letter to his Excellency, Hon. W. Wyndham, at Florence, dated the 21st of August, 1798, Sir Horatio had said, that on account of his indifferent health and his wound, he thought of going down the Mediterranean as soon as he arrived at Naples, unless he should find anything very extraordinary to detain him; and this determination had been strongly impressed on his mind by some of his friends, who doubted the effect of his going into winter-quarters at Naples [where the modern Anthony would find his Cleopatra, in the person of the then charming Lady Hamilton] might have on a mind by no means adapted to cope with the flattery of the Sicilian Court.   He also informed Mr. Wyndham, that *L'Orient certainly struck her colors*, and had not fired a shot for a quarter of an hour before she took fire."

Admiral Ganteaume resumed his duties as a naval officer immediately after his escape, repairing to Cairo, where Napoleon then was, to put himself under the orders of the Great Captain.   He returned with his distinguished chief to France, in the frigate *Le Muiron*. The British Government did not demand him of the French Government as a prisoner of war. This case was almost precisely similar with my own. Both ships struck their colors; both ships were destroyed before the enemy could take possession of them, and both commanders escaped; the only difference being that Admiral Ganteaume escaped in one of his own boats, to one of his own brigs of war, and thence to Alexandria, and I escaped by swimming to a neutral ship, and to the cover of a neutral flag; which, as before remarked, was the same thing as if I had swum to neutral territory. Mr. Lancaster could no more have thrust me back into the sea, or handed me over to the *Kearsarge*, than could the keeper of the Needles light, if I had landed on the Isle of Wight.

I have presented several contrasts in these pages; I desire to present another. The reader has seen how Mr. Seward, a civilian, insisted that beaten enemies, who were struggling for their lives in the water, should be permitted to drown, rather than be rescued from the grasp of his naval commander by a neutral. I desire to show how a Christian admiral forbade his enemies to be fired upon, when they were engaged in rescuing their people from drowning; even though the consequence of such rescue should be the escape of the prisoners. I allude to Lord Collingwood, a name almost as well known to American as to English readers; the same Lord Collingwood, who was second in command to Nelson at the famous battle of Trafalgar. This Admiral, from his flag-ship, the *Ocean*, issued the following general order to the commanders of his ships: —

" Ocean, September 19, 1807.

" In the event of an action with the enemy, in which it shall happen that any of their ships shall be in distress, by taking fire, or otherwise, and the brigs and tenders, or boats which are attached to their fleet, shall be employed in saving the lives of the crews of such distressed ships, they shall not be fired on, or interrupted in such duty. But as long as the battle shall continue, his Majesty's ships are not to give up the pursuit of such, as have not surrendered, to attend to any other occasion, except it be to give their aid to his Majesty's ships which may want it."— *Collingwood's Letters*, 235

But the American war developed " grand moral ideas," and Mr. Seward's, about the drowning of prisoners, was one of them.

CHAPTER LV.

THE FEDERAL GOVERNMENT AND THE BRITISH STEAM-
YACHT DEERHOUND — MR. SEWARD'S DESPATCH, AND
MR. LANCASTER'S LETTER TO THE "DAILY NEWS" —
LORD RUSSELL'S REPLY TO MR. ADAMS ON THE SUBJECT
OF HIS COMPLAINT AGAINST MR. LANCASTER — PRESEN-
TATION OF A SWORD TO THE AUTHOR, BY THE CLUBS IN
ENGLAND — PRESENTATION OF A FLAG BY A LADY.

THE howl that went up against Mr. Lancaster, the owner
of the *Deerhound,* for his humane exertions in saving my
crew and myself from drowning, was almost as rabid as that
which had been raised against myself. Statesmen, or those
who should have been such, descended into the arena of coarse
and vulgar abuse of a private English citizen, who had no
connection with them or their war, and no sympathies that I
know of, on the one side or the other. Mr. Welles, in one of
those patriotic effusions, by which he sought to recommend
himself to the extreme party of the North, declared among
other things, that he was "not a gentleman!" Poor Mr. Lancaster, to have thy gentility questioned by so competent a
judge, as Mr. Gideon Welles! If these gentlemen had confined themselves to mere abuse, the thing would not have been
so bad, but they gave currency to malicious falsehoods concerning Mr. Lancaster, as truths. Paid spies in England reported these falsehoods at Washington, and the too eager Secretary of State embodied them in his despatches. Mr. Adams
and Mr. Seward have, both, since ascertained that they were
imposed upon, and yet no honorable retraxit has ever been
made. The following is a portion of one of Mr. Seward's
characteristic despatches on this subject. It is addressed to
Mr. Adams: —

"I nave the honor to acknowledge the receipt of your despatch of the 21st of June, No. 724, which relates to the destruction of the pirate-ship *Alabama*, by the *Kearsarge*, off Cherbourg. This event has given great satisfaction to the Government, and it appreciates and commends the bravery and skill displayed by Captain Winslow, and the officers and crew under his command. Several incidents of the transaction seem to demand immediate attention The first is, that this Government disapproves the proceedings of Captain Winslow, in paroling and discharging the pirates who fell into his hands, in that brilliant naval engagement, and in order to guard against injurious inferences which might result from that error, if it were overlooked, you are instructed to make the fact of this disapprobation and censure known to her Majesty's Government, and to state, at the same time, that this. Government, adhering to declarations heretofore made, does not recognize the *Alabama* as a ship of war of a lawful belligerent power."

Mr. Seward, when this despatch was penned, had hopes that the "pirates" would be given up to him, and the *caveat*, which he enters, may give some indication of the course the Yankee Government intended to pursue toward the said "pirates," when they should come into its possession. It did not occur to the wily Secretary, that, if we were "pirates," it was as competent for Great Britain to deal with us as the United States; and that, on this very ground, his claim for extradition might be denied, — a pirate being *hostis humani generis*, and punishable by the first nation into whose power he falls. But these *mistakes* were common with Mr. Seward.

Laying aside, therefore, all his trash and nonsense about piracy, let us proceed with that part of his despatch which relates to Mr. Lancaster : —

"Secondly, the presence and the proceedings of a British yacht, the *Deerhound*, at the battle, require explanation. On reading the statements which have reached this Government, it seems impossible to doubt that the *Deerhound* went out to the place of conflict, by concert and arrangement with the commander of the *Alabama*, and with, at least, a conditional purpose of rendering her aid and assistance. She did effectually render such aid, by rescuing the commander and part of the crew of the *Alabama* from the pursuit of the *Kearsarge*, and by furtively and clandestinely conveying them to Southampton, within British jurisdiction. We learn from Paris that the intervention of the *Deerhound* occurred after the *Alabama* had actually surrendered. The proceeding of the *Deerhound*, therefore, seems to have been directly hostile to the United States. Statements of the owner of the *Deerhound* are reported here, to the effect that he was requested by Captain Winslow to rescue the drowning survivors of the battle, but no official confirmation of this statement is found in the reports of Captain Winslow. Even if he had made such a request, the owner of the *Deerhound* subsequently abused the right of interference, by secreting the rescued pirates, and carrying them away beyond the pursuit of the *Kearsarge*. Moreover, we are informed from Paris, that the *Deerhound*, before going out, received from Semmes, and that she subsequently conveyed away to England, a deposit of money, and other valuables, of which Semmes, in his long piratical career, had despoiled numerous American merchantmen."

There was not one word of truth in this cock-and-a-bull story, of concert between Mr. Lancaster and myself, as to his going out to witness the combat, as to his receiving money or anything else from the *Alabama*, or as to any other subject whatever. We had never seen each other, or held the least communication together, until I was drawn out of the water by his boat's crew, and taken on board his yacht, after the battle.

It was quite natural that Mr. Seward's Yankee correspondents in London and Paris, and Mr. Seward himself, should suppose that money and stealings had had something to do with Mr. Lancaster's generous conduct. The whole American war, on the Yankee side, had been conducted on this principle of giving and receiving a "*consideration*" and on "*stealings*." Armies of hired vagabonds had roamed through the Southern States, plundering and stealing — aye, as the reader has seen, stealing not only gold and silver, but libraries, pianos, pictures, and even the jewelry and clothing of women and children! The reader has seen into what a mortal fright the lady-passengers, on board the captured steamship *Ariel*, were thrown, lest the officers and crew of the *Alabama* should prove to be the peers of Yankee rogues, epauletted and unepauletted. These men even laid their profane hands on the sacred word of God, *if it would pay*. Here is a *morceau*, taken from the "Journal of Commerce" of New York, a Yankee paper, quite moderate in its tone, and a little given, withal, to religious sniffling. It shows how a family Bible was stolen from a Southern household, and sold for a "consideration" in the North, without exciting so much as a word of condemnation from press or people : —

"*An Old Bible Captured from a Rebel.*—H. Jallonack, of Syracuse, New York, has exhibited to the editor of the 'Journal' of that city a valuable relic—a Protestant Bible, printed in German text, 225 years ago, the imprint bearing date 1637. The book is in an excellent state of preservation, the printing perfectly legible, the binding sound and substantial, and the fastening a brass clasp. The following receipt shows how the volume came in Mr. Jallonack's possession:—

"'NEW YORK, Aug. 21, 1862.

"'Received of Mr. H. Jallonack $150 for a copy of one of the first Protestant Bibles published in the Netherlands, 1637, with the proclamation of the King of the Netherlands. This was taken from a descendant Hollander at the battle before Richmond, in the rebel service, by a private of the Irish Brigade.

"'JOSEPH HEIME, M. D., 4 Houston Street.'"

"Semmes, in his long piratical career," scarcely equalled these doings of Mr. Seward's countrymen. He certainly did not send any stolen Bibles, published in the Netherlands or elsewhere, to the *Deerhound*, to be sold to pious Jallonacks for $150 apiece.

But to return to Mr. Lancaster, and the gross assault that was made upon him, by the Secretary of State. Mr. Lancaster, being a gentleman of ease and fortune, spent a portion of his summers in yachting, as is the case with a large number of the better classes in England. Being in France with his family, he ordered his yacht, the *Deerhound*, to meet him, at the port of Cherbourg, where it was his intention to embark for a cruise of a few weeks in the German Ocean. A day or two before the engagement between the *Alabama* and the *Kearsarge*, a steam yacht, under British colors, was reported to me, as having anchored in the harbor. Beyond admiring the beautiful proportions of the little craft, we paid no further attention to her; and when she steamed out of Cherbourg, on the morning of the engagement, we had not the least conception of what her object was. With this preface, I will let Mr. Lancaster tell his own story. He had been assaulted by a couple of Yankee correspondents, in the London "Daily News," a paper in the interests, and reported to be in the pay of the Federal Government. He is replying to those assaults, which, as the reader will see, were the same that were afterward *rehashed* by Mr. Seward, in the despatch already quoted.

"THE DEERHOUND, THE ALABAMA, AND THE KEARSARGE.

"To the Editor of the 'Daily News.' Sir:—As two correspondents of your journal, in giving their versions of the fight between the *Alabama* and the *Kearsarge*, have designated my share in the escape of Captain Semmes, and a portion of the crew of the sunken ship as 'dishonorable,' and have moreover affirmed that my yacht, the *Deerhound*, was in the harbor of Cherbourg before the engagement, and proceeded thence, on the morning of the engagement in order to assist the *Alabama*, I presume I may trespass upon your kindness so far as to ask an opportunity to repudiate the imputation, and deny the assertion. They admit that when the *Alabama* went down, the yacht, being near the *Kearsarge*, was hailed by Captain Winslow, and requested to aid in picking up the men who were in the water; but they intimate that my services were expected to be merely ministerial; or, in other words, that I was to put myself under the command of Captain Winslow, and place my yacht at his disposal for the capture of the poor fellows who were struggling in the water for their lives.

"The fact is, that when we passed the *Kearsarge*, the captain cried out, 'For God's sake, do what you can to save them,' and that was my warrant for interfering, in any way, for the aid and succor of his enemies. It may be a question with some, whether, without that warrant, I should have been justified in endeavoring to rescue any of the crew of the *Alabama;* but my own opinion is, that a man drowning in the open sea cannot be regarded as an enemy, at the time, to anybody, and is, therefore, entitled to the assistance of any passer-by. Be this as it may, I had the earnest request of Captain Winslow, to rescue as many of the men who were in the water, as I could lay hold of, but that request was not coupled with any stipulation to the effect that I should deliver up the rescued men to him, as his prisoners. If it had been, I should have declined the task, because I should have deemed it dishonorable—that is, inconsistent with my notions of honor—to lend my yacht and crew, for the purpose of rescuing those brave men from drowning, only to hand them over to their enemies, for imprisonment, ill-treatment, and perhaps execution.

"One of your correspondents opens his letter, by expressing a desire, to bring to the notice of the yacht clubs of England, the conduct of the commander of the *Deerhound*, which followed the engagement of the *Alabama* and *Kearsarge*. Now that my conduct has been impugned, I am equally wishful that it should come under the notice of the yacht clubs of England, and I am quite willing to leave the point of honor to be decided by my brother yachtsmen, and, indeed, by any tribunal of gentlemen. As to my legal right to take away Captain Semmes and his friends, I have been educated in the belief that an English ship is English territory, and I am, therefore, unable, even now, to discover why I was more bound to surrender the people of the *Alabama* whom I had on board my yacht, than the owner of a garden on the south coast of England would have been, if they had swum to such a place, and landed there, or than the Mayor of Southampton was, when they were lodged in that city ; or than the British Government is, now that it is known that they are somewhere in England.

"Your other correspondent says that Captain Winslow declares that 'the reason he did not pursue the *Deerhound*, or fire into her was, that he could not believe, at the time, that any one carrying the flag of the royal yacht squadron, could act so dishonorable a part, as to carry off the prisoners whom he had requested him to save, from feelings of humanity.' I was not aware then, and I am not aware now, that the men whom I saved *were, or ever had been his prisoners*. Whether any of the circumstances which had pre-ceded the sinking of the *Alabama* constituted them prisoners was a question that never came under my consideration, and one which I am not disposed to discuss even now. I can only say, that it is a new doctrine to me, that *when one ship sinks another, in warfare, the crew of the sunken ship are debarred from swimming for their lives, and seeking refuge wherever they can find it;* and it is a doctrine which I shall not accept, unless backed by better authority than that of the master of the *Kearsarge*. What Captain Wins-low's notion of humanity may be is a point beyond my knowledge, but I have good reason for believing that not many members of the royal yacht squadron would, from 'motives of humanity' have taken Captain Semmes from the water in order to give him up to the tender mercies of Captain Winslow, and his compatriots. An-other reason assigned by your correspondent for that hero's for-bearance may be imagined in the reflection that such a performance as that of Captain Wilkes, who dragged two 'enemies' or 'rebels' from an English ship, would not bear repetition. [We have here the secret of the vindictiveness with which Mr. Seward pursued Mr. Lancaster. It was cruel of Lancaster to remind him of the 'seven days' of tribulation, through which Lord John Russell had put him.]

"Your anonymous correspondent further says, that 'Captain Winslow would now have all the officers and men of the *Alabama*, as prisoners, had he not placed too much confidence in the honor of an Englishman, who carried the flag of the royal yacht squadron.' This is a very questionable assertion; for why did Captain Wins-low confide in that Englishman? Why did he implore his inter-ference, calling out, 'For God's sake, do what you can to save them?' I presume it was because he would not, or could not save them, himself. The fact is, that if the Captain and crew of the *Alabama* had depended for safety altogether upon Captain Wins-low, *not one half of them would have been saved*. He got quite as many of them as he could lay hold of, time enough to deliver them from drowning.

"I come now to the more definite charges advanced by your cor-respondents, and these I will soon dispose of. They maintain that my yacht was in the harbor of Cherbourg, for the purpose of assisting the *Alabama*, and that her movements before the action prove that she attended her for the same object. My impression is, that the yacht was in Cherbourg, to suit my convenience, and pleasure, and I am quite sure, that when there, I neither did, nor intended to do anything to serve the *Alabama*. We steamed out on Sunday morning to see the engagement, and the resolution to do so was the result of a family council, whereat the question 'to go out,' or 'not to go out,' was duly discussed, and the decision in the affirmative was carried by the juveniles, rather against the wish of both myself, and my wife. Had I contemplated taking any part in the movements of the *Alabama*, I do not think I should have been accompanied with my wife, and several young children.

"One of your correspondents, however, says that he knows that the *Deerhound* did assist the *Alabama*, and if he does know this, he knows more than I do. As to the movements of the *Deerhound*, before the action, all the movements with which I was acquainted, were for the objects of enjoying the summer morning, and getting a good and safe place from which to watch the engagement. Another of your correspondents declares, that since the affair, it has been discovered, that the *Deerhound* was a consort of the *Alabama*, and on the night before had received many valuable articles, for safe-keeping, from that vessel. This is simply untrue. Before the engagement, neither I nor any member of my family had any knowledge of, or communication with Captain Semmes, or any of his officers or any of his crew. Since the fight I have inquired from my Captain whether he, or any of my crew, had had any communication with the Captain or crew of the *Alabama*, prior to meeting them on the *Deerhound* after the engagement, and his answer, given in the most emphatic manner, has been, 'None whatever.' As to the deposit of chronometers, and other valuable articles, the whole story is a myth. Nothing was brought from the *Alabama* to the *Deerhound*, and I never heard of the tale, until I saw it, in an extract from your own columns.

"After the fight was over, the drowning men picked up, and the *Deerhound* steaming away to Southampton, some of the officers who had been saved began to express their acknowledgments for my services, and my reply to them, which was addressed, also, to all who stood around, was 'Gentlemen, you have no need to give me any special thanks. I should have done exactly the same for the other people, if they had needed it.' This speech would have been a needless, and, indeed, an absurd piece of hypocrisy, if there had been any league or alliance between the *Alabama* and the *Deerhound*. Both your correspondents agree in maintaining that Captain Semmes, and such of his crew as were taken away by the *Deerhound*, are bound in honor to consider themselves still as prisoners, and to render themselves to their lawful captors as soon as practicable. This is a point which I have nothing to do with, and therefore I shall not discuss it. My object, in this letter, is merely to vindicate my conduct from misrepresentation; and I trust that in aiming at this, I have not transgressed any of your rules of correspondence, and shall therefore be entitled to a place in your columns.   JOHN LANCASTER."

"Mark how a plain tale shall put him down." There could not be a better illustration of this remark, than the above reply, proceeding from the pen of a gentleman, to Mr. Seward's charges against both Mr. Lancaster and myself. Mr. Adams having complained to Lord Russell, of the conduct of Mr. Lancaster, the latter gentleman addressed a letter to his lordship, containing substantially the defence of himself which he had prepared for the "Daily News." In a day or two afterward, Lord Russell replied to Mr. Adams as follows:—

FOREIGN OFFICE, July 26, 1864.

SIR:—With reference to my letter of the 8th inst., I have the honor to transmit to you, a copy of a letter which I have received from Mr. Lancaster, containing his answer to the representations contained in your letter of the 25th ult., with regard to the course pursued by him, in rescuing Captain Semmes and others, on the occasion of the sinking of the *Alabama;* and I have the honor to inform you, that I do not think it necessary to take any further steps in the matter. I have the honor to be, with the highest consideration, your most obedient, humble servant.   RUSSELL.

The royal yacht squadron, as well as the Government, sustained their comrade in what he had done, and a number of officers of the Royal Navy and Army, approving of my course, throughout the trying circumstances in which I had been placed—not even excepting the hurling of my sword into the sea, under the circumstances related—set on foot a subscription for another sword, to replace the one which I had lost, publishing the following announcement of their intention in the London "Daily Telegraph":—

JUNIOR UNITED SERVICE CLUB, S. W. }
June 23, 1864. }

SIR:—It will doubtless gratify the admirers of the gallantry displayed by the officers and crew of the renowned *Alabama,* in the late action off Cherbourg, if you will allow me to inform them, through your influential journal, that it has been determined to present Captain Semmes with a handsome sword, to replace that which he buried with his sinking ship. Gentlemen wishing to participate in this testimony to unflinching patriotism and naval daring, will be good enough to communicate with the chairman, Admiral Anson, United Service Club, Pall-Mall, or, sir, yours, &c.

BEDFORD PIM,

Commander R. N., Hon. Secretary.

This design on the part of the officers of the British Navy and Army was afterward carried out, by the presentation to me of a magnificent sword, which was manufactured to their order in the city of London, with suitable naval and Southern devices. I could not but appreciate very highly this delicate mode, on the part of my professional brethren, of rebutting the slanders of the Northern press and people. I might safely rely upon the judgment of two of the principal naval clubs in England,— the United Service, and the Junior United Service, on whose rolls were some of the most renowned naval and military names of Great Britain. The shouts of the multitude are frequently deceptive; the idol of an hour may be pulled down in the succeeding hour; but the approbation of my brethren in arms, who coolly surveyed my career, and measured it by the rules which had guided the conduct of so many of their own soldiers by sea and by land, in whose presence my own poor name was unworthy to be mentioned, was indeed beyond all price to me.

To keep company with this sword, a noble English lady presented me with a mammoth Confederate flag, wrought with her own hands from the richest silk. There is not a spot on its pure white field, and the battle-cross and the stars, when unfolded, flash as brightly as ever. These two gifts shall be precious heirlooms in my family, to remind my descendants, that, in the words of Patrick Henry, "I have done my utmost to preserve their liberty."

> "Furl that Banner, for 'tis *weary;*
> Round its staff 'tis drooping **dreary;**
>   Furl it, fold it, it is best:
> For there's not a man to wave it,
> And there's not a sword to save it,
> And there's not one left to lave it
> In the blood which heroes gave it;
> And its foes now scorn and brave it;
>   *Furl* it, *hide* it — let it *rest.*
> . . . .

"Furl it! for the hands that grasped it,
 And the hearts that fondly clasped it,
 Cold and dead are lying low;
 And that Banner — it is trailing!
 While around it sounds the wailing
 Of its people in their woe.

. . . .

"Furl that Banner! true 'tis gory.
 Yet 't is wreathed around with glory,
 And 't will live in song and story,
 Though its folds are in the dust ·
 For its fame on brightest pages,
 Penned by poets and by sages,
 Shall go sounding down the ages —
 Furl its folds though now we must."

Mr. Mason, our Commissioner at the Court of London, thanked Mr. Lancaster for his humane and generous conduct in the following terms: —

24 UPPER SEYMOUR STREET, PORTMAN SQUARE,
LONDON, June 21, 1864.

DEAR SIR: — I received from Captain Semmes, at Southampton, where I had the pleasure to see you, yesterday, a full report of the efficient service rendered, under your orders, by the officers and crew of your yacht, the *Deerhound*, in rescuing him, with thirteen of his officers and twenty-seven of his crew, from their impending fate, after the loss of his ship. Captain Semmes reports that, finding the *Alabama* actually sinking, he had barely time to dispatch his wounded in his own boats, to the enemy's ship, when the *Alabama* went down, and nothing was left to those who remained on board, but to throw themselves into the sea. Their own boats absent, there seemed no prospect of relief, when your yacht arrived in their midst, and your boats were launched; and he impressively told me, that to this timely and generous succor, he, with most of his officers and a portion of his crew, were indebted for their safety. He further told me, that on their arrival on board of the yacht, every care and kindness were extended to them which their exhausted condition required, even to supplying all with dry clothing. I am fully aware of the noble and disinterested spirit which prompted you to go to the rescue of the gallant crew of the *Alabama*, and that I can add nothing to the recompense already received by you and those acting under you, in the consciousness of having done as you would be done by; yet you will permit me to thank you, and through you, the captain, officers, and crew of the *Deerhound*, for this signal service, and to say that in doing so, I but anticipate the grateful sentiment of my country, and of the Government of the Confederate States. I have the honor to be, dear sir, most respectfully and truly, your obedient servant,   J. M. MASON.

.JOHN LANCASTER, *Esq., Hindley Hall, Wigan.*

Subsequently, upon my arrival in Richmond, in the winter of the same year, the Confederate Congress passed a joint resolution of thanks to Mr. Lancaster, a copy of which it requested the Secretary of the Navy to transmit to him. In the confusion incident to the downfall of the Confederacy, which speedily followed, Mr. Lancaster probably never received a copy of this resolution. Thus, with the indorsement of his own government, and with that of the yacht-clubs of England, and of the Congress of the Confederate States, he may safely despise the malicious diatribes that were launched against him by a fanatical and infuriated people, who were thirsting for an opportunity to wreak their vengeance upon the persons of the men whom he had saved.

Upon my landing in Southampton, I was received with great kindness by the English people, ever ready to sympathize with the unfortunate, and administer to the wants of the distressed. Though my officers and myself were not to be classed in this latter category, as my drafts on the house of Frazer, Trenholm & Co., of Liverpool, would have been accepted to any extent, and were as good as cash in the market, there were many generous offers of pecuniary assistance made me. I cannot forbear to speak of one of these, as it came from a lady, and if, in doing so, I trespass upon the bounds of propriety, I trust the noble lady will forgive me. This is the only means left me of making her any suitable acknowledgment. This lady was Miss Gladstone, a sister of the Chancellor of the Exchequer, who wrote me a long letter, full of sympathy, and of those noble impulses which swell the heart of the true woman on such occasions. She generously offered me any aid of which my sailors or myself might be in need. Letters of condolence for my loss, and congratulation upon my escape from the power of a ruthless enemy, came in upon me in great profusion; and, as for volunteers, half the adventurous young spirits of England claimed the privilege of serving under me, in my *new* ship. The career of the *Alabama* seemed to have fired the imagination of all the schools and colleges in England, if I might judge by the number of ardent missives I received from the young gentlemen who attended them. Mr. Mason, Captain Bullock, and the Rev. F. W. Tremlett came post-haste

to Southampton, to offer us sympathy and services. The reader
will recollect the circumstances under which I became acquainted with the latter gentleman, when I laid up the *Sumter*
at Gibraltàr, and retired to London. He now came to insist
that I should go again to my "English home," at his house, to
recruit and have my wound cared for. As I had already engaged quarters at Millbrook, where I should be in excellent
hands, and as duties connected with the welfare of my crew
would require my detention in the neighborhood of Southampton for a week or two, I was forced to forego the pleasure for
the present.

In connection with the gratitude due other friends, I desire
to mention the obligations I am under to Dr. J. Wiblin, a distinguished surgeon and physician of Southampton, who attended my crew and officers whilst we remained there, without
fee or reward. The reader may recollect, that previous to my
engagement with the *Kearsarge*, I had sent on shore, through
my paymaster, the ship's funds, and the books and papers
necessary to a final settlement with my crew. The paymaster
now recovered back these funds, from the bankers with whom
they had been deposited, paid off such of the officers and men as
were with us at Southampton, and proceeded to Liverpool,
where he was to pay off the rest of the survivors as fast as
they should present themselves. Some of the crew were
wounded, and in French hospitals, where they were treated
with marked kindness and consideration; some had been made
prisoners, and paroled by Captain Winslow, *with the approbation of Mr. Adams,* under *the mistaken idea,* as Mr. Seward afterward insisted, that they were *prisoners of war,* and some weeks
elapsed, consequently, before they could all present themselves
at the paymaster's table. This was finally accomplished, however, and every officer and seaman, received, in full, all the pay
that was due him. The amounts due to those killed and
drowned, were paid, in due time, to their legal representatives;
and thus were the affairs of the *Alabama* wound up.

CHAPTER LVI.

AUTHOR MAKES A SHORT VISIT TO THE CONTINENT —
RETURNS TO LONDON, AND EMBARKS ON HIS RETURN
TO THE CONFEDERATE STATES — LANDS AT BAGDAD,
NEAR THE MOUTH OF THE RIO GRANDE — JOURNEY
THROUGH TEXAS — REACHES LOUISIANA, AND CROSSES
THE MISSISSIPPI; AND IN A FEW DAYS MORE IS AT
HOME, AFTER AN ABSENCE OF FOUR YEARS.

I CONSIDERED my career upon the high seas closed by the
loss of my ship, and had so informed Commodore Barron,
who was our Chief of Bureau in Paris. We had a number of gallant Confederate naval officers, both in England and France,
eager and anxious to go afloat — more than could be provided
with ships—and it would have been ungenerous in me to
accept another command. Besides, my health was broken
down to that degree, that I required absolute quiet, for some
months, before I should again be fit for duty. I, therefore,
threw off all care and responsibility, as soon as I had wound
up the affairs of the *Alabama*, and went up to enjoy the hospitality of my friend Tremlett, at Belsize Park, in London.
Here we arranged for a visit, of a few weeks, to the continent,
and especially to the Swiss mountains, which was carried out
in due time. One other gentleman, an amiable and accomplished sister of my friend Tremlett, and two other ladies,
connections or friends of the family, accompanied us.

We were absent six weeks; landing at Ostend, passing hurriedly through Belgium—not forgetting, however, to visit the
battle-field of Waterloo—stopping a few days at Spa, for the
benefit of the waters, and then passing on to the Rhine; up
that beautiful and historic river to Mayence, and thence to the
Swiss lakes—drawing the first long breath at Geneva, where

we rested a few days. There, reader! I have given you my
European tour in a single paragraph; and as I am writing of
the sea, and of war, and not of the land, or of peace, this is
all the space I can appropriate to it. I must be permitted,
however, to say of my friend Tremlett, that I found him a
veteran traveller, who knew how to smooth all the difficulties
of a journey; and of the ladies of our party, that their cheerfulness, good-humor, and kind attention to me, did quite as
much as the Swiss mountain air toward the restoration of
my health. I must be permitted to make another remark in
connection with this journey. I found a number of exceedingly patriotic, young, able-bodied male Confederates, of a
suitable age for bearing arms, travelling, with or without their
papas and mammas, and boasting of the Confederacy! Most of
these carpet-knights had been in Europe during the whole war.

Returning to London, in the latter days of September, a few
days in advance of my travelling party, I made my preparations for returning to the Confederate States; and on the 3d
of October, 1864, embarked on board the steamer *Tasmanian*,
for Havana *via* St. Thomas. My intention was to pass into
Texas, through the Mexican port of Matamoras. My journey,
by this route, would occupy a little longer time, and be
attended, perhaps, with some discomfort, but I should avoid
the risk of the blockade, which was considerable. The enemy
having resorted, literally, to the starving process, as being the
only one which was likely to put an end to the war, had begun
to burn our towns, lay waste our corn-fields, run off our negroes
and cattle, and was now endeavoring to seal, hermetically, our
ports. He had purchased all kinds of steamers—captured
blockade-runners and others—which he had fitted out as
ships of war, and he now had a fleet little short of five hundred sail. Acting, as before stated, on the principle of abandoning his commerce, he had concentrated all these before the
blockaded ports, in such swarms, that it was next to impossible
for a ship to run in or out, without his permission. I preferred not to fall into the enemy's hands, without the benefit
of a capitulation. The very mention of my name had, as yet,
some such effect upon the Yankee Government as the shaking
of a red flag has before the blood-shot eyes of an infuriated

bull. Mr. Seward gored, and pawed, and threw up the dust; and, above all, bellowed, whenever the vision of the *Alabama* flitted across his brain; and the "sainted Abe" was, in foreign affairs, but his man "Friday."

At St. Thomas we changed steamers, going on board the *Solent* — the transfer of passengers occupying only a few hours. The *Solent* ran down for the coast of Porto Rico, where she landed some passengers; passed thence to the north side of St. Domingo, thence into the Old Bahama Channel, and landed us at Havana, in the last days of October. Here we were compelled to wait, a few days, for a chance vessel to Matamoras, there being no regular packets. This enforced delay was tedious enough, though much alleviated by the companionship of a couple of agreeable fellow-passengers, who had embarked with me at Southampton, and who, like myself, were bound to Mata- moras. One of these was Father Fischer, and the other, Mr. H. N. Caldwell, a Southern merchant. Father Fischer was a German by birth, but had emigrated in early youth to Mexico, where he had become a priest. He was a remarkable man, of com- manding personal appearance, and a well-cultivated and vigor- ous intellect. He spoke half a dozen modern languages, — the English among the rest, with great precision and purity, — and both Caldwell and myself became much attached to him. He afterward played a very important *role* in the affairs of Mexico, becoming Maximilian's confessor, and one of his most trusted counsellors. He was imprisoned for a time, after the fall of the Empire, but was finally released, and has since made his way to Europe, with important papers belonging to the late unfortunate monarch. and will no doubt give us a his- tory of the important episode in Mexican affairs in which he took part.

No other vessel offering, we were compelled to embark in a small Yankee schooner, still redolent of codfish, though wear- ing the English flag, to which she had recently been trans- ferred. This little craft carried us safely across the Gulf of Mexico, after a passage of a week, and landed us at a sea-shore village, at the mouth of the Rio Grande, rejoicing in the dreamy eastern name of Bagdad. So unique was this little village, that I might have fancied it, as its name imported,

really under the rule of Caliphs, but for certain signs of the
Yankee which met my eye. The ubiquity of this people is
marvellous. They scent their prey with the unerring instinct
of the carrion-bird. I had encountered them all over the world,
chasing the omnipotent dollar, notwithstanding the gigantic
war they were carrying on at home; and here was this little
village of Bagdad, on the Texan border, as full of them as an
ant-hill is of ants; and the human ants were quite as busy as
their insect prototypes. Numerous shanties had been constructed on the sands, out of unplaned boards. Some of these
shanties were hotels, some billiard-saloons, and others grog-
shops. The beach was piled with cotton bales going out, and
goods coming in. The stores were numerous, and crowded
with wares. Teamsters cracked their whips in the streets, and
horsemen, booted and spurred, galloped hither and thither.
The whole panorama looked like some magic scene, which
might have been improvised in a night. The population was
as heterogeneous as the dwellings. Whites, blacks, mulat-
tos, and Indians were all mixed. But prominent above all
stood the Yankee. The shanties were his, and the goods
were his. He kept the hotels, marked the billiards, and sold
the grog.

Pretty soon a coach drove up to the door of the *hotel* at
which we were stopping, to take us to Matamoras, a distance
of thirty miles. Here was the Yankee again. The coach had
been built in Troy, New York. The horses were all northern
horses — tall, strong, and gaunt, none of your Mexican mustangs. The Jehu was Yankee, a tall fellow, with fisherman's
boots, and fancy top-hamper. The dried-up little Mexicans
who attended to the horses, harnessing and unharnessing them,
on the road, at the different relay stations, evidently stood in
great awe of him. He took us into Matamoras "*on time*," and
at the end of his journey, cracked his whip, and drew up his
team at the hotel-door, with a flourish that would have done
honor to Mr. Samuel Weller, senior, himself.

As great a revolution had taken place in Matamoras as at
Bagdad. The heretofore quaint old Spanish town presented
the very picture of a busy commercial mart. House-rent was
at an enormous figure; the streets, as well as the stores, were

piled with bales and boxes of merchandise, and every one you met seemed to be running somewhere, intent on business. Ox and mule teams from the Texan side of the river, were busy hauling the precious staple of the Southern States, which put all this commerce in motion, to Bagdad, for shipment; and anchored off that mushroom village, I had counted, as I landed, no less than sixty sail of ships — nearly all of them foreign. Fortunately for all this busy throng, Maximilian reigned supreme in Mexico, and his Lieutenant in Matamoras, General Mejia, gave security and protection to person and property, at the same time that he raised considerable revenue by the imposition of moderate taxes.

Colonel Ford, the commandant at Brownsville, on the opposite side of the river, came over to see me, and toward nightfall I returned with him to that place. We crossed the river in a skiff managed by a Mexican, and as my foot touched, for the first time in four years, the soil of my native South, I experienced, in their full force, the lines of the poet: —

> "Where shall that *land*, that *spot of earth* be found?
> Art thou a man? — a patriot? — look around;
> Oh! thou shalt find, howe'er thy footsteps roam,
> That land *thy* country, and that spot *thy* home!"

There were no hotels at Brownsville, but I was comfortably lodged for the night, with Colonel Beldon, the Collector of the port. The next morning I breakfasted with a large party at a neighboring restaurant, who had assembled thither to welcome me back to my native land; and when the breakfast was over, a coach and four, which was to take me on my way to Shreveport, in Louisiana, drew up at the door. An escort of cavalry had been provided, to accompany me as far as King's Ranch, a point at which the road approaches the coast, and where it was supposed that some of the enemy's gunboats might attempt to ambuscade me. I found, upon entering the coach, in which I was to be the only traveller, that my friends had provided for my journey in true Texan style; my outfit being a stout pair of gray blankets, which were to form my bed on the prairies for the next hundred miles, as we should have to travel that distance before we reached the shelter of a roof; a box containing a dozen bottles of excellent brandy, and cigars at discretion! As the driver cracked his whip, to put his mustangs in motion, and my escort clattered on ahead of me, the crowd who had gathered in the street to see me depart, launched me upon the prairie, with three hearty cheers, such as only Texan throats can give.

It so happened, that my *major-domo* for the journey, Sergeant ——, was the same who had conducted my friend, Colonel Freemantle, over this route, some two years before. I found him the same invaluable travelling companion. His lunch-baskets were always well filled, he knew everybody along the road, was unsurpassed at roasting a venison steak before a camp-fire on a forked stick, and made a capital cup of coffee. I missed the Judge, whom Freemantle so humorously describes, but I found a good many judges on the road, who might sit for his portrait. And now, for want of space, I must treat this journey as I did my European tour, give it to the reader in a paragraph. We were fourteen days on the road; passing through San Patricio on the Nueces, Gonzales on the Guadalupe, Houston, Hempstead, Navasota, Huntsville, Rusk, Henderson, and Marshall, arriving on the 27th of November at Shreveport. I was received, everywhere, with enthusiasm by the warm-hearted, brave Texans, the hotels being all thrown open to me, free of expense, and salutes of artillery greeting my entrance into the towns. I was frequently compelled to make short speeches to the people, merely that they might hear, as they said, "how the pirate talked;" and, I fear, I drank a good many more mint-juleps than were good for me. At table I was always seated on the right hand of the "land-lady," and I was frequently importuned by a bevy of blooming lasses, to tell them "how I did the Yankees." Glorious Texas! what if thou art a little too much given to the Bowie-knife and revolver, and what if grass-widows are somewhat frequent in some of thy localities, thou art all right at heart! Liberty burns with a pure flame on thy prairies, and the day will yet come when thou wilt be free. Thy fate, thus far, has been a hard one. In a single generation thou hast changed thy political condition four times. When I first knew thee, thou wast a Mexican province. You then became an independent State.

In an evil hour you were beguiled into accepting the fatal embrace of the Yankee. Learning your mistake, ere long, you united your fortunes with those of the Confederate States, in the hope again to be free. You did what it was in the power of mortals to do, but the Fates were adverse, and you have again been dragged down into worse than Mexican bondage. Bide thy time! Thou art rapidly filling up with population. Thou wilt soon become an empire in thyself, and the day is not far distant, when thou mayest again strike for freedom!

At Shreveport, I was hospitably entertained at the mansion of Colonel Williamson, serving on the staff of the commanding general of the Trans-Mississippi Department, Kirby Smith. The Mayor and a deputation of the Councils waited on me, and tendered me a public dinner, but I declined. I remained with Colonel Williamson a couple of days, and the reader may imagine how agreeable this relaxation, in comfortable quarters, was to me, after a journey of fourteen consecutive days and nights, in a stage-coach, through a rough, and comparatively wild country. Governor Allen was making Shreveport the temporary seat of government of Louisiana, and I had the pleasure of making his acquaintance, and dining with him, in company with General Smith and his staff. The Governor was not only a genial, delightful companion, but a gallant soldier, who had rendered good service to the Confederacy at the head of his regiment. He had been terribly wounded, and was still hobbling about on crutches. He seemed to be the idol of the people of his State. He was as charitable and kind-hearted as brave, and the needy soldier, or soldier's wife, never left his presence without the aid they came to seek.

My object in taking Shreveport in my route, instead of striking for the Red River, some distance below, was to meet my son, Major O. J. Semmes, who, I had been informed at Brownsville, was serving in this part of Louisiana. In the beginning of the war he withdrew from West Point, where he was within a year of graduating, and offered his sword to his State — Alabama. I had not seen him since. He was now a major of artillery, commanding a battalion in General Buckner's army, stationed at Alexandria. Thither I now directed my course. The river being too low for boating, I was forced to make another land journey. The General kindly put an ambulance at my disposal, and my host, with the forethought of a soldier, packed me a basket of provisions. My friend and travelling companion, viz., the Jehu, who was to drive me, was an original. He was from Ohio, and had served throughout the war as a private soldier in the Confederate army. He had been in a good many fights and skirmishes, and was full of anecdote. If he had an antipathy in the world, it was against the Yankee, and nothing gave him half so much pleasure, as to "fight his battles o'er again." As I had a journey of four or five days before me — the distance being 140 miles over execrable roads — the fellow was invaluable to me. We passed through several of the localities where General Banks had been so shamefully beaten by General Dick Taylor, — at Mansfield, Pleasant Hill, and Monett's Ferry. The fields were still strewn with the carcasses of animals; a few, unmarked hillocks, here and there, showed where soldiers had been buried; and the rent and torn timber marked the course of the cannon-balls that had carried death to either side. The Vandals, in their retreat, had revenged themselves on the peaceful inhabitants, and every few miles the charred remains of a dwelling told where some family had been unhoused, and turned into the fields by the torch.

At Alexandria, I was kindly invited by General Buckner to become his guest during my stay, and he sent a courier at once to inform my son, who was encamped a few miles below the town, of my arrival. The latter came to see me the same afternoon. I remained in the hospitable quarters of the General a week before the necessary arrangements could be made for my crossing the Mississippi. The enemy being in full possession of this river by means of his gunboats, it was a matter of some little management to cross in safety. The trans-Mississippi mails to Richmond had been sent over, however, quite regularly, under the personal superintendence of a young officer, detailed for the purpose, and the General was kind enough to arrange for my crossing with this gentleman. The news of my passing through Texas had reached the enemy at New Orleans, as we learned by his newspapers, and great vigilance had been enjoined on his gunboats to intercept me, if possible. Our arrangements being completed, I left Alexandria on the 10th of December, accompanied by my son, who had obtained a short leave of absence for the purpose of visiting his home, and reached the little village of Evergreen the next day. Arrived at this point, we were joined by our companions of the mail service, and on the 13th we crossed both the Red and Mississippi Rivers in safety.

The journey through the swamps, leading to these rivers, was unique. We performed it on horseback, pursuing mere bridle-paths and cattle-tracks, in single file, like so many Indians. Our way sometimes led us through a forest of gigantic trees, almost entirely devoid of under-growth, and resembling very much, though after a wild fashion, the park scenery of England. At other times we would plunge into a dense, tangled brake, where the interlaced grape and other vines threatened every moment, to drag us from our saddles. The whole was a drowned country, and impassable during the season of rains. It was now low water, and as we rode along, the high-water marks on the trees were visible, many feet above our heads. From this description of the country, the reader will see how impossible it was for artillery or cavalry, or even infantry, to operate on the banks of these rivers, during a greater part of the year. Except at a few points, the enemy's gunboats were almost as secure from attack as they would have been, on the high seas. Occasionally, we had to swim a deep bayou, whose waters looked as black as those of the Stygian Lake; but if the bayou was wide, as well as deep, we more frequently dismounted, stripped our horses, and surrounding them, and shouting at them, made them take the water in a drove, and swim over by themselves. We then crossed in skiffs, which the mail-men had provided for the purpose, and caught and resaddled our horses for a fresh mount.

We reached the bank of the Mississippi just before dark. There were two of the enemy's gunboats anchored in the river, at a distance of about three miles apart. As remarked in another place, the enemy had converted every sort of a water craft, into a ship of war, and now had them in such number, that he was enabled to police the river in its entire length, without the necessity of his boats being out of sight of each other's smoke. The officers of these river craft were mostly volunteers from the merchant service, whose commissions would expire with the war, and a greater set of predatory rascals was, perhaps, never before collected in the history of any government. They robbed the plantations, and demoralized them by trade, at the same time. Our people were hard pressed for the necessaries of life, and a constant traffic was being carried on with them, by these armed river steamers, miscalled ships of war.

It would not do, of course, for us to attempt the passage of the river, until after dark; and so we held ourselves under cover of the forest, until the proper moment, and then embarked in a small skiff, sending back the greater part of our escort. Our boat was scarcely able to float the numbers that were packed into her. Her gunwales were no more than six inches above the water's edge. Fortunately for us, however, the night was still, and the river smooth, and we pulled over without accident. As we shot within the shadows of the opposite bank, our conductor, before landing, gave a shrill whistle to ascertain whether all was right. The proper response came directly, from those who were to meet us, and in a moment more, we leaped ôn shore among friends. We found spare horses awaiting us, and my son and myself slept that night under the hospitable roof of Colonel Rose. The next morning the colonel sent us to Woodville, in his carriage, and in four or five days more, we were in Mobile, and I was at home again, after an absence of four years!

CHAPTER LVII.

AUTHOR SETS OUT FOR RICHMOND—IS TWO WEEKS IN
MAKING THE JOURNEY—INTERVIEW WITH PRESIDENT
DAVIS; WITH GENERAL LEE—AUTHOR IS APPOINTED
A REAR-ADMIRAL, AND ORDERED TO COMMAND THE
JAMES RIVER SQUADRON—ASSUMES COMMAND; CON-
DITION OF THE FLEET—GREAT DEMORALIZATION—
THE ENEMY'S ARMIES GRADUALLY INCREASING—
LEE'S LINES BROKEN.

I TELEGRAPHED my arrival, immediately, to the Secre
tary of the Navy at Richmond, informing him of my intention to proceed to that capital after resting for a few days.
The following reply came over the wires, in the course of a
few hours. "Congratulate you, on your safe arrival. When
ready to come on, regard this as an order to report to the
Department." I did not, of course, dally long at home. The
enemy was pressing us too hard for me to think of sitting
down in inglorious ease, so long as it was possible that I
might be of service. At all events, it was my duty to present myself to the Government, and see if it had any commands for me. Accordingly, on the 2d of January, 1865, I
put myself *en route* for Richmond. I was two weeks making
my way to the capital of the Confederacy, owing the many
breaks which had been made in the roads by raiding parties
of the enemy, and by Sherman's march through Georgia.
Poor Georgia! she had suffered terribly during this Vandal
march of conflagration and pillage, and I found her people
terribly demoralized. I stopped a day in Columbia, the
beautiful capital of South Carolina, afterward so barbarously
burned by a drunken and disorderly soldiery, with no officer to raise his hand to stay the conflagration. Passing on,

as soon as some temporary repairs could be made on a break in the road, ahead of me, I reached Richmond, without further stoppages, and was welcomed at his house, by my friend and relative, the Hon. Thomas J. Semmes, a senator in the Confederate Congress from the State of Louisiana.

I had thus travelled all the way from the eastern boundary of Mexico, to Richmond, by land, a journey, which, perhaps, has seldom been performed. In this long and tedious journey, through the entire length of the Confederacy, I had been painfully struck with the changed aspect of things, since I had left the country in the spring of 1861. Plantations were ravaged, slaves were scattered, and the country was suffering terribly for the want of the most common necessaries of life. Whole districts of country had been literally laid waste by the barbarians who had invaded us. The magnificent valley of the Red River, down which, as the reader has seen, I had recently travelled, had been burned and pillaged for the distance of a hundred and fifty miles. Neither Alaric, nor Attila ever left such a scene of havoc and desolation in his rear. Demoniac Yankee hate had been added to the thirst for plunder. Sugar-mills, saw-mills, salt-works, and even the grist-mills which ground the daily bread for families, had been laid in ashes — their naked chimneys adding ghastliness to the picture. Reeling, drunken soldiers passed in and out of dwellings, plundering and insulting their inmates; and if disappointed in the amount of their plunder, or resisted, applied the torch in revenge. Many of these miscreants were foreigners, incapable of speaking the English language. The few dwellings that were left standing, looked like so many houses of mourning. Once the seats of hospitality and refinement, and the centres of thrifty plantations, with a contented and happy laboring population around them, they were now shut up and abandoned. There was neither human voice in the hall, nor neigh of steed in the pasture. The tenantless negro cabins told the story of the war. The Yankee had liberated the slave, and armed him to make war upon his former master. The slaves who had not been enlisted in the Federal armies, were wandering, purposeless, about the country, in squads, thieving, famishing, and dying. This was the charac-

ter of the war our *brethren* of the North—God save the mark
—were making upon us.

To add to the heart-sickening features of the picture, our
own people had become demoralized! Men, generally, seemed
to have given up the cause as lost, and to have set themselves
at work, like wreckers, to save as much as possible from the
sinking ship. The civilians had betaken themselves to speculation and money-getting, and the soldiers to drinking and debauchery. Such, in brief, was the picture which presented itself to my eyes as I passed through the Confederacy. The
Alabama had gone to her grave none too soon. If she had not
been buried with the honors of war, with the howling winds
of the British Channel to sing her requiem, she might soon
have been handed over to the exultant Yankee, to be exhibited
at Boston, as a trophy of the war.

My first official visit in Richmond was, of course, to the
President. I found him but little changed, in personal appearance, since I had parted with him in Montgomery, the then
seat of government, in April, 1861. But he was evidently
deeply impressed with the critical state of the country, though
maintaining an outward air of cheerfulness and serenity. I explained to him briefly, what, indeed, he already knew too well, the
loss of my ship. He was kind enough to say that, though he
deeply regretted her loss, he knew that I had acted for the
best, and that he had nothing with which to reproach me. I
dined with him on a subsequent day. There was only one
other guest present. Mrs. Davis was more impressed with
events than the President. With her womanly instinct, she
already saw the handwriting on the wall. But though the
coming calamity would involve her household in ruin, she
maintained her self-possession and cheerfulness. The Congress, which was in session, received me with a distinction
which I had little merited. Both houses honored me by a
vote of thanks for my services, and invited me to a privileged
seat on the floor. The legislature of Virginia, also in session,
extended to me the same honors.

As soon as I could command a leisure moment, I paid General Lee a visit, at his headquarters near Petersburg, and spent
a night with him. I had served with him in the Mexican

war. We discussed together the critical state of the country, and of his army,—we were now near the end of January, 1865,—and I thought the grand old chieftain and Christian gentleman seemed to foreshadow, in his conversation—more by manner than by words—the approaching downfall of the cause for which we were both struggling. I had come to him, I told him, to speak of what I had seen of the people, and of the army, in my transit across the country, and to say to him, that unless prompt measures could be devised to put an end to the desertions that were going on among our troops, our cause must inevitably be lost. He did not seem to be at all surprised at the revelations I made. He knew all about the condition of the country, civil and military, but seemed to feel himself powerless to prevent the downward tendency of things. And he was right. It was no longer in the power of any one man to save the country. The body-politic was already dead. The people themselves had given up the contest, and this being the case, no army could do more than retard the catastrophe for a few months. Besides, his army was, itself, melting away. That very night—as I learned the next morning, at the breakfast table—160 men deserted in a body! It was useless to attempt to shoot deserters, when demoralization had gone to this extent.

After I had been in Richmond a few weeks, the President was pleased to nominate me to the Senate as a rear-admiral. My nomination was unanimously confirmed, and, in a few days afterward, I was appointed to the command of the James River fleet. My commission ran as follows:—

CONFEDERATE STATES OF AMERICA,
NAVY DEPARTMENT, RICHMOND, February 10, 1865.

REAR-ADMIRAL RAPHAEL SEMMES.

SIR:—You are hereby informed that the President has appointed you, by and with the advice of the Senate, a *Rear-Admiral*, in the Provisional Navy of the Confederate States, "*for gallant and meritorious conduct, in command of the steam-sloop Alabama.*" You are requested to signify your acceptance, or non-acceptance of this appointment.

S. R. MALLORY,
Secretary of the Navy.

An old and valued friend, Commodore J. K. Mitchell, had been in command of the James River fleet, and I displaced him very reluctantly. He had organized and disciplined the fleet, and had accomplished with it all that was possible, viz., the protection of Richmond by water. I assumed my command on the 18th of February, 1865. My fleet consisted of three iron-clads and five wooden gunboats. I found my old first lieutenant, Kell, who had preceded me to Richmond, and been made a commander, in command of one of the iron-clads, but he was soon obliged to relinquish his command, on account of failing health. As reorganized, the fleet stood as follows : —

Virginia, iron-clad, flag-ship, four guns, Captain Dunnington.

Richmond, iron-clad, four guns, Captain Johnson.

Fredericksburg, iron-clad, four guns, Captain Glassel.

Hampton, wooden, two guns, Captain Wilson, late of the *Alabama*.

Nansemond, wooden, two guns, Captain Butt.

Roanoke, wooden, two guns, Captain Pollock.

Beaufort, wooden, two guns, Captain Wyatt.

Torpedo, wooden, one gun, Captain Roberts.

The fleet was assisted, in the defence of the river, by several shore batteries, in command of naval officers; as Drury's Bluff; Battery Brooke; Battery Wood, and Battery Semmes — the whole under the command of my old friend, Commodore John R. Tucker.

I soon had the mortification to find that the fleet was as much demoralized as the army. Indeed, with the exception of its principal officers, and about half a dozen sailors in each ship, its *personnel* was drawn almost entirely from the army. The movements of the ships being confined to the head-waters of a narrow river, they were but little better than prison-ships. Both men and officers were crowded into close and uncomfortable quarters, without the requisite space for exercise. I remedied this, as much as possible, by sending squads on shore, to drill and march on the river-bank. They were on half rations, and with but a scanty supply of clothing. Great discontent and restlessness prevailed. Constant applications were coming to me for leaves of absence — almost every one having some story to tell of a sick or destitute family. I was obliged, of course, to resist all these appeals. "The enemy was thundering at the gates," and not a man could be spared. Desertion was the consequence. Sometimes an entire boat's crew would run off, leaving the officer to find his way on board the best he might. The strain upon them had been too great. It was scarcely to be expected of men, of the class of those who usually form the rank and file of ships' companies, that they would rise above their natures, and sacrifice themselves by slow but sure degrees, in any cause, however holy. The visions of home and fireside, and freedom from restraint were too tempting to be resisted. The general understanding, that the collapse of the Confederacy was at hand, had its influence with some of the more honorable of them. They reasoned that their desertion would be but an anticipation of the event by a few weeks.

To add to the disorder, the "Union element," as it was called, began to grow bolder. This element was composed mainly of Northern-born men, who had settled among us before the war. In the height of the war, when the Southern States were still strong, and when independence was not only possible, but probable, these men pretended to be good Southerners. The Puritan leaven, which was in their natures, was kept carefully concealed. Hypocrisy was now no longer necessary. Many of these men were preachers of the various denominations, and schoolmasters. These white-cravatted gentlemen now sprang into unusual activity. Every mail brought long and artfully written letters from some of these scoundrels, tempting my men to desert. Some of these letters came under my notice, and if I could have gotten hold of the writers, I should have been glad to give them the benefit of a short shrift, and one of my yard-arms. If I had had my fleet upon the sea, it would have been an easy matter to restore its discipline, but my ships were, in fact, only so many tents, into which entered freely all the bad influences of which I speak. I was obliged to perform guard-boat duty on the river, and picket duty on shore, and these duties gave my men all the opportunities of escape that they desired.

With regard to the defence of Richmond by water, I felt

quite secure.   No fleet of the enemy could have passed my
three iron-clads, moored across the stream, in the only available channel, with obstructions below me, which would hold
it under my fire, and that of the naval batteries on shore by
which I was flanked.   Indeed, the enemy, seeing the hopeless-
ness of approach by water, had long since given up the idea.
The remainder of the winter passed slowly and tediously
enough.   A few months earlier, and I might have had something to occupy me.   For a long time, there was no more than
a single iron-clad in the lower James, the enemy being busy
with Charleston and Wilmington.   An attack on City Point,
Grant's base of operations, and whence he drew all his supplies,
would have been quite practicable.   If the store-houses at that
place could have been burned, there is no telling what might
have been the consequences.   But now, Charleston and Wilmington having fallen, and the enemy having no further use
for his iron-clad fleet, on the coasts of North and South Carolina, he had concentrated the whole of it on the lower James,
under the command of Admiral Porter, who, as the reader has
seen, had chased me, so quixotically, in the old frigate *Powhat-
tan*, in the commencement of the war.   At first, this concentra-
tion looked like a preparation for an attempted ascent of the
river, but if any attempt of the kind was ever entertained by
Porter, he had the good sense, when he came to view the
"situation," to abandon it.

I usually visited the Navy Department, during this anxious
period, once a week, to confer with the Secretary on the state
of my fleet, and the attitude of the enemy, and to receive any
orders or suggestions that the Government might have to
make.   Mr. Mallory was kind enough, on these occasions, to
give me *carte blanche*, and leave me pretty much to myself.
At length the winter passed, and spring set in.   The winds
and the sun of March began to dry the roads, and put them in
good order for military operations, and every one anticipated
stirring events.   As I sat in my twilight cabin, on board the
Virginia, and pored over the map of North Carolina, and
plotted upon it, from day to day, the approaches of Sherman,
the prospect seemed gloomy enough.   As before remarked,
Charleston and Wilmington had fallen.   With the latter, we

had lost our last blockade-running port. Our ports were now all hermetically sealed. The anaconda had, at last, wound his fatal folds around us. With fields desolated at home, and all supplies from abroad cut off, starvation began to stare us in the face. Charleston was evacuated on the 17th of February —General Hardee having no more than time to get his troops out of the city, and push on ahead of Sherman, and join General Joseph E. Johnson, who had again been restored to command. Fort Anderson, the last defence of Wilmington, fell on the 19th of the same month. Sherman was, about this time, at Columbia, South Carolina, where he forever disgraced himself by burning, or *permitting to be burned*, it matters not which, that beautiful city, which had already surrendered to his arms. The opportunity was too good to be lost. The Puritan was at last in the city of the cavalier. The man of ruder habits and coarser civilization, was in the presence of the more refined gentleman whom he had envied and hated for generations. The ignoble passions of race-hatred and revenge were gratified, and Massachusetts, through the agency of a brutal and debauched soldiery, had put her foot upon the neck of prostrate South Carolina! This was humiliation indeed! The coarse man of mills and manufactures had at last found entrance as a master into the halls of the South Carolina planter!

It was generally expected that Sherman would move upon Charlotte, North Carolina, one of the most extensive depots of the South, and thence to Danville, and so on to Richmond, to unite his forces with those of Grant. There was nothing to oppose him. In ten days at the farthest, after burning Columbia, he could have effected a junction with Grant before Petersburg. But the "great commander" seemed suddenly to have lost his courage, and to the astonishment of every one, soon after passing Winsboro', North Carolina, which lies on the road to Charlotte, he swung his army off to the right, and marched in the direction of Fayetteville! His old antagonist, Johnston, was endeavoring to gather together the broken remains of the Army of the Tennessee, and he was afraid of him. His object now was to put himself in communication with Schofield, who had landed at Wilmington and at Newbern with a large force, and establish a new base of operations at these points. He would be safe here, as his troops could be fed, and in case of disaster, he could fall back upon the sea, and upon Porter's gunboats. He effected the contemplated junction with Schofield, at Goldsboro', North Carolina, on the 21st of March. He had not touched any of Lee's communications with his depots since leaving Winsboro'; the destruction of which communications Grant had so much at heart, and which had been the chief object of his — Sherman's — "great march." At Goldsboro' he was still 150 miles from Grant's lines, and he took no further part in the campaign.

His junction with Schofield had not been effected without disaster. At Kinston, Bragg gained a victory over Schofield, utterly routing him, and taking 1500 prisoners; and at Bentonsville, Johnston checked, and gained some advantage over Sherman. As the reader is supposed to be looking over the map with me, we will now stick a pin in the point representing Goldsboro', and throw Sherman and Schofield out of view.

In the latter part of March, Sheridan, having overrun Early's small force, in the valley of the Shenandoah, found himself at liberty to join General Grant. He brought with him from 10,000 to 12,000 excellent cavalry. Grant's army was thus swollen to 160,000 men. Adding Sherman's and Schofield's forces of 100,000, we have 260,000. In the meantime, Lee's half-starved, ragged army, had dwindled to 33,000. With this small number of men he was compelled to guard an intrenched line of forty miles in length, extending from the north side of the James River, below Richmond, to Hatcher's Run, south of Petersburg. As a mere general, he would have abandoned the hopeless task long ago, extricating his army, and throwing it into the field, but *cui bono?* With Virginia in the enemy's possession, with a *beaten people*, and an army fast melting away by desertion, could the war be continued with any hope of success? If we could not defend ourselves before Richmond, could we defend ourselves anywhere? That was the question.

Grant's object was to force Lee's right in the vicinity of Hatcher's Run; but he masked this intention, as much as possible, by occasionally threatening the whole line. I had frequent opportunity, from the deck of my flag-ship, to witness terrible artillery conflicts where nobody was killed. Suddenly, on a still night, all the enemy's batteries would be ablaze, and the heavens aroar with his firing. The expenditure of powder was enormous, and must have gladdened the hearts of the Yankee contractors. I would sometimes be aroused from slumber, and informed that a great battle was going on. On one or two occasions, I made some slight preparations for defence, myself, not knowing but Porter might be fool enough to come up the river, under the inspiration of this powder-burning, and booming of cannon. But it all amounted to nothing more than Chinese grimaces, and "stink-pots," resorted to to throw Lee off his guard, and prevent him from withdrawing men from his left, to reinforce his right.

The final and successful assault of Grant was not long delayed. The lines in the vicinity of Petersburg having been weakened, by the necessity of withdrawing troops to defend Lee's extreme right, resting now on a point called the Five Forks, Grant, on the morning of Sunday, the 2d of April, made a vigorous assault upon them, and broke them. Lee's army was uncovered, and Richmond was no longer tenable!

CHAPTER LVIII

THE EVACUATION OF RICHMOND BY THE ARMY — THE
DESTRUCTION OF THE JAMES RIVER FLEET — THE
SAILORS OF THE FLEET CONVERTED INTO SOLDIERS —
THEIR HELPLESS CONDITION WITHOUT ANY MEANS OF
TRANSPORTATION — THE CONFLAGRATION OF RICHMOND
AND THE ENTRY OF THE ENEMY INTO THE CONFED-
ERATE CAPITAL — THE AUTHOR IMPROVISES A RAIL-
ROAD TRAIN, AND ESCAPES IN IT WITH HIS COMMAND,
TO DANVILLE, VA.

AS I was sitting down to dinner, about four o'clock, on the
afternoon of the disastrous day mentioned in the last
chapter, on board my flag-ship, the *Virginia*, one of the small
steamers of my fleet came down from Richmond, having on
board a special messenger from the Navy Department. Upon
being introduced into my cabin, the messenger presented me
with a sealed package. Up to this time, I was ignorant, of
course, of what had occurred at Petersburg. I broke the seal
and read as follows : —

> CONFEDERATE STATES OF AMERICA, }
> EXECUTIVE OFFICE, RICHMOND, VA., April 2, 1865. }
>
> REAR-ADMIRAL RAPHAEL SEMMES,
> *Commanding James River Squadron.*
>
> SIR : — General Lee advises the Government to withdraw from
> this city, and the officers will leave this evening, accordingly. I pre-
> sume that General Lee has advised you of this, and of his move-
> ments, and made suggestions as to the disposition to be made of
> your squadron. He withdraws upon his lines toward Danville, this
> night ; and unless otherwise directed by General Lee, upon you is
> devolved the duty of destroying your ships, this night, and with
> all the forces under your command, joining General Lee. Confer
> with him, if practicable, before destroying them. Let your people
> be rationed, as far as possible, for the march, and armed and

equipped for duty in the field. Very respectfully, your obedient servant,

S. R. MALLORY, *Secretary of the Navy.*

This was rather short notice. Richmond was to be evacuated during the night, during which I was to burn my ships, accoutre and provision my men, and join General Lee! But I had become used to emergencies, and was not dismayed. 1 signalled all my captains to come on board, and communicated to them the intelligence I had received, and concerted with them the programme of the night's work. It was not possible to attempt anything before dark, without exciting the suspicions of the enemy, as we were no more than four or five miles from his lines; and I enjoined upon my commanders the necessity of keeping their secret, until the proper moment for action should arrive. The sun was shining brightly, the afternoon was calm, and nature was just beginning to put on her spring attire. The fields were green with early grass, the birds were beginning to twitter, and the ploughman had already broken up his fields for planting his corn. I looked abroad upon the landscape, and contrasted the peace and quiet of nature, so heedless of man's woes, with the disruption of a great Government, and the ruin of an entire people which were at hand!

So unsuspicious were the Government subordinates, of what was going on, that the flag-of-truce boats were still plying between Richmond, and the enemy's head-quarters, a few miles below us, on the river, carrying backward and forward exchanged prisoners. As those boats would pass us, coming up the river, filled to overflowing with our poor fellows just released from Yankee prisons, looking wan and hollow-eyed, the prisoners would break into the most enthusiastic cheering as they passed my flag. It seemed to welcome them home. They little dreamed, that it would be struck that night, forever, and the fleet blown into the air; that their own fetters had been knocked off in vain, and that they were to pass, henceforth, under the rule of the hated Yankee. I was sick at heart as I listened to those cheers, and reflected upon the morrow.

General Lee had failed to give me any notice of his disaster, or of what his intentions were. As mine was an entirely independent command, he, perhaps, rightly considered, that it was the duty of the Executive Government to do this. Still, in accordance with the expressed wishes of Mr. Mallory, I endeavored to communicate with him; sending an officer on shore to the signal station, at Drury's Bluff, for the purpose. No response came, however, to our telegrams, and night having set in, I paid no further attention to the movements of the army. I plainly saw that it was a case of *sauve qui peut*, and that I must take care of myself. I was to make another *Alabama*-plunge into the sea, and try my luck. Accordingly, when night drew her friendly curtain between the enemy and myself, I got all my ships under way, and ran up to Drury's Bluff. It was here I designed to blow up the iron-clads, throw their crews on board the wooden gunboats, and proceed in the latter to Manchester, opposite Richmond, on my way to join General Lee. Deeming secrecy of great importance to the army, in its attempted escape from its lines, my first intention was to *sink* my fleet quietly, instead of blowing it up, as the explosions would give the enemy notice of what was going on. The reader may judge of my surprise, when, in the course of an hour or two after dark, I saw the whole horizon, on the north side of the James, glowing with fires of burning quarters, *materiel,* &c., lighted by our own troops, as they successively left their intrenchments! Concealment on my part was no longer necessary or indeed practicable.

I now changed my determination and decided upon burning my fleet. My officers and men worked like beavers. There were a thousand things to be done. The sailor was leaving the homestead which he had inhabited for several months. Arms had to be served out, provisions gotten up out of the hold, and broken into such packages, as the sailors could carry. Hammocks had to be unlashed, and the blankets taken out, and rolled up as compactly as possible. Haversacks and canteens had to be improvised. These various operations oc cupied us until a late hour. It was between two and three o'clock in the morning, before the crews of the iron-clads were all safely embarked on board the wooden gunboats, and the iron-clads were well on fire. My little squadron of wooden boats now moved off up the river, by the glare of the burning iron-clads. They had not proceeded far, before an explosion, like the shock of an earthquake, took place, and the air was filled with missiles. It was the blowing up of the *Virginia*, my late flag-ship. The spectacle was grand beyond description. Her shell-rooms had been full of loaded shells. The explosion of the magazine threw all these shells, with their fuses lighted, into the air. The fuses were of different lengths, and as the shells exploded by twos and threes, and by the dozen, the pyrotechnic effect was very fine. The explosion shook the houses in Richmond, and must have waked the echoes of the night for forty miles around.

There are several bridges spanning the James between Drury's Bluff and the city, and at one of these we were detained an hour, the draw being down to permit the passage of some of the troops from the north side of the river, who had lighted the bonfires of which I have spoken. Owing to this delay, the sun—a glorious, unclouded sun, as if to mock our misfortunes—was now rising over Richmond. Some windows, which fronted to the east, were all aglow with his rays, mimicking the real fires that were already breaking out in various parts of the city. In the lower part of the city, the School-ship *Patrick Henry* was burning, and some of the houses near the Navy Yard were on fire. But higher up was the principal scene of the conflagration. Entire blocks were on fire here, and a dense canopy of smoke, rising high in the still morning air, was covering the city as with a pall. The rear-guard of our army had just crossed, as I landed my fleet at Manchester, and the bridges were burning in their rear. The Tredegar Iron Works were on fire, and continual explosions of loaded shell stored there were taking place. In short, the scene cannot be described by mere words, but the reader may conceive a tolerable idea of it, if he will imagine himself to be looking on Pandemonium broken loose.

The population was in a great state of alarm. Hundreds of men and women had sought refuge on the Manchester side, in the hope of getting away, by some means or other, they knew not how. I was, myself, about the most helpless man in the whole crowd. I had just tumbled on shore, with their bags and baggage, 500 sailors, incapable of marching a dozen miles without becoming foot-sore, and without any means,

KELLY, PIET & CO. PUBLISHERS.

LITH. BY A. HOEN & CO. BALTO.

The Blowing up of the James River Fleet, on the night of the Evacuation of Richmond.

whatever, of transportation being provided for them. I had not so much as a pack-mule to carry a load of provisions. I was on foot, myself, in the midst of my men. A current of horsemen, belonging to our retreating column, was sweeping past me, but there was no horse for me to mount. It was every man for himself, and d—l take the hindmost. Some of the young cavalry rascals—lads of eighteen or twenty— as they passed, jibed and joked with my old salts, asking them how they liked navigating the land, and whether they did not expect to anchor in Fort Warren pretty soon? The spectacle presented by my men was, indeed, rather a ludicrous one; loaded down, as they were, with pots, and pans, and mess-kettles, bags of bread, and chunks of salted pork, sugar, tea, tobacco, and pipes. It was as much as they could do to stagger under their loads—marching any distance seemed out of the question. As I reviewed my "troops," after they had been drawn up by my captains, who were now all become colonels, I could not but repeat to myself Mr. Mallory's last words— "You will join General Lee, in the field, with all your forces."

Yes; here were my "forces," but where, the d—l, was General Lee, and how was I to join him? If I had had the Secretary of the Navy, on foot, by the side of me, I rather think this latter question would have puzzled him.

But there was no time to be lost, — I must do something. The first thing, of course, after landing my men, was to burn my wooden gunboats. This was done. They were fired, and shoved off from the landing, and permitted to float down the stream. I then "put my column in motion," and we "marched" a distance of several squares, blinded by the dust kicked up by those vagabonds on horseback, before mentioned. When we came in sight of the railroad depot, I halted, and inquired of some of the fugitives who were rushing by, about the trains. "The trains!" said they, in astonishment at my question; "the last train left at daylight this morning — it was filled with the civil officers of the Government." Notwithstanding this answer, I moved my command up to the station and workshops, to satisfy myself by a personal inspection. It was well that I did so, as it saved my command from the capture that impended over it. I found it quite true, that the "last train" had departed; and, also, that all the railroad-men had either run off in the train, or hidden themselves out of view. There was no one in charge of anything, and no one who knew anything. But there was some material lying around me; and, with this, I resolved to set up railroading on my own account. Having a dozen and more steam-engineers along with me, from my late fleet, I was perfectly independent of the assistance of the alarmed railroad-men, who had taken to flight.

A pitiable scene presented itself, upon our arrival at the station. Great numbers had flocked thither, in the hope of escape; frightened men, despairing women, and crying children. Military patients had hobbled thither from the hospitals; civil employees of the Government, who had missed the "last train," by being a little too late, had come to remedy their negligence; and a great number of other citizens, who were anxious to get out of the presence of the hated Yankee, had rushed to the station, they scarcely knew why. These people had crowded into, and on the top of, a few straggling passenger-cars, that lay uncoupled along the track, in seeming expectation that some one was to come, in due time, and take them off. There was a small engine lying also on the track, but there was no fire in its furnace, no fuel with which to make a fire, and no one to manage it. Such was the condition of affairs when I "deployed" my "forces" upon the open square, and "grounded arms,"—the butts of my rifles not ringing on the ground quite as harmoniously as I could have desired. Soldiering was new to Jack; however, he would do better by-and-by.

My first move was to turn all these wretched people I have described out of the cars. Many plaintive appeals were made to me by the displaced individuals, but my reply to them all was, that it was better for an unarmed citizen to fall into the hands of the enemy, than a soldier with arms in his hands. The cars were then drawn together and coupled, and my own people placed in them. We next took the engine in hand. A body of my marine "sappers and miners" were set at work to pull down a picket fence, in front of one of the dwellings, and chop it into firewood. An engineer and firemen were detailed for the locomotive, and in a very few minutes, we had the steam hissing from 'ts boiler. I now permitted as many of the frightened citizens as could find places to clamber upon the cars. All being in readiness, with the triumphant air of a man who had overcome a great difficulty, and who felt as if he might snap his fingers at the Yankees once more, I gave the order to "go ahead." But this was easier said than done. The little locomotive started at a snail's pace, and drew us creepingly along, until we reached a slightly ascending grade, which occurs almost immediately after leaving the station. Here it came to a dead halt. The firemen stirred their fires, the engineer turned on all his steam, the engine panted and struggled and screamed, but all to no purpose. We were effectually stalled. Our little iron horse was incompetent to do the work which had been required of it. Here was a predicament!

We were still directly opposite the city of Richmond, and in full view of it, for the track of the road runs some distance up the river-bank, before it bends away westward. Amid flames and smoke and tumult and disorder, the enemy's hosts were pouring into the streets of the proud old capital. Long lines of cavalry and artillery and infantry could be seen, moving like a huge serpent through the streets, and winding their way to State-House Square. As a crowning insult, a regiment of negro cavalry, wild with savage delight at the thought of triumphing over their late masters, formed a prominent feature in the grand procession. Alongside of the black savage marched the white savage — worthy compeers! nay, scarcely; the black savage, under the circumstances, was the more worthy of respect of the two. The prophecy of Patrick Henry was fulfilled; the very halls, in which he had thundered forth the prophecy, were in possession of the "stranger," against whom he had warned his countrymen! My temporary safety lay in two circumstances: first, the enemy was so drunk with his success, that he had no eyes for any one but himself and the population of the proud city of Richmond which he was seeking to abase; and secondly, the bridges leading across the river were all on fire. Whilst I was pondering what was best to be done, whether I should uncouple a portion of the train, and permit the rest to escape, an engineer came running to me to say that he had discovered another engine, which the absconding railroad people had hidden away in the recesses of their work-shops. The new engine was rolled out immedi-

ately, steam raised on it in a few minutes, and by the aid of
the two engines, we gave our train, with the indifferent fuel
we had, a speed of five or six miles per hour, until we reached
the first wood-pile.   Here getting hold of some better fuel, we
fired up with better effect, and went thundering, with the usual
speed, on our course.

It was thus, after I had, in fact, been abandoned by the
Government and the army, that I saved my command from
capture.   I make no charges — utter no complaints.   Perhaps
neither the Government, nor the army was to blame.   The
great disaster fell upon them both so suddenly, that, perhaps,
neither could do any better; but the naked fact is, that the
fleet was abandoned to shift for itself, there being, as before
remarked, not only no transportation provided for carrying a
pound of provisions, or a cooking-utensil, but not even a horse
for its Admiral to mount.   As a matter of course, great disorder
prevailed, in all the villages, and at all the way-stations, by
which we passed.   We had a continual accession of passengers, until not another man could be packed upon the train.
So great was the demoralization, that we picked up "unat-
tached" generals and colonels on the road, in considerable
numbers.   The most amusing part of our journey, however,
was an attempt made by some of the railroad officials to take
charge of our train, after we had gotten some distance from
Richmond.   Conductors and engineers now came forward, and
insisted upon regulating our affairs for us.   We declined the
good offices of these gentlemen, and navigated to suit ourselves.   The president, or superintendent of the road, I forget
which, even had the assurance to complain, afterward, to President Davis, at Danville, of my usurping his authority!   Simple civilian! discreet railroad officer! to scamper off in the
manner related, and then to complain of my usurping his
authority!   My railroad cruise ended the next day — April
4th — about midnight, when we reached the city of Danville,
and blew off our steam, encamping in the cars for the remainder of the night.   Our escape had been narrow, in more
respects than one.   After turning Lee's flank, at the Five Forks,
the enemy made a dash at the Southside Railroad; Sheridan
with his cavalry tearing up the rails at the Burksville Junction,
just *one hour and a half* after we had passed it.

CHAPTER LIX.

INTERVIEW WITH PRESIDENT DAVIS AND SECRETARY
MALLORY — MY COMMAND ORGANIZED AS A BRIGADE
OF ARTILLERY — BRIGADE MARCHES TO GREENSBORO',
NORTH CAROLINA — CAPITULATION BETWEEN GENERAL
JOSEPH E. JOHNSTON AND SHERMAN — DISPERSION OF
JOHNSTON'S TROOPS — AUTHOR RETURNS HOME, AND
IS ARRESTED — CONCLUSION.

MY memoirs are drawing to a close, for the career of the
Confederacy, as well as my own, is nearly ended. I
found, at Danville, President Davis, and a portion of his cabinet—the Secretary of the Navy among the rest. Here was
temporarily established the seat of Government. I called on
the President and Secretary, who were staying at the same
house, at an early hour on the morning after my arrival,
and reported for duty. They were both calm in the presence of the great disaster which had befallen them and the
country. Mr. Mallory could scarcely be said now to have a
portfolio, though he still had the officers and clerks of his
Department around him. It was at once arranged between
him, and the President, that my command should be organized
as a brigade of artillery, and assigned to the defences around
Danville. The question of my rank being discussed, it was
settled by Mr. Davis, that I should act in the capacity of a
brigadier-general. My grade being that of a rear-admiral, I
was entitled to rank, relatively, with the officers of the army,
as a major-general, but it was folly, of course, to talk of rank, in
the circumstances in which we were placed, and so I contented
myself by saying pleasantly to the President, that I would
waive the matter of rank, to be discussed hereafter, if there
should ever be occasion to discuss it. "That is the right spirit,"
said he, with a smile playing over his usually grave features.
- I did not see him afterward. He moved soon to Charlotte,
in North Carolina, and in a few weeks afterward, he fell into

the hands of the enemy. The reader knows the rest of his history; how the enemy gloated over his captivity; how he was reviled, and insulted, by the coarse and brutal men into whose power he had fallen; how lies were invented as to the circumstances of his capture, to please and amuse the Northern multitudes, eager for his blood; and finally, how he was degraded by imprisonment, and the manacles of a felon! His captors and he were of different races—of different blood. They had nothing in common. He was the "Cavalier," endowed by nature with the instincts and refinement of the gentleman. They were of the race of the Roundheads, to whom all such instincts and refinements were offensive. God has created men in different moulds, as he has created the animals. It was as natural that the Yankee should hate Jefferson Davis, as that the cat should arch its back, and roughen its fur, upon the approach of the dog. I have said that the American war had its origin in money, and that it was carried on throughout, "for a consideration." It ended in the same way. The "long-haired barbarian"—see Gibbon's "Decline and Fall of the Roman Empire"— who laid his huge paw upon Jefferson Davis, to make him prisoner, was paid in *money* for the gallant deed. A President of the United States had degraded his high office, by falsely charging Mr. Davis with being an accomplice in the murder of President Lincoln, and offered a reward for his apprehension; thus gratifying his malignant nature, by holding him up to the world as a common felon. All men now know this charge to be false, the libeller among the rest. Gentlemen retract false charges, when they know them to be such. The charge made by Andrew Johnson against Jefferson Davis has not been retracted.

Upon leaving the presence of the President, and Secretary of the Navy, I sought out my old friend, Captain Sydney Smith Lee, of the Navy, the Assistant Secretary, who had accompanied Mr. Mallory, and arranged with him, and afterward with General Cooper, the Adjutant-General of the Army, the transformation of my sailors into soldiers. There were a great many other naval officers, besides those under my command, fugitives in Danville, and the President and Secretary had been kind enough to authorize me to employ such of them in my new organization, as I might desire. But the difficulty was not in the want of officers; it was the want of men. Already my command of five hundred had dwindled down to about four hundred on my retreat from Richmond, and since my arrival in Danville. I broke these into skeleton regiments, so as to conform to the Brigade organization, and appointed Dunnington, late Captain of my flag-ship, the Colonel of one of them, and Johnston, late Captain of the *Richmond*, Colonel of the other. My youngest son, who had been a midshipman on board the School-ship at Richmond, and who had retreated thence with the School, on the night before the surrender, was ordered by Captain Lee to report to me, and I assigned him to a position on my staff, with the rank of a second lieutenant. Mr. Daniel, my secretary, became my other aide de-camp, and Captain Butt, late commander of the *Nansemond*, was appointed Assistant Adjutant-General.

We remained in the trenches before Danville ten days; and anxious, and weary days they were. Raiding parties were careering around us in various directions, robbing and mal-treating the inhabitants, but none of the thieves ventured within reach of our guns. Lee abandoned his lines, on the 3d of April, and surrendered his army, or the small remnant that was left of it, to Grant, on the 9th, at Appomattox Court-House. The first news we received of his surrender, came to us from the stream of fugitives which now came pressing into our lines at Danville. It was heart-rending to look upon these men, some on foot, some on horseback, some nearly famished for want of food, and others barely able to totter along from disease. It was, indeed, a rabble rout. Hopes had been enter-tained that Lee might escape to Lynchburg, or to Danville, and save his army. The President had entertained this hope, and had issued a proclamation of encouragement to the people, before he left Danville. But the fatal tidings came at last, and when they did come, we all felt that the fate of the Confederacy was sealed.

A new impetus was given to desertions, and before I reached Greensboro', North Carolina, to which point I was now re-moved by the orders of General Joseph E. Johnston, my command had dwindled to about 250 men. Commissioned officers slunk away from me one by one, and became deserters! I was ashamed of my countrymen. Johnston, by reason of his great, personal popularity, and of the confidence which the troops had in his ability, was enabled to gather around him the frag-ments of several armies, whilst Grant had been pressing Lee; and but for Lee's disaster would soon have been able to hold Sherman in check very effectually. But the moment the news of Lee's surrender reached him, there was a stampede from his army. It melted away like a hillock of snow before the sun-shine. Whole companies deserted at a time. Still, many true men remained with him, and with these he stood so defi-antly before Sherman, that the latter was glad to enter into negotiations with him for the *dispersion* of his troops. The reader will be pleased to pay attention to this expression. Johnston *dispersed* his troops, under the capitulation which will presently be spoken of. He never surrendered them *as pris-oners* to the enemy. The country is familiar with what oc-curred at Greensboro', between Johnston and Sherman, and I do not propose to rehearse it here. Sherman, yielding to the impulses of Johnston's master-mind, entered into an agreement with the latter, which would have achieved more fame for him in the future than all his victories, if he had had the courage and ability to stand up to his work. This agreement was that the Southern States should be regarded as *ipso facto*, on the cessation of the war, restored to their rights in the Union. The stroke was one of a statesman. It is in times of great revolutions that genius shows itself. The Federal Government, at the time that this convention was made, was prostrate be-neath the foot of the soldier, and a military man of genius might have governed it with the crook of his finger. If such a one had arisen, he might have applied the scourge to the back of the Northern people, and they would have yelped under it as submissively as any hound. They *had* yelped under the scourging of Abraham Lincoln. But Sherman was not the man to conceive the emergency, or to avail himself of it. He, on the contrary, permitted himself to be scourged by a creature like Stanton, the Federal Secretary of War, and if he did not yelp under the scourging, he at least submitted to it with most admirable docility. Stanton insolently re-

jected the convention which had been entered into between
the two generals, and, reminding Sherman that he was nothing
but a soldier, told him to attend to his own business. Stanton
knew his man, and Sherman·did, afterward, attend to his own
business; for he now entered into a purely military convention with Johnston.

The main features of that convention were, that Johnston
should disperse his army, and Sherman should, in consideration thereof, guarantee it against molestation by the Federal
authorities. It was in the interval between these two conventions, that my camp was astounded one morning, by the report
that Abraham Lincoln, President of the United States, was
dead. He had gone to a small theatre in the city of Washington, on the evening of Good Friday, and had been shot by a
madman! It seemed like a just retribution that he should be
cut off in the midst of the hosannas that were being shouted
in his ears, for all the destruction and ruin he had wrought
upon twelve millions of people. Without any warrant for his
conduct, he had made a war of rapine and lust against eleven
sovereign States, whose only provocation had been that they
had made an effort to preserve the liberties which had been
handed down to them by their fathers. These States had not
sought war, but peace, and they had found, at the hands of
Abraham Lincoln, destruction. As a Christian, it was my
duty to say, "Lord, have mercy upon his soul!" but the d——l
will surely take care of his memory.

The last days of April, and the first days of May, were employed, by General Johnston, in dispersing his army according
to agreement. Commissioners, appointed by the two Generals
to arrange the dispersion, and provide the dispersed troops
with the guaranties that had been agreed upon, met in the
village of Greensboro', on the 1st of May, 1865. On the previous evening, I had called at the headquarters of General
Johnston, where I had met Beauregard, Wade Hampton,
Wheeler, D. H. Hill, and a host of other gallant spirits, who
formed the galaxy by which he was surrounded. He was kind
enough to give me precedence, in the matter of arranging for
my departure with the Federal Commissioner. Accordingly, on
the morning of the 1st of May, accompanied by my staff, I

rode into Greensboro', and alighted at the Britannia Hotel, where the Commissioners were already assembled. They were Brevet Brigadier General Hartsuff, on the part of the Federals, and Colonel Mason, on the part of the Confederates. Each guaranty of non-molestation had been prepared, beforehand, in a printed form, and signed by Hartsuff, and only required to be filled up with the name and rank of the party entitled to receive it, and signed by myself to be complete. Upon being introduced to General Hartsuff, we proceeded at once to business. I produced the muster-roll of my command, duly signed by my Assistant Adjutant-General; and General Hartsuff and myself ran our eyes over the names together, and when we had ascertained the number, the General counted out an equal number of blank guaranties, and, handing them to me, said: "You have only to fill up one of these for each officer and soldier of your command, with his name and rank, and sign it and hand it to him. I have already signed them myself. You can fill up the one intended for yourself in like manner." "With regard to the latter," I replied, "I prefer, if you have no objection, to have it filled up and completed here in your presence." "Oh! that makes no difference," he replied. "Very well," said I, "if it makes no difference, then you can have no objection to complying with my request." He now called an aide-de-camp, and desiring him to be seated at the table where we were, told him to fill up my guaranty after my dictation. I gave him my titles separately, making him write me down a "Rear-Admiral in the Confederate States Navy, and a Brigadier-General in the Confederate States Army, commanding a brigade." When he had done this, he handed me the paper; I signed it, and put it in my pocket, and, turning to the General, said, "I am now satisfied." The following is a copy of the paper : —

GREENSBORO', NORTH CAROLINA, May 1, 1865.

In accordance with the terms of the Military Convention, entered into on the 26th day of April, 1865, between General Joseph E. Johnston, commanding the Confederate Army, and Major-General W. T. Sherman, commanding the United States Army, in North Carolina, *R. Semmes, Rear-Admiral, and Brigadier-General, C. S. Navy, and C. S. Army, commanding brigade*, has given his solemn obligation, not to take up arms against the Government of the United States, until properly released from this obligation; and is permitted to return to his home, not to be disturbed by the United States authorities, so long as he observes this obligation, and obeys the laws in force where he may reside.

R. SEMMES,
Rear-Admiral C. S. Navy, and
Brigadier-General C. S. Army.

WM. HARTSUFF,
Brevet Brigadier-General U. S. Army,
Special Commissioner.

It was well I took the precautions above described, in dealing with the enemy, for, when I was afterward arrested, as the reader will presently see, the Yankee press, howling for my blood, claimed that I had not been paroled at all! that I had deceived the paroling officer, and obtained my parole under false pretences; the said paroling officer not dreaming, when he was paroling one Brigadier-General Semmes, that he had the veritable "pirate" before him. I dispersed my command, on the same afternoon, and with my son, and half a dozen of my officers, a baggage-wagon, and the necessary servants, made my way to Montgomery, in Alabama, and, at that point, took steamer for my home, in Mobile, which I reached in the latter days of May.

Andrew Johnson, the Vice-President of the United States, had succeeded Mr. Lincoln as President. He was a Southern man, born in the State of North Carolina, and a citizen of Tennessee. He had been elected to the Senate of the United States, a short time before the breaking out of the war. He had belonged to the Democratic party, and had arisen from a very low origin—his father having belonged to the common class of laborers, and he having learned the trade of a tailor, which he practised after he had grown to man's estate. Gifted by nature with a strong intellect, he studied the law, and afterward embarked in politics. The word "embark" expresses my idea precisely, for, from this time onward, he became a mere politician. As a rule, it requires an unscrupulous and unprincipled man to succeed in politics in America. Honorable men do, sometimes, of course, make their way to high places; but these form the exceptions, not the

rule. Andrew Johnson succeeded in politics. In the earlier
stages of our troubles, he spoke and wrote like a Southern
man, demanding, in behalf of the South, some security for the
future, in the way of additional-guaranties. But when these
were all denied, and it became evident that his State would
secede, and that he would be stripped of his senatorial honors,
so recently won, if he abided by his former record, and went
with his State, he abjured his record, and abandoned his State.
Like all renegades, he became zealous in the new faith which
he had adopted, and proved himself so good a Radical, that
President Lincoln sent him back to Tennessee as a satrap, to govern, with a rod of iron, under military rule, the Sovereign State
for which he had so recently demanded additional securities.

Still growing in favor with his new party, he was elected
Vice-President, upon the re-election of Mr. Lincoln, in the fall
of 1864. The Presidential mantle having fallen upon him, by
the tragical death of Mr. Lincoln, he retained the cabinet of
his predecessor, and made his zeal still more manifest to his
party, by insisting on the necessity of making "treason odious"
—the same sort of treason enjoined upon the States by Jefferson in his Kentucky Resolutions of '98 and '99, which formed
the basis of the creed of the Democratic party, to which Mr.
Johnson had belonged—and punishing "traitors." A grand
jury in Norfolk, Va., found an indictment for treason against
General Lee, and but for the interposition of General Grant, he
would have been tried, under Mr. Johnson's administration;
and probably tried by a packed jury that would have hung
him. Mr. Davis was already in close and ignominious confinement, as has been related. Captain Wurz, of the late Confederate
States Army, who had been, for a short time, in charge of the
prison at Andersonville, was tried by a Military Commission,
in the city of Washington, under the shadow of the President's chair, convicted, and executed, notwithstanding he was
a paroled *prisoner of war*. Another Military Commission, *in
time of peace*, had convicted and executed a woman—Mrs.
Surratt—on the false charge, as is now admitted by the whole
country, that she was an accomplice in Mr. Lincoln's assassi-
nation. Mr. Johnson signed her death-warrant.

It was under these circumstances, that on the night of the

15th of December, 1865, or seven months and a half after I had received the guaranty of General Sherman, at Greensboro', North Carolina, that I should not be molested by the United States authorities, that a lieutenant of the Marine Corps, with a guard of soldiers, surrounded my house and arrested me, on an order signed by Mr. Gideon Welles, without the process of any court. I was torn from my family, under guard — the thieving soldiery committing some petty thefts about my premises — and hurried off to Washington. Arrived here, I was imprisoned, first, in the Navy Yard, and then in the Marine Barracks. I was kept a close prisoner, with a sentinel at my door, for nearly four months; the gentlemen about the barracks, however, doing everything in their power to render my confinement more endurable. It was the intention of the Government to throw me, as it had thrown Wurz, as a sop to the extreme Radicals of the New England States, whose commerce I had destroyed; and I was only saved by the circumstances which will be presently related. But before I relate these circumstances, I deem it pertinent to give to the reader the following letter addressed by me to President Johnson, from my place of confinement, charging his Government with breach of faith in arresting me.

To His Excellency Andrew Johnson,
   President of the United States.

Sir:—Being satisfied that you are anxious to arrive at a correct decision in my case,—one that shall accord, at the same time, with the honor and dignity of the United States, and with justice to myself,—I venture to address you the following brief exposition of the law and the facts of the case.

On the 26th day of April, 1865, the following military convention was entered into at Greensboro', N. C., between General Joseph E. Johnston, commanding the Confederate States Armies in North Carolina, and Major-General W. T. Sherman, commanding the United States Army in the same State, viz:—

"1. All acts of war on the part of the troops under General Johnston's command to cease from this date.

"2. All arms and public property to be deposited at Greensboro', and delivered to an ordnance officer of the United States Army.

"3. Rolls of all the officers and men to be made in duplicate, one copy to be retained by the commander of the troops, and the other to be given to an officer to be designated by General Sherman. Each officer and man to give his individual obligation, in writing, not to take up arms against the Government of the United States until properly released from this obligation.

" 4. The side-arms of officers, and their private horses and baggage, to be retained by them.

" 5. This being done, all the officers and men will be permitted to return to their homes, not to be disturbed by the United States authorities so long as they observe their obligation and the laws in force where they may reside.

[Signed]   " W. T. SHERMAN, *Major-General,*
     "*Commanding U. S. Forces in North Carolina.*

[Signed]   " JOSEPH E. JOHNSTON, *General,*
     "*Commanding C. S. Forces in North Carolina.*"

Here, Mr. President, was a solemn military convention, entered into by two generals, who had opposing armies in the field, in which convention the one and the other general stipulated for certain terms, — General Johnston agreeing to lay down his arms and disband his forces, and General Sherman agreeing, *in consideration thereof,* that the forces thus disbanded shall proceed to their homes, and there remain undisturbed by the United States authorities. I beg you to observe the use of the word "undisturbed," one of the most comprehensive words in our language. I pray you also to remark the formalities with which this convention was drawn. We were treated as officers commanding armies, representing, of course, if not a *de jure,* at least a *de facto* government. Our proper military titles were acknowledged. I was myself styled and treated in the muster-rolls, and other papers drawn up by both parties, a brigadier-general and a rear-admiral. The honors of war usual upon surrenders, upon terms, were accorded to us, in our being permitted to retain our side-arms, private horses, and baggage. In short, the future historian, upon reading this convention, will be unable to distinguish it in any particular from other similar papers, agreed upon by armies of recognized governments. At the date of, and some weeks prior to the ratification of this convention, I commanded a brigade of artillery, forming a part of the army of General Johnston. I was, of course, included in the terms of the convention. I complied with those terms, under orders received from General Johnston, by turning over my arms to the proper officer, and disbanding my forces. The convention was approved by the Government of the United States. Your Excellency may recollect that the first convention entered into between General Johnston and General Sherman, which provided, among other things, for the return of the Southern States to their functions under the Constitution of the United States, was disapproved by the Government, on the ground that General Sherman, in undertaking to treat of political matters, had transcended his authority. The armistice which had been declared between the two armies was dissolved, and hostilities were renewed. A few days afterward, however, new negotiations were commenced, and the convention with which we have to do was the second convention entered into by those

Generals, and which was a substantial readoption of the military portion of the first convention. It was this latter convention which was formally approved, both by General Grant, the Commander-in-Chief, under whose orders General Sherman acted, and by the Executive at Washington.

Confiding in the good faith of the Government, pledged in a solemn treaty as above stated, I returned to my home in Alabama, and remained there for the space of seven months, engaging in civil pursuits as a means of livelihood for my dependent family, and yielding a ready obedience to the laws. I had, in fact, become an officer of the law, having established myself as an attorney. It would have been easy for me, at any time within these seven months, to pass out of the country, if I had had any doubt about the binding obligation of the Greensboro' convention, or of the good faith of the Government. But I had no doubt on either point; nor have I any doubt yet, as I feel quite sure that when you shall have informed yourself of all the facts of the case, you will come to the conclusion that my arrest was entirely without warrant, and order my discharge. While thus remaining quietly at my home, in the belief that I was "not to be disturbed by the United States authorities," I was, on the 15th of December, 1865, in the night-time, arrested by a lieutenant and two sergeants of the Marine Corps, under an order signed by the Secretary of the Navy, and placed under guard; a file of soldiers in the meantime surrounding my house. I was informed by the officer making the arrest that I was to proceed to Washington in his custody, there to answer to a charge, a copy of which he handed me. This charge, and the protest which I filed the next day with the Commanding General of the Department of Alabama, against my arrest, your Excellency has already seen. The question for you then to decide, Mr. President, is the legality of this arrest. Can I, in violation of the terms of the military convention already referred to, and under which I laid down my arms, be held to answer for any act of war committed anterior to the date of that convention? I respectfully submit that I cannot be so held, either during the continuance of the war, (and the political power has not yet proclaimed the war ended,) or after the war shall have been brought to a close by proclamation, and the restoration of the writ of *habeas corpus*, without a flagrant violation of faith on the part of the United States. If it be admitted that I might be tried for any act *dehors* the war, and having no connection with it—as, for instance, for a forgery—it is quite clear that I cannot be arrested or arraigned for any act manifestly of war, and acknowledged as such, (as the act, for instance, for which I was arrested,) whether such act be in consonance with the laws of war or in violation thereof; and this for the simple reason that the military convention was a *condonation* and an *oblivion* of all precedent acts of war, of what nature soever those acts might be. I am "not to be disturbed," says the military convention. Disturbed for what? Why, manifestly, for any act of war theretofore committed against the United States. This is the only common-

sense view of the case; and if the convention did not mean this, it
could mean nothing; and I laid down my arms, not upon terms, as
I had supposed, but without terms.   If I was still at the mercy of
the conqueror, and my arrest asserts as much, I was in the condi
tion of one who had surrendered *unconditionally;* but it has been
seen that I did not surrender unconditionally, but upon terms —
terms engrafted upon a treaty ratified and approved by the conqueror's Government.   Nor is it consistent with good faith to qual-
ify or restrain those terms, so as to make them inapplicable to acts
of war that may be claimed to have been in violation of the laws
of war; for this would be to refine away all the protection which
has been thrown around me by treaty, and put me in the power of
the opposite contracting party, who might put his own construction
upon the laws of war.   This very attempt, Mr. President, has
been made in the case before you.   I claim to have escaped, after
my ship had sunk from under me in the engagement off Cherbourg, and I had been precipitated into the water, the enemy not
having taken possession of me, according to the laws and usages
of war, as your Excellency may read in almost every page of naval
history; the Secretary of the Navy claiming the contrary.   The true,
and the only just and fair criterion, is, was the act for which the
arrest was made an act of war?   If so, there is an end of the
question, and I must be discharged, for, as before remarked, the
convention, if it is anything, is an oblivion of all acts of war of
whatever nature.

But it may be said that, although I cannot be tried by a military
tribunal during the war, I may yet be tried by a civil tribunal after
the war.   Let us look at this question also.   I was, undoubtedly,
amenable to the civil tribunals of the country, as well after as before
the convention, for any offence of a purely civil nature, not founded
upon an act of war — to instance, as before, the crime of forgery.
If I had committed a forgery in North Carolina, I could not, upon
arraignment, plead the military convention in bar of trial.   Why
not?   Because that convention had reference only to acts of war.
I was treated with, in my capacity of a soldier and a seaman.   But,
does it follow that I may be tried for treason?   And if not, why
not?   The Attorney-General tells you that treason is a civil offence,
and in his opinion triable exclusively by the civil courts, and he
hopes you will give him plenty of occupation in trying "many
whom the sword has spared."   (See his letter to you of the 4th of
January, 1866.)   But does not that officer forget that treason is
made up of acts of war; and is it not apparent that you cannot
try me for an act of war?   The Constitution of the United States,
which the Attorney-General says he loves even better than blood,
declares, in words, that treason against the United States shall consist only in levying war against them, or in adhering to their enemies, giving them aid and comfort — all of which adherence, giving
of aid and comfort, &c., are equally acts of war.   There is no con-
structive treason in this country.   Thus I can neither be tried by a
military tribunal during the war, nor a civil tribunal after the war,

for any act of war, or for treason which consists only of acts of war.

But it may further be said that this convention, of which I am claiming the protection, is not a *continuing* convention, and will expire with the war, when, as Mr. Speed thinks, you may hand me over to the civil tribunals. Whence can such a conclusion be drawn? Not from the terms of the convention, for these contradict the conclusion; not by implication merely, but in *totidem verbis*. The terms are, "not to be disturbed, *so long as they shall observe their obligation and the laws in force where they may reside*." A misuse of terms, Mr. President, sometimes misleads very clever minds. And I presume it is by a misuse of terms that the Attorney-General has fallen into this error. (See his letter to your Excellency, before referred to.) That officer, while he admits that PAROLE protects the party paroled from trial during the war, yet contends that it does not protect him from trial by a civil tribunal, for treason, after the war. As I have shown that treason can only consist of acts of war, and that the military convention is an oblivion of all acts of war, the Attorney-General, when he says that a paroled party may be tried for treason at the end of the war, (the parole being no longer a protection to him,) must mean that the parole will have died with the war. This is entirely true of a *mere parole*, for a parole is only a promise, on the part of a prisoner of war, that if released from imprisonment, he will not take up arms again unless he is exchanged. This parole is as frequently given by prisoners of war, who have surrendered unconditionally, as by those who have surrendered upon terms. There cannot be any parole, then, without a prisoner of war, and the status of prisoner of war ceasing, the parole ceases—*cessante ratione cessat et ipsa lex*. Thus far the Attorney-General is quite logical, but by confounding in his mind the certificates given to the officers and men of General Johnston's army, stating the terms of the Greensboro' convention, and guaranteeing those officers and men against molestation, in accordance with those terms, with PAROLES, it is easy to see how the mistake I am exposing can have been made. But the convention made between General Johnston and General Sherman was not a mere release of prisoners on parole; nor, indeed, had it anything to do with prisoners, for none of the officers and men of General Johnston's army *ever were prisoners*, as may be seen at a glance by an inspection of the terms of the convention. It was a treaty between commanding generals in the field, in which the word *parole* is not once used, or could be used with propriety; a treaty in which mutual stipulations are made, one in consideration of another, and there is no limit as to time set to this treaty.

On the contrary, it was expressly stated that the guaranties contained in it were to continue and be in force, so long as the parties to whom the guaranties were given, should perform their part of the treaty stipulations. It was made, not in contemplation of a continuation of the war, but with a view to put an end to the war, and the guaranties were demanded by us as *peace guaranties*. It did, in effect, put an end to the war and pacify the whole country; General Taylor in Alabama and Mississippi, and General Buckner and others in Texas, following the lead of General Johnston. Are we to be told now by an Attorney-General of the United States, that the moment the object of the convention, to wit, the restoration of peace, was accomplished, the convention itself became a nullity, its terms powerless to protect us, and that General Johnston's army surrendered, in fact, without any terms whatever? You cannot sustain such an opinion, Mr. President. It will shock the common sense and love of fair play of the American people. But to show still further that it was the intention of the parties that this should be a *continuing* convention, the words used were, "not to be disturbed by the *United States Authorities*," these words being co-extensive with the whole power of the Government. We were not only "not to be disturbed" by General Sherman, or any other military commander or authority, but by *any authority whatever*, civil or military. Nor will it do to say that General Sherman, being merely a military man, had no authority to speak for the civil branch of the Government, for his action, as we have seen, was approved by the Administration at Washington.

One more remark, Mr. President, and I will forbear to trespass further on your time and patience. The act of war for which I was arrested, was well known to the Department of the Government making the arrest, ten months before the convention was entered into at Greensboro'. It was also well known to the same Department, that about the middle of February, 1865, I was assigned to the command of the James River Squadron, near Richmond, with the rank of a rear-admiral; being thus promoted and employed by my Government, after the alleged illegal escape off Cherbourg. If the Federal Government then entertained the design, which it has since developed, of arresting and trying me for this alleged breach of the laws of war, was it not its duty, both to itself and to me, to have made me an exception to any military terms it might have been disposed to grant to our armies? I put it to you, Mr. President, as a man and a magistrate to say, and I will rest my case on your answer, whether it was consistent with honor and fair dealing, for this Government first to entrap me, by means of a military convention, and then, having me in its power, to arrest me and declare that convention null and void, for the course recommended to you by Mr. Speed comes to this — nothing more, nothing less.

I have thus laid before you, tediously I fear, and yet as concisely as was consistent with clearness, the grounds upon which I claim at your hands, who are the guardian of the honor of a great nation, my discharge from arrest and imprisonment. I have spoken freely and frankly, as it became an American citizen to speak to the Chief Magistrate of the American Republic. We live in times of high party excitement, when men, unfortunately, are but too prone to take counsel of their passions; but passions die, and men die with them, and after death comes history. In the future, Mr. President, *when America shall have a history*, my record and that of the gallant Southern people will be engrafted upon, and become a part of your history, the pages of which you are now acting; and the prayer of this petition is, that you will not permit the honor of the American name to be tarnished by a perfidy on those pages.   In this paper I have stood strictly upon legal defences; but should those barriers be beaten down, conscious of the rectitude of my conduct, throughout a checkered and eventful career, when the commerce of half a world was at my mercy, and when the passions of men, North and South, were tossed into a whirlwind, by the current events of the most bloody and terrific war that the human race had ever seen, I shall hope to justify and defend myself against any and all charges affecting the honor and reputation of a man and a soldier.   Whatever else may be said of me, I have, at least, brought no discredit upon the American name and character.

I am, very respectfully, &c.,

RAPHAEL SEMMES.

WASHINGTON CITY, January 15, 1866.

At the time of my arrest, there was a newspaper called the "Republican," published in the city of Washington, in the interests of President Johnson.   There had been some little struggle between Congress and the President, as to who should take the initiative in the wholesale hanging of "traitors" which had been resolved upon.   The "Republican," speaking for President Johnson, declares, in the article which will be found below, *his* readiness to act.   He is only waiting, it says, for Congress to move in the matter.   Here is the article:—

"WHY DON'T CONGRESS ACT?

" As long ago as last October, the President of the United States commenced an earnest effort to initiate the trials of prominent traitors, beginning with the arch-traitor Jefferson Davis.   It is now a historical record, and officially in the possession of the Congress of the United States, that, upon application to the Chief Justice of the Supreme Court to know at what time, if any, the United States Court for the District of Virginia would be ready to try certain high crimes against the National Government, the President received an answer from Chief-Justice Chase, that the Court would not sit in that district, while that territory was under military control, and suggested the propriety of delaying action in the matter, until Congress acted.   Congress assembled.   The President referred the whole subject, respectfully, to the consideration of Congress in his annual message, and subsequently, in answer to a resolution of inquiry, he sent, by special message, the correspondence alluded to above, between himself and Chief-Justice Chase.

"All the facts were thus legitimately laid before the legislative branch of the Government *three and a half months ago!*   The President, some time in November last, stopped the work of pardoning, except in a few cases where the applications were accompanied by the most positive evidence of good intentions toward the Government. From among those who have applied for pardon, the President has reserved for trial about *five hundred* of the military and political leaders of the rebel Government—a sufficient number to begin with at least. This number, as classified by the President, we published, by permission, some time since.

"Now, in view of the above statement of facts, what has Congress done? Has Congress passed any law directing how the rebels shall be tried? No. Has Congress passed any resolution requesting the President to order a military court for the trial of Davis & Co.? No. Has Congress agitated the subject at any time, in any manner, looking to a trial of the cases referred to? No.

"But what have Congressmen done in their individual capacity? Many of them, from day to day, have spoken sneeringly of the President, because he has not done what he began to do, but which the Chief Justice of the Supreme Court prevented, by refusing to hold the court, and which the Congress of the United States has wholly neglected, or *purposely ignored*. The people, through the press of the country, and in private communication, are beginning to inquire why Congress don't act. Governors of States, ignorant of the facts, are haranguing the people about the *indisposition* or *neglect* of the *President* to try traitors. Why don't Congress act? The President is ready, and has been ready from the beginning, to co-operate with Congress in any constitutional measure by which traitors can be tried, to the end, that treason may thereby be made odious. We repeat the question with which we commenced, and which is echoed by the people everywhere, 'Why don't Congress act?'"

There is an old adage which says, "When rogues fall out, honest men get their rights." Fortunately for the "traitors" of the South, Andrew Johnson, and the Congress quarrelled. Johnson undertook to reconstruct the Southern States, in *his* interests, and Congress claimed the right to reconstruct them in *its* interests. The Constitution of the United States was equally disregarded by them both. Johnson had no more respect for it than Congress. His mode of reconstruction equally violated it, with that of Congress. It was a struggle between usurpers, which should be master—that was all. Johnson, with a single stroke of the pen, struck down all the State governments, called conventions of the people, and told the conventions what they should do. Congress might go a little further, but its violation of the Constitution could not, well, be more flagrant. The breach widened from day to day, and the quarrel at last became bitter. Neither party, opposed by the other, could afford to become the hangman of the Southern people, and the very pretty little programme, which, according to the " Republican " newspaper, had been arranged between the rogues, naturally fell to the ground.

Johnson finding that his quarrel with Congress had ruined him with his party, now set about constructing a new one— a Johnson party. His scheme was to ignore both the Democratic, and the Republican parties. If he could succeed in reconstructing the Southern States, to the exclusion of Congress, he might hope to get the votes of those States in the next Presidential election. But to conciliate these States, it would not do to hang "*five hundred* of the military and political leaders of the rebel Government," as a mere " beginning." He must pursue a different policy. He now issued first one amnesty proclamation, and then another — doling out amnesty, grudgingly, in broken doses— until he had issued three of them. By the last of these proclamations, the writer of these pages, who was true to his State, was " graciously pardoned " by Andrew Johnson, who had not only been a traitor to his State, but had betrayed, besides, two political parties. A glorious opportunity presented itself for him to show himself a statesman. He has proved a charlatan instead. He cowered in his struggle with Congress, and that body has shorn him of his prerogatives, and reduced him to the mere position of a clerk. This is the second act of the drama, the first act of which was the secession of the Southern States. The form of government having been changed by the revolution, there are still other acts of the drama to be performed.

THE END.